ADOLESCENCE

For my mother, Frances Fandel Nielsen,
as full of beauty and strength as the agates

ADOLESCENCE
A CONTEMPORARY VIEW

Second Edition

LINDA NIELSEN
Wake Forest University

HOLT, RINEHART AND WINSTON, INC.
Fort Worth Chicago San Francisco Philadelphia
Montreal Toronto London Sydney Tokyo

Publisher Ted Buchholz
Acquisitions Editor Christina N. Oldham
Senior Project Editor Dawn Youngblood
Production Manager Annette Dudley Wiggins
Art & Design Supervisor John Ritland
Text Designer Ritter & Ritter, Inc.
Cover Designer Jo Arnold

Library of Congress Cataloging-in-Publication Data

Nielsen, Linda.
Adolescence, a contemporary view / Linda Nielsen. — 2nd ed. p. cm.
Includes bibliographical references and index.
ISBN 0-03-032853-5
1. Adolescence. 2. Adolescent psychology. 3. Child development.
I. Title.
HQ796.N544 1991
305.23′5—dc20 90-46994
CIP

ISBN: 0-03-032853-5

PRINTED IN THE UNITED STATES OF AMERICA

1 2 3 4 039 9 8 7 6 5 4 3 2 1

Holt, Rinehart and Winston, Inc. The Dryden Press Saunders College Publishing

Photo Credits

1.1 p. 2 Dr. Bob Jones, **1.2 p. 6** L. Nielsen, **1.3 p. 9** The Bettmann Archive, **1.4 p. 13** Ken Heyman, **1.5 p. 15** The Granger Collection, **1.6 p. 17** The Bettmann Archive

2.1 p. 34 Dr. Bob Jones, **2.2 p. 46** Dr. Bob Jones, **2.3 p. 62** Dr. Bob Jones, **2.4 p. 69** Dr. Bob Jones, **2.5 p. 71** Wake Forest University Athletic Office

Continued on page 581

Preface

To the instructor

Given all the books you have already reviewed and the time you have invested in designing a course around your present text, why consider changing texts? Having asked myself this question each time a newly published textbook finds its way into the stack on my desk, I now find myself, as an author, wanting to answer this question for you.

In my search for the ideal textbook, I become frustrated by the same dogged dilemmas. The first is a tug-of-war between wanting my students to be captivated by the reading and simultaneously wanting them to be introduced to the most thorough, challenging scholarship available. Unfortunately, the texts that provide the most careful examinations of the research are the ones my students find the most boring. When I have adopted books of this ilk, I have been confronted with: "I don't see the relevance or the practicality of this material"; "I'm having a hard time figuring out what the author is trying to say." Taking the most "scholarly" texts further to task, my students have also subjected me to lectures on how the most talented scholars should be able to present the data and theories in an engaging manner. Under these circumstances, I wind up defending my choice of books by inviting my students to work with their classmates in devising practical applications and in discovering the relevance of the data and theories.

Safe in the privacy of my office, however, I have taken my students' criticisms to heart and adopted the second type of text—the book that students find more engaging and more pragmatic. As in any tug-of-war, however, while I too find myself more entertained by these books and while I applaud their more applied approach to adolescent psychology, I feel uneasy with several aspects of the scholarship. In examining the text's references, I find inadequacies in terms of quantity, recency, breadth, and diversity of perspective. Having counted the number of citations from the 1970s and the studies referring exclusively to college samples, I end up supplementing the text with a host of readings from the 1980s and from the burgeoning field of research on early adolescence.

More troublesome still, despite which of the two types of texts I adopt, I have encountered three other problems. First, there are too few attempts to teach students to evaluate the relative merit of various studies, to recognize the contradictions and inconsistencies in the data, or to identify significant methodological shortcomings. Consequently, I have found myself cringing when students discuss teenage pregnancy on the basis of data displayed on a full-page table entitled "Causes of adolescent pregnancy"—data derived from a 1975 correlational study with a nonrandom sample of 100 white, college freshmen volunteers. In analyzing a text's effort to summarize data for students, I have been left with the gnawing feeling that too often the data have been oversimplified by ignoring the contradictory findings and by failing to note the flaws that plague even the most compelling studies.

Second, I have been unable to find a thorough presentation of the data or the issues relevant to female adolescents or youths from minority cultures. Given that almost half of the adolescent population is female and that nearly one fifth are members of minority cultures, this disturbs me. Realizing that we have advanced beyond mere "consciousness raising" in regard to racism and sexism, I have been looking for a more rigorous, contemporary examination of the research related to female and minority youth.

Third, as a teacher who aspires to be "inspiring" and "engaging" (well, at least occasionally!), I want a text whose instructor's manual contributes to my teaching skills and whose format benefits my least successful students. I also want a fresh supply of provocative questions for class discussions and challenging test questions that distinguish between students who really understand the material and those who have merely skimmed the text and are good guessers on multiple-choice items. Finally, given the range of my students' abilities, I need a text whose study aids and writing style are suited for my most advanced studnets, as well as for their classmates whose poor study skills or whose unfamiliarity with psychology slows their understanding of the text.

Having shared my concerns with you, let me tell you how I have tried to create an adolescent psychology text that meets my own criteria. First, each of my chapters is based on data from the 1980s and focuses on adolescents between the ages of 13 and 18, rather than on college-aged youth. I invite you to examine the references for their quantity, their currency, and the variety that they represent regarding adolescents' race, sex, and socioeconomic status. I especially encourage you to examine chapter 5 on sex-role development and chapter 6 on adolescents from minority cultures, in terms of their thoroughness and empirical rigor. I think you will find them unmatched in terms of their thoroughness.

Second, each of my chapters describes many of the shortcomings, the discrepancies, and the unresolved controversies in the existing data. By explaining the advantages and disadvantages of various types of research in chapter 1 and by highlighting the limitations of our present research, I am encouraging students to interpret statistics and research with more care and sophistication. Although my strategy irritates students who want one unwavering, "correct" answer to pressing social problems, such as delinquency and teenage pregnancy, I think it creates a more mature understanding of the complexities involved in research and a more tolerant attitude toward social scientists.

I am also committed to motivating college students and to demonstrating the day-to-day value of our research and theories. Consequently, each of my chapters offers a multitude of specific examples and practical applications of theories, data, and issues. To reduce the chance of your students asking "so what?" after having read a chapter, the questions for discussion and debate and the self-administered quizzes in each chapter ask for a personal examination of controversies, such as providing abortion and contraception for minors, offering death-education classes in our schools, eliminating curricular tracking, and permitting students with AIDS to attend school. The quizzes and questions require students to apply seemingly abstract theories and concepts to their interactions with adolescents, as well as to their own adolescent and adult life.

Moreover, I have included recent news articles and writings by adolescents themselves, which breathe life into otherwise impersonal data. To provoke your students' curiosity, these materials have been set aside from the text in specially highlighted boxed inserts. For example, your students will find adolescent's own descriptions of being bisexual, of coping with a parent's death, of becoming a teenage parent, of adjusting to their parents' divorce, of living in a biracial family, of discovering incest within their family, of losing their virginity, and of attempting suicide. I have also taken care to include contemporary topics that directly affect college students themselves, such as herpes, the cervical sponge, PMS, math anxiety, anorexia, interracial dating, and date rape.

Finally, the text offers a number of features to help your students master the material: instructional objectives, a list of key terms that are then highlighted in the text, a set of review questions, and a glossary at the end of every chapter. In addition, when research concerning a particular topic is presented, it is placed within the context of the theories introduced in chapter 1, rather than as a series of isolated findings. This strategy provides students with a continuity between the chapters and fosters their understanding of the different theoretical approaches to adolescent psychology.

For your benefit, the instructor's manual offers a number of strategies for increasing students' understanding and for enlivening the time you spend together in class: topics for research projects, annotated bibliographies of supplementary readings, audiovisual aids, suggested speakers from the community, possible lecture topics, and class activities other than lectures and seminars. The manual also provides exercises that require students to examine the strengths and weaknesses of particular studies and statistics. A file of multiple-choice and essay questions is also provided for each chapter.

Features of this new edition

In this second edition, I have included a number of new features that I think you will find unique in the field. First, chapter 8 offers you the most comprehensive, up-to-date coverage of divorce, blended families, poverty, and the father's influence on his children now available in an adolescence text. Second, I have expanded my chapters on gender roles and minority adolescents, giving you the broadest possible coverage of these topics. Third, I have placed a glossary at the end of each chapter to help your students master difficult concepts and have added "limitations of the research" sections to help the students understand the discrepancies and contradictions in our findings. Finally, I have added and expanded upon topics not found, or treated only peripherally, in other texts: steroids, death and dying, homosexuality, at-risk students, premenstrual syndrome, date rape, adult children of alcoholics, codependency, incest, poverty, joint custody, "ice" and "ecstasy," neo-Nazism. I invite you to thumb through the index at the end of the book and compare its contents to the contemporary issues affecting today's adolescents.

In closing, I feel simultaneously frustrated and satisfied. The deluge of newly published data, which challenge our once-revered theories and our "conclusions" about adolescence, remind me that, even as this book goes to press, it is already in some sense outdated. In striving to be current, I am already part of the past. In striving to be comprehensive, I am still confined by the limitations of time, personal energy, and manuscript length. In trying to be objective, I am nonetheless influenced, as we all are, by my own past. These reservations about my own work notwithstanding, I am convinced that this book can provoke your students' passions, hone their critical thinking, deepen their understanding of adolescence, debunk many of the myths surrounding today's adolescents, and leave you with the satisfaction of having presented material that is both engaging and intellectually demanding.

To the student

Would you like to be 14 again? If given the choice of supervising either adolescents or younger children for a weekend, which would you choose? Would you be more likely to write an article entitled "The adolescent years: A survival guide for parents" or "Adolescence: Time of love and laughter"? Your answers to such questions depend both on your own adolescent experiences and on the accuracy of your information about adolescents. Obviously, neither you nor I have the power to alter your adolescence. We do, however, have the power to examine your assumptions and your convictions about the adolescents of today and yesterday. With this in mind, my primary objective in writing this book is to introduce you to the most recent data and the most prevalent controversies in the field of adolescent psychology. I am hoping to alter many of your images of adolescents, as well as to reinforce some of the feelings and opinions that you presently cannot defend with statistical data or research.

Because we all tend to generalize on the basis of our own personal experiences, a number of myths and misperceptions regarding adolescence continue to thrive, despite the absence of data to support them. Indeed, I have found it frustrating and sometimes poignantly touching that my own students often defend their opinions by citing their own personal experiences, totally disregarding the data from national surveys or from carefully designed experimental research. With reams of data and statistics in hand, I am often trying to jar students into understanding that their personal experiences do not necessarily reflect the realities of most Americans: "Just because the earth looks flat from your view out this window, are you willing to discount the photographic and navigational data that disprove your personal vision of reality?" I invite you to give your most careful consideration to the data and theories that contradict your personal experiences and that challenge some of your most heartfelt convictions—a feat that, in and of itself, will require considerable selflessness and a certain kind of courage on your part.

My second goal is to engage you in an examination of your own adolescence—to recognize its impact on your present life and to appreciate the differences between your adolescence and that of thousands of other young people in our society. I have provided questions with each chapter to provoke discussions about your adolescence and to heighten your awareness of the diversity within our society. If your instructor does not allot time in class for discussing these questions, I hope you will share them with friends and relatives as a way of better understanding yourself and others. I also invite you to attend with care to the voices of adolescents that appear in the chapters' boxed inserts—voices that speak poignantly and powerfully to those willing to listen.

Finally, as you embark on this study of adolescence, your attention will probably wander to an aspect of the course that can arouse considerable anxiety—your grade. Confronted with a 700-page book, you may be asking, as do most of my students, "How should I prepare for the tests?" Having heard too many students lament, "I studied but it sure didn't show in my grade," I have provided special features throughout my book to guide you in preparation for your exams.

First, each chapter is prefaced by a detailed outline, a statement of the main objectives, and a list of technical terms and concepts. These concepts and terms are also highlighted in the chapter and are defined in the glossary at the end of each chapter. Before beginning to read a chapter, examine the outline, the list of concepts, and the objectives. Most important, read the questions at the end of the chapter at least twice *before* you begin reading. As you read, attend carefully to the highlighted terms, take notes on the material relevant to the study questions, and read the boxed inserts and tables carefully. After completing the reading, define each of the concepts listed at the chapter's beginning and write your answers to the review questions.

My hope is that, having finished my book, you will decide to keep it as a permanent part of your personal library, rather than rushing back to the bookstore in anticipation of a sizable refund. In any event, I would value your recommendations for improving the text, as well as your comments regarding what you found most provocative or most entertaining. I invite you to write to me at my university address—Box 7266, Wake Forest University, Winston-Salem, NC, 27109.

Acknowledgments

Although I still have not gotten over my anxiety when reading my reviewers' initial critiques of each chapter, I would like to thank each of them for their candid comments and for their useful suggestions: Dolores Jenerson, California State University, Fullerton; Carole Krauthamer, Trenton State College; James A. Boytim, Dickinson College; Edward Lonky, State University of New York at Oswego; Shalia Frances, Kearney State College; Juanita Collier, Wayne State University; Leslie Fisher, Cleveland State University; Robert Schell, State University of New York at Oswego; Frederic Medway, University of South Carolina; Frank Vitro, Texas Woman's University; Jim Steinberg, Wright State University, Lake Campus; Joan Corell, Westfield State College; Fredda Blanchard-Fields, Louisiana State University; Tim Cavell, Texas A&M University; Jean Ann Linney, University of South Carolina; and Richard Fabes, Arizona State University.

I'd also like to express my appreciation to my editor, Tina Oldham, for her encouragement and her attentiveness to my project. Her assistant, Susan Pierce, and Molly Shepard, photo research editor, also deserve credit for their work in pulling together the artwork.

My special thanks go to Bob Jones, research director for Appalachian State University's BIABH study center and long-time friend, whose creative eye and sensitive heart captured the spirit of the adolescents in many of the photographs in this book. Then, too, I thank Peggy, Marty, Sarah, and Mary for understanding the many times I had to back out at the last minute to meet another deadline—patience is only one of their many virtues.

Finally, I am indebted to my mother and to Steve. Thanks, Mom, for showing me how much you loved me and believed in me that night we saw the Northern Lights together—and time and time and time again. And thank you, Steve, for bringing me to the laughter, the gentleness, and the chutzpa I needed to bring me out from under the shadow of the Cosmic Centipede.

Linda Nielsen

About the Author

Linda Nielsen has written extensively about adolescents and adolescent psychology. Her other publications include *How to Motivate Adolescents: A Guide for Parents, Teachers, and Counselors* (Prentice-Hall, 1982); *Understanding Sex Roles and Moving Beyond* (U.S. Department of Education, 1979), and numerous articles and textbook chapters. A high-school teacher for 5 years and an educational psychologist for 15 years, Dr. Nielsen currently teaches at Wake Forest University and conducts workshops for counselors, parents, and teachers. Her work with public schools and federal research projects has included delinquent, learning-disabled, and unmotivated adolescents. She was the winner of the 1980 author's award from the U.S. Center for Women Scholars and a postdoctoral fellowship in 1981 from the American Association of University Women. She is a member of the American Psychological Association.

Contents

10

Adolescent Sexuality 368

12

Adolescent Moral, Religious, and Political Development 446

13

Adolescents and Drugs 472

1 Adolescence: Theories and Research

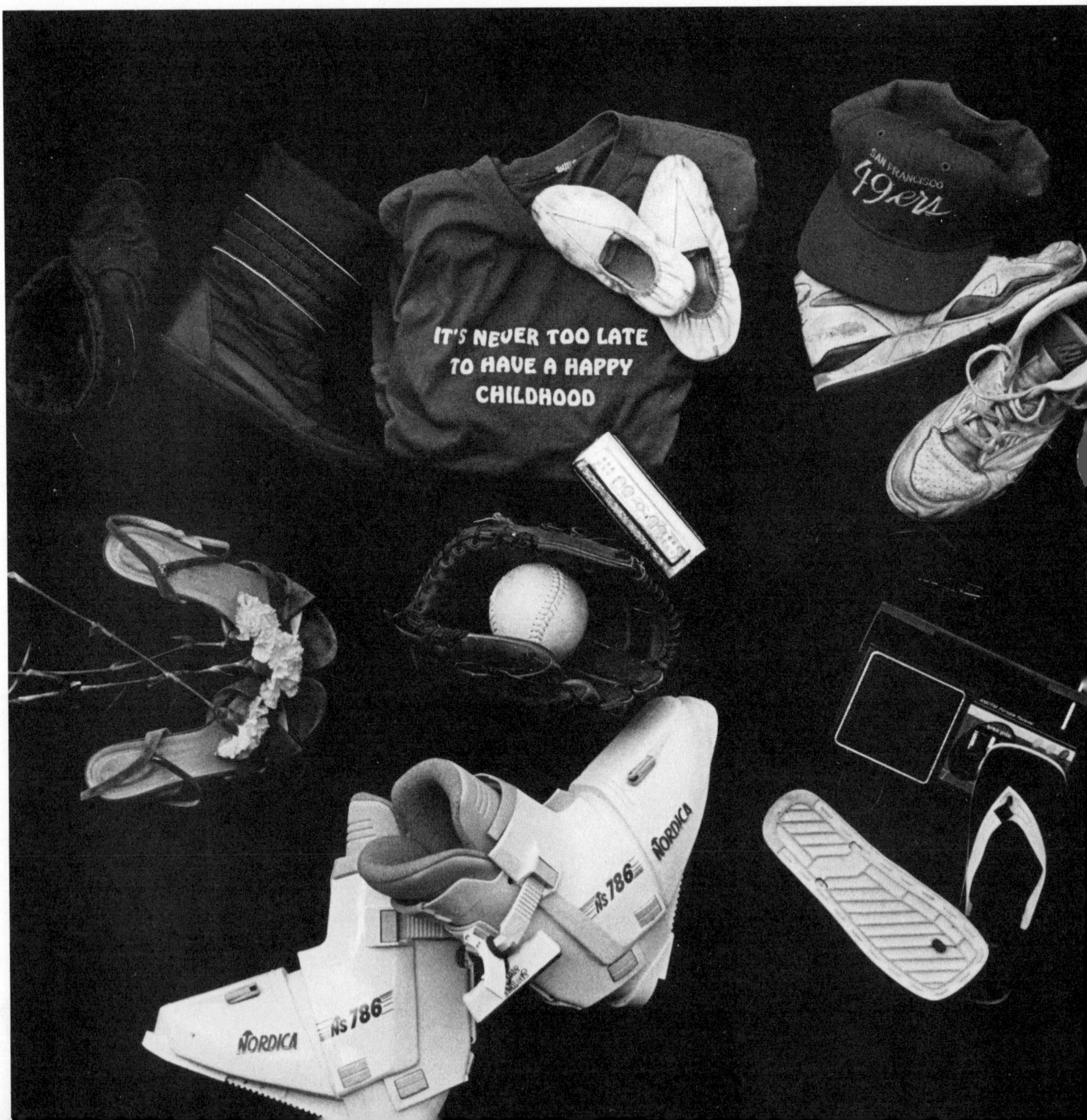

CHAPTER OUTLINE

A HISTORICAL VIEW OF ADOLESCENCE

THEORIES OF ADOLESCENCE

Biological Theories
Sociological and Anthropological Theories
Psychoanalytic Theories
Cognitive-Developmental Theories
Behavioral and Social Learning Theories
A Synthesis of Theories

CONDUCTING RESEARCH ON ADOLESCENCE

Survey Research
Field Research
Correlational Research
Experimental Research
Misinterpreting the Research

CONCLUSION

GOALS AND OBJECTIVES

This chapter is designed to enable you to:

- Discuss the historical development of the concept of adolescence
- Delineate the major differences among the various theoretical perspectives on adolescence
- Enumerate the distinctions between descriptive, experimental, and correlational research
- Explain the benefits of the various types of research designs employed in the study of adolescence
- Identify in various types of research the methodological shortcomings that might lead to misinterpretation of the data regarding adolescents

CONCEPTS AND TERMINOLOGY

aggregate data
behaviorism
biosocial theories
cohort
confounding variable
continuous culture
control group
correlation coefficient
correlational research
cross-sectional studies
dependent variable
discontinuous culture
ecological fallacy
empirical data
environmental theories
experimental group
experimental research
extraneous variable
field research
Freudian theory
independent variable
inverse correlation
longitudinal study
mean
negative correlation
neo-Freudian theories
operant psychology
operational definitions
organismic theories
panel studies
psychoanalytic theory
random sample
representative sample
Skinnerian psychology
social learning theory
stage theories
survey research

"Leave me the hell alone, you old lop-eared heifer!" And so began my relationship with 6-ft, 200-lb Joe Romines, who at the age of 18 indignantly refused my requests for him to complete just one of the exercises on short vowel sounds that I had so proudly designed for the class. As those early winter months passed with Joe and his classmates, I came to understand that "far" was what caused things to burn, that "Jews are people who don't believe in God," and that "using coca-cola after sex will keep you from getting pregnant." I was to be continually perplexed by students like the tow-headed Troy Meyers, who year after year signed up for my reading classes, despite having told me several times to "go to hell" in front of the whole class—but only when he had become frustrated with the "silent *e*'s" or when his stepfather had given him another black eye. How was I to explain to myself why, during his senior year, Troy—who had by then become infamous for his delinquency and encounters with the police—still carried in his wallet a complimentary letter that I had written about him to his mother four years earlier?

Believing that love and empathy were essentially what my adolescent clients and students needed, I spent hours listening to their woeful tales and reassuring them that I cared about their well-being. Yet the impact of my efforts seemed to me both unpredictable and inexplicable, for each time I succeeded in convincing one sexually active student to use contraceptives or in preventing one frustrated student from dropping out of school, I failed in convincing two others. Baffled by the seemingly unpredictable and sometimes serendipitous outcomes of my work with adolescents, I resigned from my teaching and counseling job and embarked on the formal study of psychology, which I hoped would enhance my effectiveness with adolescents.

For personal or vocational reasons of your own, you have decided to undertake a similar journey—one that will begin with our glancing back into the early part of the 20th century, when the concept of adolescence was in its infancy. Without examining the ways in which adolescence, as we now know it, is distinct from adolescence as it has traditionally been perceived, we are unable to appreciate fully the dramatic transformations that have occurred. Moreover, in our quest for a more accurate and more complete understanding of contemporary adolescents, we must examine the five approaches that have traditionally been employed to study and to hypothesize about young people. Although this chapter will present only a brief overview of these theoretical approaches, subsequent chapters will elaborate upon each in detail as it applies to the myriad issues involved in adolescent development.

Finally, our journey into adolescent psychology requires that we equip ourselves with some rudimentary information regarding the manner in which research is conducted. Accordingly, this chapter examines the relative shortcomings and benefits of the various kinds of research employed by the researchers whose findings underlie our present knowledge about adolescents.

Whether you intend to apply the information in this text to your own interactions with adolescents or to achieve greater insight into your own adolescence, it is my hope that the adolescents' own commentaries will lend a special dimension to your understanding of adolescents.

A HISTORICAL VIEW OF ADOLESCENCE

Derived from the Latin verb *adolescere,* adolescence literally means "to grow to maturity." Yet, although the verb from which it is derived is old, the concept of adolescence as we now know it has only recently come into being. The idea of adolescence as a period of life that is somehow distinct from childhood or adulthood did not exist before the 19th century (Demos & Demos, 1979). Indeed, researchers paid relatively little attention to adolescence until recent decades. For example, in the 1950s and 1960s fewer than 2% of the articles published about human behavior included teenagers (L'Abate, 1971).

The leading historian of adolescence, Joseph Kett, explains that our modern perception of adolescence as a distinct period of life has developed only recently in conjunction with changes in our society's educational system and labor market (1977). In the 18th century in the United States, formal schooling was limited almost exclusively to male children from upper-class families, the only members of society who were preparing themselves for professional occupations. Furthermore, since school attendance was not compulsory, young people between the ages of 12 and 17 seldom congregated in groups, which would have enabled them to form a subculture distinct from that of their elders. Indeed, most young people in the past grew up in agricultural communities where age segregation was atypical. Working alongside their elders, children grew into adolescence in a society where one's participation in work did not mark the advent of adulthood, as it does in our present social structure. In contrast to our own highly technical urban environment, in a predominantly agrarian society most adolescents interacted with both younger and older members of the community and passed relatively unobtrusively from their roles as children into their roles as workers and parents.

Although the percentage of teenage people was higher in 1890 than at any other period in our country's history, these 19th-century youths were not perceived as "adolescents" in the contemporary sense. Several factors account for this lack of identification as members of a specific age group. In addition to the ramifications of living in an agricultural society, adolescents developed physically at a later age than today's young people. Pubescence, literally meaning "development of hair," did not occur as early in life as it does today. As Kett commented, "If adolescence is defined as the period after puberty during which a young person is institutionally segregated from casual contacts with a broad range of adults, then it can scarcely be said to have existed at all, even for those young people who attended school beyond age 14" (1977, p. 36).

After the 1860s the period of life now known as adolescence underwent a dramatic redefinition as a consequence of two events: compulsory education and industrialization (Kett, 1977). Between 1852 and 1918 all states enacted compulsory education laws. As a result, although only about a third of the young people

If you had to be an adolescent at any other time in history, which place and period would you choose? Why?

between 14 and 17 were enrolled in school in 1920, enrollment has hovered near 90 percent since 1960. To account for such phenomenal growth in school attendance, it must be noted that the unavailability of jobs during the Great Depression and the fact that our industrialized society needed young workers with more formal education to perform technological jobs encouraged adolescents to remain in school. Once valued for their labor on the family farm, adolescents became less necessary in the labor market as the society became more technologically advanced. The creation of restrictive child-labor laws reflected the country's new attitudes toward adolescents in the labor market. Thus, over time, adolescence was gradually delineated as a period distinct from childhood or adulthood—a period in which the young were assembled in large numbers on a daily basis for a formal education.

Indeed, a recent analysis of journal articles published during periods of economic depression and wartime demonstrates how our society's economy influences theorists' views of adolescents (Enright, Levy, Harris, & Lapsley, 1987). In times of economic depression, theories of adolescence portrayed teenagers as immature, psychologically unstable, and in need of extended education—all of which work to discourage adolescents from entering the labor force. During wartime, however, the journal articles portrayed adolescents as psychologically mature and as less in need of extended formal education. That is, young people were considered ready for the adult responsibilities of wartime service. Simply put, this study reiterates that our supposedly "objective" theories about adolescents can indeed be influenced by our society's prevailing economic or political needs.

Another factor contributing to our evolving views of adolescence is the transformation that has occurred in the size and composition of secondary schools (Elder, 1980). Between the 1930s and the 1960s the average size of a high school more than doubled, increasing from approximately 700 to approximately 1,600 students. The far-ranging implications of this educational phenomenon are addressed in books of the period, such as *The Lonely Crowd* published in 1950, *The Social System of the High School* in 1957, and *The Adolescent Society* in 1961, all of which highlighted the growing importance of the adolescent's peer group and the segregation that had occurred between young and old (Elder, 1980).

Another factor that has focused increasing attention on adolescents was the unparalleled demographic change during the 1960s. Born to parents after the end of World War II, members of the "baby boom" generation reached adolescence during the 1960s. As Figure 1.1 shows, the number of individuals between the ages of 14 and 24 increased by an unprecedented 52% between 1960 and 1970. Not unexpectedly, given their high percentage in the population in comparison to previous decades, adolescents captured the attention of industries and retailers. Members of the business community were eager to sell them the records, cosmetics, clothes, athletic equipment, and other commodities that the young, both increasingly numerous and more affluent, could potentially purchase. Similarly, problems such as drug use, out-of-wedlock pregnancies, delinquency, and political dissent became more apparent as the adolescent population grew dramatically in proportion to the adult population. This proportional increase in relative numbers contributed to both social scientists' interest in and the general public's attention to the needs and behavior of adolescents (Elder, 1980).

By recognizing and appreciating the recent development of the concept of adolescence, we can more fully comprehend the basis for the current confusions and contradictions that appear in the literature. As we shall see, the collection of actual data has lagged behind the development of theories about adolescence. Thus, our views of adolescents have been influenced more by theories than by theoretical descriptions of adolescents' behavior.

THEORIES OF ADOLESCENCE

To get a simplified overview of the theories that we will examine in detail throughout this text, we can examine two basic questions that underscore the theories' different views of adolescence: Do environmental factors or do processes occurring within the adolescent primarily determine adolescent behavior? Is adolescence a stage of life with its own unique characteristics that occurs in a

FIGURE 1.1
Secular trends in population aging and school enrollment

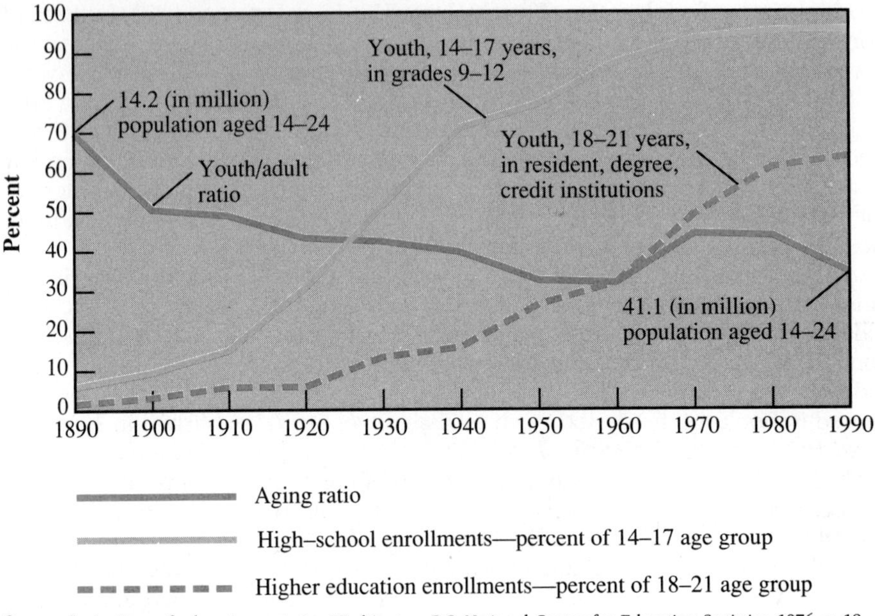

Source: Projections of education statistics. Washington, DC: National Center for Education Statistics, 1976, p. 18.

relatively predictable fashion for all individuals? As Table 1.1 illustrates, theorists and researchers have adopted quite different positions in regard to these two controversial questions.

Organismic theories contend that processes within the individual, not environmental factors, are primarily responsible for human conduct. Organismic theories differ, however, in regard to which internal processes they hold responsible for an adolescent's behavior and attitudes. For this reason, organismic theories can be further categorized as psychoanalytic, biological, or cognitive. Although most organismic theorists would agree that environmental events do exert some influence over our behavior, they argue that cognitive, physiological, or psychological variables within us are in large part responsible for our behavior as children, adolescents, or adults.

In contrast, **environmental theories** contend that factors external to us, such as reinforcement and punishment from other people, are primarily responsible for our behavior. Within the field of psychology, environmental theorists identify themselves as either social learning theorists or behaviorists. Cultural anthropologists and sociologists who study adolescence would also be classified as environmental theorists in that they focus on relationships between an individual's behavior and external factors, such as membership in specific groups or cultures.

A second dimension for categorizing theories is whether their advocates perceive adolescence as a stage of life that has distinct characteristics and occurs in a predictable and universal way for all adolescents. **Stage theories** maintain that

Do these adolescents make you laugh? Which of your own teenage customs and clothes do you now find amusing?

adolescence is one of the many distinct stages in life during which specific types of development occur. Stage theories also contend that there are abrupt changes in our behavior and attitudes from one stage to the next and that our stages can be distinguished from one another on the basis of this unique behavior. Moreover, advocates of this theory contend that we cannot advance to a higher stage without having moved successfully through the previous stages and that some of our most

Table 1.1

Theories of Adolescent Development

	PRIMARY INFLUENCES ON ADOLESCENT BEHAVIOR	SAMPLE RESEARCH QUESTIONS
ORGANISMIC THEORIES Premise: Processes within the adolescent are primarily responsible for his or her behavior and attitudes.		
Biological Theories	Physiological factors—rate of maturation, hormonal levels, inherited abilities, type of diet, exposure of the fetus to chemicals and hormones in the uterus.	How do the increases in testosterone and estrogen at puberty affect adolescent behavior? How does an adolescent's diet affect his or her cognitive performance? How do the hormones to which an individual is exposed while in the mother's womb affect his or her sexual preferences during adolescence?
Anthropological and Sociological Theory	The culture, community, and groups to which adolescents belong	How do different cultures' definitions of adolescence influence the behavior of young people in a society? How do the roles that adolescents assume in large high schools differ from their roles in small high schools?
Psychoanalytic Theories	Psychosexual stages, instincts, unconscious thoughts, defense mechanisms	How do an adolescent girl's sexual feelings about her father affect her later relationships with men? What are the subconscious motives of adolescents who overeat or abuse drugs?

important advancements are made during our adolescence. For example, Erik Erikson's theory stated that we will experience the "crisis" of forming an identity only during our adolescence, not during our adult lives. Stage theorists differ, however, in their perspective—biological or psychoanalytic or cognitive—on the stages of human development. For example, Sigmund Freud, a stage theorist, believed that each stage of our development is related to psychological and sexual issues. In contrast, Jean Piaget, also a stage theorist, contended that our stages of development are determined by our cognitive skills, not by psychosexual issues.

Those who are not stage theorists are said to hold a *continuous developmental*

Table 1.1 *(continued)*

Theories of Adolescent Development

	PRIMARY INFLUENCES ON ADOLESCENT BEHAVIOR	SAMPLE RESEARCH QUESTIONS
ORGANISMIC THEORIES *(continued)*		
Cognitive-Developmental Theories	Cognitive stage of development, specifically the transition from concrete to formal operational thought	What specific mental skills permit adolescents to reason abstractly, unlike younger children? Do adolescents in different cultures develop the same reasoning skills at approximately the same ages?
ENVIRONMENTAL THEORIES Premise: Influences external to the individual are primarily responsible for human behavior and attitudes.		
Behavioral Theory	Reinforcement and punishment from people or experiences in the environment	What types of teacher behaviors help underachievers make the greatest academic gains in school? Is advertising contraceptives on television more effective than sex education programs at school in increasing adolescents' use of contraceptives? What aspects of the family environment discourage adolescents from abusing drugs?
Social Learning Theory	Reinforcement, punishment, modeling, and the individual's cognitive beliefs	How does watching violent television programs affect adolescents' aggressive behavior at school and at home? Which adults do adolescents choose to model themselves after, and how can we encourage adults to develop these traits?

view of human behavior. These theorists see our behavior as a gradual, continuous unfolding, without distinct stages that differ qualitatively from one another. According to this viewpoint, each of us experiences our adolescence somewhat differently in that we do not all undergo predictable "stages" in our development. In addition to undergoing physical changes, we will all change socially, cognitively, and morally, and our development may differ quite considerably. You, for example, may not deal with issues related to your vocational or your religious "identity" until you are in your late 20s. The person sitting next to you, however, may have established his or her identity at the age of 18.

Although no current theory of adolescence denies the influence of organismic or environmental factors, the environmental perspective emphasizes the importance of factors external to the adolescent, while the organismic approach emphasizes the individual's internal processes. The following introduction to the various theories of adolescence will further illuminate these differences.

Biological Theories

According to the biological or **biosocial theories,** adolescent behavior is primarily a consequence of the physiological changes that accompany puberty. An oversimplified, humourous version of this view might be described as the "raging hormones" view of adolescence: Once Mother Nature takes over and changes a person physiologically from a child into an adolescent, the youngster's behavior is in her hands.

Exemplified by the theory of psychologist Stanley Hall (1904), often acclaimed as the "father of adolescence," biological views dominated the field of adolescent psychology during the early part of the century. Strikingly, in his theory of *recapitulation* Hall asserted that our individual development reflects the development of the human species throughout its entire evolution. Just as the earliest human inhabitants of our planet lived in ways that modern society considers primitive or animallike, so do infants and young children behave in animalistic ways.

According to Hall, since children are dominated by instinct and are beyond the bounds of environmental influence, they are in the "animal" stage of development. Later, at the onset of adolescence, an evolutionary mechanism makes it possible for the individual to behave in more sophisticated, although still primitive, ways. Furthermore, as time progresses, their susceptibility to environmental influences makes adolescents more manageable and somewhat more "civilized" than children. During this transitional period from primitive to civilized behavior, Hall assumed, all adolescents experience an extended period of upheaval, rebellion, and suffering. It was through such pronouncements that Stanley Hall established the long-standing assumption that adolescence is inevitably and unalterably a stage of "storm and stress" dictated by nature's physiological control over hormones and physical growth. Although this lacks support by empirical data (see page 20) many people still hold this view of adolescents today.

Despite the criticisms leveled against it, the biological perspective continues to exert its influence on our study of adolescent behavior and to fan the fires of controversy in the ranks of psychoanalytic, cognitive, and behavioristic psychologists. In subsequent chapters the relevance of biosocial perspectives will become clearer in regard to questions such as: Does the age at which a girl starts to menstruate influence her heterosexual behavior? How do adolescents who become physically mature at an early age differ from those who mature later? How do estrogen and testosterone affect male and female behavior? Do delinquents and aggressive youths differ in certain biological respects from their peers? Are the differences in adolescents' IQ scores primarily the consequence of genetic endowment or of environmental influences?

Sociological and Anthropological Theories

Although biological theories dominated the field of adolescent psychology in the early 1900s, their premises were initially challenged and discredited by sociological and anthropological theorists. In contrast to biological approaches, sociological and anthropological approaches stress the importance of cultural influences. Comparing adolescents in different cultures, in different periods of history, and in different socioeconomic situations within a culture has demonstrated the impact that social structures and cultural mores have on adolescents' behavior and attitudes. Some of the earliest illustrations of this view are found in the work of Ruth Benedict, Margaret Mead, and Kingsley Davis.

In his 1940 treatise on the etiology of parent-youth conflicts, the sociologist Kingsley David (1941) argued that modern society changes so rapidly that each new generation experiences a social milieu almost totally distinct from its predecessor. In socializing and interacting with their children, David noted, parents naturally rely upon the experiences relevant to their own generation. Since, however, these experiences are now relatively irrlevant to their children in a more modern society, a certain amount of conflict must inevitably arise between the young and their elders.

From a similar perspective, cultural anthropologist Ruth Benedict (1934) argued that different societies impose on the young their own unique expectations and social roles, which create distinct, not universal, adolescent experiences. According

Margaret Mead 1901–1978

to Benedict, adolescents' behavior primarily reflects whether they are living in a **continuous** or a **discontinuous culture.** In continuous cultures the young are expected to work from childhood throughout adulthood, with a gradual increase in responsibilities with age. There are no dramatic transitions during adolescence and no strict lines of demarcation separating the young and the old in this regard. Furthermore, children are permitted to be dominant over others within their areas of expertise, rather than relegated to positions of submissiveness to all adults, as is the case in discontinuous cultures. In addition, within continuous cultures, children and adolescents are allowed to express their sexuality as they are growing up, rather than being expected to restrict sexual experimentation to their adult years, as is expected in discontinuous cultures. Given these differences, U.S. culture is considered to be more discontinuous than continuous in its tone and expectations.

A contemporary of Benedict, Margaret Mead also acknowledged the culture's role in defining adolescence. In her classic study, *Coming of Age in Samoa,* Mead (1961) noted that Samoan adolescents did not experience the emotional distress associated with their U.S. counterparts. Mead attributed these differences to the fact that Samoans did not expect adolescence to be a critical period for making economic, social, sexual, and vocational decisions. She further noted that Samoans did not present the young with conflicting, hypocritical standards of sexual morality, a practice that creates anxiety and confusion among youths in the United States. The work of Mead and Benedict represents the anthropological perspective that cultural influences, rather than biological or psychological factors, primarily determine adolescent behavior.

As an adjunct to the anthropological perspective, the sociological view of adolescence was ably presented in Hollingshead's *Elmstown's Youth*—a 1949 study of young people in a quiet midwestern town. Hollingshead's focus was on the changing status and new roles associated with physical growth during adolescence. His data showed that adolescence is influenced more by external social forces, such as socioeconomic status, than by biological forces. Hollingshead's research is noteworthy because it was instrumental in helping to change the prevailing view of adolescence as a universal, stressful period controlled by biological forces.

Some time later Robert Havighurst (1952) elaborated on Hollingshead's findings by conducting longitudinal research on children and adolescents from various social classes. Havighurst's results further supported the sociological view: Social class is strongly related to a person's adolescent and adult behavior. Confirming much of the recent data, which will be presented in succeeding chapters, Havighurst found that children from lower income families are more likely to quit school, to behave aggressively, to become delinquent, to marry early, and to experience stress during adolescence than children from wealthier backgrounds.

The sociological and anthropological perspectives espoused by theorists such as Havighurst, Hollingshead, Mead, and Benedict challenge the long-standing notions of adolescence as a period dominated exclusively by biological forces.

Psychoanalytic Theories

Like sociological and anthropological perspectives, the psychoanalytic approach contends that forces other than the physiological changes of puberty are primarily responsible for behavior that distinguishes adolescence from other periods of life (Adelson & Doehrman, 1980). Unlike the environmentalists, however, psychoanalytic theorists attribute adolescents' behavior primarily to internal, psychological struggles related to their achieving independence from their parents. While Sigmund Freud and his daughter Anna are surely the most renowned psychoanalytic theorists, other respected theorists like Peter Blos and Erik Erikson have contributed much to the study of contemporary adolescence (Blos, 1962; Erikson, 1968; Freud, 1953; A. Freud, 1958).

According to the psychoanalytic viewpoint, one can understand an adolescent's behavior only by having a sufficient understanding of that adolescent's personal past. Within this context, behavior that appears to be motivated by environmental factors is often found to be related to the individual's past, with a particular relevance attached to previous interactions within the family. More specifically, the psychoanalytic approach has traditionally maintained that internal drives and

Sigmund Freud 1856–1939

the inevitably resulting psychological conflicts are at the core of adolescent development. Thus, a primary task of adolescence involves controlling the expression of these internal drives that, if unbridled, would result in unacceptable behavior.

In addition to learning to control their instinctual urges, adolescents have the task of overcoming their childhood attachments to parents. According to psychodynamic theory, this process is called "individuation" and is a prerequisite for achieving a healthy adult personality. From the psychodynamic perspective, there must be a shift from reliance on parents to appreciation of peers; hence, the growing importance of the peer group is viewed as a healthy and inevitable aspect of individuation. Indeed, among the most crucial tasks of adolescence are those that involve overcoming sexual and emotional attachments to parents. Furthermore, it is recognized that as a family attempts to come to terms with a youngster's increasing independence, both adolescent and parent will occasionally regress to behavior characteristic of earlier periods in their lives. As a consequence, adolescence can evoke unresolved parent-child conflicts from a parent's own youth.

For both Freud and his followers, referred to as **neo-Freudians,** developing an independent identity is a task delegated to the "ego." Thus, one of the chief contributions of Erik Erikson and James Marcia has been to describe the various stages an adolescent's ego passes through as he or she develops an identity (Erikson, 1968; Marcia, 1980). As conceived by these neo-Freudian psychologists, adolescence is a time for young people to experiment with various ideologies, vocational roles, and social identities. Adolescents who use this period of life for such experimentation and who become individuated from their parents form independent identities. Others, less fortunate, either remain in a state of identity confusion or adopt an identity prematurely. These aspects of ego development will be carefully examined in chapter 4 and chapter 11.

Cognitive-Developmental Theories

Although psychoanalytic and cognitive-developmental theories of adolescence are similar in that they both represent the organismic perspective, their many differences will become apparent in chapters 3 and 4. Most renowned among the cognitive or developmental theorists is Jean Piaget, an eminent scholar whose developmental-stage theory has provided the basis for the work of contemporary researchers such as David Elkind and Lawrence Kohlberg (Piaget, 1971).

As a stage theorist, Piaget contended that adolescence is a qualitatively unique period of life, set apart from childhood by our expanding cognitive abilities. While we are experiencing the joys and lessons of childhood, our abilities to reason abstractly, to develop moral principles on a sophisticated level, and to empathize with others are restricted by our cognitive abilities. During adolescence, however, our cognitive abilities presumably advance from what is known as the "concrete operation" level of reasoning to the more advanced stage known as "formal operational" thought. According to cognitive psychologists, this cognitive advance is responsible for the many new behaviors and attitudes that accompany adolescence: the ability to reason abstractly, to formulate and test hypotheses, to assume the perspective of another person, to recognize incongruities and hypocrisy, to behave less self-consciously, to recognize the motivations underlying other people's behavior, and to appreciate wit and satire.

Jean Piaget 1896–1980

Cognitive-developmental psychologists differ from other theorists in that they emphasize the importance of the cognitive stage in determining an individual's behavior and attitudes. From the cognitive-developmental perspective, it is the adolescent's cognitive stage—not the psychodynamics of the relationship with parents, not the stage of ego development, and not the culture's influences—that exerts the strongest hold over the adolescent's behavior.

Behavioral and Social Learning Theories

Although social learning theorists and behaviorists do not couch their theories in terms of an explicit "theory of adolescence," their principles of learning are both critical and relevant to our understanding of adolescence. As future chapters will demonstrate, the social learning and behavioral psychologists have contributed many of the most pragmatic and most successful strategies for therapists, teachers, and parents who relate to adolescents. Having critiqued the literature on child and adolescent development, Robert Muuss (1975) concluded that social learning theorists are responsible for some of the most influential research in the field.

Behaviorism, or **Skinnerian psychology,** includes both the radical behavioral theory, generated by the controversial psychologist B. F. Skinner, and modifications of the behavioral perspective known as **social learning theories,** exemplified by researchers such as Walter Mischel and Albert Bandura. From Skinner's strictly behavioristic approach, human behavior and attitudes depend primarily on the reinforcement and the punishment that an individual receives from other people or from actual consequences of experiences in the environment (Skinner, 1953). Within this context, the adolescent's behavior and attitudes are not attributed to internal processes, such as Piaget's cognitive stage, Erikson's stages of ego development, or Freud's notions about the id, ego, and superego. Instead, according to Skinnerian psychologists, the attitudes and actions of people at all ages are primarily determined by the positive or negative consequences that follow their behavior in particular types of situations. From the Skinnerian perspective, conduct or attitudes that are rewarded are likely to be repeated, and those that are punished or ignored are unlikely to be repeated.

Expanding upon these behavioristic or Skinnerian views, social learning theorists contend that our behavior is also influenced by the models—both live and vicarious—we observe in our daily activities. For example, some research shows that children who are exposed to violent television programs behave more aggressively thereafter than those exposed to nonviolent programs (Mischel, 1981). Social learning theorists acknowledge, however, that internal factors, such as our expectations and selective perceptions, interact with our rewards, punishments, and modeling. Hence, predicting any single adolescent's behavior in a particular situation is a difficult, if not impossible, task.

Despite these distinctions between Skinnerian and social learning theorists, both focus on the environmental influences that shape adolescents' behavior. As future chapters will demonstrate, the social learning and behavioral approaches have proved themselves to be the most empirical of all adolescent theories in terms of being able to provide operational definitions, testable hypotheses, and replicable results. Nevertheless, you will see that these theories are not without their critics.

A Synthesis of Theories

During recent decades the life-span approach to human development has become increasingly popular (Baltes & Reese, 1984). Rather than viewing change as a characteristic solely of childhood and adolescence, life-span theorists consider change an inevitable process that occurs throughout adult life as well. Therefore, some life-span theorists are suggesting that the theories applicable to understanding behavior during one period of our lives may be relatively less important for understanding behavior in another period. For example, biological theories may be more applicable to explaining behavior during infancy and childhood than to explaining the behavior of adolescents or adults.

Taking advantage of the merits of each of the theoretical theories, researchers are increasingly using a multivariate approach to the study of human behavior.

The multivariate approach integrates biological, psychological, social, and cultural variables into the study of adolescents' behavior and attitudes. For example, projects are now under way that assess the relationship between daily fluctuations in adolescents' hormone levels and their social behavior in school and at home (Nottelmann et al., 1986). Similarly, cross-cultural research is examining adolescents' rates of physical maturation, their cognitive development, and each society's methods for transmitting adult skills to its young (Burbank, 1988).

Demanding a greater collaboration between the disciplines of medicine, sociology, psychology, biology, and anthropology, the multivariate approach also encourages the use of cross-cultural data. Although rare, multidisciplinary, cross-cultural studies of adolescents are in progress. As data from multivariate projects such as these accumulate, we will be afforded a unique view of adolescence that incorporates biological, environmental, and organismic perspectives of human development.

CONDUCTING RESEARCH ON ADOLESCENCE

Whether you ultimately adopt the perspective of psychoanalytic, biosocial, or behavioristic theorists, you will most likely find yourself frustrated, at various points throughout this text, by the discrepancies between the conclusions of various research studies. For instance, you will encounter a convincing study that persuades you of the merits of high-school sex education programs, but in the very next paragraph, your head will be turned by an equally impressive study that concludes that sex education has virtually no bearing on adolescents' attitudes or behavior. Why? With our sophisticated statistics and computerized methods for conducting research, why can we authors and researchers not offer you straightforward, unequivocal answers—at least to those questions that we have studied so diligently, such as delinquency and teenage pregnancy?

Part of the answer, as we have already seen in our discussion of theories, is that psychologists, anthropologists, biologists, and sociologists are each approaching the study of adolescence from a different perspective. Their focus of attention, the questions they are pursuing, and their methods for conducting research differ. Each is pursuing "truth," but usually each is asking a different set of questions. To paraphrase an old story, if both of us are blindfolded and you are holding the elephant's leg while I hold its trunk, we are going to form different hypotheses about the creature—even though each of us, in a manner of speaking, has truth and fact and logic on our side, neither of us has *the* truth. As our research methods become more refined, we are "capturing more truths" about adolescence. If, however, you expect this book—or other sources of research information—to offer you *the* truth about a particular issue regarding adolescents, you are more apt to be disappointed than not.

One reason for your disappointment may be your inclination to reduce complex social phenomena and complex human behavior to a single cause. This tendency, which also victimizes researchers and authors, is known as reductionism. A common example of reductionism is to use data from individuals to explain the behavior of entire groups. For example, if today's adolescents use more drugs and watch more television than their counterparts in the 1950s, you could try to reduce the complex problem of drug abuse to television viewing. Yet complex phenomena, such as drug abuse and delinquency, cannot be reduced to the effect of an individual attribute, such as low self-esteem or poverty.

Your frustration with the contradictory or ambiguous findings in the research on adolescence may also be related to your confusion about how research is conducted. Each of the research strategies described in the next section is scientific in that each is trying to formulate hypotheses and to collect and interpret observable data, rather than to rely on abstract concepts that cannot be tested by a scientific method. Social scientists, in other words, try to use **empirical data,** meaning that they base their conclusions on observable, replicable evidence. Yet what they observe must be clearly defined and precisely measured—neither of which is any simple feat when the subjects are human beings rather than cells under a microscope.

Indeed, much of the confusion in our research on adolescence stems from the difficulties involved in agreeing on our definitions for particular concepts. For example, what comes to mind when you hear the term "aggressive" youth? Do you envision a knife-wielding boy? a girl who bad-mouths her teachers? a youngster who refuses to obey his parents' household rules? Once you have clearly defined the term, how will you measure a youth's aggressiveness—by a written test administered to the youngster? reports from the parents? observations of the child's behavior in math class? reports from the school principal?

As social science research has become more sophisticated, we have attempted to define and to measure our concepts more specifically. That is, we try to provide operational definitions for ambiguous concepts, such as "aggressive," "middle class," "underachiever." An **operational definition** is one that specifies ways of measuring a concept so that other observers can replicate the measurements. For example, what empirical observations could we make in order to study the "underachiever"? We might operationally define "underachiever" as someone whose grades do not coincide with his or her IQ scores, or we might choose another operational definition by counting the number of incomplete homework assignments and days absent from school.

The point is that since researchers often use different operational definitions for the same concepts, the results of their studies can contradict one another. Thus, one researcher may conclude that academic underachievers did not profit from a special tutoring program, whereas another researcher may find that underachievers profited immensely from tutoring. To understand this contradiction, you would need to know how each researcher operationally defined the terms "tutoring," "underachievement," and "improvement."

By the time you finish this text, you will probably appreciate that there is never a simple way of collecting raw "facts" and compiling them "objectively" into a "finding." In this spirit, the information in the following sections is intended to help you feel less frustrated by the contradictions in our research by introducing you to the various kinds of research that are taking hold of the "trunks and legs" of adolescence: survey research, field research, correlational research, and experimental research.

Survey Research

Survey research describes the attitudes and behaviors of adolescents by selecting a representative sample of young people and collecting their responses to a specific set of questions. One of the larger scale surveys of adolescents was undertaken by James Coleman to determine whether public or private high schools were more successful in educating adolescents (Coleman, Hoffer & Kolgore, 1982).

Using a representative sample of nearly 60,000 students, the extensive surveys concluded that public schools did not live up to their image as environments where a wide mix of students become more similar in their talents over time—results that we will explore in greater detail in chapter 7. Following the old adage that "if you want to know something, ask," survey research uses specific questions about their behavior and attitudes to get adolescents to describe themselves.

One of the most obvious limitations of survey research is its reliance on the honesty of the respondents. Particularly in cases where adolescents may feel there is a socially "correct" response, their answer may not accurately reflect their actual behavior or attitudes. For example, adolescents who have never had sexual intercourse and those who have racist attitudes may both respond less than candidly to the surveyor's questions, fearing, in the first case, that it is unacceptable to be a virgin and, in the second, that it is unacceptable to admit openly to racist attitudes. Moreover, the surveyor's questions must be designed to make precise and accurate assessments. Finally, in cases where surveys are conducted through personal interviews or through telephone conversations, the interviewer must be skillful enough to elicit honest and complete responses.

Field Research

Some social scientists contend that the most meaningful way to study human behavior is to become a participant in a particular social setting. Such **field research** attempts to explain how an entire social unit operates on its own terms. In this pursuit, most field researchers have to immerse themselves personally in the day-to-day life of a specific social unit, trying to keep their presence from altering the environment or the people being observed. In a recent study, for example, researchers observed adolescents interacting in a summer camp. As the author himself commented, "I make no claim that the participating adolescents are normal or representative of anything. There is no reliance on new methodological ploys; rather, psychology's most basic procedure, observations of behavior, is used" (Savin-Williams, 1987, p. viii).

Field studies often read much like novels in that they describe individuals and their environments in detail, without the researchers' attempting to impose a specific set of predetermined questions on their subjects. Rather than entering the setting with specific questions, the field researchers usually begin with a few general questions and then let the experiences in the natural setting direct the course of research. Moreover, talented field researchers must be able to gain the confidence of their subjects in order to elicit their candid responses and to observe their natural behavior.

Like survey research, field research is not without its critics. Field researchers are open to the charge that the situations they have chosen to observe are not representative of the environment and individuals they are trying to portray. For example, a critic might ask field researchers how they know whether adolescents they are observing at the local hamburger hangout are characteristic of other adolescents. In response, field researchers claim that their primary purpose is more to explore the intricacies of a particular situation than to generalize their observations. Despite its shortcomings, however, field research does present a sensitive, detailed view of individuals' feelings and personal lives. In this spirit, most of the information in the "Adolescent Voices" boxes throughout this text is a form of field research intended to provide intimate glimpses of individual adolescents.

Correlational Research

Correlational research extends beyond field research in that it attempts to draw conclusions about the relationship between two or more variables in the adolescent's life. Although a correlational study often employs written surveys to gather data from the subjects, statistical procedures are applied to the surveys in order to determine how two variables are related to one another. For example, you might pursue these questions with correlational statistics: How is an adolescent's socioeconomic status related to his or her grades in school? How is smoking cigarettes correlated with adolescents' drinking alcohol, having friends who smoke, and having parents who smoke? What is the relationship between the age at which an adolescent girl begins to menstruate and the age at which she first has sexual intercourse? Each of these questions is trying to establish whether a relationship exists between two or more variables.

In determining whether there is a significant relationship between the variables, correlational statistics yield a number called a **correlation coefficient.** The coefficient is a number ranging from .01 to 1.00 and is accompanied by either a positive (+) or a negative (−) sign. The further the coefficient is from .0, the stronger the relationship between the variables. That is, if a correlation coefficient of +.80 is obtained between adolescents' smoking and their parents' smoking and a coefficient of +.20 is found between adolescents' smoking and their friends' smoking, we would conclude that the relationship between parents' and adolescents' smoking is stronger than that between adolescents and their friends. The closer the correlation is to −1.00 or to +1.00, the more confident we can be that a strong relationship exists between the variables.

A negative sign in front of the coefficient indicates that the variables are **inversely** or **negatively correlated.** In other words, an increase in one variable is related to a decrease in the other. As is the case with a positive correlation, the closer to the whole number, in this case a −1.00, the stronger the correlation between the variables. Thus, a coefficient of −.85 between church attendance and socioeconomic status would indicate a strong, but inverse, correlation meaning that as income increases, church attendance decreases.

The major limitation of correlation research is that the results cannot be used to establish causality. Correlational studies do not imply that one factor has "caused" the other to increase or decrease. For instance, if you found a correlation of −.98 between an adolescent's grades and the number of cigarettes he or she smoked each day, you would be committing a heinous error to conclude that cigarette smoking causes poor grades. All that you could reasonably conclude is that smoking is inversely related to good grades. Further investigation might show that the heavy smokers are also those whose parents have the least education, who get the least sleep every night, and whose self-confidence is lowest—any of which might affect a person's academic performance. Deciding which of these variables might be causing poor grades is the goal of experimental research.

Experimental Research

Unlike correlational research, **experimental research** attempts to establish causality. That is, experimental research tries to establish that a cause and effect exists between specific variables in the adolescent's life and his or her feelings and behavior. To prove causality, an experimental study must arrange conditions in such a way that the people being studied, called the **experimental group,** are subjected to a specific treatment without being influenced by other variables outside the experiment that might influence their behavior or attitudes. The behavior or attitudes being measured are referred to as the **dependent variables.** The variables that the experimenter believes might be influencing these dependent variables are referred to as the **independent variables.**

In well-designed experimental studies, the experimental group's reactions are compared to the reactions of another group, called the **control group,** whose members are not exposed to any treatment but who are similar to the subjects in all other regards. Since the control group and the experimental group are selected on the basis of their being similar, they should both respond in similar ways to a researcher's questions or observations. As a consequence, when we manipulate certain variables with our experimental group while leaving our control group untouched, we are able to determine whether our independent variables are actually causing changes in our subjects. Without a control group, we have no way of determining whether factors other than our independent variables are influencing our subjects. The other "outside" variables that could confuse or confound the results of an experiment are called the **confounding variables** or **extraneous variables.**

To demonstrate the experimental method, let's assume you want to see whether adolescents' attitudes about using drugs can be changed by exposing them to a 6-week drug education program (your independent variable). First, you select a representative sample of 200 students from a local high school, randomly assigning 100 of them to the 6-week program (your experimental group) and the other 100 to your control group. Before your drug program begins, you administer a 20-item test (your dependent variable) to all 200 students to assess their attitudes toward drugs. Once your drug program is completed, you will administer the test again to both groups to determine whether your independent variable had any impact on your dependent variable. Tragically, during the third week of your study, one of the school's most popular students dies from a drug overdose. Many of the students in your experimental group and in your control group are overwrought by the tragedy. At this point in your experiment, the student's tragic death becomes an extraneous variable that could have a sizable impact on your experimental group's attitudes toward drug use. Since your control group and your experimental group have both been exposed to this extraneous variable, however, your experiment is not ruined. You can still determine how much impact your drug program will have on students' attitudes. At the end of your experiment, you will use statistical formulas to compare the test scores of the control group with those of the experimental group. Although the student's death might have influenced all the subjects in your study, if your experimental group's scores have improved more than the control group's, you can still claim that your independent variable (the drug program) was responsible for the improvement, since both groups were exposed to the same extraneous variables.

Misinterpreting the Research

Whether our information about adolescents is derived from experimental, correlational, or survey research, a number of shortcomings exist that make some studies far more trustworthy than others. Unfortunately, too many of us base our

Table 1.2

Methods for Studying Adolescence

ADVANTAGES	DISADVANTAGES
Survey Research (Interviews and Questionnaires)	
Relatively easy and quick. Provides information from large samples. Can elicit detailed responses from subjects.	Dishonest responses from subjects. Poorly constructed or vague questions. Requires skilled interviewers.
Field Studies	
Personal, detailed descriptions of individuals. In-depth information about people in their natural environment.	Subjects may not behave naturally when being observed. Situations may not be representative and results not generalizable. Researcher must be a skilled observer and recorder.
Correlational Studies	
Establishes the degree of relationship between variables. Provides clues for further experimental research. Can be used to predict future behavior or performance.	Too easily misinterpreted as cause-and-effect studies.
Experimental Studies	
Identifies cause-and-effect patterns.	Uses group averages and therefore overlooks individual change. Can distort results through improper use of statistics. Time-consuming and complicated in trying to control for extraneous variables.
Longitudinal Studies	
Demonstrates changes in people over time. Identifies societal trends. Controls extraneous variables and cohort effects better than cross-sectional studies do.	Does not control for extraneous variables as well as experimental studies do. More time-consuming and complicated than cross-sectional research.

assumptions about adolescents on studies riddled with methodological problems. We thus fall victim to what has playfully been termed the "Whoozle" effect (Gelles, 1980). The Whoozle effect occurs when a study's conclusions are repeatedly cited by researchers and practitioners without considering its limitations and without trying to replicate its findings. As a consequence, over the years the study's conclusions are passed along as "facts," while its methodological errors continue to be ignored and, ultimately, forgotten.

How are you most likely to be "whoozled" by the research on adolescence? Among the most common mistakes we make in trying to understand the research are ignoring the limitations of the hypothesis-testing procedure, generalizing from nonrandom samples, misinterpreting correlational data, and misconstruing the results of longitudinal and cross-sectional research (Baker, 1988; Kupfersmid, 1988).

Limitations of hypothesis testing Most data that are collected are subjected to the hypothesis-testing procedure. In this procedure, the researcher formulates a hypothesis that states that no difference exists between groups or variables. A hypothesis stated in this form is called a "null hypothesis." Statistical formulas are then applied to the data in order to determine whether to accept or to reject the null hypothesis. Significance testing involves selecting a level of probability, or a level of significance (p value), to determine how improbable an event could be under the null hypothesis. If the data collected from the various groups are different enough from one another, the statistical formula will show that the results are statistically "significant." If this is the case, the null hypothesis is rejected, showing that there is a difference between the groups. If, however, the data from each group do not differ enough from one another, the results will fail to reach "levels of significance" and the null hypothesis will be accepted. This is what is meant by achieving or failing to achieve statistical significance.

Although the hypothesis-testing procedure is utilized in almost all published studies on adolescence, what is significant statistically and what is significant in a practical sense may be contradictory. Why? First, since small samples require a greater disparity between groups in order to reach the same level of significance as large samples, studies with large sample sizes are more likely to achieve "significant" findings than those with smaller samples. That is, when you read that a study involving 20,000 adolescents found girls to be "significantly" more promiscuous than boys, the results may actually be less trustworthy than those of a study that found no significant differences between the sexual behavior of only 50 girls and boys. Unfortunately, studies with large sample sizes often lead readers to place a greater confidence in their results and researchers to believe they have made a startling discovery when, indeed, they have not (Kupfersmid, 1988).

A second limitation of the hypothesis-testing procedure is its exclusive reliance on group data; the group **mean** or mathematical average. Statistical equations combine each individual's data with the data of all other individuals in the group in determining whether the null hypothesis should be accepted or rejected. Data that sum everyone's data together as a group are referred to as **aggregate data.** The disadvantage of using aggregate data is that useful information about any one individual is lost in the statistical analysis—a loss of information that is of utmost importance to practitioners working with individual adolescents (Barlow, Hays, and Nelson, 1984).

For example, let's assume that the school board is trying to decide whether to invest $4,000 dollars to purchase a series of anti-smoking films. In trying to reach a decision, the board members compare the mean [average] number of cigarettes smoked by 100 students before viewing the films to the average number of cigarettes these students smoke after the film series ends. Although the statistical tests may show that there were no significant differences between the average number of cigarettes smoked before and after the film series, 15 of the 100 students may actually have quit smoking. Consequently, the school board saves $4,000 by accepting the null hypothesis, but the fact is lost that the films were effective in helping 15 students quit smoking. Here again, "practical significance" and "statistical significance" may be at odds. For these reasons, some argue that statistical significance testing should be replaced by measures that will show changes in the individual's behavior (Jacobson, Follette, & Revenstorf, 1984).

A final problem related to hypothesis testing is that a bias exists among most editors and reviewers toward publishing studies that reject the null hypothesis.

Because reputations are often associated with publication records and therefore researchers might feel the need to write what is more likely to be printed, published articles do not portray adolescence as accurately as if studies were published on the basis of sound methodology, rather than on the basis of their finding significant differences (Kupfersmid, 1988). This means that you, the general public, and other researchers are more likely to encounter articles that report differences between groups of adolescents than to encounter those showing no differences.

Generalizing from random samples In addition to overlooking the limitations of hypothesis testing, we are often apt to generalize the results from a single study inappropriately. In attempting to apply the results from a particular study to adolescents who were not in the study itself, we must first note the characteristics of the subjects in the researcher's sample. A **representative** or a **random sample** is one whose characteristics, such as age, socioeconomic status, race, and gender, are similar to the characteristics of the group to whom we are generalizing the study's results. Unfortunately, our generalizations about adolescents are often predicated upon information from nonrepresentative groups. For example, as chapters 5 and 6 will demonstrate, most of our information about adolescents is derived from studies whose samples did not include female or minority subjects.

Misinterpreting correlational data Another way in which research can dupe you is by construing correlational data as if they were the results of experimental studies. Although people often incorrectly assume that correlational data establish cause and effect, this is a gross misuse of correlational statistics. Only experimental studies can establish causality, and even then, the study must be designed in such a way that the confounding variables are reduced.

For example, assume you want to determine whether sex education programs "cause" sexually active youths to make better use of contraceptives. Going to the school records, you randomly select 100 students who have had sex education classes and 100 students who have not yet attended the classes. Then you administer an anonymous survey to all 200 students to determine how often those who are sexually active use contraceptives. Using correlational statistics, you find a +.86 correlation between frequency of contraceptive use and participation in sex education. Have you proved that sex education "causes" adolescents to use contraceptives more effectively? No. Why? Because, in order to demonstate causality, you would have to design an experimental study. One example of such an experimental study would require you to collect data from a control group and compare their contraceptive use to that of the students who have taken a sex education course, measuring both groups before and after the course.

The mistake often made in interpreting correlational data is to base your conclusions on an ecological fallacy. An **ecological fallacy** is the drawing of conclusions from aggregated (group) data and trying to apply them to an individual or to a smaller unit. For example, assume you have the high-school dropout rates and the per capita incomes of 10 states, and you note that those states with the higher dropout rates also have higher per capita incomes. You would be committing an ecological fallacy if you concluded that rich people are more likely to drop out of school than poor people, since you do not have information about the individual incomes of people who dropped out of school. In this particular case, it might well be that poor people in the richest states are the most likely to drop out of school.

Misconstruing developmental research We encounter a different type of research error when we try to identify changes in people's attitudes or behavior across a period of time. Given that adolescence is a time during which many changes are assumed to occur, researchers are particularly interested in studying the ways in which aging affects our behavior and attitudes between childhood and our adult years. In our attempts to examine the impact of time, we rely primarily on two types of research designs: cross-sectional studies and longitudinal studies. In **cross-sectional studies,** researchers gather data at a single point in time and then make comparisons between groups. For example, suppose you want to know whether aging affects adolescents' cigarette smoking habits: Do adolescents become more opposed to cigarette smoking as they age? If you are like many other researchers, you may not have the time, circumstances, or wherewithal to wait several years for one group of young adolescents to age. Instead, you might administer a "smoking habits and attitudes" questionnaire to a group of high-school freshmen and to another group of high-school seniors. In analyzing the results from each group, you might find that the seniors have more negative attitudes toward smoking and smoke less than the freshmen. You might then be tempted to interpret your results to mean that as adolescents age, they become more negative about smoking and less likely to smoke. In reaching this conclusion, however, you have overlooked an important shortcoming of cross-sectional research: Because you have measured two different groups of teenagers, you cannot be certain that the passage of time is the only difference between them. In other words, the two groups may be different in ways besides their age. For example, how do you know whether the seniors in your study were actually more opposed to cigarette smoking when they were freshmen than they are now as seniors? Perhaps they are even smoking more now than when they were freshmen, even though they are more opposed to smoking than the group of freshmen you measured. The point is that in cross-sectional research we are comparing groups who may be different in significant ways other than age, yet we are running the risk of attributing their differences only to age.

The obvious way to overcome this shortcoming is to take **cohorts;** a group all approximately the same age, measure their behavior or attitudes now, and then measure them again in the future by asking the same questions or making the same observations. This approach, called a **longitudinal study,** or a **panel study,** enables us to measure the same subjects over a period of time. Understandably, longitudinal research is rare because it is more complicated, more time-consuming, and more expensive than cross-sectional research, since the researcher has to keep track of the same individuals over a period of months or years. It is, however, one of the most effective ways to measure change, and for your purposes in interpreting research accurately, you should be mindful of the superiority of panel research in contrast to cohort and trend studies.

CONCLUSION

Having begun this chapter with an explanation of the reasons underlying my initial involvement in adolescent psychology, let me now conclude with similar tales regarding the role of empirical research and theory. Convinced that a knowledge of the empirical data and theory would enhance my relationships with adolescents, I embarked on my studies, as do all graduate students, with the intent of being both scholarly and open-minded. While I enthusiastically spent the next several years in school, becoming more familiar with the empirical data on adolescence, I remained totally oblivious to the fact that I was committing several fundamental errors—errors that, in my years of college teaching, I have observed repeatedly in the comments and in the writing of my own graduate and undergraduate students.

First, in failing to apply my knowledge of research and statistics consistently as a graduate student, I inadvertently presumed that the results of most studies in prestigious journals deserved equal merit and equal consideration. I attended too little to what seemed to me at the time the less significant "details" of a study, such as the research design and the representativeness of the sample. In this regard, therefore, I have tried within this text to devote additional attention to those studies that are most compelling and noteworthy in terms of their methodology. However, given my desire to acquaint you with as much research as possible and my decision to emphasize the practical applications of the empirical and theoretical data, you are inevitably left with the responsibility for independently evaluating many of the studies cited throughout the remaining chapters. I hope that you will continue to draw upon the information in this first chapter as you embark upon your independent evaluation of the research.

Given the independence you have now been accorded, my second shortcoming as a former student will perhaps appear all the more relevant. Having spent several years teaching and counseling adolescents, I was naively confident that my personal experiences were the nexus for my understanding of adolescents. While still able to join other graduate students in academic debates over the relative merits of various theories and empirical studies, I nonetheless tended to discount, to deemphasize, or to discredit data that contradicted either my own experiences as an adolescent or my own interactions with adolescents as a teacher and counselor. In other words, I found it difficult to put aside the "fact" that the earth is flat because that is exactly how it appeared from my window and to accept the "fact" offered by satellites and navigators that the earth is pear-shaped.

As evidenced by my scores on written exams, I could on an abstract and intellectual level examine data and theories that contradicted or were not part of my personal experiences. I continued to gravitate, however, toward data that supported my own preconceived views of adolescents. My first method of discounting data that contradicted my personal feelings, convictions, and ideologies was to compare the data to my own personal experience: "Well, I never knew an adolescent who felt that way"; "Nobody I ever knew behaved like that"; "I really don't think things could be that bad on the basis of what I've seen and heard." Although such comparisons were not, in and of themselves, reprehensible or illogical, I had grossly inflated the validity of convictions derived exclusively from firsthand experiences—convictions based upon my having taught fewer than 2,000 of the 22 million adolescents in the United States—notions based on working with adolescents from only two racial groups in one region of a very large country—views based on my own life as an adolescent whose socioeconomic background alone gave her little in common with most of the country's youths.

My second method for discounting data that failed to support my views was considerably more sophisticated than the first. Armed with the knowledge of statistics and research that supposedly ensured objectivity, I would subject certain studies to far more thorough scrutiny than others. Although honestly unaware of my behavior at the time, I nonetheless imposed stricter standards of scholarship in evaluating the studies whose conclusions were in least accord with my own.

Unfortunately, it was inevitably easier for me to recognize the methodological shortcomings and to question the underlying premises of data or theory that contradicted my visions of adolescence or of related social issues. Depite my best intentions, I seldom approached the various studies with equal objectivity, equal willingness to scrutinize the results, and equal proclivity to lay aside my own feelings about the matter at hand.

Although I was once convinced that my own behavior as a student of adolescent psychology was atypical, my years as a college teacher have persuaded me that both my cohorts and my students share—to greater or lesser degrees—my own difficulties in regard to encountering empirical data. Moreover, I continue to struggle against the inadvertent oversights, the ethnocentricity, the lack of objectivity, or the overreliance on the validity of my personal experiences. It is my hope that in reading this text you will encounter theories and empirical data that will arouse discomfort, surprise, and, on occasion, anger. It is my further hope that, when such feelings arise, you will accept the challenge of scrutinizing data that confirm your own experiences and convictions as carefully as data that dispute them.

QUESTIONS FOR DISCUSSION AND REVIEW

Basic Concepts and Terminology

1. How has the concept of adolescence developed historically?
2. In what major ways do the biological, sociological, psychoanalytic, cognitive, and behavioral theories differ with regard to adolescence?
3. How do organismic and environmental theories of adolescence differ? What, if anything, do they share in common?
4. What are the limitations and the advantages of survey research, field research, correlational research, and experimental research?
5. How do correlational, and experimental studies differ in terms of their purpose, limitations, and relevance to the study of adolescence? Which kinds of research questions can each legitimately answer?
6. Give a specific example and definition of each of the terms listed in the overview of this chapter. Then explain why each needs consideration in our study of adolescence.
7. How are stage theories distinct from environmental theories?
8. Considering both their sign and their numerical value, how are correlation coefficients to be interpreted?
9. What are the possible limitations of the hypothesis testing procedure?
10. Give an example of how each of the following might cause someone to misinterpret the data regarding adolescence: nonrepresentative samples, reductionism, ecological fallacy, correlational data, confounding variables.

Questions for Discussion and Debate

1. How relevant is Havighurst's description of developmental tasks for today's adolescents? What are the potential consequences associated with failing to complete each of these developmental tasks during adolescence?
2. Which theoretical perspective do you feel most adequately explains your own adolescent development? Least adequately? Why?
3. Forced to align yourself with only one of the five theoretical perspectives on adolescence, which would you choose? Why?
4. How would you design the best possible correlational study and the most convincing experimental study to answer a question of your choice regarding adolescents' behavior? Consider the importance of your research design and the presence of confounding variables in each of your studies.

5. Find a correlational study and an experimental study in a recent journal on adolescence and discuss the merits and limitations of each.
6. Given the information on conducting research, how have you formerly misinterpreted data relevant to the study of adolescent behavior?
7. Given the fact that the meaning of adolescence differs from culture to culture, what changes would you recommend be made with regard to our own culture's expectation of adolescents?
8. Is the concept of adolescence still evolving? What constancies might remain by the year 2050?
9. What significant aspects of adolescence have not been addressed by any of the theories to date?
10. Why have you embarked upon this study of adolescent psychology? What experiences in your past and present influenced your decision? What do you hope to have gained as a consequence of completing this course? What kinds of interactions with your fellow students or your professor might help you achieve these goals?

GLOSSARY

aggregate data The summing of each person's data together to form group averages.

behaviorism A school of psychology that examines only observable behavior and that believes our personalities and attitudes are primarily determined by how we are rewarded and punished.

biosocial theories Beliefs that human behavior is determined by biological influences, such as genes and hormones.

cohort A person who has experienced the same events during the same interval of time as another person; generally refers to people born at about the same time.

confounding variable Factor other than the experimental treatment that might account for changes in the subject's attitudes or behavior.

continuous culture A society in which children move gradually from childhood to adulthood without defined periods such as adolescence being marked along the way.

control group The group of people who are not exposed to any treatment in an experiment.

correlation coefficient The number that indicates the strength of the relationship between two variables in correlational studies.

correlational research Studies comparing the strength of the relationship between two or more variables but not able to determine cause and effect.

cross-sectional studies A way of designing research in which subjects from two or more age groups are measured at the same point in time on the same dependent variables.

dependent variable The variable that changes as a consequence of the treatment being administered by the experimenter.

discontinuous culture A society, like the United States, in which childhood, adolescence, and adulthood are clearly delineated in terms of roles and responsibilities for each age group.

ecological fallacy Drawing conclusions from group data and trying to apply them to an individual or to a smaller group.

empirical data Data that can be confirmed by experiments or gathered in surveys.

environmental theories Theories contending that factors external to the individual are primarily responsible for human behavior.

experimental group The people who are subjected to a specific treatment in an experiment.

experimental research Studies that are designed in such a way that cause and effect can be examined.

extraneous variable *See* confounding variable.

field research Studies in which the researcher observes and describes the behavior of a group in its natural social environment.

Freudian theory Theory contending that human behavior is primarily determined by childhood conflicts, primarily sexual in nature, within the family.

independent variable A factor that remains constant throughout a study, such as the subject's gender or race.

inverse correlation A relationship in which as one factor increases, the other decreases.

longitudinal study Research in which people from the same cohort group are measured on the same dependent variables over a period of time.

mean The mathematical average. Example: 10 is the mean of the numbers 12, 2, 13, 8, and 15.

median The number that divides a group of scores in half, with half the scores falling above the median and half falling below the median. Example: 10 is the median for the numbers 12, 2, 8, 15.

neo-Freudian Freudian theories that deviate from Freud's original ideas in that they place less emphasis on early childhood and unconscious sexual conflicts as the explanations for human behavior.

negative correlation A relationship in which an increase in one variable is related to a decrease in the other variable.

operant psychology *See* behaviorism.

operational definitions Concepts that are defined in terms of specific, observable behavior, rather than in terms of abstractions that cannot be specifically measured.

organismic theories Theories that attribute human behavior and attitudes primarily to influences within the individual, rather than in the environment.

panel study *See* Longitudinal study.

psychoanalytic theory *See* Freudian theory.

random sample Sample of people participating in a study who possess characteristics similar to those of people to whom the results are going to be generalized. Also called a representative sample.

representative sample *See* random sample.

Skinnerian psychology *See* behaviorism.

social learning theory The view that our behavior and attitudes are primarily the consequence of reinforcement, punishment, and modeling but are also influenced by such cognitive variables as our preconceived expectations.

stage theories Theories contending that human behavior changes as a consequence of maturation occuring in distinct, universal stages that are basically unaffected by environmental influences.

survey research Gathers information through written or personal questionnaires but cannot establish cause and effect.

REFERENCES

Adelson, J. & Doehrman, M. (1980). The psychodynamic approach to adolescence. In J. Adelson (Ed.), *Handbook of adolescent psychology* (pp. 99–117). New York: Wiley.

Baker, T. (1988). *Doing social research.* New York: McGraw-Hill.

Baltes, P. & Reese, H. (1984). The life span perspective in developmental psychology. In M. Bornstein & M. Lamb (Eds.) *Developmental psychology* (pp. 493–531). Hillsdale, NJ: Lawrence Erlbaum.

Barlow, D., Hays, S., & Nelson, R. (1984). *The scientist practitioner: Research and accountability in clinical and educational settings.* New York: Pergamon Press.

Benedict, R. (1934). *Patterns of culture.* Boston: Houghton Mifflin.

Blos, P. (1962). *On adolescence.* New York: Free Press.

Burbank, V. (1988). *Aboriginal adolescence.* New Brunswick, NJ: Rutgers University Press.

Coleman, J., Hoffer, T., & Kilgore, S. (1982). *High school achievement.* New York: Basic Books.

Davis, K. (1941). The sociology of parent youth conflict. *American Sociological Review, 5,* 523–525.

Demos, J., & Demos, V. (1979). Adolescence in historical perspective. *Journal of Marriage and the Family, 31,* 628–632.

Elder, G. (1980). Adolescence in historical perspective. In J. Adelson (Ed.), *Handbook of adolescent psychology* (pp. 3–46). New York: Wiley.

Enright, R., Levy, V., Harris, D., & Lapsley, D. (1987). Do economic conditions influence how theorists view adolescents? *Journal of Youth & Adolescence, 16,* 541–559.

Erikson, E. (1968). *Identity: Youth and crisis.* New York: Norton.

Freud, A. (1958). *Adolescence: Psychoanalytic study of the child.* New York: International Universities Press.

Freud, S. (1953). *A general introduction to psychoanalysis.* New York: Permabooks.

Gelles, R. (1980). Violence in the family: A review of the research in the seventies. *Journal of Marriage and the Family, 42,* 873–885.

Hall, S. (1904, 1905). *Adolescence: Its psychology and its relations to physiology, anthropology, sociology, sex, crime, religion and education.* Englewood Cliffs, NJ: Prentice-Hall.

Havighurst, R. (1952). *Developmental tasks and education.* New York: McKay.

Hollingshead, A. (1949). *Elmstown's youth.* New York: Wiley.

Jacobson, N., Follette, W., & Revenstorf, D. (1984). Psychotherapy outcome research: Methods for reporting variability and evaluating clinical significance. *Behavior Therapy, 15,* 336–352.

Kett, J. (1977). *Rites of passage: Adolescence in America 1790 to the present.* New York: Basic Books.

Kupfersmid, J. (1988). Improving what is published. *American Psychologist, 43,* 635–642.

L'Abate, L. (1971). The status of adolescent psychology. *Developmental Psychology, 4,* 201–205.

Marcia, J. (1980). Identity in adolescence. In J. Adelson (Ed.), *Handbook of adolescent psychology* (pp. 159–188). New York: Wiley.

Mead, M. (1961). *Coming of age in Samoa.* New York: William Morrow.

Mischel, W. (1981). *Introduction to personality.* New York: Holt, Rinehart and Winston.

Muuss, R. (1975). *Theories of adolescence.* New York: Random House.

Nottelmann, E., et al. (1986). Gonadal and adrenal hormone correlates of adjustments in early adolescence. In R. Lerner & T. Foch (Eds.), *Biological-psychosocial interactions in early adolescence.* Hillsdale, NJ: Erlbaum.

Piaget, J. (1971). The theory of stages in cognitive development. In D. Green (Ed.), *Measurement and Piaget* (pp. 184–215). New York: McGraw-Hill.

Savin-Williams, R. (1987). *Adolescence: An ethological perspective.* New York: Springer-Verlag.

Skinner, B. F. (1953). *Science and human behavior.* New York: Free Press.

2 Adolescent Physical Development

CHAPTER OUTLINE

PUBERTY: WHAT, WHEN, AND WHY?

PHYSICAL TRANSFORMATIONS

- The Sequence of Growth
- The Head and Face
- Height
- Muscle Tissue
- Adipose Tissue
- Basal Metabolism Rate
- Breast Development
- Male Reproductive System
- Female Reproductive System

ABNORMAL DEVELOPMENT OF THE REPRODUCTIVE SYSTEM

ISSUES RELATED TO ADOLESCENT PHYSICAL DEVELOPMENT

- Early and Late Maturation
- Appearance and Personality
- Food, Nutrition, and Dieting
- Advantages and Disadvantages of Sports
- Steroids and the Adolescent Athlete

CONCLUSION

GOALS AND OBJECTIVES

This chapter is designed to enable you to:

- Describe the physical changes that occur during adolescence
- Explain the factors that influence adolescent growth and appearance
- Examine the physiological and developmental difference between males and females
- Explore adolescents' reactions to their physical changes
- Identify some common adolescent diseases and genetic abnormalities
- Discuss the advantages and disadvantages of organized sports
- Consider the impact of air pollution, diet, exercise, hormones, and early maturation on adolescent behavior
- Examine the relationship between appearance and personality

CONCEPTS AND TERMINOLOGY

adipose tissue
amenorrhea
androgen
anovulatory
areola
basal metabolism rate
cervix
circumcised
clitoris
dysmenorrhea
ectomorph
endomorph
endorphins
estrogen
Fallopian tubes
foreskin
glans
gonadotropins
gonads
hymen
hypothalamus
Klinefelter's syndrome
labia
mammary glands
menorrhagia
mesomorph
nocturnal emissions
os
ovulation
premenstrual syndrome (PMS)
prepuce
progesterone
prostate gland
protein loading
scrotum

Key terms continued

Key terms continued

semen	Turner's syndrome
seminal fluid	urethra
seminal vesicles	uterus
shaft	vagina
steroids	vas deferens
testicles	vasectomy
testosterone	vulva
tubal ligation	zygote

PUBERTY: WHAT, WHEN, AND WHY?

Between the ages 9 and 16 it happens to everyone—puberty begins. Literally meaning "to be covered in fine hair," the word is derived from the Latin verb *pubescere,* which means "to grow hairy or mossy." In a more contemporary context, the term "puberty" has come to signify the period of life during which a young person becomes physically capable of sexual reproduction. Given the dramatic rise in hormonal levels, which are responsible for the adolescent's sexual maturity, it is not surprising that researchers have devoted considerable attention to the impact that adolescents' hormones might have on their moods and behavior, as Box 2.1 indicates. (Lerner & Foch, 1986).

Puberty technically begins when the part of the upper brain stem known as the **hypothalamus** signals the pituitary gland to release the hormones known as **gonadotropins.** (All physiological data in this section are from Higham, 1980, & Katchadourian, 1977, unless otherwise noted.) Heralded as the "master gland" in our endocrine system, the pituitary releases the gonadotropins into the adolescent's body during sleep, a year or so before any of the physical changes associated with puberty actually become apparent. These gonadotropins cause the ovaries and the testes, both referred to as the **gonads,** to increase their production of **estrogen** and **androgen.** Consequently, the ovaries increase their production of estrogen sixfold in a girl's body, and the testes produce 20 times the amount of **testosterone** formerly present in a boy's body. When released in sufficient amounts, **testosterone** increases muscle mass, body hair, and the size of the vocal cords. Similarly, the elevated estrogen levels in a girl's body are accompanied by such changes as breast development, menstruation, and extra fat tissue around the hips and abdomen, resulting in the loss of her younger, boyish figure.

From birth, both the male's body and the female's body produce androgen and estrogen. The distinction between the sexes is that during adolescence a boy's androgen level becomes 20–60 percent higher than a girl's, while her estrogen

A CLOSER LOOK 2.1

Do Hormones Influence Adolescents' Behavior?

Do the dramatic increases in hormones that accompany puberty affect adolescents' behavior and emotions? Can daily fluctuations in these hormones influence adolescents' interactions with their parents and peers? According to longitudinal data being collected by monitoring the daily hormone levels and behavior of adolescent boys and girls, the answer to these questions is yes (Inoff-Germain, Arnold, Nottelmann, & Susman, 1988; Susman, Inoff-Germain, Nottelmann, & Loriaux, 1987).

One of the most consistent findings thus far is that boys' obsessive-compulsive, aggressive, and hyperactive behavior is correlated with days when androgen levels were higher and steroid levels were lower. In contrast, on days when androgen levels in girls were lower, the girls were more likely to show signs of depression or withdrawal, as well as aggression. On these days, boys and girls were more likely to defy their parents and to express anger. On a more optimistic note, when their steroid levels were high, both boys and girls reported feeling more self-confident and competent. Also noteworthy is that boys whose androgen levels were higher than their same-age peers' were more interested in dating and sexuality. What implications might such findings have for our relationships with and perceptions of adolescents?

level becomes 20–30 percent higher than his. Although the level of estrogen varies with a female's age and with the phase of her menstrual cycle, the ovaries produce both estrogen and androgen throughout her lifetime. Interestingly, however, it has not yet been determined whether the estrogen in a male's body is produced by the testes or whether the male body somehow converts testosterone into estrogen. Nevertheless, the two hormones that influence masculine or feminine appearance are produced by the bodies of both sexes.

The obvious physical differences among adolescents of the same chronological age underscore an endocrinological fact: The hypothalamus does not relay the message to release gonadotropins at the same time in each adolescent's life. Some 11-year-olds' bodies are responding to the commands of the hypothalamus, while some 15-year-olds have not yet begun to respond to the hormonal changes within them. The factors that activate the hypothalamus are still undetermined. According to some theorists, the hypothalamus monitors the adolescent's body weight and releases the necessary hormones when the body is heavy enough (Frisch, 1984). This hypothesis would explain why youngsters in richer communities, where nutritional and medical benefits increase their weight, reach puberty before children from poorer communities. Further corroborative evidence shows that girls whose body weight drops below a certain level stop menstruating (Frisch, 1984). Despite the evidence suggesting a relationship between messages from the hypothalamus and weight, most biologists still contend that an adolescent's weight is a response to—not the cause of—the hypothalamus's activity (Peterson & Taylor, 1980).

In addition to the activity of the hypothalamus, puberty appears to be affected by certain environmental factors. For example, adolescents living in higher altitudes and those from small families mature earlier than those in lower altitudes and those from large families (Beau, Baker, & Haas, 1977; Malina, 1979). Children who are malnourished, emotionally deprived during infancy, or financially impoverished also mature more slowly. Two facts suggest that seasonal changes may somehow influence puberty: Fewer girls start to menstruate in the spring than in any other season, and most adolescents grow tallest during the springtime and gain the most weight during the autumn. Although environment seems to influence certain aspects of puberty, genetic endowment still asserts primary control over when and how quickly a youngster will mature. In sum, if a 10-year-old girl is curious about how quickly she will mature, her most reliable predictor is her own mother's pattern during adolescence. In general, adolescents whose parents are tall and thin mature more slowly than those whose parents are short and stocky.

Over the last century the age of puberty has steadily decreased, although the trend is now slowing. The average U.S. boy now begins puberty around the age of 12 and completes his growth by 19. Most girls mature about 2 years earlier than boys, beginning around the age of 11 and reaching the end of growth around the age of 17. The height spurt starts in most girls between 9.5 and 14.5 years and between 10.5 and 16 years for boys. Pubic hair generally appears around 11 in girls and 12 in boys. By the end of the teenage years, most males and females have entirely completed the growth that has transformed them physiologically from children to adults.

PHYSICAL TRANSFORMATIONS

The Sequence of Growth

Although the age at which puberty begins differs among adolescents, the sequence of physiological changes is relatively predictable. Most adolescent girls develop pubic hair before their breasts develop and thereafter experience rapid growth in weight and height. Menstruation and the growth of other body hair generally occur last in the growth sequence. Most adolesent boys first experience enlargement of the penis and testicles, followed by the growth of pubic hair, voice changes, and a rapid spurt in height and weight. A boy's facial and underarm hair develop last in the growth sequence, because these areas have the highest tolerance for testosterone.

The fact that boys produce more testosterone and less estrogen than girls accounts for a number of sexual differences, which manifest themselves during adolescence. Testosterone is responsible for boys' hairier bodies, their higher ratio of muscle to fat tissue, and their larger number of sweat glands. Although a girl's voice undergoes some change during adolescence as her vocal cords grow, a boy's vocal cords nearly double in length, thus causing his voice to drop nearly an octave. Similarly, blood volume and lung size increase more significantly in boys than in girls during adolescence. This larger blood volume permits most boys to exchange oxygen more efficiently than girls. Before puberty a girls' shoulders are proportionately larger than a boy's in comparison to the size of the hips, but during adolescence this ratio of shoulder-to-hip size reverses—boys' shoulders grow larger than their hips, while girls' grow smaller. As information later in this chapter will demonstrate, however, these differences do not mean that boys are necessarily stronger or more athletically talented than girls.

The Head and Face

Both male and female adolescents undergo a host of other physical alterations. The lymphatic tissues, which increase in size throughout childhood, begin to decrease during adolescence. This shrinkage in the tissues of the tonsils and adenoids accounts for adolescents' "growing out of" the allergic reactions, colds, and sore throats that so often plague them during childhood. Unfortunately, this gain is offset by a new loss—the loss of vision. Rapid changes in the eye between the ages of 11 and 14 often produce myopia, or shortsightedness, which diminishes a youngster's long-range vision. As a consequence, many young adolescents who have had perfect vision during childhood suddenly need glasses.

Another change accompanying adolescence is the loss of a childlike face. As the hairline recedes and the facial bones grow in such a way that the nose and chin become more prominent, the adolescent's face assumes its permanent adult features. The one feature of the head that changes relatively little during adolescence is the brain. Having attained 90 percent of its weight by the time we are 5 and 95 percent by the time we are 10, it grows little during our adolescence.

Height

Familiar questions from our own adolescence are reminders that most of us are concerned over our weight and height during the years of most rapid growth: How tall am I going to be? Will I ever gain weight or will I look like a scarecrow forever? Why do I still have all this "baby fat" when everyone else looks so muscular and lean? Why do I feel that I am all hands and feet? Why are my legs so long compared to my arms?

These questions reflect the confusing but relatively predictable pattern that the human body follows as it matures. Both adolescents who fear that their body's awkward appearance is permanent and those who hope that adolescence will somehow magically bestow an entirely new body upon them are in error. Because the body grows at different rates throughout the course of a given year and because certain parts of the body grow faster than others, adolescents may sometimes feel ungainly. Such anxieties might be relieved if adolescents were acquainted with several physiological realities: Legs grow to their full length before arms, and hands and feet reach their full size before arms and legs. Because human beings grow tallest in the spring and gain the most weight during the autumn, adolescents may feel especially lanky and skinny during the summers, when their bodies have not yet added the weight that corresponds more closely to their height. These uneven patterns of growth inevitably make some adolescents feel physically awkward, but the assumption that adolescence causes graceful human beings to suddenly become clumsy oafs is unfounded. People who are uncoordinated and clumsy during adolescence were uncoordinated and clumsy as children.

Another consoling or perhaps disconsoling fact is that an individual will generally have the same basic body type after adolescence as before. In other words, the short, stocky 9-year-old is generally going to be a short, stocky 20-year-old, and the girl who is taller and skinnier than her peers in the 3rd grade is still likely to be taller and skinnier than her peers in the 12th grade. Furthermore, despite what adolescents look like at the moment, they are likely to resemble their parents in terms of weight and height by the end of puberty. Youngsters who wonder how tall or how heavy they will be as adults should simply look at their own parents. Although there are exceptions to this rule, genetics generally dictate our adult height and weight.

Between the ages of 11 and 17 most males and females grow taller by about 11 inches. During the fastest year of growth a youngster grows 3 to 5 inches in height, and by the end of adolescence most boys are about 5 inches taller than girls. The average U.S. female grows to be about 5′ 5″ tall, while the average boy grows to be about 5′ 10″. Although in the 1890s only 5% of the boys grew taller than 6 ft., nearly 25% of today's boys will exceed that height. In trying to predict children's adult height, we can assume that they will be about 20% taller at the end of puberty than at the beginning. More accurate predictions can be gleaned from x-rays, which demonstrate how far the bones have progressed in their process of calcification. From x-rays of the hand and wrist, a specialist can determine skeletal or "bone" age and thereby estimate the amount of additional height the adolescent can expect.

Muscle Tissue

Although height usually increases by only about 20% during adolescence, weight may actually double. By the end of adolescence most boys weigh about 25 lbs more than girls. Besides the additional weight of the organs, bones, and blood, boys generally outweigh girls because of their higher proportion of muscle to fat tissue. The average boy's muscle tissue doubles during adolescence, while a girl's increases by only 50%. During childhood about 16% of a boy's or a girl's weight is accounted for by fat tissue, but by the end of adolescence, only about 12% of a boy's body is fat tissue, in contrast to 20–25% of a girl's. Because muscle tissue weighs more than fat tissue, the average male is heavier than a female.

The ramifications of these gender differences are both fascinating and controversial: How can adolescent girls compete athletically with boys when they do not have equal muscle tissue? Is one sex any better suited than the other for specific types of activities such as long-distance swimming and running? Should girls abstain from rigorous physical activity or contact sports with boys? Why encourage girls to develop their muscles like boys?

Addressing such questions, physiologists have accumulated considerable evidence refuting traditional assumptions about the differences between males' and females' physical abilities (Peterson & Taylor, 1980). For example, the notion that adolescent boys are better suited than girls for sports and strenuous physical tasks is overly simplistic when the overlapping abilities of the sexes are considered. First, there are enough small, overweight, or poorly exercised males and enough large, muscular, well-conditioned girls to undermine gross generalizations about strength solely on the basis of a youngster's sex. Second, recent evidence suggests that when adolescent boys and girls exercise alike, their percentages of body fat and their physical abilities become much more similar.

Unfortunately, girls have traditionally been discouraged from exercising as rigorously or as frequently as boys. As a consequence, adolescent and adult females are generally less physically fit than their male peers. For example, the National School Population Fitness Survey found that girls aged 6 to 17 generally scored lower than boys on all tests of fitness except flexibility (Raithel, 1987).

Indeed, empirical data already lend support to this contention about the differences that similar exercise would effect (Marshall, 1981). For example, athletic girls have higher oxygen intake, more stamina, more strength, and a lower percentage of body fat than unathletic boys. In addition, girls are generally more loose-jointed than boys, which enables girls to perform certain physical tasks more easily, such as touching the floor with the palms of the hand. (Unfortunately, wearing high-heeled shoes contracts the heel muscles and necessitates special stretching exercises to reinstate the muscles to their more naturally limber state.) Furthermore, a girl's lighter bones, smaller shoulders, and additional fat tissue are assets in activities like long-distance running and swimming. As the information in Box 2.2 demonstrates, many erroneous assumptions about females' physical abilities are slowly falling by the wayside.

Data on females' physical potential, however, should not be misconstrued to mean that the physiological differences between the sexes have no impact whatsoever on the motor performance of adolescent males and females. For example, an analysis of 176 studies revealed that since most adolescent boys are larger and have a higher percentage of muscle tissue than their female peers, they generally have a biological advantage in motor skills that depend on size and muscle strength. Moreover, after the onset of puberty, a girl and a boy who engage in similar amounts of exercise will not develop the same muscular appearance because the male's body has less fat tissue covering the muscles and because muscle mass is partially dependent on the higher level of testosterone in the boy's body. Before puberty, however, the differences in male and female motor performance appear to be socially induced by parents, peers, teachers, and coaches. In other words, the studies suggest that if boys and girls were subjected to equal expectations and equal opportunities, their physical performances would be similar before puberty, and the differences in their performance would be less exaggerated during adolescence (Thomas & French, 1985).

ARE YOU SURE? 2.2

Myths About Females and Physical Exercise

If a female adolescent seeks your counsel on physical exercise, which of the following beliefs would you endorse?

1. If girls lift weights, they will develop muscles as large as boys'.
2. Jogging causes the breasts and facial muscles to sag.
3. Exercising decreases the size of the breasts.
4. Rigorous exercises aggravate menstrual cramps.
5. A girl is incapable of performing as well athletically during her period as she can before or after menstruation.
6. Being injured on the chest during sports causes permanent damage to a girl's breast tissue.
7. A girl's reproductive organs are more vulnerable to athletic injuries than a boy's.
8. Girls are less well equipped physically than boys to cope with high temperatures or humidity.
9. Rigorous athletic competition during adolescence creates complications in pregnancy and childbirth later in a girl's life.
10. Girls have less stamina and muscle power relative to their size than boys.

Answers: All of the above are false.

Sources: J. Marshall. (1981). *The sports doctor's fitness book for women.* New York: Delacorte; S. Twin. (1979). *Out of the bleachers: Writings on women and sports.* New York: McGraw-Hill.

Adipose Tissue

Adolescents often become confused about the relationship between the fat and muscle tissues in their bodies, as Box 2.3 illustrates. This confusion provokes a number of naive questions: How can I get rid of all the fat inside my body? Why am I not losing weight now that I am exercising more? How much food do I need to eat each day so I can gain some weight? Why is my tummy still fat, even though I have lost ten pounds? Why is my best friend skinnier than I am, when she eats so much more? Why do I not feel stronger, even though I made my muscles bigger through special training? Questions like these reflect adolescents' lack of information about their fat and muscle tissues.

Purposes of fat Despite our derogatory comments about adipose tissue, fat is essential for our health and survival. Everyone's body contains three kinds of fat or **adipose tissue:** essential fat, subcutaneous fat, and storage fat. The essential fat protectively covers our nerves, organs, and cells. Lying just underneath the skin, subcutaneous fat envelops the entire body, protecting us from extremes of heat and cold. Storage fat is distributed around the abdomen, thighs, hips, and underarms.

During adolescence, girls develop more storage fat than do boys, causing them to lose their "boyish" childhood bodies as this adipose tissue distributes itself

ARE YOU SURE? 2.3

Physical Exercise: Facts and Fairy Tales

How accurately could you answer adolescents' questions about physical exercise? To assess your knowledge, determine which of the following statements are false:

1. You need to lose weight before you start to exercise.
2. Exercise makes you hungry afterwards.
3. Some diets cause you to lose muscles instead of fat.
4. Exercise raises your basal metabolic rate.
5. Exercise can improve your posture, relieve menstrual cramps, and decrease your need for sleep.
6. There is a possibility that exercise early in life restricts the total number of fat cells or will alter their size.
7. The fatter and more out of shape you are, the more slowly you should exercise in the beginning.
8. Exercise is more effective than a diet for losing fat quickly.
9. If you stay busy all day long, you do not need to exercise.
10. The best fitness program is to exercise 60 min daily 3 days a week instead of 20 min every day.
11. The best way to determine the benefit of an exercise for your heart is to take your pulse afterwards.
12. Exercising can make you look skinnier without your losing any weight.
13. Your body burns calories more quickly in the hours after you exercise than if you had not exercised at all.
14. Your muscles get as much benefit from 15 min of jogging as from 2 hr of tennis.
15. Two vigorous 6-min exercises burn up more fat than one slow, continuous 12-min exercise.

Answers: All are true except 1, 2, 9, 10, and 15.

around the hips, thighs, upper arms, abdomen, and breasts. No matter how much weight a girl loses, these parts of her body remain fleshier and fuller than a boy's because of this different distribution of adipose tissue. This extra adipose tissue does not, however, mean that girls are "fat" and need to diet. Unfortunately, too many adolescent girls expect their bodies to look straight and lean like a ten-year-old's or a boy's body; thus the adolescent girl's primary complaint about her body is that it's "too fat" (Gunn & Peterson, 1984). Even among competitive swimmers whose bodies are well-conditioned, adolescent females are more dissatisfied with their weight than are adolescent males (Dummer, 1987). As the data in chapter 14 will demonstrate, girls with this false perception of "fatness" are prime candidates for anorexia nervosa—a psychological disorder in which a girl's refusal to eat enough food can become life threatening. In less extreme forms, the adolescent girl's perception of herself as too fat can lead to other unhealthy habits, such as going on dangerous diets and taking diet pills, which will be examined later in this chapter.

Although some adolescent boys also consider themselves too fat, they more commonly complain about their lack of musculature (Bell, 1988). The boy's adipose tissue typically accumulates around his abdomen rather than on his hips, breasts, and thighs. Consequently, too much adipose tissue causes a "pot-bellied" look. Like girls, boys sometimes mistakenly assume that they have too much fat tissue. Although the most popular way of determining whether an adolescent is too fat is to compare his or her weight to standardized charts, this method is far less reliable than more recent methods for measuring fat and muscle tissue.

Measuring fat tissue What does it mean to say that a youngster "lost weight"? Many people erroneously assume that if an adolescent loses 10 lb, he or she has lost 10 lb of fat tissue, though this is not the case. For example, suppose Juan notices after his 4-mi run on a hot afternoon that he weighs 5 lb less than before he jogged. Likewise, Susan notices that in the week before menstruation she weighs 4 lb more than during the week following her period. Despite what their scales show, neither Juan nor Susan has lost or gained any fat. In these two examples the scales are measuring the amount of water in the adolescent's body. When Juan runs several miles on hot afternoons, his body sweats profusely by releasing pints of water stored in his tissues. For every pint of water that Juan sweats, he loses about 1 lb on the scales (Bailey, 1978). If he weighs 5 lb less after his run, he has lost about 5 pt of water, not fat, and will regain this weight once he replenishes his liquids.

Typically, boys lose more weight than girls after rigorous exercise, because their sweat glands release more water than girls' (Marshall, 1981). Therefore, if Susan is not sweating as much as Juan after her 4-mi run, do not assume that she has not exerted just as much effort or done just as much exercise! In addition, her weight will probably change more than Juan's from week to week, no matter what she eats or how she exercises, depending on her menstrual cycle. Just before and during menstruation most girls retain more liquids in their tissues and weigh more than at other phases of their cycle. Once again, weight on the scales has changed, but the percentage of fat or muscle in the adolescent's body remains unaltered.

There is one other reason why adolescents should not rely on the bathroom scales to determine how fat or muscular they are. Consider this situation: Samantha decides to build up her arm and leg muscles and to get rid of some fat by lifting

A CLOSER LOOK 2.4

The Younger Generation: Failing in Fitness?

Despite the growing concern over physical fitness among their elders during the 1980s, the younger generation appears less physically fit than their peers in previous decades. In 1956, President Eisenhower was concerned enough over the poor physical fitness of the youth of the United States to create the President's Council of Youth Fitness, which reached its zenith of popularity during President Kennedy's administration. Since that time, it appears that the fitness of U.S. youth has been on the decline.

Since traditional fitness tests like the standing long jump have been replaced with more sophisticated, modern tests of cardiovascular endurance and measurements of factors such as cholesterol levels, comparisons from decade to decade are somewhat confounded. Nevertheless, in a 3-year National Child and Youth Fitness Study released in 1985, measures like the skinfold test revealed that representative samples of children and adolescents in the 1980s are fatter than those in the 1960s. Similarly, 10-year-old boys averaged only 2.7 chin-ups and on average took more than 10 min to run 1 mi. Other tests conducted in various parts of the country confirm the study's results: Contemporary youths are losing ground in terms of physical fitness.

Although some may trivialize the unfit physical condition of today's youth as an issue related to vanity or limited to "health nuts," the ramifications of physical fitness go far beyond the bounds of physical appearance. Kinesiologist Guy Reiff of the University of Michigan espouses the view

continued

weights. After 6 weeks of lifting, she is angry because her weight has increased by 4 lb and she presumes the exercises have made her fatter. She is wrong. She has indeed been converting her fat into muscle tissue and is unquestionably "skinnier" in terms of having less fat inside her body; but muscle tissue weighs more than fat tissue, so she does indeed weigh more on the scales. If she had one measuring cup full of her muscle tissue and one cup of her fat tissue, she could put them on the scales and see that the cup of muscle weighs almost two and a half times as much as the cup of fat. Thus, a physically fit adolescent like Samantha can weigh more than her flabby, out-of-shape classmates who have more fat but less muscle than she does. Generally the most athletic and well-conditioned adolescents will weigh more than unathletic youngsters of similar stature. Moreover, the stomach holds 2 or 3 lb of food, so everyone weighs slightly more at the end of a full day of eating than in the morning (Bailey, 1978).

Losing fat Although adolescent girls need to maintain their adipose tissue at about 12%, boys can reduce their adipose tissue to 6% without any ill effects (Edelstein, 1980). Reducing the body's supply of fat below these limits can pose health hazards. The body converts all food into sugar or glucose. This converted sugar, as well as raw sugar contained in foods such as candies and cake, provides the energy for breathing, pumping blood, digesting food, and all other bodily functions: Sugar also enables a body to move. Thus, if an adolescent eats a sandwich containing 800 calories' worth of carbohydrates and then goes out to play basketball

Box 2.4 continued

of other health-care professionals by saying that "cardiovascular disease starts by the first grade." Poor eating habits and the lack of physical exercise contribute to high cholesterol levels, high blood pressure, and poor cardiorespiratory functioning. In addition, evidence suggests that students who exercise regularly improve their academic skills and their self-concepts.

Several hypotheses have been offered to explain the poor condition of today's young people. First, budget cuts have forced many school districts to dismantle or to drastically reduce their physical education programs. Second, the demands on working parents often result in poorer eating habits, when children come home from school unsupervised and spend hours snacking in front of the televsion set, prepare their own makeshift dinners, or rely on fast-food industries to provide their meals.

Projects like "Shapedown" in San Francisco are designed to help overweight adolescents learn new eating and exercising habits. Initiated in 1980 by the University of California, Shapedown is available at 400 medical centers throughout the country. During the 12-week programs, which cost from $80 to $200, adolescents discuss their reasons for overeating, keep records of their eating and exercise habits, and learn to institute daily changes in their behavior. Parents are required to attend two sessions, in which they examine their own weight problems and discuss bad habits to which they are contributing, such as buying sweet foods and forcing their children to eat everything on the plate. Data collected months after a program's completion suggest that Shapedown is successful in helping adolescents change their eating and exercising habits on a permanent basis.

Source: J. Carey & M. Hager. (1985, April 1). Failing in fitness. *Newsweek*, pp. 84–87.

for 2 hr, everything is fine, because playing ball requires only about 350 calories of energy each hour. If, however, that youngster wants to play basketball for 4 hrs, the body relies on the body's supply of fat for the necessary sugar. Conversely, if youngsters consume more calories than their bodies need to complete their daily activities, the extra calories are converted to fat.

Each pound of fat can be converted into 3,500 calories' worth of energy (Bailey, 1978). Hence, youngsters who want to eliminate 1 lb of fat from their bodies have to exercise rigorously enough to burn up 3,500 calories more than the calories contained in the food they have eaten. Put another way, to lose 1 lb of adipose tissue in 1 week, an adolescent must be physically active enough to burn 500 more calories each day than he or she eats. Since most of us do not exercise enough to burn up more calories than we consume, losing fat tissue is a slow process.

Food and fat How should an adolescent eat and exercise for the healthiest balance of fat and muscle tissues? Consider this situation: Agatha is aggravated because she is fatter and less muscular than her friend Rosie, despite Agatha's best efforts to lose weight and build muscles. She cannot understand why this is so, when she bowls 6 hrs a week, never eats breakfast, eats only a bag of potato chips and drinks a coke for lunch, and includes plenty of protein-packed red meat in her dinners, as a way of building muscle tissue. In contrast, lean, muscular Rosie eats three hearty meals a day and jogs only 20 min each afternoon.

How physically fit were you as an adolescent? How much emphasis should males and females place on developing their muscles?

In assessing her physical fitness, Agatha has failed to consider four essential physiological facts. First, even though Rosie eats more food than Agatha, Rosie may be consuming fewer calories. Second, 20 min of daily jogging consumes far more calories than 6 hr a week of bowling. As Table 2-1 illustrates, the physiological value of various activities differs considerably. Third, Agatha is confused about the impact of protein on muscles. Muscle tissue is only 22% protein; the remainder is water. Hence, the idea of **"protein loading"** as a way of building muscles has limited value. While protein is necessary for maintaining muscles, exercise is the vital ingredient for building muscles (Bailey, 1978). Fourth, and most important, Agatha has overlooked the fact that the most efficient way to lose weight and to build muscle is through exercising, not through dieting.

In assessing their caloric needs, adolescents should first determine whether they are inactive, moderately active, or extremely active physically. Those who are inactive should multiply their ideal weight by 12 to determine their daily caloric needs, the moderately active by 15, and the extremely active by 18 (Edelstein, 1980). For example, if Roy wants to weigh 140 lb and he presently categorizes himself as inactive, he needs only about 1,680 calories a day to maintain a weight of 140 lb. If Roy presently weighs 150 lb, he has two options for losing his extra

Table 2.1

Scorecard on 14 Sports for Adolescents

Below is a summary of how seven experts rated 14 sports. A score of 21 indicates maximum benefit. Ratings were based on exercising four times a week for 30 min to 1 hr.

	Stamina	*Muscular Endurance*	*Muscular Strength*	*Flexibility*	*Balance*	*Weight Control*	*Muscle Definition*	*Digestion*	*Sleep*	*Total Score*
Jogging	21	20	17	9	17	21	14	13	16	148
Bicycling	19	18	16	9	18	20	15	12	15	142
Swimming	21	20	14	15	12	15	14	13	16	140
Skating	18	17	15	13	20	17	14	11	15	140
Handball	19	18	15	16	17	19	11	13	12	140
Squash										
Skiing	19	19	15	14	16	17	12	12	15	139
Basketball	19	17	15	13	16	19	13	10	12	134
Tennis	16	16	14	14	16	16	13	12	11	128
Calisthenics	10	13	16	19	15	12	18	11	12	126
Walking	13	14	11	7	8	13	11	11	14	102
Golf	8	8	9	8	8	6	6	7	6	66*
Softball	6	8	7	9	7	7	5	8	7	64
Bowling	5	5	5	7	6	5	5	7	6	51

*Ratings for golf are based on the fact that most people use a golf cart or caddy. If walking, the fitness value increases.

Source: U.S. Department of Health and Human Services. (1980). *Children and youth in action: Physical activities and sports.* (p. 29). Washington, DC: Author.

10 lb: Exercise more to burn more calories every day without dieting or reduce his calories to 1,680 a day without becoming more physically active.

Adolescent obesity Despite the importance of physical exercise in maintaining the proper balance of fat and muscle tissue, most adolescents exercise very little and presume that dieting is the most efficient way to lose weight. Even more unfortunately, as indicated in Box 2.4, recent data suggest that adolescents in the 1980s are less physically active than their counterparts in the 1960s and 1970s (Carey & Hager, 1985).

Contrary to most adolescents' notions, the most effective way to lose weight is by exercising, not by dieting. The major difference between fat and thin people is that the overweight people engage in considerably less physical exercise and activity. Indeed, overweight adolescents often consume fewer calories than their thinner peers (Edelstein, 1980; Thompson, Jarvie, Lahey, & Cureton, 1982). For example, in one experiment with obese adolescents, the group members who performed exercises before lunch lost more weight than the group members who restricted their calories at lunch. The youths who were exercising reduced their intake at lunch voluntarily to about the level that their nonexercising friends were forced to accept (Thompson et al., 1982). Moreover, fat youngsters are more likely than their thin peers to skip meals, underestimate their caloric intake, overestimate their level of physical activity, snack between meals, eat their food hurriedly, and

ARE YOU SURE? 2.5

Fictions About Fat and Food

How accurately could you advise adolescents who want to lose or gain weight? Which of the following statements would you endorse?

1. Eating grapefruit helps the body burn calories quickly.
2. Dieting is a better way to lose fat than exercise.
3. Younger adolescents are generally not as fat as older adolescents.
4. Most overweight people have thyroid problems.
5. People on diets should avoid as many carbohydrates as possible.
6. Amphetamines decrease appetite.
7. Diet pills deplete the body of water, not of fat.
8. The best way to measure the loss of fat is on the bathroom scales.
9. You can eat as much as you want of certain kinds of food, such as fruit, and never gain weight.
10. A person will lose about 1 or 2 lb of fat tissue per week on a good diet and exercise program.
11. Most adolescents can lose weight by consuming about 1,200 calories a day.
12. Eating a big breakfast, a medium-sized lunch, and a small supper is the best pattern for weight loss.
13. Fruit-flavored yogurt is a low-calorie food.
14. Dill pickles and other sour foods tend to decrease the desire for sweet foods.
15. A plain baked potato is a nutritious, low-calorie food.
16. If you get a headache after eating chocolate or drinking a cola, it is probably the caffeine that is bothering you.
17. Milk is the food that is most likely to cause allergies.
18. Food eaten before you go to bed is more likely to make you gain weight than food eaten at other times of the day.
19. Cellulite is just plain old fat tissue.
20. Exercising reduces appetite.

Answers: 1, 2, 4, 5, 8, 9, 13, and 18 are false.

Sources: C. Bailey, *Fit or fat?* (1978). Boston: Houghton Mifflin; B. Edelstein. (1980). *The woman doctor's diet for teen-age girls.* New York: Ballantine.

choose the least nutritional and most caloric foods (Carey & Hager, 1985; Edelstein, 1980).

The most successful programs for helping obese adolescents lose weight employ daily exercise, a change in diet, and behavior modification techniques (Hoerr, Nelson, & Essex, 1988; Johnson & Corrigan, 1987). Among the techniques that help adolescents maintain their exercise program and new eating habits are setting explicit daily goals and using behavioral contracts in which parents or other adults consistently reward the young people for their progress. Charging adolescents a minimal fee for attending a weight loss program also seems to help them take their weight loss more seriously. Ironically, it now appears that the parents of both anorexic (self-starvation) and obese adolescents may be overprotective and may create a sense of enmeshment within the family—the sense that nobody has an identity of his or her own. As a consequence, adolescents may develop a poor sense of self and a feeling of powerlessness to which they respond by overeating or self-starvation (Brone & Fisher, 1988). Whatever the underlying causes of adolescent obesity, however, the sad fact remains that most obese adolescents are unable to lose their excess weight and remain overweight throughout their lives (D. Freedman, 1987).

A CLOSER LOOK 2.6

Adolescent "Couch Potatoes"

Attacked for years as an intellectual wasteland, television is now being considered a possible culprit in the declining rates of physical fitness among today's adolescents. Studying the television-viewing habits of 397 high-school boys, a health scientist has found that the biggest "couch potatoes" were in the worst physical shape. Although the TV addicts were no more obese than those who watched TV infrequently, they performed worse on pull-ups, push-ups, sit-ups, side steps, long jumps, and the jog-walk. Since adolescents typically spend more time in front of a television than in front of a teacher, are they learning poor eating habits from the boob tube? Are the food advertisements and the passive act of couch warming contributing to adolescents' flabbiness? Although Tucker's study does not prove that television viewing causes physically fit youngsters to lose their tone and verve, it is plausible that poor physical fitness and excessive television viewing reinforce one another in a way that handicaps those adolescents who most need to be exercising and eating less caloric foods. If so, the question then becomes: How can we wean the couch potatoes away from their televisions?

Source: L. Tucker. (1987). The relationship of television viewing to physical fitness and obesity. *Adolescence, 21,* 797–806.

Basal Metabolism Rate

In addition to undergoing changes in the proportions of fat to muscle tissue, the adolescent body also experiences changes in its **basal metabolism rate.** An inherited feature, the metabolic rate is the speed at which a body converts calories into energy. Because their bodies burn calories faster, people with a high basal metabolism can eat more food without creating fat tissue than can people with a low rate. Since the basal metabolism rate declines between the ages of 11 and 20, adolescents must either eat less or exercise more in order to maintain a normal weight. Moreover, since the basal metabolism rate continues to decline as we age, many adults find themselves getting fatter, even though their exercise and diet habits are no different from those they practiced as adolescents. Since, however, a male's metabolic rate is usually higher than a female's, boys can consume more calories than girls without gaining weight. Similarly, athletic people of either sex can consume more calories than their nonathletic peers, because muscles have a higher metabolic rate than does adipose tissue and because exercise raises the metabolic rate (Bailey, 1978).

Breast Development

Why don't males develop breasts like females, since their bodies produce estrogen? How can a girl increase the size of her breasts? Can a girl who is not pregnant still produce milk? What is wrong with a boy whose breasts start to swell? Questions like these reflect the concern that many youngsters have about their breasts during adolescence.

Although the male body produces estrogen, its levels are too low to augment breast tissue substantially. In contrast, the female body produces enough estrogen to stimulate the growth of adipose tissue on the chest, hips, thighs, and upper arms. Because breasts are primarily composed of adipose tissue, their size diminishes or increases with the amount of overall fat in the girl's body. In other words, a girl who loses 30 lb will have smaller breasts as well as smaller hips, thighs, and abdomen. Boys' breasts fail to grow like girls' also because they lack mammary glands. The **mammary glands** are milk-producing glands with ducts through which the milk travels to the nipple. Milk is produced only during pregnancy and during the period of time the mother is nursing her child. Although some adolescent girls may occasionally produce a milky substance, this is merely a cleansing liquid to keep the nipples' ducts open.

During adolescence the breasts develop in stages. First the **areola,** the area around the nipple, becomes thicker and darker. Depending on the amount of pigment in the skin, the areola can range from light pink to very dark brown. Because the nipples grow before the breast tissue, many girls feel embarrassed by their prominence. Furthermore, once the breast tissue does start growing, it may develop at different rates in the two breasts, leaving girls embarrassed by their unbalanced appearance. Breast size is genetically determined and—contrary to advertisers' claims—cannot be augmented by physical exercise. Certain exercises may increase the size of the pectoral muscles, which underlie the breast tissues, thereby giving the breasts a more uplifted appearance; but the amount of fat tissue in a breast can be altered only through gaining or losing weight.

Because adipose tissue retains water, the breasts can become swollen and tender just before or during menstruation, when the body tends to retain fluids. This tenderness and swelling diminish naturally at the end of each menstrual period. Although normal breast tissue is somewhat lumpy, adolescents should be taught to examine their breasts for unusual lumps, which may be early signs of malignant growths. When a girl becomes familiar with her own breast tissue, she can more easily detect new lumps that are not part of her natural tissue. Although lumps sometimes disappear on their own and although most are merely benign cysts, one that remains for more than several weeks should be examined by a physician.

A CLOSER LOOK 2.7

Eating Poultry and Breast Development: A Link?

For the last few years an epidemic of premature "telarche," the medical term for breast enlargement in girls between 6 months and 8 years old, has been spreading in Puerto Rico. According to an endocrinologist at the University of Puerto Rico, 2,000 to 3,000 girls are now afflicted with telarche. Some of the experts suspect that the epidemic on the island is caused by the estrogen that farmers feed chickens to fatten them. Poultry is a staple of the Puerto Rican diet. In 1977 a similar problem arose in Milan, Italy, where boys developed enlarged breasts. The Italian researchers suspected poultry and veal as the culprits. Although premature telarche usually goes away in a year or two, some young Puerto Rican girls have developed more hazardous conditions—ovarian cysts and signs of premature puberty, such as menstruation and rapid bone development. Some researchers suspect that the estrogen in poultry is also causing these abnormalities.

Source: A. Bongiovani. (1983). An epidemic of premature telarche in Puerto Rico. *Journal of Pediatrics, 103,* 245–246.

In a society that has traditionally placed great emphasis on the size of the female breast, many adolescent girls still worry about being too big or too flat chested (Bell, 1988). Although the size of the breast has no relationship to her ability to nurse children or to any health hazards, the dissatisfied girl who can afford the fees sometimes opts to have cosmetic surgery to decrease or increase breast tissue. Like an adolescent boy who may worry about his penis being too small, an adolescent girl may experience considerable distress over the size of her breasts.

Male Reproductive System

The first sign of reproductive maturation for young men is usually the growth of the penis and testicles. Although it is not invariant, the most common sequence is enlargement of the penis and testicles, appearance of pubic hair, and ability to produce active sperm.

Basic components The two parts of the penis are the **glans,** or rounded head, which is the most sensitive area, and the **shaft,** which becomes engorged with blood during an erection (see Figure 2.1). Most boys who are now in their adolescence have a **circumcised** penis, meaning that the skin covering the glans (the **foreskin**) was surgically removed shortly after their birth. Circumcision has historically been performed as a religious rite and as a measure for preventing

FIGURE 2.1
Male pelvic organs

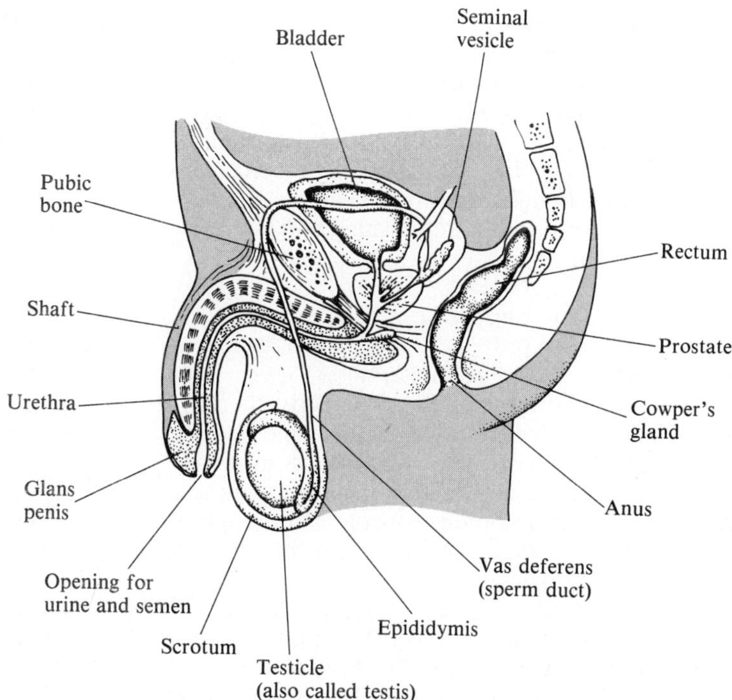

infections that might develop from bacteria trapped underneath the foreskin. Although this is our nation's most common surgical procedure, by the 1970s both the American Academy of Pediatrics and the American College of Obstetricians and Gynecologists concluded that there was no medical justification for routine circumcision—a message that is obviously taking hold in our society. In 1985, the most recent year for which statistics are available, only 59% of newborn boys were circumcised, a decrease of almost 10% from 1979 (Doubts, 1987). Given current doubts about the necessity of circumcision, it is possible that the majority of adolescent boys in future decades will not share this feature in common with today's youth.

At the onset of adolescence the young male's reproductive glands, the **testicles,** grow, causing the skin sack that houses them, the **scrotum,** to enlarge. The left testicle generally hangs slightly lower than the right, creating the false impression that one gland is larger than the other. In fact both testicles are the same size. The scrotum's primary functions are to maintain the proper temperature for sperm production and to offer protection against injury to the testicles. In cold weather or in situations of impending physical danger, the scrotum contracts, pulling the testicles nearer to the body for additional warmth and protection. In warmer weather or after hot showers, the scrotum relaxes, causing the testicles to descend further from the body, thereby maintaining a cool enough temperature for sperm production.

Inside the testicles the **vas deferens** tubes transport sperm from the testicles to the **seminal vesicles** for storage. If the vas deferens tubes were unwound, they would stretch the length of several football fields. The seminal vesicles and the **prostate gland** produce **semen,** the fluid ejaculated during orgasm. The semen, also called **seminal fluid,** is primarily composed of protective fluids that ensure the sperm's survival in the acidic environment of the vagina. During a **vasectomy** the vas deferens is surgically severed, rendering it impossible for sperm to be added to the seminal fluids that will be ejaculated. The diverted sperm are then absorbed by the male's body, although his testicles continue to produce new sperm and he continues to ejaculate seminal fluids during orgasms. Semen is ejaculated through the **urethra,** the tube that also transports urine from the bladder. Popular beliefs notwithstanding, it is physiologically possible for a male to have an orgasm without ejaculating and, conversely, to ejaculate without having had an orgasm.

Impregnation A single ejaculation of semen contains about 400 million sperm, which during intercourse propel themselves rapidly through the cervical opening, past the uterus, and into the Fallopian tubes. Sperm swim more slowly and are few in number during the early years of puberty, thereby decreasing the chances of a boy's impregnating a girl during this time. Nevertheless, live sperm are present in young adolescents' semen, as well as in the drops of fluid that escape from the penis before ejaculation. The pragmatic significance of this physiological fact is that a female can become pregnant even though ejaculation never occurs, if these sperm reach her Fallopian tubes as a consequence of sexual foreplay.

Emotional reactions As the information in Box 2.8 indicates, the experiences that accompany the reproductive system's maturation create anxiety and confusion in most boys at one time or another during adolescence (Bell, 1988). Among boys' concerns are worries about exhausting their supply of sperm by ejaculating too

2.8

ADOLESCENT VOICES

Boys' Feelings About Puberty

"My dad is always bugging me to go on a diet. I think it's because he was fat and unpopular as a kid. I'm heavy, but not that heavy. But when he looks at me with that look in his eyes, I feel like I weigh 300 pounds."

"Where I go to school, I'd say 80 percent of the boys work out with weights. It's pointless, because what happens is the standards just go up. If no one worked out, then the people who had less manly chests would be just as unhappy as they are now. It escalates. Now everybody spends an hour a day working out, when they could be doing something far more enjoyable and useful."

"Well, for me it was weird, because I didn't even start growing until last year. Everybody thought there was something wrong with me, because I still looked like a 10-year-old up until I was 15 or 16. That has been really a bad experience for me, because everybody was changing around me and I was standing still. I was changing in my head but not in my body. My parents were even going to take me to the doctor to see if I was deformed or something like that, but they didn't, and finally last year I started to grow. My voice started changing and everything, so I guess I'm normal after all. But I think it's going to be a while before I stop feeling like I'm different from everybody else."

"I had to shave a lot earlier than most of my friends. I was already shaving every day by the time I was 15, and even though I felt macho about it, it really was a pain in the neck. My dad's the same way—he has to shave twice a day to look good."

"When I was 14 I went around for about two weeks with this dirty smudge on my upper lip. I kept trying to wash it off, but it wouldn't wash. Then I really looked at it and saw it was a mustache. So I shaved! For the first time."

"You feel self-conscious, especially talking to a girl. I hear my brother talking on the phone with his girlfriend and he seems to be controlling his voice. He doesn't let himself sound angry or really happy or surprised. Your voice usually goes high when you get emotional or angry. So you try not to get too emotional. That way your voice will keep steady and low."

"All of a sudden I realized my voice was low. On the telephone people started thinking I was my father, not my mother!"

Source: Ruth Bell et al (1988). *Changing bodies, changing lives.* New York: Random House, Inc.

often. This worry is unfounded, since the male body continually produces fresh supplies of seminal fluid and sperm, although there are fewer sperm in the fluid after several successive ejaculations. Boys may also be embarrassed by erections that occur at inopportune moments. Sometimes just having to urinate or feeling the friction of clothes against the penis can produce an erection. Others worry that becoming aroused but being prevented from ejaculating can cause physical problems. Although the testicles may ache slightly from the blood that is draining away from the aroused penis (a condition that boys sometimes refer to as "blue balls"), the discomfort dissipates without physiological damage of any sort. Ejaculating while asleep, called "wet dreams" or **nocturnal emissions,** can also be a source of embarrassment, despite the fact that these are a normal, unpreventable aspect of a boy's adolescence.

Still another source of numerous jokes, good-natured teasing, and occasional cruelty, the size of his penis can cause a boy considerable consternation and alarm. Falling prey to locker-room comparisons and numerous myths about penis size, a boy may feel that his penis is too small. Despite the fact that almost every male's penis expand to 5 or 6 in. when aroused, the differences in size of the flaccid penis (as it most often appears in locker rooms and showers) can lead adolescent males to believe that they are poorly endowed in comparison to other males. Furthermore, most adolescent males know too little about female sexuality or anatomy to appreciate the fact that the length of the penis is almost totally irrelevant to a woman's sexual pleasure.

Many boys are concerned with the physical appearance of their genitals, but very few have been instructed to examine this part of the body for disease. Although cancer rarely afflicts adolescents, cancer of the testicles can occur during puberty. Just as medical practitioners urge girls to examine their breasts regularly, they urge boys to examine their testicles for unusual lumps. The best time to examine the testes is after a hot bath or shower, when the scrotum is most relaxed and the testicles are suspended farthest from the body. Each testicle should be examined gently with the fingers of both hands. If a boy discovers any lumps, he should contact a doctor for a more thorough examination (Testes test, 1981).

Female Reproductive System

Although the sequence is not universally predictable, female maturation generally proceeds in distinct phases: the appearance of pubic hair; the addition of adipose tissue on the breasts, thighs, hips, and abdomen; and finally the onset of menstruation.

Basic components During adolescence many girls discover their primary sexual organ—the **clitoris** (see Figure 2.2). Like the penis, the clitoris has a glans and a shaft containing the same type of spongy tissue responsible for a male's erection. The glans is covered by a protective hood of skin, the **prepuce,** and the shaft is buried beneath the skin, rather than exposed above the surface like the shaft of the penis. During sexual arousal, blood rushes into the genital tissues, causing the clitoris and surrounding area to swell. In the event an orgasm does not ensue, a sexually aroused girl sometimes experiences the same physical discomfort as boys whose testicles ache until the extra blood in these tissues is reabsorbed by the body. Unlike the penis, which serves urinary and sexual purposes, the clitoris serves exclusively to provide sexual pleasure. Although researchers have argued since Freud's time about whether females can experience two kinds of orgasm, clitoral and vaginal, most empirical data show that female orgasms are caused by direct or indirect clitoral stimulation. The debate continues, however, since reports during the early 1980s indicated that some women experience an orgasm from stimulation of an area inside the vagina, referred to as the "G spot." Despite the continuing controversy, the physiological fact remains that the area near the entrance to the vagina is more abundantly supplied with nerves than are the deeper vaginal areas.

Next to the clitoris is the **urethra,** the tube that carries urine from the bladder. The extremely small urethral opening is almost invisible because it is surrounded by the **labia,** the folds of skin that protect the genital area. The more noticeable opening is the vaginal entrance. Contrary to many adolescents' beliefs, the vagina

FIGURE 2.2
Female pelvic organs

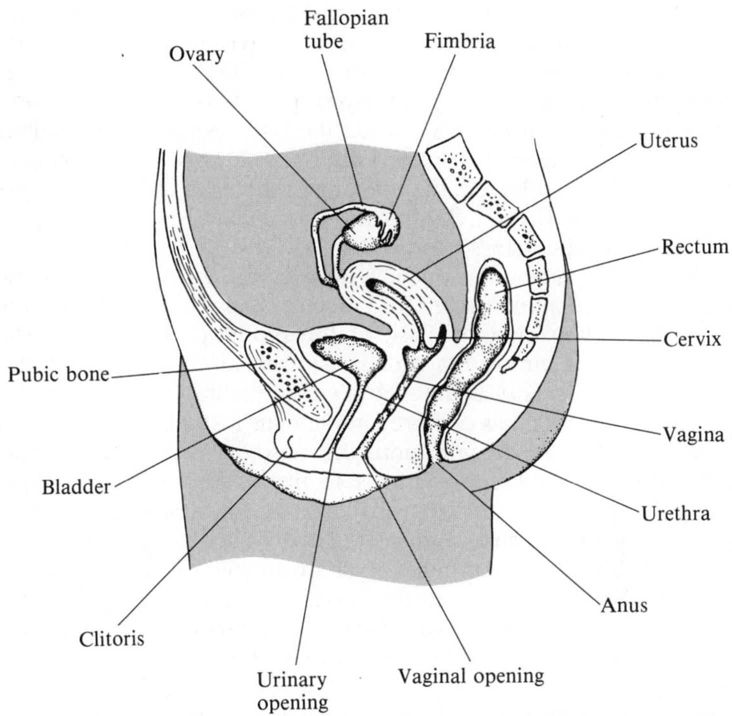

is not where the baby is housed. The **vagina** is the pasageway through which the baby passes as the uterus contracts and through which the menstrual blood flows after being shed from the uterine walls. It is also the area that accommodates the penis during intercourse. To the surprise of ill-informed adolescents, the vagina is not an endless "open space." On the contrary, the walls of the vagina are touching one another unless an object, such as a penis, a tampon, a finger, or a baby, is separating them. In this sense the vagina is more like an envelope than like the open space inside an inflated balloon. Misunderstanding their own anatomy, many girls believe that a tampon can get lost inside the vagina if pushed too far. The vagina, however, is a clearly limited space whose contours can be explored by touching the walls with the fingers. Even the end of the cervix is clearly discernable by touching it with the end of a finger.

Other myths surround the part of the vagina called the **hymen.** The hymen, also called the "cherry" or the "maidenhead," is a thin membrane that partially blocks the vaginal opening. The crucial word here is "partially." Except in the case of a physical abnormality, the hymen never entirely covers the vaginal opening, since an unobstructed opening is necessary for the flow of menstrual blood and vaginal secretions. Although often heralded as the sign of a girl's virginity, the hymen is often stretched unknowingly during childhood play or by inserting tampons. Furthermore, some girls are born without hymens. Its stretching is seldom accompanied by any bleeding or discomfort, contrary to stories about a girl's first sexual experiences to which many naive adolescents are subjected.

Near the farthest end of the vagina is the bottom portion of the uterus, the **cervix.** The cervical opening, called the **os,** is the passageway between the vagina and the uterus. The position of the os within the vagina changes throughout the menstrual cycle as the uterus changes its position. Early and late in the monthly cycle the os is easy to touch from outside the body because it is slanted toward the vaginal opening, rather than toward the back of the vagina. During midcycle, when the egg has been released, the opening of the os is widest and is positioned far back in the vagina. During childbirth the os expands to a width of 10 cm to allow the passage of the baby's head.

The walls of the vagina produce a liquid, called "mucus," on most days throughout a girl's monthly cycle. This mucus changes both in quantity and in appearance, depending on the phase of the monthly cycle. Immediately after menstruation there is almost no mucus. As ovulation approaches, the mucus becomes more profuse and assumes a stretchy quality similar in appearance to egg whites. After ovulation has occurred, the mucus loses its stretchy texture, turns white, and diminishes in quantity until the onset of menstruation. The vaginal walls also produce a lubricating mucus in preparation for intercourse, which adolescent girls may notice during sexual arousal. Because vaginal infections and venereal diseases often cause a mucus-like discharge, girls need to learn to distinguish their body's normal mucus cycle from atypical secretions.

The reproductive organs beyond the cervix extend too far up inside the body for a girl to touch or see them. Only the size of a walnut and located low in the abdominal area (not some large empty cavity in the intestinal area that extends up to the belly button, as some girls erroneously imagine!), the **uterus,** or womb, is an organ whose walls are composed of thick muscles. During pregnancy the womb houses the infant until the uterine muscles contract, forcing the child out through the os and the vagina. It is these same uterine muscles whose contractions are responsible for the sensations referred to as menstrual "cramps." At the top of the uterus a **Fallopian tube** leads to each ovary, where eggs have been stored since the girl's birth. In a **tubal ligation** these tubes are surgically cauterized or clamped, thereby making pregnancy impossible since the sperm and egg cannot unite once their bridge has been severed. Unlike sperm, which are freshly produced on a continual basis, each female egg is "old" in the sense that it has been inside the ovaries since the girl's birth.

Menstruation Beginning between the ages of 11 and 16, menstruation is the shedding of the uterine lining when no fertilized egg has implanted itself in the uterine wall. In the United States, half of all white girls start their periods before the age of 12.8 years, and half of all black girls at 12.5 years (Eveleth, 1986). Although the menstrual fluid is referred to as blood, it is in fact the mixture of tissue, mucus, and blood that lined the uterus during the previous month. If fertilization occurs, the **zygote** (fertilized egg) implants itself in the uterine lining, which then becomes the placenta, which nourishes the infant for 9 months. Some adolescent girls erroneously believe they lose a lot of blood during menstruation, somehow contributing to anemia. However, the 2 or 3 tbsp of menstrual fluid are not extracted from the body's supply of circulating blood, and unless some physiological disorder is causing excessive bleeding, menstruation does not create anemia.

Most females' menstrual cycles are approximately 28 days long, with menstruation lasting 3 to 4 days. During the first year or two of menstruation, the adolescent's cycles are often irregular. She may occasionally skip a period altogether, a condition referred to as **amenorrhea,** which can be caused by tension, illness, dietary changes, certain medications, or excessive weight loss (Gunn & Peterson, 1984). Similarly, some athletes temporarily stop menstruating if their adipose tissue falls to excessively low levels (Frisch, 1984). Some adolescents experience the opposite condition, **menorrhagia,** in which an excessively heavy, prolonged menstrual flow can cause a temporary state of anemia. Avoiding aspirin and taking vitamin K have alleviated this condition in many cases (Wollman & Lotner, 1983).

Particularly during the first few years of menstruation, adolescent girls may be less likely to become pregnant because their ovaries occasionally fail to release an egg into the Fallopian tubes. An **anovulatory** period means that the ovaries have not released an egg during that menstrual cycle, although menstruation still occurs. During adolescence, when the reproductive system is approaching maturity, neither amenorrhea nor anovulatory periods are causes for alarm (Gunn & Peterson, 1984).

Menstrual "cramps" occur when the uterine muscles contract to expel the uterine lining from the body. Recent evidence suggests that the decrease in the body's calcium level before menstruation may contribute to the headaches, swollen tissues, or cramps that some girls experience. Taking calcium tablets sometimes alleviates these discomforts. Myths to the contrary notwithstanding, the majority of adolescent and adult females report minimal or no discomfort during menstruation. Fewer than 10% of all females report that their menstrual discomfort is severe enough to interfere with their daily activities. **Dysmenorrhea,** or painful menstruation, is the exception, not the rule (Gunn & Peterson, 1984). For those who do experience moderate or severe pain while menstruating, a number of options are now available to reduce their discomfort (see Box 2.9).

Emotional reactions to menstruation Why do some girls feel depressed and physically uncomfortable before their periods while others do not? Are menstrual cramps and mood swings caused by physiological factors or are these feelings "all in the head"? Understandably, such questions have stirred controversy among researchers, as well as among females themselves. Given the difficulties involved in designing experimental studies to test these hypotheses (how do you define "lots of pain" or "feeling blue"?), the debate remains unsettled. In general, however, it appears that a girl's reactions to her period are determined both by physiological and by environmental factors (Delaney, Lupton, & Toth, 1988; Buckley & Gottlieb, 1988).

On the one hand, girls who have been taught that menstruation causes intense pain, depression, and irritability tend to experience more of these negative side effects than do girls who are taught that their periods will be relatively pain free and uneventful (Gunn & Peterson, 1984; Pillemer, 1987; Whitehead, 1986). From this social learning theorists' perspective, our attitudes about and reactions to menstruation are primarily determined by the ways in which our society reinforces us and by the types of models it offers us. Consider, for example, the images presented to you by the media and the jokes you have heard related to menstruation, as well as the ways in which feminine hygiene products are advertised. How were you first introduced to the topic of menstruation, and what impact did these first impressions have on your teenage attitudes and behavior?

A CLOSER LOOK 2.9

Relieving Menstrual Cramps

1. Eat more wisely. Cut down on salty foods the week before and during the menstrual period. Also eat less red meat.
2. Avoid certain liquids. Beer, caffeine, and wine can increase cramping and headaches.
3. Take additional vitamins the week before and during menstruation. Some girls find that supplements of dolomite, calcium, vitamin C, vitamin B, and magnesium reduce menstrual cramping.
4. Apply heat. A hot water bottle or heating pad on the stomach or lower back may help. Sometimes curling up in a knee-to-chest position with a hot water bottle against the back relaxes the muscles.
5. Use aspirin. Many girls find that aspirin brings fast and complete relief from cramping. Other pain relievers are also available for menstrual discomfort.
6. Exercise! An extremely effective way to relax muscles is regular, vigorous aerobic exercise, like running or swimming. There is no exercise that is dangerous for girls during their periods.
7. Take birth-control pills. In cases of extreme menstrual pain, some doctors will prescribe birth-control pills, although this poses several dangers for adolescent girls.

On the other hand, physiological studies demonstrate that premenstrual tension and mood swings are not always determined solely by what we expect to happen or what we have learned from society (Debrovner, 1982; Ojeda, 1983). Irritability, depression, cramps, and headaches appear to be related to the amount of calcium, progesterone, and prolactin in the body. Some girls may indeed suffer more pain and mood swings than others as a result of these chemical fluctuations. In their extreme form, these adverse and emotional reactions to menstruation are referred to as **premenstrual syndrome,** or **PMS.** Since American females report having PMS far more frequently than females in other Western countries, especially the Scandinavian countries, it appears that life-style, exercise, diet, and self-fulfilling prophecies do play a part. Similarly, in a series of studies, college students stated that a girl's positive behavior and good moods during the premenstrual or menstrual period were caused by "her personality," whereas they stated that her angry moods or negative behavior were caused by "her period" (Koeske, 1983).

Although we do not know how much of a girl's reactions to menstruation are influenced by physiological factors, we do know that many young males and females still receive the message that menstruation is "dirty," "embarrassing," and "depressing" (Bell, 1988; Gunn & Peterson, 1984; Lander, 1988; Shuttle & Redgrove, 1988; Taylor, 1988). Many parents, educators, and merchants still direct our attention to the negative aspects of menstruation. For example, in a sample of 135 advertisements from teenage magazines, menstruation was typically portrayed as a "hygienic crisis" that was best coped with by an effective "security system" for "peace of mind." Moreover, males were noticeably absent in these advertisements (Havens & Swenson, 1988). Is it particularly surprising, then, that so many girls still feel embarrassed by the normal incidents that accompany menstruation, such as buying tampons or letting a boyfriend know that she is having her period?

In addition to creating feelings of shame, the attitude that menstruation is "unclean" can contribute to health problems (Bell, 1988). Believing that the body's natural odors and menstrual fluids are repugnant, many girls use vaginal deodorants and deodorized tampons or sanitary napkins that irritate the genital tissues and create infections. Likewise, douching can cause infections by interfering with the vagina's cleansing secretions that maintain a proper balance of yeasts and bacteria. Worse yet, douching can spread infections by flushing harmful microorganisms from the vagina into the uterus.

Impregnation Despite the fact that girls' reactions to menstruation may differ, their bodies all undergo similar hormonal changes during a monthly cycle. Approximately 5 days after menstruation begins, the pituitary gland signals the ovaries to prepare for ovulation. The ovaries' increased production of estrogen causes the uterine lining to thicken with blood vessels and tissue in preparation for the possible implantation of a zygote. Near the 14th day of a 28-day cycle **ovulation** occurs, releasing one or more mature eggs into one of the Fallopian

2.10 ADOLESCENT VOICES

Girls' Feelings About Puberty

"Every morning when I was in eighth grade my mother would meet me at the door and ask if I was going to put on lipstick that day. Couldn't she see I didn't want to? Why was she so attached to my looking a certain way?"

"Sometimes when I'm all alone I stand in front of the mirror and stare at myself. I stare at all the things I can't stand about myself, like I absolutely can't stand my legs. They're so short and my thighs are huge. And the worst part is my chest. I'm so flat-chested I look like a boy."

"There were some days in high school when I'd shave under my arms and then cover my armpits with adhesive tape. It wasn't much good for my skin, but on those days I knew for sure I wouldn't perspire on my blouse!"

"How about guys whistling at you and bugging you on the street? I hate that. And it's pretty scary, too, people whistling at you when you're walking home at night."

"My mom and I are really close and when I first started getting breasts she took me out to celebrate. It was around my tenth birthday, and I remember feeling very grown-up about it."

"I started maturing physically when I was very young and I never wanted to. When I was about 9 I already started having breasts and I hated it. I was still a tomboy and I used to do anything to hide my chest, like wear baggy shirts and overalls all the time. Now that I'm older I realize that I just didn't feel ready to grow up then. My body was leading the way and my feelings about changing were about a mile behind."

"There's a difference between what you want and what you think other people want. I don't think hairy legs are that bad. It doesn't bother me on me, and it doesn't bother me on other girls."

"I'm glad I haven't gotten my period yet. I'm still a kid. No way do I want to worry about that every month."

"I got my period early, when I was in fourth grade, and all my friends were jealous. They wanted to get theirs too."

Source: Ruth Bell et al. (1988). *Changing bodies, changing lives.* New York: Random House, Inc.

tubes. Some girls feel a slight twinge or lower back pain when they ovulate. As the egg moves down the Fallopian tube toward the uterus, the ovaries release **progesterone,** causing the uterine lining to become more receptive to implantation. When no fertilization occurs, the egg disintegrates inside the uterus, the supplies of estrogen and progesterone dwindle, and the uterine lining detaches itself and is expelled from the body.

Because the egg survives only from 24 to 48 hours, a girl is fertile for a maximum of 2 days per month. Given this amazingly short period of fertility, how do so many thousands of adolescent girls (and women) become accidentally pregnant? The answer resides in the amazing tenacity and long lives of sperm. In the 3 or 4 days preceding ovulation, the vaginal mucus becomes less acidic and extremely stretchy in texture. These two changes ensure the survival of any sperm deposited into the vagina during the preovulatory days. Yet even under these receptive conditions, sperm can survive only 5 or 6 hours in the vagina. If the couple has placed a spermicide within the vagina before sperm are released, many of these sperm will die on contact with the chemicals. If a spermicide is being used along with a diaphragm, cervical cap, or cervical sponge, additional protection is afforded, since the os is covered and sperm cannot travel into the uterus. (Note the warning on all barrier methods of contraception that these devices must *not* be removed from the girl's body for at least 6 hours after intercourse.) Unfortunately, most adolescents do not understand that without spermicide the sperm rapidly propel themselves through the os, past the uterus, and into the Fallopian tubes, where they can patiently survive for almost a week. Consequently, a couple who has intercourse any time during the week before ovulation is introducing millions of sperm into the Fallopian tubes, where only one is needed to penetrate the egg during the brief fertile period.

A second reason many adolescent girls become pregnant is the erroneous assumption that pregnancy is impossible unless a girl has already started having menstrual periods. Because ovulation occurs 2 weeks before menstruation, a girl is unknowingly fertile before she has her first period. Intercourse or foreplay can thus result in pregnancy. (Remember there are live sperm in the pre-ejaculatory fluids on the penis.) Misguided by uninformed adults or friends, too many adolescents discover these physiological facts too late through the trauma of unplanned pregnancies.

ABNORMAL DEVELOPMENT OF THE REPRODUCTIVE SYSTEM

Although in most cases physical development proceeds normally, some adolescents undergo ordeals created by their chromosomal abnormalities. Two such conditions that affect the adolescent's sexual development are Klinefelter's and Turner's syndromes. Both are caused by an abnormal division of X and Y chromosomes on the 23rd chromosomal pair at the time of conception.

In **Klinefelter's syndrome** a male is born with an extra X chromosome on the 23rd pair. Although the boy has a penis and testicles, he develops female characteristics as well. His genitals may be quite small and his body less muscular than those of normal boys. Most boys with the extra X chromosome are sterile. The opposite condition, being born with an extra Y chromosome, creates other kinds of problems for the adolescent male. The XYY pattern tends to make boys mature sooner, to be slightly taller, and to suffer from more acne than boys with the normal XY pattern. The extra Y chromosome causes the adrenal glands to secrete too much androgen, causing earlier puberty and additional acne. However, evidence has failed to support the hypothesis that the extra Y chromosome causes boys to be more aggressive (Hamburg & Trudeau, 1981).

A similar condition in females, **Turner's syndrome,** causes the child to be born with female genitals but without ovaries. Consequently, her body cannot produce the estrogen necessary for the development of her secondary sex characteristics during adolescence. Through hormone injections, estrogen is introduced into her body to enhance the development of female characteristics.

Early studies generally concluded that children with abnormal sex chromosomes would be mentally retarded and that the males would be predisposed to criminal behavior and the females to psychosis. Current data on more representative samples, however, show that although many adolescents with these genetic disorders need extra help in school, have low self-esteem, and have difficulties with social relationships, these children can succeed and do not generally develop the serious behavioral abnormalities that had originally been predicted (Berch & Bender, 1987).

Despite their potential for social and academic success, girls with Turner's syndrome do tend to be hyperactive and inattentive in school. As adolescents, these girls also have difficulty establishing friendships, a problem that may be partially explained by their difficulty in interpreting people's facial expressions. Moreover, many of these girls do have specific cognitive deficiencies, especially in the areas of math and spatial skills (McCauley, Kay, Ito, and Treder, 1987). Likewise, boys with Klinefelter's syndrome often have problems with language and reading skills and are unassertive, inactive, and withdrawn (Berch & Bender, 1987).

Although genetic factors clearly predispose these children to cognitive and behavioral disorders, the quality of their environment is now seen as an important factor in the final outcome. That is, children from stable families tend to develop mental skills similar to their chromosomally normal siblings, while those from stress-filled families develop more cognitive and social problems than their siblings (Berch & Bender, 1987).

ISSUES RELATED TO ADOLESCENT PHYSICAL DEVELOPMENT

Early and Late Maturation

What impact does the age at which puberty begins have on an individual's behavior during adolescence and in later life? Is early physical maturation advantageous or disadvantageous?

In approaching these questions, most researchers have found that early maturation is advantageous for boys (Peterson & Taylor, 1980). Those who mature early often have an athletic advantage over less physically mature boys in our society, a culture where popularity is often predicated upon success in sports. Early maturers usually have higher self-esteem and more sophisticated social skills

Were you an early or a late maturer? How did your physical development make you feel about yourself?

than boys who mature later. In addition, adults often rate them as more masculine, more relaxed, and more attractive and afford them more freedom and responsibility than less physically mature boys. Men who matured early in adolescence have also been found to be more poised, more successful vocationally, and more socially active than men who matured late in adolescence.

In contrast, other studies indicate that whatever advantages might accrue to boys who mature early do not extend beyond adolescence. Accordingly, these data have failed to find a significant relationship between a male's adult personality and the timing of his physical maturation during adolescence (Peterson & Taylor, 1980). Furthermore, some evidence suggests that early maturation can be disadvantageous to the adolescent boy. Because adults tend to treat the boy who matures early like an older adolescent and to base their expectations on his physical maturity, they may deny him the time to develop his social and mental skills at a normal rate. Adults may also inadvertently force him into adopting a vocational and personal identity before he has had adequate time to explore and to experiment with his options. Despite these possible disadvantages, most boys say they would prefer to mature earlier than their male peers, if given the chance (Bell, 1988; Peterson & Taylor, 1980).

In contrast, the research generally acknowledges that the impact of early maturation is less favorable for girls (Gunn & Peterson, 1984). Girls who mature early usually date more often, express more dissatisfaction with their bodies, make lower grades, and express less self-confidence than girls who mature at an older age. Moreover, their physical maturity imposes sexual responsibilities that most are ill-equipped to handle, given their mental, social, and emotional immaturity. With these disadvantages, it is perhaps not surprising that, unlike boys, most girls say they do not want to mature earlier than their peers.

Appearance and Personality

While it might be heartening to believe that "beauty is only skin deep," most empirical data fail to support the maxim. Physical appearance affects not only how adolescents feel about themselves but also how adults and peers respond to them.

Investigations of the relationship between physical appearance and personality are hardly recent. Decades ago Harvard scientist W. H. Sheldon (1940) presented his theories regarding the relationship between body types and personality. According to Sheldon, an individual's personality is related to his or her body type: endomorphic, ectomorphic, or mesomorphic. **Endomorphs** are stocky, short, overweight people who are generally outgoing, sociable, and good-natured, in contrast to the tall, skinny **ectomorphs,** who tend to be introverted, intellectual, and inhibited. Most desirable in this typology are the **mesomorphs**—athletic, muscular individuals who are presumably assertive, energetic, extroverted, and courageous.

Is there any validity to Sheldon's hypotheses? Do adolescents' physiques affect their personalities? Although contemporary research discounts Sheldon's notion that our physique determines our personality in a predictable fashion, some of his assertions are credible—at least in a modified form. First, both adolescents and adults in our culture generally consider tall, muscular males and relatively tall, somewhat muscular females more attractive than their skinnier, shorter, or fatter peers. In other words, most of us do prefer mesomorphs. Second, our appearance as adolescents and as adults does influence the way people behave toward us. On the basis of appearance only, most of us judge tall, muscular people of all ages to be more influential, more outgoing, more popular, and more self-disciplined in comparison to skinny, overweight, or short people. Social psychologists have provided us with ample documentation of this view (Gillis, 1982; McConnell, 1983).

Moreover, this research consistently demonstrates that attractive people of all ages enjoy certain benefits that are generally denied to their unattractive peers. That is, we perceive attractive people as more friendly, intelligent, dependable, independent, and competent than their less attractive friends, even when their actual behavior contradicts our perception. Similarly, extremely thin people are often prejudged as being nervous and taciturn, whereas obese people are prejudged as slovenly and undisciplined. As a consequence of our preconceptions, attractive adolescents and adults often receive the benefit of the doubt in academic, social, and employment situations (McConnell, 1983). For instance, teachers and employers are more apt to overlook the inappropriate conduct and the mistakes of attractive adolescents than of those who are unattractive. In this sense, then, Sheldon's hypotheses have some bearing on today's adolescents, since the ways in which people behave toward an adolescent will inevitably exert some influence over his or her self-esteem and behavior. Since most of us consider mesomorphic physiques to be the most attractive, our behavior may indeed help these adolescents develop an outgoing, self-confident, poised personality.

Moreover, when young people begin dating, it becomes clear that some people are, quite literally, "beyond your reach." Given our society's definitions of attractiveness, height represents an important factor in our social and vocational lives. Indeed, the term "heightism" has been introduced as a way of pointing out that our height often influences the jobs we get, our sexual options, our self-esteem, and the power we ascribe to other people. For example, tall males tend to be seen as more intelligent, good looking, extroverted, and likeable than short males. Similarly, most of us submit to the unwritten "height rule" in dating or marrying: The boy has to be at least as tall as the girl—and preferably taller. In brief, short males and tall females are usually at a disadvantage in the dating game, both as adolescents and as adults. Indeed, the short man paired with a tall woman is often even used as the target of humor in comic strips and television programs (Gillis, 1982).

Given our feelings about height, it is not particularly surprising to find that adolescents' height has a considerable influence on their self-esteem and self-confidence (Gillis, 1982). Although there has been about a 4-in. shift upward in our society's opinions since the 1960s, most girls above 5′9″ are still considered too tall. Likewise, most boys under 5′5″ are still considered too short. Consequently, tall girls and short boys often feel embarrassed by their height—an embarrassment that can lead to defensive or aggressive behavior or to shyness and social withdrawal. Extremely tall boys may even develop what has been termed the "friendly giant syndrome." Trying hard not to intimidate other people by their size, very tall boys may be reluctant to assert themselves in a normal fashion for fear of appearing too dominant or aggressive. Some short boys and tall girls seek hormone treatments during adolescence in hopes of altering their adult height (Gillis, 1982). Given that this treatment is costly, is sometimes dangerous, and usually alters height by only 2 or 3 in., we are left to wonder: At what price are we teaching our young people to try to make themselves fit the "ideal" height?

The relationship between physical appearance and self-esteem is especially disadvantageous for adolescent girls. In our society, where physical beauty is highly valued, it comes as no great surprise that most adolescents—male and female—are dissatisfied with some aspect of their appearance. However, physical appearance tends to take a heavier toll on girls' self-esteem than on boys'. Girls consistently report being more dissatisfied with their bodies than are boys (Gunn & Peterson, 1984; McConnell, 1983; Simmons & Blyth, 1987). Specifically, most girls see themselves as too fat, even though their actual weight is normal or below normal (R. Freedman, 1989; Levinson & Powell, 1986; Seid, 1989). Since we will explore this sex difference more thoroughly in chapter 5, suffice it to say at this point that, especially for girls, most adolescents do not accept the old adage that "beauty is only skin deep." Quite simply, most of us, as adolescents and as adults, are "judging the book by its cover" by allowing physical appearance to influence our judgments and expectations of others and of our own selves.

Food, Nutrition, and Dieting

Given the role that our physical appearance plays in our self-esteem and popularity, it is not particularly surprising that most adolescents are dissatisifed with their weight. Most teenage boys, under the thumb of our present notions of "masculinity," want to be heavier and more muscular. On the other hand, most girls want to be skinnier. Unfortunately, in attempts to alter their weight, too many young people jeopardize their health through dangerous diets like those described in Box 2.11.

Not only are these diets dangerous, they ignore the teenage body's requirements for normal growth. During his peak growing years, a teenage boy needs 2,500 to 3,000 calories a day, and the average girl needs 2,000 to 2,500. The time for cutting back our calories is during our early adult years, not during our adolescence. Unfortunately, poor eating habits and too little exercise have taken their toll on today's teenage bodies. As the National Youth Fitness Study of 1985 demonstrated, adolescents are now more overweight and less physically fit than teenagers in the 1960s (Carey & Hager, 1985; see Box 2.4). Likewise, a 1989 nationwide sample of more than 12,000 students revealed that today's teens live a more sedentary lifestyle, have less physical stamina, and are more overweight than teenagers in 1980, with our average 13-year-old boy needing to lose 9 lb (Amateur Athletic Union, 1989).

Advantages and Disadvantages of Sports

Despite the fact that most adolescents are more physically out of shape than their peers in earlier decades, most would agree that physical exercise has its benefits. In addition to its many physiological benefits (lowering blood pressure and the basal metabolic rate and reducing excess fat tissue), regular physical exercise has psychological benefits. Regular exercise has been found to reduce depression and elevate the spirits, supposedly by increasing the body's production of endorphins. **Endorphins** are chemicals released by the brain as a natural anesthetic when the body is severely injured. Some evidence suggests that these endorphins are released during rigorous exercise as well, thereby acting as an antidepressant by reducing tension and anxiety (Carr, 1981). Although the role of endorphins in reducing depression is still being debated, there is general agreement that regular exercise helps adolescents build self-confidence and improve their mood.

A review of the research also shows that physically competent youths are more popular than their physically inept peers (Evans & Roberts, 1987). Developing their physical skills through sports, then, could become a pathway for less popular or socially awkward adolescents to enhance their social status and improve their peer relationships.

Males and sports More relevant to adolescents is the ongoing controversy regarding the role that organized sports should play in their lives. How much time should adolescents devote to interscholastic sports? Do the advantages of

A CLOSER LOOK 2.11

Dangerous Diets for Adolescents

Fasting: Fasting is a poor method for losing weight, since the body that receives no food can last only a few days without weakening. Fasting causes dizziness, lethargy, and headaches. Once a fast ends, you are still left with the problem of how to control fattening habits.

Macrobiotic Diets: The macrobiotic diet progresses through six increasingly severe stages that limit the kinds of foods you can eat. In the final stage the diet consists only of brown rice and tea. Some physicians consider this diet the most dangerous, because it lacks most vitamins and the critically important mineral, iron.

Liquid-Protein Diets: The fad started as a beauty-shop diet marketed as NaturSlim, a powder added to skim milk for breakfast and lunch. When you add a sparse dinner, you consume about 750 calories a day. These protein products are now sold in drug and grocery stores under many brand names. While they do take weight off, they are nutritionally unbalanced and fail to provide the kind of calories necessary for adolescent growth.

Low-Carbohydrate Diets: Low-carbohydrate diets permit you to eat as much protein and fat as desired, but no carbohydrates. These high-protein diets put the body into a state that can be dangerous to diabetics and hard on the kidneys. The initial weight loss is mostly a loss of the body's fluids, not fat. Without carbohydrates most people feel listless.

continued

being a high-school athlete outweigh the disadvantages? How are our adult attitudes about professional sports influencing our young people?

On the one hand, it is argued that participating in interscholastic team sports builds a young man's character by teaching him the value of cooperation, self-discipline, self-sacrifice, competition, and concentration (Sabo & Runfola, 1980). In this vein, sports teach boys to overcome obstacles they will encounter in other areas of their lives and to compete successfully in the world off the courts and playing fields. Furthermore, athletic success can underwrite the cost of a college education for the fortunate few who excel in high-school sports.

As a counter to the argument that participating in sports will undermine an athlete's academic performance, in the mid-1980s high schools and colleges began imposing more stringent academic requirements on athletes. Under the National Collegiate Athletic Association (NCAA) standards, a ruling known as "Proposition 48" requires high-school athletes to score at least 700 out of a possible 1600 on the Scholastic Aptitude Test (SAT) or 15 out of 36 on the American College Tests (ACT) and to have at least a 2.0 grade point average in 11 mandatory courses. Most of the high-school athletes who have been barred from intercollegiate athletics by the NCAA standards are black, leading critics to contend that the SAT and ACT tests are culturally biased in favor of white, middle-class students.

Nevertheless, Proposition 48 has led to changes in high-school athletic requirements as well. In high schools, "no pass, no play" rules require athletes to pass their classes in order to participate in extracurricular activities. Two years after

Box 2.11 continued

Higher-Fiber Diets: According to the advocates of the high-fiber diet, you should load your diet with high-fiber foods like bran, fruits, and vegetables. The fiber supposedly "speeds" food through your intestines and minimizes the chances for the body to absorb the calories. Nonsense! These diets do make you feel full and they are not harmful to the body, but they do not cause weight loss unless the feeling of fullness causes you to eat less.

Diet Pills: Most nonprescription diet pills are a combination of chemicals that cause the body to lose fluids, not fat. Because some bodies may contain as much as 10 lb of water, these pills do cause immediate weight loss and do make people feel thinner. These diets, however, are the equivalent of squeezing out a big sponge, since all the body loses is water. The danger is that the body needs water to keep itself cool, get rid of waste products, lubricate the joints, digest food, and carry nutrients to the cells. To accomplish these tasks, the body needs about 3 qts of water a day. Most of us "eat" 1 or 2 qt of water in fruits and vegetables. Using diet pills to rid the body of water is potentially dangerous and does not cause us to lose fat.

Another kind of diet pill, prescribed by physicians, contains amphetamines. Amphetamines were originally created to control mental depression, but people soon discovered that the drug also diminished their appetites. Although this is true, amphetamines also raise blood pressure, cause headaches, create restlessness, and are addictive. Amphetamines are hazardous enough for the federal government to regulate their sale and put warning labels on the bottles.

Source: B. Edelstein. (1980). *The woman doctor's diet for teen-age girls.* New York: Ballantine.

imposing these rules, the Dallas Independent School District reported that the percentage of students in grades 7–12 who failed one or more classes fell from 55.6% in 1985 to 46.4% in 1986 (No pass, 1987). Critics have pointed out, however, that both high-school and college athletes can circumvent the new standards by simply avoiding difficult classes or by seeking out teachers who make special concessions for outstanding athletes. Moreover, even as the ruling enters its fifth year, the Texas legislature and school boards continue to battle with adolescent athletes and coaches over the ruling, and legislatures in at least six other states have refused to establish no-pass, no-play standards (Mathis, 1989).

The argument that sports interfere with a young man's academic development is one among many for those against interscholastic athletics (Sabo & Runfola, 1980). Critics contend that the present system permits only a handful of male students to make the team, leaving the majority of boys and traditionally all the girls sitting inactively on the sidelines, cheering the few who play. Thus, whatever benefits might accrue from sports, few adolescents get the opportunity to enjoy them. If interscholastic sports are so worthwhile, why not disperse the school's funds and facilities among more students, rather than limiting the benefits to a few outstanding athletes?

Some have also questioned what kind of "character" sports are building. What attitudes are we encouraging by the kind of emphasis on winning that provokes violent, aggressive behavior among both fans and players? What values are we endorsing by creating a social hierarchy in high schools (and beyond) where "jocks" are elevated in status and given preferential treatment by their peers? In this vein, some evidence suggests that male athletes become less sensitive to other people's needs and overly concerned with proving their masculinity (Sabo & Runfola, 1980).

And the physical benefits of sports? It is reported that 12 million children suffer permanent physical damage from sports before the age of 18 and that these injuries are disproportionately high among young adolescents. The risk of permanent bone and joint damage, as well as damage to immature hearts, kidneys, and muscles, is especially critical among those whose bone and muscle development is not yet complete. In high-school football alone during 1988, 14,000 of the 503,706 injured players required surgery—most often on the knee (National Athletic Trainers' Association, 1988). Moreover, this study, which the National Athletic Trainers' Association described as the most thorough ever conducted, found that the number of serious injuries had increased between 1987 and 1988. Critics of interscholastic sports also worry that boys are operating under a delusion regarding the odds of their making it in the pros, since only 1 in 10,000 high-school athletes ever becomes a professional athlete.

One of the most extensive recent studies of high-school athletes, which followed 13,000 students over a 6-year period, dispels some of these concerns and affirms others (Women's Sports Foundation, 1989). Most high-school athletes fare no worse than other students academically, thus dispelling the stereotype of the "dumb jock." Participation in sports, however, did not improve most athletes' grades. Moreover, participating in sports did little to further the higher educational gains of minority youth. In fact, for black urban females, only 5% of the former athletes eventually entered "high status" jobs, in comparison to 60% of the girls who were not high-school athletes. Also, being an athlete had no effect on the dropout rate of urban males and females, although athletes in rural and suburban areas were somewhat less likely to drop out of school than other students at the same schools.

Females and sports If team sports and interscholastic athletics do more good than harm, girls are less likely than boys to reap these rewards. When girls play sports, they generally engage in individual exercises such as skating, gymnastics, or tennis, in contrast to boys, who are typically involved in competitive team sports. As a consequence, girls are more apt to be deprived of the opportunities in team sports for learning competitiveness, assertiveness, and physical self-discipline. Team sports can also teach players how to accept criticism, how to relate to authority figures, and how to express opinions and emotions without resorting to tears—areas in which adolescent girls could benefit, as we will see in future chapters.

Considering these potential benefits, why are more girls not active in competitive team sports? The most evident reason is that our society has traditionally discouraged girls from participating in rigorous exercise of any kind—especially in competitive team sports. Although our attitudes may slowly be changing, traditional beliefs and misconceptions about the female body die hard. For example, some people still fear that vigorous exercise will disrupt a teenage girl's maturational processes, although a review of the research shows that carefully monitored sports participation and intensive training have no effect on a girl's growth or maturation (Zimmerman, 1987).

Why aren't girls more athletically active?

Unlike their male counterparts, those girls who do venture into sports are not generally esteemed for their roles as athletes. Even among today's "liberated" teenagers, girls who participate in "unladylike" sports, such as basketball or soccer, usually encounter more disapproval than those who compete in less "masculine" sports, such as gymnastics and tennis—a disapproval, by the way, that comes from girls as well as from boys (Colley, Nash, O'Donnell, & Restorick, 1987; Kane, 1988). Similarly, high-school girls who are athletes have reported feeling more role conflict than nonathletes (Desertrain & Weiss, 1988).

Girls' participation in sports is also discouraged by an unequal distribution of money, facilities, publicity, scholarships, and coaching. Most schools accord boys preference in terms of facilities, publicity, schedules, pep rallies, booster clubs, and special services, such as academic tutoring. Boys' coaches are also generally paid more than girls' coaches (Carpenter & Acosta, 1982; Parkhouse & Lapin, 1980).

In 1975 the federal government approved Title IX, a law intended to ensure that male and female citizens would be treated more equitably. In regard to school athletic programs, Title IX states that "no person in the United States shall, on the basis of sex, be excluded from participation in, be denied the benefits of, or be subjected to discrimination under any education program or activity receiving federal financial assistance" (Title nine, 1978). Despite this legislation, resistance to athletic equity has been prevalent at both the high-school and the college level. Indeed, girls' participation in sports actually declined after the passage of Title IX, reminding us that more than legislation is needed to encourage our adolescent women to become more athletic (Parkhouse & Lapin, 1980).

Steroids and the Adolescent Athlete

Whether you adopt the position of those who oppose or those who endorse interscholastic sports, one fact is indisputable: Too many adolescent and college athletes are abusing drugs in order to enhance their athletic performance. Perhaps the most serious in terms of their popularity and their side effects are steroids. **Steroids** are drugs that closely resemble the male sex hormone testosterone. Either injected into muscle tissue or ingested in pill form, steroids increase the body's muscle mass in the same way that boys' muscle tissue naturally increases in response to their higher levels of testosterone during adolescence. Males or females who use steroids, therefore, develop excessive muscle tissue at a rapid rate and appear somewhat puffy and swollen around the face and neck.

Steroid use among athletes is not a new phenomenon, despite the fact that the substance has been banned from major athletic events, such as professional and collegiate sports and the Olympics. Since the 1950s, athletes have been using hormone-like drugs to build their muscle tissue and cut their training time. The alarming news lies, not in their existence, but in their increasing popularity among both the adolescent and the adult populations. Although steroids are illegal except when prescribed by doctors for the treatment of specific diseases (severe asthma and Klinefelter's syndrome, for example), adolescent athletes have relatively easy access to them through private gymnasiums, other athletes, unscrupulous doctors and coaches, and mail-order companies. The federal Food and Drug Administration estimates that annual illegal sales of steroids may total $100 million (Flax, 1988), and Congress is considering a bill that would make unauthorized steroid sales a felony instead of a misdemeanor.

The potential side-effects of steroids are more far-reaching than puffy, swollen skin: Cancer, heart disease, impotence, stunted growth, and even death may result. Yet, despite these dangers, the first national study of adolescent steroid use showed that almost 7% of the 3,403 high-school athletes questioned had tried or were currently using steroids (Yesalis, 1988). Of these, 3% were heavy users who had taken steroids for at least a year, some in quantities higher than those consumed by professional football players, and 44% had "stacked" (used more than one kind at once) steroids. More alarming still, half of the boys said they would continue using steroids even if they were proved to cause sterility, and 42% said they would not quit even if steroids were found to cause cancer or increase the risk of heart attack. After conducting his study, Yesalis warned that "the appetites for these drugs are created solely by society because we have a win-at-all-costs philosophy and we put an emphasis on appearance. Any coach who says you could make the first string if you were 15 pounds heavier and any parent who says sports is more than a pastime is encouraging steroid use" (Schmidt, 1989, p. 25).

Similarly, in a smaller study of 12th-grade boys in 39 schools across the nation, 8% claimed to have used steroids at least once during the previous month. On a national level, from 250,000 to 500,000 adolescents are estimated to have used or to be using steroids (Flax, 1988). Moreover, it appears that as many as one third of steroid users are nonathletes who are merely taking the drug to improve their physiques for social reasons (Schmidt, 1989).

These statistics are particularly disturbing given that teenagers using steroids may unintentionally stunt their growth since their development is not yet complete (Flax, 1988). Moreover, adolescents may become psychologically dependent upon these drugs to give them feelings of self-esteem, security, and popularity among

Should female athletes take steroids to improve their performance as do many male athletes?

their admiring peers. Nevertheless, adolescents who use steroids rationalize their decision by claiming that it is a victimless crime whose side-effects are minimal—and whose payoffs in the world of sports are part of a "commitment to the sport" (Fuller & LaFountain, 1988). Unfortunately, many high-school coaches still question the medical evidence against steroids or know little about them, thereby undermining attempts by the media or by parents to stop adolescents from using the drug (Schmidt, 1989).

CONCLUSION

In this chapter we have examined the physical changes that occur during adolescence. We have also considered the impact that many of these changes have on a youngster's personality, moods, and self-esteem. While no two adolescents react to their physical growth in exactly the same manner, all emerge from the years of puberty with the awareness that their child's body is gone forever. The body that will house them for the rest of their lives has completely matured by the age of 20. Many adolescents enjoy their bodies, care well for them, and undergo the physical changes of puberty with relatively little trauma. The less fortunate suffer the humiliation or anxiety that can accompany illness, unattractiveness, premature development, or genetic disabilities. As adolescents live through these years of rapid growth, one of our primary responsibilities is helping them accept, understand, and care for their physical selves in ways that will bring them the greatest pleasure and the least pain.

QUESTIONS FOR DISCUSSION AND REVIEW

Basic Concepts and Terminology

Cite specific statistics, research studies, or physiological data to support each of your answers.

1. Which factors influence an adolescent's rate of physical maturity?
2. How do male and female adipose and muscle tissues differ?
3. What impact do estrogen and testosterone have on male and female development?
4. What methods have proved successful in helping overweight adolescents lose fat and build muscle tissue?
5. What changes during adolescence account for the transformation of the face from that of child to that of adult?
6. What misconceptions about impregnation, fertility, and menstruation can result in unwanted pregnancies?
7. Describe the typical pattern of growth during adolescence for males and females. Take into consideration the reproductive system, height, weight, voice, muscles, adipose tissue, and secondary sex characteristics.
8. Which factors determine how much fat or muscle tissue an adolescent develops?
9. What advantages and disadvantages accompany early maturation for males and for females?
10. How much influence do hormones exert over adolescent behavior?
11. How can adolescents' diets affect their behavior?
12. Why do more adolescent girls not participate in sports?
13. How should male and female adolescents examine themselves for cancer?
14. What are the potential side-effects of using steroids?
15. In what ways are sports and physical exercise advantageous and disadvantageous to adolescent male and female development?

Questions for Discussion and Debate

1. What arguments might people offer against adolescent girls participating in sports?
2. How did your own physical development affect your personality during adolescence?
3. What were the wisest and most foolish habits you developed during your adolescence in terms of your own physical fitness and health?
4. What information presented within this chapter might have an impact on the way you are presently caring for yourself physically?

5. How does your own appearance differ from what you consider "the ideal," and how has this affected your social, athletic, academic, and personal development?
6. How do you feel secondary school athletic programs should be designed?
7. What are your happiest and unhappiest memories associated with your physical development during adolescence? In regard to your physical development, how might an adult have helped alleviate some of your anxiety or disappointment?
8. Given the benefits of a muscular, athletically competitive body, how would you convince adolescent athletes not to use steroids?
9. Given our society's preference for the mesomorphic physique and the benefits that accrue to attractive people, how would you help unattractive adolescents or those with endomorphic and ectomorphic physiques deal with these social realities?

GLOSSARY

adipose tissue Fat.

amenorrhea The cessation of the menstrual period.

androgen Any of the steroid hormones that develop and maintain masculine secondary sex characteristics.

anovulatory When the ovaries do not release an egg during the monthly cycle.

areola The dark-colored area of skin around the nipple.

basal metabolism rate The rate at which the body converts calories into sugar for energy.

cervix The tip of the uterus; extends into the vagina.

circumcised When the skin covering the penis glans is surgically removed.

clitoris The female's center of sexual excitation and source of orgasms whose small, pea-shaped glans (head) is protected by a small covering of skin within the folds of the labia; swells during sexual excitation. Slang/synonyms: "joy button," "clit."

dysmenorrhea Excessive pain during menstruation.

ectomorph Tall, skinny body type.

endomorph Stocky, short, round body type.

endorphins Chemicals released by the brain that act as natural pain killers and mood elevators.

estrogen The hormone in both males and females that, at high enough levels, produces female secondary sex characteristics in either sex.

Fallopian tubes The small tubes that connect the ovaries to the uterus and through which the egg passes midway through each monthly cycle. The place where the egg is fertilized by sperm during a pregnancy. Synonym: oviducts.

foreskin The skin that covers the end of the penis and is cut and folded back during a circumcision.

glans The head of the penis or the tip of the clitoris.

gonadotropins Hormones released by the pituitary gland that cause the ovaries and the testes to increase the amounts of estrogen in girls and testosterone in boys during puberty.

gonads The ovaries and the testes.

hymen The fold of mucous membrane partially closing the external opening to the vagina. Slang/synonyms: "maidenhead," "cherry."

hypothalamus The upper brain stem, which signals the pituitary gland to release the hormones that begin puberty.

Klinefelter's syndrome Chromosomal abnormality in males that prevents their secondary sex characteristics from developing at puberty.

labia The folds of skin surrounding the vulva.

mammary glands The milk-producing glands in the breast.

menorrhagia Excessively heavy menstrual flow.

mesomorph Muscular, relatively tall body that is not too heavy or too lean.

nocturnal emissions Male ejaculation during sleep. Synonym: "wet dreams."

os The opening in the cervix through which menstrual fluid flows and which expands during birth for the baby's passage.

ovulation The release of the egg from the ovary each month, usually occurring about two weeks after menstruation.

premenstrual syndrome (PMS) A condition causing an extreme shift in mood and behavior in some females before each menstrual cycle.

prepuce The protective hood of skin covering the end of the clitoris or the end of the penis.

progesterone Female hormone secreted before implantation of the fertilized egg in the uterine lining.

prostate gland The male gland that produces semen.

protein loading Consuming large quantities of proteins in the erroneous belief that it will build muscles.

scrotum The pouch of skin that contains the testes.

semen The fluid, containing both sperm and seminal fluids, that is released when a male ejaculates. Not synonymous with sperm.

seminal fluid Semen.

seminal vesicles Tubes where the sperm is stored.

shaft The part of the penis below the glans that becomes engorged during an erection.

steroids Sex hormones that contribute to muscle bulk.

testicles The male sex glands that hang inside the scrotum. Slang/synonyms: "balls," "nuts," "family jewels," "rocks."

testosterone The hormone in males and females that, at high enough levels, produces male secondary sex characteristics in either sex.

tubal ligation A method of birth control in which the female's Fallopian tubes are either clamped shut or cauterized so that the egg, after it is released from the ovary, cannot meet with a sperm. Synonym: a tubal.

Turner's syndrome A chromosomal abnormality in females that prevents the development of secondary sex characteristics at puberty. The equivalent of Klinefelter's syndrome in males.

urethra In the female, the tube that carries urine from the bladder to the outside of the body; in the male, the tube that carries both urine and seminal fluid to the outside of the body.

uterus The organ, about the size of a fist and the shape of an upside-down pear with a thick wall of strong, stretchy muscles, in which the fetus develops during pregnancy. Synonym: womb.

vagina The passageway from the uterus to the outside of the body whose walls touch unless separated by an external object, such as a tampon or a penis; produces mucous for cleansing the body and for lubrication during intercourse. Synonym: birth canal.

vas deferens The tubes that carry sperm from the testicles to the seminal vesicles.

vasectomy A method of birth control in which the vas deferens are surgically cut or cauterized so that sperm cannot be mixed with the seminal fluid before ejaculation.

vulva The external female genitals.

zygote An egg that has been fertilized by the sperm.

REFERENCES

Amateur Athletic Union. (1989). *Physical fitness trends in American youth, 1980–1989.* Washington, DC: Author.

Bailey, C. (1978). *Fit or fat?* New York: Houghton Mifflin.

Beau, C., Baker, P., & Haas, J. (1977). The effects of high altitude on adolescent growth. *Human Biology, 49,* 109–124.

Bell, R. (1988). *Changing bodies, changing lives.* New York: Random House.

Berch, D., & Bender, B. (1987, December). Margins of sexuality. *Psychology Today,* 54–57.

Blacks are hit hardest by N.C.A.A. academic eligibility rule. (1988, September 21). *Education Week,* p. 24.

Bongiovani, A. (1983). An epidemic of premature telarche in Puerto Rico. *Journal of Pediatrics, 103,* 245–46.

Brone, R., & Fisher, C. (1988). Determinants of adolescent obesity. *Adolescence, 23,* 155–169.

Buckley, T., & Gottlieb, A. (1988). *Blood magic: The anthropology of menstruation.* Berkeley: University of California Press.

Carey, J., & Hager, M. (1985, April 1). Failing in fitness. *Newsweek,* pp. 84–87.

Carpenter, L., & Acosta, R. (1982). College athletes. *Chronicle of Higher Education, 26,* 4.

Carr, D. (1981). Physical conditioning facilitates the exercise induced secretion of beta endorphin and beta lipotropin. *New England Journal of Medicine, 305,* 560–563.

Colley, A., Nash, J., O'Donnell, L., & Restorick, L. (1987). Attitudes to the female sex role and sex typing of physical activities. *International Journal of Sport Psychology, 18,* 19–29.

Debrovner, C. (Ed.) (1982). *Premenstrual tension: A multidisciplinary approach.* New York: Human Sciences Press.

Delaney, J., Lupton, M., & Toth, E. (1988). *The curse: A cultural history of menstruation.* Urbana: University of Illinois Press.

Desertrain, G., & Weiss, M. (1988). Being female and athletic: Cause for conflict? *Sex Roles, 18,* 567–582.

Dietz, W., & Gortmaker, S. (1985). Do we fatten our children at the television set? *Pediatrics, 75,* 807–812.

Doubts about Circumcision. (1987, March 30). *Newsweek,* p. 74.

Dummer, G. (1987). Pathogenic weight control behaviors of young competitive swimmers. *Physician and Sports Medicine, 15,* 75–78.

Edelstein, B. (1980). *The woman doctor's diet for teenage girls.* New York: Ballantine.

Evans, J., & Roberts, G. (1987). Physical competence and the development of children's peer relations. *Quest, 39,* 23–35.

Eveleth, P. (1986). Timing of menarche. In J. Lancaster & B. Hamburg (Eds.), *School age pregnancy and parenthood: Biosocial dimensions* (pp. 39–52). Hawthorne, NY: Aldine de Gruyter.

Flax, E. (1988, September 21). Steroids: Few demanding that high school athletes just say no. *Education Week,* p. 25.

Freedman, D. (1987). Persistence of juvenile onset obesity over eight years: The Bogalusa heart study. *American Journal of Public Health, 77,* 588–592.

Freedman, R. (1989). *Bodylove: Learning to like our looks: A guide for women.* New York: Harper & Row.

Frisch, R. (1984). Fatness, puberty and fertility. In J. Gunn and A. Peterson (Eds.), *Girls at Puberty.* New York: Plenum Press.

Fuller, J., & LaFountain, M. (1988). Performance enhancing drugs in sport: A different form of drug abuse. *Adolescence, 22,* 969–976.

Gillis, J. (1982). *Too tall too small.* Champaign, IL.: Institute for Personality and Ability Testing.

Gunn, J., & Peterson, A. (Eds.). (1984). *Girls at puberty: Biological, psychological and social perspectives.* New York: Plenum Press.

Hamburg, D., & Trudeau, M. (Eds.). (1981). *Biobehavioral aspects of aggression.* New York: Alan Liss.

Havens, G., & Swenson, I. (1988). Imagery associated with menstruation in advertising targeted to adolescent women. *Adolescence, 23,* 89–97.

Higham, E. (1980). Variations in adolescent psychohormonal development. In J. Adelson (Ed.), *Handbook of adolescent psychology* (pp. 472–495). New York: Wiley.

Hoerr, S., Nelson, R., & Essex, D. (1988). Treatment and follow up of obesity in adolescent girls. *Journal of Adolescent Health Care, 9,* 28–37.

Inoff-Germain, G., Arnold, G. Nottelmann, E., & Susman, E. (1988). Relations between hormone levels and observational measures of aggressive behavior of young adolescents in family interactions. *Developmental Psychology, 24,* 129–139.

Johnson, W., & Corrigan, S. (1987). The behavioral treatment of child and adolescent obesity. *Journal of Child and Adolescent Psychotherapy, 4,* 91–100.

Kane, M. (1988). The female athletic role as a status determinant with the social systems of high school adolescents. *Adolescence, 23,* 253–264.

Katchadourian, H. (1977). *The biology of adolescence.* San Francisco: W. H. Freeman.

Koeske, R. (1983). Premenstrual emotionality. *Women and Health, 8,* 1–16.

Lander, L. (1988). *Images of bleeding: Menstruation as ideology.* New York: Orlando Press.

Lerner, R., & Foch, T. (Eds.), (1986). *Biological-psychosocial interactions in early adolescence: A life span perspective.* Hillsdale, NJ: Erlbaum.

Levinson, R., & Powell, R. (1986). Social location and body image among adolescents. *Social Psychology Quarterly, 49,* 330–337.

Malina, R. (1979). Secular changes in size and maturity: *Monographs of the Society for Research in Child Development, 44* (Serial No. 179).

Marshall, J. (1981). *The sports doctor's fitness book for women.* New York: Delacorte.

Mathis, N. (1989, May 17). No pass, no play. *Education Week,* p. 12.

McCauley, E., Kay, T., Ito, J. & Treder, R. (1987). The Turner syndrome: Cognitive deficits, affective discrimination and behavior problems. *Child Development, 58,* 464–473.

McConnell, J. (1983). *Understanding human behavior* (pp. 418–422). Fort Worth: Holt, Rinehart and Winston.

National Athletic Trainers' Association. (1988). *High school football injuries.* Oak Park, IL: Author.

Nielsen, L. (1983). Putting away the pom poms: A psychologist's view of females and sports. In B. Postow (Ed.), *Women, philosophy and sports* (pp. 115–130). Metuchen, NJ: Scarecrow Press.

No pass, No play. (1987, April 29). *Education Week,* p. 3.

Ojeda, L. (1983). *Exclusively female: A nutrition guide for better menstrual health.*New York: Hunter House.

Parkhouse, B., & Lapin, J. (1980). *Women who win: Exercising your rights in sports.* Englewood Cliffs, NJ: Prentice-Hall.

Peterson, A., & Taylor, B. (1980). The biological approach to adolescence. In J. Adelson (Ed.), *Handbook of adolescent psychology* (pp. 117–158). New York: Wiley.

Pillemer, D. (1987). Flashbulb memories of menarche and adult menstrual distress. *Journal of Adolescence, 10,* 187–199.

Raithel, K. (1987). Are girls less fit than boys? *Physician and sports medicine, 15,* 156–163.

Sabo, D., & Runfola, R. (Eds.). (1980). *Jocks: Sports and male identity.* Englewood Cliffs, NJ: Prentice-Hall.

Schmidt, P. (1989, May 17). Officials are aware of steroid use. *Education Week,* p. 8.

Seid, R. (1989). *Never too thin: Why women are at war with their bodies.* New York: Prentice-Hall.

Sheldon, W. (1940). *Varieties of human physique.* New York: Harper & Row.

Shuttle, P. & Redgrove, P. (1988). *The wise wound.* New York: Grove Press.

Simmons, R., & Blyth, D. (1987). *Moving into adolescence: The impact of pubertal change and school context.* New York: Aldine de Gruyter.

Susman, E., Inoff-Germain, G., Nottelmann, E., & Loriaux, L. (1987). Hormones, emotional dispositions and aggressive attributes in young adolescents. *Child Development, 58,* 1114–1134.

Taylor, D. (1988). *Red flower: Rethinking menstruation.* Freedom, CA: Crossing Press.

Testes test. (1981, September 21) *Time,* p. 69.

Thomas, J., & French, K. (1985). Gender differences across age in motor performance: A meta-analysis. *Psychological Bulletin, 98,* 260–282.

Thompson, J., Jarvie, G., Lahey, B., & Cureton, K. (1982). Exercise and obesity: Etiology, physiology and intervention. *Psychological Bulletin, 91,* 55–79.

Title nine and intercollegiate athletics: Nondiscrimination on the basis of sex in education programs (1978). Washington, DC: Office of Civil Rights.

Tucker, L. (1987). The relationship of television viewing to physical fitness and obesity. *Adolescence, 21,* 797–806.

Twin, S. (1979). *Out of the bleachers: writings on women and sports.* New York: McGraw-Hill.

U.S. Department of Health (1980). *Children and youth in action.* Washington, DC: Department of Health and Human Services.

Viadero, D. (1986, November 19). Lead in water poses major health risk to schoolchildren. *Education Week,* p. 12.

Whitehead, W. (1986). Social learning influences on menstrual symptoms and illness behavior. *Health Psychology, 5,* 13–23.

Wilson, D. (1987). IQ and height. *Pediatrics, 78,* 646–650.

Wollman, L., & Lotner, L. (1983). *The complete guide to sexual nutrition.* New York: Pinnacle Books.

Women's Sports Foundation. (1989). *Minorities in sports.* New York: Author.

Yesalis, C. (1988, December 16). High school steroid use. *Journal of the American Medical Association,* pp. 126–134.

Zakus, G. (1979). A group behavior modification approach to adolescent obesity. *Adolescence, 14,* 481–94.

Zimmerman, D. (1987). Maturation and strenuous training in young female athletes. *Physician and Sports Medicine, 15,* 219–222.

3 Adolescent Cognitive Development

CHAPTER OUTLINE

GOALS AND OBJECTIVES

This chapter is intended to enable you to:

- Identify the similarities of and differences between the psychometric, Piagetian, and information-processing approaches to cognitive development
- Enumerate the strengths and weaknesses of IQ tests
- Examine the cognitive changes that typically occur during adolescence
- Describe ways to encourage adolescents' creativity and special talents

CONCEPTS AND TERMINOLOGY

accommodation
assimilation
associativity
brain lateralization
class inclusion
concrete operations stage
conservation
convergent thinking
disequilibrium
divergent thinking
egocentrism
eidetic memory
flashbulb memory
formal operations stage
information processing approach
metacognition
neo-Piagetian
object permanence
Piagetian theories
preoperational stage
psychometric approach
reliability
reversibility
rule of equivalence
schema
sensorimotor stage
serialization
stage theories
Stanford-Binet
state-dependent memory
SOMPA (System of Multicultural Pluralistic Assessment)
validity

Key terms continued

Key terms continued

WAIS (Wechsler Adult Intelligence Scale)

WISC-R (Wechsler Intelligence Scale for Children-Revised)

THEORIES OF COGNITIVE DEVELOPMENT

Why do adolescents think more maturely than young children? How can we measure an adolescent's intellectual potential in order to predict what he or she is capable of achieving? How is intelligence related to creativity? Can we improve adolescents' cognitive skills and IQ scores through training, or are these abilities unalterable? Why do some adolescents have higher IQs than others? Are our intellectual skills primarily determined by our genetic inheritance or by the environments in which we are raised?

In their attempts to answer questions such as these, psychologists approach the study of adolescent cognitive development from three different viewpoints: the psychometric, the information processing, and the **Piagetian.** The **psychometric approach** focuses its attention on defining, measuring, and comparing individuals' intellectual abilities. This approach quantifies intelligence by converting our performance on written and oral tests into IQ scores. Although useful, as well as controversial, this approach does not help us explore how the minds of children, adolescents, and adults differ from one another. For this, we must turn to either the information-processing or the Piagetian (developmental stage) views of cognitive development.

The Psychometric Approach

Defining intelligence Which adolescent is the most intelligent? Sarah, who can quickly compute quadratic equations; Larry, who adapts easily to new situations and displays an acute understanding of people's feelings and motives; or Sam, who writes sonnets and speaks with a vocabulary far beyond his years? When trying to choose who is the most intelligent, you are confronting one of the fundamental dilemmas of the psychometric approach: How should intelligence be defined?

When you hear an adolescent described as "intelligent," specific images come to mind. If you are like most other people in our society, including the academicians who conduct research on human intelligence, your definitions of intelligence will include at least these three aspects of human behavior: (1) practical problem-solving skills—reasoning logically, seeing many sides of a problem, and keeping an open mind; (2) verbal skills—being a good conversationalist, reading often and well; (3) social skills—being sensitive to social cues, admitting mistakes, and displaying interest in the world at large. In particular, we make judgments about one another's intelligence on the basis of our verbal abilities (Weinberg, 1989). Beyond accepting these broad definitions, however, researchers are unable to agree on a unified definition of intelligence or on the ways in which intelligence can be measured.

Moreover, theorists disagree on whether intelligence is a single trait or is composed of many separate mental abilities. In this regard, theorists can be categorized as either "lumpers" or "splitters" (Mayr, 1982). Lumpers define intelligence as a general, unified capacity to acquire knowledge, to reason, and to solve problems. Those who advocate the use of IQ tests would, therefore, be classified as lumpers since they presume we have a general intelligence factor that IQ tests can accurately measure.

Other psychologists, the splitters, contend that our intelligence is composed of many mental abilities that operate more or less independently of one another. In this vein, Howard Gardner (1983) rejected the idea that IQ tests alone can measure our intellectual skills. Instead, he contended that we have seven "multiple intelligences": linguistic, mathematical, spatial, musical, interpersonal (understanding others), intrapersonal (knowing one's self and having a sense of identity), and bodily kinesthetic (exhibiting fine motor movement). Moreover, each of these kinds of intelligence follows a somewhat different path of development. For example, our kinesthetic intelligence presumably appears early in our lives, whereas our linguistic intelligence, exemplified by the poet, requires a longer period of apprenticeship and imitation. Gardner is among those who believe that our understanding of human intelligence will come from studying the interactions of people in their everyday environments, not from IQ testing.

In a similar regard, many psychologists argue that our existing definitions of and ways of measuring intelligence are culturally biased (Anastasi, 1988; Williams, 1975). That is, our definitions of "intelligent" and "unintelligent" behavior are limited by our racial and cultural perceptions. Who is to say, for example, that those of us who are the most verbally articulate are more intelligent than those of us who are verbally awkward but adept at other tasks less valued in our particular culture? From this viewpoint, IQ tests are especially dangerous in that they deny most minority and poor white youngsters the opportunity to demonstrate their intelligence according to the standards and experiences of their own cultures. As Box 3.1 demonstrates, defining intelligence exclusively on the basis of IQ test scores can be perceived as a form of racism.

Simply put, what is "intelligent" in one environment may be irrelevant, or even "stupid," in another. In Robert Sternberg's triarchic theory of intelligence, for example, our ability to adapt to the particular environment in which we find ourselves is one measure of our intelligence (1985). From this viewpoint, intelligence cannot be understood outside the person's sociocultural context. The problem for researchers then becomes how can we measure each individual's ability to adapt to his or her particular environment, since the environments in which we are raised often differ so considerably? Specifically, if an African American adolescent from the ghetto is "smart" in his or her environment but scores poorly on measures of intelligence that are designed for people raised in a middle-class culture, how can we accurately measure that adolescent's intelligence?

A CLOSER LOOK 3.1

Scientific Racism and Intelligence Testing

When Robert Williams was 15, his school counselor suggested that he become a bricklayer, because he was "good with his hands" and he had scored only 82 on an IQ test (3 points above the track for the special education class). Ignoring this advice, Williams earned a doctorate in psychology, became one of the founders of the American Association of Black Psychologists, and established a successful career as a college professor and researcher in the area of intelligence testing. According to Williams, "scientific racism is part of silent racial war and the practitioners of it use intelligence tests as their hired guns. Intelligence and achievement tests are nothing but updated versions of the old signs down South that read 'For Whites Only.'" Williams believes that the testing industry refuses to admit the truth about tests for fear of going bankrupt. The economic survival of the industry depends on defending their tests and convincing public schools and colleges that the tests are necessary.

Williams feels that we need to examine our beliefs about intelligence. First, he contends that intelligence cannot be inherited. Second, IQ test scores do not measure a person's ability to succeed in the world. The tests are simply designed to predict school success, and only children who attend good schools will be prepared to do well on the test. Third, the IQ test measures literacy and cultural background—not intellect. IQ tests do not measure a person's capacity to learn. Finally, the questions on IQ tests do not reflect the skills or mental potential of individuals who have grown up in ghetto environments.

Concerned about the placement in special education classes of minority students, Williams urges whites to be equally worried about the educational uses of IQ scores with white youngsters from impoverished environments. "As with every other manifestation of racism, the scientific variety threatens to destroy us all."

Source: R. Williams. (1974). The silent mugging of the black community. *Psychology Today, 12,* 32–42.

Efforts of psychologists such as Sternberg, Gardner, and Williams will likely result in new forms of assessing human intelligence in coming years. In the meantime, however, standard IQ tests remain the popular means for determining an adolescent's intelligence. Children's scores on conventional IQ tests continue to be a crucial factor for placement in the school curriculum and for assigning life-long labels, such as "retarded" or "gifted and talented." Since IQ test scores have played such a pivotal role in our society in allocating educational and vocational opportunities, they are well worth your careful examination, whether or not you ultimately agree with their definitions of intelligence or endorse their use.

Measuring Adolescents' Intelligence The psychometric approach assumes that we can define and can measure intelligence. In their quest to measure our intelligence, psychometricians rely primarily on two intelligence tests: the Stanford-Binet test and the Wechsler Intelligence Scales.

Originally designed by the French psychologist Alfred Binet and revised by the American psychologist Lewis Terman at Stanford University in 1916, the **Stanford-Binet** has been updated several times, most recently in 1985 (Terman & Merrill,

1985). The test primarily examines our verbal skills by asking us to define words, interpret proverbs, explain abstract terms, complete sentences, and explain analogies.

Believing that the Stanford-Binet relied too heavily on verbal skills and was not well designed for measuring adults' intelligence, David Wechsler developed his intelligence scales in 1939. Like the Stanford-Binet, these scales have been updated several times since their inception (Wechsler, 1952, 1975). The **Wechsler Adult Intelligence Scale** (the **WAIS**) is usually given to older adolescents and adults, and the 1975 revision of the **Wechsler Intelligence Scale for Children,** the **WISC-R,** is administered to young adolescents and children. Unlike the Stanford-Binet, which provides one total score, the Wechsler Scales provide a verbal IQ score, a performance IQ score, and an overall IQ score. Wechsler's IQ test asks us to solve arithmetic problems, define words, explain similarities between concepts, arrange pictures in the proper sequence to tell a logical story, reproduce designs with colored blocks, assemble cutouts into whole pictures, and answer an assortment of questions on "general topics." Both the Stanford-Binet and the Wechsler employ the same scale for classifying us on the basis of our scores (see Table 3.1).

What is "intelligence"? How should we measure it?

Table 3.1

LQ Ranges and Classification Labels

IQ RANGE	LABEL	PERCENT IN POPULATION
130 and above	Very superior	2.2
120–129	Superior	6.7
110–119	Bright-normal	16.1
90–109	Average	50.0
80–89	Dull-normal	16.1
70–79	Borderline	6.7
69 or below	Mental defective	2.2

Source: D. Wechsler. (1955). *Manual of the Wechsler Adult Intelligence Scale.* New York: Psychological Corporation. Reprinted by permission.

The pros and cons of IQ tests As previously mentioned, one of the major criticisms levied against IQ tests is that these measures lack **validity** (Anastasi, 1988). To be considered valid, a test must measure only the concept it proposes to measure and not some other concept. For example, if I want to test your marriage success potential, I might try to determine what percentage of the people you meet ask you out and what percentage of your dates have asked you out a second time. You might argue, however, that this is not a valid measure of whether you will make a good marriage partner, although it may be a valid measure of your present popularity.

Similarly, opponents of IQ tests argue that these instruments are not valid measures of our intelligence, although they may be valid measures of academic achievement, aptitude for school success, or knowledge of middle-class culture. In short, it is argued that intelligence is not limited to what intelligence tests test. How do you feel, for example, about the "Chitling Test" and the standard IQ test questions in Box 3.2? Does your score depend on who has designed the test questions and whether you share the cultural perspective that the test endorses? In this regard, it is noteworthy that Alfred Binet's IQ tests dovetailed with the social values and needs of Western society at the time he devised them (Wigdor & Garner, 1982). Subsequently, however, the growth of industrial economies, the need to extend formal education, and the demands of two world wars contributed to society's need for a new tool of measurement for making decisions in job and school placement. Nevertheless, the tests' advocates contend that IQ scores do reflect our inherent intellectual capacities, not merely our cultural knowledge (Jensen, 1985).

A second criticism is that IQ test scores may have too little practical significance. For example, a recent survey from 14 countries showed an average gain of 15 IQ points during the past 30 years (Flynn, 1988). According to the advocates of IQ tests, such gains should mean that the younger generation would be outperforming their elders. However, although the Netherlands has almost 60 times more "potential geniuses" (people with IQ scores higher than 150) now than in 1952, the number of scientific discoveries has not increased dramatically. Indeed, the number of patents granted to its citizens each year decreased by one third during the period in which the nation's average IQ scores rose by 15 points. Such findings lead

ARE YOU SURE? 3.2

The Chitling Test of Intelligence

Adrian Dove, an African American sociologist, has devised an intelligence test that emphasizes the impact of a person's culture on intelligence-test scores. Dove believes his test is "culturally biased," like standard intelligence tests used to assess minority children's abilities. Dove's Chitling Test is culturally biased in favor of individuals raised in an African American ghetto, rather than in favor of those from white, middle-class environments. See how you score on a few of the questions from the Chitling Test:

1. A "handkerchief head" is (a) a cool cat (b) a porter (c) an Uncle Tom (d) a hoddi (e) a preacher.
2. Which word is most out of place here? (a) splib (b) blood (c) gray (d) spook (e) black.
3. A "gas head" is a person who has (a) a fast-moving car (b) a stable of "lace" (c) a "process" (d) a habit of stealing cars (e) a long jail record for arson.
4. If you throw the dice and seven is showing on the top, what is facing down? (a) 7 (b) snake eyes (c) boxcars (d) little Joes (e) 11.
5. "Jet" is (a) an East Oakland motorcycle club (b) one of the gangs in *West Side Story* (c) a news and gossip magazine (d) a way of life for the very rich.
6. T-Bone Walker got famous for playing (a) trombone (b) piano (c) "T-flute" (d) guitar (e) "Hambone."
7. If a pimp is uptight with a woman who gets state aid, what does he mean when he talks about "Mother's Day"? (a) second Sunday in May (b) third Sunday in June (c) first of every month (d) none of these (e) first and fifteenth of every month.

Answers: 1. c 2. c 3. c 4. a 5. c 6. d 7. e

Source: A. Dove. (1968, July 15). Taking the Chitling Test. *Newsweek*, pp. 51–52.

many to wonder how the skills needed in order to score well on IQ tests are related to solving real-world problems.

Further, attacks on IQ tests have underscored the unfairness of the test-taking situation itself (Anastasi, 1988). The examiner may inadvertently administer the test differently to two individuals or make errors in scoring. Unknowingly, the examiner may also add to or detract from the individual's score by offering verbal or nonverbal prompts and hints. Extraneous factors, such as the noise level in the room or the rapport established between the examiner and the test taker, can also affect test scores. Then, too, some of us will have an advantage because we are more relaxed about taking tests than our test-anxious peers. In fact, some students who scored poorly on IQ tests improve their scores after learning how to relax and how to approach questions during a test (Whimbey & Whimbey, 1975). Moreover, there is strong evidence that our IQ test scores are influenced by a variety of motivational and personality variables that have little to do with formal cognition or achievement (Zigler & Seitz, 1982).

The tests are also criticized because an individual's score may change dramatically depending on extenuating circumstances (Anastasi, 1988). Although most of our IQ scores remain relatively stable from elementary school through adulthood, some youngsters' scores have been reported to change by as much as 50 points.

Divorce in the family, prolonged illness, and experiences at school have all been associated with gains and losses in a student's IQ score. Also, our IQ scores tend to fluctuate more during childhood than during adolescence, which should make us more cautious about forecasting performance or potential on the basis of these childhood scores.

Finally, it is argued that IQ scores are not reliable enough predictors of our intellectual abilities to be used for placing students in classes for the "retarded," the "average," or the "gifted" (Boehm, 1985; Wigdor & Garner, 1982). IQ scores must be interpreted within the context of a student's total record, including actual behavior in class and outside of school. If parents and educators are going to continue using IQ scores, they must be well informed about the characteristics of the tests and able to take account of the individual student's cultural background.

Given these criticisms and the long-lived popularity of the tests, it is not surprising that IQ tests have been placed on trial in federal courts during the past decade. For example, in the *Larry P.* case (1979), the California federal district court banned the use of IQ tests scores as the major basis for placing students in classes for the retarded. The lengthy court battle began in 1971 when a group of African American parents filed a class action suit charging that their children had been inappropriately placed in classes for the educable mentally retarded. The suit charged that IQ tests failed to account for the differences among children's cultural backgrounds and home experiences. In fact, when psychologists retested Larry P. and his classmates, several of the students scored as much as 38 points higher on alternative methods for assessing intelligence and, as a result, were not assigned to special education classes.

If there is so much controversy surrounding IQ tests, why do we continue to use them? First, IQ scores are reliable predictors for how well most of us will perform in school. The tests can also serve as a useful diagnostic tool in identifying which students need assistance and in which types of skill. In this regard, IQ scores can be useful in helping teachers decide which teaching techniques would be most effective for each individual student. In these ways, IQ scores could help schools individualize instruction by matching specific teaching techniques with a student's particular skills and deficits (Snow, 1982).

The tests' defenders also argue that IQ scores can protect minority youth from subjective or discriminatory assessments (Anastasi, 1988). In response to the charge that IQ tests are culturally biased, their supporters contend that since success in our society does depend on a mastery of white, middle-class skills and values, minority youths need to know where they stand regarding these criteria. Armed with this knowledge, youths who score poorly on the tests could then seek help to equip themselves with the skills necessary for success in our society.

Improving adolescents' IQ scores: The nature/nurture debate Inevitably, the controversies surrounding IQ tests have led to even more debatable questions: Can IQ scores be improved? If so, how? If not, why not? Those who support the genetic (or organismic) argument contend that our IQ scores are primarily determined by our inherited traits: "You can't make a silk purse out of a sow's ear." In contrast, the environmentalistic theorists argue that our IQ scores are primarily a reflection of environmental factors, such as socioeconomic status, diet, and cultural bias within the tests themselves: "As the wind blows, so will the tree grow."

One of the most publicized proponents of the genetic viewpoint, Arthur Jensen created a ruckus by asserting that racial differences in IQ scores are primarily the consequence of genetic, not environmental, differences (1969, 1985). In short, he and his supporters contend that there is nothing our society can really do to improve the low IQ scores of minority youth. From this perspective, enrichment programs such as Head Start and the Beethoven Project (which we will examine in chapter 6) are a waste of taxpayers' money in that they cannot substantially improve the intellectual abilities of children with low IQ scores. At their extreme, hereditarian arguments have been used to defend notions of racial inferiority and to attack intervention programs aimed at helping poor young people catch up with their more affluent peers (Plomin, 1986).

Countering these arguments, the environmentalists contend that factors other than genes are primarily responsible for our IQ scores. Environmentalists do not argue that our genetic inheritance has no impact whatsoever on our mental abilities. Clearly, for example, children born with Down's syndrome have a genetic condition that severely limits their intellectual development and that cannot be eradicated through environmental enrichment. Nevertheless, environmental theorists point out that most of our intellectual abilities—particularly the types of ability assessed on conventional IQ tests—are shaped by our environments, not by our genes (Anastasi, 1988; Spitz, 1986).

How do these warring sides defend their respective positions? First, the genetic theorists point out that the IQ scores of identical twins are more similar than the scores of fraternal twins. Since identical twins are developed from the same egg, while fraternal twins develop from two separate eggs, this is interpreted as evidence for the genetic argument. Similarly, the IQ scores of children raised in foster homes are more similar to the scores of their biological parents than to those of their foster parents. Finally, the proponents of the biological viewpoint cite the failure of enrichment programs, such as Head Start, to raise IQ scores substantially as evidence that intelligence is unalterable because it is inherited (Plomin, 1986).

On the other side, environmentalists point out these findings: The IQ scores of poor, minority children who are adopted and raised in upper-middle-class homes improve significantly, especially when the children are adopted at an early age. African Americans who moved north from the South and those earning high incomes score better on IQ tests than African Americans in rural southern communities and those earning low incomes. Moreover, firstborn children and children from small families usually have higher IQ scores than later-born siblings and children from large families. These findings indicate that the extra attention and time devoted to firstborns and to children in small families has a positive impact on their IQ scores.

Environmental research also underscores the impact of early childhood nutrition on a child's future IQ score and academic performance (Drotar, 1985; Galler, 1984; Lozoff, 1989). For example, a longitudinal study with a large sample of children who suffered from severe protein malnutrition in the first year of life (a critical time for brain growth) showed that these children failed to catch up with their peers intellectually even during adolescence (Salt, Galler, & Ramsey, 1988). Even though enriched diets helped these children catch up in physical growth to their well-nourished peers, their IQ scores remained 12 points lower, and even at the age of 18, they had more academic problems. Although such results were initially interpreted to mean that the brain had been permanently damaged by early malnutrition, reports now show that undernourished children adopted into advantaged families can develop normal academic and intellectual skills. In sum, it now appears that environmental enrichment and family nurturance may allow children to recuperate, at least in most part, from the damaging impact of childhood malnutrition.

In a similar vein, recent studies indicate that early exposure to lead may be linked to lower IQ scores and to learning disabilities (Viadero, 1986). The lead poisoning suffered by poor children after eating the sweet-tasting flakes of lead paint in older, rundown houses and tenements has long been recognized by scientists and health officials. More recently, however, emissions from leaded gasoline have been identified as a major source of exposure for children living in heavily populated, urban environments—the neighborhoods in which most of our nation's poor and minority children live. High levels of lead have also been found in drinking water where pipes have been repaired with lead solder. Understandably, environmental hazards such as these lend further support to the hypothesis that differences in our IQ scores are indeed influenced by the environment into which we happen to be delivered at birth.

Despite the evidence supporting the environmentalists' position, however, one of the most remarkable changes in psychology during the 1980s was the increasing acceptance of heredity's influence on our behavior, including our intellectual abilities (Plomin, 1989). This is not to say that psychologists now contend that our genes operate independently of our environment in determining our intellectual abilities. Although one gene determines the color of your hair, there is no firm evidence that single genes affect any complex human behavior, such as intelligence. Nevertheless, psychologists are more willing than they were in recent decades to acknowledge the role of heredity in our intellectual abilities.

Establishing the role of heredity and environment, however, is impossible in terms of conducting a true "experiment," since none of us lives in a vacuum free from environmental influences. Our best attempts to measure the relative impact of heredity and environment, therefore, have had to rely on studies of identical twins raised in separate homes. Ironically, these studies offer support for both the environmental and the genetic arguments. On the one hand, these studies show high correlations between the grades, IQ scores, and vocational achievements of twins raised in different homes (Bouchard, 1984; Pedersen, McClearn, Plomin, & Friberg, 1985; Plomin, et al., 1988). On the other hand, these same studies show that twins and other siblings raised in the same family are not very similar in terms of IQ or personality variables (Plomin, 1986, 1989; Scarr & Saltzman, 1982). In short, we have not yet established the relative power of "nature" versus "nurture."

Alternatives to traditional IQ tests In response to the criticism leveled against IQ tests, attempts have been made to develop more valid, culturally fair instruments for assessing intelligence. These tests attempt to avoid questions that reflect one culture's values over another's. Consequently, all individuals should have an equal chance of scoring well on the test. Other researchers are pursuing the option of developing tests that will measure an individual's intelligence by asking questions that reflect the skills being taught in his or her particular culture. For instance, Adrian Dove's Chitling Test (Box 3.2) is "culturally fair" to African American youngsters from ghetto neighborhoods but not to Mexican Americans from rural communities. Like conventional IQ tests, culture-free and culture-fair tests assume that if they are well designed, they can measure native intelligence.

Reflecting this contemporary approach to IQ testing is **SOMPA**—the System of Multicultural Pluralistic Assessment (Mercer & Lewis, 1978). SOMPA was designed to prevent minority children from being misclassified as mentally retarded on the basis of traditional IQ tests. Although the SOMPA is suitable only for children under 11, adolescents' school records may contain SOMPA scores. The SOMPA evaluates a child's intelligence by comparing individuals from the same ethnic group and by measuring other variables that may affect an IQ test score. For example, the test includes an interview with the child's parents, an examination for neurological problems, and assessments of the child's behavior at home and at school. The final score, called the Estimated Learning Potential, is obtained by adjusting the child's actual score on the Weschler IQ test on the basis of the information from the SOMPA. According to one of the nation's leading experts on psychological testing, Anne Anastasi, the SOMPA offers a powerful corrective for the routine, superficial misuse of test scores in isolation (Anastasi, 1982).

Finally, even among those who contend that our intelligence is primarily determined by our environment, a question arises of whether adolescents are "too old" to benefit from programs intended to improve IQ scores. Traditionally, we have invested our time and money almost exclusively in programs for young children, assuming that by adolescence it is simply "too late to teach an old dog new tricks." Research has demonstrated, however, that adolescents' IQ scores and cognitive skills can be improved despite early childhood deprivation (Hobbs & Robinson, 1982).

Admidst the controversy, the opponents of IQ testing continue to demonstrate how IQ scores perpetuate social and economic injustice in our society (Kaplan, 1985; Oakland & Parmelee, 1985); and the tests' advocates continue to demonstrate that IQ scores are relatively reliable predictors of which of us are most likely to succeed in school and, as a consequence, succeed in the marketplace (Jensen, 1985). Although you will have to decide for yourself which arguments about IQ tests and the nature/nurture controversy are most convincing, you may nonetheless feel confident in this: Both genetic and environmental factors determine our intellectual abilities during adolescence and adulthood. Moreover, an IQ test score should not be used as the primary criterion for determining any adolescent's educational or vocational future.

The Developmental Approach

In contrast to the psychometric approach, the developmental perspective is predicated on the theories of the Swiss psychologist Jean Piaget. Assuming that cognitive skills develop in predictable, invariant, sequential stages as an individual matures physically, the **Piagetian theories** exemplify the **stage theories** of adolescence described in chapter 1. In keeping with other stage theorists, psychologists who endorse Piaget's developmental perspective attribute adolescents' more advanced mental skills to their maturational stage, rather than to environmental variables. Despite the fact that Piaget's theories are being disputed by many contemporary researchers, an understanding of his model is imperative in order to appreciate the developmental viewpoint that has dominated the study of adolescents' cognition throughout recent decades.

A CLOSER LOOK 3.3

IQ: The Genetic Differences Are Real

In 1969, Arthur Jensen created an uproar with his article on racial differences and IQ. According to Jensen's analysis of the research, genetic factors are about twice as important as environmental factors in determining a person's intelligence. Differences such as education, income, or nutrition are inadequate explanations for the fact that African Americans score lower on IQ tests than do whites. Amidst the controversy and criticism, Jensen said, "The civil rights movement that gained momentum in the 1950's required liberal academic adherence to the theory that the environment was responsible for any individual or racial behavior differences. Thus when I questioned such beliefs I, and my theories, quickly acquired the label 'racist.' I resent this label and consider it unfair and unaccurate" (p. 80).

Jensen is one of the researchers who defends several unpopular conclusions: (1) African Americans score an average of 15 points lower than whites on intelligence tests, but this cannot be blamed on "culturally biased" tests. If the tests were culturally biased, African Americans would not be performing relatively better on the more culture-loaded questions than on the culture-fair ones. Neither would people, regardless of their race, tend to miss the same questions on IQ tests. If the tests favor people raised in the Anglo society, Chinese children who have recently immigrated to the United States would not be scoring higher than whites. And if environmental factors controlled IQ scores, Native Americans, who are the most economically and educationally disadvantaged citizens, would not be scoring higher than African Americans. (2) IQ tests are valid predictors of academic and vocational performance and of the ability to compete in many aspects of American life. Ap-

continued

The cognitive stages between birth and adolescence According to Piaget, children advance through three cognitive stages between birth and adolescence: the sensorimotor stage from birth to 18 months, the preoperational stage from 18 months to 7 years, and the concrete operations stage from 7 to 12 years (Inhelder & Piaget, 1958).

During the **sensorimotor stage,** children develop simple, generalized responses to objects and people. A major advance during this stage is the child's acquisition of the concept of **object permanence.** Initially confused by the relationship between what they see and what exists beyond their vision, young children fail to understand that objects or people still exist even when they are out of immediate sight. Without the capability to form mental symbols to represent that which is not immediately visible, young children are greatly amused by games such as hide-and-seek, which older children quickly understand as being just a game. Once children develop the ability to represent the external world with symbols, however, they can hold an object in mind and realize it still exists even though it is no longer in sight. Acquiring this skill is, according to Piaget, a mental landmark that signifies the end of the child's sensorimotor stage.

Box 3.3 continued

titude, IQ, and vocational tests predict whites' and minorities' abilities equally well. IQ scores reliably indicate that whites have about seven times as many talented people (those with IQs over 115) and seven times as few mentally retarded people as do African Americans. (3) Since each race's physical characteristics are inherited, there is a logical reason to presume that mental abilities are also inherited and that races differ. (4) The race and language of the examiner do not inhibit the performance of African American youngsters on IQ tests. When the tests are given by African American examiners who translate the questions into ghetto dialect, African American youngsters' scores remain unchanged. (5) Even though minorities and whites in the same soioeconomic class score more similarly than those with dissimilar incomes, this does not demonstrate that IQ is primarily controlled by environmental factors. These studies fail to consider that African Americans in the upper income brackets usually have lighter skin than those in the lower economic classes, indicating that genetic traits are influencing the IQ scores of people in the same economic groups. (6) Malnutrition has little if any impact on an individual's IQ score. Even the victims of severe famine in the Netherlands during World War II had IQ scores similar to their fellow citizens who had not been exposed to the famine.

The conclusions of researchers like Arthur Jensen inevitably fuel impassioned debate. Jensen, however, adheres to his theories and fends off his critics with steadfast confidence:

> The orthodox environmental theories have been accepted, not because they have stood up under proper scientific investigation, but because they harmonize so well with our democratic belief in human equality. . . .
>
> True liberals and humanists, on the other hand, want to learn the facts. They do not wish to expend their energies sustaining myths and illusions. They wish to face reality, whatever it may be, because only on the level of reality can real problems be effectively confronted (p. 86).

Source: A. Jensen. (1973, December). The differences are real. *Psychology Today, 7,* 80–86.

During the second, or **preoperational stage,** children's cognitive skills advance rapidly because they have acquired language, which permits the mental manipulation of meanings as well as objects. Children also develop the capability to use objects as symbols for other objects. For example, the child can pretend a doll is a real baby. Preoperational children, however, interpret reality exclusively on the basis of their own perceptions and experiences without being able to consider anyone else's point of view. Stated differently, children cannot be objective or terribly empathetic since they are viewing the world from an extremely subjective, personal viewpoint. This inability to see things from another person's point of view and to be able to imagine several different perspectives to solve a problem is referred to as **egocentrism** (see Table 3.2).

As they advance to the third stage of **concrete operations,** children become capable of perceiving relationships between objects and ideas and of recognizing general rules that apply to these relationships. For instance, the child is able to understand the **rule of equivalence**: If *A* is equal to *B* in some way (length or weight), and if *B* is equal to *C*, then *A* and *C* are also equal. The child also realizes that objects can belong to several categories simultaneously and that categories

Table 3.2

Piaget's Stages: Concrete and Formal Operational Thinking

CONCRETE OPERATIONAL THINKING

New skills acquired roughly between the ages of 7 and 11

Equivalence

The ability to grasp that if $A = B$, and $B = C$, then $A = C$.

If you notice that your sister's boots are smaller than your boots and if, later that afternoon, you notice that your cousin Gert's boots are bigger than yours, you can figure out that Gert can't wear your sister's boots. But you have to see the boots!

Reversibility

The ability to work backward and forward, rotate objects in your mind, and undo activities that have been completed in actuality or in thought.

You can understand that you can add alcohol and cocaine to equal "drugs" but also that you can subtract "cocaine" from "drugs" in order to get "alcohol."

Class Inclusion

The ability to reason simultaneously about the parts of a whole as well as about the whole itself.

You understand that when you have 10 candy bars, 8 of which are chocolate, you do not have more "chocolate bars" than you have "candy bars."

Associativity

The idea that the sum is independent of the order in which things are added.

You understand that $4 + 2 + 6 = 12$, but so does $6 + 4 + 2$.

FORMAL OPERATIONAL THINKING

Abstract Reasoning

The ability to solve problems and understand situations without having to see the actual objects or people involved.

After your dad has mentioned that your feet are bigger than your sister's but Freda's feet have outgrown yours, even without setting eyes on anyone's boots, you can finally understand that your cousin Freda is not going to be able to borrow your sister's boots.

Combinational Analysis

The ability to formulate several combinations in figuring out solutions: either *A* or *B* or *C* caused *X*, or *A* and *B* and *C* caused *X*, or any combination of *A, B,* and *C* caused *X*, or none of the above occurred.

After glancing at the recipe, you bake a cake. After 40 minutes in the oven, it comes out flat as a pancake and hard as a rock. You are able to figure out that you (a) either left out an ingredient or (b) put in too much of something or (c) had the oven on too low or (d) any combination of (a), (b), and (c).

Table 3.2 *(continued)*

Piaget's Stages: Concrete and Formal Operational Thinking

CONCRETE OPERATIONAL THINKING

Propositional Thinking

The ability to generalize from propositions based on one kind of content to other kinds of content.

A few weeks after your cake mishap, you are in the kitchen trying to bake bread. You are able to figure out that since both bread and cake have to rise, some of the lessons you learned from your last fiasco might apply to this new situation.

Perspective Taking

The ability to take the view of others and to understand that others may not view events, or feel, the same way you do.

You feel depressed after seeing a movie about world hunger and poverty because you can empathize with the victims in the film. You also can put yourself in your parents' place and understand how frightened they feel when you stay out late at night without telling them where you are.

---

can be ranked in relation to one other. In other words, a 7-year-old can understand that a puppy belongs to the categories "dog" and "pet" and that "dog" is a part of a larger category called "animals." The child also masters the concept of **reversibility.** This mental skill permits the young child to see that if we take four apples out of a bowl of six apples, divide these four into two equal groups, and then put all the apples back into the bowl again, we still have six apples despite the divisions.

In a related skill, children learn to reason simultaneously about parts of a whole and the whole itself. This comptenency enables them to solve problems of **class inclusion.** If we show children in the preoperational stage a box containing eight white buttons and two green ones, they are likely to tell us that there are more white buttons than there are buttons; but children in the concrete operations stage are able to discern that there are more buttons than there are white buttons.

In the concrete operations stage, youngsters also master the principles of conservation and serialization. **Conservation** is the idea that liquids and solids can be changed in shape without changing their volume or mass. Not until about the age of 7 can a child understand that when we pour liquid from a large glass into two smaller glasses, we still have the same amount of water. **Serialization** is the ability to arrange objects in proper order according to some abstract dimension. For instance, the child can arrange objects in correct order from shortest to longest. When individuals are thinking at the concrete operational stage, they are reasoning in terms of concrete realities and direct personal experiences. They do not yet have the ability to think about abstract ideas.

Cognitive stages during adolescence According to Piaget's theories, most youngsters advance to the stage of **formal operations** near the age of 12 (Inhelder & Piaget, 1958). During this stage, thinking becomes more logical, more abstract, and less egocentric than in childhood. Without having to rely solely on concrete objects or personal experiences, the adolescent is able to think about abstract concepts and to discuss hypothetical situations and problems. Although youngsters in the stage of concrete operations can create hypotheses, they are limited in terms of being able to generate only one possible explanation for a problem and are often ready to accept a hypothesis as true without examining its premises. Formal operational thinking also enables a young person to discard an initial hypothesis more quickly than younger children can when the evidence proves the initial reasoning to be incorrect. Furthermore, adolescents become more adept at solving verbal problems that are beyond the limits of younger children's concrete thinking: "If Alan is taller than Bear, but Alan is shorter than Paul, who is the tallest of the three?"

A conversation with a 10-year-old boy and his 15-year-old brother exemplifies several distinctions between concrete and formal operational thinking. The 15-year-old is more likely than his younger brother to consider other people's opinions, to modify his initial hypotheses, to comprehend abstractions, and to generate alternatives. As the research in chapters 4 and 12 will demonstrate, 15-year-olds are also more apt to empathize with others, to reason from a less egocentric view, and to become engaged in religious and political issues formerly beyond their interest or comprehension.

Developing new cognitive stages Given Piaget's descriptions of the more advanced skills that presumably accompany each stage of our intellectual development, we might well ask how we humans make the transition from one stage to another. Put a little more bluntly, we might also wonder why some of us do not seem to use formal operational reasoning very often even after we have left adolescence. In order to appreciate the Piagetian perspective on how we advance from one cognitive stage to another, we have to understand four concepts: schema, assimilation, disequilibrium, and accommodation (Flavel, 1985; Ginsburg & Opper, 1988).

A **schema** is a collection of data organized in a way that helps us interpret the new data and new experiences with which we are continually bombarded in the world around us. When we encounter new information, we rely on our existing schema to plot our course of action and to interpret new situations. Our schemata are actively selecting and interpreting environmental information in the construction of knowledge. Our mind is reconstruing and reinterpreting the environment to make new data fit in with our existing mental framework—our schema. **Assimilation** is the process of interpreting or construing these external events in terms of our present ways of thinking. Sometimes, however, new information from the environment does not fit into our existing schema and we experience the unpleasant feeling of **disequilibrium.** In order to reduce our feelings of disequilibrium, we change our existing schema. **Accommodation** is the act of noticing the differences between our existing schema and new data and of adjusting our schema accordingly.

For example, assume that Howard has gone to his new girlfriend's house for dinner. Using his existing schema, after he sits down he reaches for the nearest bowl of mashed potatoes, just as he does at home. With flushed embarrassment, he notices that everyone is staring at him with their heads bowed and their hands clasped. Howard (in a definite state of disequilibrium by now) quickly withdraws his hands and bows his head. Accommodating this new information into his outmoded schema, when he joins another friend's family for dinner, he reaches for the pork chops only after having glanced around the table to be sure everyone else's hands are extended.

Piaget's model stresses the constant interaction and collaboration between our internal (cognitive) processes and our external environment. Both the cognitive and the environmental factors contribute to the construction of our new schema and to the advancement from one cognitive stage to another.

Weaknesses in Piaget's stage theories Although Piaget's stage theories have been invaluable as a catalyst for research in cognitive development, they no longer represent the leading edge in cognitive psychology (Flavel, 1985). To begin with, psychologists face a number of problems in trying to diagnose our developing cognitive abilities. How, for example, can we determine when a given adolescent has or has not acquired formal operational reasoning? Since most subjects in the research engage in certain formal operational reasoning skills in some tasks but not in others, is this evidence that they have achieved formal reasoning? Similarly, suppose an adolescent actually does possess the abilities to reason at the formal operational level but shows no evidence of this on the laboratory test. Given the nature of Piagetian experiments, this might happen for any number of reasons: The subject fails to understand the instructions, fails to attend to the right aspects of the problem, or is disinterested in playing the experimenter's "game." Further, the youngster may possess the cognitive ability, but not possess the verbal communication skills necessary to explain to the experimenter how he or she is working through the experimental problem. In this vein, the adolescent's cultural background seems to affect his or her performance on Piagetian tasks, making our attempts to test Piaget's theories in cross-cultural studies especially troublesome.

In addition to exhibiting these shortcomings in diagnostic procedures, stage theorists such as Piaget assume that the transitions from one cognitive level to another are clear-cut and that, once in a stage, an adolescent's ways of reasoning will be fairly predictable. The transition from one cognitive stage to another, therefore, would be expected to emerge over a relatively brief period of time, followed by several years of stability. These assumptions, however, are not borne out by the research. In fact, our most important cognitive developments seem to proceed slowly and gradually. Moreover, we do not gain complete command of the skills associated with each stage without a considerable amount of seesawing. That is, even when adolescents have been diagnosed as being in the stage of formal operational thinking, they revert to concrete operational thinking. In short, we cannot predict adolescents' (or our own) reasoning abilities on the basis of their being diagnosed as either "concrete" or "formal" operational thinkers—a failure that undermines the value of any stage theory such as Piaget's.

This is not to say that Piaget's theories should be discounted. Indeed, they still form the basis of some of the most current theories in the field of cognitive development, as the next section will demonstrate. Moreover, despite the weaknesses of any type of stage theory, those theories still have their advocates, as you will see in future chapters. Given the current state of affairs, John Flavel probably best sums up Piagetian theory for us: "Whether the concept of stage will continue to figure importantly in scientific work on cognitive growth in decades to come is difficult to predict" (1985, p. 295).

A CLOSER LOOK 3.4

The Two Sides of the Brain

How does an adolescent's brain affect his or her abilities in mathematics and language? Is the female adolescent's brain different from the male's? What happens to an adolescent's cognitive skills if the brain is damaged? What relationship is there between being left-handed and being mathematically talented?

Researchers who study the brain have discovered fascinating answers to questions like these. The human brain is divided into two cerebral hemispheres, each of which controls different mental and physical functions. **Brain lateralization** is the separation of mental and physical functions into one side of the brain or the other. The left half of the brain receives messages from and controls the right side of the body. The right side of the brain does the same for the left side of the body. In most people the left hemisphere is the site of language ability, and the right hemisphere is the site of spatial skills, visual imagery, and musical abilities. Therefore, if the left hemisphere of an adolescent's brain is damaged, the youngster may be paralyzed on the right side of the body or may develop speech disorders. Likewise, youngsters with damage to the right hemisphere may find it difficult to draw, to find their way from one place to another, or to build a model from a plan. They may also respond inappropriately in social situations because they misinterpret other people's emotions. For instance, they often mistake another person's joking for hostility.

The two hemispheres process information differently. The left hemisphere uses logical strategies, while the right uses intuitive strategies. This does not mean, however, that each half of the brain can process only certain kinds of information. It simply means that each half is more efficient than the other in such processing. The left hemisphere's proficiency in language skills is probably due to the fact that it processes

continued

The Information-Processing Approach to Adolescent Cognition

At the present time, the **information-processing approach** is the leader in the field of cognitive development (all information in this section is from Flavel, 1985, unless otherwise noted). Advocates of this approach view the mind as being similar to a computer. Like a computer, our mind processes information from the environment in combination with data already stored in its system. The processing of information involves encoding and decoding new data, comparing or combining data, storing and retrieving data from memory, and focusing on particular bits of information while ignoring others. The primary goal of the information-processing approach is to provide a detailed understanding of what our mind actually does when confronted with a task or problem. As a consequence, it attempts to answer questions such as, Why do adolescents have better memories than younger children? What strategies do adolescents use in solving problems, and how can we help them to learn more efficient strategies? How does damage to a particular part of the brain affect our information-processing skills? Are the differences in

Box 3.4 continued

information faster than the right hemisphere, but the right hemisphere can also process language. The two halves of the brain also seem to store different kinds of informtion. Because they are connected by a cable of neural tissue, however, the information is passed back and forth between the two sides. If this cable is surgically cut (as surgeons sometimes do to control a patient's epileptic seizures), each half of the brain functions independently. For example, after this kind of surgery, a patient who is shown an object only in front of the left eye (the message is sent to the right brain) reports having seen nothing.

The relationship between the sides of the brain and left- or right-handedness is unclear, but we do know that right-handed people tend to do better on language tasks and left-handed people do better on spatial tasks. For example, Benbow and Stanley found that 20 percent of the students who scored above 700 on the math portion of the SAT exam were left-handed, which is twice the national average.

There also seems to be a relationship between brain lateralization and certain cognitive differences between males and females. Females tend to be more proficient in language tasks and less proficient in mathematical tasks than males. When portions of the left hemisphere are surgically removed, males often develop language disturbances; when portions of the right hemisphere are removed, they often develop problems in spatial skills. This does not happen with females. Findings like these suggest that lateralization may be greater in males than in females. Females may use both hemispheres in language and mathematical skills, while males may rely more on just one hemisphere to perform these tasks. These differences between male and female brains are relatively unimportant for practical purposes, because the average differences in mathematical and language skills are so small. The sex differences may eventually be extremely useful, however, in helping us understand more about how the human brain functions.

Sources: E. Hall (1983). The brain and behavior. In *Psychology today: An introduction* (pp. 59–61). New York: Random House; C. Benbow and J. Stanley. (1983). Sex differences in mathematical reasoning ability: More facts. *Science, 222,* 1029–1031.

male and female cognitive skills linked to the different ways in which each hemisphere of the brain processes information (see Box 3.4)?

Information processing also emphasizes that the adolescent's cognitive abilities are restrained by certain processing limitations. For example, an adolescent is able to remember more units of information than a younger child and therefore has a greater processing capacity. An adolescent, however, may encounter a task that requires a greater capacity for memory than he or she possesses and will then fail at the task. In trying to test their hypotheses about how our cognitive system functions, advocates of the information-processing approach use a variety of analytic methods. For example, as Boxes 3.5 and 3.6 illustrate, they will ask subjects in their experiments to verbally explain how and why the subjects arrived at their conclusions. By observing the patterns of our mistakes and the ways in which we adopt new strategies for solving problems, these researchers are trying to discover the conscious plans and strategies we use in problem solving. Similarly, by studying our eye movements as we try to solve problems, they observe the ways in which our visual attention patterns relate to what we can remember at a later time.

A CLOSER LOOK 3.5

Intuitions About Physics Die Hard

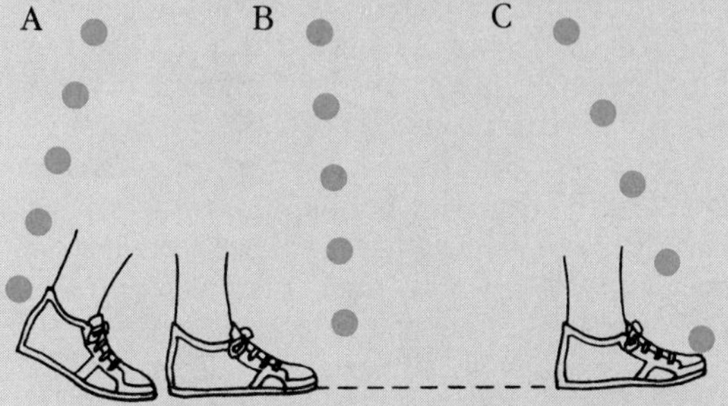

If you are strolling along and drop a ball from shoulder height, what path will the ball follow as it falls, as you keep walking—*A, B,* or *C*?

When researchers at Johns Hopkins University asked students to answer questions like this, surprising results occurred. Half of the college students guessed incorrectly that the ball would fall straight down and hit the ground directly beneath where it was released (*A*), In fact, the ball continues moving forward and then slightly downward as gravity exerts pressure. The ball then hits the ground in front of where it was dropped, following a parabolic arc (*B*). Why do so many of the students, even those who have had a physics course, misunderstand the laws of physics? And why do young children answer the physics questions more accurately than older children?

The researchers believe that visual illusions and the ability to think at the abstract level contribute to our misperceptions about the laws of motion. For example, when we see a walking person drop a ball, we may concentrate on the person as the frame of reference against which we view the falling ball. Since the ball does fall straight down relative to the moving person who dropped it, we may think that it has fallen straight down relative to the floor. A similar illusion occurs when clouds that are moving to the right across the moon make us believe that the moon is moving to the left.

A second explanation for people's success or failure at solving these problems may be their level of cognitive development. The youngest children probably deal with the problems on a concrete level by thinking about other identical situations in which they have seen the object move in exactly the same way. Older children, however, have developed the ability to think abstractly and to generalize from previous situations to new ones that are somewhat similar. For instance, noticing that a toy car continues rolling in the direction in which it was pushed, the child may create the abstract hypothesis that every object set in motion keeps moving in the direction it was set going.

And the consequence of these misperceptions and abstract reasoning? Consider the person who steps from the roof 20 ft aboveground to the ladder. Unfortunately, the ladder slips. The person tries to push away from the roof to avoid landing in the bushes directly below. Basing the shove on faulty assumptions about physics, he or she ends up on the cement sidewalk 9 ft away from the side of the house!

Source: M. McCloskey. (1983). Intuitive physics. *Scientific American, 248,* 122–130.

Much of the work in information processing builds on Piagetian principles. In this sense, these theories might be classified as **"neo-Piagetian,"** although they dispute Piaget's basic premises about "stages" of development. Instead, cognitive growth is seen as the acquisition of increasingly efficient rules for solving problems. Based in part on Piaget's predictions, certain types of problem-solving strategies are studied in children of different ages in order to identify the ways in which they discard less efficient strategies for more efficient ones. By presenting carefully selected types of problems, such as those described in Boxes 3.5 and 3.6, to subjects of different ages, we explore such questions as: How do we learn our more sophisticated reasoning skills as we age? Do females reaon differently than males? If so, why?

Not only are adolescents acquiring new problem-solving strategies, they are acquiring more refined methods for storing and retrieving information; that is, their memory is improving. For example, adolescents can recall more words from a list than can 10-year-olds, in part because they have learned a new method of "rehearsal." In trying to memorize a list of words, 10-year-olds typically try to memorize each word in isolation. After reading the word *cat,* they will say "cat, cat, cat" to themselves, then go on to read and rehearse the next word. In contrast, adolescents will combine several words, trying to find a pattern to help them remember the words' connections. It is also worth noting, however, that how well and how much any of us remember is often influenced by our physical or emotional condition at the time we are entering the data into our memory (see Box 3.7).

Even more important, the studies in information processing demonstrate that adolescents "think better" than younger children, not because the adolescents have entered a new stage of cognition, but because they have acquired more knowledge in certain specific areas. As a consequence adolescents are then able to attend to more details simultaneously, to remember more information, and to solve problems more efficiently; that is, the more knowledge we have about a topic, the "smarter" and more "cognitively mature" we will appear. Does this sound like just garden-variety common sense to you? In a way it is, in that not many psychologists or people in line at your local "Hop and Shop" market would exactly be shocked by the idea. Nevertheless, this hypothesis is demanding serious attention in psychology because it is finally being tested through experimental research in ways that allow its proponents to do more than just offer it up as common sense.

What is the practical significance of this common-sense hypothesis for your relationships with adolescents? Essentially this: If you adopt the position that the cognitive differences between children and their elders is primarily due to differences in knowledge, you cannot also adopt the notion that adolescents are in a different cognitive stage than we adults are in. For example, if 14-year-old Joshua knows a great deal about chemistry, he will employ very advanced reasoning skills and an excellent memory in this domain, yet he may simultaneously appear immature or even slow when you ask him to solve math problems. Moreover, unless you are as knowledgable about chemistry, you (and other adults) will come across as a less mature, less logical thinker than Joshua—or than any other 14-year-old who is operating in a domain in which you have less expertise. So who is "smarter," you or Joshua?

In contrast, Piagetian theories predict that we will apply similar levels of maturity (or immaturity) in our problem-solving strategies, regardless of the types of problem we are trying to resolve. Further, a Piagetian model suggests that we adults have a basically different kind of mind than do children or young adolescents, whereas information processing assumes we all have one kind of mind with varying amounts of accumulated knowledge. As a consequence, neither we nor adolescents function consistently "in" a stage of concrete or of formal reasoning. In short, whether you are 14 or 40, you will function above your typical cognitive level (you will look "smarter" to the rest of us) in those domains in which you

A CLOSER LOOK 3.6

An Experiment in Information Processing

Blocks *A* and *B* are the same size. Block *B* weighs twice as much as Block *A*. Which block will make the water go up higher, or will they both make it go up the same?

When confronted with experiments such as this, how will adolescents respond? If the results of the experiment contradict their preexisting expectations, will they, as Piaget theorized, accommodate the new data into their existing schema? Will males outperform females on this test? What is the best method for helping adolescents learn the appropriate reasoning strategies for tasks such as this?

In pursuing the answers to these questions, researchers presented 166 students aged 12, 13, and 14 with eight questions from the Predicting Displaced Volume test, one of which is the example above. One group of students was asked to make predictions about how much water would be displaced by objects of varying size, shape, and weight. They were then asked to test their predictions by actually immersing the different objects in the water. The second group was presented with the same questions and also given the opportunity afterwards to test their predictions, but they were given the chance beforehand to examine the objects and to generate alternative hypotheses regarding the possible outcomes. In both groups most students made the wrong predictions because they incorrectly focused on the weight of the various objects. Only gradually did most youngsters change their predictions and begin to consider volume rather than weight.

Not only were most of the students reluctant to change their predictions in the face of the contradictory new evidence, but they changed

continued

are quite knowledgable. Put less delicately, even the brightest, most well-educated adults often fail to process information adequately or to reason intelligently (Nisbett & Ross, 1980).

This is not to say that we cannot identify any important cognitive-developmental changes that occur between childhood and adolescence or between adolescence and adulthood. The concept of stages, particularly Piaget's stages, has been hotly contested and often discounted in recent years, and the question is still controversial: Do we undergo stages in our development or not? Moreover, it is not at all clear that all the developmental changes, especially in our early childhood, can be adequately explained by the "accumulation of knowledge" hypothesis. Indeed, substantial changes in our reasoning abilities do occur during middle childhood and adolescence, which suggests at the very least, that we do see trends in our cognitive skills during these periods of our lives.

Box 3.6 continued

their opinions in unpredictable ways. Many abandoned their original strategy erratically, rather than passing through any logical sequence of weight only; weight, then volume; volume, then weight; and volume only. Moreover, most subjects made errors on problems exactly identical to ones they had answered correctly just minutes before. Most students seemed to be guessing randomly, sometimes failing more often than they had on their initial trials. Although a few changed their strategy immediately and completely, others persisted through repeated contradictions. One boy, for example, said after the very first experiment, "Weight doesn't matter—I just thought about it." After a later error, he slapped his forehead and said, "There I go with the weight again."

In general, however, most students were unable to explain how they went about changing their strategies, despite repeated probing from the experimenters. In some cases the students began to focus on completely irrelevant features, such as how the object was submerged in the water or the type of hooks on top of the objects. In short, most of the students applied different rules at different times—they just "muddled through." Even by just muddling along, however, 90% were able to apply the correct rule, and 70% were able to make the right predictions by the end of the 20-minute experiment.

The girls were more ill at ease with the apparatus and with the act of conducting experiments than the boys. While several boys commented that "I used to do this as a kid," only one girl mentioned any experience in her past that was similar to the scientific experiments. When given a little time beforehand to familiarize themselves with the equipment, however, the girls made greater gains than the boys.

Taken together, the results suggest two specific recommendations for us in working with adolescents: First, the best way to help students improve their scientific reasoning is to give them hands-on science activities whose results contradict their expectations. Second, when adolescents say, "I understand that principle," we should not take their statement at face value. We need to see them apply the principle consistently in a number of actual problem-solving situations.

Source: N Burbules & M. Linn. (1988). Response to contradiction: Scientific reasoning during adolescence. *Journal of Educational Psychology, 80,* 67–75.

DEVELOPMENTAL TRENDS DURING ADOLESCENCE

Although it is still being debated whether the Piagetian or the information-processing theories are more correct in their views of cognitive development, theorists from both camps at least concur that certain cognitive changes do occur for most of us during adolescence. Not surprisingly, there is no such thing as a list of adolescent cognitive changes upon which all developmentalists agree. Nevertheless, the following adolescent trends represent those that have made the list for a number of prominent psychologists (Flavel, 1985).

In regard to memory, our short-term memory improves with age. For instance, as 4-year-olds we usually had a memory span of only about four digits, while by age 12, we could remember six or seven digits. Similarly, we gradually acquire a larger variety of problem-solving strategies as we pass through adolescence, being

A CLOSER LOOK 3.7

If an Elephant Never Forgets, Why Do Adolescents?

What determines whether adolescents will remember what they see or hear? In answering this question, researchers suggest that state-dependent memory and flashbulb memory may be partially responsible for remembering and forgetting. In **state-dependent memory,** information that the individual memorizes in one mood is difficult to retrieve unless the individual is in a similar mood. For example, students who memorized a list of words while smoking marijuana recalled more of the words when they were using the drug again than when they were undrugged. The reverse was also true: Those who had memorized the words while undrugged could not recall them very well when they smoked grass. In another study, college students in happy or sad moods memorized lists of words. The students recalled the words best when they were in the same kind of mood as they had been when they first memorized the words.

The impact of emotions on memory is also demonstrated in research about events such as the *Challenger* disaster. Almost all adolescents and adults remember exactly where they were and what they were doing when they heard about it. Many even remember minute details such as what objects they were holding or the taste of the food they were eating when they heard the news. The memory of brief, highly emotional moments from the past is called eidetic, or flashbulb, memory, because it seems like a photograph taken with a flashbulb. Flashbulb memories are usually incomplete, and more experiments are needed to determine their accuracy. Flashbulb memories occur when a person undergoes an emotionally shocking experience, such as hearing about a friend's death. According to some researchers, the shock releases a substance, perhaps a neurotransmitter, into the central nervous system at the same moment that the substance crosses the brain's cortex, causing it to store the highly vivid memory for later use.

Sources: G. Bower. (1981). Mood and memory. *American Psychologist, 36,* 129–148; R. Brown & J. Kulik. (1977). Flashbulb memories. *Cognition, 5,* 73–99.

able to complete many cognitive tasks faster and more efficiently. As adolescents, we are also more apt to try to solve problems by imagining the various alternatives and then examining the reality of the present situation before arriving at our decisions. In contrast, as younger children we usually began with a concrete reality and were reluctant to move to the unseeable possibilities.

During adolescence we learn to inspect the problem data, hypothesize about correct answers, and deduce our answers in order to predict outcomes. This kind of thinking begins with the possible rather than with the real; therefore, it is referred to as "hypothetico-deductive reasoning," in contrast to the nontheoretical, or "empirico-inductive" reasoning we rely upon as young children. In conjunction with this new type of reasoning ability, adolescents come to understand that a person does not have to believe something is either true or right in order to argue reasonably on its behalf. Adolescents who are approaching a problem from this position of formal operational reasoning understand that logical arguments can stand on their own without having to have our personal endorsement.

Finally, during adolescence we become more adept at metacognition. **Metacognition,** literally meaning "to think about thinking," is the knowledge you accumulate about how the human mind—yours and others people's—operates. For example, you may have become aware by the age of 16 that you had a poor memory and that you needed prompts, such as a calendar and a homework assignment notebook, to keep you from making a fool of yourself. Or you may have discovered some universal principles about other people's thinking—for example, that everybody else also has a problem remembering things from time to time. Another example of metacognition is the adolescent's realization that everybody occasionally misunderstands or misinterprets what is being said or done. These metacognitive strategies, unlike cognitive strategies that help you complete a specific task or goal, serve to monitor your progress as you think through a task. An example would be double-checking the answers on a test or skimming the entire test before you begin in order to get a rough idea of which questions to devote the most time to. During adolescence, our "thinking about our thinking" becomes increasingly more sophisticated.

Conclusion By now you may be feeling frustrated or overwhelmed by the contradictory data offered by the information-processing and the Piagetian theorists. One response to this confusion may be the "what does it matter which approach I adopt" attitude. If you are tempted to brush aside the controversies regarding adolescents' cognitive development as being insignificant from any practical standpoint, let me urge you to read Box 3.8 especially carefully. The ongoing debate about whether to grant teenage girls the right to abort unwanted pregnancies is but one of many real-life problems that are intricately linked to our beliefs about adolescents' cognitive maturity.

A second response to the contradictory data—the one that I frankly hope you will adopt—is that of the developmental psychologist John Flavel, who has devoted his career to the study of human cognition:

> When I read in the popular press about some new medical claim or discovery, I nod approvingly at this Latest Advance in Our Understanding of Nature. When the claim or discovery is in the area of cognitive development, on the other hand, I usually have two reactions. The first is that, as always, the reporter has partly misunderstood what the developmental psychologist was trying to tell him. The second is that the developmental psychologist who told it to him is just old Bleatworthy, peddling "that" view again, and that Bleatworthy herself is probably just as conscious as I am of all the unresolved questions and problems that shroud it (Flavel, 1985, p. 272).

CREATIVITY AND GIFTEDNESS

Defining Creativity and Giftedness

Much like the concept of intelligence, creativity and giftedness provoke considerable debate regarding their definitions. Despite these disagreements, however, experts on creativity generally agree that creativity and intellectual giftedness are not synonymous; that is, creative adolescents are not necessarily the ones who score high on IQ tests or perform ahead of their peers academically, nor are the most intelligent and successful students necessarily creative (Bloom, 1985). While intellectual giftedness depends upon the individual's skills in convergent thinking, creativity requires skillfulness in divergent thinking. **Convergent thinking** strategies lead us to the discovery of a single, correct answer to a problem. For

A CLOSER LOOK 3.8

Adolescents' Cognitive Maturity and Abortion Rights

Are adolescent girls cognitively mature enough to decide whether to abort their accidental pregnancies? This controversial legal question, now being hotly debated among legislators and their constituents, is a powerful example of the relevance of the research on adolescents' cognitive development. To resolve this legal quandary, lawyers and legislators have posed the following question to psychologists: Can adolescent girls reason as well as adult women in regard to the issue of abortion? Those who advocate giving adolescent girls the legal right to decide the outcome of their pregnancies have adopted the Piagetian viewpoint that most adolescents have acquired the necessary reasoning skills that accompany formal operational thinking. In other words, adolescent girls can generate several solutions to a problem, think about each alternative hypothetically, imagine the future consequences of each option, and weigh each factor before reaching their decision.

Not all psychologists agree, however, that the research presently available warrants these conclusions. First, only two studies have actually compared adolescent and adult decision making on abortion or health issues. In one, 16 adolescents and 26 women were given hypothetical situations regarding abortion. The adolescents resembled the adults in legal knowledge, in reasons mentioned for choosing either motherhood or abortion, and in their final decisions (Lewis, 1981). In the second study, adolescents as young as 14 reached decisions similar to those of adults in hypothetical situations involving general medical dilemmas (Weithorn & Campbell, 1982). Nevertheless, the researchers cautioned against generalizing their results, given that the sample sizes were small and that the situations were hypothetical, rather than actual decisions in each female's life.

Second, recent cognitive developmental theory has turned away from stage theories, thus undermining the legal assumption that adolescents have reached an irreversible stage of maturity. Indeed, the studies cited by those who supported giving adolescents and adult women equal abortion rights were primarily from the 1960s and 1970s, a time during which Piaget's stage theories were popular.

Third, the legal briefs did not take account of researchers' unanswered questions regarding adolescent and adult cognition. For example, do adolescents and adults react similarly to stress and to emotional upheaval when making their decisions? Can adolescents focus on essential data when confronted with too much information, as can most adults?

Despite an absence of data, research does at least make this much clear: We cannot automatically assume that adolescents are too incompetent to make logical decisions regarding issues as complex as abortion. Nevertheless, the assertion that adults and adolescents have equal decision-making skills is unwarranted, given our present lack of research in this domain. Given this conundrum, would you approve of giving adolescent women the same legal rights as adults in determining the outcomes of their pregnancies?

instance, mathematically talented students usually employ convergent thinking in their problem solving, since mathematics typically involves finding the single correct answer to each problem. In contrast, **divergent thinking** is the act of producing a variety of unusual solutions for problems that have no single correct answer. Creative adolescents use divergent thinking, for example, when imaging 10 possible ways to use paper clips other than for clamping paper together.

Which of your skills are you proudest of? How much have your family and teachers contributed to your skills?

To assess an adolescent's creativity, three aspects of divergent thinking are measured on standardized tests: fluency, flexibility, and originality. Fluency is the ability to produce a large number of responses, and flexibility is the ability to create different categories of response. Three of the most popular tests for assessing these aspects of an adolescent's thinking are Guilford's Creativity Tests for Children (1967), Torrance's Tests for Creative Thinking (1966), and the Khatena-Torrance Creative Perceptions Inventory (1976).

Like those of creativity, the definitions of giftedness have been so nebulous and nettlesome that some experts have concluded that "giftedness is a concept that we invent, not something we discover; it is what one society or another wants it to be, making it, therefore, subject to change according to time and place" (Sternberg & Davidson, 1986, p. 4). Despite the ongoing dispute over its exact definition, most would at least be willing to agree that a "gifted" youth has above-average intelligence, creativity, and task commitment (Horowitz & O'Brien, 1985; Sternberg & Davidson, 1986; Tannenbaum, 1986).

Whether we can agree on exact definitions for giftedness and creativity, 47 states have now recognized the need for special educational programs for gifted and talented youth, a category including both the creative and the intellectually gifted adolescent. Indeed, the field of education for the gifted and talented has enjoyed overwhelming growth in the past 30 years. Almost 5% of the students in public schools received special educational services through their states' gifted and talented programs in 1987. Although this support is encouraging, most programs for gifted students focus only on the academically successful and provide little or no services for artistically talented youngsters or those with high potential who are underachieving academically. To compound the problem, most teachers are not trained to tailor their teaching methods or the curriculum to meet the needs of gifted students. Moreover, many who have no knowledge of the field are assigned to positions of directing or providing consulting for programs for the gifted (Reis, 1989).

Increasing Creativity

However the needs of our nation's gifted and creative adolescents are ultimately cared for, many of us are asking an even more pressing question: How can a young person's creativity and special talents be encouraged? In studying the families and childhood experiences of creative and gifted adults, researchers are helping us answer this intriguing question (see Box 3.9). As you might expect, the parents and teachers of creative and talented adolescents do figure significantly in the ultimate success of these young people.

What do the parents of creative adolescents have in common? First, they actively encourage their children's independence, curiosity, and nonconformity. Themselves relatively indifferent to social status and conformity, these parents tend not

A CLOSER LOOK 3.9

Increasing Adolescents' Creativity

Teachers and parents can increase adolescents' creativity by

- Encouraging spontaneous expression and accepting novel ideas
- Relying less on memory activities and asking provocative questions
- Providing a stimulating, nonthreatening environment
- Reducing anxiety and rewarding nonconformity
- Emphasizing the value of working alone rather than in groups
- Discouraging sex-role stereotypes
- Encouraging controversy and disagreement without hostility
- Discouraging the need to be perfect and to never make mistakes
- Granting responsibility and independence
- Respecting fantasies, daydreaming, and other imaginative activities
- Encouraging disagreements and discussions of controversial ideas
- Providing opportunities for hypothesizing, exploring, and experimenting
- Deferring judgment and evaluation of the adolescents' ideas and work
- Helping the youngsters learn to trust their own senses and intuitions
- Showing respect for emotion, ambiguity, and imperfections
- Providing games and books that demand creative responses and playfulness

to have an overly symbiotic relationship either with one another or with their children. These parents tend to be vocationally and socially successful and to relate democratically, rather than authoritatively, to their children. Rather than stressing high grades, these parents encourage their children to experiment and to learn through making mistakes. By treating their children with respect and by providing enough distance to foster self-reliance, these adults help their offspring become adventuresome and nonconforming.

Certain factors within the society at large—formal education, war, political unrest, role models, and civil disobedience—have also been found to influence young people's creativity (Simonton, 1978). Although a degree of civil disobedience and political disagreement seem to encourage creativity among citizens, war and government upheaval cause too insecure a milieu for creativity to thrive in. To foster creativity, a society also needs to provide young people with role models of creative adults who are respected and financially rewarded by their fellow citizens. According to Simonton's analysis, however, too much formal education detracts from our creativity by encouraging us to conform to too many traditions. In the opinion of social critics like Simonton, our adolescents would be more creative if we deemphasized the importance of formal education and invested as much attention and money in our creative artists as on our sports heroes.

In a similar vein, a team of researchers has been examining how talented people in our society have been helped to develop their special abilities by their parents and teachers (Bloom, 1985). These researchers have found striking similarities in the backgrounds of gifted adults who have achieved prominence as concert pianists, sculptors, mathematicians, neurologists, and Olympic athletes. First, most talented adults began with merely a recreational, childhood interest in their field, followed by a long period of intense training and a tremendous investment of time. During adolescence, these young people invested 25 to 30 hours a week practicing their special talent, in lieu of other recreational activities and many of the typical interests of other teenagers.

And the parents? These adults emphasized the work ethic and the importance of an individual's doing his or her best at all times. Regardless of their educational levels or vocations, these parents were models of the work ethic in their own lives in that they were regarded as hard workers and did their best in their own endeavors. Moreover, they delegated responsibilities to their children in a way that would teach them self-discipline. Although the parents varied greatly in their own levels of education and financial success, they were all genuinely concerned about their children and wanted to do the best for them at all stages of their development. In this sense, these adults were child oriented, willingly devoting their time and money for the development of their children's special talents.

Although first teachers played an important role in the development of the children's talents, these adults were not the most outstanding people in their field; that is, becoming an outstanding pianist or athlete did not require having an exceptionally talented pianist or athlete as a first teacher. The major quality these teachers did share was that they made the initial learning pleasurable and rewarded their students often. Rarely critical, these teachers set high standards that they helped their pupils reach through reinforcement, rather than through punishment or humiliation. Many teachers kept records of the students' weekly or daily progress and used these as motivational tools to encourage more daily practice. As the students' skills improved, the teachers raised their expectations accordingly. In part, these young people maintained their rigorous practice schedules because of the rewards for progress that parents and teachers provided. Yet, during the initial

How creative do you consider yourself to be? What is "creativity"?

years of formal instruction, the children's own motivation and effort seemed to count far more than the particular talent itself.

As the children progressed into adolescence, teachers with more expertise became increasingly important in helping them hone their exceptional skills. Similarly, as the talented children aged, support and reinforcement from their peers became an important element in maintaining their motivation. "Birds of a feather flocked together" in that these talented young people typically developed friendships with other similarly talented youths. Indeed, learning often took place by making comparisons with more advanced students.

Interestingly, only about 10% of these gifted individuals had progressed far enough by the age of 11 or 12 to be recognized as exceptionally talented. Why was it so difficult to identify and to predict the high levels of success of these highly accomplished individuals by the beginning of adolescence? The answer, it appears, is that it takes those adolescent years to provide the time needed to amass the knowledge and to do the rigorous practicing required to become truly outstanding in a field. Being good as a young student is only partially related to the eventual development of an exceptional talent. This is not to say that some adolescents' talents are not clearly recognized well before their teenage years. Nevertheless, it seems that most gifted children need their adolescent years for the enormous amount of practice and instruction that their talent must have for its unfolding. Bloom and his colleagues, therefore, are among those who contend that no aptitude test or predictive instrument can enable us to identify which children will become exceptionally talented adults. Put differently, "genius is 1% inspiration and 99% perspiration." It is hard to predict which talented children will have the wherewithal to sweat it out.

CONCLUSION

Given the disagreements among researchers and the different approaches to studying cognition examined in this chapter, you may be wondering whether you can live up to anyone's definition of intelligence. Although each theoretical approach to cognitive development is beset by its own particular limitations, each is, at least in part, accurate in its descriptions of children's and adolescents' thought. Assuming an eclectic perspective will permit us to appreciate the theoretical assumptions upon which each approach is predicated and to utilize the pragmatic recommendations that each offers for our interactions with adolescents.

The next chapter will expound upon the ways in which cognitive growth affects adolescents' personalities, and chapter 7 will examine the impact of cognitive abilities on adolescents' academic performance. The data in several later chapters will allude to Piaget's model when presenting other theorists' views on adolescents' political, social, sexual, religious, moral, and vocational development. Similarly, much of the empirical data cited in subsequent chapters is interpreted or disputed in relation to adolescents' IQ scores. For these reasons, clearly understanding the concepts listed for you in this chapter's overview will enhance your ability to critique the data in following chapters with more wisdom.

QUESTIONS FOR DISCUSSION AND REVIEW

Basic Concepts and Terminology

Cite specific research studies and statistics to support your answers to each of the following:

1. How do the psychometric, developmental, and information-processing approaches to adolescent cognition differ?
2. Describe each of Piaget's stages of cognitive development by providing specific examples of children's behavior that demonstrate the major advances within each stage.
3. What are the major criticisms leveled against traditional IQ tests?

4. Explain each side of the nature/nurture argument as it relates to the IQ controversy by describing the research supporting each perspective.
5. How reliable a measure of intelligence is an adolescent's IQ score?
6. Why must validity, chronological age, race, and ability all be considered before interpreting a youngster's IQ score?
7. According to Piaget's theories, how do youngsters advance from one stage of cognitive development to another?
8. According to information-processing theories, why does the thinking of children, adolescents, and adults appear to be different?
9. In what ways do the functions of the left and right hemispheres of the brain differ?
10. What specific changes generally occur during adolescence in our cognitive abilities? How do these changes affect our abilities in school and in social situations?
11. How do the problem-solving strategies and memory of adolescents differ from those of younger children?
12. How can parents and teachers encourage young people to develop their creativity or special talent?

Questions for Discussion and Debate

1. How would you go about helping young adolescents develop formal operational thinking?
2. What do you consider the major strengths and weaknesses of each approach to the study of adolescent cognition?
3. How do you feel about using IQ tests to measure an individual's intellectual potential?
4. Considering the experts' suggestions for improving IQ tests, how would you determine an adolescent's intelligence?
5. How can we increase adolescents' creativity at home and in school?
6. If given the choice between being extremely creative or extremely intelligent during your adolescence, which would you choose and why?
7. What experiences contributed most to the development or diminishment of your own creativity and intelligence during childhood and adolescence?
8. In regard to an individual's intellectual skills, how would you defend or refute the maxim, "You can't make a silk purse out of a sow's ear"?

GLOSSARY

accommodation As used by Piaget, the change in an existing schema to one that enables us to understand a new concept or new experience.

assimilation As used by Piaget, the process of fitting new concepts or new experiences into our existing schema.

associativity According to Piaget, the idea that the sum is independent of the order in which things are added. $4 + 2 + 3 = 9$, and so does $2 + 3 + 4$.

brain lateralization The separation of mental and physical functions between the left and right hemispheres of the brain. Synonyms: hemisphericity, left and right brain thinking.

class inclusion The ability to reason simultaneously about parts of a whole and the whole itself.

concrete operations stage According to Piaget, the cognitive stage between the ages of 7 and 11 during which we learn the rules of equivalence, reversibility, class inclusion, and associativity.

conservation According to Piaget, the concept grasped by about age 7 that the amount of something stays the same regardless of changes in its shape or the number of parts into which it is divided.

convergent thinking Thinking along conventional lines in order to find a single best answer or solution.

disequilibrium In Piagetian theory, the unpleasant feeling that arises when we encounter new information that contradicts the information in our existing schema.

divergent thinking Thinking that is creative and original in that it deviates from the obvious and produces several solutions or answers.

egocentrism The inability to see things from another person's point of view or to imagine several different perspectives simultaneously

eidetic memory Memory of the explicit details of an event as a consequence of the emotionally charged nature of the situation.

flashbulb memory See eidetic memory.

formal operations stage In Piagetian theory, the fourth stage of cognitive development, which is supposed to occur during adolescence and in which we become capable of logical reasoning and abstract thinking.

information processing approach An approach concerned with how we process the information and experiences around us; it involves perception, memory, thinking, and problem solving.

metacognition The ability to think about the strategies we use in thinking.

neo-Piagetian The updated or modified theories based on the work of Piaget.

object permanence In Piagetian theory, the awareness that comes before the age of 7 that even when an object or person is out of view, it still exists.

Piagetian theories Theories contending that our cognitive skills advance in relatively predictable, universal stages, each of which is associated with specific new skills, primarily determined by our chronological age, not by environmental influences.

preoperational stage According to Piaget, a stage of cognitive development between the ages of 2 and 7 in which we develop such new skills as object permanence but during which we are still handicapped by our egocentristic thinking.

psychometric approach A method of studying human intelligence through measurements such as IQ tests.

reliability The ability of a measuring device or a test to yield consistent scores or results over time.

reversibility The ability to work backward or forward, rotate objects in your mind, and undo activities that have been completed in actuality or in thought.

rule of equivalence According to Piaget, the ability to understand the equivalent relationships between seemingly different objects or ideas (if $A = B$, and $B = C$, then $A = C$) acquired during the stage of concrete operations.

schema The existing mental framework (ideas, ways of analyzing data) into which new information or new experiences are integrated as we mature.

sensorimotor stage According to Piaget, the earliest cognitive stage, from birth to 2 years, in which we learn to use primitive symbols.

serialization The arrangement of objects in proper order according to some dimension, such as weight or length, attained during the concrete stage of thought, according to Piaget.

stage theories Any theories that explain human behavior or cognition as the consequence of clearly delineated, universal stages that are basically unaffected by environmental influences.

Stanford Binet An IQ test.

state-dependent memory Information that the individual memorizes in one mood is difficult to retrieve unless the individual is in a similar mood.

System of Multicultural Pluralistic Assessment (SOMPA) An IQ test that takes account of ethnicity and environmental variables, such as family income.

validity The ability of a test or an instrument to measure accurately what it claims to be measuring.

Wechsler Adult Intelligence Scale (WAIS) An IQ test.

Wechsler Intelligence Scale for Children-Revised (WISC-R) An IQ test.

REFERENCES

Anastasi, A. (1988). *Psychological testing.* New York: Macmillan.

Benbow, C., & Stanley, J. (1983). Sex differences in mathematical reasoning. *Science, 222,* 1029–1031.

Bloom, B. (Ed.). (1985). *Developing talent in young people.* New York: Ballantine.

Boehm, A. (1985). Educational applications of intelligence testing. In B. Wolman (Ed.), *Handbook of intelligence* (pp. 933–964). New York: Wiley.

Bouchard, T. (1984). Twins reared together and apart. In S. Fox (Ed.), *Individuality and determinism* (pp. 147–178). New York: Plenum Press.

Bower, G. (1981). Mood and memory. *American psychologist, 36,* 129–148.

Brown, R., & Kulik, J. (1977). Flashbulb memories. *Cognition, 5,* 73–99.

Burbules, N., & Linn, M. (1988). Response to contradiction: Scientific reasoning during adolescence. *Journal of Educational Psychology, 80,* 67–75.

Dove, A. (1968, July 15). Taking the chitling test. *Newsweek,* pp. 51–52.

Drotar, D. (Ed.). (1985). *New directions in failure to thrive.* New York: Plenum Press.

Feuerstein, R. (1979). *The dynamic assessment of retarded performers.* Baltimore: University Park Press.

Flavel, J. (1985). *Cognitive development.* Englewood Cliffs, NJ: Prentice-Hall.

Flynn, J. (1988). IQ in 14 countries. *Psychological Bulletin, 101,* 171–191.

Galler, J. (Ed.). (1984). Human nutrition: A comprehensive treatise. New York: Plenum Press.

Gardner, H. (1983). *Frames of mind: Theory of multiple intelligence.* New York: Basic Books.

Gardner, W., Scherer, D., & Tester, M. (1989). Asserting scientific authority: Cognitive development and adolescent legal rights. *American Psychologist, 44,* 895–902.

Ginsburg, H., & Opper, S. (1988). *Piaget's theory of intellectual development.* Englewood Cliffs, NJ: Prentice-Hall.

Guilford, J. (1967). *The nature of human intelligence.* New York: McGraw-Hill.

Hall, E. (1983). The brain and behavior. In E. Hall (Ed.) *Psychology today.* New York: Random House.

Hobbs, N., & Robinson, S. (1982). Adolescent development and public policy. *American Psychologist, 44,* pp. 212–223.

Horowitz, F. (1987). *Exploring developmental theories.* Hillsdale, NJ: Erlbaum.

Inhelder, B., & Piaget, J. (1958). *The growth of logical thinking from childhood through adolescence.* New York: Basic Books.

Jensen, A. (1969). How much can we boost IQ and scholastic achievement? *Harvard Educational Review, 39,* 1–123.

Jensen, A. (1973). The differences are real. *Psychology Today,* pp. 80–86.

Jensen, A. (1973). *Educability and group differences.* New York: Harper & Row.

Jensen, A. (1985). Methods and statistical techniques for the study of mental abilities. In C. Reynolds & V. Willson (Eds.), *Methodological and statistical advances in the study of individual differences* (pp. 51–116). New York: Plenum Press.

Kaplan, R. (1985). The controversy related to the use of psychological tests. In B. Wolman (Ed.), *Handbook of intelligence* (pp. 465–504). New York: Wiley.

Khatena, J. (1982). *Educational psychology of the gifted.* New York: Wiley.

Khatena, J., & Torrance, E. (1976). *Khatena-Torrance creative perceptions inventory.* Chicago: Stoelting.

Larry P. v. Wilson Riles, 495 F. Supp. 926 N.D. Cal. 1979.

Lewis, C. (1981). Minor's competence to consent to abortion. *American Psychologist, 42,* 84–88.

Linn, M., & Petersen, A. (1986). A meta analysis of gender differences in spatial ability. In J. Hyde & M. Linn (Eds.), *The psychology of gender: Advances through meta analysis* (pp. 67–101). Baltimore: Johns Hopkins University Press.

Lozoff, B. (1989). Nutrition and behavior. *American Psychologist, 44,* 231–236.

Mayr, E. (1982). *The growth of biological thought.* Cambridge, MA: Belknap Press.

Mercer, J., & Lewis, J. (1978). *System of Multicultural Pluralistic Assessment.* New York: Psychological Corporation.

Nisbett, R., & Ross, L. (1980). *Human inference: Strategies and shortcomings of social judgment.* Englewood Cliffs, NJ: Prentice-Hall.

Oakland, T., & Parmelee, R. (1985). Mental measurement of minority group children. In B. Wolman (Ed.), *Handbook of intelligence* (pp. 699–736). New York: Wiley.

Pedersen, N., McClearn, G., Plomin, R., & Friberg, L. (1985). Separated fraternal twins. *Behavior Genetics, 15,* 407–419.

Plomin, R. (1986). *Development, genetics and psychology.* Hillsdale, NJ: Erlbaum.

Plomin, R. (1989). Environment and genes: Determinants of behavior. *American Psychologist, 44,* 105–111.

Plomin, R., Pedersen, N., McClearn, G., Nesselroade, J., & Bergemen, C. (1988). EAS temperaments during the last half of the life span. *Psychology and Aging, 3,* 43–50.

Reis, S. (1989). Reflections on policy affecting the education of gifted and talented students. *American Psychologist, 44,* 399–408.

Salt, P., Galler, J., & Ramsey, F. (1988). The influence of early malnutrition on subsequent behavioral development. *Development and Behavioral Pediatrics, 9,* 1–5.

Scarr, S., & Saltzman, L. (1982). Genetics and intelligence. In R. Sternberg (Ed)., *Handbook of human intelligence* (pp. 792–896). New York: Cambridge University Press.

Simonton, D. (1978). The eminent genius in history. *Gifted Child Quarterly, 22,* 187–195.

Snow, R. (1982). Education and intelligence. In R. Sternberg (Ed.), *Handbook of human intelligence* (pp. 493–559). New York: Cambridge University Press.

Snyderman, M., & Rothman, C. (1987). Survey of expert opinion on intelligence and aptitude testing. *American Psychologist, 42,* 137–144.

Spitz, H. (1986). *The raising of intelligence: A selected history of attempts to raise retarded intelligence.* Hillsdale, NJ: Erlbaum.

Sternberg, R. (1985). *Beyond IQ: A triarchic theory of human intelligence.* Cambridge, England: Cambridge University Press.

Sternberg, R., & Davidson, J. (Ed.). (1986). *Conceptions of giftedness.* New York: Cambridge University Press.

Tannenbaum, A. (1986). *Gifted children: Psychological and educational perspectives.* New York: Macmillan.

Terman, L., & Merrill, M. (1985). *Stanford Binet Intelligence Scale: Manual for the third revision.* Boston: Houghton Mifflin.

Torrance, P. (1966). *Torrance tests for creative thinking.* Princeton, NJ: Personnel Press.

Viadero, D. (1986). Lead in water poses major health risk to schoolchildren. *Education Week, 6,* 12.

Wechsler, D. (1952; 1975). *Wechsler intelligence scale for children.* New York: Psychological Corporation.

Wechsler, D. (1955) *Manual of the Wechsler Adult Intelligence Scale.* NJ: Psychological Corporation.

Weinberg, R. (1989). Intelligence and IQ: Landmark issues and great debates. *American Psychologist, 44,* 98–104.

Weithorn, L., & Campbell, S. (1982). The competency of children and adolescents to make informed treatment decisions. *Child Development, 53,* 1589–1599.

Whimbey, A., & Whimbey, L. (1975). *Intelligence can be taught.* New York: Dutton.

Wigdor, A., & Garner, W. (Eds.). (1982). *Ability testing: Uses, consequences and controversies.* Washington, DC: National Academy Press.

Williams, R. (1975). The bitch 100: A culture specific test. *Journal of Afro-American Issues, 3,* 103–116.

Zigler, E., & Seitz, V. (1982). Social policy and intelligence. In R. Sternberg (Ed.), *Handbook of human intelligence* (pp. 586–641). Cambridge, England: Cambridge University Press.

4 Adolescent Identity and Personality

CHAPTER OUTLINE

PERSONALITY THEORIES

TRADITIONAL FREUDIAN THEORIES

The Personality's Structure
Psychosexual Stages
Applications to Adolescents
Criticisms of Psychoanalytic Theories

NEO-FREUDIAN THEORIES

Erikson's Psychosocial Stages
Marcia's Identity Statuses
Individuation During Adolescence
Criticisms of Neo-Freudian Theories

COGNITIVE STAGE THEORIES OF PERSONALITY

Hypocrisy and Idealism
Egocentrism
Pseudostupidity

TRAIT THEORIES

Assessing Personality Traits
Applications to Adolescents
Criticisms of Trait Theories

PHENOMENOLOGICAL THEORIES OF PERSONALITY

Rogers and Maslow's Theories
Field Theories
Measuring Adolescents' Self-Concepts
Applications to Adolescents
Criticisms of Phenomenological Theories

BEHAVIORISTIC THEORIES OF PERSONALITY

Traditional Behavioral Theories
Social Learning Theories
Applications to Adolescents
Criticisms of Behavioristic Theories

CONCLUSION

GOALS AND OBJECTIVES

This chapter is designed to enable you to:

- Describe the different approaches for studying the adolescent personality
- Evaluate the advantages and disadvantages of each theoretical viewpoint
- Consider the different methods suggested for altering an adolescent's personality
- Examine the variables that seem to affect the development of personality
- Explore the new aspects of personality that appear during adolescence

CONCEPTS AND TERMINOLOGY

achieved identity
anal stage
attribution theories
behaviorism
behavior modification
classical conditioning
client-centered therapy
contingency contract
counter conditioning
defense mechanisms
denial
desensitization
diffused identity
displacement
Electra complex
external locus of control
extinction
field theory
foreclosed identity
free association
generativity
genital stage
Gestalt psychology
humanistic psychology
id, ego, superego
identity status
imaginary audience
individuation
internal locus of control
latency stage
learned helplessness
life space
locus of control
Maslow's hierarchy of needs
Minnesota Multiphasic Personality Inventory (MMPI)

Key terms continued

Key terms continued

modeling
moratorium
neo-Freudians
observational learning
Oedipus complex
operant conditioning
operant psychology
oral stage
personal fable
phallic stage
primary reinforcers
projection
projective techniques
pseudostupidity
psychosexual stages
psychosocial stages
Q-sort technique
rationalization
reaction formation
regression
reinforcement
repression
Rogerian counseling
Rorschach test
secondary reinforcers
self-actualization
semantic differential
Skinnerian psychology
Thematic Apperception Test (TAT)

PERSONALITY THEORIES

How can two adolescents from the same family have such different personalities? Does adolescence have much impact on our personalities or are we essentially who we are long before puberty? Do adolescents have certain traits, such as shyness or aggressiveness, that influence their behavior no matter what the situation? How much do unconscious motives control the adolescent's personality? Do personality traits run in families, and if so, does this mean that certain aspects of our personalities are genetically determined?

In attempting to answer questions such as these about the development of our personalities, researchers have adopted different theoretical approaches: the Freudian and neo-Freudian theories, developmental stage theories, phenomenological theories, trait theories, and social learning/behavioristic theories. Despite the differences among them, each approach is attempting to answer several of the same essential questions: What determines the type of personality we each develop? What special role, if any, does adolescence play in the development of our personalities? What are the most effective methods for changing undesirable aspects of our personalities or the personalities of those around us?

Until you decide where you stand on each of these theories of personality development, you will be handicapped in your dealings with adolescents. Many of the day-to-day decisions we make in relating to adolescents rest on our beliefs about what is shaping (or what has shaped) their personalities. For example, assume that as a counselor you are working with 15-year-old Larry, who is so aggressive and hot tempered that he is on the verge of being expelled from school for beating up other students. He also has a record in juvenile court for being involved in several neighborhood fights. How would you counsel with him? Would you show him films and tell him stories depicting the gruesome consequences for others like him who have been kicked out of school or who live in juvenile detention centers—in other words, the scare tactic? Would you administer a series of psychological tests trying to determine the underlying, unconscious causes of Larry's aggressive behavior? Would you ask his parents to come in to discuss situations within the family that might be causing Larry to vent on his peers the anger he feels against his family? Would you explore the possibility that in his fights with his peers Larry is modeling physical abuse occurring in the family?

The ways in which you relate to Larry, and to other adolesents, will depend in large part on your own beliefs about how our personalities develop and how, or if, they change. Each of the theories of personality presented in this chapter will offer its own unique explanations for Larry's behavior and its own recommendations for helping young people change certain aspects of their personalities. Whichever theoretical position you ultimately endorse, an understanding of each viewpoint will help you appreciate the complexities involved in other issues we will be examining in future chapters. Indeed, debates about issues such as drug abuse and teenage pregnancy rest squarely on our differing assumptions regarding the ways in which a personality is developed—and the ways in which it can, or can not, be changed.

TRADITIONAL FREUDIAN THEORIES

Indisputably, the most influential theorist in the field of personality is Sigmund Freud (1856–1939), whose work has provided the basis around which most controversies regarding adolescent and adult development revolve. To date, some of the most comprehensive explanations of how the psychoanalytic approach applies to adolescents have been written by Freud's daughter, Anna. Despite the fact that both Anna Freud and contemporary adolescent psychologists such as Joseph Adelson admit that psychoanalytic theorists have devoted too little attention to the period of adolescence, classical Freudian theories continue to exert a significant influence over our views of the adolescent personality (Freud, 1946, 1977).

The Personality's Structure

According to the Freudian perspective, the adolescent's personality is determined by interactions among the id, the ego, and the superego. We might be led to envision the rational, self-controlled ego as some sort of entity that tries to exert its control over the irrational, impulsive id and the harsh, moralistic superego. In fact, however, Freudians use these terms to refer to motivational forces underlying our behavior, not to suggest three separate entities or any type of physical structure residing somewhere within the brain.

As conceived by Freudians, the **id** (which means *it* in German) represents our unconscious biological drives and instincts. The id supplies the ego and superego

How would you describe your personality?

with the psychic energy, referred to as the *libido*, that propels the entire personality throughout life. The id's two main instincts are *Eros* (Greek for *love*) and *Thanatos* (Greek for *death*). Eros motivates us to fulfill our basic needs, such as our desires for food and sex, and is also responsible for artistic and productive work. In contrast, Thanatos is the motivating force that underlies our aggressive and self-destructive behavior.

Since Freudians presume that the id operates on the basis of the *pleasure principle*, the ego is necessary to counter the id's impulses with the *reality principle*. The **ego** (meaning *I* in German) is the part of your personality that you consciously acknowledge as the self. Using memory, logic, preplanning, education, discrimination, and judgment, the ego tries to satisfy the id's needs without jeopardizing the individual. For example, Sue's sexual impulses (id) may be urging her to have sex with her boyfriend, although neither of them thought to bring any contraceptives. Realistically appraising the situation (the ego), she tells herself: "It is not logical to take the risk of getting pregnant for a few minutes of pleasure—be rational."

The **superego** (meaning *over the I* in German) refers to the part of your personality that imposes society's moral codes—in other words, your conscience. Like the id, your superego ignores certain objective realities and functions on the basis of values and abstract moral ideals instilled by society—above all, by your parents. Therefore, for example, although Sue may be rational next time and bring contraceptives with her on her date, her conscience (superego) may still control her behavior by whispering in her ear at the crucial moment: "Even though you won't get pregnant because you brought a contraceptive, you shouldn't do this because you're not that kind of girl—your parents would be so ashamed of you if they found out."

Within the Freudian context, most of our behavior is an attempt to reduce anxieties created by the contradictory needs of the id, ego, and superego. Our behavior is an attempt to maintain and to restore *homeostasis*—a relaxed condition without conflict among id, ego, and superego. When anxiety becomes so acute that there is no readily available way to reduce it, the individual may resort to defense mechanisms. **Defense mechanisms** are strategies by which a person attempts to reduce his or her anxiety by denying or distorting reality. The ways in which adolescents might employ defense mechanisms are explained in Box 4.1

Psychosexual Stages

According to Freudian perspectives, your personality is primarily determined by the ways in which you resolve the psychological conflicts you encounter during various **psychosexual stages** of childhood and adolescence. If, however, you do not resolve these psychosexual conflicts at each stage, you will encounter personality problems later in life. The transitions between these psychosexual stages are presumed to occur at approximately the same age in our lives as the transitions between Piaget's stages of cognitive development, between Erikson's stages of ego development, and between Hall's stages of biological development.

The **oral stage,** occurring during the first year of life, is so named because the child's mouth is presumed to be the primary source of pleasure. During this stage the personality is immature, dependent, and in need of nurturance. Consequently, weaning is the crucial conflict to be resolved. According to Freudians, adolescents who are fixated at the oral stage are likely to develop overly dependent relationships and to expect people to "mother" them.

During the second and third years of life, a child's libido supposedly shifts from the oral to the anal region. In this **anal stage** the child is expected to develop self-control, particularly with bowel and bladder functions. From the Freudian perspective, toilet training becomes a metaphorical act of society's triumph over

A CLOSER LOOK 4.1

Adolescents' Defense Mechanisms

Repression is a defense mechanism that involves forgetting unpleasant incidents or information by pushing them into the recesses of the unconscious. For example, an adolescent boy may be unable to cope with the fact that he was sexually molested as a child. Consequently, he may repress these memories and be unable to recall the sexual incidents. Youngsters may also temporarily repress information, such as the name of a teacher they dislike.

Denial is refusing to believe that an event is true. A young girl may pretend that her hostile, unloving father is actually friendly and supportive, or a boy whose mother dies can refuse to believe she is dead for months following the funeral. Daydreaming is sometimes a form of denying an unpleasant circumstance from which the individual cannot escape.

Regression is a return to an earlier stage of development in response to a threatening or frustrating situation. When adolescents are failing to elicit the response they want from other people, they may regress to more infantile behavior that was once effective in controlling other people's reactions. When a calm, rational discussion is failing to change her mother's opinion, a daughter may throw a temper tantrum like a 3-year-old child. According to contemporary theorist Peter Blos, occasional regression is a normal part of developing new coping strategies during adolescence.

Reaction formation is the process of replacing an anxiety-producing feeling or impulse with its opposite feeling or impulse. Generally, the stronger the impulse to behave in ways that

continued

the child's undisciplined self. Consequently, if a child willingly becomes toilet trained, he or she has supposedly developed the basis for future self-control. In contrast, children who try to counter-attack society's wishes by protesting against toilet training may develop an anal aggressive personality as they age.

During the fourth and fifth years of life, most children do become interested in exploring their genitals, masturbating, and asking sexual questions. According to Freudian views, such behavior is indicative of the **phallic stage,** during which the child's essential conflict is between the unconscious sexual desires toward the opposite-sexed parent and jealousies directed toward the same-sexed parent. This dilemma, referred to as the **Oedipus complex** in relation to the mother-son relationship, causes the son unconsciously to perceive his father as a rival for his mother's sexual attentions. Secretly harboring the jealous desire to eliminate his father, the son fears his father's retaliation—specifically, castration. Once the son represses his incestuous desires by identifying with his father and thereby vicariously possessing his mother by becoming "just like Daddy," the Oedipus complex is presumably resolved.

In regard to the father-daughter relationship, Freudians contend that daughters must resolve their incestuous desires for their fathers by overcoming their **Electra complex.** Like sons, daughters first fall in love with their mothers. Upset, however, by her discovery that she lacks a penis, the daughter assumes she must have been

Box 4.1 continued

society designates as inappropriate, the stronger the reaction formation. For instance, an extremely religious girl, who vehemently crusades against all literature, movies, or jokes with sexual overtones, may be concealing her genuine desire to look at or read these materials. Or a boy who hates his younger sister may shower her with gifts and affection, since society would condemn him for expressing his hatred.

Projection is attributing one's own feelings to other people, rather than claiming responsibility for these impulses or sentiments. When using this defense mechanism, adolescents reject or ignore the objective evidence in favor of their own projected wishes. According to Freudian psychologists, a boy who accuses his classmates of cheating without any evidence to support his accusation, when in fact he is wanting to cheat, is projecting his dishonest desires onto others.

Displacement is similar to projection in that the adolescent attributes feelings to the wrong source. A youngster who accurately recognizes his or her feelings may inaccurately identify the source from which these feelings emanate. Hence, a boy who has been bawled out by his track coach comes home and starts yelling at his younger brother for "messing with" his stereo. Because the older brother cannot express his anger or defend himself to the coach, he displaces his frustration by getting angry at his defenseless younger brother.

Rationalization is the act of creating reasons that are not indicative of true motives in order to justify behavior. According to the Freudian perspective, rationalizing is a device by which the superego or conscience is overridden in order to satisfy some of an individual's less-than-admirable desires. The boy who breaks up with his girlfriend because he is bored with her and wants to date the cute new girl on his block is rationalizing if he tells himself "it's for my ex-girlfriend's own good, since she shouldn't be getting tied down to just one boy anyway."

castrated and unconsciously blames her mother. Simultaneously, the daughter harbors sexual desires for her father and jealousy toward her mother as a supposed sexual rival. According to Sigmund Freud, once the daughter unconsciously comes to terms with the fact that her incestuous desires cannot be fulfilled, she represses them by identifying with her mother. In disagreement with her father's theory on this point, Anna Freud argued that daughters identify with their mothers out of fear of losing their love.

How does a girl resolve her Electra complex? This was problematic for Freud. Indeed, he believed this complex was never completely resolved for girls as it was for boys. As we will see later in this chapter and in chapter 5, Freudian theories share a limitation in common with many other theories of personality in that they fail to account as well for female development as for male development. Parenthetically, in case you have now been provoked to wonder why you do not remember your own sexual desires for your opposite-sexed parent, Freudians contend that we suppress our memories of the Oedipus or Electra complex as part of resolving the conflict.

Once beyond the phallic stage, children enter the **latency stage,** which spans the years from 6 to 11. In the Freudian context, this is the stage for strengthening one's identifications with the same-sexed parent through interacting almost exclusively with members of one's own sex. Neither sex has much interest in sexual issues during this stage, and the superego supposedly exerts increasing influence over the child's behavior. In short, the boys do not like the girls, and the girls think the boys are undesirable, too.

Freudians perceive adolescence as the final phase of psychosexual development, the **genital stage.** The individual's libido is once again focused on the genital area, as during the phallic stage. As adolescents, however, we seek our sexual gratification with other people, rather than by ourselves, as we did in the phallic stage of our early childhood. Furthermore, the superego becomes somewhat more flexible as adolescents examine and modify the rules and mores that they learned as children. As we shall see later in this chapter, this process—called individuation (see page 132)—is an essential component of adolescence, according to Freudian and neo-Freudian theories. Freudians maintain that adolescents who successfully resolve the conflict associated with each psychosexual stage can develop adult personalities that are free of neuroses.

Applications to Adolescents

Given that Freudian psychologists view adolescence as the genital stage of our personality development, how are their views actually applied to interpreting adolescents' behavior? According to the neo-Freudian Peter Blos (1979), the Oedipal and Electra conflicts recur during the early years of adolescence. Once again we find ourselves, as young adolescents, jealous of our same-sex parent because of the sexual attention he or she is receiving from our other parent. To overcome our jealousy and liberate ourselves from this kind of incestuous desire, we turn our sexual attention elsewhere: to our favorite young teacher, to a rock star, or to another adult object of our crushes. As young adolescents, we may also cope with our Oedipal urges by pulling away from our parents and choosing to be by ourselves rather than to participate in activities with them. Both strategies, according to Blos, are our ways of redirecting our sexual urges away from our parents toward other adults and, eventually, toward people our own age.

In their work with adolescents, therapists often apply Freudian principles beyond the realm of the family. Guided by classical Freudian concepts, psychotherapists try to uncover their adolescent clients' unconscious motives and conflicts, which are presumed to be frequently disguised by the youngsters' defense mechanisms. The therapists' task is to help the adolescents achieve insights into the motives underlying their behavior and attitudes. Only when such insights have been achieved are the young people presumed capable of permanently changing their behavior. In contrast to social learning and behavioral theories, psychoanalytic counseling is predicated on the assumption that merely modifying the adolescents' problematic behavior will result in other inappropriate acts, since the underlying motives are still unresolved. For instance, Freudian therapists presume that if a behavioral psychologist helps an adolescent overcome his or her stuttering solely through behavior-modification strategies, the adolescent may then develop a facial tick, since he or she will have failed to gain an understanding of the unconscious motives that underlay the stuttering.

Since psychoanalytic theories assume that we exhibit our unconscious motives indirectly rather than directly through our overt behavior, they frequently use **projective techniques** in order to find out what is unconsciously motivating our behavior. Two of the most popular projective tests are the Rorschach and the

Thematic Apperception Test. The **Rorschach** consists of a series of complex inkblots similar to the one illustrated in Figure 4.1. As the subject explains what each inkblot resembles, the examiner poses questions and interprets the responses. On the basis of the information gleaned in this manner, the therapist arrives at his or her judgment of the adolescent's unconscious motives and personality.

In a similar fashion, the **Thematic Apperception Test (TAT)** is administered by showing adolescents a series of pictures about which they are then asked to create a story. Subjects are told to create as dramatic and as interesting a story as they can, including an explanation of what preceded the event in the picture, what the characters feel, and what the outcome of the pictured event will be. On the basis of the responses, the examiner diagnoses each youngster's personality. Like the Rorschach, the TAT is presumed to reflect the youngsters' own unconscious motives and unresolved conflicts.

In addition, two other projective strategies were popularized by Freud—dream analysis and free association. **Free association** is the process whereby the therapist presents a list of words or phrases and interprets the youngsters' answers in accord with Freudian assumptions about the personality. For example, an adolescent girl might complete the phrase "my mother" by saying, "My mother reminds me of a vampire I saw once in a movie." Upon further questioning from the therapist, she might add, "Just like the vampire, she sneaks up on you, making you believe she's your friend until she sucks the life out of you." From a Freudian perspective, hostile responses of this sort might be interpreted as manifestations of an unresolved Electra complex.

The use of projective techniques and the continued practice of psychoanalytic counseling testify to the fact that Freudian theories still maintain their importance in adolescent psychology. The remaining chapters of this book will introduce you to many contemporary theorists, such as Peter Blos, whose research on adolescence is predicated on Freudian notions of personality development.

FIGURE 4.1

An inkblot of the type employed in the Rorschach technique

What do you see in this inkblot?
How might your response be interpreted
as a reflection of your personality?

Criticisms of Psychoanalytic Theories

Regardless of what the ultimate judgments of Freud's hypotheses about the role of adolescence in personality development prove to be, many of his assertions have been challenged. To begin with, research has consistently failed to uphold the Freudian hypothesis that adolescence is a period of considerable turmoil and tension between parents and children (Adelson & Doehrman, 1980; Josselson, 1980). Since this research will be discussed in detail in chapters 8 and 9, suffice it to say at this point that the comments of Ruth Josselson represent the consensus among even those scholars who are psychoanalytically oriented:

> Identity is a result of minute, seemingly inconsequential choices: whom one chooses for friends, what school one attends, what courses one takes, what one reads or does not read, whether one learns to play tennis or fly airplanes, whether one takes drugs or robs a store. This "turmoil" theory of ego development was so widespread that it misled a generation of adolescent researchers (Josselson, 1980, p. 202).

Another criticism leveled against traditional Freudian theories is their inaccuracy and incompleteness regarding female development. Such criticisms are by no means recent, as evidenced by the fact that in the 1920s the renowned psychoanalyst Karen Horney (1967) was criticizing many Freudian hypotheses about females. According to neo-Freudian critics such as Horney, the traditional psychoanalytic model fails to consider the fact that our society, as well as Freud's, accords greater status, privileges, and power to males. Therefore, the female tendency to develop nurturant, dependent personalities is a response to societal influences, rather than an outgrowth of psychosexual phenomena such as "penis envy" (Josselson, 1980). From this perspective, both males' and females' personalities are more powerfully affected by societal influences than classical Freudian theories acknowledge.

The psychoanalytic approach is also criticized for its subjectivity and for the lack of empirical data in support of its hypotheses (Adelson & Doehrman, 1980; Mischel, 1981). According to critics, projective techniques and personal judgments based on the psychotherapist's sessions with the client are too subjective for a reliable appraisal of an individual's personality or for an appraisal of the motives underlying his or her behavior. They are also criticized for their reliance on untestable hypotheses. For example, what behavior would allow us to conclude with some assurance that a particular adolescent is fixated at the anal stage? Or what evidence do we look for to substantiate the hypothesis that an adolescent girl has finally resolved her Electra complex? In short, Freudians have had a more difficult time than developmental or social learning theorists in testing their hypotheses empirically.

Furthermore, psychoanalytic therapy has been criticized on grounds that it is prohibitively expensive and requires an extensive investment of time. Since the goal of Freudian therapy is to help clients uncover their unconscious motivations and to resolve their unresolved psychosexual conflicts from childhood, the process typically involves months or years of work with a psychotherapist. In contrast, social learning and behavioral strategies have proved themselves successful in changing adolescents' behavior in a relatively short period of time and in the adolescents' natural setting, such as the school, rather than requiring visits to a therapist's office.

Finally, but perhaps most important from the standpoint of the methodological problems associated with research on adolescence, almost all Freudian theories are predicated upon therapists' individual judgments based on psychotherapy with

Which has had more influence over your personality, heredity or environment?

upper-middle-class, white, adult males, many of whom have voluntarily sought counseling (Adelson & Doehrman, 1980). In terms of clients' socioeconomic status, race, gender, age, and self-selection, the absence of random sampling remains one of the most serious challenges to psychoanalytic hypotheses. As discussed in chapter 1, without data derived from random samples, generalizing theories to the adolescent population is unwarranted.

NEO-FREUDIAN THEORIES OF PERSONALITY

Neo-Freudians differ from traditional Freudians in that they acknowledge the importance of environmental factors in affecting our personalities. They are also less likely than classical Freudians to emphasize early childhood experiences or to view adolescence as the final stage of our personality's development. Neo-Freudians see our personalities developing throughout the course of our lifetimes, rather than ending with our adolescence. In regard to the role of adolescence, two of the most prominent neo-Freudians are Erik Erikson and James Marcia.

Erikson's Psychosocial Stages

Like Freud, Erik Erikson (1968) contended that we pass through clearly delineated stages in which we have to resolve specific types of conflict if we are to enter the next stage successfully. Also like Freud, Erikson believed that the way in which we resolve these conflicts as children and adolescents will influence our adult personalities. Unlike Freud, however, Erikson viewed our personalities as developing throughout our lifetimes, rather than as being primarily determined in childhood. Moreover, Erikson did not see each stage in our development as being a matter of resolving sexual issues, as do the Freudians. Instead, Erikson saw our conflicts within each stage as being **psychosocial**. As Table 4.1 illustrates, although Freud, Erikson, and Piaget are all "stage theorists," they defined their stages differently in terms of the basic goals and conflicts associated with each part of our development. Piaget's stages are cognitive. Freud's are sexual. Erikson's are psychosocial.

According to Erikson, our major task during the first few years of life is to learn to trust other people and to develop a sense of security. This trust enables us to feel secure enough to explore the environment and to feel comfortable with the new and the unfamiliar as we age. In the next stage, our task is to establish a sense of autonomy and self-control in our growth toward independence. Between the ages of 3 and 5, we then enter the stage of "initiative versus guilt," which

Table 4.1

Stages of Personality Development

	PSYCHOANALYTIC	NEO-FREUDIAN	COGNITIVE DEVELOPMENTAL
	Freud	***Erikson***	***Piaget***
Birth–1 year	Oral	Trust versus mistrust	Sensorimotor
1–3 years	Anal	Autonomy versus shame	Preoperational
3–5 years	Oedipal	Initiative versus guilt	Preoperational
5–puberty	Latency	Industry versus inferiority	Concrete operations
Puberty	Genital	Identity versus confusion	Formal operations
Adulthood		Intimacy versus isolation	Formal operations
		Generativity versus stagnation	
		Integrity versus despair	

parallels Freud's Oedipal stage in several respects. While in this stage, we have to overcome our feelings of rivalry with our same-sex parent for the opposite-sex parent's attention. In large part, we overcome our jealousy by establishing relationships with our same-age peers. In other words, by the age of 5 we should be "cutting the apron strings" and moving into the world of our peers.

Wanting to be accepted by our peers, between the ages of 6 and 12 we should be motivated to acquire new social and intellectual skills. We want to overcome our feelings of inferiority and to gain status among our peers. Overcoming our

Which aspects of your personality do you most and least enjoy?

A CLOSER LOOK 4.2

Havighurst's Developmental Tasks of Adolescence

Task One: Acquiring More Mature Social Skills

Before adolescence most friendships are formed with members of the same sex. During early adolescence the young begin to interact with the opposite sex within the security of group settings where members of the same sex are present. As they become more confident in their social skills, the young are also gaining the cognitive abilities that permit a more complete understanding of social roles and friendships. Heterosexual relationships thus become more frequent and more intimate as adolescents age.

Task Two: Achieving a Masculine or Feminine Sex Role

The maturational changes of puberty exacerbate the physical differences between males and females. In addition, the culture encourages each sex to assume specified social, sexual, and vocational roles. Consequently, adolescence becomes a time for adopting, rejecting, or modifying cultural expectations regarding male and female behavior and attitudes.

Task Three: Accepting the Changes in One's Body, Using the Body Effectively, and Accepting One's Own Physique

In a culture that often exaggerates the value of physical appearance, adolescents whose bodies fail to fit our culture's expectations of "beauty" confront the difficult tasks of learning to value themselves physically. For the fortunate ones whose bodies conform to our society's notions of beauty, the task is limited to brief periods of time when the body's rapid growth may make its owner feel awkward, ungainly, and unattractive. If adolescents are able to accept themselves physically without being overly critical, their anxieties about physical appearance should diminish considerably by the end of adolescence.

Task Four: Achieving Emotional Independence From Parents and Other Adults

Increased social skills and physical maturation motivate adolescents to be less reliant on adults. Although their desires for independence are culturally sanctioned in the sense that all children must eventually become self-reliant, adolescents often expect to be granted independence before their elders feel they are emotionally, intellectually, or socially prepared. Parents must relinquish their former roles as protectors of dependent children, and the family must establish new relationships reflecting the adolescent's increasing self-reliance. Understandably, the successful completion of this developmental task often creates conflict between young and old.

continued

sense of inferiority also demands, however, that we learn to assess our own strengths and weaknesses honestly. In other words, part of the psychosocial task is to learn to "see ourselves as others see us." If these four stages of development are successfully completed, we will enter our teenage years prepared to develop an identity. If, however, we have not mastered the goals in these childhood stages, these unfinished tasks will interfere with our establishing an identity of our own during adolescence. For example, as a consequence of years of academic failure and frustration, adolescents with learning disabilities have been found to lack a sense of "industry and competence" (Pickar & Tori, 1986).

Box 4.2 continued

Task Five: Preparing for Sex, Marriage, and Parenthood

As physical maturation is completed and emotional attachments to the opposite sex become more intimate, older adolescents must develop ideologies and behavior that allow them to incorporate aspects of sexuality into their lives. This involves developing realistic attitudes about sex, love, marriage, and parenthood and casting aside many mythical beliefs that were part of early adolescence.

Task Six: Selecting and Preparing for an Occupation

As older adolescents advance toward independence from their parents, they confront the inevitable questions related to financial self-reliance. These include whether to continue one's education beyond high school, what vocation to pursue, and how to overcome whatever obstacles may lie in the path of accomplishing these vocational goals. For females in contemporary society, this task may now also involve deciding whether to postpone marriage for a career, deciding whether to have children in one's early 20s or to postpone motherhood until the 30s, and deciding whether to pursue a profession that might somehow interfere with men's perceptions of the females' social desirability.

Task Seven: Developing a Personal Ideology and Ethical Standards

As cognitive growth enables older adolescents to think more abstractly and less egotistically than younger people, questions related to morality, religion, philosophy, and politics are more likely to arise. Through their interactions with people outside their own families and their observations of the world around them, older adolescents often come to question their elders' ethical standards and to experiment with other beliefs. This experimentation may involve joining religious sects, becoming active in political parties, or interacting with people from other cultures whose views challenge their own. By accepting, rejecting, or modifying the beliefs that they readily accepted as younger children, older adolescents are confronted with the task of developing their own ethical standards and philosophies of life.

Task Eight: Assuming Membership in the Larger Community

As independence from parents and other elders grows, older adolescents must learn to recognize their roles in and responsibilities to a community beyond the school, neighborhood, or family. Rather than defining themselves exclusively through their roles in the school and family, young adults learn to derive self-satisfaction and identity from their roles within the community.

Source: R. Havighurst. (1972). *Developmental tasks and education.* New York: McKay.

During adolescence, however, our primary task is to develop an identity of our own. According to Erikson, and also according to Robert Havighurst, whose theory is presented in Box 4.2, two aspects of our identity that assume primary importance during adolescence are our vocational roles and our sex roles; that is, What do I want to be when I grow up, and what does it mean to be "feminine"? "masculine"? "a woman"? "a man"? Our attitudes about sex, love, marriage, parenthood, and future employment are being formed in conjunction with our beliefs about what is appropriate behavior for males and females. Since this aspect of Erikson's work has added to the controversy regarding male and female personalities in our society, it is discussed in detail in chapter 5. Suffice it to say at this point that Eriksonian psychologists believe that males and females behave differently primarily as a consequence of biological, rather than environmental, influences.

One of the most controversial aspects of Erikson's model is this belief that males and females develop different personalities primarily as a consequence of biological, not environmental, factors. Because this controversy will be presented in detail in Chapter 5, suffice it to say at this point that Eriksonian psychologists believe that our gender has an influence over our personalities independent of what our particular society teaches us about masculinity or femininity.

Finally, Erikson believed that our personalities are shaped by our confronting a new task in our early adult years: the task of developing intimate relationships with other people. According to Eriksonian psychologists, only after we have formed a vocational and sex role identity during adolescence are we ready to establish truly intimate friendships with members of both sexes. Having accomplished this task, as older adults we shape our personalities by the way we come to terms with the task of **generativity**—the need to guide the younger generation and leave something of value behind in our lives. Those of us who fail to master the conflicts in each of life's eight psychosocial stages will feel a sadness and despair in our old age. In contrast, those of us who successfully resolve the crises in each of these stages will experience feelings of "integrity."

Marcia's Identity Statuses

Elaborating on Erikson's model, James Marcia described four different types of identity that adolescents may adopt: identity diffusion, foreclosure, moratorium, and identity achievement. Marcia referred to each of these options as an **identity status** (Marcia, 1980) (see Box 4.3).

According to Marcia, young people with **diffused identities** have not yet chosen any vocational or ideological direction, even though they may have experimented with various roles and ideologies. For example, a male with a diffused identity might say he has no idea what to do after graduation or that "one political view is just about as good as any other, I guess." Without clear identities or values, these youngsters are the least likely of the four identity-status groups to have close relationships with friends of either sex. Identity diffusion has often been found characteristic of adolescents who feel rejected and detached from their parents.

Similar to identity-diffused youth in that they have not yet adopted an identity, adolescents in the **moratorium** identity status are currently struggling with their identities. In Marcia's model, the moratorium youth's lack of defined goals or clear values contributes to feelings of anxiety. Nevertheless, these young people tend to be characterized by sophisticated levels of moral reasoning, self-esteem, self-directiveness, curiosity, social activity, and emotional expressiveness.

In contrast, an individual with a **foreclosed identity** has adopted an identity and a system of clearly defined values. Unfortunately, from Marcia's and Erikson's perspectives, these adolescents have prematurely endorsed the viewpoints of their parents and society's other authorities in lieu of examining alternative roles and values. For example, a boy with a foreclosed identity may, without ever exploring any other vocational option, acquiesce to his parents' expectations that he become a physician. Or a girl whose identity is foreclosed may embrace the religious and

A CLOSER LOOK 4.3

Marcia's Identity-Status Interview

The following are samples of the types of response representing the various identity statuses proposed by James Marcia. Which type of identity status characterized your adolescence? Which identity status characterizes your present personality?

OCCUPATIONAL AREA

"How willing do you think you'd be to give up going into _____ if something better came along?"

- *Achievement:* "Well, I might, but I doubt it. I can't see what something better would be for me."
- *Moratorium:* "I guess if I knew for sure, I could answer that better. It would have to be something in the general area—something related."
- *Foreclosure:* "Not very willing. It's what I've always wanted to do. The folks are happy with it and so am I."
- *Diffusion:* "Oh, sure. If something better came along, I'd change just like that."

RELIGIOUS AREA

"Have you ever had any doubts about your religious beliefs?"

- *Achievement:* "Yeah, I even started wondering whether there is a God. I've pretty much resolved that now, though. The way it seems to me . . ."
- *Moratorium:* "Yes, I guess I'm going through that now. I just don't see how there can be a God and yet so much evil in the world or . . ."
- *Foreclosure:* "No, not really. Our family is pretty much in agreement on these things."
- *Diffusion:* "Oh, I don't know. I guess so. Everyone goes through some sort of stage like that. But it really doesn't bother me much. I figure one's about as good as the other."

Source: J. Marcia. (1966). Development and validation of ego-identity status. *Journal of Personality and Social Psychology, 3,* 551–558.

political policies of her family without ever discussing or reading about different perspectives. These adolescents seldom defy the wishes of authorities. Yet because young people with foreclosed identities tend to have a greater need for social approval than youths in the other identity statuses, they are often the most susceptible to persuasion by others—especially by those whom they perceive as authority figures, such as religious leaders, teachers, or parents.

The fourth identity status, and the one Marcia considered most ideal, is the **achieved identity.** Those of us who form an achieved identity by the end of adolescence are more likely to be emphathetic, reflective, resistant to authority, self-confident, and academically successful than our peers who adopted other identity statuses. Adolescents who have an achieved identity also seem to be more willing to reveal their thoughts and feelings and to focus on other people, while those with diffused identities are the most self-focused (Adams, Abraham, & Markstrom, 1987). Unfortunately, the process of becoming identity achieved involves a certain amount of struggle—experimenting with different identities and attitudes and trying on new social, vocational, political, and religious values in hopes of discovering which ones best represent the "real" individual.

Not surprisingly, Marcia and other researchers have found that our parents have considerable influence over which identity status we adopt (Baumrind, 1989; Grotevant & Cooper, 1986; Hauser, et al 1987; Hill, 1987). Those of us in the moratorium stage generally have parents who encourage our autonomy, expressiveness, and independence. Similarly, most identity-achieved youths come from nurturant, supportive families where independence and nonconformity are encouraged. Their parents are authoritative, meaning that they do not regard themselves or their standards as infallible. Although these parents set clear limits and punish their children for overstepping those limits, they are also willing to discuss family rules with children in a democratic fashion, rather than imposing rules and punishment unilaterally. In contrast, the parents of adolescents with foreclosed identities are generally authoritarian. In these households, obedience is an overriding virtue, and children are expected to abide unquestioningly by their parents' standards—standards often derived from religious leaders or other outside authorities.

Although research generally supports Marcia's and Erikson's theories of identity statuses with regard to male development, female development defies many of their predictions; that is, males' and females' personalities do not follow a similar path of development, an issue we will examine more carefully in chapter 5.

Individuation During Adolescence

Although neo-Freudians and Freudians may disagree on the types of stage we go through as children and adolescents, they do nonetheless agree that the component of our personality that they refer to as the ego undergoes an important change during adolescence. From their viewpoint, adolescence is a crucial part of our personality development in that it is the period during which individuation needs to occur. **Individuation** is the process whereby our childhood ego separates itself from the egos of our parents (Blos, 1979); that is, during adolescence our ego should become "individuated" from, or independent of, our parents and other adult authorities. More simply put, the task of the ego during adolescence is to learn to differentiate "me" from "them" by establishing an identity of its own, rather than merely reflecting the identities (egos) of parents and, ultimately, of our peers.

Many psychoanalytic scholars consider individuation to be a lifelong process of discovering "who am I," a process of struggling to answer "who is the real me and who is the 'me' the rest of you are telling me I have to be?" Although our ego is engaged in this task well beyond adolescence, the teenage years are especially important in that they are the initial period during which we begin to truly define "me" as separate from our parents. Not surprisingly, in our initial attempts as young adolescents to become individuated from our parents, we occasionally defy adult authority. Contrary to researchers' earlier assumptions about individuation, however, adolescents do not reject all their parents' values or become emotionally detached from their parents in the process of developing a more autonomous ego. Current data show that adolescents do not reject their parents as individuation occurs (Josselson, 1980).

Although individuation is the process of becoming more autonomous from our parents, it also affects our relationships with our adolescent peers (Blos, 1979; Josselson, 1980). In early adolescence, we are still conforming to the peer group and seeking peer approval as ways of supporting the newly individuated parts of our ego. Not really sure of who "I" am, I have to verify it on a regular basis with my friends. The ego is still too insecure and separation from our parents is still too frightening to enable us to have the courage to be ourselves without peer approval. As our ego becomes more sure of itself, however, we become more willing to define ourselves without the constant approval of others. Consequently, in contrast to young adolescents, older adolescents are generally less willing to think or to behave like everyone else in order to win peer approval. The ego, as it has become more autonomous, has also become more self-assured.

Similarly, individuation affects our superego, or conscience. Young adolescents are more willing than older adolescents to adopt the "shoulds and should nots" of their parents and other authorities, rather than determining for themselves what is right and wrong; that is, 13-year-olds are apt to feel guilty after getting drunk because they have been told by their parents and preachers that doing so is sinful and wrong, whereas 18-year-olds are likely to feel guilty after getting drunk because they have decided, of their own accord, that abusing alcohol is dangerous and socially embarrassing. Both have a conscience (superego) influencing their behavior, but the younger adolescents' superego, being less individuated, is based on the voice of authorities, while their older counterparts' superego is based on their own values and ideals.

According to some ego theorists, young people who devote themselves zealously to religious leaders are trying to avoid the somewhat discomforting task of developing their own individuated superego (Blos, 1979; Josselson, 1980). By adopting a prepackaged set of rules and values espoused by "the authorities," these young people are failing to assume the responsibility for forming their own ethical codes by refusing to question the established order. Unfortunately, this failure to examine our superego's values and to replace them, when necessary, with our own standards may result in the lifelong feeling of never being good enough. In such cases, we resemble a young child in that we are always trying (and failing) to "be good" in terms of the superego's unrealistic expectations.

Criticisms of Neo-Freudian Theories

Although neo-Freudian theories have contributed to our understanding of ego development and identity statuses during adolescence, they have their limitations. Even James Marcia himself has admitted that most of the research on identity status has been limited to white college students and may not be generalizable to other adolescents. Likewise, although white males seem to follow the patterns of identity development described by ego psychologists, females and minority youths seem to follow different patterns of development, as we will see in chapters 5 and 6 (Marcia, 1980).

Another shortcoming of Erikson's and Marcia's theories is that they assume that identity achievement is superior to the other identity statuses, although people with foreclosed identities have many appealing attributes that may in fact be well adapted to their life circumstances. They are not generally as daring, adventuresome, and independent as those with achieved identities but are nonetheless cooperative, steadfast, and committed to their principles. Likewise, although they have not achieved an identity of their own, identity-diffused people usually have the attributes of being quite charming and carefree. Indeed, given the rapidity with which our society and our individual life circumstances change, perhaps having a more flexible and more ambiguous identity has certain advantages over having an achieved identity.

As is the case with stage theories, Marcia's and Erikson's theories have also been criticized for their assumption that later we move from one identity status into another and remain fixed in that later identity status from then on. In fact, some research already indicates that college students sometimes "regress" to an earlier identity status even after they have presumably achieved their independent identity (Adams, Abraham, & Markstrom, 1987). Furthermore, since our identity status is determined by our answers and self-descriptions during an interview, we may not give an accurate representation of what we really believe and how we actually behave. In order to impress our interviewer, we may hedge on our answers, describing ourselves as we would like to be rather than as we are (see Box 4.3).

COGNITIVE STAGE THEORIES

As already shown in chapter 3, cognitive stage theorists assume that adolescents' more advanced mental skills are primarily the consequence of their entering the formal operations stage of reasoning. Guided by these concepts, cognitive psychologists contend that formal operational thinking is responsible for many of the changes that personalities undergo during adolescence. The theories of David Elkind, a renowned psychologist in the field of adolescent cognition, illustrate the applicability of the cognitive stage perspective to adolescents' personalities.

Hypocrisy and Idealism

In the Piagetian tradition, Elkind contended that adolescents' newly acquired ability to differentiate between reality and ideals permits them to perceive hypocrisy for the first time in their lives (Elkind, 1970, 1978). This cognitive awareness often means that parents who previously appeared totally good and marvelously knowledgable suddenly fall from grace and appear disappointingly human, much to the dismay of their adolescent children. Disappointed by the contrasts between ideals and reality, young people may react to criticizing both "the system" and their parents. Others may rebel against the institutions they view as responsible for the hypocrisy in our society.

Elkind believed that this disillusionment also motivates some adolescents to construct their own idealistic, theoretical visions of how society ought to function. Hence, adults often witness the phase in which younger adolescents appear overly optimistic and idealistic. Yet, in the midst of condemning the hypocrisy surrounding them, adolescents are typically unable to recognize the hypocrisy in much of their own behavior. Although able to think abstractly, most adolescents lack the experience necessary to practice their own principles. As a consequence, a young adolescent might chastise his or her parents for not donating money to clean up the community's polluted lake, while nonchalantly tossing a candy wrapper out the car window.

Egocentrism

In addition to being influenced by this form of hypocrisy and idealism, young adolescents' personalities are also supposedly affected by their egocentrism (Elkind, 1978). As you recall from chapter 3, egocentrism is the inability to take another's perspective or to see several sides of an issue. Since psychologists such as Elkind believe that egocentrism declines as we age, young adolescents are presumed to be less empathetic and more self-centered than older adolescents or adults. Although there may be a certain appeal to envisioning ourselves as more emphathetic and more unselfish than we were as young adolescents, recent studies have called this assumption into question (DeRosenroll, 1987; Lapsley, 1986). For the present, then, we might best reserve our judgments about the egocentrism of young adolescents.

The evidence is more convincing, however, for another of Elkind's assumptions about the adolescent personality, that it believes in an **imaginary audience.** Young adolescents do tend to behave as though "everyone" is watching them, as though they are on stage in front of an audience. According to Elkind, this belief in the imaginary audience underlies the excessive self-consciousness of early adolescence. Feeling that the world is noticing and judging their every move, young adolescents tend to be more hypersensitive about aspects of their appearance or behavior than are older adolescents. Assuming that everyone else is as critical or as approving of them as they are of themselves, young adolescents let their imaginary audience inflate or deflate their self-confidence with the slightest remark.

For example, a 13-year-old boy may refuse to run into the grocery store for his dad, arguing vehemently that he cannot go into a store wearing jeans that are an inch too short because "everyone will notice and laugh at me." Similarly, a father's joking around in front of his son's friends may be misconstrued by the overly self-conscious youth: "Dad, don't embarrass me like that in front of my friends. Can't you just stay kind of quiet, you know, like a grown-up?" Although we may or may not agree with Elkind's hypothesis of the imaginary audience, studies have demonstrated that young adolescents are shyer and more self-conscious than are older adolescents or adults (Hauck, Martens & Wetzel, 1986; Hudson & Gray, 1986). In consequence, they are often hypersensitive to gestures or remarks that may be misconstrued to mean that we are observing or judging them.

Furthermore, young adolescents' personalities appear to be quite influenced by the **personal fable,** the belief that an individual is so unique and special that he or she is protected from harm and that nobody else can possibly understand that individual's feelings and experiences. Unfortunately, under the spell of this personal fable, young people too often risk their own health or well-being: "I can't get pregnant even though I didn't take any precautions with birth control. That only happens to other kids." "I can have a few beers and still drive safely—I'm not one of those drunk drivers." "Young people don't die, so why worry about smoking cigarettes?" Moreover, the young adolescent has difficulty understanding that other people have shared experiences like theirs—the sorrows of a broken heart or the shame of public humiliation—for to understand that all humans share these feelings and experiences, the adolescent would have to abandon his or her sense of being unique.

In contrast, older adolescents are more likely to see their own frailties and to understand that they, too, are subject to the same kinds of consequence and experience that befall all of us as mortal, fallible creatures. Consequently, the older adolescent is not nearly as shocked as the 14-year-old to discover that mom and dad also cry and feel afraid. As we approach the end of adolescence, most of us learn to put aside our personal fable, recognizing that our own suffering, disappointments, or anger does not make us special or different from other human beings—that, indeed, having these feelings is part of our shared human condition.

Pseudostupidity

Finally, ego psychologists such as Elkind offer us an explanation for why adolescents sometimes seem to behave so "stupidly." Why is it, for example, that when faced with a simple, straightforward decision, adolescents will mull it over so thoroughly that they are unable to make any decision at all? Why is it that adolescents often attribute complicated, hidden motives to other people's behavior when none exist? According to Elkind, such behavior is not a consequence of real stupidity, hence the term **"pseudostupidity"** (meaning "not genuine stupidity"). Elkind contended that this kind of behavior is the consequence of cognitive growth in combination with a lack of experience, neither of which the adolescent can control. Having acquired more advanced reasoning skills, adolescents will literally think too much about simple problems and about the motives underlying other people's behavior. As they age, however, experience will catch up with their cognitive skills and the pseudostupidity will disappear.

In sum, psychologists such as Elkind believe that the new aspects of our personalities that appear during adolescence are related to the cognitive changes accompanying formal operational thinking. From this perspective, adolescents' personalities are being heavily influenced by their egocentrism, their beliefs in the imaginary audience and the personal fable, and their idealism and hypocrisy. Once we are beyond adolescence, these dimensions of our personalities supposedly subside.

TRAIT THEORIES

A third approach to the study of adolescents' personalities, trait theories, presumes that we all behave in a relatively consistent manner as a consequence of our innate "traits" (Kenrick & Funder, 1988; Mischel, 1981). According to some trait theorists, our personalities are based on a very few basic traits, such as introversion or extroversion, dominance or submissiveness. Others argue, however, that a number of traits direct our behavior. Despite this disagreement, trait theorists agree that our personality traits can be identified on the basis of written tests. Once identified, these traits can supposedly be used as blueprints to predict how we will behave in future situations. For example, if a personality test assesses you as shy and introspective and assesses your adolescent brother as domineering and extroverted, we should be able to predict which of you will do most of the talking and most of the directing at your family get-togethers. Moreover, as Box 4.4 illustrates, some researchers are pursuing the possibility that certain personality traits may be inherited.

Whether personality traits are ultimately found to have a hereditary basis, most of us nonetheless apply trait theories in our everyday lives. In a sense, when you read a description of your personality from an astrology book, you are applying trait theories: "Oh, yes, she's a Scorpio, so of course she's going to be intense, mysterious, and passionate. But since I'm a Libra, I should be able to get along with her." Even if you have never thumbed through an astrology book, you probably base many of your reactions and expectations on trait theories without being particularly cognizant of their ramifications. For example, when you hear someone describe her 16-year-old daughter as friendly and self-confident, you are probably already presuming to know how the girl will behave when she is on a

A CLOSER LOOK 4.4

Do We Inherit Our Personalities?

Is it possible that we inherit certain aspects of our personalities, such as sociability and shyness? Can we inherit an attitude, such as the willingness to follow rules and obey authorities? While such notions would be unlikely to find many advocates among social learning theorists and behaviorists, sociobiologists have presented evidence suggesting that our emotionality, activity levels, and sociability may indeed have a genetic component. These three traits have been proposed as the most heritable components of personality from infancy to adulthood (Plomin, 1986). Surprisingly, some attitudes and beliefs show almost as much genetic influence as these three behavioral traits. One focus of recent interest is the trait of "traditionalism:—the tendency to follow rules and authorities, to embrace high moral standards, and to impose strict discipline—which, from studies of twins reared apart, seems to have a genetic basis" (Tellegen, Lykken, Bouchard, Wilcox, Segal, & Rich, 1988). Moreover, some evidence suggests that even juvenile delinquency may be influenced by genetic factors (Wilson & Hernstein, 1985). What other aspects of our adolescent and adult personalities might sociobiologists ultimately credit to our genetic influences?

date, in her math class, or at a ball game; that is, most of us presume that people's traits remain relatively constant despite the particulars of the settings in which they find themselves. Similarly, when we use descriptors such as timid or outgoing about ourselves or others, we are attempting to analyze and to predict human behavior using the assumptions of trait theorists.

Assessing Personality Traits

A description of the standardized tests that trait theorists might use to identify an adolescent's personality traits is beyond the scope of this text, but a cursory description of one such test, the **Minnesota Multiphasic Personality Inventory** (**MMPI**), can serve to exemplify the trait theorists' approach (Hathaway & McKinley, 1943). Composed of 550 statements to which the individual responds "true," "false," or "undecided," the MMPI was initially devised to classify mental patients into various categories of psychiatric disorder. The scale is frequently used, however, with people who have no apparent psychiatric problems, in an attempt to compare their traits with those of other people from similar backgrounds or circumstances.

Like a number of other personality tests, the MMPI combines the adolescent's responses into categories, permitting an overall "profile" of the personality to emerge. For instance, if a statement on the MMPI, such as "I cry easily," is typically affirmed by adolescents who have been hospitalized for psychiatric problems but rarely affirmed by high-school students who have never been treated for psychiatric problems, the statement could be used as part of the test for identifying certain kinds of adolescent maladjustment. The individual's overall profile is then coded in a way that permits a general description of his or her personality or specific dimensions of personality. For example, a young person's MMPI score might yield this description: "This person avoids close relationships with other people, tends to be resentful, often feels tense, manifests anger through somatic illnesses, is very dependent on other people's opinions, and aspires to unrealistic goals for self and others."

Research on the validity and reliability of personality inventories such as the MMPI is extensive. Just for the MMPI alone, almost 100 studies are conducted each year (Mischel, 1981). Although the MMPI is only one among dozens of popular personality scales, it serves as the model for many others, such as the California Psychological Inventory (CPI), the Taylor Manifest Anxiety Scale (MAS), and the Hackson Personality Inventory.

Applications to Adolescents

Since we often behave toward adolescents in accord with the traits that we—correctly or incorrectly—have ascribed to them, it becomes incumbent upon us to reexamine our own behavior and attitudes in terms of the questions that trait theorists explore: Are we correct in expecting an adolescent to behave according to traits that have been ascribed to him or her? Do personality traits determine an adolescent's behavior or attitudes across different situations? Do idiosyncratic situational factors influence the youngster's behavior more than personality traits? Can we modify an adolescent's behavior, or is it fundamentally controlled by his or her intrinsic traits? Do tests or descriptions from other people reliably identify an adolescent's traits or permit us to predict his or her behavior? Such questions reflect the quest of trait theorists.

Unlike cognitive, Freudian, or neo-Freudian theorists, trait theorists approach adolescents' problems without much attention to concepts such as ego stages, identity statuses, formal operational thought, or individuation. As an illustration, if two adolescent boys are suspended from school for fighting, a trait theorist might approach the situation by administering a personal inventory in order to identify the traits that seem to characterize each boy's personality. Once having established a personality profile for each boy on the basis of the test data, the trait theorist might pursue other questions in an attempt to resolve the problem: Was the fight atypical or typical behavior, given each boy's personality profile? Is there behavioral evidence other than the fight to corroborate the test results? Do the descriptions of each boy from friends, family, and teachers confirm or dispute the test results? Given the test results and behavioral reports, do specific traits appear to be influencing each boy's behavior across a number of situations? If the test results contradict the descriptions of these boys' personalities from other people, which source is correct?

Criticisms of Trait Theories

Despite the fact that many of us behave like trait theorists in our interactions with and expectations of adolescents, trait theories have been criticized on a number of grounds (Hogan & Nicholson, 1988; Kagan, 1988; Kenrick & Funder, 1988). First, critics point out that the tests on which trait theorists assess our personalities are not reliable methods for assessing our actual behavior. In answering questions about ourselves, both as adolescents and as adults, we tend

What troubled you most about yourself when you were an adolescent? What about now?

to describe ourselves as we would like to be or as we think other people would like us to be, rather than as who we really are. How many of us, for example, are willing to admit that we would rather have things our own way than compromise with someone? Knowing that answering "yes" to such questions will probably categorize us as domineering or selfish, how many of us are willing to confess? Moreover, even if we are willing to describe ourselves honestly, we may have only a limited awareness of our own moods, motives, and behavior.

In addition, although there is a strong intuitive appeal to the assumption that we have consistent traits, the research often shows that we behave differently

Which aspects of yourself did you spend the most time thinking about as a teenager? And now?

depending on the situation in which we find ourselves. An adolescent, for instance, may be very shy and insecure in math class, but very outspoken and self-assured with his girlfriend. Which is he, shy or outspoken? In a similar fashion, his scores on the MMPI may show him to be assertive and noncompliant, while his actual behavior may be sheepish and deferent. Which is true, the personality test results or his behavior?

It might seem that one way around the shortcomings of self-report tests would be to solicit other people's opinions of our personality. That is, if you want to know whether Siegfried is shy and withdrawn or aggressive and domineering, ask his teachers, his friends, and his parents to describe him. However, this approach has also been criticized. First, we tend to make unwarranted judgments based on our expectations of which traits seem to go together. That is, if you have observed Siegfried being aggressive, you may also describe him as selfish, inconsiderate, insensitive, and insincere, although you have not actually observed those traits in his behavior.

For these reasons, many trait theorists recommend that assessments of an adolescent's personality include observations of his or her actual behavior in a variety of situations, as well as the results of written personality tests. Indeed, when data have been collected from a number of independent observers and from personality tests, the descriptions that emerge tend to be relatively reliable and valid (Kagan, 1988; Mishel, 1981). Applied in this way, the trait theorists' approach can be useful in helping us explain and predict adolescents' behavior.

PHENOMENOLOGICAL THEORIES

In contrast to trait theories, phenomenological theories maintain that adolescents play many different roles, rather than behaving in accord with an identifiable set of personality traits (Mischel, 1981). Phenomenological psychologists reject the notion that a youngster's personality is controlled by psychosexual or psychosocial conflicts, cognitive stages, or internal traits. From their viewpoint, the adolescent's personality is directed by the "self," which interprets experiences on the basis of its own private, idiosyncratic concepts and the self-image. Hence, adolescents' personalities depend on the way they perceive the self and the way the self perceives other people and experiences. Phenomenologists contend that we can never completely understand another person's behavior, because we never completely know his or her "internal frame of reference" in any particular situation. Adolescents' interpretations of the phenomena in the world—including their interpretation of the self—are too private and too complex for other people to comprehend or to predict.

Rogers' and Maslow's Theories

Two of the best-known advocates of the phenomenological view are Carl Rogers and Abraham Maslow. They refer to their collective theories as **humanistic psychology.** According to Rogers and his advocates, the adolescent's personality is determined by conceptualizations he or she has of the self—the self-concept (Rogers, 1969).

Rogers developed **client-centered** therapy, sometimes referred to as **Rogerian counseling,** as a way of helping us examine our self-concepts. The Rogerian counselor must be emphathetic, friendly, honest, trustworthy, nonthreatening, nonjudgmental, and unconditionally accepting of the client's feelings and behavior—an attitude Rogers referred to as *unconditional positive regard.* Under these conditions, we will supposedly disclose our self-concepts, feelings, and perceptions. Unlike psychoanalytic counseling, Rogerian counseling refrains from interpreting a client's motives and from advising the client to adopt any particular course of action. Client-centered therapists assume that clients—even adolescent clients—

possess the abilities necessary for resolving their own problems, if helped to disclose and to accept the self.

According to Rogerian theories, "reflective listening" is a crucial component of effective counseling and effective communication. Reflective listening is repeating or reflecting the client's comments without judgment or interpretation. For example, Leon might say, "I feel like adults are ganging up against me and that nothing I do is right." The counselor might then respond, "So you feel that no matter what you do, you can't make adults happy."

In a similar vein, Abraham Maslow believes that we are all motivated by an intrinsic tendency called **self-actualization** (Maslow, 1968). According to Maslow, we want to "actualize" ourselves and behave in ways that make self-actualization possible. Before we can develop the traits of a self-actualized personality, however (see Table 4.2), we must fulfill other more basic needs. As Figure 4.2 demonstrates, Maslow presumed that we are all motivated by the same needs and, further, that these needs are arranged in a hierarchical order: physiological needs, safety needs, needs for love and belongingness, need for self-esteem, and need for self-actualization.

From Maslow's viewpoint, for example, adolescents who are tired, hungry, or cold will behave in ways that lead toward fulfilling these basic physiological needs. Until these needs are satisfied, the adolescents will not be motivated to behave in ways to meet their needs for self-esteem or other higher-order needs in the hierarchy. Similarly, adolescents who feel inferior to their peers and rejected by

FIGURE 4.2
Maslow's hierarchy of needs

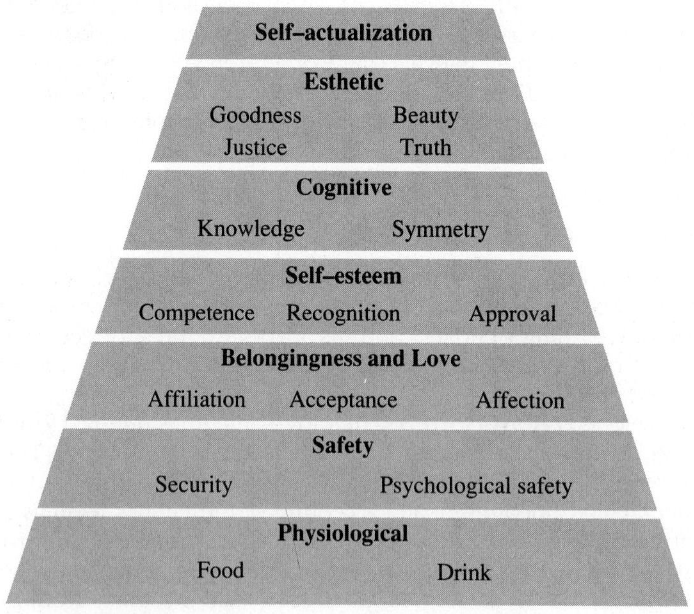

Source: A. Maslow, *Toward a psychology of being.* New York: Van Nostrand, 1968.

their parents cannot develop self-actualized personalities, because their needs for safety and self-esteem are unmet. In regard to our interactions with adolescents, therefore, Maslow would recommend our arranging experiences and environments that assure the fulfillment of their needs as designated in his hierarchy. We must then trust that youngsters' intrinsic desires to become self-actualized will direct their personalities in ways that are beneficial to them and to others.

How do we know when adolescents are becoming or have become self-actualized? From Maslow's perspective, specific behaviors and attitudes characterize the self-actualized personality. On the basis of his observations of adults whom he considered self-actualized, Maslow compiled the profile presented in Table 4.2.

Field Theories

The phenomenological approach also includes psychologists like Kurt Lewin, who developed many aspects of **field theory.** According to field theorists, the adolescent has a life space that determines behavior (Lewin, 1935). The **life space** includes the youngster's self-concept, his or her ways of perceiving the world, and the experiences occurring in the environment at the moment. Within this life space are many fields of force, as there are in physics, which interact with one another to influence behavior. Altering one part of the force field causes the entire field to change. In other words, an adolescent's interpretation of reality can change dramatically from moment to moment, since some dimensions of his or her life space are inevitably changing.

According to field theorists, the adolescent's perceptions may or may not coincide with objective data or with another person's interpretation of reality. This

Table 4.2

Qualities of Maslow's Self-Actualized Person

How many of the following qualities of the self-actualized person did you embody as an adolescent? How many of these traits characterize your present personality?

1. Creative and inventive
2. Aware of the need for change and improvement
3. Ethical, unprejudiced, and respectful of others
4. Independent and spontaneous
5. Appreciative of solitude and privacy
6. Accepting of self, others, and the world
7. Realistic in perceiving experiences and people
8. Concerned with problems of others
9. Aware of simple, commonplace experiences, such as sunsets and flowers
10. Thoughtful, good-humored, and philosophical
11. Emotionally bonded to relatively few people in profound ways
12. Democratic and broad-minded
13. Capable of "mystical" feelings or "peak experiences," in which one feels separate from ordinary reality and part of nature

Source: A. Maslow. (1968). *Toward a psychology of being.* New York: Van Nostrand.

principle is demonstrated by people's different reactions to gestalts like the one in Figure 4.3. Literally translated from German, a gestalt means "shape or outward form" hence the term **Gestalt psychology.** As used by phenomenological psychologists, the gestalt demonstrates the principle of our idiosyncratic interpretations of all phenomena. Looking at Figure 4.3, some of us will see a black vase against a white background, and others will see two white silhouettes against a black background, depending upon which part of the picture we attend to first. Similarly, Gestalt theorists contend that adolescents' personalities and their behavior in any given situation depend on their unique interpretations of a phenomenon—interpretations that will not necessarily reflect any other person's conceptualization of that phenomenon.

According to Gestalt psychologists, adolescents' personalities may differ from situation to situation as a consequence of the ways in which they perceive a gestalt at any given moment. For example, Joyce may get home from school and, finding her father in a bad mood, interpret his surliness as a sign that he no longer loves her. Given her interpretation of the situation (the gestalt), she feels depressed and angry for the rest of the week. If the same situation recurs next week, however, she may interpret the gestalt differently and assume that her dad's surly mood has nothing to do with her. Her mood and behavior remain unchanged. Our ways of perceiving situations, in turn, influence our self-concepts and our beliefs about other people. Thus, from a Gestalt psychologist's perspective, if we can change adolescents' self-concepts, their personalities will undergo transformations as a consequence. One of the primary goals of Gestalt therapy, therefore, is to help adolescents refashion some of their perceptions of themselves and of other people in order to enhance their self-concepts.

FIGURE 4.3
A "gestalt"

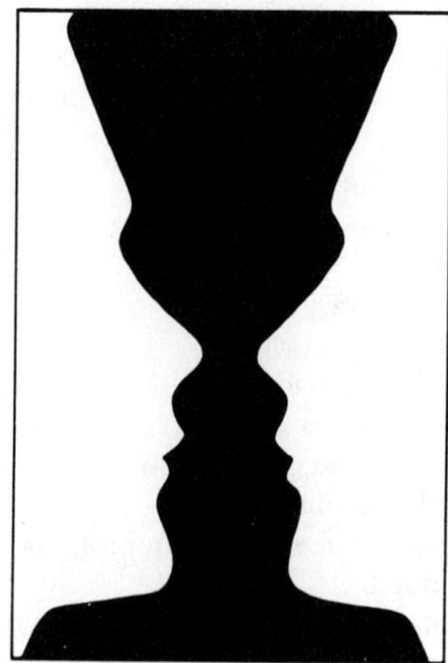

What do you see in this gestalt—two white silhouettes or a black vase?

How have your race, gender, and socioeconomic class influenced your self-esteem and personality?

Measuring Adolescents' Self-Concepts

Since phenomenologists assume that our self-concepts directly shape our personality, they rely on standardized tests for assessing our perceptions of self and others. In addition to Carl Rogers's client-centered interviews, tests like the Q-sort technique and the semantic differential can be used to asess our perceptions of ourselves and of other people.

The **Q-sort technique** consists of cards on which are inscribed statements such as "I am likable," "I am a thoughtful person." Adolescents are told to sort the cards into stacks according to which statements are most and least descriptive of themselves. Another way of using the Q-sort is to have a youngster sort the cards into two stacks—one containing the cards that describe the "ideal" self and the other, the cards that describe the "real" self. The Q-sort is also sometimes used to determine whether certain kinds of therapy have improved youngsters' self-concepts or have brought their ideal and real self-concepts closer together.

The **semantic differential** is another technique for assessing adolescents' perceptions of others and of themselves. The test consists of phrases, such as "my father" or "my ideal self," each next to a 7-point scale between two opposite words, such as "strong-weak" or "pleasant-unpleasant." Respondents assign a numerical rating to each phrase, according to how they feel about the concepts being evaluated.

Applications to Adolescents

Assume that Leon has been sent to you for counseling because he was caught robbing the local Seven-Eleven store. His hostile behavior toward authorities has also earned him a reputation as a troublemaker at school. As a Gestalt psychologist, your first step might be to assess Leon's self-concept with a Q-sort technique. Presumably this test would show you that Leon has certain beliefs about himself and certain ways of interpreting other people's behavior that undermine his sense of self-esteem. On the basis of these results, you might proceed with one of several Gestalt counseling techniques (Higgins, 1987).

In the "empty chair" technique, for example, you would ask Leon to imagine that the person he robbed is seated in the empty chair in front of him. You then ask him to carry on a conversation with this imaginary merchant, playing both his role and that of the merchant, moving back and forth between the two chairs as his roles shift. You might also ask him to imagine his ideal self in one chair and his real self in the other, having each carry on a conversation about why he behaves as he does and having the real self decide what he might do to change into someone closer to his ideal. The purpose of such Gestalt exercises is to help adolescents gain insights into the ways in which they choose to interpret situations, their self-concepts, and other people's behavior.

Criticisms of Phenomenological Theories

Critics have raised numerous objections to phenomenological theories of personality (Mischel, 1981; Weiner, 1980). First, relatively little evidence supports the notion that raising an individual's self-concept score appreciably alters his or her behavior. Moreover, social learning theorists and behaviorists present ample evidence that self-concepts often improve as a consequence of behavioral changes, rather than being prerequisities for behavioral change (Mischel, 1981; Skinner, 1974; Weiner, 1980). For example, if you want to help an overweight teenager with a low self-concept improve her self-image, which approach should you adopt—the social learning theorists' view, according to which you should first change her eating and exercising behavior, thereby assuming that her self-concept will improve as a consequence of her losing weight, or the phenomenologists' view, according to which you should first try to improve her self-concept so that she will become motivated enough to lose weight?

Phenomenological theorists have also been criticized for failing to provide operational definitions and for relying on abstract concepts that cannot be empirically tested. For example, how can it be empirically demonstrated that "José has a hostile, uncooperative personality because his self-concept is poor and his needs for self-esteem and love have not been met"? How are abstractions such as self-actualization and the self to be measured and tested?

Finally, many psychologists disagree with phenomenologists like Rogers and Maslow for maintaining that the self is an entity that can evaluate and alter itself. Furthermore, the belief in an innate drive for self-actualization overlooks the fact that many people behave in destructive, unproductive ways, even when their basic needs have been met. For these reasons, many critics feel that while Rogers's and Maslow's hypotheses may introduce ideals for human behavior, their views fail to offer empirical data about the human personality. Representing this view, an expert on human motivation, Bernard Weiner, asserts that "although worthy of discussion, in my opinion humanistic theory has not greatly advanced our knowledge of human motivation" (1980, p. 408).

BEHAVIORISTIC THEORIES

In recent years two theories—traditional behavioral and social learning—have provided the basis for many successful programs aimed at helping adolescents change problematic aspects of their personalities and for understanding adolescents' behavior. Both of these viewpoints maintain that our personalities, as adolescents and as adults, are primarily fashioned by the rewards and punishments we receive from other people and from our experiences. Unlike Freudian or neo-Freudian theorists, behavioral psychologists strive to identify the types of reward and punishment that shape our behavior and our attitudes. Moreover, behaviorists and social learning theorists reject the notion that adolescence is a distinct stage of development during which we must resolve certain psychosocial or psychosexual conflicts.

Traditional Behavioral Theories

Traditional behavioral theories, whose most renowned proponent is B. F. Skinner, are also referred to as **Skinnerian psychology** or **operant psychology** (1974). According to behavioral psychologists, our personality is actually a collection of attitudes and acts learned as a consequence of punishment and reinforcement. In other words, adolescents' personalities—just like children's and adults'—are primarily determined by the positive or negative consequences that follow their behavior in particular types of situations. Behavior that is followed by rewarding consequences is likely to be repeated, thereby becoming part of our personality. From the behavioral perspective, understanding an adolescent's personality is primarily a matter of observing his or her behavior and its consequences. The behaviorist's goal is to identify the pleasurable consequences that maintain our behaviors and attitudes, as well as to identify the types of punishment that will eliminate undesirable behaviors. This process of eliminating or creating behavior through reinforcement and punishment is called **operant conditioning.**

For example, rather than attributing a boy's fighting to his aggressive personality or to an unresolved Oedipal complex, behaviorists would record data about the circumstances under which this boy fights. Through careful observation, the observer may find that this boy's inappropriate behavior is being maintained by several positive reinforcers: peer approval, the status associated with being "masculine," attention from adults who otherwise ignore him, and freedom from being bullied by other boys.

According to the behavioral model, anything that the adolescent considers pleasurable enough to cause him or her to change or maintain a particular behavior is **reinforcement.** For example, one adolescent may consider the prospect of watching the World Series reinforcing enough to cause him to agree to do homework every night for the privilege of viewing the games. Another adolescent, however, may not consider the ball games reinforcing, and, therefore, his or her behavior will be unaffected by the offer to watch the World Series. The criticism that behaviorists can manipulate other people through reinforcement is undermined by the fact that reinforcers are subjectively determined by our ever-changing preferences, thereby rendering surreptitious control over another person highly unlikely.

Experiences or things that are innately pleasurable to human beings, such as food or sex, are referred to as **primary reinforcers.** In contrast, **secondary reinforcers** are experiences or items that are reinforcing only as a consequence of their being paired with primary reinforcers or as a consequence of our having been taught by our society to value them. For example, dollar bills are secondary reinforcers in our society because their power comes from the fact that they can be exchanged for primary reinforcers like medical aid, food, and clothes. Our currency has no intrinsic value as a primary reinforcer in and of itself, as demonstrated by the fact that a 2-year-old would just as soon tear it up or try to eat it, while a 5-year-old has learned from society to put it in a piggy bank for future purchases.

According to behaviorists, aspects of an adolescent's behavior that do not appear to be the consequence of punishment or reinforcement may be the result of prior **classical conditioning.** In classical conditioning, a neutral stimulus is paired with a pleasant or an unpleasant stimulus. After repeated presentations of the two stimuli together, individuals react to the neutral stimulus just as they do to the one with which it has been paired. This principle can be illustrated by fears that have been conditioned during childhood. For instance, a teenage girl whose mother repeatedly hit her as a young child in the presence of bearded men may develop an excessive fear of all bearded men. Her fear is then a classically conditioned response, which resulted from pairing a neutral stimulus—bearded men—with an aversive stimulus—being hit.

Social Learning Theories

In recent years, the principles of Skinnerian psychology have been expanded upon by social learning theorists (Bandura, 1977; Mischel, 1981). Although agreeing that our personalities are shaped by rewards and punishments, social learning theorists have incorporated many aspects of cognitive theories into their model. Thus, social learning theorists assume, as do cognitive psychologists, that our ways of processing information and our attitudes have a profound effect on the ways in which we respond to rewards and punishments.

For example, within the realm of social learning theory are the **attribution theories** (Phares, 1973; Rotter, Chance, & Phares, 1972). According to this model, each of us attributes our successes and failures (including the negative or positive responses we get from other people) to either external or internal causes. External causes include any source over which we have no personal control, such as "God's will," chance or luck, someone else's disliking us, bad weather. In contrast, internal attributions include anything over which we have control: not studying hard enough, being mean to another person, overeating. Each of us carries a set of beliefs, known as our **locus of control** attitudes, regarding these external or internal causes of what befalls us. For example, **external locus of control** is demonstrated when obese adolescents attribute the cause of their obesity to factors beyond their control, such as a thyroid problem, whereas, in reality, their obesity is caused by too much food and too little exercise. Likewise, an adolescent athlete who wins a race could attribute the victory to an external factor, such as good coaching, luck, or poor competition, when in reality the success was due to his or her own hard work and nutritious diet. In this case, the athlete needed to have a more **internal locus of control** attitude.

Those of us who attribute what happens to us (including our successes) to external factors often come to feel powerless or helpless; hence the term **"learned helplessness"** has been applied to people with extremely external locus of control attitudes (Seligman, 1975). Depending upon our locus of control attitude, we will each respond differently to reward and punishment; that is, those of us with an external locus of control are less apt to recognize the connections between our own behavior and the types of reward or punishment we receive. For example, if you have an extremely external locus of control attitude, you may not read this text or study the night before your exam, since you are convinced that whatever grade you make in this course is contingent on factors beyond your control. Even if you do study and do receive a reward (a good grade on the test), your external locus of control attitude may remain intact since you will attribute your good grade to, for example, luck or easy test questions.

As Table 4.3 illustrates, adolescents' locus of control attitudes can be assessed with a written questionnaire in hopes of identifying which young people feel "helpless" (Nowicki & Strikland, 1973). Having identified those adolescents who feel that the rewards and punishments in their lives are beyond their control, counselors and teachers have devised methods for helping them develop a more internal locus of control attitude (see Box 4.5).

Social learning theorists have also extended Skinnerian psychology to include the importance of **observational learning.** More commonly known to us as **modeling** (being a copycat), observational learning occurs when we observe and emulate other people's behavior. Not surprisingly, adolescents and adults are most likely to model their behavior after people whom they respect and people whom they see receiving rewards. For instance, you would probably be far more successful in changing an athlete's attitudes toward steroids if you asked a rich, prominent athlete to talk about steroid use than if you asked a hell and brimstone preacher to do the same. Likewise, you have a much better chance of convincing adolescents to quit smoking by displaying a sexy, teenage model on an antismoking poster than by showing one with a stern-looking adult warning against the dangers of tobacco.

Applications to Adolescents

The various ways in which social learning theories and traditional behavioristic theories can be applied to adolescents will become more apparent in the remaining chapters of this book, since most of the effective programs for dealing with

Table 4.3

Nowicki's Locus-of-Control Inventory for Adolescents

Answer the following questions and then score yourself to assess your locus-of-control attitude:

1. Do you believe that most problems will solve themselves if you just do not fool with them?
2. Are you often blamed for things that just are not your fault?
3. Do you feel that most of the time it does not pay to try hard because things never turn out right anyway?
4. Do you feel that most of the time parents listen to what their children have to say?
5. When you get punished, does it usually seem that it is for no good reason at all?
6. Most of the time do you find it hard to change a friend's opinions?
7. Do you feel that it is nearly impossible to change your parents' minds about anything?
8. Do you feel that when you do something wrong there is very little you can do to make it right?
9. Do you believe that most students are just born good at sports?
10. Do you feel that one of the best ways to handle most problems is just not to think about them?
11. Do you feel that when a student your age decides to hit you, there is little you can do to stop him or her?
12. Have you felt that when people were mean to you it was usually for no reason at all?
13. Most of the time do you feel that you can change what might happen tomorrow by what you do today?
14. Do you believe that when bad things are going to happen they are just going to happen, no matter what you try to do to stop them?
15. Most of the time do you find it useless to try to get your own way at home?
16. Do you feel that when somebody your age wants to be your enemy there is little you can do to change matters?
17. Do you usually feel that you have little to say about what you get to eat at home?
18. Do you feel that when someone does not like you there is little you can do about it?
19. Do you usually feel that it is almost useless to try in school because most other children are just plain smarter than you?
20. Are you the kind of person who believes that planning ahead makes things turn out better?
21. Most of the time do you feel that you have little to say about what your family decides to do?

Directions for scoring: Give yourself 1 point for answering "no" to questions 4, 13, and 20 and 1 point for answering "yes" to all other questions. A score of 21 reflects the highest possible external locus-of-control attitude, while a score of 1 indicates the highest possible internal locus-of-control attitude.

Source: S. Nowicki & B. Strickland. (1973). A locus-of-control scale for children. *Journal of Consulting and Clinical Psychology, 40,* 148–154. Copyright 1973 by the American Psychological Association. Reprinted by permission of the authors.

problems such as drug abuse and school failure are predicated on these theories. For the moment, let's examine desensitization and contingency contracting, two of the more popular techniques used by behaviorists and social learning theorists in their work with adolescents.

A CLOSER LOOK 4.5

Changing Adolescents' Locus-of-Control Attitudes

"I only passed that test because it was given on my lucky day."; "I lost that track meet because the coach doesn't like me." An external locus-of-control attitude often underlies expressions like these. Feeling powerless to control the good or the bad in their lives, some adolescents believe "there's no use trying because nothing I do makes any difference." This pessimistic attitude, known as external locus of control, often undermines adolescents' academic success as well as their self-confidence. The attitude causes many youngsters to behave "helplessly," when in fact they could have an impact on what is happening to them. In order to increase internal locus-of-control attitudes, researchers have implemented a number of strategies for helping adolescents recognize the relationship between their own conduct and the consequences that follow.

Reading or hearing stories about people who have taken control of their lives by changing their own behavior lessens some adolescents' feelings of external control. Contingency-management programs, where youngsters are systematically rewarded or punished for their behavior, also diminish feelings of helplessness. In contrast, unstructured classes, an open curriculum, and peer competition tend to increase feelings of external control and helplessness. Programs that have helped externally oriented adolescents teach them how to set reasonable goals and how to measure their own behavior and its consequences. For example, when a youngster succeeds, an adult might ask, "What do you think you did differently this past week that caused that improvement on your math test grade and a change in the way your mother is responding to you?" Questions like this can help adolescents learn how to perceive the relationships between their conduct and outcomes.

Of course, all people are sometimes at the mercy of circumstances that are truly beyond their control. There are times when it is surely appropriate for an adolescent to feel that external sources are in control of the outcomes. The ideal attitude is neither to constantly blame other people for the outcomes nor to constantly blame the self. In other words, "Grant me the serenity to accept the things I cannot change, the courage to change the things I can, and the wisdom to know the difference."

Source: L. Nielsen. (1982). *Motivating adolescents: A guide for parents, teachers and counselors.* Englewood Cliffs, NJ: Prentice-Hall.

Desensitization, or **counter conditioning,** is a procedure in which a counselor helps the client overcome fears or anxieties through relaxation exercises. First, the client ranks his or her emotional responses to the fear-producing event. For example, an adolescent who is terrified of math exams might rank her nervousness like this: thinking about the exam, hearing people talk about exams, walking to class, going into the classroom, seeing the teacher with the test booklets, taking the exam. The counselor then teaches the youngster how to use relaxation techniques, such as deep breathing or muscle relaxation exercises. Once the client learns to relax, the counselor begins to describe each fear-producing stimulus on the client's list, beginning with the least threatening. When the client is able to remain calm while hearing a particular description, the counselor moves on to describe the next most fearful situation on the list.

Desensitization techniques are often combined with modeling as a way of increasing their effectiveness. To illustrate, a number of experimenters have demonstrated the success of this method in teaching people to overcome their fear of snakes (Mischel, 1981). In these experiments individuals are shown films and live demonstrations of people becoming progressively more friendly with snakes. Models of people interacting with snakes are also presented. Gradually the fearful subjects are encouraged to touch a snake and, eventually, to hold a snake. Through this combination of modeling and desensitization, most subjects completely overcome their snake phobias. Similar procedures have been employed to help adolescents and adults overcome their fears of taking tests, speaking out in class, speaking to large audiences, flying in planes, and dating.

Behavior modification programs often apply the principles of contingency management in modifying adolescents' inappropriate behavior. By reinforcing desirable conduct and ignoring or punishing undesirable conduct, contingencies are arranged in ways that increase the likelihood that an adolescent's behavior will change. One method typically used in contingency-management programs is a **contingency contract**—an agreement between the adolescent and another person that specifies the rewards and punishments for particular behaviors. For example, a father and son might agree verbally that every grade above a C will be rewarded by a weekly allowance increase of $2. Even more impressive, adolescents have been taught to modify their own behavior, as well as the behavior of other people such as their parents and teachers, by designing their own contingency-management strategies.

Contingency-management programs also try to eliminate unwanted behavior through a method known as extinction. **Extinction** is withholding all forms of reinforcement by completely ignoring the undesirable behavior. If you totally ignored an adolescent who constantly interrupted your telephone conversation and you just kept talking as if the interruption had never occurred, you practiced extinction. In other words, "just ignore it and it will go away."

Criticisms of Behavioral Theories

Despite their success and popularity, behavioristic theories are not without their critics (Mischel, 1981; Weiner, 1980). Reflecting the psychoanalytic position, one criticism is that behavior modification ignores the underlying psychological causes of our inappropriate or destructive conduct. As a consequence, we may temporarily appear to be "cured" of a bad behavior after being retrained through behavioristic methods, only to have our emotional or psychological problems crop up later in some other form of bad behavior. A second criticism is that, in our efforts to modify adolescents' behavior, we may inadvertently get them "hooked" on our external reinforcements and punishments, rather than helping them develop their own internal systems for controlling their own behavior. Third, it is argued that offering reinforcement to people is a form of "bribery" and that, as a matter of ethics, we should not offer such incentives to get people to do what they themselves are not motivated to do.

Behaviorists and social learning theorists counter these criticisms by pointing out that the ultimate goal of any behavior modification program is to wean people from reliance on external rewards by gradually moving them toward more internal forms of reinforcement. For instance, if Henry detests math, you might initially have to offer him a little incentive to do his math homework, like an extra dollar added to his weekly allowance for each math assignment he completes. In terms of the ethics involved in this kind of bribery, it can be argued that your monetary

A CLOSER LOOK 4.6

The Little Engine That Could: Self-Efficacy and Your Personality

"You cannot prevent the birds of worry and care from flying over your head. But you can stop them from building a nest in your hair."

"I think I can, I think I can" puffed the little red engine—and so goes the children's story "The Little Engine That Could," about an engine that huffed and puffed its way to success on the basis of its positive self-image. But psychologists who study human agency, or self-efficacy, are now telling us that it is not just little red engines that succeed or fail on the basis of their internal beliefs (Bandura, 1989). Children who grow up literally visualizing themselves as successful and believing that they control, at least in large part, the outcomes in their lives, are the most likely to become the James Baldwins, Vincent van Goghs, and Alice Walkers of the future. Indeed, the striking characteristic of people who have achieved eminence in their fields is their steadfast sense of personal efficacy and a firm belief in the worth of what they are doing in the face of rejection, criticism, and ridicule from the people around them (White, 1982). Yet even those of us who never achieve eminence are more innovative, more sociable, more relaxed, and healthier acting, like the little red engine, than those of us who tell ourselves, "I think I can't, I think I can't."

As children and as adults, how much effort we exert, how long we are willing to persevere in the face of obstacles, and even which vocations we are willing to pursue are often determined by how much control we think we have over the events that affect our lives. Our beliefs regarding our self-efficacy also influence how threatened we feel and how motivated we are in taxing situations. Indeed, even our immune systems can be weakened by the stress we create by our own pessimistic, external locus of control attitudes (Coe & Levine, 1990). Given the same reinforcement and punishments as those with a positive sense of personal efficacy, those of us who have a limited sense of personal agency will be the most likely to fail, to be depressed, and to dwell on our past failures and disappointments.

payoff is a more ethical option than letting Henry fail math because he will not do his homework. Your ultimate goal, however, is to wean Henry from the money onto his own internal forms of reward, like being able to feel proud of himself for having done his assignments (which, by the way, the behaviorists contend is just another form of reinforcement, since Henry is engaged in self-reinforcement when he says to himself, "I'm a good guy for doing this work"). Doing his homework should also improve Henry's math grades, which, in and of itself, will become a form of reinforcement that can eventually replace the allowance.

CONCLUSION

As Table 4.4 summarizes, there seems little doubt that the development of our personalities involves more than just reinforcement and punishment. On the basis of today's more advanced biomedical and genetic research, it now appears that our genetic makeup and our hormones may play at least some small part in the personalities we ultimately develop. Particularly during our adolescent years, when our bodies are undergoing dramatic hormonal shifts, our moods and behavior

Table 4.4

Theories of Personality

	CAUSES OF BEHAVIOR	DATA BASE	APPROACH TO PERSONALITY CHANGE
BIOLOGICAL THEORIES	Biological factors, such as hormones, genetic makeup, structural differences in the brain (brain lateralization), or chemicals from the environment, such as lead and asbestos	Measurements of physiological factors that might influence behavior: genetic structure, hormone levels, exposure to hormones in utero, amounts of lead in the air or water	Altering, if possible, the chemicals or hormones that are influencing behavior
FREUDIAN/PSYCHOANALYTIC THEORIES	Unconscious psychosexual conflicts and motives; conflicts between the id, ego, and superego	Interpretations by expert clinicians based on projective tests and dreams; therapists' case studies	Gaining insight into psychosexual motives and unconscious conflicts
NEO-FREUDIAN THEORIES	Processes involved in individuation, psychosocial motives and conflicts	Clinicians' interpretations of ego development from written tests, interviews, and therapy	Gaining insight into psychosocial motives
COGNITIVE THEORIES	Stage of cognitive development—concrete or formal	Tests and experiments that assess cognitive stage	Natural maturation, interactions with more cognitively advanced peers
TRAIT THEORIES	Consistent, stable traits, some of which may be genetically influenced	Written tests and questionnaires	Not as concerned with change as with the search for consistent characteristics
PHENOMENOLOGICAL THEORIES	Self-concepts, feelings, and personal interpretations of the phenomena around us; an innate drive toward self-actualization	Self-disclosure or tests that disclose self-concepts	Increased personal awareness and self-acceptance
BEHAVIORAL THEORIES	Past and present reinforcement and punishment	Direct observations of behavior	Alter the rewards and punishments
SOCIAL LEARNING THEORIES	Past and present reinforcement and punishment, observational learning from models, personal beliefs regarding the likelihood of success or failure.	Direct observations of behavior; responses on tests assessing expectations of success and locus of control	Alter the rewards, punishments, and models; provide experiences that modify expectations

may be affected from time to time by factors other than the ways in which those around us are reinforcing, punishing, or extinguishing our behavior. On the other hand, there is ample evidence to refute the trait theorists' assumption that we carry fixed and immutable traits with us from birth throughout our adolescent and adult lives. In this regard, social learning theorists can muster ample research support for their beliefs that our personalities are powerfully shaped by the models, the reinforcement, and the punishments to which we are subjected throughout our lifetimes.

Rather than perceiving these behavioristic theories as being totally at odds with cognitive theories, we can see the two viewpoints as complementary. That is, while our adolescent personalities are certainly influenced by rewards and punishments, our personalities are also being influenced by our new cognitive abilities—abilities that are not altogether dependent on our external world. Since adolescence is the time during which we become able to think more abstractly and to reason less egocentrically, our personalities may indeed appear to "change" in these regards. Although it is debatable whether these cognitive changes actually represent any clearcut stages in our development, it is evident that our personalities are influenced by these cognitive changes. In sum, then, we might best see our personalities as evolving throughout our lifetimes—an evolution that is a consequence of physiological, genetic, cognitive, and environmental factors, as well as of the ways in which the people in our individual worlds punish, reward, and offer models for us.

QUESTIONS FOR DISCUSSION AND REVIEW

Basic Concepts and Terminology

1. In what respects do Freudian and neo-Freudian views of the adolescent's personality differ?
2. How do Freudian, neo-Freudian, cognitive, and behavioristic theories account for the changes in an individual's personality during adolescence?
3. By providing specific examples of adolescent behavior, explain each of the defense mechanisms according to the Freudian view.
4. How is each of the following used in the assessment of adolescents' personalities: the MMPI, TAT, Rorschach test, Q-sort, locus-of-control inventories, and semantic differential?
5. How do Rogerian, behavioristic, and psychoanalytic counseling differ in regard to their goals, methods, and assumptions about changing adolescents' attitudes and conduct?
6. How are Erikson's psychosocial stages, Piaget's cognitive stages, and Freud's psychosexual stages interrelated?
7. Citing specific examples of adolescent behavior as illustrations, explain the phenomenological perspective of personality in regard to locus of control, attribution theory, self-concepts, and gestalts.
8. In what respects do social learning theories differ from more traditional behavioral theories in regard to adolescents' behavior?
9. What are the strengths and limitations of behavioral, psychoanalytic, cognitive, and phenomenological theories?
10. According to cognitive psychologists, how can each of the following influence an adolescent's personality: egocentrism, the imaginary audience, the personal fable, and pseudostupidity?

Questions for Discussion and Debate

1. How do Marcia's identity statuses apply to your own adolescence and to your present life?
2. What evidence do you see of the following in adolescents' behavior: locus-of-control attitudes, cognitive dissonance, the imaginary audience, and the personal fable?
3. Using the principles of behavioristic theories, how would you design a program to change these aspects of an adolescent's personality: fear of going to school, shyness, test-taking anxiety, poor communication with a parent, temper tantrums, and alcoholism?

4. If forced to choose only one of the five theoretical approaches to the study of adolescents' personalities, which would you choose and why?
5. Which of the criticisms levied against each theoretical approach to personality do you consider most significant? What additional criticisms would you add to those presented in this chapter?
6. How have you inadvertently used trait theories in describing and interacting with adolescents and with your own friends? In what ways has this been advantageous and disadvantageous for you?
7. How have the Freudian concepts of individuation and the Oedipal complex affected your development or the development of any adolescent you know?
8. How does your score on the locus-of-control inventory in Box 4.3 coincide with your present behavior and your feelings of personal powerlessness or control?
9. How closely aligned is Maslow's description of a self-actualized person with your own views of the ideal or mature personality? How did you measure up to Maslow's description in Table 4.2?
10. How do you presently employ defense mechanisms in comparison to the ways you employed them during your adolescence?

GLOSSARY

achieved identity An independent identity that we acquire as a consequence of experimenting with different roles and values during adolescence and early childhood.

anal stage According to Freudians, the period, usually between 2 and 3 years old, when the child makes the shift from deriving pleasure from defecating to learning self-control.

attribution theories Theories that assign responsibility for one's own successes or failures either to oneself (internal attributions) or to something outside oneself (external attributions). These beliefs then influence our responses to reinforcement and punishment. Related concepts: learned helplessness, locus of control, self-efficacy.

behaviorism Theories of psychology which contend that most human behavior is primarily determined by the ways in which we are punished and rewarded for various kinds of behavior.

behavior modification Altering a person's attitudes or behavior through the rearrangement of reinforcements and punishment. Related concepts: contingency management, operant conditioning, behaviorism, Skinnerian methods.

classical conditioning A form of learning by association that involves pairing a "conditioned stimulus" (such as a bell ringing) with an "unconditioned stimulus" (such as food), thereby eliciting a "conditioned response" (such as salivation) to the conditioned stimulus. Example: Pavlov's dog experiment.

client-centered therapy *See* Rogerian counseling.

contingency contract A written or verbal agreement in which the parties agree to certain goals stated in terms of specific behaviors and in which the rewards and punishments for achieving or failing to achieve these behaviors are clearly specified. A behavior modification technique.

counter conditioning *See* desensitization.

defense mechanisms According to Freudians, the methods by which the ego protects itself from threatening ideas or from external dangers: denial, projection, rationalization, reaction formation, regression, repression, and sublimation.

denial A defense mechanism in which we refuse to believe that something that threatens or offends us is true.

desensitization A form of behavior therapy that helps a person overcome a fear by presenting the threatening stimuli in small doses and then gradually increasing the doses, while simultaneously teaching the person to relax.

diffused identity An identity that is based on not yet having chosen one's values or goals ("diffused" literally means being spread widely or thinly).

displacement A defense mechanism in which the person attributes his or her feelings to the wrong source.

ego The part of the personality that attempts to balance the id's unconscious drives and the superego's unrealistic rules and regulations.

Electra complex A daughter's unconscious desire to have sex with her father and her consequent jealousy toward her mother.

external locus of control The belief that the successes or failures in our lives are primarily determined by sources beyond our personal control, resulting in a "why bother" attitude. Related concepts: attribution theory, learned helplessness.

extinction The weakening of a particular behavior by withholding reinforcement.

field theory A set of theories developed from Gestalt psychology that views human behavior as a consequence of the interactions between the field of our psychological forces and the field of our environment.

foreclosed identity A person who has adopted an identity based on the viewpoints and values of their parents and other authorities without first examining other roles and values.

free association The process whereby a therapist presents a list of words or phrases and the therapist interprets the client's answers in accord with Freudian theory.

generativity According to Erikson's personality stages, the last stage in life when we want to guide and advise younger people and leave something of value to others before we die.

genital stage In Freudian theory, the final stage, lasting from puberty throughout adulthood, in which we focus our sexual energy on love and work.

Gestalt psychology A type of field theory, formed in reaction against behaviorism, contending that our experiences are like "gestalts" (pictures) that can be interpreted differently depending on the viewer's particular perspectives. See Figure 4.3.

humanistic psychology Largely the creation of Abraham Maslow, the view that psychology should be concerned with higher human motives such as self-actualization.

id The part of the personality that houses those drives that are most in touch with a person's biological nature—above all, sex and aggression.

identity status In Erikson's and Marcia's theories, the four types of identity statuses—foreclosed, achieved, diffused, and moratorium—that people can adopt in the process of creating their adult personalities.

imaginary audience The false belief that a person is continually being noticed and critiqued by other people; hypersensitive self-consciousness.

individuation According to Freudians, the process, typically occurring during adolescence, of forming a more independent identity by examining and modifying the contents of the superego, particularly the values adopted in childhood from our parents.

internal locus of control The belief that the successes and the failures in our lives are primarily determined by sources within our personal control. Synonym: self-efficacy.

latency stage The fourth stage in Freud's theory (roughly ages 6–12) in which the child concentrates on forming satisfying peer relationships and identifying with the same-sex parent.

learned helplessness The view that depression and lack of motivation arise from prolonged exposure to failure and losses over which we have no control, resulting in the belief that whatever good or bad happens to us is beyond our control: "Why bother trying?"

life space In field theories, the field that includes the individual and all significant other people.

locus of control The beliefs we carry with us about who or what controls the successes or failures in our lives. *See* external locus, internal locus. Synonyms: attribution theory, self-efficacy.

Maslow's hierarchy of needs According to Maslow, the set of basic and more sophisticated needs that motivate an individual.

Minnesota Multiphasic Personality Inventory (MMPI) A written test used to identify personality traits.

modeling Learning that occurs by our watching the ways in which other people are reinforced or punished and, on that basis, deciding whether we want to copy their behavior. Synonym: observational learning.

moratorium According to Marcia, the stage in which an individual has not yet adopted any specific identity.

neo-Freudian Theories that modify Freud's original ideas while still maintaining a basically Freudian viewpoint.

observational learning *See* modeling.

Oedipus complex In Freudian theory, the son's unconscious desire to have sex with his mother and his jealousy and hatred toward his father.

operant conditioning *See* behaviorism, behavior modification.

operant psychology *See* behaviorism.

oral stage According to Freudians, the first psychosexual stage (birth to 12 months), in which we must learn to be less dependent on our mothers.

personal fable The erroneous belief, typifying early adolescence, that we are immune from any type of harm.

phallic stage The Freudian stage (ages 4–5) in which our essential conflict is created by our sexual desire for our opposite-sex parent and by our jealousies toward our same-sex parent.

primary reinforcers Objects or activities, such as food and sex, that naturally motivate us because they satisfy our biological needs.

projection Denying one's own feelings or tendencies by ascribing those traits or feelings to other people.

projective techniques Any test or procedures designed to provide insight into an individual's personality by allowing him or her the chance to respond in an unrestricted manner to ambiguous objects or situations.

pseudostupidity The seemingly "stupid" behavior of adolescents that ego psychologists believe is the consequence of their rapidly expanding cognitive abilities in combination with their lack of experience.

psychosexual stages According to Freudians, the stages of childhood and adolescence during which we must resolve certain psychological conflicts of a sexual nature in order to form a healthy adult personality.

psychosocial stages According to Erikson, the stages people undergo in which the personality is shaped primarily by the interaction between the person and the physical and social environment.

Q-sort A technique used in personality assessment based on a series of statements which the subject sorts into categories from "most characteristic of me" to "least characteristic of me."

rationalization A defense mechanism in which a person creates reasons to justify his or her behavior and attitudes but that conceals the person's true motives.

reaction formation A defense mechanism in which a person replaces his or her anxiety-producing feeling with its opposite feeling.

regression A defense mechanism in which a person who feels threatened or frustrated reverts to ways of behaving that were characteristic of a less mature stage of development.

reinforcement Any object or activity that increases the likelihood that a person will repeat a particular behavior.

repression The defense mechanism of forgetting unpleasant incidents.

Rogerian counseling A type of therapy developed by Carl Rogers in which clients can presumably resolve their own problems without the counselor's advice through self-disclosures and feeling accepted without any judgments by the counselor. Synonym: client-centered therapy.

Rorschach test The "ink-blot" projective test for diagnosing unconscious traits or problems. See Figure 4.1.

secondary reinforcers Activities or objects that become rewards only as a consequence of someone's teaching a person that they are important or because that person discovers that he or she can exchange the activities or objects for primary rewards.

self-actualization In Maslow's theory of personality, the final level of psychological development that can be achieved when all the basic and higher level needs are fulfilled and the "actualization" of the person's full potential occurs.

semantic differential A technique in which subjects reveal their feelings by rating specific words along a scale of opposite words such as "strong-weak."

Skinnerian psychology *See* behaviorism.

superego According to Freud, the part of the personality that has internalized society's values, particularly the values of one's parents, and controls behavior by invoking guilt feelings. Synonym: the conscience.

Thematic Apperception Test A psychoanalytic technique in which the therapist asks the client to tell a story based on viewing a series of pictures and then interprets the story from a Freudian viewpoint.

REFERENCES

Adams, G., Abraham, K., & Markstrom, C. (1987). The relations among identity development, self-consciousness and self-focusing during middle and later adolescence. *Developmental Psychology, 23,* 292–297.

Adams, G., & Fitch, S. (1983). Ego stage and identity status development. *Journal of Personality and Social Psychology, 43,* 574–583.

Adelson, J., & Doehrman, M. (1980). The psychodynamic approach to adolescence. In J. Adelson (Ed.), *Handbook of adolescent psychology* (pp. 99–116). New York: Wiley.

Bandura, A. (1977). *Social learning theory.* Englewood Cliffs, NJ: Prentice-Hall.

Bandura, A. (1986). *Social foundations of thought and action: A social cognitive theory.* Englewood Cliffs, NJ: Prentice-Hall.

Bandura, A. (1989). Human agency in social cognitive theory. *American Psychologist, 44,* 1175–1184.

Baumrind, D. (1989). Rearing competent children. In W. Damon (Ed.), *New directions for child development.* San Francisco: Jossey-Bass.

Blos, P. (1979). *The adolescent passage: Developmental issues.* New York: International Universities Press.

Cattell, R. (1965). *The scientific analysis of personality.* Baltimore: Penguin Books.

Coe, C., & Levine, S. (1990). Psychoimmunology. In P. Barchas (Ed.), *Social physiology of social relations.* Oxford, England: Oxford University Press.

DeRosenroll, D. (1987). Early adolescent egocentrism: A review of six articles. *Adolescence, 22,* 791–802.

Douvan, E., & Adelson, J. (1966). *The adolescent experience.* New York: Wiley.

Elkind, D. (1970). *Children and adolescents: Interpretive essays on Jean Piaget.* New York: Oxford University Press.

Elkind, D. (1978). *The child's reality: Three developmental themes.* Hillsdale, NJ: Erlbaum.

Elkind, D., & Bowen, R. (1979). Imaginary audience behavior in children and adolescents. *Developmental Psychology, 15,* 38–44.

Erikson, E. (1968). *Identity: Youth and crisis.* New York: Norton.

Freud, A. (1946). *The ego and the mechanisms of defense.* New York: International Universities Press.

Freud, A. (1977). *Normality and pathology in childhood: Assessment of development.* New York: International Universities Press.

Freud, S. (1927). *The ego and the id.* London: Hogarth.

Freud, S. (1949). *Group psychology and the analysis of the ego.* London: Hogarth.

Grotevant, H., & Cooper, C. (1986). Individuation in family relationships. *Human Development, 29,* 82–100.

Hathaway, S., & McKinley, J. (1943). *MMPI Manual.* New York: Psychological Corporation.

Hauck, W., Martens, M., & Wetzel, M. (1986). Shyness, group dependence and self concept: Attributes of the imaginary audience. *Adolescence, 21,* 529–534.

Hauser, S., Powers, S., Noam, G., & Bowlds, M. (1987). Family interiors of adolescent ego development trajectories. *Family Perspectives, 21,* 263–282.

Havighurst, R. (1972). *Developmental tasks and education.* NY: David McKay.

Higgins, G. (1987). *Gestalt psychology and the theory of emotional growth.* New York: American Institute of Psychiatry.

Hill, J. (1987). Research on adolescents and their families. In E. Irwin (Ed.), *Adolescent social behavior and health* (pp. 13–31). San Francisco: Jossey-Bass.

Hogan, R., & Nicholson, R. (1988). The meaning of personality test scores. *American Psychologist, 43,* 621–626.

Horney, K. (1967). *Feminine psychology.* New York: Norton.

Hudson, L., & Gray, W. (1986). Formal operations, the imaginary audience and the personal fable. *Adolescence, 21,* 751–765.

Josselson, R. (1980). Ego development in adolescence. In J. Adelson (Ed.), *Handbook of adolescent psychology* (pp. 188–211) New York: Wiley.

Kagan, J. (1988). The meanings of personality predicates. *American Psychologist, 43,* 614–620.

Kendrick, D., & Funder, D. (1988). Profiting from controversy: Lessons from the person-situation debate. *American Psychologist, 43,* 23–34.

Kolligian, J., & Sternberg, R. (Eds.) (in press). *Competence considered: Perceptions of competence and incompetence across the lifespan.* New Haven, CT: Yale University Press.

Lapsley, D. (1986). Adolescent egocentrism and formal operations. *Developmental Psychology, 22,* 800–807.

Lewin, K. (1935). *A dynamic theory of personality.* New York: McGraw-Hill.

Loevinger, J. (1976). *Ego development.* San Francisco: Jossey-Bass.

Marcia, J. (1966). Development and validation of ego identity status. *Journal of Personality and Social Psychology, 3,* 551–558.

Marcia, J. (1980). Identity in adolescence. In J. Adelson (Ed.), *Handbook of adolescent psychology* (pp. 159–188) New York: Wiley.

Martin, N., Eaves, L., Heath, A., Jardine, R., Feingold, L., & Eysenck, H. (1986). Transmission of social attitudes. *Proceedings of the National Academy of Sciences, 83,* 4364–4368.

Maslow, A. (1968). *Toward a psychology of being.* New York: Van Nostrand.

Mischel, W. (1981). *Introduction to personality.* New York: Holt, Rinehart and Winston.

Nielsen, L. (1982). *Motivating adolescents: A guide for parents, teachers and counselors.* Englewood Cliffs, NJ: Prentice-Hall.

Nisbet, R., & Ross, L. (1980). *Human inference: Strategies and shortcomings of social judgment.* Englewood Cliffs, NJ: Prentice-Hall.

Nowicki, S., & Strickland, B. (1973). Locus of control scale for children. *Journal of Consulting and Clinical Psychology, 40,* 148–154.

Phares, E. (1973). *Locus of control: A personality determinant of behavior.* Morristown, NJ: General Learning Press.

Pickar, D., & Tori, C. (1986). The learning disabled adolescent: Eriksonian psychosocial development, self concept and delinquent behavior. *Journal of Youth and Adolescence, 15,* 429–440.

Plomin, R. (1986). *Development, genetics and psychology.* Hillsdale, NJ: Erlbaum.

Rogers, C. (1969). *Client centered therapy.* Boston: Houghton Mifflin.

Rotter, J., Chance, J., & Phares, E. (1972). *Applications of a social learning theory of personality.* New York: Holt, Rinehart and Winston.

Seligman, M. (1975). *Helplessness: On depression development.* New York: Freeman.

Skinner, B. F. (1974). *About behaviorism.* New York: Knopf.

Snyder, M. (1986). *The psychology of self-monitoring.* New York: Freeman.

Tellegen, A., Lykken, D., Bouchard, T., Wilcox, K., Segal, N., & Rich, S. (1988). Personality similarity in twins reared apart and together. *Journal of Social and Personality Psychology, 54,* 1031–1039.

Weiner, B. (1980). *Human motivation.* New York: Holt, Rinehart and Winston.

White, J. (1982). *Rejection.* Reading, MA: Addison-Wesley.

Wilson, J., & Hernstein, R. (1985). *Crime and human nature.* New York: Simon and Schuster.

Wylie, R. *The self-concept: Theory and research.* Lincoln: University of Nebraska Press, 1979.

5 Sex Roles and Adolescent Development

CHAPTER OUTLINE

GOALS AND OBJECTIVES

This chapter is designed to enable you to:

- Understand gender roles and the effects of gender stereotyping
- Identify the shortcomings in the research on sex differences
- Explain the major theories of gender differences
- Demonstrate the impact of gender roles on adolescent development
- Understand the controversies surrounding gender roles and differences
- Identify methods for eliminating gender stereotypes
- Enumerate the cognitive, personal, and academic differences between adolescent males and females

CONCEPTS AND TERMINOLOGY

androgyny
bilateralized
brain lateralization
fear of success
gender roles
gender schema theory
hemisphericity
mental rotation
meta-analysis
nonconscious ideology
sociobiology
spatial perception
spatial visualization
Title IX

GENDER ROLES AND ANDROGYNY

Why will more adolescent males than females become mathematicians, doctors, and engineers, while more adolescent females will become teachers, nurses, and secretaries? Are there significant differences between males' and females' cognitive abilities, and if so, what causes them? Do the increased levels of estrogen and testosterone during adolescence affect "masculine" and "feminine" behavior? Do the brains of males and females function differently, resulting in adolescent girls being more intuitive, more verbal, and more musical than adolescent boys?

Such questions are at the heart of the ongoing and heated controversies regarding gender differences and gender role development. Indeed, perhaps no other issue in adolescent psychology has aroused such debate and public attention during the past 20 years. One of the most dramatic changes in psychology in recent decades has been the shift in attitudes toward gender role socialization. In the early 1970s most psychologists, parents, and educators believed children should be socialized to conform to our society's prescribed gender roles, whereas by the 1980s most psychologists disapproved of socializing "boys to be boys" and "girls to be girls" (Cook, 1985; Huston, 1984).

As part of this transition, the concept of androgyny has gained increasing acceptance among psychologists as a standard for male and female mental health (Cook, 1985; Huston, 1984). Derived from the Greek words *andro* (meaning *man*) and *gyne* (meaning *woman*), **androgyny** means a combination of traits traditionally considered either masculine or feminine. During the 1970s the literature on gender roles typically assumed that masculine and feminine traits were opposite and mutually exclusive. In other words, if you possessed a certain so-called feminine trait such as nurturance, you could not simultaneously possess its opposite masculine trait, independence. In contrast, recent research has demonstrated that we can simultaneously embody traits that are characteristic of both the male and the female gender roles. For example, a mathematically precocious teenage girl can be just as ambitious about her future career as an engineer as she is about learning to be nurturant toward others. Likewise, an athletic, 6-ft 2-in. boy can be as assertive, daring, and rational (masculine) as he is affectionate, emotional, and talkative (feminine).

Unfortunately, the term *androgyny* is often confused with other concepts. Androgyny does not mean an absence of any sex role differences, nor does it mean being bisexual or being a hermaphrodite (someone born with both male and female sex organs). Androgyny means possessing certain positive aspects of masculinity and femininity, for example, being both independent and affectionate, assertive and nurturant. This combination of masculine and feminine traits is thus considered more desirable for both males and females than having to choose between the two, for example, having to choose between being either assertive or nurturant or being either independent or affectionate. From this perspective, the more of both masculine and feminine traits you possess, the better off you are.

Gender roles, or sex roles, are terms referring to those characteristics, interests, and activities that a society defines as appropriate for members of one sex. In our society, for example, being the primary breadwinner for a family is generally considered part of the male gender role, while assuming primary responsibility for raising the children is still assigned to the female gender role. As Table 5.1 demonstrates, the expectations and descriptions of male and female behavior are remarkably similar throughout the industrialized world—and are surprisingly unchanged from gender roles in earlier decades (Williams & Best, 1982).

Margaret Mead's classic study of preliterate societies underscores the distinctions between the terms *gender role* and *sex differences* (Mead, 1935). Mead observed that both males and females in the Arapesh tribe behaved in a feminine manner, by our society's gender role definitions of femininity. That is, all Arapesh were socialized to be cooperative, nurturant, and nonaggressive. In contrast, the nearby Mundugunore tribe socialized both sexes to behave in a masculine manner by U.S. standards. The Mundugunore females were as aggressive, ruthless, and nonnurturant toward their children as were the males. Then again, the Tchambuli socialized its males to behave in ways we would consider appropriate only for females, such as applying makeup and coiffing their hair, whereas the females were the aggressive, independent, rational members of their tribe. Although such findings are not particularly surprising to us today, in the 1930s Mead's research was eye-opening in that it refuted the long-standing notion that male behavior

Table 5.1

Adjectives Highly Associated With Males or Females

Which of the following characteristics do you associate with each gender?

ADJECTIVES ASSOCIATED WITH MALES		ADJECTIVES ASSOCIATED WITH FEMALES	
Active	Humorous	Affectionate	Poised
Adventurous	Lazy	Appreciative	Sensitive
Aggressive	Logical	Attractive	Softhearted
Assertive	Masculine	Changeable	Sophisticated
Autocratic	Rational	Dreamy	Submissive
Boastful	Reckless	Emotional	Sympathetic
Coarse	Robust	Excitable	Talkative
Confident	Rude	Feminine	Timid
Courageous	Sentimental	Frivolous	Warm
Cruel	Severe	Fussy	Weak
Daring	Stern	Gentle	Whiny
Dominant	Strong	High-strung	Worrying
Enterprising	Tough	Inventive	
Forceful	Unemotional	Mild	
Handsome	Unexcitable	Nagging	

Source: J. Williams & D. Best. (1982). *Measuring sex stereotypes: A 30-nation study* (p. 28). Beverly Hills, CA: Sage.

and female behavior were determined by our genes or hormones. Cross-cultural research such as Mead's underscored a new and upsetting reality: that the ways males and females behave are heavily influenced by their own society's particular expectations.

As Mead, among others, demonstrated, our gender is a constant, but our sex role is defined by the particular society and the time into which we are born. What is macho in one society may be effeminate in another, and what is masculine in one decade may be feminine in the next. In 1954, a 16-year-old boy who wore a gold necklace and a pastel floral shirt was violating his generation's sex role standards for masculinity; but by the 1980s, he could have donned the same clothes, worn a pierced earring, and still been considered the epitome of masculine style. Moreover, in a society as heterogeneous as that of the United States, sex roles can differ in relation to our ethnic affiliations or geographic location. That is, a boy sporting a pierced earring may still be considered less masculine in Arkansas than in California and more or less masculine depending upon whether he is growing up in a Mormon, Hispanic American, or Chinese American culture.

Few psychologists would disagree that we are socialized to adopt certain attitudes and behaviors that reflect our society's sex role expectations. Psychologists disagree vehemently, however, about the extent to which this socialization accounts for the differences between males and females—differences that often manifest themselves for the first time during adolescence. In our quest to understand sex differences and sex role socialization, we continue to do battle with unresolved questions whose political and personal implications are far-reaching: How much do nature and nurture contribute to male and female behavior? How different are males and females in their cognitive abilities and personalities? Which environmental factors are most influential in determining our masculinity or femininity?

LIMITATIONS OF THE RESEARCH

Given that the questions regarding sex roles and sex differences are emotionally and politically charged, it behooves us to recognize the shortcomings in the existing research before examining the data (Epstein, 1988; Huston, 1984; J. Hyde & Linn, 1986; Lewin, 1984; McHigh, Koeske, & Frieze, 1986; O'Leary, Unger, & Wallston, 1985; Wittig, 1985). With these limitations in mind, you can examine the data more cautiously and appreciate the difficulties involved in conducting research on sex differences and gender roles.

Absence of Data

First and foremost, our understanding of male and female behavior is restricted by the scarcity of studies that have included females. In constructing our hypotheses and generalizing about male and female development and sex differences, we have had to rely on research conducted primarily on white males. As chapter 1 demonstrated, much of our research in adolescent psychology and in the social sciences has excluded females and minorities. As a consequence, scholars such as the renowned adolescent psychologist Joseph Adelson have lamented that "adolescent" psychology is, more accurately, "the psychology of adolescent boys" (1980). This imbalance of information about males and females has resulted in a number of once well-established theories being discredited in terms of their inappropriateness or inaccuracies regarding female development and behavior.

Publication Biases

Of further concern, studies demonstrating sex differences are more likely to be published, publicized, and used as the basis for public policy than are studies demonstrating the similarities between males and females. Publication policies have traditionally resulted in preferences being given to studies that found differences between groups (males and females, delinquents and nondelinquents, rich and poor, and so forth). Although efforts are under way to redress this publication bias, this long-standing policy has resulted in an exaggeration of the differences between the sexes in the literature from which we draw our conclusions about males and females. As equal attention and publicity are accorded to studies that find similarities between the sexes, our understanding of the sexes will inevitably become more accurate and more complete.

Statistical Procedures

Along similar lines, the traditional method for assessing sex differences (and differences among other groups) has been to tally the number of published studies that found differences and compare them to the number of published studies that found no differences. Applying statistical methods, the researcher then asks whether the number of studies that reported a difference between males and females is statistically different from the number of studies reporting no difference. The disadvantages of this statistical method are apparent: the reliance only on published studies (which exaggerates group differences) and the failure to consider the size of the group differences in each individual study before making a statistical comparison.

In order to redress these problems, a new statistical approach known as **meta-analysis** has been developed. As you will see throughout this chapter, this statistical breakthrough has allowed researchers to reexamine some of our former assumptions about gender differences (Glass, McGaw & Smith, 1981; Hedges & Olkin, 1985). Meta-analysis enables us to compare the size of the differences between groups in each study before comparing the separate findings to one another. More impressively, the studies can be grouped into categories on the basis of variables other than the size of the differences. For instance, studies can be categorized into separate groups depending on whether the design was experimental or correlational and whether the subjects' age was included as a variable.

Sampling Errors

As you recall from chapter 1, researchers should never generalize their results to people who are not represented in their study's sample. Nevertheless, inappropriate generalizations do frequently occur in social science research. This error is particularly important in the area of gender research, where a number of investigators have inappropriately generalized their results on the basis of non-representative samples. For instance, generalizations about normal males and females have too often been derived from research conducted with people with genetic or hormonal abnormalities. Moreover, some researchers generalize to humans from their observations of insects and animals, a shortcoming we will explore in the section on biological theories. In addition, interpretations of sex-related research often overlook that large samples are more likely than small samples to reveal statistically significant differences between groups. Given the frequency of these errors in sampling and generalizing, some reviewers of the literature have concluded that "essentially all of the variability in the reported sex differences can be explained as a function of the publication date and the selectivity of the sampling used in the studies" (Becker & Hedges, 1984, p. 583).

Expectations of Subjects and Observers

In addition to trying to find representative samples, researchers are confronted with the problem of finding objective observers to gather their data. A wealth of evidence shows that sex role stereotypes are difficult to disconfirm because we select and remember information from our environment that is consistent with our preformed expectations and beliefs (Halpern, 1985). As a consequence, gathering data about males and females is often influenced by the observer's or the experimenter's own sex role expectations. Given that we usually see what we expect to see and that all of us have preconceived notions about male and female behavior, objective measurements in sex-related research are understandably hard to come by.

For instance, in trying to determine whether male or female infants are more aggressive, psychologists asked college students to watch a videotape of a baby reacting to different stimuli. Half of the student observers were told that the baby was a girl and half were told it was a boy. One of the most important scenes on the videotape was the baby's reaction to a jack-in-the-box. In the first sequence, the baby appears startled, and in the second, the baby becomes agitated and starts to cry. Students who thought the baby was a boy described the baby's crying as "anger," while those who thought it was a girl described the crying as "fear" (Condry & Condry, 1976). Similar results with older children, adolescents, and adults call into question the subjectivity involved in collecting data about male and female behavior.

Likewise, the subjects' own sex role beliefs can influence their behavior while data are being collected, thereby giving us inaccurate information about males' and females' actual abilities and attitudes. Assume, for example, that Elmo thinks doing math is masculine, while doing English is feminine. If you, as the researcher, try to assess Elmo's skills, you might find that he has more potential or ability in math than in English. In reality, however, what you have probably measured is Elmo's motivation, which is being held hostage by his sex role attitudes—a dilemma for researchers who are trying to identify male and female aptitudes.

Situational Context and Sex-Typed Behavior

Also keep in mind that our behavior usually depends on the situation in which we find ourselves. Different situations will evoke different aspects of our personalities, male and female alike. (Remember the critique of trait theories in chapter 4?) Moreover, when we behave in ways that people expect of us on the basis of characteristics such as our race, height, or gender, they attribute our behavior to our "personality," whereas when we behave contrary to their expectations, they generally attribute our conduct to a peculiarity of circumstance or other temporary causal factor (D. Kaufman & Richardson, 1982; Mischel, 1984). In regard to sex-typed behavior, this is particularly relevant since males and females have historically been restricted to very different types of activities. In this vein, a recent analysis of sex differences in 11 different cultures concluded that "we are the company we keep." That is, the kinds of people we interact with elicit masculine or feminine behavior from us. Specifically, whether male or female, individuals who spent time with infants tended to behave nurturantly in all 11 cultures (Whiting & Edwards, 1988).

Suppose, for example, you want to know whether adolescent boys are more sensitive and emotionally expressive than girls. Hiding yourself in the theater, you count the number of teenage boys and girls who cry during the tear-jerking love story. Crying girls outnumber crying boys 10 to 1. Now assume that you repeat your study at a championship football game in which the "Cinderella team" (the hard-working underdog) loses by a mere point. In this situation, you might find that male crying among the players outnumbers female crying among the spectators 10 to 1. Moreover, you might be tempted to label the girls' tears as signs of sensitivity and the boys' tears as signs of frustration. The point is that it is very difficult to establish gender differences given the types of situation in which researchers generally gather their data and the various ways in which the same behavior might be interpreted differently in males than in females.

Experimental Versus Correlational Studies

Assume that you could do what most researchers thus far have failed to do: collect data from representative samples, find observers and subjects whose own expectations will not interfere with your data collection, and gather data about your subjects in a variety of situations. Smug as you may be about having achieved these feats, you are now confronted with yet another problem: establishing causality. Unless you can design an experimental study, you are still stuck with correlational data that do not grant you license to draw inferences about whether a person's sex is the "cause" of his or her behavior. Unfortunately, most of our hypotheses about sex differences are based on correlational data, leaving us in a lurch when it comes to determining the causes of what we observe.

Assume, for instance, you are studying a group of adolescent girls who, due to chromosomal abnormalities, have excessively high levels of testosterone during puberty. Having interviewed parents and teachers, you discover that these girls are reported to be more physically aggressive and more athletic than girls with normal testosterone levels. (Remember that all normal males and females have both testosterone and estrogen in their bodies throughout their lives.) Can you conclude that excessive testosterone causes girls to be more masculine in terms of their athletic and aggressive behavior? Can you conclude that normal girls are generally less aggressive and less athletic than boys because their testosterone levels are lower than those of boys? No, because your research is correlational, not experimental. You have merely demonstrated a correlation between testosterone levels, aggression, and athletic activity. You have not proved that high levels of testosterone "cause" anything.

It is possible, for instance, that girls with excessively high levels of testosterone look somewhat more masculine than other girls, thereby inadvertently influencing the ways in which others interact with them. Likewise, knowing that these girls have abnormally high levels of testosterone, people in their lives may respond to them as if they were more masculine than other girls. As social learning theorists would predict, such expectations could then shape the girls' aggressive and athletic behavior. In order to prove that testosterone causes alterations in such behavior, you would have to conduct an experimental study by administering varying concentrations of androgens to your subjects and controlling for environmental variables, such as their parents' and teachers' behavior—an unethical option, to be sure.

Interpreting and Disseminating Data

Finally, we are confronted with the problem of interpreting and disseminating the data that many historians, researchers, and philosophers have pointed out, unfortunately often reflect the values and concerns of the dominant group in a society (McHigh, Koeske, Frieze, 1986; O'Leary, Unger, & Wallston, 1985; Wittig, 1985). This has meant that social science has traditionally been androcentric (male centered) in its ways of choosing a research question, collecting data, and interpreting and disseminating findings. Perhaps one of the most taxing tasks of a social scientist is to become disengaged from the shared assumptions of his or her culture. Yet, despite our best intentions, very few of us are able to achieve this kind of objectivity in terms of our research, especially in areas related to gender issues, where so much is at stake politically and personally. What social scientist can approach a research study without having had a lifetime of personal experiences molding his or her beliefs about male and female behavior? In this respect, we social scientists do not "discover" a fixed "reality" that is waiting for us out there somewhere; rather, we "invent" reality, at least in part, from our own subjective viewpoints (Hare-Mustin & Marecek, 1988; Scarr, 1985; Watzlawick, 1984). Like you, we researchers have personal, political, and religious beliefs and experiences that actively influence what we see and how we interpret it, what we are willing to accept as fact and what we reject as balderdash.

Moreover, our beliefs and expectations influence which research findings are most widely publicized. In general, we are less critical of, and more willing to accept as "fact," those findings that confirm our personal ideologies and preconceptions. A case in point: In the early 1980s' *Time* magazine chose to disseminate research findings in which the investigators concluded that male superiority in mathematics was linked to testosterone. The article included a cartoon that portrayed a girl and a boy at the blackboard. The puzzled girl is frowning as she looks directly at the reader, with the unsolved multiplication problem 7 × 8 in front of her. The boy is smiling at his teacher, having written the correct answer to his problem, 632 × 7,683 (The gender factor, 1980). Leaving aside the fact that the article did not give equal attention to data supporting other viewpoints or the shortcomings of the research in question, the cartoon and the headline perpetuated the belief that the differences in male and female math skills are sizeable and genetic—neither of which has ever been agreed upon by researchers. In contrast, a *Newsweek* article chose to focus differently on the same topic. The article featured research showing that the gender gap in mathematics is declining and allocated little space to the research that had been the basis for *Time*'s cartoon. Moreover, *Newsweek*'s photographs showed male and female students learning math together, with captions underneath saying "Nurture over nature" and "Equality in class" (Begley, 1988).

The point here is not which article is correct or whether controversial research should be disseminated to the public. The point is that writers' and cartoonists' representations of the data shape public opinion—opinion that, in the case of gender issues, ultimately affects our laws and public policies. For example, although meta-analyses reveal that males are generally more aggressive than females (S. Hyde, 1986), the media has not introduced this research to the public through a cartoon depicting male politicians and military leaders setting off an atomic bomb. If this hypothetical example seems somewhat absurd, it might be helpful to note that George Gilder, an unofficial spokesperson for former President Ronald Reagan's economic policies, wrote that "the hard evidence is overwhelming that men are more aggressive, competitive, risk taking and combative than women," and, therefore, having equal rights in the armed services might endanger our nation's security (Gilder, 1979, p. 44). Similarly, Gilder argued in his book on wealth and poverty that "the biological factor of male aggressiveness and competitiveness fully explains all gaps in earning between males and females in our society" (Gilder, 1979, p. 137). Again, the issue is, not whether Gilder has the right to express his viewpoint, but the manner in which research findings are misinterpreted before the public.

Summary

Before drawing your own conclusions about male and female adolescents on the basis of the research that will be presented in this chapter, keep these shortcomings in mind: (1) the relative scarcity of research on females compared to that on males; (2) the exaggeration of sex differences in the published research; (3) the failure of statistical techniques, with the exception of meta-analysis, to take account of the magnitude of sex differences and other confounding variables before generalizing about sex differences; (4) inappropriate generalizations from nonrepresentative samples, from exclusively male samples, from subjects with physiological abnormalities, or from animal research; (5) bias from experimenters' and subjects' expectations regarding sex-related behavior; (6) the impact that different situations have on eliciting contradictory types of behavior in any one individual; (7) the inconsistency of any personality "trait" that remains constant across situations or across a lifetime; (8) the overreliance upon and misinterpretation of correlational studies; and (9) an androcentric bias in interpreting and disseminating data.

THEORIES OF SEX DIFFERENCES

From the time scientists and philosophers began observing male and female behavior, two assumptions have guided their conclusions: first, that males and females are more different than they are alike in their ways of thinking and behaving, and, second, that we must choose between one of two explanations for these differences—a biological explanation or a psychosocial explanation. Ironically, neither of these two assumptions has withstood the test of modern data analysis. Research now demonstrates that we males and females are far more alike than we are different. Similarly, we need not be forced to choose either a biological or a psychosocial explanation for those differences that do exist (Epstein, 1988; Fausto-Sterling, 1985; Halpern, 1986).

Biological Theories

Nevertheless, both modern and traditional researchers approach the study of males and females from the two positions of biological theories or psychosocial theories. It is the shopworn nature/nurture debate: Is our masculine and feminine behavior primarily determined by our hormones, our chromosomes, our brain structure, and our evolutionary past or primarily by the ways in which we are socialized in our particular environment? It is important to note that neither the biological nor the psychosocial theorists would completely dismiss the others' viewpoint; that is, even as adamant a behaviorist as B. F. Skinner himself would not deny that biology plays some part in influencing our behavior. Nor would sociobiologists deny that environmental factors are partially responsible for our behavior. The question is one of degree; it is not an either-or decision.

Evolutionary theories Within the biological camp, the viewpoints of sociobiologists have fanned the nature/nurture issue to new levels of public controversy in recent years. According to the theory of **sociobiology,** all social behavior among humans is primarily determined by biological factors that have developed from our evolutionary past (Barash, 1979; Wilson, 1975). According to this view, evolutionary principles can explain whatever differences we observe between male and female behavior, just as evolutionary principles can explain animal behavior. Accordingly, there are genetically programmed universal traits that have evolved in order to ensure the survival of our species—"Darwin with a twist."

From this Darwinian viewpoint, today's females, as a consequence of their genetic predisposition for nursing and raising children, are less competitive, less aggressive, less sexually promiscuous, less financially successful, and less skilled in certain cognitive domains than males. From this evolutionary perspective, our male and female predispositions are a consequence of males hunting the game, protecting their families, and mating with numerous females in order to ensure survival of our species. The dominance of men today in politics, the family, and the economy thus supposedly arose out of the divisions of labor necessary for the species to flourish.

Some sociobiologists also extrapolate from observations of animals and insects in their attempt to explain the behavior of human males and females. Likewise, they use human behavior to draw inferences about animals by attributing animal behavior to human motivations and by describing animal behavior with human terms (anthropomorphism). For example, sociobiologists refer to "gang-rape," "promiscuity," "monogamy," and "harem-keeping" in describing animal behavior and in explaining the inevitability of such acts among humans (Lewontin, Rose, & Kamin, 1984).

As you might expect, these hypotheses have come under heavy fire (Bleir, 1984; Fausto-Sterling, 1985; Gould, 1984; Kitcher, 1985; Lewontin, Rose & Kamin, 1984). Critics of the evolutionary hypotheses are quick to point out that archaeological and fossil records show that our early ancestors were more likely to have been gatherers and scavengers than hunters, with males and females sharing the food-gathering task. Morever, the aggressive, domineering male "killer ape," presumed forebear of humans, was predominantly vegetarian. In short, the myth of "man the hunter and woman as nothing in particular" seems to have bitten the archaeological dust (Gould, 1984).

Recent studies have also led many sociobiologists to amend their hypotheses. For example, male owl monkeys and marmosets usually carry the infants, giving them to the mothers only for nursing, while many female primates are far from "monogamous," copulating, even when pregnant, with any number of males. Likewise, among forest-dwelling baboons, the bigger, stronger males are the first up the trees to safety when the troop is startled, leaving females and infants lagging behind (Epstein, 1988; Fausto-Sterling, 1985). In brief, sociobiologists who extrapolate from animal studies provide us with interesting information about the social lives of insects, birds, and mammals but not much of relevance for our own behavior.

Why, then, have I presented you with these aspects of sociobiology? How are they relevant to our study of adolescence? Quite simply because despite the lack of data in their support, many of these assumptions are still very much alive in the minds of some adolescents and of the adults who influence their attitudes. Indeed, published authors are still offering evolutionary hypotheses as explanations for such behaviors as juvenile delinquency, boys' reckless driving, and rape:

> It makes good biological sense that juvenile delinquency is more common among boys than among girls and that males are more prone than females to commit violent crime. . . . Automobile insurance is also revealing, with the highest rates being charged to unmarried male drivers under twenty-five. . . . The rates reflect the predictions of evolutionary biology (Barash, 1979, pp. 170, 192).

Similarly, some sociobiologists contend that rape is a reproductively adaptive trait for males who do not have the economic resources or social status to attract and, therefore, to reproduce with desirable females (Thornhill & Thornhill, 1983). Unless you understand enough about these theories to refute them, you will be of little use in helping adolescents sort facts from fiction.

Brain lateralization Although hypotheses derived from observations of animals and from evolutionary theory have generally been discredited, other aspects of sociobiology continue to receive more serious attention. Among these, comparisons of male and female brains have a long history of capturing the interest of researchers and the public. During the early part of the century, scientists reached a number of fascinating conclusions about the female brain in their attempts to explain why girls and women were in positions of lesser power in our society, among them being that since male brains are larger than female brains, females are the less intelligent sex and that since women cannot consume as much food as men, their brains have fewer nutrients to convert into thought, and, therefore, males will always think more than females (Fausto-Sterling, 1985).

While scientific conclusions such as these now seem ludicrous, the quest for establishing differences between male and female brains is very much alive and well. Indeed, some contemporary scientists are pursuing hypotheses with striking similarities to those of yesteryear: that male and female behavior differs as a consequence of our different patterns of brain lateralization. **Brain lateralization,** or brain **hemisphericity,** refers to the fact that each side of the brain appears to be specialized to perform different functions. The left hemisphere seems to be responsible for our verbal activities, analysis, computation, and sequential tasks, while the right hemisphere controls our artistic, musical, emotional, and nonanalytic abilities.

Since sex differences have most frequently been found between males' and females' visual-spatial skills (see Figure 5.1), and since the brain's hemispheres seem to differ with regard to these two abilities, it seems reasonable to hypothesize that these particular sex differnces may be due to cerebral lateralization. As a consequence, scientists have conducted countless studies trying to establish a link between brain lateralization and our verbal and visual-spatial skills. The theory most favored at the present time was proposed by Jerry Levy in the early 1970s (1972; 1981). According to her theory, female brains are more **bilateralized** than those of males, meaning that females have the capacity for processing verbal information in both hemispheres. In contrast, the male brain is supposedly more lateralized, meaning that its verbal abilities are contained exclusively in the left hemisphere. As a result, females are more skilled than males at tasks requiring verbal processing and less skilled than males at tasks requiring visual-spatial processing.

A number of studies, however, have challenged these hypotheses about gender and brain lateralization (Fausto-Sterling, 1985; J. Hyde, 1985). First, these analyses of the literature conclude that female brains have not been proved to be more bilateral than those of males, although girls do tend to rely more than boys on verbal processing when solving visual-spatial problems. This reliance may, however, result from the types of reinforcement most girls receive: Since little girls talk somewhat earlier than boys, we may, in turn, encourage girls to use a more verbal style in solving problems. More important, however, critics point out that male and female verbal and spatial abilities are not as different as we had once presumed. Moreover, verbal and visual-spatial differences between the sexes appear to be diminishing in recent decades as a consequence of girls' and boys' educational and cultural experiences becoming more similar (Feingold, 1988; Rosenthal & Rubin, 1982). Meta-analyses also show that the kinds of experience we encounter both in and out of school influence our visual-spatial skills (Baenninger & Newcombe, 1990). Complicating matters further, even if we could prove that the male brain is more lateralized, how could we separate the influence of environment from that of brain lateralization? Since males and females grow up in such different environments, it will be difficult ever to establish that brain lateralization is more influential than the environment in determining our cognitive skills.

Then, too, research on brain lateralization may have overstepped its bounds in terms of our limited understanding of the human brain. Roger Sperry, the Nobel Prize-winning neurobiologist whose experiments helped establish our theories on brain lateralization, has lamented that "the left-right dichotomy is an idea with which it is very easy to run wild"(1982, p. 1224). As Sperry himself pointed out, the brain operates as a closely integrated whole, not as two absolutely separate and distinct halves. For example, when a child's brain is damaged on one side, the undamaged hemisphere assumes all the functions of an uninjured brain. (This is not the case when the adult brain is damaged.)

On the other hand, the biological arguments cannot be completely dismissed (Halpern, 1986). For example, in comparison to right-handed males, females and left-handed males rely more on verbal skills than on visual-spatial skills in solving problems. These findings support brain lateralization hypotheses in that left-handed males and females are supposedly right-brain dominant. Since handedness is related to brain lateralization, these correlations suggest that our cognitive skills may be linked to brain lateralization. Moreover, there are 3 to 4 times more male stutterers than female and 10 times more boys than girls with dyslexia (a severe

FIGURE 5.1
Tests of visual-spatial abilities

SPATIAL VISUALIZATION Imagine folding and unfolding a piece of paper. The figure below represents a square piece of paper being folded. After being folded, a hole is punched through all of the thicknesses. Which figure is correct when the paper is unfolded—A, B, C, D, or E?

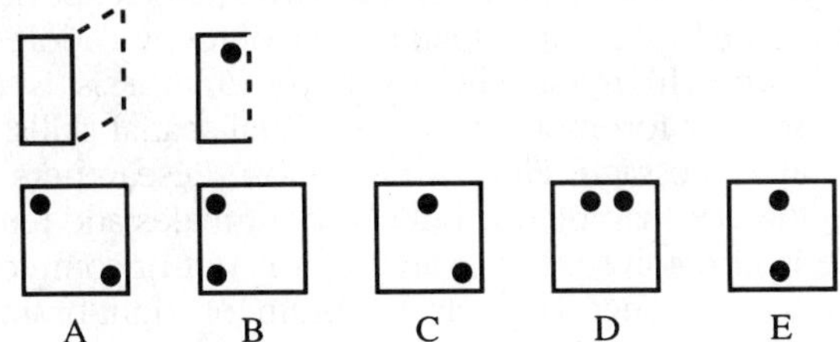

SPATIAL PERCEPTION Piaget's "Water Level Test"—Assume that the two glasses below are half filled with water. Which glass represents the correct water line—A or B?

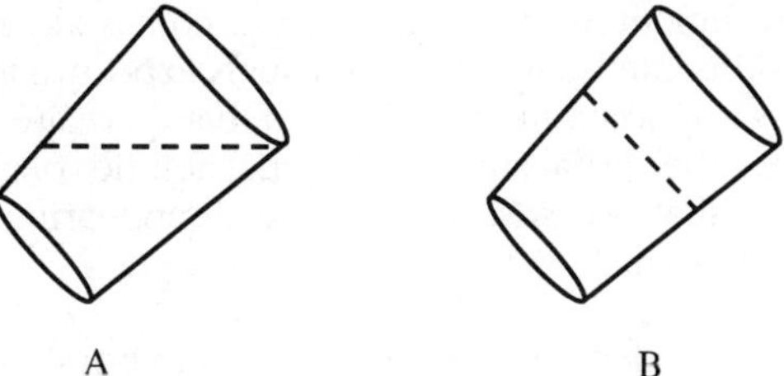

MENTAL ROTATION Can either of these pairs of three-dimensional objects be made congruent by rotation?

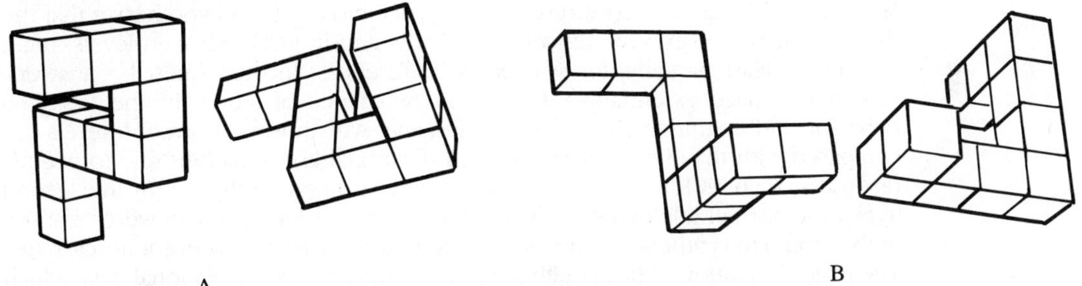

reading disability), suggesting that boys' verbal abilities in these regards are too inferior to those of girls to be adequately explained by environmental factors (Skinner & Shelton, 1985). In sum, there is research suggesting that our cortex is specialized for the processing of language and of spatial-related information and that these innate differences in the left and right hemispheres of males' and females' brains may influence the ways in which we process information.

Sociobiologists have also proposed that adolescents' hormonal changes might affect brain lateralization, thereby influencing the cognitive skills of males and females. For example, both boys and girls who mature early tend to have somewhat better verbal than visual-spatial skills. These correlations have been construed to suggest that the differences in males' and females' verbal or spatial skills may be due to the fact that girls mature earlier than boys, and therefore their brains are more bilateralized. From this viewpoint, although it is not gender per se that determines brain lateralization, girls will generally be more bilateral and less adept at visual-spatial skills because they mature sooner (Waber, 1977). However, the data have been too inconsistent for us to embrace these hypotheses without reservation (Linn & Petersen, 1988). For example, since girls now start to menstruate at a much earlier age than did their mothers, who also experienced earlier menarche than their mothers, the visual-spatial skills of today's adolescent females should be on the decline. In reality, however, the antithesis is true: Today's adolescent girl surpasses her foremothers in her visual-spatial skills.

What is the bottom-line message? First and foremost: Researchers' speculations about brain lateralization are shaping our beliefs about males and females, despite the fact that the issue is unresolved. For example, it is not uncommon for people to believe that, as a consequence of their left-brain or right-brain dominance, females are more intuitive and males are more analytical and rational. Second, if research does some day demonstrate that our brain lateralization has an impact on our verbal or visual-spatial skills, this will not be reason enough to discredit the impact of our environment. In this regard, research has already demonstrated that our visual-spatial skills can be improved through exposure to certain types of experience. Finally, it is important to keep in mind that there are more similarities than differences between the verbal and visual-spatial abilities of males and females and that the differences that do exist seem to be disappearing (Fausto-Sterling, 1985; Feingold, 1988; Halpern, 1985).

Sex hormones Why is it that differences in girls' and boys' mathematical skills do not emerge until adolescence? Why do adolescents tend to engage in more sex-typed behavior than younger children? Such questions stem from the observation that during adolescence, sex differences tend to become more, rather than less, defined. These observations have led sociobiologists to hypothesize that the dramatic increases in boys' testosterone levels and in girls' estrogen levels might account, at least partially, for sex-related differences. In their quest for answers, researchers have essentially relied upon two types of study. In the first, the behavior and cognitive abilities of adolescents with normal hormone levels are compared with those of adolescents with hormonal abnormalities due to genetic disorders, such as Klinefelter's syndrome and Turner's syndrome. In the second approach, normal adolescents are compared with adolescents who were exposed in the womb to synthetic sex hormones their mothers took to prevent miscarriage. The major limitation of both methods is their reliance on correlational data, which negates generalizations about cause and effect. Another limitation is that adolescents with genetic disorders or prenatal exposure to androgens are not a representative sample from which we can generalize to normal adolescents. Nevertheless, we are forced to rely on these correlational studies since it would be unethical to conduct experiments in which we tampered with normal adolescents' hormones. What, then, do these correlational studies tell us?

Some studies have found correlations between prenatal exposure to synthetic androgens (masculinizing hormones) and adolescents' aggressive behavior. Also, prenatal hormones and low levels of female hormones have been correlated with girls' higher visual-spatial skills. Along similar lines, boys with androgen deficiencies have been found to be less proficient in visual-spatial skills than boys with normal androgen levels. Other studies, however, have failed to replicate these correlations.

Is our "masculine" or "feminine" behavior learned or is it biologically determined?

Moreover, even when a correlation is found between prenatal sex hormones and cognitive abilities, it is difficult to distinguish between the impact of life experiences and biological factors. For example, girls with Turner's syndrome (low levels of both female and male hormones) are typically quite short, flat chested, and thick necked, which contradicts our society's image of a feminine body. As a consequence, these girls may perceive themselves as less feminine than other girls, as may the people who interact with them. These environmental influences may then contribute to those girls' avoiding any types of activity that might be construed as masculine—the types of activity that contribute to the development of visual-spatial skills. Given such complicating factors, the influence of prenatal or hormonal abnormalities on adolescents' cognitive abilities or aggressive behavior has not yet been clearly established (Fausto-Sterling, 1985; Halpern, 1986).

In a further effort to understand the relationship between sex hormones and adolescent behavior, three large-scale studies are under way (Eccles, et al., 1988; Susman et al., 1987; Udry, 1988). To date, their results indicate that the variation in adolescents' hormone levels may exert a stronger influence over the adolescents' behavior than do the absolute amounts of circulating hormones. For example, adolescent boys and girls whose testosterone levels fluctuate considerably from day to day are more likely to behave aggressively than those whose testosterone levels remain relatively constant. It also appears that the same hormone may affect males and females differently. For example, high levels of androgen are correlated with hyperactivity and aggression in boys but not in girls.

Among the shortcomings of these hormone studies, however, is their failure to account for those behavioral differences that have been observed in males and females during infancy and early childhood—ages when male and female hormones are virtually identical. Second, since adolescence is the time when most boys and girls are encouraged to don their masculine and feminine roles, society's influence cannot be separated from the impact that hormones may or may not have during our adolescence. Third, research has not shown that girls' cognitive abilities or behavior differs considerably as their hormones fluctuate during each monthly cycle, a finding that undermines the hormone hypotheses (Halpern, 1986).

Similarly, when males imprisoned for violent, aggressive crimes have been castrated on the assumption that testosterone causes violence and aggression, the procedure has not been particularly effective in improving their behavior (Whitehead, 1981). To confound hormone studies even further, evidence now suggests that testosterone levels may, in fact, change as a result, rather than as a cause, of aggressive behavior. That is, behaving aggressively seems to raise our testosterone levels as males or females, rather than the other way around (Fausto-Sterling, 1985). In sum, the research is still too contradictory and too fraught with methodological problems for us to conclude that our behavior or cognitive skills are determined by our sex hormones.

Scientific evidence notwithstanding, the conviction that hormones control male and female behavior survives, as evidenced by the late Hubert Humphrey's medical advisor who warned against women's participation in public affairs because of their "raging hormones" (Berman, 1982). Similarly, some authors still argue that adolescent girls' premenstrual hormonal changes cause them to perform poorly at school, to become slovenly and disobedient, and to develop a "nymphomaniac [uncontrollable sexual desire] urge that may be responsible for young girls running away from home, only to be found wandering in the park or following boys" (Dalton, 1983, p. 78).

The influence of chromosomes In addition to studying adolescents' hormones, researchers have studied adolescents who were raised as one sex, only later to be discovered to be chromosomally the other sex. Consider these real-life situations: Several weeks after birth, a baby boy has convulsions, a situation that leads the attending doctors to discover that the child has two *X* chromosomes, ovaries, oviducts, and a uterus. After further examination, the doctors discover that "he" is actually a girl whose vaginal lips have fused to look like a scrotum and whose clitoris has developed to the size of a penis. After genital surgery, the child is raised as a girl and eventually marries and has children. Another child, raised as a girl, changes as an adolescent. "She" grows a beard, "her" voice deepens, and "her" clitoris enlarges into a penis. Eventually the individual gets married and fathers children (Money & Ehrhardt, 1972).

Chromosomal abnormalities such as these have further fueled the nature/nurture controversy. In the one camp are psychologists such as John Money and his associates, who argue that our behavior depends primarily on the ways in which we are socialized, rather than on whether we are chromosomally male or female (Money & Ehrhardt, 1972). From his longitudinal studies with children whose correct chromosomal sex was discovered months or even years after their birth, Money concluded that the ways in which these children were socialized, not their actual biological sex, determines their behavior. For example, a child raised as a boy until the age of 12 opted to have a double mastectomy when he developed breasts and to continue his life as a male, although he was chromosomally a female.

Representing the opposite view, Julianne Imperato-McGuinley and her coworkers have reached a different conclusion from data similar to Money's (1979). Of the 38 people in her study, 18 were raised as females. At puberty, each of these "girls" developed a deep voice, a penis, and a scrotum, indicating that they were chromosomally male. This surprising phenomenon, by the way, was common enough among the rural villages in Santo Domingo to have been given a name, translated as "penis-at-12." Sixteen of the 18 "girls" chose to adopt the male gender role as adolescents, eventually marrying and fathering children. On the basis of these "girls" changing to boys. Imperato-McGuinley concluded that biological factors influence our behavior more than environmental ones. Two complicating factors, however, call her conclusions into question. First, these Dominican adolescents lived in a society in which males were accorded far more freedom and status than females. As a consequence, the opportunity to become a "male" at the age of 12 could be extremely appealing to these young "female" teenagers. Second, if the parents or others in the community suspected that these children might possibly develop the penis-at-12 syndrome, they may have raised their children in ways that prepared them for a future transition to maleness. In that event, Imperato-McGuinley's observations support Money's conclusion: Socialization, not chromosomes, determines our male and female behavior.

In sum, these studies lead us to the same conclusion we settled for in regard to adolescents' hormones: inconclusive, contradictory, not enough evidence to vote for nature over nurture. Perhaps the conundrum might be resolved if we could find a society in which children raised as boys but later discovered to be girls chose to become female, even when their culture accorded greater advantages to males than to females.

Psychosocial Theories

Although the impact of biological factors has yet to be determined, there is little doubt that adolescents' sex-related attitudes, behavior, and cognitive skills are heavily influenced by environmental factors. The questions then become: How do girls' and boys' different life experiences and our ways of socializing children into their sex roles influence their cognitive and social development? Which experiences are most influential in fashioning male and female attitudes and cognitive skills? What changes might our society make in order to expand the intellectual, vocational, and personal development of male and female youths?

According to social learning theorists, the pressure to conform to our society's prescribed sex roles is so prevalent and so ingrained in our daily lives that we scarcely recognize its presence. The toys you were given as a child, the bedtime stories and fairytales you heard, the clothes you wear, the television programs you watch, the lyrics of the songs you hear, and the language you speak all work toward shaping the course of your life regarding the shoulds and should-nots for your gender and for the "opposite" sex (a term that, in and of itself, conveys the message that we males and females are more different than alike). The term **nonconscious ideology** has been coined to describe this situation of being so inundated by our society's sex role messages that we fail to see the pressure to which we are being subjected (Bem & Bem, 1976). Like fish in a pond, we are "unaware that the water is wet." As Table 5.1 illustrates, our society, like that of other industrialized nations, still has clearcut notions about how we should and should not behave as a consequence of being either male or female (Williams & Best, 1982). We might then wonder how adolescents actually acquire the sex roles we have prescribed for them?

Freudian theories According to Freudian theorists, we begin acquiring our sex roles during early childhood through the process of identifying with our same-sex parent in order to overcome our Oedipal or Electra complex. Briefly stated, Freudians contend that around the age of 4 or 5 we enter our phallic stage. We are then jealous of the attention that our opposite-sex parent is bestowing upon our same-sex parent. Simultaneously, the young boy recognizes that he has a penis and that girls do not—an unsettling discovery that leads him to conclude that the girls' penises were cut off for some terrible reason. He then assumes that he might also be castrated for the sexual feelings he is secretly harboring toward his mother. Likewise, the young girl discovers that she does not have a penis and she somehow concludes that her mother is responsible. As a consequence, the girl temporarily shifts her affections to her father but, fearing reprisal from her mother, eventually shifts her allegiance back to her mother and begins to imitate her behavior.

As you might expect, Freudians have been taken to task on several counts for these views (Alpert, 1986; Bernay & Cantor, 1986). Most notably, children in the phallic age range have not yet acquired an understanding of the physical differences between the sexes, which undermines the Freudian assumptions regarding penis envy or castration anxiety. Freudian theory has also been chastized for its androcentric (male-centered) assumption that boys and girls automatically regard a penis as superior to a vagina. A less androcentric explanation is that both boys and girls want to be boys because they have seen that males are accorded greater power and greater freedom in our society, as well as in other societies. Moreover, data have discredited the Freudian notion that children from single-parent families will develop inappropriate sex role behaviors since they have no same-sex parent in the home to imitate. Indeed, most scholars have rejected the traditional assumption that identifying with, and modeling ourselves after, our same-sex parent is the crucial variable influencing our sex-typed behavior (Huston, 1984).

Cognitive theories In contrast to Freudian views, cognitive theories are based on the assumption that our sex roles are acquired at specific developmental stages during our childhood (Kohlberg, 1966). From this viewpoint, our understanding of what is appropriate and inappropriate for each sex changes as we age. Around the age of 3, we begin to identify ourselves as either male or female. Once having estabished this fact, during the next 2 years we learn how to identify other people's gender correctly. For example, by the age of 5 we have learned that even if a man is decked out in women's clothes, he is still male. The cognitive viewpoint assumes that we become aware of our gender before we develop a desire for the specific rewards associated with being a boy or a girl: "I am a boy so I want to do boy things; therefore the chance to do boy things is rewarding to me." In contrast, social learning theorists argue that our desire for certain rewards motivates us to identify ourselves as either male or female: "I want to be rewarded. People reward me for doing girl things; therefore, I want to be a girl."

A more recent variant of cognitive theory is **gender schema theory** (Bem, 1981; Liben & Signorella, 1987). Information-processing theories show that we are routinely exposed to more incoming information than we can reasonably handle;

therefore, we screen out certain information. In the process, we attempt to understand new information in light of our previously held beliefs, which are organized by our internal cognitive structures, our schemata. A "schema" is a set of ideas or an organizational framework that helps us categorize, process, interpret, and remember new information.

According to Bem's theory, we remember incidents and information that conform to our existing beliefs about males and females, while we usually ignore or discount experiences that contradict our notions about each gender. As children we learn from society what traits are appropriate for each sex, and we evaluate our own adequacy as individuals in terms of the gender schema we have developed. Those of us who continue to conform to society's gender roles have schema that organize all incoming information in terms of our culture's traditional definitions of masculinity and femininity. In contrast, those of us who become more androgynous by stepping outside our culture's gender roles have schemata that organize incoming information on bases other than gender stereotypes. In other words, sex-typed people differ from more androgynous people primarily in terms of whether their schemata are organizing information on the basis of gender.

Social learning theories As you recall from previous chapters, social learning theorists contend that we learn our attitudes and behaviors as a consequence of the ways in which we are rewarded and punished. Additionally, we learn how to behave, how to think, and what to expect from ourselves and from others as a result of modeling what we see and hear in the world around us. These rewards, punishments, and models come into our daily lives in a multitude of subtle, blatant, trite, and ingenious forms: a smile, a frown, a television program, a rock star, magazine ads, the lyrics of a song, physical punishment, a good grade, fairytales, public humiliation, salaries, promotions, special parking spaces, membership in exclusive clubs, exclusion from the group, an affectionate touch, no touch at all, terms of endearment, epithets (abusive, contemptuous words: dyke, wop, nigger, bitch). Thus, having been exposed to different models and having been rewarded and punished differently, boys and girls learn to behave differently, to use their cognitive skills differently, and to expect different things from life—lessons that are well in place by the onset of adolescence. Social learning theorists are thus confronted with the perplexing question: how do we go about socializing our children and adolescents into adopting our society's prescribed sex roles?

SEX ROLE SOCIALIZATION

Parental Influence

Among the many ways through which we are socialized is the family. How your mother and father have interacted with you from the moment of your birth has had a major impact in shaping your beliefs about masculinity and femininity. Their verbal and nonverbal responses helped mold your views regarding the types of cognitive skills, vocations, social behavior, and sexual conduct that are appropriate for you, as well as for other males and females. Although parents' notions about what is appropriate for males and females naturally differ somewhat from family to family, studies have consistently demonstrated that parents treat their male and female children differently (Lamb, 1987). For example, in contrast to their

A CLOSER LOOK 5.1

Nature/Nurture: The Conflicting Evidence

SUPPORT FOR PSYCHOSOCIAL HYPOTHESES

Sex ratios in prestigious occupations—If females excel in verbal abilities, why do males dominate the most prestigious occupations (writers, lawyers, professors) requiring these skills?

Academic choices—Why has the number of females entering the math and science fields been increasing dramatically?

Increasing similarities—Why have males' and females' cognitive skills become increasingly similar if biological factors determine these skills?

Spatial skills training—Why do girls' scores on spatial ability tests improve with training if their brain lateralization, chromosomes, or hormones determine cognitive differences?

SUPPORT FOR BOTH HYPOTHESES

Events at puberty—Since our hormones undergo dramatic changes at puberty and since our society increases its pressure on us to behave "like a woman" and "like a man" during adolescence, how can we determine which has the greater influence on our behavior?

Mathematically precocious youth—Since the largest disparities are found between the ratios of male to female students who are mathematically precocious, how can we account for this with psychosocial theories?

SUPPORT FOR BIOLOGICAL HYPOTHESES

Sex by handedness—How can psychosocial factors account for the correlations between spatial and verbal abilities and right- or left-handedness, suggesting a link between skills and brain lateralization?

Spatial abilities tests—How can environmental factors account for males scoring better only on particular tests of visual-spatial skills?

Source: Adapted from D. Halpern. (1986). Sex differences in cognitive abilities (p. 155). Hillsdale, NJ: Erlbaum.

interactions with male infants, parents generally talk more to female infants, restrict their roaming and physical activity, and pick them up more frequently when they cry. Similarly, girls are given fewer toys or gifts that require mathematical, scientific, and visual-spatial skills (Liss, 1983; Tracy, 1987).

That being the case, it is not particularly surprising to find that adolescent boys are more likely than girls to play, for example, billiards and video games. Although the differences may at first seem trivial, they become relevant when we realize that toys and leisure activities often teach us skills and attitudes that carry over into our academic and vocational aptitudes. For example, video games and billiards require repeated practice in visual-spatial skills that appear to transfer into academic disciplines such as science and math (Greenfield & Lauber, 1985). Similarly, boys' childhood experiences with such toys as erector sets, building blocks, levers, and science kits prepare them for related experiences in school, experiences that, in turn, prepare them for entrance to better colleges and higher paying jobs.

Unfortunately, most parents interact with a daughter in ways that undermine her cognitive and vocational development, while interacting with a son in ways that enhance his development in these domains (Lamb, 1986, 1987; Sandberg, 1987; Young, 1988). Both mothers and fathers are more likely to encourage their sons' independence, vocational aspirations, and educational achievements than their daughters'. Furthermore, when a family suffers economic setbacks, parents are more apt to lower their educational goals for their daughters than for their sons (Elder, Nguyen, & Caspi, 1985; Galambos & Silbereisen, 1987; Mott & Haurin, 1982).

Written and Spoken Language

Written and spoken language also helps shape adolescents' ideas regarding gender roles: "Attending his last class, the medical student heard the professor lecture in his same raspy voice about the ways in which a Nobel Prize-winning scientist should conduct his research." Is the first image in your mind a female student, her female professor, and a female Nobel laureate? Although the issue may initially seem trivial, it has been estimated that the generic pronoun *he* is used more than 1 million times throughout our lifetimes and that most of us think of a male whenever *he* is used (Schulz & O'Barr, 1984). As Box 5.2 demonstrates, our language molds our expectations and self-images, and it needs revision in order to present less stereotypical views of males and females (Maggio, 1989; Schulz & O'Barr, 1984; Thorne, Kramarae, & Henley, 1983).

A CLOSER LOOK 5.2

The Power of Nonsexist and Sexist Language

Pejorative terms: What words are used when referring to the other gender's counterpart for spinster, battle-ax, henpecked, housewife, chick, stud, coed?

The generic "he": Which words can be substituted for those underlined?

- The fireman relies on the average man in the street to man this post.
- The spokesman continued his lecture about our forefathers.
- These manmade products have saved mankind hundreds of man-hours.
- The average adolescent lets his parents clean his room.

Gratuitous or irrelevant modifiers: Reword these sentences to eliminate the unnecessary references to gender or to equalize references to gender.

- The attractive lady attorney and confident young lawyer teamed up. (As written, what sex is the young lawyer?)
- Walt Whitman was a male nurse during the Civil War.
- Joan Adams, a female physician, and Dr. Carter, her colleague, talked.
- Mrs. Orr, our music teacher, and Adam Smith, our math teacher, wept.
- Dr. Smith, wife of a local lawyer and mother of three, joined Dr. Sam Jones, our science professor, at the podium.

Parallel treatment: Reword the following so that each gender is accorded equal status:

- The college students, three girls and a man, were laughing.
- Our high school has a large custodial staff of men and maids.
- That fine-boned, well-dressed woman is dining with the hotel and real-estate millionaire.
- The pioneers moved westward, taking their wives and children.

Sources: C. Miller & K. Swift. (1980). *The handbook of nonsexist writing.* New York: Lippincott & Crowell; R. Maggio. (1989). *The nonsexist word finder.* Boston: Beacon Press.

The Media and Literature

By the age of 4, most children in our country have spent between 2,000 and 3,000 hours watching television (Nielsen, 1988). With few exceptions, television still depicts females and males in stereotypical roles. Men and boys are overwhelmingly portrayed as active, industrious, vocationally ambitious, and financially self-sufficient, while most women and girls are still depicted in roles related to childcare, food preparation, housework, helpmate, marriage, and sexual partner. This is particularly unfortunate given that adolescents' attitudes become less stereotypical when males and females in nontraditional roles are presented to them on television (Johnston & Attema, 1982; Liebert & Sprafkin, 1988; Morgan, 1987; Wroblewski & Huston, 1988).

These messages from TV and other media are further reinforced through childrens' and adolescents' literature. A sample of adolescent romance novels written from 1942 to 1982, for example, shows the "good girl" as being dependent on boys to make her happy (Christian-Smith, 1987). Similarly, a survey of 113 recently published books for children and adolescents found females receiving far more help from others than did males. Boys and men were generally the rescuers and help givers (White, 1986). The practical significance of such findings is underscored by a study with 4th-, 7th-, and 11th-graders who read stories in which males and females were portrayed in nontraditional roles. These students were more likely to believe that females and males could succeed at nonstereotypical activities than were those who had read the versions with traditional sex-typed characters (Scott, 1986).

What about the fairytales and nursery rhymes to which most children in our culture are exposed? These, too, send powerful messages about gender roles (Bettelheim, 1976; Bottigheimer, 1987). Think for a moment about the messages in "Little Miss Muffet," "Jack and the Beanstalk," "Sleeping Beauty," "Snow White," and "Cinderella." (Do not overlook the portrayals of stepmothers and biological fathers—what, no stepfathers?) Now turn your attention to "Henny Penny" ("The sky is falling, the sky is falling!") and "The Little Engine That Could" ("I think I can, I think I can!"). What sex is the little engine? What sex is Henny Penny? How does each respond to "crisis"? In and of themselves, our nursery rhymes and fairytales might be viewed as harmless entertainment; but in conjunction with the media, parents, our language, and our literature, fairytales and nursery rhymes are yet another influential source reinforcing sex role stereotypes and restricting children's expectations. As a consequence, new fairytales are now being offered as a way to expand young children's visions about males and females (Binchy, 1988; Crowley, 1989; Gander, 1985; Kelly, 1988; Molloy, 1989).

Teachers and Schools

We might expect that an adolescent's gender, like his or her race or religion or height, would have no bearing on the ways in which teachers and counselors behave. We might also expect that our schools' policies and curriculums would give all students equal encouragement to develop and to expand their cognitive abilities, vocational interests, and physical talents. Unfortunately, this is generally not the case.

In an attempt to provide equal job and educational opportunities for males and females in our society, Title IX legislation was instituted in the early 1970s (Title

IX, 1976). **Title IX** mandates that "no person in the United States shall, on the basis of sex, be excluded from participation in, be denied the benefits of, or be subject to discrimination under any educational program or activity receiving federal financial assistance" (see Table 5.2). Despite this legislation, however, many schools have failed to adopt sex-fair policies and curriculum (Bornstein, 1985). Study after study underscores the disquieting reality: For the development of mind, body, and self-esteem, schools are generally better for boys than for girls (Carelli, 1989; Dusek & Joseph, 1985; Good & Brophy, 1984; Klein, 1985; Wilkinson & Marrett, 1985).

Interactions with teachers These recent studies show us that from elementary school through college, male students generally receive more attention, more praise, more questions, and more feedback from their teachers than do their female classmates. Most teachers also give male students more remedial help, explaining why the students' answers are incorrect and offering specific suggestions for improvement. Teachers are also more likely to reprimand girls for calling out answers without raising their hands. These patterns appear to hold true whether the teachers are male or female, white or minority, urban or suburban. Despite the stereotypical image of females as the more talkative sex, male students talk more and interrupt others more frequently than females. Parenthetically, this situation holds true for most adult males as well (Eakins & Eakins, 1978).

Likewise, teachers' methods generally appeal more to boys than to girls in that the methods are more compatible with the male gender role. Since males are generally more comfortable than females in competitive situations, teaching techniques relying on competition tend to make females more uneasy. The "I win, you lose" philosophy is the basis for many of our traditional teaching strategies. While boys also might prefer a less competitive environment if given a say in the matter, their sex role socialization generally prepares them to cope with competition more effectively than do girls. Further complicating the situation, girls are expected not only to be at ease about competition, they are expected to be comfortable competing against boys—an expectation at odds with most teenage girls' social concerns: "How are the boys in my class going to feel about dating me if I am beating them in math class or outrunning them on the track?" In short, the competitive atmosphere in most classrooms is often more debilitating to girls than to boys.

Curriculum and role models Similarly, the school curriculum is typically more relevant and engaging for boys. The content of textbooks, the photographs used to illustrate the text, the questions asked on tests, and out-of-class assignments are more likely to reflect male interests and viewpoints. As a consequence, male students tend to be more motivated by the material, finding the curriculum more relevant to their personal goals and experiences. For example, the required reading lists for public, Catholic, and independent high schools in both urban and nonurban schools have changed very little since 1963 in that the authors are predominantly white males. Efforts to expand the required reading to include more works by female and minority authors have been virtually ineffective (Applebee, 1989). This is not to say classics by white male authors should be excluded, but that the curriculum should be expanded and diversified to include materials that reflect the interests and experiences of female and minority students.

Table 5.2

Title IX Regulations

Which of the following are true statements based on the federal regulations legislated by Title IX in 1972?

1. All schools receiving federal money must keep records of plans to rectify sexual inequities.
2. Victims of discrimination may file complaints directly to the Department of Health, Education and Welfare.
3. Recipients of federal money must provide grievance procedures for any student or employee who wants to file a complaint.
4. In publicly supported schools students may not be denied admission to any course on the basis of their sex.
5. Limited enrollment percentages for males or females may not be set for entrance to schools or programs.
6. You may not ask students or employees questions about their marital status, pregnancy, termination of pregnancy, or their sex in order to discriminate against them in any way.
7. Residential schools must have the same dormitory rules for both sexes.
8. Separate toilets, locker rooms, and shower facilities for males and females are illegal.
9. Classes on human sexuality may not be taught separately to males and females.
10. Males and females must be admitted to the same teams for contact sports (football, hockey, basketball, rugby, wrestling).
11. Single-sex physical education classes must end.
12. If a course is disproportionately of one sex, the school is obliged to determine whether this is the consequence of biased counseling or testing.
13. Schools that provide full-coverage health services must offer gynecological care.
14. If a student leaves school because of pregnancy, she must be reinstated to her former status when she returns.
15. Both sexes must be allowed on the same teams for noncontact sports.
16. Athletic expenditures must be equal for males and females.
17. Title IX prohibits discrimination in employment, recruitment, and promotion, as well as in education.

Statements 8, 9, 10, and 16 are false.

Source: Title IX of the Education Amendments of 1972. (1976). Washington, D.C.: Resource Center on Sex Roles in Education.

Coeducational versus single-sex schools Given these shortcomings in coeducational schools, researchers have investigated the possibility that single-sex schools may have certain advantages for adolescent girls and college women. In exploring this question, two limitations arise: First, most of our data has been gathered from college samples or from high schools outside the United States. As a consequence, our generalizations about U.S. high-school students are based on relatively few studies. Second, since single-sex schools are almost always private schools, and since private schools are usually more selective than public schools, it is difficult to make accurate comparisons between the academic performance of females in the two settings.

Nevertheless, some evidence suggests that adolescent girls may reap certain benefits from single-sex education. In these comparisons, girls in single-sex schools had higher achievement scores than their counterparts in coeducational schools (Rierden, 1985). Girls in single-sex schools have also been found to have higher educational aspirations, greater achievement gains, and less stereotypical attitudes about gender roles (Lee & Bryk, 1986).

In contrast, however, one of the most methodologically sophisticated studies to date has reached different conclusions (Marsh, 1989b). In this longitudinal study, a boys' school and a girls' school serving the same suburb merged into two coed high schools. No changes occurred in either boys' or girls' achievement levels across the 5 years of the study. Moreover, the students overwhelmingly preferred the coed schools, and both males' and females' self-concept scores improved. In sum, it appears that, once preexisting conditions such as prior academic achievement, motivation, and socioeconomic status are taken into account, few differences have been found between female achievement in single-sex or coeducational schools (Marsh, 1989b).

Extracurricular activities The extracurricular activities in most secondary schools also reinforce traditional sex role stereotypes. For example, male athletes are center stage as they compete with a cheering crowd supporting their achievements. In contrast, cheerleaders, who are almost always female, remain on the sidelines as observers whose primary roles are to look pretty and to offer emotional support for the players and the crowd (Elder & Parker, 1987). While there is nothing wrong with encouraging adolescents to be supportive of their classmates' accomplishments, the problem is that there are so few situations in which male students are encouraged to cheer for their female classmates.

Computer technology The school's reinforcement of stereotypical gender roles is further reflected in students' use of computers. Given our society's increasing dependence on the machines, many adolescents' future vocational options are closely linked with their mastery of computer technology. Also, as more and more schools begin using computers as teaching aids, students' access to and comfort with these machines can be a critical factor in their intellectual development. Especially in areas, such as mathematics, where frequent, repetitive practice is essential, students who are ill at ease with computers will be academically disadvantaged.

Unfortunately, female students are not faring as well as males in this domain. Although the use of microcomputers varies widely across the country, boys generally have more exposure than girls to computers both at home and at school. Moreover, when girls do have access to computers, it is usually in stereotypically female roles. Just as girls have historically dominated our schools' typing classes, they now fill almost every desk in word-processing classes. In contrast, boys account for most of the enrollment in the computer programming classes that prepare them for a greater array of future careers (Chen, 1986; Hess & Miura, 1985). It also appears that the type of software offered to students affects their interests in computers and in the subject matter; that is, when girls are given software that appeals more to female interests, they have expressed more enthusiasm for the material, as well as in the computers themselves (Hawkins, 1985). Given the current state of affairs, however, it is hardly surprising to find that in the adult work force 92% of entry-level computer operators are women, whereas 96% of electrical engineers and 72% of computer specialists are men (Chen, 1986).

The college environment What about the college environment? Are male and female students not treated in the same manner at this advanced level of education? We have, of course, witnessed a growth in the percentage of young women attending postsecondary schools, now accounting for about half of this enrollment. However, female students are more likely than males to be enrolled in publicly funded or junior colleges than in the more prestigious private or 4-year colleges—a reality that might be accounted for partially by the fact that females receive less financial aid than do males. Perhaps more important, although women earn half the bachelor's and master's degrees awarded each year, those degrees remain predominantly in the fields with lower status and lower pay that have historically been dominated by females. Many young women report that college has discouraged them from pursuing nontraditional occupations, has lowered their self-esteem, and has undermined their career aspirations (Bogart, 1984).

Given these studies and the statistics on government cutbacks for educational equity, some educators are expressing the view that "equity is not merely out of fashion in the U.S. Department of Education, it has been declared an enemy" (Shakeshaft, 1988).

SEX DIFFERENCES: HOW MUCH AND HOW MANY?

In the early 1970s the first major review of the literature on sex differences was presented by Eleanor Maccoby and Carol Jacklin (1974). Although many of their conclusions about sex-related differences have now been discounted, their findings are worth noting because they continue to shape many of our opinions about males and females and because their conclusions generated further exploration of gender issues. In their review of nearly 2,000 studies with children and adolescents, Maccoby and Jacklin found only four sex differences: Girls had greater verbal skills, boys had greater mathematical and visual-spatial skills, and boys were more aggressive. No differences were found in regard to self-esteem, sociability, suggestibility, analytical thinking, achievement motivation, or auditory versus visual preferences. More sophisticated statistics and more recent data have now enabled us to examine these supposed sex differences more accurately. Although a complete review of sex differences is beyond the scope of this chapter, we can examine several of greatest relevance to our study of adolescents: visual-spatial abilities, math and science achievement, aggression, achievement attitudes, and self-esteem.

Visual-Spatial Abilities

The term *visual-spatial abilities* probably has little meaning to most of us, with the exception of cognitive psychologists. Indeed, even among psychologists its definition is ambiguous in that many different tests are used to assess this skill. In general, visual-spatial ability refers to three types of skill: spatial perception, mental rotation, and spatial visualization. **Spatial perception** tasks require subjects to locate the horizontal or the vertical while ignoring the distracting cues. **Mental**

Would you rather be male or female? Why?

rotation involves the ability to imagine what a two- or three-dimensional figure would look like from different angles or in its mirror image if it were rotated in space. **Spatial visualization** requires the subject to analyze the relationship between different spatial representations of an object (see Figure 5.1 on page 165).

The practical relevance of such research is that visual-spatial skills are used extensively in jobs such as engineering, architecture, chemistry, and the building trades, as well as in mathematics and science problems. Since females are greatly underrepresented in math and science fields and since girls' math and science skills fall behind those of boys during adolescence, sociobiologists contend that girls have fewer visual-spatial skills than boys as a consequence of differences in their brain lateralization and hormones. In contrast, social learning theorists argue that we socialize girls in such a way that their visual-spatial skills are less well developed than those of boys.

One of the major obstacles in comparing the visual-spatial abilities of males and females is that experimenters have used too many different tests to measure this construct. As a consequence, male and female performance often depends on the type of test used, leading some researchers to conclude that the entire notion of spatial abilities is questionable, given the lack of any clearcut definition (Caplan, MacPherson & Tobin, 1985). Some tests of visual-spatial ability reveal no sex differences, while on others males generally outperform females. For example, males typically outperform females on Piaget's Water Level Test (see Figure 5.1). The subject is shown an upright bottle partially filled with water and is then asked to predict where the water level will be when the bottle is tipped. According to Piaget, until about the age of 12, children erroneously believe that the water level will also "tilt" as the bottle is tilted. It seems, however, that while most boys learn this principle when Piaget predicted, girls acquire the concept at a much later age. In fact, it has been estimated that half of all college women still have not grasped the water-level principle (for review see Harris, 1978). Such findings have been used to argue that either hormones or brain lateralization is primarily responsible for the differences between males and females in certain visual-spatial tasks.

In contrast, ample evidence shows that nurture, not nature, is primarily responsible for gender differences in visual-spatial skills; that is, boys develop better visual-spatial skills than girls as a consequence of childhood experiences. These male experiences include playing with "boys' " toys, such as building blocks and erector sets, as well as participating in leisure activities, such as playing video games, billiards, and ball, from which girls are typically excluded. Indeed, when girls are allowed to engage in activities involving visual-spatial skills, their test performance improves (Baenninger & Newcombe, 1990).

Moreover, several meta-analyses have failed to find a relationship between sex differences in visual-spatial ability and sex differences in math or science achievement. Further undermining hormonal hypotheses, male and female spatial abilities do not change magnitude during adolescence, when hormones change most dramatically. Nevertheless, meta-analyses have found that males generally do outperform females in spatial perception and mental rotation, although not in spatial visualization. Furthermore, these sex differences appear among students as young as 7 years old and persist across the life span. In sum, it is not altogether clear why males outperform females in certain visual-spatial tasks. What is clear, however, is that our childhood and adolescent experiences do affect our visual-spatial proficiencies (Linn & Petersen, 1988).

Mathematical Achievement

In the early 1980s a series of articles by Carol Benbow and John Stanley created a stir in both the popular press and the research community (1983). Describing math scores for a large population of mathematically precocious youth, they reported that boys outscored girls in every study. What made their findings especially controversial and newsworthy, however, was that the authors suggested that biological sex differences were responsible for the diversity in the students' mathematical skills. Since their findings seemingly supported the popular myth that boys have "more mathematical minds" than do girls, those findings were especially suited to capture the media's and the public's attention. Nevertheless, critics have been quick to point out a number of shortcomings. Among them, the results were reported as ratios of girls to boys, using only the highest scores, a statistical procedure that exaggerates actual group differences. The studies also excluded all students except those who had been classfied as mathematically precocious. Perhaps most significantly, the researchers failed to take account of the students' different math-related experiences (Eccles & Jacobs, 1986; Lips, 1988).

At the time that Benbow and Stanley's studies were capturing the public's attention, Joyce Eccles and her colleagues were gathering data for a large-scale study of math achievement in 7th-, 8th-, and 9th-grade students (Eccles & Jacobs, 1986). Given the media's national coverage of Benbow and Stanley's findings, the Eccles studies were able to assess the impact of the media's presentations on parents' and adolescents' attitudes. Eccles and her colleagues found that adolescents' math anxiety, their parents' beliefs about female mathematical abilities, and the value a student places on mathematics account for most of the sex differences in mathematical performance. Moreover, the students' attitudes were most strongly related to their mothers' beliefs concerning the difficulty of mathematics, a finding that has also been reported for younger children (Entwisle & Baker, 1983).

In further contrast to the impressions created by Benbow and Stanley's research, the Eccles studies found that starting at a very young age, females outperform males on mathematical computations—an advantage that disappears during adolescence. Similarly, males begin outperforming females in certain aspects of mathematical problem solving after the age of 14. In short, it is not until adolescent girls begin to enroll in fewer math classes than do boys that the girls start falling behind mathematically. An equally discouraging finding is that girls also participate in fewer out-of-school activities that build mathematical skills, such as computer camps and math clubs (Fox, Brody, & Tobin, 1984).

Adolescent girls who enroll in science and math courses and who later pursue nontraditional careers often tell us that the most significant factor influencing their academic decisions was encouragement from the significant people in their lives (Eccles, 1983; Houser & Garvey, 1985). Unfortunately, teachers, counselors, and parents too often discourage girls from developing their mathematical talents. For example, many studies show that even when girls do enroll in the same math classes as boys, they generally receive less encouragement and less help from their teachers. Many teachers have also expressed the belief that females have less mathematical "potential" than males and have, as a consequence, discouraged their female students from pursuing further math courses or math-related careers. Given this state of affairs, it is perhaps not too surprising that girls with the same mathematical abilities as boys tend to underestimate their abilities, while males tend to overestimate theirs.

Does this mean that Benbow and Stanley's findings are without merit? Are girls' and boys' math achievement scores equivalent? In a word, no. Most adolescent boys still outperform most adolescent girls in mathematics. Comparisons of adolescents' scores on aptitude tests between 1947 and 1980 and on the Preliminary Scholastic Aptitude Tests (PSAT) between 1960 and 1983 show that girls score higher than boys on grammar, spelling, and perceptual speed; boys score higher on spatial visualization, high-school mathematics, and mechanical aptitude; and boys and girls score equivalently on verbal reasoning, arithmetic, and figural reasoning. By 1980, boys had completely closed the gender gap on the PSAT-Verbal scores and cut in half the difference in clerical speed and accuracy. Similarly, girls closed the gap on verbal reasoning, abstract reasoning, and numerical ability and cut in half the gender difference on mechanical reasoning, space relations, and PSAT-Math. Although these results are encouraging, boys still outperform girls at the highest levels of mathematics, a difference that has remained constant since 1960 (Feingold, 1988).

In sum, although the gender gap is narrowing, female adolescents are still behind their male classmates in mathematical performance. Taken together, the research makes clear that our best hope for helping adolescent girls develop their mathematical talents is to begin encouraging their math interests and skills at a very early age. While the debate continues over the possible links between biological factors and math performance, it is already within our power to change our schools and our own behavior in ways that will help girls become more confident and more proficient in their mathematical skills.

Science Achievement

As the story in Box 5.3 illustrates, female adolescents certainly have the ability to become capable scientists. Unfortunately, adolescent girls generally score lower than boys on science achievement tests. These tests typically include two kinds of items. One assesses scientific information with such questions as; What is evaporation?, and the other assesses "scientific reasoning" by asking students to design experiments and to draw conclusions about specific scientific principles. Overall, adolescent males score about 5 percentage points higher than females on the science information questions. Girls, however, are more knowledgable about biology and health questions than about physical and earth sciences, a strong indication of the impact of socialization. Interestingly, there are no significant gender differences on scientific reasoning, although girls tend to have more difficulty with problems involving proportional reasoning, a mathematical aspect of scientific problem solving (Linn & Petersen, 1986; Meehan, 1984; Steinkamp & Maehr, 1983).

It is worth noting, however, that girls perform better on proportional reasoning problems when the tasks involve familiar experiences. That is, rather than giving girls the "balance beam" problems that typify tests of proportional reasoning, researchers give them proportional reasoning tasks involving shopping for groceries and clothes. In these experiments, girls' proportional reasoning skills improve (Meehan, 1984). Similarly, in national testing girls score higher than boys on questions related to scientific responsibility and public safety, that is, to matters of altruism (Hueftle, Rakow, & Welch, 1983). Such findings suggest that science teachers and science books should expand their classroom examples, assignments, and exam questions to include values and experiences that appeal to girls as well

A CLOSER LOOK 5.3

The "Mad" Scientist Is a Girl?

Who could save America $4 billion a year in fertilizer costs without exhausting any of the country's supply of petroleum or natural gas? Eighteen-year-old Elisabeth Bryenton! While working in her homemade laboratory 2 hours a night and most weekends during her high-school years, she invented a natural fertilizing agent that could some day save all the energy, natural gas, and petroleum now used for synthetic fertilizer production—an estimated savings of $18 billion worldwide and $4 billion in the United States alone. In addition to the interest expressed by several foreign governments in her scientific discovery, Ms. Bryenton was awarded prizes from the U.S. Department of Agriculture, the U.S. Air Force, General Motors, and the 1979 International Science and Engineering Fair.

Source: M. Fisher. (1980, July). Teenage scientist. *Ms.*, p. 23.

as to boys. Perhaps these findings also give us a clue about why fewer girls than boys enroll in high-school science classes.

In addition to the science curriculum's being geared more toward boys' values and interests, males also have more science-related experiences outside the classroom, such as visits to science museums and enrollment in summer science or scouting programs. Given these differences, it is not especially unexpected that boys express more self-confidence than girls when tackling science problems, even when both sexes have equal ability, or that most boys perceive their science classes more positively than do girls (Linn & Petersen, 1986). Simply put, adolescent girls need more encouragement from us to engage in activities related to science, both in and out of school.

Aggression

One of the few gender differences that have held up under recent meta-analyses is aggression. In general, males are more aggressive than females for all types of aggression and across all age groups. Males also behave more aggressively than females after being exposed to an aggressive model. Before jumping to the conclusion that adolescent boys are more aggressive than adolescent girls, however, we need to take heed of several other findings. First, there are significant variations in males and females depending on the kind of aggression being measured, the method of measurement, and the design of the study. In experimental studies where aggression is being stimulated in some way, there are fewer gender differences than in naturalistic studies where we are generally observing spontaneous aggression. This might be interpreted to mean that females are relatively low in spontaneous aggression but are increasingly aggressive when provoked. Then, too, males may control their aggression more in the experimental situations where an observer is present. Second, age and education appear to play some part in our aggressive behavior. For example, college males and college females are more similar in regard to their aggression than are preschoolers (Eagly, 1987; Hyde, 1986).

Perhaps more important, the research repeatedly demonstrates that male and female aggression varies with the situations in which the subjects find themselves, as well as with their beliefs about the likelihood of being punished for aggressiveness. For example, in her role as brigade commander of West Point's Corps of Cadets, 21-year-old Kristin Baker is probably more aggressive than many women her age living outside the military (see Box 5.4).

Finally, it bears repeating that although most males do behave more aggressively than most females, these differences are not causally related to their higher testosterone levels, to prenatal hormones, or to an extra *Y* chromosome (Fausto-Sterling, 1986). On the basis of our current research, our best bet for narrowing this particular gender gap is to encourage girls to throw themselves into the world of competitive contact sports; to teach them to resolve their disputes through physical aggression rather than through "sissy" behavior, such as walking away from a fight; and to offer them more role models of verbally and physically aggressive women. On the other hand, we could elect another option: to reinforce boys' and men's nonaggressiveness through noncompetitive and noncontact sports, verbal rather than physical resolutions to their disputes, and role models who say, "I'm sorry, it's my fault" or who walk away from a fight as the way to prove their manhood.

A CLOSER LOOK 5.4

Top Gun: West Point's First Female Brigade Commander

When Kristin Baker told her high-school friends that she had been admitted to the United States Military Academy at West Point, New York, one classmate remarked, "Isn't that a boys' school?" Although West Point began admitting female students in 1976, its enrollment is still 90% male. Nevertheless, Kristin has become the first woman ever to serve the Academy as brigade commander and first captain of the Corps of Cadets, a position previously held by Douglas MacArthur and William Westmoreland. As West Point's highest ranking cadet, Baker will be responsible for almost all aspects of life to 4,400 cadets. A philosophy major, Baker was awarded the post as a consequence of her athletic prowess, her ability to inspire others, and her strong academic record. Commenting on her position, Baker remarked, "Some people try to lead by fear. My style is to explain first and then correct. That's how people learn." As she walks across campus, cadets stand at attention and salute, "Good afternoon, ma'am." "No slack," she barks back.

Source: "No slack": A woman's touch at West Point. (1989, August 21). *Newsweek,* p. 20.

Achievement Attitudes

In trying to explain why most adolescent girls achieve less academically and vocationally than boys, researchers have offered two other hypotheses. The first is that girls, unlike boys, have a **"fear of success"** that causes them to avoid situations in which they might become successful and to downplay their intellectual talents. The concept of fear of success was derived from Matina Horner's studies, in which high-school and college students were presented with hypothetical stories about women who were succeeding in masculine endeavors. When asked to elaborate on these stories, most female students imagined negative consequences for the successful female. Specifically, the females assumed that the successful women in the stories would be socially rejected by males or would lose their femininity (Horner, 1972). The concept was enthusiastically embraced as an attitude that distinguished females from males and that helped account for females' lesser achievements.

Further studies, however, cast doubts upon the interpretations of Horner's findings. To begin with, females' fear of success scores fell when the hypothetical stories put the successful females in situations that involved other females. Moreover, when male students were given stories in which males succeeded in feminine activities, they also expressed fear of success. That is, if Joe was described as the top student in his nursing class, males expressed fear of success attitudes just as their female classmates did when Jane was described as the top student in her medical class. In addition, the relationship between fear of success scores and a girl's academic or vocational success has not been established. In short, fear of success is not an attitude that sets females apart from males. To the contrary, it appears that both sexes have anxieties about participating or succeeding in endeavors that have traditionally been reserved for the other gender (Fogel & Paludi, 1984; Mednick, 1990).

Unfortunately, some researchers and therapists continue to use fear of success as an explanation for female's achievement anxieties (Moulton, 1986). The concept seems to survive on intuitive appeal, even though most researchers have discarded the concept on the basis of the actual data. Our best tack, then, is to recognize that most adolescents, whether male or female, are anxious or fearful of entering nontraditional spheres in the classroom, on the playing fields, in the work force, or on the dance floor, as Box 5.5 illustrates. Our task is to recognize that both sexes need our encouragement to engage in activities that have been declared off limits to anyone but the "sissies" and the "tomboys."

In contrast to fear of success attitudes, adolescent boys and girls generally do have different attitudes about the role that external or internal factors play in their successes and failures. As explained in chapter 4, adolescents with internal locus of control attitudes feel personally responsible for and in control of most of the events in their lives ("I failed the math test because I didn't study hard enough"). In contrast, those with external locus of control attitudes generally feel powerless over their successes or failures, attributing both to external factors over which they have no control ("I failed the test because the teacher doesn't like me. Besides, I just don't have a mathematical mind").

In general, adolescent girls are more likely than boys to attribute their failures to shortcomings within themselves over which they feel they have no control. Adolescent boys, on the other hand, are more likely to attribute their successes to their own abilities and their failures to "bad luck" or to lack of effort. Moreover, it appears that girls do feel less confident about their abilities than do boys, especially after failing at a task (Dweck, 1984; Simmons & Blyth, 1987; Whitley, McHugh, & Frieze, 1986).

Self-Esteem and Self-Expectancies

Given these differences in locus of control attitudes, it stands to reason that adolescent girls tend to have less self-esteem than boys of the same age group. From the research on sex differences and self-esteem, four findings stand out: First, adolescent girls base more of their self-esteem on their appearance, their social standing, and the approval of other people and less on their academic or athletic accomplishments than do boys. Second, even among the most academically talented students, teenage girls often devalue their own skills and underestimate their abilities, unlike their male classmates with comparable skills. Third, both sexes generally value male skills and male accomplishments more than female skills and female accomplishments. That is, boys and girls who have masculine skills generally have higher self-esteem and are more popular than those who are successful at feminine skills. Fourth, girls are more dissatisfied with their appearance and have less self-esteem regarding their physical and mental skills than boys (Cate & Sugawara, 1986; Cook, 1985; Huston, 1984; Marsh, 1989a; Offer, Ostrov, Howard, & Atkinson, 1988; Piers, 1984; Robison, Kehle & Jenson, 1986; Simmons & Blyth, 1987).

Although not all studies have found differences in male and female self-esteem, when differences do exist, the girls feel inferior to the boys. In terms of both their physical appearance and their intellectual abilities, adolescent girls are less satisfied with themselves and less confident than boys (as are adult women and men). Moreover, girls are more likely than boys to want to be a member of the other sex. That is, both adolescent boys and girls tend to view being male as more

A CLOSER LOOK 5.5

Male Dancers: Where Are All the Men?

Dance companies are looking for a few good men but are not having much luck. "Where's the prince?" asks an editorial in *Dance Magazine.* A recurrent problem, more urgent than ever these days, is the scarcity of classically trained male dancers. The shortage has reached such proportions that the *New York Times* ballet critic laments, "We are back to the same old story—forced to acknowledge that the United States is less receptive to the development of male classical dancing than it should be." Given the social and sexual revolutions of recent years, we might assume that such stereotypes as "only homosexuals become male ballet dancers" would be out of fashion. But, sadly, the notion of adolescent boys or men dancing ballet still embarrasses people. Even in our supposedly "liberated" times, very few parents support their sons' taking ballet, despite the muscle, prowess, and stamina that ballet demands of male dancers. While nobody minds seeing girls or women display their bodies on stage in white tights and provocative costumes, seeing a male's body similarly highlighted by ballet tights often sends an embarrassing shudder or snickers through the audience. Although some male dancers are gay, as are some males in every other profession, our assumptions about homosexuality and our discomfort with some of the graceful movements required of male dancers ensure that almost every young boy will squelch any desire to don a pair of ballet shoes. Until we get beyond this aspect of our homophobia and sex stereotyping, boys in our society will continue to be deprived of the joys of ballet, either as an art form or as a future profession.

Source: L. Shapiro. (1989, April). Where are all the men? *Newsweek,* pp. 62–63.

What comes into your mind as you look at this picture? Why?

desirable than being female. In regard to their self-esteem relative to that of boys, girls today have changed surprisingly little from girls in the 1970s (Massad, 1981; Nicholson & Antil, 1981; Offer, Ostrov, & Howard, 1981; Wylie, 1979). It would appear that the women's movement and other efforts to equalize opportunities have not yet raised girls' self-esteem to match that of boys. The sobering reality is that, even among today's adolescents, masculine traits are more often valued and more often associated with self-esteem than are feminine attributes.

Body Image

Not only do adolescents generally value masculine traits more than feminine traits, teenage girls generally feel worse than boys about their physical appearance. One of the most consistent findings in the research is that most teenage girls dislike their bodies—above all, they see themselves as fat or overweight when, in reality, they are either of average or below-average weight for their age and height. For example, in a study of nearly 6,000 adolescents between the ages of 12 and 17, 70% of the girls wanted to be thinner. Moreover, the most popular girls were the most concerned about being thin, suggesting that popularity is closely and tenuously linked to being skinny (Duncan, 1985). Likewise, in a survey of 1,000 competitive swimmers whose bodies were in excellent shape, the teenage girls were more dissatisifed with their bodies than the boys were with theirs and wanted, more than any other change, to lose weight (Dummer, 1987). This indicates that even among athletes, whom we might expect to be more reasonable in terms of healthy attitudes toward weight, many girls are still dominated by the notion that a woman can never be too thin. In sum, boys are generally more satisfied with themselves physically than are girls and seldom judge themselves as being overweight (Cohn, 1987; Desmond, Price, Gray, & O'Connell, 1986; Dummer, 1987; R. Levinson, Powell, & Stellman, 1986; Rierden, Koff, & Stubbs, 1988; Storz & Greene, 1983).

These gender differences are especially disturbing given that millions ofteenage girls are subjecting themselves to dangerous diets or developing the life-threatening disease anorexia nervosa in their quest to fit our society's physical image of femininity. Unlike boys, many girls are literally killing themselves in order to reduce their maturing bodies to our culture's definition of "sexiness" and "womanliness"—a body with the thighs, hips, and stomach of a prepubescent child. Unfortunately, by adolescence girls have learned all too well that in our society the thin female body conjures up traits traditionally considered desirable in women: sweetness, dependence, fragility, sexiness, nurturance, adorability, and girlishness.

This is not to say that teenage boys are never dissatisfied with their bodies. The increasing use of muscle-building steroids and body-building equipment is clear testimony that sometimes they are. In fact, most teenage boys and men say they want to be taller, more muscular, and heavier (Mishkind, 1987). In this sense, then, males are also held hostage to their gender role in that masculinity is equated with being bigger, taller, and more muscular than other males—and certainly bigger, taller, and bulkier than females. Indeed, the research consistently shows that we tend to ascribe more masculine personality traits to males who fit our stereotypical image of the tall, muscular he-man. Without knowing him, we expect the mesomorph (lean, muscular) to be more independent, competitive, self-confident, active, daring, and invulnerable than the male with a smaller, slighter build (Hatfield & Spencer, 1989; Lakoff & Scherr, 1984).

In our society, self-esteem and self-confidence are closely linked to our being satisfied with our physical appearance. It is also well documented that our society's particular definitions of beauty and handsomeness do influence the ways people treat us. Those of us lucky enough genetically to fit our society's notions of what is good-looking at the period of history into which we happen to be born are generally treated better than those of us who did not get this lucky break genetically. From preschool through adulthood, "attractive" people are more popular, are treated better by their teachers and employers, are considered more intelligent, are more likely to receive help from others, and have better chances of getting jobs and receiving higher salaries (Hatfield & Spencer, 1989; Lakoff & Scherr, 1984). Where, then, do our sex role stereotypes regarding "beauty" leave girls whose genetic makeup does not allow them to squeeze into our cultural image? Like Cinderella's sisters, are they left sitting home from the ball because their feet are too big to fit into the prince's glass slipper? Where do our stereotypes of masculinity leave boys whose bodies are shorter or slighter or less muscular than our knight in shining armor ideal? Are they left behind in the dust while the John Waynes and Rambos ride off into the sunset with the pretty women—left in the band and the Latin Club while the cheerleaders turn their attention to the "jocks"? In accepting society's notions of masculine and feminine bodies, what have we done to ourselves and to our young people?

ADOLESCENTS' ATTITUDES TOWARD GENDER ROLES

As these findings on body image demonstrate, gender roles are still very much alive and well, although both male and female adolescents seem to be somewhat more willing than their counterparts in earlier decades to step outside these roles. Vocationally most teenagers still restrict their choices on the basis of gender stereotypes. Young women still overwhelmingly choose to enter the historically feminine fields, even in graduate school. Likewise, most males still take the more highly paid and more prestigious jobs that have historically been restricted to men. Since these issues will be explored in chapter 11, suffice it to say at this point that our work force is still sex segregated and that most teenagers are still restricting their choices on the basis of gender stereotypes.

In regard to more personal matters, such as childcare and housework, today's adolescents also endorse many traditional gender roles. For example, 85% of the 3,000 high-school seniors in a nationally representative sample disapproved of a woman's being the breadwinner while her husband stayed home to raise the children. More than two thirds of these seniors also opposed a mother's being employed while her children were preschoolers (Herzog, Bachman & Johnston, 1983). Similar surveys from the 1980s have also shown that adolescents' attitudes about gender roles are more traditional than we might expect in the midst of our supposedly more liberated society (Hansen & Darling, 1985; Hertsgaard & Light, 1984; Lewin & Tragoso, 1987; Lueptow, 1984; Simmons & Blyth, 1987).

Moreover, boys' gender roles may be just as restrictive as girls'. Indeed, it is still more acceptable for a girl to be a tomboy than for a boy to be a sissy. The restrictiveness of the male gender role is comically portrayed in Feirstein's definitions of "real men": "Real men don't smoke low tar cigarettes or drink light beer. They still pass in the no-passing zone; they don't settle with words what can be settled with a flame-thrower, and they don't eat quiche, yogurt, broccoli, or tofu" (1982). In a less comic vein, researchers have noted that teenage boys and men are still restricted to roles that contribute to their high death rates from murder, drunk driving, and stress-related illnesses. Most males are also still discouraged from exploring careers in such fields as cosmetology and dance, where many people in our society question their "manhood." Even the human response of crying jeopardizes the self-image of many boys and men (see Box 5.6). More sadly still, most males are reluctant to ask for help or to admit weakness,

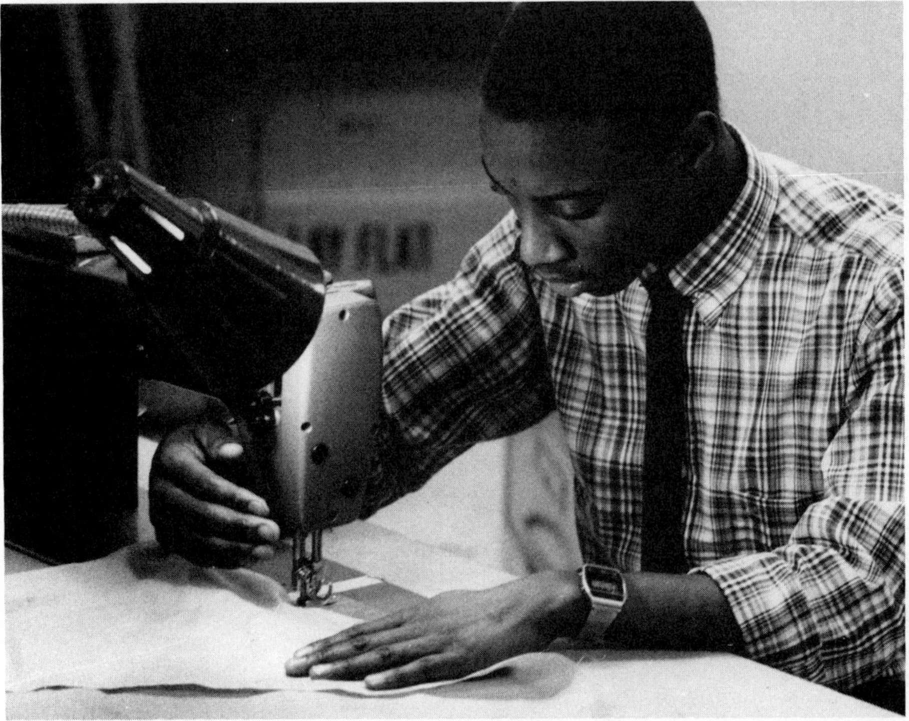

How do you feel about males sewing? being kindergarten teachers? being cosmetologists?

often concealing physical or emotional pain to the point of harming themselves physically and psychologically (Gerzon, 1984; Goldberg, 1987).

This is not to say that no changes whatsoever have occurred in adolescents' gender role attitudes. Nevertheless, the research shows that the changes lag behind what we might assume on the basis of our society's presumed support for less restrictive roles. In this light, it is important to note that just as women's studies courses are trying to help teenage girls and college women examine the restrictions of the female role, men's studies courses are urging males to reexamine their notions of masculinity. Men's studies takes masculinity, as it has been traditionally defined, and asks boys and men to reconsider their roles in terms of the physical, sexual, and emotional disadvantages—the pressures to perform, to lead, to conceal emotions, to be decisive, to dominate, to be assertive, to be athletic, to be financially powerful, to be in control (Brod, 1987, 1988; Franklin, 1984; M. Kaufman, 1987; Kimmel, 1987; Seidler, 1989). In this vein, specific programs have been designed to help teenage boys reexamine their gender roles in hopes of helping them live more fulfilling, less restricted lives as men (Gerzon, 1984; Thompson, 1985).

THE DEVELOPMENT OF MALE AND FEMALE IDENTITY

Given that most boys and girls are still socialized to don a prescribed gender role, it is understandable that the paths by which each sex establishes an identity also differ (Josselson, 1987; Marcia, 1981). As you recall from chapter 4, adolescents

A CLOSER LOOK 5.6

Big Boys Should Cry!

"Act like a man! Don't cry! Only sissies and girls cry!" Such enjoinders to young boys and adolescent males notwithstanding, David Goodman at the Newport Neuroscience Center in California has shown that weeping may be therapeutic for males of any age. Convulsive weeping is a rare experience for most American males, given our society's sex role stereotypes of masculinity. Yet Dr. Goodman encouraged a group of men to weep intensively and uncontrollably whenever they needed to release tension during the course of the experiment. Goodman found that men with initially high levels of testosterone who cried regularly, as instructed, lowered their testosterone levels. More surprisingly, men whose testosterone levels had been below the male average before the experiment experienced a rise in testosterone level after several weeks of intensive weeping. In some cases, testosterone levels rose or fell by as much as 30% during the 4-week period, bringing these men's hormonal levels closer to the male population's average. In addition, the men whose testosterone levels fell as a consequence of their crying reportedly felt less "driven." Conversely, those whose testosterone levels had risen reportedly felt more "assertive." Goodman noted that he asked the men to cry in intense ways that resembled the crying of newborns and young children because he was "looking for an extraordinarily stressful way of releasing tension." According to Goodman, as boys enter adolescence, their testosterone levels rise to levels that might make crying more difficult than in their childhood years.

Source: D. Goodman. (1984, October). *Biochemical changes during a dacrystic regimen.* Paper presented at the meeting of the Society of Neuroscience, Anaheim, CA.

with foreclosed identities make premature decisions regarding their goals and values. Without questioning the expectations or values of their parents and other authority figures, young people who adopt a foreclosed identity conform to the wishes of others without developing their own standards and identities. In contrast, adolescents who experiment with various roles and ideologies, question authorities, and reject some of their elders' ideas can develop an independent identity. These young people with achieved identities enter their adult years with a clearer sense of who they are and what they believe than those who have foreclosed identities.

Unfortunately, adolescent girls are more likely than adolescent boys to adopt a foreclosed identity. Achieving an identity of one's own involves experimentation, a certain amount of defiance of authority, and a self-reliant, independent spirit—traits more congruent with the traditional male gender role than with the female role. Indeed, some of the very characteristics necessary for forming an independent identity are at odds with our notions of femininity: assertiveness, defiance, self-reliance, and a certain willingness to define ourselves without the approval of those who love us. In this vein, adolescent girls who dare to fashion their own identities report feeling more anxious than girls who accept a foreclosed identity and often pay the price for having defied our traditional definitions of femininity.

In contrast to adolescent males, most adolescent girls are encouraged to postpone developing their own identities until they have honed their skills in the areas of intimacy and interpersonal relationships. They are then rewarded for doing so.

Moreover, many girls are still encouraged to remain "flexible" about their future goals to fit into their roles as wives and mothers. For example, girls receive more encouragement than boys to prepare themselves for jobs, such as nursing or teaching, that fit more easily into the demands of child rearing than professions such as law or medicine. Adolescent boys, on the other hand, are usually encouraged to develop their vocational potential and their personal ideologies before thinking of settling down into a relationship. As a consequence, most young women end up with more well-developed interpersonal skills, but with a more poorly defined sense of self, than most young men.

Given these different paths to identity, whether 18 years old or 30, a male is more likely than a female to be working on issues related to intimacy and interpersonal relationships: "How do I share my feelings with another person?" "How can I figure out when my children are mad and when they're hurt?" "How can I learn to empathize with and listen attentively to other people?" Likewise, the 30- or 40-year-old woman is more likely to be working on issues that most men confronted as adolescents: "What kind of work do I really want to do?" "How competent am I to take care of myself on a day-to-day basis?" "How can I establish my independence and be less overly dependent on everyone else's approval?" In short, the various aspects of identity that we pursue as adolescents are often mirrored later in our lives in our different paths as men and women (Baruch, Barnett, & Rivers, 1983; Josselson, 1987; D. Levinson, 1978; Sheehy, 1982; Smelser & Erikson, 1980).

Erik Erikson, upon whose theories many of our hypotheses about adolescents' identity development were based, assumed that both males and females advanced through the same stages in forming an identity (1968). Erikson further assumed that, as adolescents or young adults, we must form an identity of our own before we can learn how to establish an intimate relationship with another person. Put differently, we must decide who and what we are before we can attempt to be connected in intimate relationships with others. While Erikson's hypotheses appear to hold true for most males in our society, they fail to explain female development.

As Erikson predicted, most adolescent boys and young men develop their sense of self through their personal achievements and through their separateness or independence from other people. Contradicting Erikson's predictions, however, most adolescent girls and young women develop a sense of identity through their relationships with and "connectedness" to other people. While the teenage girl's identity is primarily organized around establishing and maintaining relationships, the teenage boy's identity is primarily a movement from dependence on others to autonomy. Unlike those of a girl, a boy's relationships play a secondary, rather than a primary, role in his definition of self. As an adult, then, he derives more of his identity from his personal achievements than from his relationships with friends or family. Females, on the other hand, generally derive their identities from their sense of what they mean to others. Even in her vocation, the young woman's work generally has to matter to someone who matters to her in order for her to feel fulfilled. Likewise, while the adolescent girl may be preparing herself for a career, she is still more likely than a boy to attach her personal sense of self to her future roles as a wife and mother. Unfortunately, this means that many teenage girls forfeit their chance to establish their own identity (Josselson, 1987).

For those adolescent males and females who do establish an identity of their own, the challenge of forming intimate relationships awaits them in their adult years. While these young men and women will still suffer through the pain and self-doubt that accompany losing a relationship with someone they love, they will not forfeit their entire sense of self in the process. To those who have not achieved an identity of their own, however, the end of a relationship is the loss of self. Without the ability to stand alone, without any identity separate from another person, these young men and women will continually turn to others for self-validation and caretaking. Questing for a self-confidence and an independence that never took root during their youth, they seek to find a self by looking exclusively into the eyes of others, hoping, in vain, to find a reflection there of their own forever elusive identity.

CONCLUSION

Amidst the ongoing debates related to sex differences and gender roles, what can we conclude? At the very least, that both male and female adolescents are still constrained by our society's sex role stereotypes, that the sexes are far more similar than they are different in their intellectual and vocational abilities, and that a number of unfounded beliefs about each sex are still deeply rooted in our society's institutions. We can also safely conclude that most adolescents' attitudes are more sex typed than we might assume, given the women's movement and other efforts to equalize opportunities. Moreover, although the nature/nurture debate has not been resolved, we cannot altogether discount the possibility that biological factors may influence certain aspects of our male and female behavior, nor can we discount the reality that our childhood and adolescent experiences shape our gender attitudes and behavior. Finally, male and female adolescents do differ in a number of domains that are worthy of our attention in the following chapters—among them, differences in their moral and vocational development, delinquency, suicide and depression, eating disorders, sexual behavior, drug use, and relationships with friends and family.

QUESTIONS FOR DISCUSSION AND REVIEW

Basic Concepts and Terminology

1. What are the methodological problems encountered in conducting research on sex-related behavior?
2. According to sociobiologists, why do males and females behave or think differently? What data support and what refute their hypotheses?
3. How do social learning theorists explain the behavioral differences between males and females? What data support and refute their hypotheses?
4. How "liberated" are today's adolescents in regard to sex role stereotypes and sex-typed behavior? Cite data to support your answer.
5. How do male and female adolescents differ in regard to academic achievement, vocational choices, aggression, and self-esteem?
6. How do schools and parents influence adolescents' sex-typed behavior and gender role attitudes?
7. In what ways can teachers, counselors, and parents help children and adolescents develop their athletic, intellectual, and vocational skills without regard to gender?
8. How do males and females generally differ in regard to developing an identity?
9. How do gender schema theory, Freudian theory, and social learning theory account for the adoption of gender roles?
10. How do males' and females' fear of success and locus of control attitudes compare?

Questions for Discussion and Debate

1. How would your own adolescence and your present life be different if you were a member of the other sex?
2. In what ways did your parents and teachers respond to you that did and did not reinforce traditional sex role expectations?
3. In what ways have your gender role attitudes been advantageous and disadvantageous to your academic, vocational, physical, social, and sexual development?
4. How do you feel about the sociobiologists' and the social learning theorists' viewpoints on sex-typed behavior? Which of their hypotheses do you find most convincing and least convincing?
5. Looking at Table 5.1, how would you describe yourself as you are now? How does this differ from your personality as a 15-year-old? What accounts for the similarities and the differences?
6. To what degree are your present behavior and attitudes influenced by sex role stereotypes?
7. Recall your favorite fairytales and nursery rhymes. How are the male and female characters (or animals or inanimate objects) portrayed? Which fairytales or nursery rhymes present male and female characters in nonstereotypical ways?
8. Recall several television ads, several popular television series, and the lyrics of several of the most popular songs now being played on the radio. What messages about males and females does each convey? In what ways does each support or refute sex stereotypes?
9. Who has the greater advantage in today's society—male or female adolescents? Why?
10. What information most surprised you in this chapter? Why? What information most upset you? Why?

GLOSSARY

androgyny State of possessing masculine and feminine personality traits simultaneously. Example: being both nurturant and independent.

bilateralized The brain's capacity to process certain types of information in either hemisphere.

brain lateralization The separation of mental and physical functions between the left and right hemispheres of the brain. Synonym: hemisphericity.

fear of success Being afraid to succeed at tasks or in jobs that have traditionally been considered appropriate for the other gender.

gender roles The behaviors and attitudes prescribed by a society as appropriate for males and for females. Synonym: sex roles.

gender schema theory A cognitive theory stating that sex-typed behavior is influenced by fitting our experiences into our existing systems of beliefs (schema).

hemisphericity The brain's organization in which each side of the brain is generally responsible for a specific type of motor or cognitive task.

mental rotation The result of imagining what a two- or three-dimensional figure would look like from different angles or in its mirror image if it were rotated in space. See Figure 5.1.

meta-analysis A statistical technique that permits more sophisticated analyses of data by considering variables such as gender and socioeconomic class that influence the results.

nonconscious ideology Values and beliefs so ingrained in a society's institutions and habits that people are unaware of being subjected to them.

sociobiology The study of theories contending that human behavior is in large part determined by biological factors, such as hormones, and by genetic changes that have evolved for the good of a species.

spatial perception The ability to locate the horizontal or the vertical while ignoring other distracting, irrelevant visual cues. See Figure 5.1.

spatial visualization The ability to analyze the relationship between different spatial representations of an object. See Figure 5.1.

Title IX Federal law passed in 1972 stating that no person in the United States shall, on the basis of sex, be excluded from participating in, be denied the benefits of, or be subjected to discrimination under any educational program or activity receiving federal money. See Table 5.2.

REFERENCES

Adelson, J. (Ed.). (1980). *Handbook of adolescent psychology.* New York: Wiley.

Alpert, J. (1986). *Psychoanalysis and women: Contemporary reappraisals.* New York: Erlbaum.

Applebee, A. (1989). *A study of book length works taught in high school English courses.* Albany, NY: State University of New York, Center for the Learning and Teaching of Literature.

Baenninger, M., & Newcombe, N. (1990). The role of experience in spatial test performance: A meta-analysis. *Sex Roles, 17,* 80–93.

Barash, D. (1979). *The whispering within.* New York: Harper and Row.

Baruch, G., Barnett, R., & Rivers, C. (1983). *Lifeprints.* New York: Basic Books.

Becker, B., & Hedges, L. (1984). Meta-analysis of cognitive gender differences. *Journal of Educational Psychology, 76,* 583–587.

Begley, S. (1988, April 11). Closing the gender gap. *Newsweek,* p. 73.

Bem, S. (1981). Gender schema theory: A cognitive account of sex typing. *Psychological Review, 88,* 354–364.

Bem, S., & Bem, D. (1976). Training the woman to know her place: The power of a nonconscious ideology. In S. Cox (Ed.), *Female psychology* (pp. 180–190). Chicago: Science Research Associates.

Benbow, C., & Stanley J. (1983). Sex differences in mathematical reasoning ability. *Science, 222,* 1029–1031.

Berman, E. (1982). *The complete chauvinist.* New York: Macmillan.

Bernay, T., & Cantor, D. (Eds.). (1986). *The psychology of today's woman: New psychoanalytic visions.* New York: Analytic Press.

Bettelheim, B. (1976). *The uses and abuses of enchantment: The meaning and importance of fairytales.* New York: Knopf.

Binchy, M. (1988). *Rapunzel's revenge.* Greenwood, SC: Attic Press.

Bleir, R. (1984). *Science and gender: A critique of biology and its theories on women.* New York: Pergamon Press.

Block, J. (1984). *Sex role identity and ego development.* San Francisco: Jossey-Bass.

Bogart, K. (1984). *Toward equity: An action manual for women in academe.* Washington, DC: Project on the Status and Education of Women.

Bornstein, R. (1985). Ambiguity as opportunity and constraint: Evolution of a federal sex equity education program. *Educational Evaluation and Policy Analysis, 7,* 99–114.

Bottigheimer, R. (Ed.). (1987). *Fairytales and society.* Pittsburgh: University of Pennsylvania Press.

Brod, H. (1987). *The making of masculinities: The new men's studies.* New York: Allen & Unwin.

Brod, H. (Ed.) (1988). *A mensch among men: Explorations in Jewish masculinity.* Freedom, CA: Crossing Press.

Caplan, P., MacPherson, G., & Tobin, P. (1985). Do sex related differences in spatial abilities exist? *American Psychologist, 40,* 786–799.

Carelli, A. (1989). *Sex equity in education.* New York: Charles Thomas.

Cate, R., & Sugawara, A. (1986). Sex role orientation and dimensions of self-esteem among middle adolescents. *Sex Roles, 13,* 145–158.

Chen, M. (1986). Gender and computers. *Journal of Educational Computing Research, 2,* 265–282.

Christian-Smith, L. (1987). Gender, popular culture, and curriculum: Adolescent romance novels as gender text. *Curriculum Inquiry, 17,* 365–406.

Condry, J., & Condry, S. (1976). Sex differences: A study in the eye of the beholder. *Child Development, 47,* 817.

Cook, E. (1985). *Psychological androgyny.* New York: Pergamon Press.

Cohn, L. (1987). Body preferences in male and female adolescents. *Journal of Abnormal Psychology, 96,* 276–279.

Crowley, E. (1989). *Sweeping beauties: Fairytales for feminists.* Greenwood, SC: Attic Press.

Dalton, K. (1983). *Once a month.* Claremont, CA: Hunter House.

Desmond, S., Price, J., Gray, N., & O'Connell, J. (1986). The etiology of adolescents' perceptions of their weight. *Journal of Youth and Adolescence, 15,* 461–473.

Dummer, G. (1987). Pathogenic weight control behaviors of young competitive swimmers. *Physician and Sports Medicine, 15,* 75–78.

Duncan, P. (1985). The effects of pubertal timing on body image. *Journal of Youth and Adolescence, 14,* 227–235.

Dusek, J., & Joseph, G. (Eds.). (1985). *Teacher expectancies.* Hillsdale, NJ: Erlbaum.

Dweck, C. (1984). Attribution theory. In P. Mussen and M. Hetherington (Eds.) *Child development handbook* (pp. 210–285). New York: Wiley.

Eagly, A. (1987). *Sex differences in social behavior.* Hillsdale: NJ: Erlbaum.

Eakins, B., & Eakins, G. (1978). *Sex differences in human communication.* Boston: Houghton Mifflin.

Eccles, J. (1983). Expectancies, values and academic behaviors. In J. Spence (Ed.), *Achievement and achievement motives* (pp. 75–146). San Francisco: W. H. Freeman.

Eccles, J., & Jacobs, J. (1986). Social forces shape math attitudes and performance. *Signs, 11,* 367–389.

Eccles, J., et al. (1988, March) *Hormones and their effect at early adolescence.* Paper presented at the meeting of the Society for Research on Adolescence, Alexandria, VA.

Elder, D., & Parker, S. (1987). The cultural production and reproduction of gender. *Sociology of Education, 60,* 200–213.

Elder, G., Nguyen, T., & Caspi, A. (1985). Linking family hardship to children's lives. *Child Development, 56,* 361–375.

Entwisle, D., & Baker, D. (1983). Gender and young children's expectations for performance in arithmetic. *Developmental Psychology, 19,* 200–209.

Epstein, C. (1988). *Deceptive distinctions: Sex, gender and the social order.* New York: Russell Sage Foundation.

Erikson, E. (1968). *Identity: Youth in crisis.* New York: Norton.

Fausto-Sterling, A. (1986). *Myths of gender: Biological theories about women and men.* New York: Basic Books.

Feingold, A. (1988). Cognitive gender differences are disappearing. *American Psychologist, 43,* 95–103.

Feirstein, B. (1982). *Real men don't eat quiche: A guidebook to all that is truly masculine.* New York: Simon and Schuster.

Fisher, M. (1980, July). Teenage scientist. *Ms.,* p. 23.

Fogel, R., & Paludi, M. (1984). Fear of success and failure. *Sex Roles, 10,* 431–434.

Fox, L., Brody, L., & Tobin, L. (Eds.). (1984). *Women and the mathematical mystique.* Baltimore: Johns Hopkins University Press.

Franklin, C. (1984). *The changing definition of masculinity.* New York: Plenum Press.

Galambos, N., & Silbereisen, R. (1987). Income change, parental life outlook and adolescent expectations of job success. *Journal of Marriage and the Family, 49,* 141–149.

Gander, F. (1985). *Father Gander nursery rhymes: The equal rhymes amendment.* Santa Barbara, CA: Advocacy Press.

The gender factor. (1980, November 15) *Time,* p. 46.

Gerzon, M. (1984). *A choice of heroes: The changing faces of American manhood.* Boston: Houghton Mifflin.

Gilder, G. (1979, January). The case against women in combat. *New York Times Magazine,* p. 44.

Gilligan, C. (1982). *In a different voice: Psychological theory and women's development.* Cambridge, MA: Harvard University Press.

Glass, G., McGaw, B., & Smith, M. (1981). *Meta-analysis in social research.* Beverly Hills, CA: Sage.

Goldberg, H. (1987). *The inner male: Overcoming roadblocks to intimacy.* New York: New American Library.

Good, T., & Brophy, J. (1984). *Looking in classrooms.* New York: Harper & Row.

Gould, S. (1984, August 12). Similarities between the sexes [Review of *A Critique of Biology and Its Theories on Women*]. *New York Times Book Review,* p. 7.

Greenfield, P., & Lauber, B. (1985, March). *Cognitive effects of video games.* Paper presented at the Claremont Conference on Applied Cognitive Psychology, Claremont: CA.

Halpern, D. (1985). The influence of sex role stereotypes on prose recall. *Sex Roles, 12,* 363–375.

Halpern, D. (1986). *Sex differences in cognitive abilities.* Hillsdale, NJ: Erlbaum.

Hansen, S., & Darling, C. (1985). Attitudes of adolescents toward division of labor in the home. *Adolescence, 77,* 61–71.

Hare-Mustin, R., & Marecek, J. (1988). The meaning of difference. *American Psychologist, 43,* 455–464.

Harris, L. (1978). Sex differences in spatial ability. In M. Kinsbourne (Ed.), *Asymmetrical functions of the brain* (pp. 405–522). Cambridge, MA: Cambridge University Press.

Hatfield, E., & Spencer, S. (1989). *Mirror, mirror: The importance of looks in everyday life.* New York: State University of New York Press.

Hawkins, J. (1985). Computers and girls. *Sex Roles, 13,* 165–180.

Hedges, L., & Olkin, I. (1985). *Statistical methods for meta-analysis.* New York: Academic Press.

Hertsgaard, D., & Light, H. (1984). Junior high girls' attitudes toward the rights and roles of women. *Adolescence, 19,* 847–853.

Herzog, A., Bachman, J., & Johnston, L. (1983). Paid work, child care and housework: A national survey of high school seniors' preferences for sharing responsibilities between husband and wife. *Sex Roles, 9,* 109–135.

Hess, R., & Miura, I. (1985). Gender differences in enrollment in computer camps and classes. *Sex Roles, 13,* 193–203.

Horner, M. (1972). Toward an understanding of achievement related conflicts in women. *Journal of Social Issues, 28,* 157–175.

Houser, B., & Garvey, C. (1985). Factors that affect nontraditional vocational enrollment among women. *Psychology of Women Quarterly, 9,* 105–117.

Hueftle, S., Rakow, S., & Welch, W. (1983). *Images of science.* Minneapolis: University of Minnesota Press.

Huston, A. (1984). Sex typing. In P. Mussen & M. Hetherington (Eds.), *Child development handbook* (pp. 388–467). New York: Wiley.

Hyde, J. (1985). *Half the human experience: The psychology of women.* Lexington, MA: D. C. Heath.

Hyde, J., & Linn, M. (Eds.). (1986). *The psychology of gender: Advances through meta-analysis.* Baltimore: Johns Hopkins University Press.

Hyde, J. (1986). Gender differences in aggression. In J. Hyde & M. Linn (Eds.), *The psychology of gender:*

Advances through meta-analysis (pp. 51–67). Baltimore: Johns Hopkins University Press.

Imperato-McGuinley, J. (1979). Androgens and the evolution of male gender identity among male pseudohermaphrodites. *New England Journal of Medicine, 43,* 236–237.

Johnston, J., & Ettema, J. (1982). *Positive images: Breaking stereotypes with children's television.* Beverly Hills, CA: Sage.

Josselson, R. (1987). *Finding herself: Pathways to identity development in women.* San Francisco: Jossey-Bass.

Kaufman, D., & Richardson, B. (1982). *Achievement and women: Challenging the assumptions.* New York: Free Press.

Kaufman, M. (1987). *Beyond patriarchy: Essays by men on pleasure, power and change.* New York: Oxford University Press.

Kelly, M. (1988). *Ms. Muffet and others.* Greenwood, SC: Attic Press.

Kimmel, M. (Ed.). (1987). *Changing men: New directions in research on men and masculinity.* Beverly Hills, CA: Sage.

Kitcher, P. (1985). *Vaulting ambition: Sociobiology and the quest for human nature.* Cambridge, MA: MIT Press.

Klein, S. (Ed.). (1985). *Handbook for Achieving Sex Equity Through Education.* Baltimore: Johns Hopkins University Press.

Kohlberg, L. (1966). A cognitive development analysis of children's sex role concepts and attitudes. In E. Maccoby (Ed.), *The development of sex differences* (pp. 82–133). Stanford, CA: Stanford University Press.

Lakoff, R., & Scherr, R. (1984). *Face value, the politics of beauty.* Boston: Routledge & Kegan Paul.

Lamb, M. (Ed.). (1986). *The father's role.* New York: Wiley.

Lamb, M. (Ed.). (1987). *The father's role: Cross cultural perspectives.* Hillsdale, NJ: Erlbaum.

Lee, V., & Bryk, A. (1986). Effects of single sex secondary schools on student achievement and attitudes. *Journal of Educational Psychology, 78,* 381–395.

Levinson, D. (1978). *The seasons of a man's life.* New York: Knopf.

Levinson, R., Powell, R., & Stellman, L. (1986). Social location, significant others and body image among adolescents. *Social Psychology Quarterly, 49,* 330–337.

Levy, J. (1972). Lateral specialization of the human brain. In J. Kiger (Ed.), *The biology of behavior* (pp. 315–324). Eugene: University of Oregon Press.

Levy, J. (1981). Lateral specialization. *International Journal of Women's Studies, 4,* 318–328.

Lewin, M. (Ed.). (1984). *In the shadow of the past: Psychology portrays the sexes.* New York: Columbia.

Lewin, M., & Tragoso, L. (1987). Has the feminist movement influenced adolescent attitudes? *Sex Roles, 16,* 125–135.

Lewontin, R., Rose, S., & Kamin, L. (1984). *Not in our genes.* New York: Pantheon Books.

Liben, L., & Signorella, M. (Eds.). (1988). *Children's gender schemata.* San Francisco: Jossey-Bass.

Liebert, R., & Sprafkin, J. (1988). *The early window: Effects of television on children and youth.* New York: Pergamon Press.

Linn, M., & Petersen, A. (1988). Meta-analysis of gender differences in spatial ability. In J. Hyde & M. Linn (Eds.), *The psychology of gender* (pp. 67–101). Baltimore: Johns Hopkins University Press.

Lips, H. (1988). *Sex and gender.* Mountain View, CA: Mayfield Publishing.

Liss, M. (Ed.). (1983). *Social and cognitive skills: Sex roles and children's play.* New York: Academic Press.

Lueptow, L. (1984). *Adolescent sex roles and social change.* New York: Columbia University Press.

Maccoby, E., & Jacklin, C. (1974). *The psychology of sex differences.* Stanford, CA: Stanford University Press.

Maggio, R. (1989). *The nonsexist word finder: A dictionary of gender free usage.* Boston: Beacon Press.

Marcia, J. (1981). Identity in adolescence. In J. Adelson (Ed.), *Handbook of adolescent psychology* (pp. 197–243). New York: Wiley.

Marsh, H. (1989a). Age and sex effects in multiple dimensions of self-concept. *Journal of Educational Psychology, 81,* 417–430.

Marsh, H. (1989b). Effects of attending single sex and coeducational high schools on achievement, attitudes, behaviors and sex differences. *Journal of Educational Psychology, 81,* 70–85.

Massad, C. (1981). Sex role identity and adjustment during adolescence. *Child Development, 52,* 1290–1298.

McHigh, M., Koeske, R., & Frieze, I. (1986). Issues to consider in conducting nonsexist psychological research. *American Psychologist, 41,* 879–890.

Mead, M. (1935). *Sex and temperament in three primitive societies.* New York: American Library.

Mednick, M. (1990). Fear of success. In H. Tierney (Ed.), *Women's studies encyclopedia* (205–231). Westport, CT: Greenwood.

Meehan, A. (1984). A meta-analysis of sex differences in formal operational thought. *Child Development, 55,* 1110–1124.

Mischel, W. (1984). Convergence and challenges in the search for consistency. *American Psychologist, 39,* 351–364.

Mishkind, M. (1987). The embodiment of masculinity. In M. Kimmel (Ed.), *Changing men: New directions in research on men and masculinity* (pp. 37–51). Beverly Hills, CA: Sage.

Molloy, F. (1988). *Mad and bad fairies.* Greenwood, SC: Attic Press.

Money, J., & Ehrhardt, A. (1972). *Man woman, boy girl.* Baltimore: Johns Hopkins University Press.

Morgan, M. (1987). Television, sex role attitudes and sex role behavior. *Journal of Early Adolescence, 7,* 269–282.

Mott, F., & Haurin, R. (1982). Variations in the educational progress and career orientations of brothers and sisters. In F. Mott (Ed.), *The employment revolution* (pp. 19–44). Cambridge, MA: MIT Press.

Moulton, R. (1986). Professional success: A conflict for women. In J. Alpert (Ed.), *Psychoanalysis and women* (pp. 161–181). New York: Erlbaum.

Nicholson, S., & Antil, J. (1981). Personal problems of adolescents and their relationship to peer acceptance and sex role identity. *Journal of Youth and Adolescence, 10,* 309–325.

Nielsen, A. (1988). *1988 Nielsen report on television.* Northbrook, IL: A. C. Nielsen Co.

No slack: A woman's touch at West Point. (1989, August 21). *Newsweek,* p. 20.

Offer, D., Ostrov, E., & Howard, K. (1981). *The adolescent: A psychological self portrait.* New York: Basic Books.

Offer, D., Ostrov, E., Howard, K., & Atkinson, R. (1988). *The teenage world: Adolescents' self-image in ten countries.* New York: Plenum Press.

O'Leary, V., Unger, R., & Wallston, B. (Eds.). (1985). *Women, gender, and social psychology.* Hillsdale, NJ: Erlbaum.

Piers, E. (1984). *Piers-Harris children's self-concept scale: Revised manual.* Los Angeles: Western Psychological Services.

Rierden, J., Koff, E., & Stubbs, M. (1988). Gender, depression, and body image in early adolescents. *Journal of Early Adolescence, 8,* 109–117.

Robison, P., Kehle, T., & Jenson, W. (1986). But what about smart girls? *Journal of Educational Psychology, 78,* 179–183.

Rosenthal, R., & Rubin, D. (1982). Further meta-analytic procedures for assessing cognitive gender differences. *Journal of Educational Psychology, 74,* 708–712.

Sandberg, D. (1987). The influence of individual and family characteristics upon career aspirations of girls during childhood and adolescence. *Sex Roles, 16,* 11–13.

Scarr, S. (1985). Constructing psychology: Making facts and fables for our times. *American Psychologist, 40,* 499–512.

Schulz, M., & O'Barr S. (Eds.). (1984). *Language and power.* Beverly Hills, CA: Sage.

Scott, K. (1986). Effects of sex fair reading materials on pupils' attitudes, comprehension, and interest. *American Educational Research Journal, 23,* 105–116.

Seidler, V. (1989). *Rediscovering masculinity.* New York: Routledge.

Shakeshaft, C. (1988). *Wild patience: The story of women in school administration.* Beverly Hills, CA: Sage.

Sheehy, G. (1982). *Pathfinders.* New York: Bantam Books.

Simmons, R., & Blyth, D. (1987). *Moving into adolescence.* New York: Aldine de Gruyter.

Skinner, P., & Shelton, R. (1985). *Speech, language and learning.* New York: Wiley.

Smelser, N., & Erikson, E. (Eds.). (1980). *Themes of work and love in adulthood.* Cambridge, MA: Harvard University Press.

Sperry, R. (1982). Some effects of disconnecting the cerebral hemispheres. *Science, 217,* 1223–1226.

Steinkamp, M., & Maehr, M. (1983). Affect, ability and science achievement: A synthesis of correlational research. *Review of Educational Research, 53,* 369–396.

Storz, N., & Greene, W. (1983). Body weight, body image and fad diets in adolescent girls. *Journal of Nutritional Education, 15,* 15–18.

Thompson, D. (1985). *As boys become men: Learning new male roles.* New York: Irvington.

Thorne, R., Kramarae, D., & Henley, C. (1983). *Language, gender and society.* Rowley, MA: Newbury House.

Thornhill, R., & Thornhill, N. (1983). Human rape: An evolutionary analysis. *Biology and sociobiology, 4,* 137–154.

Title IX of the Education Amendments of 1972. (1976). Washington, DC: Resource Center on Sex Roles in Education.

Tracy, D. (1987). Toys, spatial ability and science and mathematics achievement. *Sex Roles, 17,* 115–138.

Udry, R. (1988). *Biological and social determinants of behavior change in early adolescent boys.* Paper presented at the meeting of the Society for Research on Adolescence, Alexandria, VA.

Waber, D. (1976). Sex differences in mental abilities and rate of physical growth at adolescence. *Developmental Psychology, 13,* 29–38.

Watzlawick, P. (Ed.). (1984). *The invented reality: Contributions to constructivism.* New York: Norton.

White, H. (1986). Damsels in distress: Dependency themes in fiction for children and adolescents. *Adolescence, 21,* 251–256.

Whitehead, T. (1981). Sex hormone treatment of prisoners. In P. Brain & D. Benton (Eds.), *Approaches to aggression research* (pp. 503–511). Amsterdam: Elsevier.

Whiting, B., & Edwards, C. (1988). *Children of different worlds: The formation of social behavior.* Cambridge, MA: Harvard University Press.

Whitley, B., McHugh, M., & Frieze, I. (1986). Assessing the theoretical model for sex differences in causal attributions of success and failure. In J. Hyde & M. Linn (Eds.), *Psychology of gender* (pp. 102–136). Baltimore: Johns Hopkins University Press.

Wilkinson, L., & Marrett, C. (Eds.). (1985). *Gender influences in classroom interaction.* New York: Academic Press.

Williams, J., & Best, D. (1982). *Measuring sex stereotypes: A 30 nation study*. Beverly Hills, CA: Sage.

Wilson, E. (1978). *Sociobiology: The new synthesis.* Cambridge, MA: Harvard University Press.

Wittig, M. (1985). Metatheoretical dilemmas in the psychology of gender. *American Psychologist, 41,* 800–811.

Wroblewski, R., & Huston, A. (1988). Televised occupational stereotypes and their effects on early adolescents. *Journal of Early Adolescence, 7,* 283–298.

Wylie, R. (1979). *The self concept: Theory and research.* Lincoln: University of Nebraska Press.

Young, R. (1988). Activities and interpersonal relations as dimensions of parental behavior in the career development of adolescents. *Youth and Society, 20,* 29–45.

6 Adolescents From Minority Cultures

CHAPTER OUTLINE

GOALS AND OBJECTIVES

This chapter is designed to enable you to:

- Describe the problems that confront minority youths
- Refute the stereotypes associated with various racial groups
- Identify the unique characteristics of different racial minorities
- Examine the various ways of resolving the problems of minority youth
- Discuss the controversies related to the schooling of minority students
- Examine the reasons underlying the conditions of minority adolescents

CONCEPTS AND TERMINOLOGY

acculturation
assimilation
banana syndrome
bicultural
bilingual
Bureau of Indian Affairs (BIA)
English as a second language (ESL)
ethnocentrism
limited English proficiency (LEP)
machismo
multicultural
neo-Nazi
skinheads

OUR MULTICULTURAL SOCIETY

Although many white Americans still consider issues related to Hispanic Americans, African Americans, Native Americans, and Asian Americans to be "minority" concerns, these groups have long since ceased to represent only a small segment of our population. At present these minority groups account for about 22% of our society—1% Native American, 2% Asian American, 9% Hispanic American and 10% African American. Although African Americans, now numbering approximately 28.9 million, are our largest minority group, the 17.5 million Hispanic Americans will become our largest minority within the next 40 years. Looking ahead, the percentages of minority youths are projected to rise to 15% African American, 4% Native and Asian American, and 13% Hispanic American by the year 2000. Although representing only about 2% of our present population, Asian Americans are our fastest growing minority, having increased in number between 1980 and 1985 by 36% to 7.3 million people (U.S. Bureau of the Census, 1989b).

As a result of this expanding diversity in our society, white students are already in the minority in many school systems (See Figure 7.1 in chapter 7). For example, only 49% of the public school students in California, 40% in New Mexico, and 7% in Washington, D.C., are white. Moreover, within the next 30 years, the number of white children will decline by about 13%, while the number of African American children will increase by 25% and the number of Hispanic children will more than triple. This means that within the next decade minority students will account for one third of our school-age population. With half of all Hispanic Americans now under the age of 25, they already represent the group with the highest percentage of young people in our society (McKenna & Ortiz, 1988). In short, for any of us to be viewing these minorities as a small or insignificant part of our adolescent population is to be living with the realities of the 1950s, not the 1990s.

LIMITATIONS OF THE RESEARCH

Ethnocentrism

The primary limitation of the research on minority adolescents is that there is so little of it. Given that most research and statistics have focused on white youths, our understanding of Hispanic, African American, Native American, and Asian American teenagers is based on relatively recent information. For example, between 1930 and 1980 virtually all the studies published in the popular journal *Child Development* were conducted with white, middle-class subjects (Super, 1982).

Likewise, by 1978 only 250 articles about Mexican Americans had been published in all journals, with 210 of the articles appearing only after 1970 (Hispanic Mental Health Bibliography, 1978). Noting this exclusion of minorities from our research, a number of psychologists and sociologists have lamented that "even the laboratory rat was white!" (Guthrie, 1976; Wing Sue, 1981).

Another shortcoming is that we have too often been ethnocentric in our interpretations of the research regarding minorities. **Ethnocentrism** is the belief in the superiority of one's own ethnic group. Being ethnocentric means that we interpret another group's customs, literature, art, music, humor, physical appearance, families, politics, and general ways as inferior or less advanced or less sophisticated than our own group's. For example, defining beauty as having a thin nose, thin lips, rounded eyes, straight hair, and a tall, skinny body can be seen as ethnocentric if the person doing the defining is unable to perceive any other physical features or body shapes as attractive. Likewise, it is ethnocentric to believe that the only ideal, natural, or healthy family is one with two parents, two or three children, and no other relatives living in the home and that any other type of family is abnormal, dysfunctional, deficient, or disadvantaged.

Perhaps one of the most powerful examples of ethnocentrism in terms of its impact on public opinion was the 1965 Moynihan Report. Headed by Senator Daniel Moynihan, a U.S. Senate committee studied African American family structure, incomes, and marital status. Having interpreted these statistics, the committee announced that, unlike white families, African American families were matriarchal in that women, not men, ran the households and were dominant. The report accused the women of "emasculating" men and, in so doing, of perpetuating poverty among African Americans: "The weakness of the negro family structure is the principal source of most of the aberrant, inadequate and anti-social behavior that perpetuates poverty and deprivation. The matriarchal structure retarded progress of the group as a whole and imposes a crushing burden on the negro male" (Moynihan, 1965). In short, Moynihan's committee told the American public that if African American women were not so domineering, African American men would be able to make greater economic gains. The report also told us that African American families were "unstable" and "broken down" because many did not have two married parents present in the household.

The Moynihan committee's interpretations of reality shaped white Americans' opinions of African American families and poverty for years after its appearance in the press. In the decade that followed this highly publicized report, numerous research studies refuted the committee's conclusions, criticized its ethnocentric interpretations of the data, and lambasted its faulty methodology (Billingsley, 1968; Ladner, 1971; Staples, 1982; Wallace, 1978). Nevertheless, the damage had been done because millions of Americans embraced the Moynihan Report's conclusion that poverty was primarily the fault of the African American family structure, rather than a consequence of racism in our society. Not only did the committee demonstrate its ethnocentrism, so, too, did the American public in its willingness to judge family structures that differed from the white, middle-class norm as deviant, unstable, and deficient.

As part of the backlash to the Moynihan report, during the 1960s and 1970s nearly 500 articles about African American families appeared—five times more than in the entire century that preceded the report. Its critics argued that while many African American families were indeed different from the white nuclear family, the difference was not dysfunctional or pathological. Many scholars also attacked Moynihan's report as an example of blaming the victim (Ryan, 1972). Blaming the victim is the process of blaming victimized people for problems that actually arise from the attitudes, policies, and institutions that uphold the status quo. Blaming the victim is a way of rationalizing cruelty, injustice, discrimination, and prejudice by placing the responsibility on the victims rather than on the societal policies and attitudes that perpetuate unequal treatment. For example, if a woman is raped, she might be blamed for causing the attack by wearing "provocative" clothing. Or, as was the case in the Moynihan Report, if African Americans are poor, it is the fault of African American women for being "too strong" and "emasculating their men." In blaming the victim, we ascribe the problems of victimized people to supposed "defects" within the victims themselves, rather than to the actual causes that reside in the dominant group's own policies of self-interest. Thus, the people who are most likely to engage in blaming the victim are those who benefit personally from the system as it is.

Moynihan's committee was also ethnocentric in that it chose to ignore or to overlook certain relevant data. For example, when family incomes are equivalent, African American women and white women are about equally likely to be married and living with their husbands. Likewise, the committee failed to point out that the welfare laws penalized poor families when the husbands lived in the same households with their wives. That is, the welfare system paid larger benefits to children when their fathers were not living at home. It is understandable, then, why many African American couples chose to live apart. Then, too, the committee failed to note any of the strengths of African American families. Why, for example, were African American women accused of being "domineering" when white women have also made most family decisions related to child rearing and budgets but without being accused of "emasculating" their husbands? Why, too, were African American families judged to be "unstable" solely on the basis of a husband's not being present, when the extended family offered a powerful source of support and nurturance for African American children? And why were African American women accused of being "too powerful" in relation to men when 85% of these women earned less money than their husbands?

Although the Moynihan Report ethnocentrism occurred nearly three decades ago, even in the 1990s ethnocentric research is alive and well (Rogoff & Morelli, 1989; Tharp, 1989; Tharp & Gallimore, 1988). Since almost all researchers and writers are from the white middle or upper class, ethnocentric attitudes toward nonwhites or toward people from lower income brackets is of particular concern in our understanding of adolescence. This is not to say that only white people can be ethnocentric, nor that all research conducted by whites shares this bias. To the contrary, people of any racial group can and do have ethnocentric views, and more and more studies are succeeding in overcoming ethnocentrism. Nevertheless, the fact remains that racial minorities and people from lower income backgrounds do not have nearly the control over gathering and interpreting our data as do whites. Nevertheless, all of us, regardless of race or gender, are ethnocentric to greater or lesser degrees. In this light, we need to be asking ourselves as we read the research, are the methods of collecting and of interpreting this information biased in favor of one particular group's values and behavior? Do I see any evidence of negative judgments against another culture because it differs from the white, middle-class norm? Could this researcher's data be conceived more favorably if someone from another culture had interpreted the information?

Race and Income

Another problem we often encounter when trying to make generalizations about minority youths is that race is so closely affiliated with socioeconomic status in our society. In our attempts to compare adolescents from various racial groups, therefore, we have too often made the mistake of ascribing differences to race rather than to income. In reality, however, when differences do exist between the behavior or attitudes of white and nonwhite youths, they are often a consequence of family incomes, not of racial differences.

For example, as you will see in chapter 8, the problems that we once believed were a consequence of being raised by a single mother are associated more with poverty than with not having two parents in the home. Since most single mothers are living in poverty, it is not particularly surprising to find their children having more problems than children from two-parent families. Yet, when upper-income children are raised by a divorced or a single mother, most of the disadvantages supposedly caused by not living with two parents disappear. Similarly, the racial differences in teenage pregnancy, delinquency, drug use, and academic failure become negligible when adolescents come from the same income levels. In other words, poor white children are more likely than higher income African American or Hispanic children to abuse drugs, become teenage parents, drop out of school, and commit crimes.

Since parents' incomes are primarily determined by their educational levels, being an African American, a Hispanic, or a Native American child has almost become synonymous with being poor in our society. As Figure 6.1 illustrates, when we speak about minority adolescents, we are usually referring to children living in poverty or in very low-income families. Similarly, since the least educated parents are the most likely to have had children as teenagers, to have larger families, and to have never been married, minority children are more likely to be growing up in relatively large, single-parent homes with young, uneducated mothers. Keep in mind, however, that minority adolescents from middle- and upper-income families will not share many characteristics in common with low-income minority youths. In other words, the special concerns of poor nonwhite youths are also concerns of most poor white children. A teenager does not have to be African American, Hispanic American, or Native American to know poverty.

SPECIAL CONCERNS OF MINORITY YOUTH

Poverty

The working poor As a consequence of the relationship between race and income, the greatest obstacle faced by most minority children is poverty (Children's Defense Fund, 1985; Lee, 1985; Moore & Pachon, 1985; Slaughter, 1990). For both whites and nonwhites, more poverty exists now than at any time during the 1960s or 1970s. With the median family income for four people being $36,800, the poverty line is now about $12,000. Minority children, however, who comprise only about 25% of our youth population, account for 65% of all children living in poverty (Bane & Ellwood, 1989).

FIGURE 6.1
Poverty rates of 16–21-year-olds, 1985

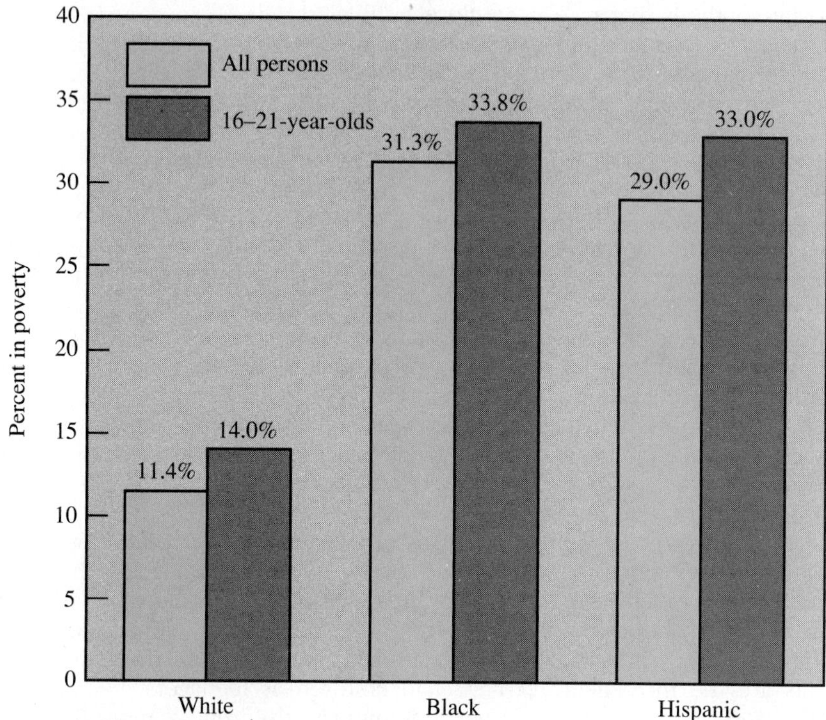

Source: W. T. Grant Foundation. (1986). *Youth and America's Future.*

Contrary to popular belief, however, most of our nation's poor children are not living in single-parent families with an unemployed mother or living in an inner-city slum (Bane & Ellwood, 1989). In fact, nearly a third of all poor children live in rural areas and another third in suburban areas. Fewer than 9% of our poor children live in large central cities. Moreover, 44% of all poor children are white, and roughly half live in two-parent homes where one or both adults have a job. During the 1970s and 1980s, as the number of poor children in our society grew, the poverty rates for female-headed families remained constant at about 50%. By contrast, poverty among children in two-parent homes jumped dramatically.

How can it be that so many parents are working without being able to keep their families above the poverty level? Part of the answer lies in the overall decline in our economy during the 1980s. In the 1960s, the poverty rates for children in two-parent homes fell dramatically, leveled off in the 1970s, then jumped in the 1980s. After rising during the 1960s, our real wages (what our money is worth after adjustments for inflation) have been almost stagnant since the early 1970s. If, for example, the minimum wage were restored to the level it was worth during the 1960s and 1970s, it would have to be raised to $5.40 by 1992. The present congressional debate has focused on a minimum of between $4.25 and $4.55, which would still leave a family of three with a full-time minimum wage worker $2,000 below the poverty line. In short, money is worth less than it was in 1973,

How would you go about resolving the problems that confront so many minority youths?

which has thrown millions of two-parent families into poverty. Although unemployment also has some impact on family incomes, pay rates have had a far more powerful role in raising our poverty rates.

Another factor hurting two-parent working families is that most do not qualify for financial assistance other than food stamps, and most do not even collect these. Lack of medical protection is the most costly problem, since these families have limited coverage from their employers and no coverage under Medicaid. As a consequence of our society's overall economic decline and our welfare policies,

A CLOSER LOOK 6.1

The Widening Gap Between White and Black Children's Well-Being

- In 1983, 13.8 million children were living in poverty—the highest level since the mid-1960s.
- Half of all African American children and one-third of all Hispanic children are poor, compared with one-sixth of all white children.
- Eight out of every 10 white children live in two-parent families, compared with 4 out of every 10 African American children.
- About 67% of all african American children have an employed parent, compared with 86% of white children.
- Approximately 2 out of every 5 African American children are living in a household headed by an adult without a high-school diploma—a rate twice that of white children.
- Each month in 1982, 3,000 girls under the age of 15 had babies—60% of whom were born to African American females.
- White children are four times as likely as African American children to grow up in families headed by college graduates.
- African American students are twice as likely as white students to be suspended from school and to be subjected to corporal punishment.
- The unemployment rate of African American college graduates is almost as high as that of white high-school dropouts.
- African American children are three to four times as likely as white children to be murdered.

Source: Children's Defense Fund. *Black and white children in America: Key facts.* (1984). Washington, DC: Author.

low-income two-parent families with a full-time worker have fallen further below the poverty line on average than any other type of family, including unmarried mothers on welfare. The harsh reality is that having a job no longer guarantees that parents can keep their children out of poverty (Bane & Ellwood, 1989; Cottingham & Ellwood, 1989; C. Johnson & Sum, 1988).

What about welfare benefits? Have we not increased poverty in our society by giving "easy handouts" to unmarried mothers and their children? Although this belief is widespread, it is unfounded. Although welfare benefits rose dramatically during the 1960s, the inflation-adjusted welfare benefits fell by 25% during the following two decades. Eligibility rules were also tightened. Yet these major cuts in benefits and eligibility had no apparent effect on the number of single-parent families. If welfare were encouraging or even allowing people to form single-parent households, why were welfare rolls unchanged while the number of children in single-parent homes rose? Indeed, some of the states with the lowest welfare benefits have the highest rates of unmarried mothers and vice versa. Moreover, no state has welfare benefits high enough to keep a family out of poverty, as evidenced by the fact that 90% of the unemployed mothers on welfare live below the poverty level (Bane & Ellwood, 1989). In short, we cannot blame our rising poverty rates on our welfare policies.

Is it not a fact that many unmarried mothers choose not to work? Yes, and many with good reason. The welfare system in most states is structured in such a way that it is economically foolish for many poorly educated single mothers to work

(Bane & Ellwood, 1989). A woman working full-time at a job paying 50% above the minimum wage will have only $1,500 more disposable income per year than a woman who does not work at all but receives welfare. In other words, she is working for 75 cents an hour, without counting the Medicaid benefits she loses because she is employed. Part-time work, the norm for married mothers, has no benefit for the unmarried mother. She is still on welfare and has no more money. Put differently, working full-time makes financial sense only if a woman can earn at least $6 or $7 an hour, get good medical benefits from her employer, and find inexpensive day care.

African American poverty The disparities in the economic situations of African American and white adolescents have widened during the past decade (Children's Defense Fund; 1985; National Resource Council, 1989). For example, although 80% of white children and 70% of African American children who live with both parents enjoy a family income of at least $20,000, nearly 60% of all African American children live with a divorced or never-married mother, in contrast to only 17% of white children (Hernandez, 1988. See Table 6.1). This has meant that nearly half of all African American children are now growing up in poverty, since the poverty rate in single-parent families hovers around 50%. More disturbing still, nearly 85% of all African American children are now likely to spend at least part of their childhood in a single-parent family, in comparison to only 40% of white children (Bane & Ellwood, 1989). While the percentage of African American families with incomes above $35,000 rose from 18% to 22% between 1970 and 1980, the proportion with incomes of less than $10,000 grew from 25% to 30% (National Research Council, 1989). In short, the economic gains that many African American families made during the 1960s have stagnated or deteriorated.

Table 6.1

Racial Differences in Children's Living Arrangements

	LIVING WITH ONE PARENT	LIVING WITH TWO PARENTS*
White	17%	80%
African American	42%	43%
Native American	40%	42%
Asian American	11%	85%
Chinese	6%	
Japanese	12%	
Korean	10%	
Vietnamese	14%	
Filipino	10%	
Hispanic	20%	71%
Cuban	14%	78%
Mexican	15%	75%
Puerto Rican	40%	51%

Sources: D. Hernandez. (1988). Demographic trends and the living arrangements of children. In E. Hetherington & J. Arasteh (Eds.), Impact of divorce, single parenting and stepparenting on children (pp. 3–22). Hillsdale, NJ: Erlbaum; U.S. Bureau of the Census. (1983). *Marital status and living arrangements.* Washington, DC: U.S. Government Printing Office; Bureau of Indian Affairs. (1989). *Population and family status.* Washington, DC: Author.

* This includes adults who have remarried.

Hispanic poverty Economically, Hispanic adolescents do not fare much better. For example, almost 75% of all Hispanic children living only with their mother live below the poverty level, in contrast to only 45% of white children. Similarly, the median income for Hispanic heads of household has declined by 30% since 1973. Taken together, such statistics mean that nearly half of all Hispanic children are now living in poverty (Hernandez, 1988). Hispanic poverty is now comparable to that of African Americans and is expected to exceed African American poverty by the year 2000. Indeed, in 1985, Hispanic per capita income had already fallen below that of African Americans, with $6,613 for Hispanics, $6,840 for African Americans, and $11,671 for whites and Asian Americans (Miller, et al., 1988).

Native American poverty Poverty among Native Americans is even worse (Reeves, 1989). Their median family income is only $14,000—more than $6,000 less than the median income for all other American families. The poverty rate, at nearly 30%, is more than double the national rate and approaches 50% on the reservations where nearly one-fourth of all Native Americans live. Indeed, nearly 15% of those living on reservations survive on annual incomes of less than $2,500. Moreover, 40% of all Native Americans (or American Indian) children are living in one-parent families. Although the percentage of African American children living with only one parent is higher, Native American children are more likely than any other racial group to be living with neither parent.

Health

Many minority children born into poverty pay the price with their health (Children's Defense Fund, 1988). As a result of poor prenatal care, malnutrition, unsanitary living conditions, lack of immunization, and inadequate medical services, minority youths are at a serious disadvantage in terms of their overall health. For example, twice as many Native American children die from heart disease, influenza, and pneumonia as other children. Likewise, Chicano children have four times as much amoebic dysentery and twice as many cases of measles, mumps, tuberculosis, and hepatitis as other children. Not surprisingly, minority children die from illness at a 25% higher rate than white children.

Given these distressing statistics, it has been recommended that we expand and remodel our medical services for the poor and the culturally different. With doctors preferring to practice and to live in higher income communities, poor communities where many minorities live have a difficult time attracting physicians. Additional financial incentives could be established to attract doctors to these communities, at least on a rotating basis. Above all, our society needs to furnish the type of comprehensive medical coverage that permits the unemployed and the working poor to provide their children with medical services (Bane & Ellwood, 1989). As former Surgeon General Everett Koop stated:

> An estimated 30 million Americans, 15% of our population, have poor or no access to medical care. Basically a change needs to be made in the structure of the system. Not just a little change here and a little change there. We need a profound change across the board in the way we make medical and health care available to all our citizens (Koop, 1989).

Education

Academic deficits Living in such poverty, minority students understandably have more than their share of problems in school. As chapter 7 will explain in detail, minority students are at higher risk than white students of dropping out of school or of graduating from high school without adequate skills to qualify for good jobs. Minority students continue to lag behind white students in their reading, math, and science skills (National Assessment of Educational Progress, 1988). Likewise, nearly 50% of Native Americans and 20% of African Americans and Hispanic Americans quit high school before graduating, in contrast to only 12% of white students (U.S. Bureau of the Census, 1988). For committing the same types of infraction as whites, minority students are also more likely to be suspended and to be the victims of corporal punishment in our schools (Children's Defense Fund, 1985; National Coalition of Advocates for Students, 1988).

Ethnocentric curriculum Moreover, in most schools the needs and perspectives of minority students, regardless of their economic backgrounds, are excluded from the curriculum. From first grade through graduate school, most of the curriculum is still designed for only one group of students in that it is centered on the needs, the history, the literature, the goals, and the perspectives of white, middle-class males (Bennett, 1986; Gollnick & Chinn, 1986; Tiedt & Tiedt, 1986). For example, the required reading lists for high-school English classes show almost no change in the past 30 years in terms of including more female or minority authors (Center for Learning and Teaching Literature, 1988). In addition to finding little or nothing about your own racial group's history, literature, or cultural viewpoints in your school's curriculum, imagine, too, that you have never had a teacher of your same race at any point in your education. This is the reality for most minority students, given that only 12% of our public school teachers are minorities. Worse yet, by the year 2000 this number is predicted to dwindle to a mere 5% as a consequence of federal cutbacks in college aid for low-income students (Holmes, 1989).

Ethnocentric teaching methods Just as the curriculum is still primarily oriented toward white male students, so, too, are the methods that most teachers use to teach and to evaluate their students. That is, most teachers still use techniques that work against the learning styles and cultural values of many minority students. Our most prevalent teaching methods rely on noncooperative, individual, competitive methods of learning and grading. Students are seldom permitted, let alone encouraged, to work cooperatively with one another, to work in small groups, or to help tutor one another. Most teachers also expect their students to be outspoken, to ask questions without hesitation, to respond quickly to questions, to get directly to the point, to share opinions voluntarily, and to learn material primarily through the written word or through the teacher's verbal explanations.

While these methods may be well suited to the experiences and cultural values of most white, middle-class students, they are not the most effective ways of teaching minority students (Bennett, 1986; Gollnick & Chinn, 1986; Tiedt & Tiedt, 1986). For example, Hispanic and Native American students generally perform best in cooperative situations and in small groups. Rather than competing against other students in the "I win, you lose" game, these students learn best when working with one another toward a mutually beneficial goal—much like a basketball or football team. As you will see in chapter 7, these cooperative classroom methods have been extremely successful with both minority and white students, with males and females, and with the least and most skilled students.

Moreover, psychologists have discovered that our cultural backgrounds influence the ways in which we teach, learn, and respond to our teachers. For example, Native Americans tend to emphasize holistic learning in which meaning is derived from the pattern of the whole and in which visual cues tend to be more important than verbal cues. Thus, one Native American teacher explained that when she was learning from her mother how to prepare salmon, she was taught to speak up and ask questions only if she could not learn through silently observing. While watching her mother, she spoke up only at the point where she did not understand how to do "the backbone part." Rather than responding with words, her mother quietly picked up another whole fish and repeated the entire deboning process. Most white teachers would have relied on their own cultural style and begun to explain verbally how to take out the backbone, whereas the Native American parent or teacher presents "the backbone part" within the context of the whole fish. Within most Native American communities, learning and teaching occur through observing, not through constant questioning and talking (Tharp & Gallimore, 1988). A similar point has also been made about African American learning styles: Many African American children are expected to show or demonstrate what they know, rather than to tell it (Heath, 1989).

The point here is not whether the white, Native American, or African American method is correct or better, but that each culture has its own ways of teaching and learning. Since more than 88% of our teachers are white and since most have not been prepared for multicultural teaching, they often use culturally inappropriate methods in their classrooms. In contrast to ethnocentric teaching, **multicultural** teaching and a multicultural curriculum incorporate students' different cultural experiences and preferences. In other words, our schools need to be making more of an effort to achieve "cultural compatibility" between students, teachers, and the curriculum.

A major source of information about culturally compatible methods of teaching and learning is the Kamehameha Early Education Program (KEEP). Over a 20-year period KEEP has developed and studied a culturally compatible language arts program for kindergarten through third-grade children of Hawaiian ancestry, who are among the lowest achieving minorities in the United States. In KEEP classrooms, more than 2,000 Hawaiian children are educated each year by methods that are compatible with their culture. For example, most students work in small groups, teaching and learning from one another, while the teacher is interacting with another small group. In contrast to Hawaiian children with similar backgrounds in traditional public schools, the KEEP students approach national norms on their achievement tests. The KEEP model has also been in operation on the Navajo reservation of northern Arizona for 6 years, using methods compatible with Navajo students' culture. For example, researchers discovered that male and female students could not be assigned to work together since the Navajo admonish their children for playing or working with members of the other sex. Especially during adolescence, this sex segregation is extremely important in Navajo culture (Tharpe & Gallimore, 1988; Vogt, Jordan, & Tharp, 1987).

Among other studies (Atkinson & Hackett, 1988; Wing Sue, 1981), KEEP's data also remind us of the importance of the seemingly insignificant cultural differences in our communication styles. In actuality enormous differences exist between cultures regarding the courtesies and conventions of conversation—differences that can work to the detriment of minority students in a predominantly white school. For example, the time that teachers wait for a student's answer to a question varies considerably between white and Navajo teachers. Culturally conditioned to expect a quick response, white teachers wait less time than Navajo teachers, often going on to another student before the Navajo student has completed his or her response. When given a little longer to answer the question, however, the Navajo students participate more often and more enthusiastically, thus not leading their white teachers to believe they have low verbal abilities. On the other hand, native Hawaiian students have the opposite pattern: They frequently interrupt the teacher before he or she has even finished asking the question. Unfortunately, white teachers often misinterepret this cultural style as rudeness or impatience (Rowe, 1987; Tharp, 1989).

Once again, the issue is not which teachers or students are "right." The issue is to be aware of our students' cultural differences before misdiagnosing minority youths with such derogatory terms as slow, rude, uncommunicative, or inattentive. Unfortunately, however, most teachers are not trained in multicultural teaching techniques, and most of our schools do not offer white and minority students the benefits of a multicultural curriculum. Not surprisingly, many minority students feel ignored, misunderstood, excluded, or unwelcomed in our schools. In conjunction with our society's growing poverty rates, our ethnocentric teaching methods and curriculum too often leave minority students without the academic skills that would permit them to achieve a higher standard of living later in life. For these millions of young people, the "American dream" of being able to achieve a better standard of life than their parents is quickly vanishing (Children's Defense Fund, 1988).

Bilingualism and African American Dialect

Hispanic and Native American languages Unlike African American teenagers, many Hispanic and Native American adolescents do not speak English as their native language. As a consequence, these children, referred to as **limited English proficiency (LEP) students,** have special educational needs in terms of learning to speak **English as a second language (ESL).** Since mastery of the English language is closely aligned with educational and financial success in our society, having limited proficiency puts these Hispanic and Native American students at a disadvantage, both in school and in the marketplace. Perhaps partially as a consequence of these linguistic problems, Hispanic and Native American students are more likely than African Americans to quit school and to be further behind in terms of their academic skills (Miller, 1988; National Assessment of Educational Progress, 1988).

The problems associated with learning English as a second language and with **bilingual** education have been carefully delineated by educational researchers and linguists (Asher, 1984; Association for Supervision and Curriculum Development, 1987; Hakuta, 1986; National Clearinghouse for Bilingual Education, 1985, 1986; Willig, 1985). To begin with, some teachers still discriminate against students who speak English poorly or speak with a pronounced accent. These teachers attribute traits such as low intelligence, poverty, and low educational goals to their

LEP students. Moreover, many teachers providing English instruction to nonnative speakers are poorly qualified. For example, a national study of elementary schools showed that only one third of the teachers who were teaching English to LEP students had been trained in ESL techniques, and nearly half were unable to speak the students' native language (National Clearinghouse for Bilingual Education, 1985). Such findings raise serious questions about our schools' commitment to LEP students.

Although in 1973 the U.S. Supreme Court ruled that our public schools have to provide special programs for students who cannot speak English, there has been an ongoing and heated debate on how bilingual education should be designed. Before the Court's 1973 ruling, Native American and Hispanic students were often severely reprimanded, mocked, and punished for speaking their native languages in school. For example, many older Native Americans can still remember the humiliating experiences of having their mouths washed out with soap and being forced to sew buttons on the knees of their pants and then kneel for hours for having spoken their tribal language on school grounds (McDonald, 1989). While such cruelty is now illegal, a number of controversial questions related to bilingual education still plague us: Should all courses be offered in both languages? If so, how should this be arranged in the school curriculum? How long should students stay in a bilingual program? What is the least confusing way to teach English as a second language, especially to older students who do not want a babyish curriculum?

While many of these questions remain unanswered, recent research has at least helped dispel a number of earlier assumptions about bilingual education and bilingual children (Association for Supervision and Curriculum Development, 1989; Nielsen & Fernandez, 1982; Willig, 1985). Contrary to the long-standing belief that knowing one language somehow gets in the way of mastering a second language, we now know that being proficient in a native language paves the way for proficiency in a second language. In fact, students who are proficient in their native language and become proficient in a second are superior to monolingual students in terms of cognitive development, academic achievement, and linguistic awareness. In this vein, there is a certain irony to the fact that we spend billions of dollars trying to teach English-speaking students a second language, while we spend virtually no money trying to maintain the native languages of those students learning to speak English as a second language. Research has also shown us that skillfully implemented bilingual programs do result in higher academic performance, although far too few LEP students receive this quality instruction.

African American dialect In a somewhat similar vein, many African American students speak a nonstandard dialect that has created considerable controversy among educators and minority parents (Foster, 1986; Golb, 1980). Although African American adolescents are native English speakers, a number speak a particular dialect that renders their speech almost unintelligible to outsiders. As Box 6.2 illustrates, this African American dialect, while innovative and creative, has a cadence, metaphors, conjugation of verbs, and use of pronouns that distinguish it from standard English. The problems thus become: Should we discourage African American adolescents from using this dialect in school? Does this dialect interfere with African American students' learning standard English or with mastering other academic skills? If we encourage this dialect in schools, how should it be incorporated into the curriculum?

On the one hand, there are those who argue that this dialect should be encouraged and built upon in the school curriculum. In this regard, linguistic studies of inner-city African American youths have found that their speech is not haphazard or unstructured but is governed by specific rules and organization (Baugh, 1983; Labov, 1972). On the other hand, even African American parents and educators themselves have argued that this street vernacular and its nonstandard dialect are an educational, social, and financial handicap to African American youths. From this perspective, we are doing a disservice to African American adolescents by encouraging them to use this dialect in school or work settings. For example, one former math teacher and author concluded, after her lifelong career teaching African American students, that black dialect is an impediment to learning math in that it lacks the prepositions, conjunctions, and pronouns necessary to learn basic mathematical principles, such as "from" and "between" in subtraction and "by" and "into" in division (Orr, 1987). In general, however, the research is inconclusive, leaving both educators and parents in the midst of the continuing debate.

Segregated Neighborhoods and Schools

A number of social scientists have argued that if we permitted poor families to live in wealthier neighborhoods, the negative impact of poverty on children would be less severe (W. Wilson, 1987). According to this viewpoint, if children grow up in a community where many of their neighbors commit crimes, abuse drugs, and have children out of wedlock, they will be more likely to model their own behavior accordingly. Since these kinds of behavior are less common in higher income neighborhoods, poor children would have better role models and more reinforcement for good behavior if they could live alongside wealthier neighbors. Likewise,

6.2 ADOLESCENT VOICES

African American Dialect

The Three Little Pigs "The wolf came to the big house. And the wolf say, 'let me in!' And the pig say, 'no, no, no my shinny shin shin!' He huff, and he puff, and he tough, and he rough, but he couldn't knock the house down. And ol wolf say, 'I'm a jump down you chimney!' And that ol pig put some water on the fire till when you could jump in it, and the lil pig had cook greens. Yeah, he fool him! He jump in the hot water, and the pig, he had greens and wolf! Greens and wolf!"

Source: S. Houston. (1974, March). Black English. *Psychology Today,* p. 45.

Dialogue "Aw, man, you trying to show you grandma how to milk ducks. Best you can do is to confidence some kitchen mechanic out of a dime or two. Me, I knocks de pad with them cack broads up on Sugar Hill and fills 'em full of melody. Man, I'm quick death and easy judgment. Youse just a home boy. Jelly, don't try to follow me."

Source: H. Foster. (1986). *Ribbin and jivin and playin the dozens: The persistent dilemma of inner city schools* (p. 220). Cambridge, MA: Ballinger.

schools in affluent neighborhoods are generally superior to those in poor communities, so poor children would receive the benefit of a better education under this plan. Others, however, contend that living in the same neighborhoods as, and going to the same schools with, richer children would provoke resentment among the poor. Being less successful in these more demanding schools and having fewer material goods, low-income children might become more hostile and less motivated as a consequence of being constantly reminded of the disparities between themselves and their wealthier classmates and neighbors.

Reviews of the research on integrated schools and integrated neighborhoods offer some partial answers (Cook, 1984; Mayer & Jencks, 1989; McKenna & Ortiz, 1988). It appears that poor teenagers who live in higher income neighborhoods or attend schools with higher income classmates do attain more schooling and achieve more academically than teenagers from similar families who live in lower income neighborhoods or who attend predominantly nonwhite schools. In other words, minority students are more likely to stay in school and to achieve more academically when they attend predominantly white schools where families' incomes are higher. A student body's average family income, therefore, does seem to have some impact on how much the average student learns.

Given these findings, it is discouraging to discover that most of our neighborhoods are still highly segregated by race and income. The poor live among the poor, the rich among the rich. For example, residential segregation of whites and African Americans in large metropolitan areas remains nearly as high now as in the 1960s (National Research Council, 1989). It is also discouraging that most minority students still attend predominantly minority schools. (Children's Defense Fund, 1985; Lee, 1985; McDonald, 1989; National Research Council, 1989). For example, nearly 70% of Hispanic American students attend schools with at least half minority enrollment, and more than 25% attend schools with at least 90% minority enrollment (Vincent & Drum, 1984). Despite efforts to integrate schools, racial isolation of Hispanic students actually increased from 1972 to 1980, regardless of the area of the country, the socioeconomic status of the students, or the type of school (Rock, 1985). As a consequence of our segregated schools and the inferior quality of education in most predominantly minority schools, many educators and researchers have concluded that our schools generally perpetuate, rather than reduce, the racial, economic, and social inequalities in our country (Apple, 1982; Children's Defense Fund, 1985, 1988; Ogbu, 1978).

Racism: Prejudice and Discrimination

Even those minority adolescents who are successful students, however, often share a common experience with low-income minority youth: racial discrimination and prejudice. Although we have undeniably made strides toward becoming a less racist society, racism is by no means extinct. In fact, more than 25 years after the enactment of the landmark Civil Rights Act of 1964, schools are experiencing what many educators characterize as a disturbing resurgence of racism. Racist incidents have included racist graffiti, disputes over Confederate flag waving, and fistfights. For example, in Water Valley, Mississippi, trouble started when a group of white students waved the Confederate flag during an African American history program at the high school. The incident prompted African American athletes to boycott the school's teams. Likewise, in Falls Church, Virginia, Asian American students have been the victims of racial hostility. As one white male student said, "We just don't like them. There's so many of them, you just can't get away from them ('gooks,' 'chinks')." In the midst of the hostility, many minority teenagers report that those who will "act white" are subjected to less discrimination and ostracism than those who maintain their racial or ethnic identities (Viadero, 1989). Indeed, African American teenagers have reported that acting "raceless" is essential for gaining their teachers' and their peers' acceptance (Fordham, 1988).

In some communities, racial incidents have been attributed in part to hate groups, notably the young people known as **skinheads** (Viadero, 1989). These loosely organized gangs range in age from 13 to 25 and are known for shaving their heads, wearing **neo-Nazi** insignia, and preaching violence against racial minorities and Jews. The Jewish Anti-Defamation League of B'nai B'rith estimated that in 1989 there were 2,000 skinheads active in 21 states—up from 1,000 in 12 states just 8 months earlier. What concerns many educators is the escalation in more subtle brands of prejudice, such as name calling, racist jokes, and social segregation. While some feel that the Reagan administration's reversals of earlier civil rights legislation are the primary cause of the rise in racism among the young, others feel the rapid growth of racial minorities in our society is largely responsible.

ARE YOU SURE? 6.3

Recognizing Racism in Books

1. Does the author assume all readers are white and Christian?
2. Are facts romanticized to glorify the white culture's perspective and to gloss over cruelty and inequity toward minorities?
3. Are minorities mentioned as social problems rather than as contributors to society?
4. Are minorities described in degrading terms (the "roaming, ferocious, primitive Indians")?
5. Are words used to support a Caucasian perspective without presenting other views (Indians "massacred," but whites "fought battles"; white leaders are "assertive and outspoken," but minority leaders are "aggressive and rebellious")?
6. Are the contributions of other cultures ignored? (Is Africa mentioned only in relation to slavery, but not in relation to its rich civilizations?)
7. Do evolutionary charts end with a white man, as if he were somehow more truly "evolved" than anyone else?
8. Are oversimplified generalizations perpetuated (fat, eye-rolling Chicano; sombrero-wearing, fiesta-loving bandito; inscrutable, slant-eyed Oriental; switchblade-toting Puerto Rican)?
9. Does the minority person progress by adapting to white standards? Is success defined only by white-male values?
10. Is the oppression of minorities accurately and candidly represented?
11. Does a white person consistently resolve the problems for the minority group member?
12. Are the only nonwhite heroes and heroines people who avoided serious conflict with or contributed to white society?
13. Does the book encourage the passive, patient acceptance of injustice?
14. Do portrayals of nonwhite cultures create a genuine respect or perpetuate the "quaint natives in costume" syndrome?
15. If authors and illustrators are not members of the groups being written about, is there anything in their background that specifically qualifies them to write this book?

Source: National Education Association. *How fair are your children's textbooks? 1975. Hyattsville, MD: Author.*

Is this young woman beautiful? How ethnocentric are your definitions of "beauty" and "ugliness"?

Whatever the underlying reasons, a congressional committee studying racial incidents concluded that racial bigotry is on the rise among the young (House Select Committee on Children, Youth and Families, 1987).

Cultural Standards of Beauty

Another subtle form of prejudice that can affect minority adolescents is our ethnocentric standards of beauty. As the research in chapter 2 demonstrated, our physical appearance has a considerable impact on our self-esteem and on the ways in which other people respond to us, especially during adolescence when we are so very aware of the physical changes we are undergoing and when we are trying to establish our sexual and social self-confidence. In a society where racism and ethnocentrism still exist, our standards of beauty often reflect a purely Caucasian viewpoint. Considering what we see on television and in magazines, which are touted as more "beautiful": thin noses; thin lips, rounded eyes; long legs; a relatively tall, slender body; and straight hair or full, thick lips; slanted eyes; dark skin; coarser, curly hair; and a fuller figured or short body? Not surprisingly, television has been found to convey a highly ethnocentric world view in which being youthful and beautiful by white standards is more valuable than being dark skinned or having distinctly ethnic features (Berry & Mitchell, 1982; Greenberg, 1986; Liebert & Sprafkin, 1988).

In one of the earliest studies to examine the self-concepts of minority children, African American preschoolers were shown white dolls and black dolls. Then they were asked to answer a series of questions. In this highly publicized study, most of the African American children wanted to play with the white dolls because they perceived the black doll as bad and ugly (Clark & Clark, 1947). More recent studies have also demonstrated that some adolescents from minority cultures try to look "white," believing that their own racial features and body types are uglier. Some Chicanos, for example, powder their necks to look lighter skinned, and some Asian Americans undergo plastic surgery to give their eyes a less slanted and more rounded look. Similarly, some Asian American males have mocked females of their own race for being too flat chested or too short legged by white standards of beauty (Wing Sue, 1981). This is not to say that all minority adolescents feel bad about their racial features. It is, nonetheless, a reality that our standards of physical beauty still tend to be restricted to white features and body types.

UNIQUE CHARACTERISTICS OF MINORITY CULTURES

Before examining the characteristics of minority cultures, it's essential to avoid the tendency to stereotype. Although certain traits tend to be representative of each racial group, some adolescents of every race and socioeconomic class do not conform to their group's norm. Particularly since socioeconomic factors play such a large role in our behavior and attitudes, racial differences may be less important in distinguishing adolescents from one another than are their parents' income and educational experiences. Before characterizing adolescents on the basis of their race, therefore, we must, at the very least, consider their socioeconomic backgrounds and their parents' life-styles.

Members of the same racial groups also differ from one another as a result of their varying degrees of assimilation into white, middle-class culture. **Assimilation** is the process of taking on the values, behaviors, and perspectives of the dominant, or majority culture. For example, some Asian American teenagers have become so assimilated into white culture that they have little sense of a separate ethnic or racial identity; a situation that has been alluded to as the **banana syndrome,** meaning that while yellow skinned on the outside, these young people are white on the inside in regard to their behavior and values (Mindel, 1981). Whether assimilation is good or bad and to what degree minorities should or should not strive to become assimilated into white culture are matters of personal opinion. Should we work toward eliminating our cultural differences, or should we work toward preserving our unique racial or ethnic heritage and perspectives? Minorities as well as whites have different opinions on this "melting pot" issue. As Box 6.4 illustrates, some minority parents believe their children have become too assimilated into white culture, forgetting their own history and heritage (Roots III, 1985). On the other hand, an Asian American father expressed the other perspective: "I don't worry whether my children feel 'banana' or not as long as they are top banana in this rat race" (Mindel & Habenstein, 1976, p. 120).

A CLOSER LOOK 6.4

African American Parents Bemoan Too Much Assimilation

Are African American adolescents growing up without an adequate awareness of their parents' struggles against racism and without an awareness of the racism that still exists in our society? Have middle-class African American youths become too assimilated into white culture, thereby losing all sense of racial identity? According to some African American professionals and parents, the answers to these questions are a resounding—and disappointing—yes. In the words of one African American 15-year-old from Bethesda, Maryland, whose parents are both lawyers, "Look, I know I didn't come here on the Love Boat, but racist thought is disappearing."

Such attitudes among African American youngsters, however, have aroused concern among a number of parents whose hard-fought, firsthand battles against racism in the 1950s and 1960s seem like irrelevant, ancient history to their upper-middle-class offspring. These parents fear that in the process of becoming assimilated into white culture, their children have learned too little about African American history and culture and have had too few experiences with racism to understand how to handle discrimination when it occurs. Further, in seeking to protect their children from the hardships and prejudice that they themselves endured, these well-educated, financially successful parents now worry that their children will be unable to cope with the racism they will eventually encounter in their adult years—being denied promotions in leading corporations, being called "niggers," being disapproved of for marrying whites. Without an awareness of racism in the world at large or of the stereotypes of African Americans that still prevail, young African Americans may not have the resources to understand or to cope with discrimination when it arises.

Some older adolescents have begun to share their parents' perspectives, as evidenced by the comments of African American students in several universities. A young man at Harvard commented that although he himself had no problems dating white girls in high school, his relationships seldom prevailed in the face of objections from the girls' parents. On the basis of his high-school experiences, this young man chose to attend Harvard, where he felt there would be a large enough African American student population, and where he now dates only African American girls who he said, "are even prettier than white girls." Similarly, a female African American student maintained that despite having been raised in a predominantly white suburban environment, her self-confidence has improved as a consequence of having chosen to attend an all-African American college.

In sum, it appears that a certain segment of the African American middle class is seeking to reaffirm its racial heritage and to recapture a lost sense of racial identity that distinguishes it from the white middle class.

Source: Roots III: Souls on ice: A post civil-rights generation struggles for identity. (1985, June 10). *Newsweek* pp. 82–84.

In addition to considering the degree to which minority adolescents are assimilated, we want to be careful not to lump all members of a single racial group together as one people. For example, although Native Americans comprise less than 1% of our population, there are 200 languages and more than 500 tribes with vast differences in customs, wealth, and political organization among them (Reeves, 1989). Similarly, the category "Hispanics" refers to, among others, people from Cuban, Mexican, or Puerto Rican origins. Although these groups share certain Hispanic characteristics, they also differ markedly from one another along a number of dimensions. For example, more than twice as many adolescents of Puerto Rican origin live in single-parent families as do those of Cuban or Mexican origins. Similarly, twice as many Japanese American as Chinese American children are growing up in single-parent families, yet both groups are typically lumped together and discussed as Asian Americans (Laosa, 1988).

Unfortunately, most of our generalizations about adolescents from various racial groups are not based on data from the individual subgroups within each racial category. This shortcoming needs to be kept in mind, therefore, as you read and generalize about African, Hispanic, Native, and Asian American youths and their families. It is beyond the scope of this chapter to consider the differences within each of these four groups. In this spirit, the brief descriptions that follow focus on characteristics that tend to typify each group.

African American Adolescents

Demographics With a population of 28.9 million, African Americans represent our largest racial minority. Half live in the South, comprising more than 30% of the population in Mississippi, Louisiana, and South Carolina; and 10% live in the metropolitan New York area (U.S. Bureau of the Census, 1988). Unlike their parents, today's African American adolescents are more likely to live in urban than in rural areas, a shift that has had far-reaching ramifications for the types of family and community environment in which most African American adolescents now live (Slaughter, 1990; Spencer, Brookins, & Allen, 1985; M. Wilson, 1989).

The family As African Americans migrated away from rural communities to urban areas to find work and improve their living conditions, the family's influence over children diminished. The extended family, which has historically provided emotional and economic support for African American children and their parents, has virtually disappeared in urban areas. The African American family's exodus to urban areas particularly weakened its influence on teenage children, who have increasingly become the victims of the neighborhood influences in high crime, high poverty neighborhoods. Many impoverished urban parents now worry that street gangs, drugs, unemployment, and poverty have destroyed the influence of the extended family. While some urban African American parents may talk nostalgically about going home to rural communities, the economic realities of the future ensure that by the year 2000 virtually all African American adolescents will be growing up in urban, not rural, areas (House Select Committee on Children, Youth and Families, 1983).

In conjunction with the extended family's diminishing influence, the number of one-parent households has skyrocketed, leaving African American teenagers in an even more precarious situation in terms of money, adult supervision, and

If you could not be the race you are now, which race would you choose to be? Why?

familial support. Almost 60% of all African American children are now living with a divorced or never-married mother, and nearly 85% will spend at least a part of their childhood in a single-parent home. Sadder still, children in these female-headed families have only 25% of the total income of all African American families (National Resource Council, 1989. See Figure 8.1 in chapter 8).

Male and female roles Although socioeconomic status has a greater impact than race on our male and female sex roles, historical influences have contributed to somewhat different notions of masculinity and feminity among African Americans (Gary, 1982; McAdoo, 1981; Myers, 1980; Rose, 1980; Staples, 1982; Willie, 1981).

Historically, slavery and racism have forced African American females to be more economically independent than white females. This heritage, coupled with the financial plight of many African American men in our present-day society, contributes to the self-reliant attitudes that many of the adolescent females have toward their own education and employment. Unlike white females who have historically been socialized to depend on males for financial support and social status, African American females have not been socialized to view their own financial or educational success as a threat to their femininity. In this sense, then, African Americans have historically had less restrictive sex roles than whites in that females are encouraged to be economically self-sufficient.

Another important factor influencing the community is the shortage of African American males (Gibbs, 1988). One-fourth of all African American males are in prison, and 1 in 20 is murdered, nearly 50% of the time by another African American male in incidents involving drugs, robbery, or gang fights. For example, in 1977 more young African American men were murdered than were killed from 1963 to 1972 in the Vietnam War. Then, too, suicide rates among African American teenage males and young men have tripled since 1960. A common thread connecting these statistics is the use of drugs and alcohol, which is rampant in ghetto areas where most African American males are growing up. This tragic situation has been explained by a number of factors in addition to poverty and racism: the media's glamorization of violence and drugs, easy access to handguns, and strained relationships between police and African American communities. African American females are faced with a unique and troublesome dilemma: dating and marrying in a society where males of their race are increasingly in short supply and where racial prejudice still puts the African American female at a greater social disadvantage than Asian American or Hispanic girls.

Hispanic American Adolescents

Demographics Of the 16.9 million Hispanics in our society, nearly 50% live in California or Texas with another 20% living in Florida and New York (U.S. Bureau of the Census, 1988). A highly urbanized population, 75% of all Hispanic Americans live in metropolitan areas in the Southwest. Within our nation's Hispanic population, the 10.3 million Mexican Americans represent the largest share, with the next most populous group being our Puerto Rican population of 2.6 million. Although comprising only 8% of our present population, Hispanics will become the largest within the next 30 years. Of special importance to those of us interested in adolescents, Hispanics already constitute the largest racial minority in terms of young people, since more than half of all Hispanics are under the age of 25. Given the youthfulness of Hispanic Americans, our school population and young work force will increasingly become more Hispanic than African American.

The family In contrast to the white middle-class emphasis on competition and independence, Hispanic families have traditionally encouraged cooperation and interdependence (Camarillo, 1984; Martinez & Mendoza, 1984; Moore & Pachon, 1985). Striving for individual gain at the expense of others is considered selfish and egotistical. This cooperative, less self-centered attitude is demonstrated, for example, in classroom studies showing that Hispanic students are generally more cooperative than their white peers from similar socioeconomic backgrounds (D. Johnson & Johnson, 1985). Hispanic families have also traditionally placed greater emphasis than white families on familial loyalty, respect for the elders, and obedience to parents.

Although most Hispanic parents place a high value on their children's education, very few have a college degree and many are not proficient in English. For example, in the five states with the highest concentration of Hispanic families, only 5% of the parents have a college degree (McKenna & Ortiz, 1988). This has meant that many Hispanic parents are unable to help their preschool children in the basic skills of reading, writing, and language. Nevertheless, even among less assimilated and less well-educated parents, many enroll their children in Catholic schools at great financial sacrifice in order to obtain what they believe to be the best possible education (McKenna & Ortiz, 1988; Sanchez & Cordoza, 1985).

Migrant families Although only a small percentage of the entire Hispanic population is involved in migrant agricultural work, this life-style still affects about 800,000 children. Of all migrant families, only 6% are African American, only 13% are white, and nearly 70% are Hispanic. As a consequence of disease, malnutrition, and the physical strains of stoop labor, migrant workers die 20 years earlier than the average white American. Given their frequent moves and sporadic attendance,

---

A CLOSER LOOK 6.5

Recommendations for Educating Hispanic Adolescents

- Eliminate curriculum tracking.
- Be sensitive to the indirect, less assertive manner in which they may express their need for help or their confusion.
- Use more cooperative teaching methods, such as peer tutoring and small group projects, instead of so many individualistic, competitive techniques.
- Offer more students an effective bilingual education program taught by teachers trained in teaching English as a second language.
- Enroll in a special summer language program those Hispanic students who fail an English proficiency test taken before entering high school.
- Keep Hispanic students literate in Spanish as a way of enhancing their English skills and their future marketability as bilingual employees.
- Appeal to students' sense of family pride as a motivational tool.
- Provide them with immediate reinforcement and feedback.
- Deemphasize the lecture approach in favor of a more direct, experiential, and personal approach.
- Do not rely too heavily on activities that require verbal assertiveness, such as debating, criticizing other classmates' ideas, or oral presentations in front of large groups.
- Make the curriculum more multicultural and avoid textbooks that are racist or ethnocentric.
- Correct prejudicial stereotypes and offer positive role models.
- Provide multicultural counseling that avoids ethnocentric or racist practices and assumptions.
- Do not pressure or punish students when their family responsibilities prevent them from completing homework or from attending class.
- Don't Anglicize their names (for example, Joe for Jose).

Sources: Grossman, H. (1984). *Educating Hispanic students.* Springfield, IL: Charles Thomas; National Commission on Secondary Schooling for Hispanics. *Make something happen: A report on secondary schooling for Hispanics.* New York: Author.

most adolescents in migrant families are also years behind other teenagers academically. Furthermore, since migrant families are often forced to rely on adolescent children's incomes for their family's survival, attending school often has to come second to working. Then, too, given their own academic deficiencies and poor English skills, most migrant parents are unable to offer their children much assistance in learning how to read, write, or do math at home (Diaz, Rivera, & Trotter, 1989; Interstate Migrant Education Council, 1987).

A number of suggestions have been offered for improving the educational plight of these migrant teenagers. One is to provide more teachers who will travel to migrant camps to give special tutoring in the workers' homes. Disseminating a monthly bilingual newsletter, offering toll-free hotlines for counseling and referral services, and providing more computerized instruction for individual tutoring have also been recommended. More efficient methods for keeping up-to-date academic records of each student's skills and needs and for transferring this information rapidly from school to school are also being devised. Descriptions of these exemplary programs and procedures are now available from the Interstate Migrant Education Council (1987).

Male and female roles Non-Hispanics have often assumed that the ethic of **machismo** creates a male hierarchy in Hispanic families. According to the popular stereotypes, Hispanic males, unlike non-Hispanic males, try to prove their manhood through aggression and domination, especially of females. As was the case with the Moynihan Report's descriptions of African American matriarchy and the subjugation of African American males, however, the concept of machismo is more fiction than fact (Camarillo, 1984; Martinez & Mendoza, 1984; Moore & Pachon, 1985). Like some non-Hispanic males, certain Hispanic men try to establish their masculinity through physical aggression, acts of daring, and the subjugation of girls and women. These types of "macho" behavior in any group, however, are more closely aligned with education and income than with race or ethnicity. Moreover, among Hispanics the concept of machismo includes more than aggression and domination. It also involves taking care of one's responsibilities, providing emotionally for all family members, and protecting one's children, especially girls, while making sure that children respect their mother and give her due status.

This is not to say that sexism does not exist in Hispanic families. Indeed, as in many non-Hispanic families, it does. For example, both Hispanic and white parents generally have higher educational goals for their sons than for their daughters. Yet contrary to stereotypes, more Hispanic than white parents want their daughters to go to college (Sanchez & Cordoza, 1985). Moreover, gender roles have become less restrictive in Hispanic families in response to our society's more liberal views. Indeed, like African American females, Hispanic girls are now enrolling in and graduating from college at higher rates than Hispanic males (Zambrana, 1982). In short, once family income and parents' education are taken into account, gender roles within Hispanic families seem to be far more similar to than different from gender roles in non-Hispanic families.

Native American Adolescents

Like that of Hispanics, the Native American population is remarkably young. Although accounting for less than 1% of our population, half of our Native American population of 1.5 million is under the age of 20. Underscoring the fact that Native

Americans are not one people with identical life-styles or needs, however, it is worth reiterating that 200 separate languages are spoken among nearly 500 different Indian tribes. The Pueblo Indians, for example, are known to be among the most peaceful cultures in the world and are renowned for their skills in making jewelry and pottery. Even among the Pueblo, however, differences exist between the Hopi, the Zuni, and the Santo Domingo tribes.

Like African American and Hispanic adolescents, but unlike their own parents' generation, most Native American teenagers now live in urban areas. Indeed, only one fourth of the Indian population still live on reservations, the largest of which, the Navajo, has approximately 104,500 residents. As Figure 6.2 illustrates, nearly half of the total Native American population live in Arizona, New Mexico, California, and Oklahoma—the state with the largest percentage of Native Americans (U.S. Bureau of the Census, 1989a).

The family As Native Americans have migrated from their reservations to cities in search of work and education, their families have fallen victim to worse economic and social conditions. Almost 40% of the children now live in one-parent families, and the median family income of $13,600 falls more than $6,000 below our national

FIGURE 6.2
Number of American Indians, Eskimos, and Aleuts, 1980

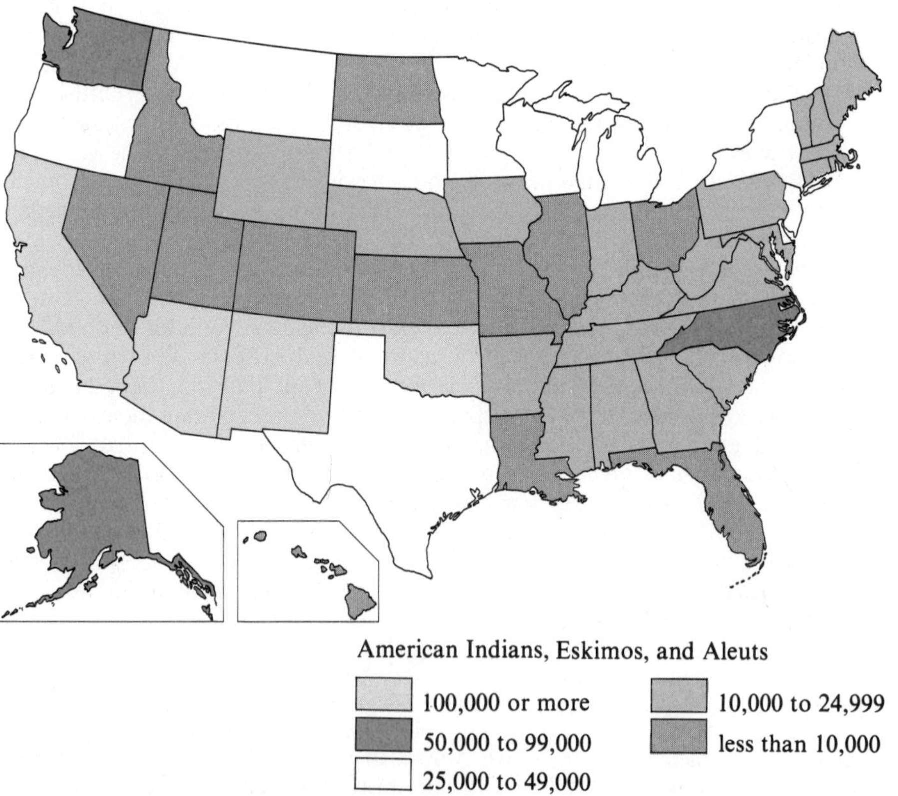

Source: U.S. Department of Commerce. (981). Bureau of the Washington, DC: Census.

family average. Although the percentage of African American children living with only one parent is higher, no other racial group has as many children living with neither parent as do Native Americans. Moreover, the unemployment rate of nearly 30% is almost twice the national average. One third of the adults who live on reservations have less than an eighth-grade education, while the average Native American adult has completed only 9.6 years of school, the lowest of any racial group in comparison to the national average of 10.9 years. Nearly one third of these adults are classified as illiterate, and only one fifth of the men have a high-school education. Sadly, a 1988 report by the Bureau of Indian Affairs indicates that many Native American parents do not have as high expectations as other minorities for the educational achievements of their children, at least in part because of their own negative school experiences and poor academic skills (Reeves, 1989).

Many Native American adolescents are also growing up in homes where alcoholism has disrupted the family. Native American leaders and health experts have long identified alcoholism as a pervasive and entrenched problem in their communities, estimating that 60% of all Native American children are now affected by their parents' alcoholism. Of every 10 deaths among Indians, 4 are alcohol related, and recent research has found that up to 25% of infants in some tribes are born mentally and physically impaired by fetal alcohol syndrome. Given these circumstances, it is not surprising that Native American adolescents are the most deprived racial minority in our society. In comparison to any other minority group, these youths have the highest dropout rates and the highest rates of poverty, unemployment, suicide, alcoholism, nutritional deficits, disease, and learning disabilities (Harras, 1987; LaFromboise, 1988; Reeves, 1989; Watts & Lewis, 1988). More than 50% of urban Native American teenagers and 80% of reservation teenagers are involved in heavy alcohol or drug use, as compared to 23% of their urban, non-Native American counterparts (U.S. Senate Committee on Indian Affairs, 1985).

Despite these hardships, many adolescents are still socialized within the family to adopt certain traditional Native American values. Like Hispanic Americans, Native American youths are socialized to respect their elders, to esteem old age, and to be less assertive, less verbal, and less boastful than white children. Talking about your own accomplishments, asking too many questions, talking too much, or looking your elders too directly in the eyes is considered rude and self-centered. Similarly, unless the group can benefit, competing against your peers or trying to win at someone else's expense is viewed as vain and egotistical.

Education Unfortunately, the family's values and traditions sometimes work against their children's success in school (Carnegie Foundation, 1989; Deloria, 1978, 1988; McDonald, 1989). Given the family's emphasis on humility, community service, and nonverbal communication, Native American students are often viewed as too unassertive, too timid, or unambitious by their non-Indian teachers. Unlike their white classmates, most of these students are less interested in acquiring personal status, competing against others, setting long-term goals, delaying gratification, adhering to strict time schedules, asserting their opinions publicly, questioning their teachers, or being put in situations where their personal accomplishments are made public. For example, Native American students who are asked a question that a classmate has missed might choose not to answer in order not to embarrass the other student. Likewise, Native Americans who are taught to respect their elders by avoiding direct eye contact and by not speaking unless spoken to are caught in a dilemma when they are expected to raise their hands, participate in lengthy class discussions, and look their teachers in the eyes when speaking or listening. Because most schools rely almost exclusively on verbal modes of learning, they may actually work against the strengths of Indian students, such as their keen analytical skills and unusually refined spatial abilities.

Indian students can also be made to feel out of place in school when they are expected to engage in classroom activities that defy their religious traditions. For example, planting seeds as part of a science project is considered taboo in some tribes, as is touching certain revered animals. In a similar vein, some Indian religions still believe in reincarnation and in physical illnesses being caused by a person's own misdeeds. Without a sensitivity to these cultural differences, educators put Indian students in difficult and embarrassing situations.

In comparison to the education of African American and Hispanic students, the education of Native American students is also somewhat more complicated due to its unique history and subsequent political complications (Deloria, 1978; 1988; McDonald, 1989; Reeves, 1989). Unlike other minority students, most Native American children have historically attended schools operated by the **Bureau of Indian Affairs (BIA).** Operated as boarding schools, these BIA schools forced children to live away from their own families and subjected them to a number of humiliating experiences designed to assimilate them into white culture. In 1924, when the U.S. government finally granted citizenship to Native Americans, a California court was the first to rule that the children must be allowed to attend public schools, even if a BIA school was located nearby. Thus, by 1943 almost half of all Native American children were attending public schools, and most BIA schools had been converted to day schools. Although 90% of the children now attend regular public schools, an ongoing debate has continued regarding the role of local tribes and the BIA in the educational process.

In order to maintain their traditions, many Indians have wanted control of their own schools in their own communities. In 1966, this wish finally became legally possible when the federal government granted the Navajo control of their own school system. This policy was further expanded under President Richard M. Nixon's administration, which ruled that any Native American community wishing to control its schools must be allowed to do so. These Education Amendments of 1972 also provided funding for culturally relevant programs for Native American students in public schools. Yet, while many Indian leaders say they want greater control over their own schools, they are simultaneously fearful that this federal policy of self-determination is a guise for reducing federal support (Reeves, 1989).

The tradition of educating Native Americans in BIA boarding schools, in combination with the high rates of alcoholism and of poverty and the ethnocentric teaching techniques, has placed these students at a tremendous educational disadvantage. As a result, somewhere between 30% and 50% of all Native Americans quit school without earning a high-school diploma. Of those few who do attempt to go to college, nearly 80% drop out (Carnegie Foundation, 1989). Recognizing the severity of the situation, in 1989 Secretary of Education Lauro Cavazos called for a national study of the problems afflicting Native American students (West, 1989).

Asian American Adolescents

Demographics About the only two similarities between Asian and Native American adolescents are the size of their population and their geographic location.

Like Native Americans, Asian Americans are a small group, numbering only approximately 7.3 million, about 2% of our population. Most Asian Americans also live in the West, with almost half residing in California and Hawaii. Although small in number, Asian Americans are our fastest growing minority group and will probably represent about 3% of our population by the year 2000 (U.S. Bureau of the Census, 1989b). This rapid growth came about primarily as a consequence both of the federal government's relaxing our immigration laws in 1965 and of the wars in Cambodia and Vietnam, which brought a new surge of immigrants from Hong Kong, Taiwan, South Korea, India, Vietnam, Cambodia, and the Philippines.

The "model" minority? What has distinguished Asian Americans from other minorities, however, is not their rapid growth but their amazing financial and educational success. By almost every educational measure, young Asian Americans are outpacing everyone else. Not only do they take more advanced high-school courses and graduate with more credits than other American students, they finish in the top ranks of Scholastic Aptitude Test scores, national achievement tests, and high-school grade point average. Asian American students also have the highest rates of college and high-school graduation of all American students, including whites. For example, in the fall of 1987, Asian Americans accounted for 14% of the entering freshmen at Harvard, 25% at Berkeley, and 20% at the Massachusettes Institute of Technology (Brand, 1987). As a consequence of their splendid academic performance and subsequent financial status, Asian Americans are often referred to as our society's model minority—a model against which Hispanic, African, and Native Americans are often compared. Yet a closer look at our nation's history and recent statistics casts a somewhat different light on this "ideal minority."

To begin with, Asian Americans, like other nonwhite minorities, have encountered racism in our society (Phillips, 1981). As the numbers of Japanese and Chinese immigrants grew on the West Coast during the early part of this century, animosity and suspicion increased among whites. As a consequence, Asian Americans were legally barred from attending white schools, from citizenship, from intermarrying with whites, and from owning property. In 1924 the Federal Immigration Act denied immigration rights to Asians, and not until 1954 did the U.S. government grant them the right to become citizens. Furthermore, Asian Americans were disliked and suspected for practicing their "heathen" religions and for continuing to speak their native languages.

Worse yet, when America became engaged in World War II with Japan, we forced Japanese Americans into "relocation camps." A historical fact that many of us would prefer to forget, nearly 110,000 Japanese Americans were forced to leave their homes and businesses and to live in isolated camps until the war's end. Our racism against Asians was further highlighted by the fact that citizens of Italian and German descent were not "relocated" into these camps, despite our being at war with their ancestral homelands also. Not surprisingly, this imprisonment ruined many Japanese American families financially. Yet the new generation of Japanese Americans who emerged from this experience were tremendously motivated to achieve upward mobility in our society once they were permitted to leave the camps.

Although most Asian Americans of Chinese, Japanese, and Korean backgrounds are educationally and financially successful, not all Asian American teenagers are now part of an ideal minority group. Many who have immigrated more recently from Southeast Asia live in poverty and are not succeeding in school or in the

A CLOSER LOOK 6.6

Children of the Rainbow: Interracial families

Between 1970 and 1980 the number of racially mixed marriages in the United States rose from 310,000 to 613,000. Today the 1 million children of these marriages—sometimes referred to as *rainbow children*—must often confront difficulties that extend beyond the racism in our society at large: What should children do when they prefer one parent's racial heritage and culture over the other's? How should parents show respect for one another's culture when they may feel that the children are rejecting one in favor of the other? How should rainbow children relate to those relatives who disapprove of their parents' marriage?

Among other difficulties, interracial dating becomes particularly problematic for many rainbow children. In trying to explain, one clinical psychologist with an African American father and a white mother remembers feeling that his family was perfectly normal until he became a teenager: "It didn't hit me until I was 13 and asked a white girl for a date. Then one of my black buddies pulled me aside and told me the facts of life." It also goes without saying that many rainbow children encounter racial prejudice from both racial groups, although this often depends on the shade of the child's skin. Adolescents with white-Hispanic or white-Asian backgrounds are generally more easily assimilated into the majority culture and experience less racism than those with one African American parent. Even when their skin is light, children with African American heritage are generally perceived and treated by our society as if they are African American.

With our high divorce rate, interracial children can be put in an especially volatile situation if their parents' marriage ends. Since one parent usually assumes the primary responsibility for raising the children, how is he or she to acculturate the child into the second culture without the former spouse? As one white mother whose child's father is African American admitted. "I'm not a black person and I'm not going to indulge my daughter in something that's not natural to me." Yet are such decisions fair to the racially mixed child?

Despite the experts' concerns, not all adolescents from racially mixed marriages feel that their lives have been complicated by being biracial. For example, Aminta Steinback, 15, and her 13-year old sister, Tirien, whose father is white and whose mother is African American, claim that being biracial is "no big deal." Aminta said she does not prefer to be with other interracial youngsters any more than someone with red hair prefers other redheads. "It's not like we cling together," she explained, "though we might say, 'Oh, we're both mixed—that's neat.' " As for Tirien, she said that her white friends do not comment on her mixed heritage "except to say that I'm lucky I've got a year-round tan."

Sources: Children of the Rainbow. (1984, November 19). *Newsweek*, pp. 120–122.

work place. For instance, at least 50% of the Indochinese immigrants in California are on welfare, as are more than 35% of all Vietnamese families nationwide (U.S. Bureau of the Census, 1988). Moreover, many of these war-scarred adolescent immigrants still struggle with learning English, adapting to Western ways, and overcoming the horrifying experiences of war in their former homelands (Brand, 1987). Given that asking for help is not easy for most Asian Americans, these teenagers are likely to suffer in silence, while believing that somehow their own willpower and stoicism can resolve their problems (Wing Sue, 1981).

Moreover, even among those Asian American adolescents who are successful students, the stereotype of the ideal minority falls somewhat short of the reality. First, some parents may be pushing their children too hard, contributing to depression, stress, and suicide. Many of these parents even dictate their children's college courses with an eye to a prosperous future. As one college student recalled, when she changed her major from pre-med to a doctoral program in psychology, her parents were disappointed that they would not have a "real doctor" in the family (Brand, 1987).

This excessive pressure to succeed also contributes to stereotyping Asian American teenagers as "grade grinds" who do nothing but study. In fact, however, Asian American teenagers are as involved in extracurricular activities as are other teenagers, with nearly a third competing on varsity athletic teams and more than one fifth participating in their student governments (Peng, 1984). Nevertheless, the stereotype of the Asian American teenager as the relentless bookworm persists. Although we might initially think such a positive stereotype is harmless, it can actually produce racism and discrimination. In some schools, for example, students resent their Asian classmates on the basis of the stereotypical assumption that they are star students who will always outperform non-Asians. Not only have Asian American students in some schools encountered their classmates' racial slurs—chink, gook, chop suey—they have also been harassed, threatened, ostracized, and physically attacked (House Select Committee on Children, Youth and Families, 1987; Viadero, 1989).

It also appears that Asian American students are being discriminated against on the basis of their race in college admissions. Given that these students typically surpass whites in academic skills and college entrance exam scores, some colleges have set quotas on the number of Asian students they will admit. As a consequence of activists' racial discrimination charges, some universities—notably Stanford—have eliminated these quotas and agreed to admit students on the basis of their academic credentials without regard to race. The quota problem is not confined to colleges, however. At San Francisco's competitive and prestigious Lowell High, Chinese Americans constitute 45% of the student body; but since no city school is legally permitted to have more than 45% of its students from any single ethnic group, Lowell is having to turn away qualified Chinese American students—to the dismay of the students, parents, and staff (Brand, 1987).

In sum, most Asian American teenagers are more fortunate than Hispanic, Indian, or African American adolescents in terms of their educational and financial success. This does not mean, however, that they are a model minority in terms of having escaped racial discrimination in the past or in the present. Neither does the remarkable success of many of these young people mean that their lives are without certain stresses that are directly related to their being a member of a racial minority.

The family Although not all Asian Americans have achieved academic and financial success, a number of distinctive aspects of their families do appear to contribute to their children's academic motivation (Levine & Rhodes, 1981; Phillips, 1981). Asian American children are socialized to be quiet, self-disciplined, and respectful toward their elders. Since the extended family has traditionally exerted a major influence over the young, these adolescents are often more motivated to succeed in order to bring honor to the family. Traditionally, Asian parents have also discouraged their children from expressing their emotions publicly, from being too assertive, or from being too self-disclosing. Indeed, self-disclosure is considered rude and boastful, rather than as a mark of intimacy or esteem for another person. The unrestrained displays of physical affection that characterize most non-Asian families in our society are perceived by many Asian parents as insincere and socially inappropriate. For example, one Asian American college student explained that she did not hug or kiss her parents publicly, as she did her white friends, in order not to embarrass her family (Wing Sue, 1981).

Given this family training, Asian American adolescents, although far less traditional in most cases than their parents, still appear somewhat less assertive, less physically demonstrative, and less self-disclosing than their non-Asian peers. Being socialized to rely less heavily on verbal interaction and verbal assertiveness, Asian American students generally achieve higher scores in their mathematics and science skills than in their verbal and language skills. As a result, they predominate in the fields of engineering, the sciences, and mathematics. For example, since 1981, Asian American teenagers have won 20 of the 70 scholarships awarded by the Westinghouse Science Talent Search, our nation's oldest and most prestigious high-school science competition. Nevertheless, the data do not warrant our creating a new stereotype of Asians as students whose interests and talents are narrowed to mathematics and science. To the contrary, many Asian students excel in the arts and in languages. New York's famed Juilliard School of the Arts, for example, has a student body estimated to be 25% Asian American (Brand, 1987).

As is the case with Hispanic and Native American teenagers, Asian American adolescents are generally more assimilated into white, middle-class culture than were their parents and older relatives. For instance, during the 1970s many Asian American college students defied their parents' sanctions against public displays of emotion and assertively participated in civil rights protests alongside other students. Noted for their academic and vocational achievement, some Asian youths are causing their elders further concern by questioning our society's emphasis on money, social status, and competition (Wing Sue, 1981).

COUNSELING MINORITY YOUTH

Because of the diversity among minority youths, psychologists and counselors are urging mental health practitioners to be trained in multicultural counseling (Atkinson & Hackett, 1988; LeFrambois, 1988; Pedersen, 1985; Ramirez, 1990; Shultz, 1982). Multicultural counseling involves a sensitivity to the cultural differences in communication styles, values, religions, and traditions that each individual brings from his or her own family and culture. As Box 6.7 illustrates, multicultural counseling demands an awareness of the distinctions between our society's various racial and religious groups.

This multicultural awareness, however, goes beyond merely respecting each adolescent's racial heritage or cultural traditions. It demands that we alter our own behavior and our own interpretations of the adolescent's attitudes and behavior. Indeed, we will be challenged to suspend our own visions of reality in order to see the realities of others. For example, when interacting with Native American teenagers who may not look us directly in the eyes during a conversation, we have the choice to interpret this behavior ethnocentrically as a sign of shyness, guilt, discomfort, disinterest, disrespect or to interpret their behavior from a

A CLOSER LOOK 6.7

Counseling an Adolescent from a Minority Culture

John C. is a 21-year-old student majoring in electrical engineering. He first sought counseling because he was failing courses. These academic difficulties became apparent during the first quarter of his senior year and were accompanied by headaches, indigestion, and insomnia. Since he had been an excellent student in the past, John felt that his lowered academic performance was caused by illness. However, a medical examination failed to reveal any organic disorder. He was difficult to counsel because he would respond to inquiries with short but polite statements and would seldom volunteer information about himself. He avoided any statements that involved feelings and presented his problem as a strictly educational one.

As the sessions progressed, John became less anxious and more trusting of the counselor. Much of his earlier difficulty in opening up was caused by his feelings of shame and guilt at having to come to a counselor. He was concerned that his family might discover this help and that it would disgrace them. He was also embarrassed by his academic failures. However, when the counselor informed him that many Chinese students experienced similar problems and that these sessions were completely confidential, John seemed relieved. As he became increasingly able to open up, he revealed problems typical of Chinese students who have strong traditional cultural values and whose self-worth and identity are defined with the family.

John's parents had always had high expectations of him and constantly pressured him to do well in school. They seemed to equate his personal worth with his ability to obtain good grades. This pressure caused him to spend endless hours studying, and generally he remained isolated from social activities. This isolation did not help him to learn the social skills required in peer relationships. His background was in sharp contrast to the informality and spontaneity demanded in Caucasian relationships. Therefore, his circle of friends was small, and he was never really able to enjoy himself with others.

John experienced a lot of conflict, because he was beginning to resent the pressure his parents put on him. He had always harbored secret wishes about becoming an artist but was pressured into engineering by his parents. His deep-seated feelings of anger toward his parents resulted in failure in school and in his physical symptoms.

The case of John C. illustrates some of the following conflicts encountered by many Chinese students attempting to maintain traditional Chinese values: (a) there is often a conflict between loyalty to the family and personal desires for independence; (b) the self-restraint and formality in interpersonal relationships often result in a lack of social experience and subsequent feelings of loneliness; (c) the family pressure to achieve academically accentuates feelings of shame and depression when the student fails.

Source: D. Wing Sue (Ed.). (1981), *Counseling the culturally different.* New York: Wiley Interscience. Reprinted by permission.

multicultural perspective as a sign of respect, courtesy, and cultural tradition. Likewise, when interacting with adolescents whose cultures respect silence and observation more than assertion and talking, we have the choice of judging these attitudes as less mature and passive or as attentive and sophisticated.

Developing this kind of awareness and respect requires more of us than merely discussing or reading about cultural, religious, or racial differences. It also requires more than just our good intentions. Indeed, it is an arduous undertaking and challenge to move beyond our own racial, religious, or ethnic culture—whatever

A CLOSER LOOK 6.8

Nationwide Successes in Improving Minority Education

Although we still have a long way to go in improving education for minority students, we have had countless successes in hundreds of projects nationwide:

Perry Preschool Program One of the most carefully evaluated and best-known early childhood efforts is the Perry Project in Ypsilanti, Michigan. Low IQ, poor children were placed in a 2-year preschool program in the mid-1960s and followed through age 19. Compared to children from similar backgrounds not enrolled in a preschool, these children gained 11 points in IQ scores, had 20% greater high-school graduation rates, were half as likely to be arrested, and were 60% more likely to be employed. A similar program now under way in Texas that provides comprehensive 9-month training for Hispanic parents and their children under age 4 is showing both parents returning to school to earn their high-school diplomas and children more advanced in their verbal skills and more eager to learn.

Cooperative Integrated Reading and Composition In Baltimore, cooperative learning and peer tutoring are reaching many students once written off as dropouts. The students work in small learning teams of mixed abilities, tutoring and helping one another master materials presented first by their teacher. Significant increases have occurred in these students' reading and language skills in comparison to those of the control group. In a similar approach being tried with Minnesota's Chippewa tribe, educators use traditional Indian values as building blocks for classroom techniques. For example, cooperation among students is encouraged because of the Indian belief that it is not right for one student to embarrass another by succeeding when the other fails.

continued

that culture may be—to take the perspective of another person, put aside our own cultural perceptions and interpretations of reality, and withhold judgment of those who do not share our particular truths. Should you decide to try becoming more multicultural in your interactions with others, you will be challenged to recognize and to admit your own cultural blinders—the ways in which you define good and bad behavior from your own ethnocentric perspectives, the ways in which you interpret and judge others' actions, and the ways in which you will be tempted to try to "reform them" to your own cultural ways and attitudes "for their own good."

CONCLUSION

Once again we want to remind ourselves not to create new stereotypes of adolescents from minority cultures to replace the old stereotypes. Not all Asian American teenagers are mathematical wizards. Not all Native American teenagers respect their elders. Not all African American teenagers know how to talk rap or other forms of creative dialect. Not all Hispanic teenagers speak Spanish as a native language. As we try to recognize general cultural differences, we have to keep in mind that income and parents' educations generally have more impact than race on adolescents' behavior and attitudes. Moreover, most minority youths are more

Box 6.8 continued

New Futures An alternative school for pregnant teenagers in Albuquerque, New Mexico, provides its students with pregnancy counseling, nutritional care, parental training, child care, and vocational training. The school has served more than 4,300 students since it opened in 1970, and more than 75% of its students graduate, in contrast to less than half of all teenage parents in regular high schools.

Young Black Scholars Seeking to increase the number of African American high-school graduates, 100 African American men in Los Angeles work with African American ninth graders and their parents to monitor students' schoolwork, provide after-school and Saturday tutoring, fund college scholarships, and sponsor enrichment experiences. The program seeks to have 1,000 students graduate with a grade point average above 3.0 in Los Angeles county by 1990.

Parents as Partners In Kansas City the National Council of La Raza helps Hispanic parents learn how to provide a home environment that will enhance their childrens' academic success. It also helps parents develop leadership skills so that they can participate more effectively in the local school decision-making process.

Middle College High School In Long Island City, New York, the high school is actually located on the campus of LaGuardia Community College. High-school students benefit from intensive counseling, flexible schedules, self-paced curricula, and individualized attention while gaining firsthand exposure to the world of higher education.

Madison Plan One of the most impressive college-recruitment programs is now under way at the University of Wisconsin at Madison. The university plans to double its number of minority undergraduates over a 5-year period by creating 150 new financial-aid packages for low-income students and by raising $4 million for scholarships.

Source: A. McBay. (1989c, Summer). Improving education for minorities. *Issues in Science and Technology*, pp. 41–47.

acculturated than their parents and tend, as do white adolescents, to abandon the old ways for the new.

These cautions notwithstanding, our Hispanic, Native American, and African American adolescents are far more likely than whites or Asian Americans to have a unique set of problems associated with poverty, racism, and poor education. To pretend that these differences between most whites and nonwhites are not related to racial discrimination is naive. To pretend that these differences are solely related to racial discrimination is also naive. The reasons underlying these problems are too complex for us to assign blame to any single cause. Likewise, there is no single, simple plan that will lift us out of this dilemma.

QUESTIONS FOR DISCUSSION AND REVIEW

Review questions

Cite specific statistics and research findings to justify your answers.

1. What are enthocentrism and blaming the victim? Give examples.
2. How do African American, Hispanic, and Native American teenagers compare to white and Asian American teenagers in terms of health, income, and educational skills?

3. How do the traditional values and characteristics instilled by the families of Hispanic, African American, Native American, and Asian American adolescents differ? In what ways are they similar?
4. Explain the significance of the Moynihan Report at the time it was published and at present.
5. How do the gender roles of Hispanic, white, and African American adolescents compare? What might account for their similarities or differences?
6. In what ways are adolescents from migrant families unique? What suggestions have been made for resolving their special problems?
7. In terms of size, geographic location, and rate of growth, how do each of our minority groups compare?
8. In what ways are Asian American adolescents an example of the ideal minority? In what ways is this an inaccurate stereotype?
9. In what ways are our schools ethnocentric? Specifically, what types of change in our schools would be beneficial for minority youth?
10. What are the limitations of our research regarding minorities?
11. Which factors do and which do not account for the increased poverty in our society?
12. In what ways has the education of Native American students been historically unique compared to the education of other minorities?
13. What are the controversies surrounding the issues of bilingualism and African American dialect?
14. In what ways does racism still exist in our society and in what ways has it diminished?
15. What significance docs each of these terms have regarding the well-being of minority youths: ESL, BIA, LEP, and KEEP?

Discussion questions

1. In what ways are your own behavior and attitudes ethnocentric? How have you been guilty of blaming the victim?
2. If you had to be a member of a racial group other than your own, which would you most and which would you least want to be? Why?
3. In what ways have your attitudes about different racial groups changed since your adolescence? How did these changes occur?
4. How do you feel about standards of physical beauty in terms of racial and ethnic features?
5. How assimilated do you think minorities should become? Should we all try to "melt" into the same pot? Why or why not?
6. In terms of improving the lives of minority adolescents and their families, how would you prioritize the suggestions made by economists, educators, and other experts?
7. Which of your stereotypes about minorities has this chapter dispelled? Where did your initial impressions about each group come from?
8. If you were a teacher or counselor in a high school with a large minority population, what would you do to create a motivating environment for your students or clients?
9. How were your own education and upbringing ethnocentric or racist? In what ways were they multicultural and nonracist?
10. What has most angered you while reading this chapter? What has most saddened you? What has made you feel most optimistic?

GLOSSARY

acculturation The adopting of the values and behaviors of the majority culture.

assimilation The merging of groups with different backgrounds into one group with a common identity.

banana syndrome Asian Americans who have become so assimilated into white culture that they have little sense of a separate ethnic or racial identity.

bicultural Having equal familiarity with two cultures, usually as a consequence of having been raised in a bicultural family.

bilingual The ability to speak or write in two languages.

Bureau of Indian Affairs (BIA) The federal governmental agency that oversees American Indian affairs.

English as a second language (ESL) A term referring to the study of English by people whose native language is something different.

ethnocentrism The tendency to view one's own ethnic or racial group and its standards as the basis for judging others, usually seeing others' standards and behavior as inferior.

Limited English Proficiency (LEP) Students whose abilities in writing or speaking English are limited by their having learned another language as their native tongue.

machismo Among Hispanics, the belief that men should assume responsibility for the emotional and financial well-being of their families and should instill in children a respect for their mothers. In its anglicized meaning, to be overly aggressive and dominant, to be "macho."

multicultural Reflecting the perspectives of more than two cultures simultaneously.

neo-Nazi Recently organized groups based on Hitler's Nazi doctrines that preach and practice violence against Jews and racial minorities.

skinheads Loosely organized gangs of neo-Nazi teenagers and young adults known for shaving their heads.

REFERENCES

Apple, M. (1982). *Cultural and economic reproduction in education.* Boston: Routledge & Kegan Paul.

Asher, C. (1984). *Helping Hispanic students to complete high school and enter college.* New York: ERIC Clearinghouse.

Association for Supervision and Curriculum Development. (1989). *Building an indivisible nation: Bilingual education in context.* Washington, DC: Author.

Atkinson, D., & Hackett, G. (1988). *Counseling non-ethnic American minorities.* New York: Charles Thomas.

Bureau of Indian Affairs. (1989). *Population and family status.* Washington, DC: Author.

Bane, M. & Ellwood, D. (1989). One fifth of the nation's children: Why are they poor? *Science, 245,* 1047–1053.

Baugh, J. (1983). *Black street speech.* Austin: University of Texas Press.

Bennett, D. (1986). *Comprehensive multicultural education.* Boston: Allyn Bacon.

Berry, G. & Mitchell, C. (Eds.) (1982) *Television and the socialization of the minority child.* New York: Academic Press.

Billingsley, A. (1968). *Black families in white America.* Englewood Cliffs, NJ: Prentice-Hall.

Brand, D. (1987, August 31). The new whiz kids. *Time,* pp. 42–51.

Camarillo, A. (1984). *Chicanos in a changing society.* Cambridge, MA: Harvard University Press.

Carnegie Foundation for the Advancement of Teaching. (1989). *Tribal colleges: Shaping the future of Native Americans.* Washington, DC: Author.

Center for Learning and Teaching Literature. (1988). *A study of book length works taught in high school English courses.* Albany, NY: Author.

Children's Defense Fund. (1985). *Black and white children in America.* Washington, DC: Author.

Children's Defense Fund. (1988). *Vanishing dreams: The growing economic plight of America's young families.* Washington, DC: Author.

Children of the rainbow (1984, November) *Newsweek,* pp. 120–22.

Clark, K. & Clark, M. (1947). Skin color as a factor in racial identification of Negro children. *Journal of Social Psychology, 11,* 140.

Cook, T. (1984). *School desegregation and black achievement.* Washington, DC: National Institute of Education.

Cottingham, P., & Ellwood, D. (Eds.) (1989). *Welfare policies for the 1990s.* Cambridge, MA: Harvard University Press.

Deloria, V. (Ed.) (1978). *The schooling of Native America.* Washington, DC: American Association of Colleges for Teacher Education.

Deloria, V. (1988). *Custer died for your sins.* Norman, OK: University of Oklahoma Press.

Diaz, P., Rivera, V., & Trotter, R. (1989). *The effects of migration on children.* Philadelphia, Pennsylvania Department of Education.

Fordham, S. (1988). Racelessness as a factor in black students' school success. *Harvard Educational Review, 58,* 54–84.

Foster, J. (1986). *Ribbin, jivin and playin the dozens: The persistent dilemma of inner city schools.* Cambridge, MA: Ballinger.

Gary, L. (1982). *Black men.* Berkeley, CA: Sage.

Gibbs, J. (1988). (Ed.) *Young, black and male in America: An endangered species.* Dover, MA: Auburn House.

Golb, E. (1980). *Runnin' down some lines: The language and culture of black teenagers.* Cambridge, MA: Harvard University Press.

Gollnick, D., & Chinn, P. (1986). *Multicultural education.* Columbus, OH: Charles Merrill.

Greenberg, B. (1986). Minorities and the mass media. In J. Bryan & D. Zillman (Eds.), *Perspectives on mass media effects* (pp. 165–188). Hillsdale, NJ: Erlbaum.

Grossman, H. (1984). *Educating Hispanic students.* Springfield, IL: Charles Thomas.

Guthrie, R. (1976). *Even the rat was white: A historical view of psychology.* New York: Harper & Row.

Hakuta, K. (1986). *Mirror of language: The debate on bilingualism.* New York: Basic Books.

Harras, C. (1987). *Issues in adolescent Indian health: Suicide.* Washington, DC: U.S. Department of Health and Human Services.

Heath, S. (1989). Oral and literate traditions among black Americans living in poverty. *American Psychologist, 44,* 367–373.

Hernandez, D. (1988). Demographic trends and the living arrangements of children. In E. Hetherington & J. Arasteh (Eds.), *Impact of divorce, single parenting and stepparenting on children* (pp. 3–22). Hillsdale, NJ: Erlbaum.

Hispanic mental health bibliography. (1978). Los Angeles: University of California Press.

Holmes, J. (1989, May 23). Minority teachers. *Education Week,* p. 26.

House Select Committee on Children, Youth and Families. (1983). *U.S. children and their families.* Washington, DC: U.S. Congress.

House Select Committee on Children, Youth and Families. (1987). *Race relations and adolescents: Coping with new realities.* Washington, DC: U.S. Congress.

Houston, S. (1974, March) Black English. *Psychology Today,* p. 45.

Interstate Migrant Education Council. (1987). *Migrant education.* Denver.

Johnson, C. & Sum, J. (1988). *Vanishing dreams: The growing economic plight of America's young families.* Washington, DC: Children's Defense Fund.

Johnson, D., & Johnson, R. (1985). *Learning together and alone.* Englewood Cliffs, NJ: Prentice-Hall.

Koop, E. (1989, August 28). The health care mess. *Newsweek,* p. 10.

Labov, W. (1972). *Language in the inner city.* Pittsburgh: University of Pennsylvania Press.

Ladner, J. (1971). *Tomorrow's tomorrow: The black woman in America.* New York: Anchor Books.

LaFromboise, T. (1987). Special commentary from the Society of Indian Psychologists. *American Indian Alaska Native Mental Health Research, 1,* 51–53.

LaFromboise, T. (1988). American Indian mental health policy. *American Psychologist, 43,* 388–397.

Laosa, L. (1988). Ethnicity and single parenting in the U.S. In E. Hetherington & J. Arasteh (Eds.), *Impact of divorce, single parenting and stepparenting on children* (pp. 23–49). Hillsdale, NJ: Erlbaum.

Lee, V. (1985). *Access to higher education: The experience of blacks, Hispanics and low socioeconomic status whites.* Washington, DC: American Council on Education.

Levine, G., & Rhodes, C. (1981). *The Japanese American community: A three generational study.* New York: Praeger.

Liebert, R., & Sprafkin, J. (1988). *The early window: Effects of television on children and youth.* New York: Pergamon.

Martinez, J., & Mendoza, R. (1984). *Chicano psychology.* New York: Academic Press.

Mayer, S. & Jencks, C. (1989). Growing up in poor neighborhoods: How much does it matter? *Science, 243,* 1441–1445.

McAdoo, H. (Ed.). (1981). *Black families.* Beverly Hills, CA: Sage.

McBay, S. (1989, Summer). Improving education for minorities. *Issues in Science and Technology,* pp. 41–47.

McDonald, D. (1989, August 2). Stuck in the horizon: A special report on the education of Native Americans. *Education Week,* pp. 1–16.

McKenna, T. & Ortiz, F. (1988). *The Broken Web.* Claremont, CA: Thomas Rivera Center.

Miller, S., Nicolau, S., Orr, M., Valdivieso, R., & Walker, G. (1988). *Too late to patch: Reconsidering opportunities for Hispanic and other dropouts.* Washington, DC: The Hispanic Policy Development Project.

Mindel, C. (1981). *Ethnic families in America.* New York: Elsevier.

Mindel, C., & Habenstein, R. (Eds.). (1976). *Ethnic families in America.* New York: Elsevier.

Moore, J., & Pachon, H. (1985). *Hispanics in the United States.* Englewood Cliffs, NJ: Prentice-Hall.

Moynihan, D. et al. (1965). *The Negro family: Case of national action.* Washington, DC: U.S. Department of Labor.

Myers, L. (1980). *Black women: Do they cope better?* Englewood Cliffs, NJ: Prentice-Hall.

National Assessment of Educational Progress. (1988). *The science report card. The mathematics report card.* Princeton, NJ: Author.

National Clearinghouse for Bilingual Education, (1985). Descriptive phase of national longitudinal study released. *Forum, 8,* 1.

National Clearinghouse for Bilingual Education. (1986). Academic growth of high school age Hispanic students. *Forum, 3,* 2–4.

National Coalition of Advocates for Students. (1988). *School discipline and race.* Boston: Author.

National Commission on Secondary Schooling for Hispanics. (1984). *Make something happen: A Report on secondary schooling for Hispanics.* New York: Author.

National Council of La Raza. (1985). *The education of Hispanics.* Washington, DC: Author.

National Education Association (1975). *How fair are your children's textbooks?* Hyattsville, MD: Author.

National Research Council. (1989). *A common destiny: Blacks and American society.* Washington, DC: Author.

Nielsen, F., & Fernandez, R. (1982). *Achievement of Hispanic students in high schools.* Washington, DC: National Center for Education Statistics.

Ogbu, J. (1978). *Minority education and caste: The American system in cross-cultural perspective.* New York: Academic Press.

Orr, E. (1987). *Twice as less: Black English and the performance of black students in mathematics and science.* New York: Norton.

Pedersen, P. (Ed.). (1985). *Handbook of cross cultural counseling and therapy.* Westport, CT: Greenwood Press.

Peng, R. (1984) *National longitudinal study of the high school class of 1980.* Washington, DC: U.S. Department of Health, Education and Welfare.

Phillips, V. (1981). *The abilities and achievements of Orientals in North America.* Beverly Hills, CA: Sage.

Ramirez, M. (1990). *Psychotherapy and counseling with minorities.* Riverside, NJ: Pergamon Press.

Reeves, S. (1989, August 2). The high cost of endurance. *Education Week,* pp. 2–4.

Rock, D. (1985). *Factors associated with decline of test scores in high school seniors.* Princeton, NJ: Educational Testing Service.

Rogoff, R., & Morelli, G. (1989). Perspectives on children's development from cultural psychology. *American Psychologist, 44,* 343–348.

Roots III: Souls on ice: A post-civil-rights generation struggles for identity. (1985, June) *Newsweek,* pp. 82–84.

Rose, F. (Ed.). (1980). *The black woman.* Beverly Hills, CA: Sage.

Rowe, M. (1987). Wait time: Slowing down may be a way of speeding up. *American Educator, 11,* 38–43.

Ryan, W. (1972). *Blaming the victim.* New York: Random House.

Sanchez, A., & Cardoza, D. (1985). *Educational aspirations of Hispanic parents.* Los Alamitos, CA: National Center for Bilingual Research.

Shultz, J. (1982). *The counselor or as gatekeeper.* New York: Academic Press.

Slaughter, D. (Ed.). (1990). *Black children and poverty.* San Francisco, CA: Jossey-Bass.

Spencer, M., Brookins, G., & Allen, W. (Eds.). (1985). *The social and affective development of black children.* Hillsdale, NJ: Erlbaum.

Staples, R. (1982). *Black masculinity.* San Francisco: Black Scholars Press.

Super, C. (1982). Secular trends in child development. *Newsletter of the Society for Research in Child Development,* 10–11.

Tharp, R. (1989). Psychocultural variables and constants: Effects on teaching and learning in schools. *American Psychologist, 44,* 349–359.

Tharp, R., & Gallimore, R. (1988). *Rousing minds to life: Teaching, learning and schooling in social context.* Cambridge, England: Cambridge University Press.

Tiedt, P., & Tiedt, I. (1986). *Multicultural teaching.* Boston: Allyn Bacon.

U.S. Bureau of the Census (1983) *Marital status and living arrangements.* Washington, DC: Government Printing Office.

U.S. Bureau of the Census. (1988). *School enrollment and characteristics of students: 1986.* Washington, DC: U.S. Government Printing Office.

U.S. Bureau of the Census. (1989). *Money income and poverty status in the U.S.: 1988.* Washington, DC: U.S. Government Printing Office.

U.S. Bureau of the Census. (1989b). *Projections of the population of the U.S.: 1983 to 2080.* Washington, DC: U.S. Government Printing Office.

U.S. Senate Committee on Indian Affairs (1985). *Indian juvenile alcoholism and BIA schools.* Washington, DC: U.S. Government Printing Office.

Viadero, D. (1989, May). Schools witness troubling revival of bigotry. *Education Week, 35,* 1.

Vincent, A., & Drum, L. (1984). *Selected statistics on the education of Hispanics.* Washington, DC: National Council of La Raza.

Vogt, L., Jordan, C., & Tharp, R. (1987). Explaining school failure, producing school success: Two cases. *Anthropology and Education Quarterly, 18,* 276–286.

Wallace, P. (1978). *Black macho and the myth of superwoman.* New York: Dial Press.

Watts, T., & Lewis, R. (1988). Alcoholism and Native American youth: An overview. *Journal of Drug Issues, 18,* 69–86.

West, P. (1989, October 18). Cavazos issues call for national study of problems plaguing Indian students. *Education Week,* p. 20.

Willie, C. (1981). *A new look at black families.* New York: General Hall.

Willig, A. (1985). A meta-analysis of the effectiveness of bilingual education. *Review of Educational Research, 55,* 269–317.

Wilson, M. (1989). Child development in the context of the black extended family. *American Psychologist, 44,* 380–385.

Wilson, W. (1987). *The truly disadvantaged.* Chicago: University of Chicago Press.

Wing Sue D. (Ed.), (1981). *Counseling the Culturally Different.* New York: Wiley Interscience.

Zambrana, R. (Ed.). (1982). *Work, family and health: Latina women in transition.* New York: Hispanic Research Center, Fordham University.

7 Adolescents and the Schools

CHAPTER OUTLINE

TRANSFORMATIONS IN SECONDARY EDUCATION

The School Population
Teachers
Educational Spending

ADOLESCENTS' ATTITUDES TOWARD SCHOOL

ACADEMIC ACHIEVEMENT: A NATION AT RISK?

High School Diplomas and College Degrees
National Achievement Scores
- Reading
- Mathematics
- Science

Scholastic Aptitude Test Scores

AT-RISK YOUTHS

Prevalence and Costs
Quality of Education
Educational Programs That Work
- Cooperative Learning Strategies
- Mastery Learning
- Programs That Teach Thinking
- School Within a School
- Business Funding
- Multicultural Curriculum
- Early Childhood Education

SCHOOL VIOLENCE

Truancy
Suspensions and Corporal Punishment

FACTORS INFLUENCING ACADEMIC ACHIEVEMENT

Learning Disabilities
Cognitive Styles
Overexposure to Lead
Parents' Income and Education

CONCLUSION

GOALS AND OBJECTIVES

This chapter will enable you to:
- Identify the major problems confronting adolescents and their teachers in our schools
- Assess the academic performance of today's adolescents relative to youth in former decades and in other countries
- Examine the reasons underlying students' underachievement and failure
- Discuss the various techniques, policies, and programs that have improved adolescents' academic performance and school behavior
- Describe the problems of at-risk youth
- Compare today's schools with those of yesteryear

CONCEPTS AND TERMINOLOGY

at-risk youths
attention deficit disorder
Beethoven project
cognitive style
confluence model
contingency contract
dyslexia
learning disability
mastery learning
multicultural curriculum
schools within schools
self-fulfilling prophecy
tracking

TRANSFORMATIONS IN SECONDARY EDUCATION

The School Population

In contrast to those in earlier periods in our nation's history, today's schools have assumed an unprecedented role in the lives of adolescents. Whereas in 1900 only 11% of all adolescents were enrolled in school, today 80% are attending school (Hampel, 1984). An institution once reserved almost exclusively for white males from well-to-do families, our public schools now serve a multicultural population of males and females from all socioeconomic backgrounds, including students with physical and mental handicaps. For example, nearly 60% of New Mexico's public school students are from minority cultures, as are 93% in Washington, DC, and 51% in California. Similarly, between 1976 and 1982 alone, the number of students who spoke a language other than English in their homes grew by nearly 30% (Plisko, 1984).

It is now estimated that by 2020 the number of white children will decline by about 13%, while the number of African American youths will increase by 22% and the number of Hispanic children will more than triple (Plisko, 1984. See Figure 7.1). Put differently, within the next decade minority children will account for one third of our school-age population (Holmes, 1989). In comparison to the national population increase of 3.3% between 1980 and 1985, our Hispanic American population increased by 16%. Moreover, with half of all Hispanic Americans being younger than 25, they are the youngest group in our society (McKenna & Ortiz, 1988). These changes in the schools' population have introduced adolescents to a far more varied peer group in terms of race and socioeconomic backgrounds. Our more multicultural student population has also introduced teachers to the reality that the curriculum and teaching methods must be expanded and diversified to fit the needs of our more diverse society.

Teachers' Characteristics and Attitudes

Adolescents' teachers are also a far cry from the schoolmarms of the past. Nearly half of today's teachers have bachelor's degrees, while most others have graduate degrees. As in the past, however, most adolescents' teachers are female, outnumbering male teachers by about 30% in our secondary schools. Likewise, most secondary school principals are white males, with only 7% of all principals being female and only 4% being minorities. On the average, adolescents' teachers are 37 years old, have 13 years of teaching experience, and earn about $30,000 a year (Carnegie Foundation, 1988a). Given their low salaries, it is not particularly

FIGURE 7.1
Minority enrollment in public schools, 1980

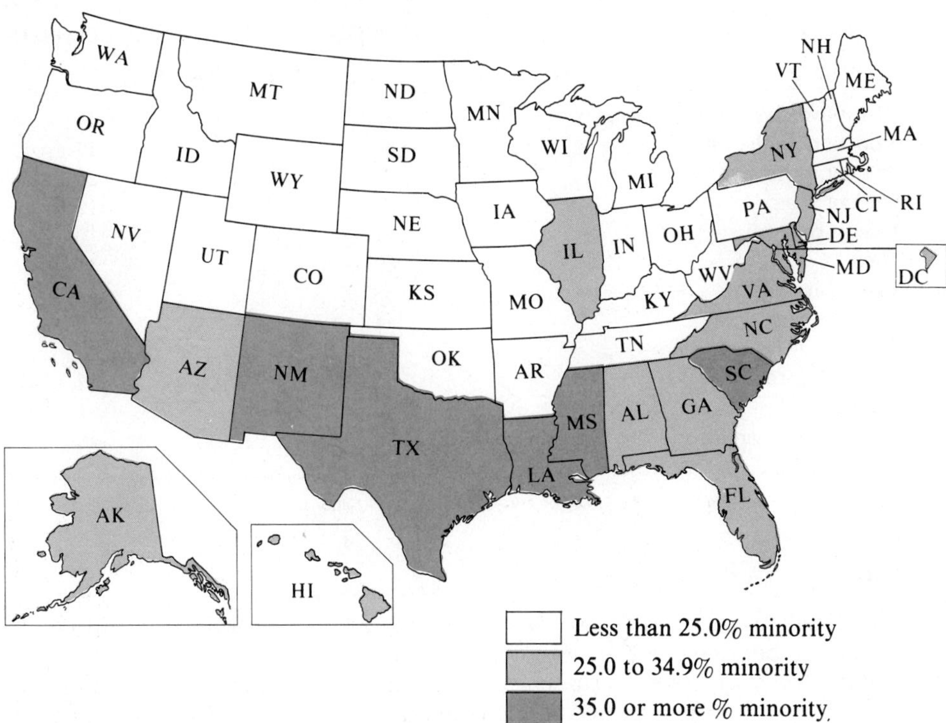

Source: V. Plisko. (1984). *The condition of education*. Washington, DC: National Center for Education Statistics, p. 19.

surprising that nearly half of our secondary school teachers have taken on a second job at some point in their career (National Center for Education Statistics, 1989a).

Despite their low wages, most teachers are satisfied with their jobs, although they express serious concerns over their working conditions and their students' attitudes. In the most comprehensive survey of teacher attitudes ever conducted, more than three fourths of the teachers said they enjoyed their work and planned to stay in the profession until retirement. Almost all, however, said that they lack parental support and that their main problems are students' apathy, absenteeism, and disruptive behavior. For example, nearly 90% were concerned about their students' apathy, whereas fewer than half felt violence was a problem in their schools. Unfortunately, more than half said morale within the profession had declined from 1982 to 1987 and that "political interference" in education is on the rise. Most teachers also felt they had no voice in determining such matters as teacher evaluation or student promotions, and most have less than an hour a day to prepare their lessons. Amazingly, despite these obstacles, most teachers are optimistic about their ability to help students learn and most believe our society can eventually help more students graduate (Carnegie Foundation, 1987. See Table 7.1).

Table 7.1

What Teachers See as Problems in Their Schools

	A PROBLEM	NOT A PROBLEM
	(% of all teachers)	
Disruptive classroom behavior	87	13
Student absenteeism	83	17
Student turnover	73	27
Student apathy	88	12
Lack of parental support	90	10
Theft	69	31
Vandalism	68	32
Violence against students	44	56
Violence agasint teachers	24	76
Racial discord	36	64
Alcohol	49	51
Drugs other than alcohol	54	46

Source: Carnegie Foundation for the Advancement of Teaching. 1987 National Survey of Public School Teachers.

Educational Spending

Although most teachers are deeply committed to their adolescent students, taxpayers' commitments are more questionable. On average nationwide, we invest only $4,216 yearly for each student's education. During the early 1990s, spending for public schools is expected to increase but at a considerably slower rate than in the 1980s. Once inflation has been taken into account, we will be investing only 13% more for education in 1993 than in 1987. A political-economic think tank has reported that our nation ranks 13th among the major industrialized nations in terms of our financial investments in precollegiate education (Economic Policy Institute, 1989). Moreover, the amount each state and local community is willing to invest in education varies widely, as Figure 7.2 illustrates. Students living in New Jersey, for example, have three times more money invested in their educations than students in Arkansas. Even within the same state, students receive unequal amounts for education since the percentage of taxes invested in education varies from one local community to another. As a consequence, adolescents living in wealthier communities generally have more modern and better equipped schools, a more varied curriculum, and better paid teachers than those living in low-income communities, where taxpayers cannot afford to invest as much in education.

ADOLESCENTS' ATTITUDES TOWARD SCHOOL

While most teachers complain that their students are apathetic, most students complain that school is boring. Not surprisingly, students who make the worst grades are the most dissatisfied with school. Likewise, those in the vocational and general tracks express more complaints than their peers in the college-bound curriculum. For example, in the largest survey yet conducted on students' attitudes

FIGURE 7.2
Education spending: Where the states stand

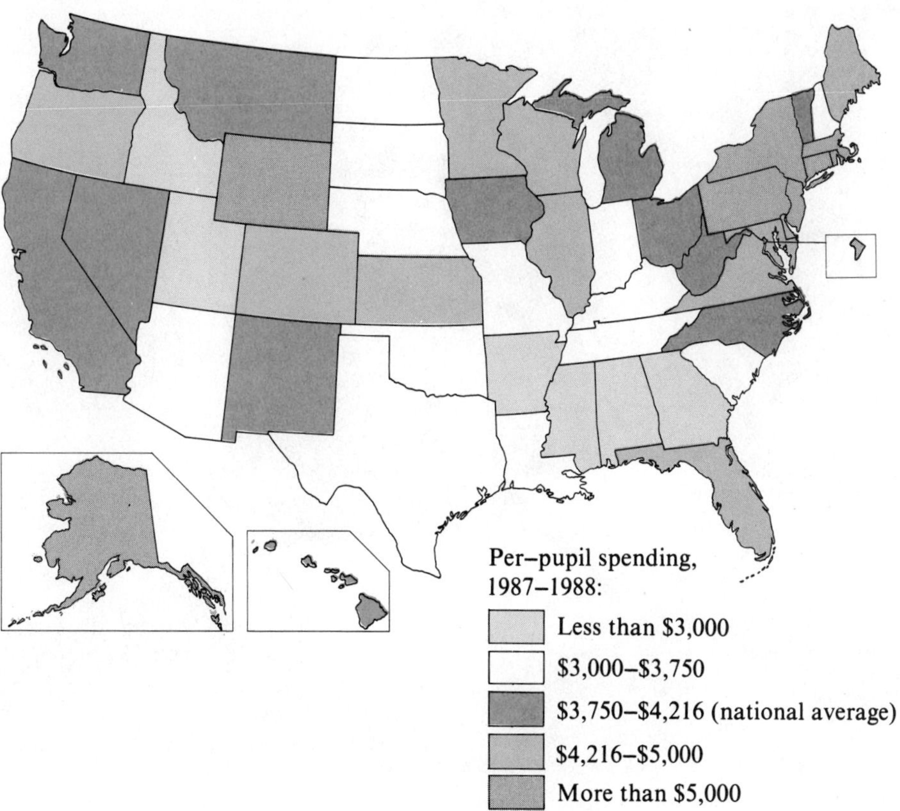

Source: National Education Association. (1988). *Ranking of the states.* West Haven, CT: Author.

toward school, only half of the 28,000 seniors and 30,000 sophomores in the general curriculum considered the quality of their instruction "good," in contrast to 75% of those in the college-bound track (Peng, Fetters & Kolstad, 1981). Even among the best students, the most frequent criticism is that teachers' methods and the curriculum are irrelevant and monotonous (Boyer, 1983; Godlad, 1983; Good & Brophy, 1984; G. Grant, 1989; Powell, Farrar, & Cohen, 1985; Sizer, 1984).

Student apathy, however, has not deterred teachers from creating innovative approaches to education that have succeeded in capturing adolescents' attention. For example, one high-school English teacher in a small Vermont farming community succeeded not only in motivating his students to read classic literature but in inspiring them to quote regularly from Homer and Shakespeare (Keizer, 1988). Likewise, Elliot Wigginton has achieved international fame with his "Foxfire" approach to teaching in a small Georgia community. His students interviewed older citizens, taped their conversations, and preserved their folk culture through putting these conversations into print, eventually in a series of four books (Wigginton, 1985). Such successes remind us that a creative teacher and a relevant curriculum can overcome student apathy.

How did you feel about high school?

ACADEMIC ACHIEVEMENT: A NATION AT RISK?

In addition to the concern over student apathy, there is growing concern regarding adolescents' academic skills and educational attainment. In assessing our young people's skills, we can examine the statistics and trends from three sources: high-school and college graduation rates, scores on national achievement tests, and Scholastic Aptitude Test (SAT) scores.

High-School Diplomas and College Degrees

Although more students are now graduating from high school than ever before, nearly 30% of Native American, 20% of African American and Hispanic, and 12% of white students quit school, their most frequent reasons being poor grades and pregnancy (V. Grant & Snyder, 1984; Plisko, 1984). The high dropout rate becomes even more evident in state-by-state comparisons. For example, in 1982, 37% of the adolescents in Mississippi, 34% in New York, and 31% in California quit school. Among Hispanic students, 80% in New York City, 70% in Chicago, and 50% in Los Angeles dropped out of school in 1983 (National Commission on Secondary

Schooling for Hispanics, 1984). Fortunately, half of those who drop out do eventually go back to school to earn their diploma, yet millions never return (National Center for Education Statistics, 1989a). Put differently, given our present rate, 12 million youngsters will become high-school dropouts by the year 2000 (Smith & Lincoln, 1988. See Table 7.2).

Moreover, of the 75% who do eventually earn a high-school diploma, only two fifths earn any type of postsecondary certificate or diploma—a percentage that represents a drop of 20% since 1972. For example, African American high-school graduates in 1982 were about 5% less likely to enroll in postsecondary education than their counterparts in 1980. In fact, African American males' college enrollment decreased by 7% between 1976 and 1986, but African American females have maintained a relatively steady college enrollment of about 5%. Similarly, Hispanics' high-school graduation rates increased by 62% between 1976 and 1985, but their college enrollment declined so that by 1986 they accounted for only 5% of the total college enrollment (American Council on Education, 1989).

These decreases in college enrollment may be related to several factors. First, the Vietnam War, which had served as an incentive for many males to attend

Table 7.2

Change in Dropout Status of 1980 Sophomores Between 1982 and 1986 by Sociodemographic and Geographic Characteristics

	PERCENT			
	Dropouts 1982	***Did Not Complete School by 1986***	***Completed School 1982–86***	***Percent of Dropouts Completed School 1982–86***
Sex				
Male	19.3	10.1	9.2	47.5
Female	15.2	8.4	6.9	45.2
Race/ethnicity				
White	14.8	7.6	7.2	48.4
African American	22.2	11.4	10.8	48.5
Hispanic	27.9	18.0	9.9	35.5
Asian	8.2	2.0	6.2	75.8
American Indian/Alaskan Native	35.5	27.1	8.4	23.7
Socioeconomic status				
Highest quartile	6.6	2.4	4.2	64.2
Second quartile	10.2	4.0	6.2	60.8
Third quartile	14.3	7.3	6.9	48.6
Lowest quartile	22.1	13.0	9.2	41.5
Unknown	78.0	48.7	29.3	37.5
Metropolitan status				
Urban	24.5	13.6	10.9	44.5
Suburban	15.1	7.1	8.0	53.0
Rural	15.6	9.5	6.1	39.0
Total	**17.3**	**9.2**	**8.0**	**46.5**

Source: National Center for Education Statistics (1988). School enrollment by age and race. Washington, DC: Author.

A CLOSER LOOK 7.1

Dropouts Lose Driving Privileges

In 1988, West Virginia became the first state to revoke the driver's licenses of high-school dropouts—a policy intended to motivate teenagers to stay in school. The West Virginia law states that if a student misses 10 consecutive or 15 total days during a semester, the state may revoke his or her license until age 18. As a consequence, school officials report that attendance rates increased by 5%, and many dropouts returned to school. Texas and Florida passed similar laws in 1989, with Colorado, Oklahoma, and South Carolina likely to follow suit. Although some lawyers believe these cases will ultimately be carried to the Supreme Court, state courts have already upheld their legality on the grounds that the state's compelling interest in education outweighs an individual's privilege of holding a driver's license.

Source: Driver's license revocation. (1989, January 25). *Education Week*, p. 16.

college, ended. Perhaps more important, as poverty has increased, so have the costs of a college education. As a result, only about 20% of the 80% who eventually graduate from high school earn a bachelor's degree, 6% a master's degree, and 2% a doctorate (Carroll, 1989; Schmitt, 1989).

In addition to our academic skills, our lifetime earnings are directly linked to the number of years of schooling we complete. For example, families headed by a college graduate earn nearly 30% more than those headed by a high-school graduate (U.S. Bureau of the Census, 1988a. See Figure 7.3). Stated differently, a male high-school dropout will earn $260,000 less than a high-school graduate and will contribute $78,000 less in taxes. A female dropout will earn $200,000 less and pay $60,000 less in taxes (Catterall, 1987). Moreover, those who take more high-school or college math courses earn higher salaries (Adelman & Alsalam, 1989).

National Achievement Scores

A second source of information on academic skills is national achievement tests, conducted yearly to help us understand how today's adolescents stand relative to their predecessors in reading, mathematics, and science (National Assessment of Educational Progress, 1988a, b, c).

Reading The good news is that students at ages 9, 13, and 17 were better readers in 1984 than students at the same ages in 1971. As in 1971, girls continue to be better readers than boys, although the gap had narrowed slightly by 1984. For example, only 35% of the 17-year-old males are reading at the "adept" level, in comparison to 45% of the females. African American and Hispanic students, as well as those living in poor communities, made sizeable improvements. For example, between 1971 and 1984 the percentage of African American 9-year-olds who had failed to acquire even *rudimentary* reading skills was reduced by nearly half, from 30 to 16.

On a more discouraging note, 9- and 13-year-olds did not show improvements in their reading skills between 1980 and 1984, as they had in the 1970s. Also

FIGURE 7.3
Median household incomes, 1987

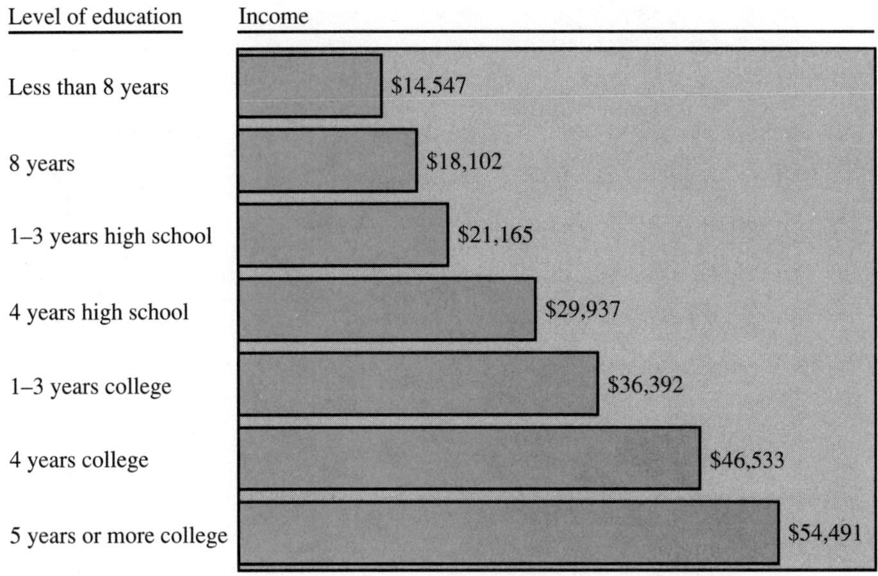

Source: *Money income of households, families and persons in the U.S.* (1988). Washington, DC: Government Printing Office.

discouraging is that 6% of the 9-year-olds in 1984 still were not reading at even the rudimentary level, 40% of the 13-year-olds had not acquired "intermediate" reading skills, and only about 5% of all students, even by the age of 17, had acquired "advanced" reading skills (see Figure 7.4).

Moreover, although minority students have made more progress than whites, the average African American or Hispanic 17-year-old is still reading only slightly better than the average white 13-year-old. Fewer than 20% of Hispanic or African American 17-year-olds demonstrated "adept" reading skills, in contrast to 45% of white students their age. Likewise, 35% of all 17-year-olds from poor communities could not read at the *intermediate* level, whereas more than half of those from advantaged urban communities read at the *adept* level.

The National Assessment of Educational Progress data also underscore the impact of academic and family variables on our reading skills. In general, students who do homework read better than students who do not. Moreover, 6 or more hours of television viewing per day is consistently and strongly correlated with lower reading skills. Unfortunately, in 1984 almost 30% of the 9-year-olds, up from 18% in 1980, fill in that category. Not surprisingly, students from homes with an abundance of reading materials are substantially better readers than those who have few books and magazines at home. Likewise, the more educated a child's parents, the better he or she is likely to read.

Mathematics As it is with reading, the news about adolescents' performance in mathematics is a mixed blessing. Although students' math skills declined between 1973 and 1978, they improved between 1982 and 1986. Nevertheless, the

FIGURE 7.4
Trends in reading skills

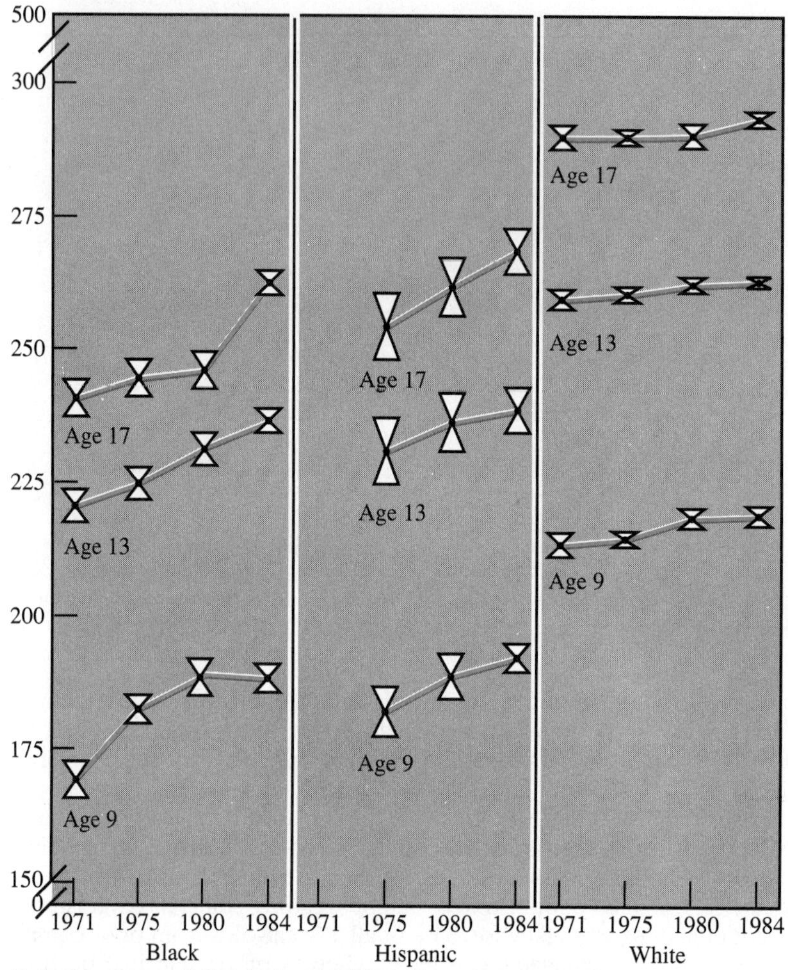

Source: National Assessment of Education Progress (1988). *The reading report card.* Princeton, NJ: Educational Testing Service.

gains have been confined primarily to lower order skills, and students in the Southeast were the only ones to make significant gains at all three age levels since 1977. These improvements are especially noteworthy given that southern states made considerable efforts to improve their schools during this period of time (Doyle & Hartle, 1985).

Despite these gains in the Southeast, however, most teenagers do not possess the breadth and depth of proficiency needed for advanced high-school mathematics, not even by age 17. In fact, only about half of all the 17-year-olds in the 1986 assessment reached the "moderately complex" level of proficiency, roughly the equivalent of junior high math courses. (For example: "Is 87% of 10 greater than 10, less than 10, or equal to 10?") In other words, nearly 1.5 million 17-year-olds were scarcely able to perform the kinds of arithmetical operation that will be required of them in their future work or daily life. Similarly, fewer than 7% of the 17-year-olds performed at the "multiple step" level. (For example: "Suppose you have ten coins and have at least one each of a quarter, a dime, a nickel and a penny. Which is the least amount of money you could have: 41¢, 47¢, 50¢, or 82¢?") In this vein, the average Japanese high-school student has better mathematical skills than the top 5% of American students enrolled in college preparatory math courses (McKnight, 1987).

As Figure 7.5 illustrates, African American and Hispanic students still fare far worse than whites in mathematical skills. Although African American students have shown a steady improvement since 1973, Hispanic students have improved only slightly. White students' skills, however, have remained relatively unchanged across

FIGURE 7.5
Adolescents' mathematics skills

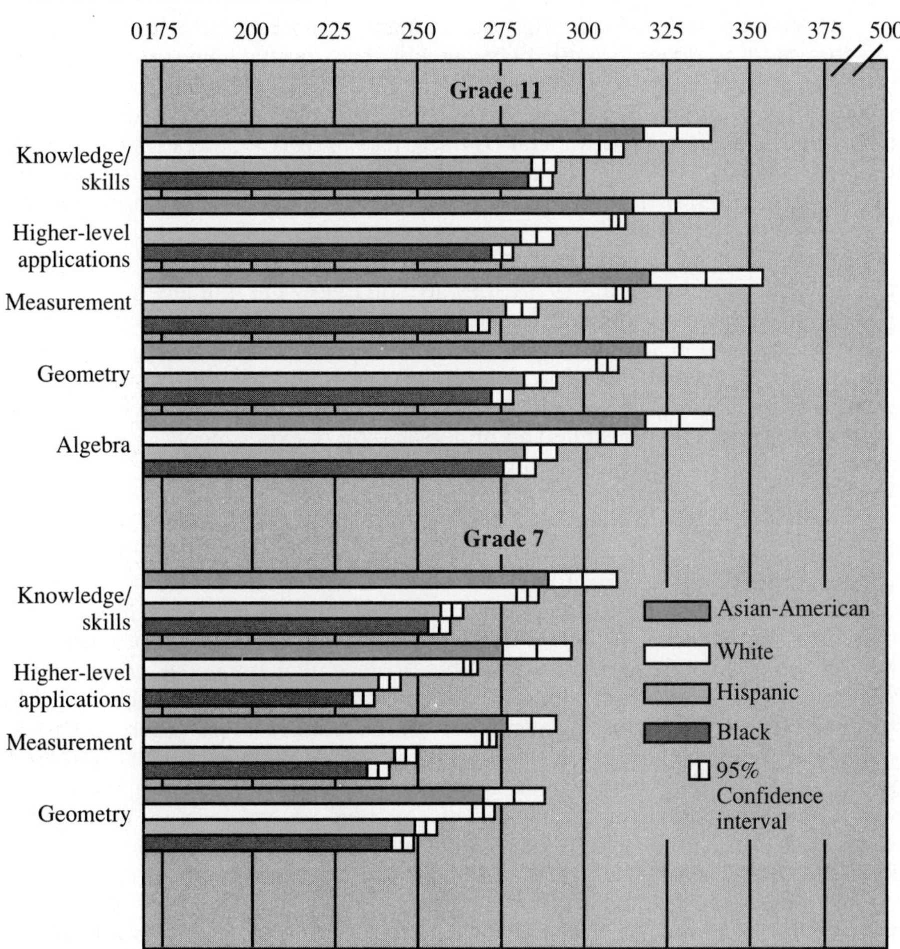

Source: National Assessment of Education Progress. (1989). *The mathematics report card.* Princeton, NJ: Educational Testing Service.

the 13-year period since 1977. In still further contrast to African Americans and Hispanics, Asian American students outperformed all groups in both the 7th and 11th grades.

In regard to gender, females outperformed males in the area of basic knowledge and skills, but males had the advantage in higher level applications. By 1986, the math skills of 13-year-old girls and boys were roughly equivalent, and boys had only slightly higher scores among the 17-year-olds. These findings represent significant gains since 1978 for boys but not for girls.

Although more high-school students took higher level mathematics courses in 1986 than in previous years, the overall percentage of students taking advanced courses remains disappointingly low. Not surprisingly, those whose parents are well educated and encourage mathematics are more proficient in math than those who lack this support at home. Students who see the relevance of math to their everyday lives also tend to have higher scores than those who see math as a waste of their time. Nevertheless, only half of the 7th- and 11-graders said they enjoyed math or felt they were good at it.

Given students' negative attitudes toward math, it is particularly discouraging to find that most students are still being taught math by the same methods used more than a decade ago—listening silently to the teacher's explanations, working problems on the board, and working problems silently at a desk. Very few students, except those in the most advanced courses, had used computers or calculators. In short, we have a long way to go before our nation's schools exploit the possibilities offered by technology and by more active methods of learning math.

Science Although students have recovered somewhat from the declines in their science skills during the 1970s, they are still below the skill levels of students in 1970. In 1985 nearly one-fifth of our 17-year-olds were unable to apply basic scientific information. (For example: "In an ordinary light bulb with a screw type base, which is the part that glows to produce the light: the thin wire, a special gas, the type of glass, the special paint that coats the bulb?") (N.A.E.P., 1988). Likewise, only 40% demonstrated an understanding of experiments or specialized knowledge in the subdisciplines of science by age 17 (For example: "What is the best indication of an approaching storm: drop in humidity, decrease in barometric pressure, clearing sky after a cold front, seismogram in a straight line?") More distressing still, only 7% were well enough prepared to enroll in college-level science courses (see Figure 7.6).

Given these findings, it is hardly surprising that our nation's youth rank poorly in comparison to those of most other industrialized societies. For example, our fifth-graders ranked in the middle of science achievement among 14 industrialized countries, whereas our ninth-graders ranked next to last. Our advanced science students ranked last in biology and performed behind most other countries' students in chemistry and physics. In physics, for example, our students answered only 44% of the items correctly, in comparison to nearly 60% for Japanese and British students. Sadly, American students in their second year of high-school science performed only slightly better than in their first year of science (International Association for the Evaluation of Education Achievement, 1988).

As with math and reading, minority students' science skills are worse than those of whites (see Figure 7.7). The skills of 13- and 17-year-old African American and Hispanic students remain at least 4 years behind those of their white peers. Only about 15% of African Americans and Hispanics were able to analyze scientific

FIGURE 7.6
Adolescents' science skills, 1986

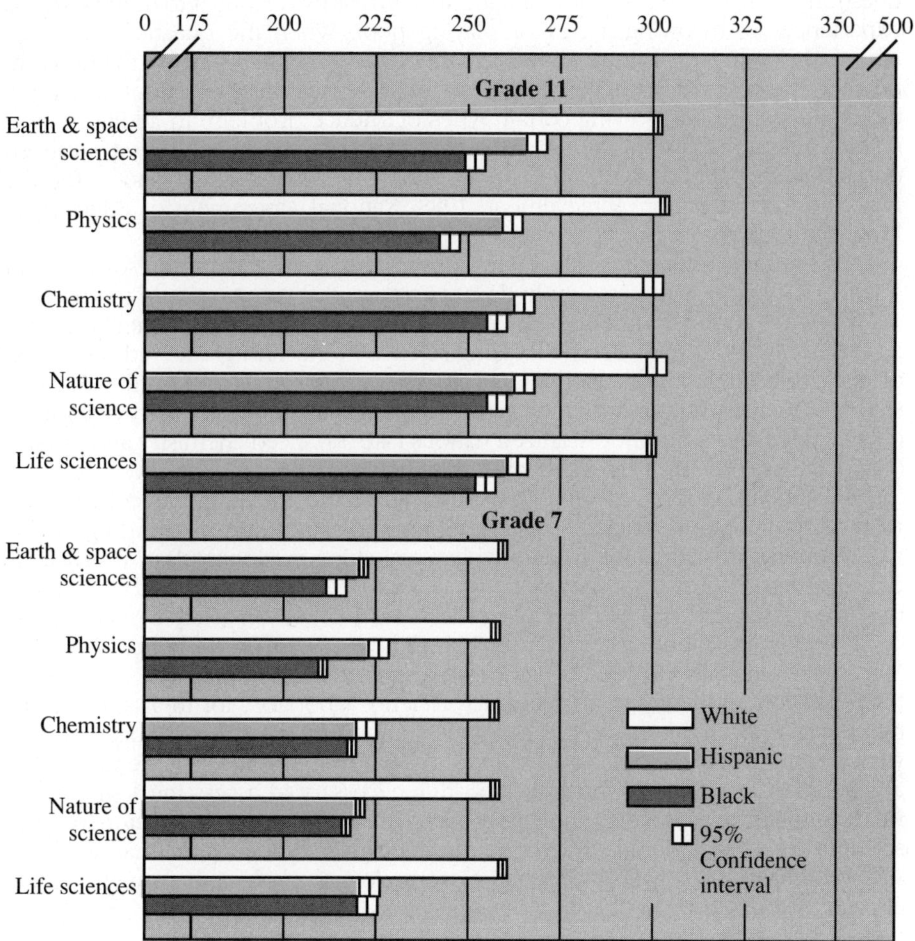

Source: National Assessment of Education Progress. *The science report card.* Princeton, NJ: Educational Testing Service.

procedures and data, compared to nearly half of the whites. African American students, unlike whites or Hispanics, surpassed their 1977 performance in 1986, however.

Unlike in mathematics, where similarities existed between the sexes, boys consistently outperformed girls in science. At age 17, roughly half the boys but only one third of the girls had the ability to analyze scientific procedures and data. In fact, the gap between males' and females' science skills has actually increased since 1977, more than doubling between 13-year-old boys and girls. Moreover, these gender differences cannot be accounted for by boys having taken more science courses than girls. Indeed, in some cases the gap between males and females actually increased when girls had taken more science courses. One hint about why these differences exist is that the greatest disparities between boys' and girls' scores were on questions involving experiences that girls did not share in common with boys. For example, more boys than girls were able to answer a question involving the reflection of light off a mirror by relating it to their boyhood experiences of throwing a ball or playing pool. When the questions involved laboratory or practical items, however, these gender differences virtually disappeared. These findings suggest that boys' experiences outside school give them the edge over girls in solving certain types of science problem. In addition, most science teachers have higher expectations for boys, ask them more advanced questions, and attend more to them in class (International Association for the Evaluation of Education Achievement, 1988; National Assessment of Educational Progress, 1988b).

These gender differences aside, why are our teenagers performing so poorly in science? To begin with, we simply do not require our young people to enroll in many science courses. Although 94% of the 7th-graders had taken a science course in 1986, only about 60% were still taking science in the 11th grade. Although 90% of our graduating seniors had studied at least 1 year of biology, only 45% had studied chemistry and only 20% had studied physics. In contrast, nearly one fourth of the students in other industrialized nations take advanced chemistry and physics (National Assessment of Educational Progress, 1988).

Our students' poor performance is also related to our antiquated classroom methods, our science teachers' qualifications, and our attitudes regarding homework. Among 7th- and 11th-graders who were taking a science class, nearly 70% did less than 2 hours of homework a week and 15% did none. Only one third of the 7th-graders and half of the 11th-graders had worked on science experiments on a weekly basis, and more than 80% had never been on a science field trip. Moreover, one fifth of the 11th-graders' science teachers were not certified to teach science, and half had no access to a science laboratory for their students. In other words, even when we can convince students to enroll in science courses, what they encounter in the classroom is sorely lacking. In short, we are producing a generation of students who lack the skills necessary to assess the logic or the validity of arguments and who are poorly informed about the nature of the scientific process. Overall, the recent trends are encouraging in that students' science scores are slowly improving. Nevertheless, it is clear that much greater effort is needed to raise our students' science skills even to their 1970 levels.

Scholastic Aptitude Test Scores

Another way of assessing adolescents' academic skills is to compare students' Scholastic Aptitude Test scores on a yearly basis (College Exam Board, 1988). These comparisons show that SAT scores fell from an average of 490 points to 445 points between 1963 and 1980 for males and females in both verbal and mathematical skills. A commission established by President Jimmy Carter came up with 79 possible reasons for these declines, among them drugs, parental neglect, poor teacher training, pollution, television, nuclear testing, and food additives. In 1980, however, the decline mysteriously began to reverse itself, even though no significant changes had taken place regarding the supposed reasons for the initial slump. Amidst our confusion about these ups and downs, even President Ronald Reagan tried to claim the improved SAT scores as one of the achievements of his administration, supposedly since the upturn began with his first election in 1980 (Zajonc, 1986)!

Reagan's hypothesis notwithstanding, among the more intriguing theories are those associated with the **confluence model,** according to which the number, order, and spacing of siblings affect their intellectual abilities and educational achievements (Blake, 1989; Zajonc, 1986). Specifically, children from smaller families supposedly have more intellectual stimulation, more verbal interaction with adults, and more intellectually stimulating experiences, such as music lessons and travel abroad, than those from larger families. Consequently, according to confluence theorists, the only child or the children from small families will have higher IQ scores, higher SAT scores, and higher educational attainments. Interestingly, family size has been correlated with the trends in SAT scores; that is, in the years when SAT scores were lowest, more students taking the test were from larger families, as the confluence model would predict. Nevertheless, the data are correlational and cannot be used to establish cause and effect. In other words, the jury is still out.

Although the reasons for the fluctuations in SAT scores are still debatable, the average scores have remained relatively constant since 1985–476 on both the mathematics portion and the verbal portion. For whatever reasons, the 1970s decline is reversing itself. Moreover, since 1978, African American students have improved their scores by an average of 30 points on math and 21 points on verbal, while Hispanics have improved by 26 points and 12 points, respectively.

Regarding sex differences, women's average score is 422 on the verbal and 455 on the math portions, while men's is 435 and 498, respectively. It appears, however, that SAT scores are more reliable for predicting males' college performance than females'. Although scoring an average of 56 points lower than males, women's first-year college grades are as good as or better than men's. Such findings suggest that the SAT questions are biased against female students. For example, a question concerning a basketball team's win/loss record was answered correctly by almost 30% more males than females (Rosser, 1988). On the other hand, men's and women's scores have become more similar over the past 20 years, thus weakening the charge of sex bias (Wilder & Powell, 1988).

While the question of sex bias continues to be debated, more male and female students are taking the SAT than before. In 1988, 1,134,364 students took the test, a 13% increase since 1986. This increase can be accounted for mainly by the growing number of minority students taking the test. In 1988, for example, 23,066 more minority students took the SAT than in 1987; and the 97,483 African Americans who took the test represented a 40% increase over 1985.

AT-RISK YOUTHS

Prevalence and Costs

In summarizing the data on achievement, it is clear that millions of adolescents, especially those from poor families and minorities, are performing poorly in math, science, and reading. It is now estimated that 30% of our nation's youths are failing to acquire the basic education and skills needed to obtain adequately paying and secure jobs (Education Commission of the States, 1988). Given that the fastest growing segments of our population are Hispanics and African Americans, who are the most likely to be growing up in poverty, the number of students who are **at risk** or truly disadvantaged is growing. In this sense, then, we are "a nation at risk." We are creating a poorly educated work force with which to compete in the world market and a large underclass of poorly educated young people who will not be able to support themselves in our society (Berlin & Sum, 1988; Wilson, 1987).

In 1983 the National Commission on Excellence in Education issued its famous report on American education, *A Nation at Risk* (1983). Following its publication, many critiques of our schools appeared, and much discussion was generated. The universal criticism of the report was its lack of sensitivity to the plight of minority, poor, at-risk students. Most of the commission's recommendations, in fact, were suitable only for relatively successful students from middle- or upper-class families. The report paid virtually no attention to the many causes of failure among our nation's millions of at-risk students.

Although economic analysts have agreed that the basic skills in our work force, particularly for entry-level jobs, are simply not good enough for our society to compete in a world economy, we are doing relatively little to help our at-risk youths. For example, only 5% of state education funds are being allocated specifically for services to students with inadequate skills. Likewise, our federal financial commitment to education declined by 23% in the 1980s once inflation is taken into account. Our present federal funding is sufficient to serve only 1 out of every 5 of the poor children in need of preschool education, 2 out of every 5 students who need remedial help, 1 out of every 4 students who need bilingual education, and 1 out of every 20 who need job training. Moreover, the 973,000 students who dropped out of school in 1981 will lose $228 billion in personal earning over their lifetime, while our society will lose $68 billion in taxes. For every $1 spent on early prevention and intervention, we would save almost $5 in costs of remedial education, welfare, and crime. Similarly, if we could raise the educational skills of our 19- to 23-year-olds by just one grade level, their lifetime earnings would increase by almost 4% and the likelihood of out-of-wedlock births, arrests, and welfare would decline by nearly 5% (Berlin & Sum, 1988; Smith & Lincoln, 1988).

Quality of Education

At-risk youths seldom receive the same quality of education as students from wealthier families. Indeed, the quality of education any student receives can be predicted, to a large degree, by his or her parents' income. Schools serving predominantly poor and minority students generally have the least qualified teachers, the poorest facilities, and the least innovative curricula and teaching techniques (Council of Chief State School Officers, 1988; Education Commission of the States, 1988; Lakebrink, 1989; Presseisen, 1988; Smith & Lincoln, 1988). Moreover, since many at-risk youths are Hispanic, they are often further handicapped by having to learn English as a second language in schools poorly prepared to offer bilingual education (Hakuta, 1986; National Commission of Secondary Schooling for Hispanics, 1984).

Of the many barriers working against at-risk students, curriculum **tracking** is easily among the worst. Almost all schools track students into the academic, general, vocational, or special education curricula on the basis of IQ scores, teachers' recommendations, and achievement test scores. Since most at-risk students are assigned to the lowest level classes in their schools, they are typically segregated from students with better academic skills throughout the school day. As a result, the students most in need of help and motivation are given less motivating activities, less engaging materials, and less positive peer role models. In lower track classes the emphasis is primarily on rote learning, workbooks, individual work kits, and teacher lectures. Moreover, teachers tend to be overly concerned with getting students in lower ability tracks to be punctual, sit quietly, and follow directions. In contrast, teachers in higher ability classes more often encourage critical thinking, independence, and creativity and are more enthusiastic, more democratic, and more creative. In short, the best teachers and the most motivating strategies and technology are reserved for the best students, who are least in need of help (Education Commission of the States, 1988; Boyer, 1983; Oakes, 1985).

Not surprisingly, once assigned to these lower track classes, students seldom advance to higher tracks. Both teachers and students in these classes come to accept the **self-fulfilling prophecy** that these students simply are not capable of doing higher level work (Insel & Jacobson, 1975; Rosenthal & Jacobson, 1968). As a consequence, the research has consistently demonstrated that the least skilled students make more academic progress in classes with students of higher abilities than when segregated into their special education or vocational classes. Even the National Education Association itself conceded more than two decades ago that tracking is an indefensible policy (1968). Moreover, the major commissions and studies assessing our nation's secondary schools during the 1980s recommended abolishing tracking (Boyer, 1983; Carnegie Council on Adolescent Development, 1989; Godlad, 1983; Powell, Farrar & Cohen, 1985).

Why, then, do we continue to track students? In large part because the parents of higher ability students fear that their children's educational progress will be impeded if slower students are in the same classes. Many teachers also support tracking because they believe they would be unable to teach students with different abilities in the same class. Some advocates of special education also argue that slower students' self-esteem will suffer if they are placed in classes with faster learners.

These arguments, however, are not supported by the research. Despite our fears about mixed-ability classes, faster students do not suffer academically as a consequence of having slower students as classmates—a finding partially explained by the fact that faster students often tutor their slower peers, thereby learning the material better. Then, too, faster students still receive the types of stimulation at home that foster their academic development whether or not slower students are in their classes. In addition, teachers tend to continue teaching as they normally would, even when slower students are present in their classes, and have available a multitude of teaching techniques and curriculum materials that have proved successful in mixed-ability classes (E. Cohen, 1986; Hargis, 1989; Johnson & Johnson, 1987; Levine, 1985; Ornstein & Levine, 1990; Slavin, 1985; Wang & Walberg, 1985).

Willing to believe these research findings, a few school systems are finally attempting to boost student achievement by abolishing the lower track remedial education classes (Rothman, 1989). Under the leadership of a program at Stanford University, 40 schools nationwide and the Denver school system are eliminating remedial classes in their efforts to boost student achievement. Taking the lead in 1987, the San Diego schools began a 7-year effort to phase out remedial courses. In the 2 years since the six San Diego high schools moved half of their students from remedial classes into regular classes, the failure rate has increased by only 4%. It is hoped that these progressive schools will serve as models for the rest of the nation to accept the reality that tracking perpetuates educational and financial inequality within our society and does little to advance the skills of either our most or our least skilled students.

Educational Programs That Work

Descriptions of a few representative programs can serve to demonstrate one simple point: We do have the means by which to help at-risk students succeed. It is especially important to keep in mind that these methods work equally well with average and advanced students.

How do you feel around deaf or blind classmates? Why?

Cooperative learning strategies Although cooperative learning strategies have been proven more effective than competitive techniques with even the most talented students, they are especially beneficial for at-risk youths. Having students of various abilities work together in teams encourages peer tutoring and enhances the self-confidence of students with lesser abilities. Within a team, students are assigned roles in which interdependence and sharing take precedence over competition and self-gain. Unlike traditional techniques that pit students against one another in ways where one student's gain is another's loss, cooperative techniques encourage students to help one another without losing anything in the process. Dividing a lesson into segments and having each team member responsible for teaching his or her segment to teammates creates a situation in which each group member has something that everyone else needs. For example, by making one person responsible for recording the group's ideas and another for checking to see that proper collaboration takes place, the teacher helps the group establish interdependence. In contrast to students in competitive classes, those in cooperative classes tend to like each other more, to experience less prejudice and ridicule, and to be more involved with the material. Even more impressive, both the fastest and the slowest students make at least as much academic progress as students in competitive classes (Johnson & Johnson, 1987; Kohn, 1986; Slavin, 1985).

Given these results, why do we not use more cooperative strategies in our schools? Because, unfortunately, most of us have been trained to equate success and doing well with beating someone. We have come to view education as a situation in which we are either winners or losers. Consequently, many educators and parents are stubbornly reluctant to adopt cooperative learning strategies in our schools, despite the research demonstrating their superiority to competitive methods.

Mastery learning In further contrast to our traditional methods of teaching and grading, **mastery learning** permits students of various abilities to work within the same classrooms. Each student is given curriculum materials matched to his or her skill level and then provided with continual feedback regarding the accuracy of the answers. The specific objectives and specific rewards for mastering each step toward a higher goal are carefully outlined at the outset. Based on social learning theories, mastery learning techniques subdivide each goal into small steps; state the learning objectives in precise, behavioral terms; and reward each small increment of progress. In terms of grading, mastery learning allows all students the opportunity to be rewarded for the material they master without competing against one another (Council of Chief State School Officers, 1988; Lakebrink, 1989; Levine, 1985).

Programs that teach thinking In contrast to more successful students, most at-risk students have not yet learned how to think; that is, many students do not know how to analyze, classify, and evaluate information or how to use strategies such as self-questioning, verbal self-instruction, or generating hypotheses. The least successful students have not yet learned how to monitor or revise their own learning strategies, even in terms of relatively simple procedures such as surveying a chapter first before reading it, attending carefully to chapter subheadings, and periodically summarizing what they have read before proceeding. A number of programs, therefore, have been developed for teaching thinking skills and have been successful with at-risk students. Among these programs are Strategic Reasoning, Odyssey, Structure of Intellect, and Instrumental Enrichment (Beyer, 1987; Chipman, Segal, & Glaser, 1985; Dillon & Sternberg, 1986; Meyers, 1986; Nickerson, Perkins, Smith, 1985; Presseisen, 1988). The success of these programs shows that, contrary to popular opinion, low achievers spend too much time being drilled on the basic skills and not enough time being taught the higher order "thinking skills" that make us competent students and life-time learners.

School within a school Another successful approach with at-risk students is the concept of a **school within a school** (Presseisen, 1988). A school within a school assigns a small group of students to a team of several teachers who stay with the students over a period of several years. Working as a team, the teachers are given greater autonomy and more control over the curriculum and teaching techniques that they deem most appropriate for their own students, and the students develop a sense of belonging and security by working with the same teachers and peers over a period of years. In contrast, the traditional school assigns adolescents to four or five new teachers and to a new set of classmates each year. As a result, many students, especially the low achievers, are left feeling unattached to their teachers, their classmates, and the curriculum. By providing continuity, the school within a school program maintains closer contact between teachers, parents, and students. As an added benefit, teachers gain a supportive team of co-workers who encourage and offer assistance to one another.

In West Germany, where the concept has been popular for years, only 1% of the students drop out of the schools within schools, in contrast to 14% in traditional German schools. Having visited the West German schools and observed their success in reducing dropout rates and raising student achievement, Albert Shanker, president of the American Federation of Teachers, believes the concept should be tried in our schools. In a program primarily for Hispanic students now under way at Los Angeles's Griffith Junior High, the teaching teams will stay with their students from the 5th through the 10th grade. Most classwork takes place in small "table groups" made up of four to six students of varying academic abilities and economic backgrounds. The Los Angeles teachers also decided to abolish the traditional letter-grade system, evaluating students instead on an achievement ladder (a mastery learning technique) that assesses each skill individually (Viadero, 1989).

Schools within schools benefit not only at-risk students but average and fast learners as well. Research shows that many adolescents experience considerable stress, a decline in academic achievement, and a loss of self-esteem when making the transition from elementary to junior high school (Carnegie Council on Adolescent Development, 1989; Jackson & Hornbeck, 1989; Kavrell & Petersen, 1985; Lipsitz, 1984). In fact, it appears that this transition to junior high school can actually have a more negative impact on young adolescents than do the maturational changes occurring at this point in their lives (Simmons & Blyth, 1987). The traditional junior high school throws young adolescents into a situation in which they must interact with a number of different teachers, none of whom they know, for only an hour at a time in large classes with new classmates. In contrast, the school within a school offers young adolescents the security and self-confidence of having continued contact with teachers and peers they have known for years.

Moreover, regardless of their age, adolescents who attend large schools often feel alienated from their teachers and classmates. Understandably, students with the weakest academic skills seem to benefit less in larger schools than in smaller schools, where they have more opportunities to succeed and to be known. On the other hand, larger schools can offer a more diverse curriculum and an array of experiences and materials that smaller schools usually cannot afford (Educational Research Information Clearinghouse, 1982). For these reasons, then, the schools within schools blend the best of both worlds: the materials and curriculum of a large school with the intimacy, security, and individualized attention of a small school.

Business funding for educational technology Some of the fourth-graders at Indianapolis's Washington Irving School are too poor to have telephones; but in 1988, 300 of these students each received a free microcomputer to use in their home (West, 1988). Funded by private businesses, this project is perceived by business leaders as an investment in a more skilled and competitive work force—an investment that will ultimately save businesses money since it will reduce their future costs of educating new employees with substandard academic skills (Berlin & Sum, 1988; Schorr & Schorr, 1988; Smith & Lincoln, 1988). It is hoped that the project will have a ripple effect on the students' parents and older siblings. With a computer at home, perhaps these parents, many of whom never completed their high-school education, and older siblings, many of whom have academic problems, will begin using the machine to improve their own educational skills.

Multicultural curriculum Members of minority cultures, a large percentage of whom are at-risk youths, often feel that the traditional school curriculum with its emphasis on white males' viewpoints and accomplishments, is irrelevant to their social, historical, and economic realities. African American, Hispanic, Native American, and female students are too often left without a sense of "ownership" in the curriculum. Where, for example, does the curriculum leave the African American teenage girl who would like to read literature by African American female writers about African American female protagonists (Mitchell, 1988)? In this vein, a national survey of required reading in high-school English classes shows almost no change in the past 30 years. Female and minority authors seldom appear in the required readings (Center for Learning and Teaching Literature, 1988).

In addition to being excluded from the curriculum materials, minority students are seldom taught by minority teachers. Although minorities made up 12% of our nation's teaching force in 1980, by the year 2000 this figure is expected to plummet to only 5%—a decline due, in large part, to the cuts in financial aid that once enabled lower income students to attend college. At the same time, minorities are expected to account for about 35% of our school-age population within the next decade (Holmes, 1989).

Given that most minority students are already struggling to master the basic skills of reading and writing, they may be especially discouraged by a curriculum designed to motivate white students. As our awareness of the importance of role models and a relevant curriculum has increased, a number of schools are trying to create a **multicultural curriculum** and teaching methods that will better meet the needs and capture the interests of at-risk minority youth (Bennett, 1986; Gollnick & Chinn, 1986; Tiedt & Tiedt, 1986. See Box 7.2).

Early childhood education Given the fact that the federal government reduced funding for preschool programs for disadvantaged children during the 1970s and 1980s, it is especially discouraging to learn that well-designed programs

A CLOSER LOOK 7.2

Multicultural and Gender-Fair Curricula

As part of a nationwide trend toward eliminating biases in school instruction, Minnesota now requires schools to develop multicultural and gender-fair curricula. As part of the effort to reduce the high dropout rates among minority students, Iowa became, in 1979, the first state to mandate such instruction throughout the curriculum. Under Iowa's legislation, schools must incorporate multicultural and nonsexist approaches into all curricular and program areas, including the placement of students in special education and gifted education classes. Developing multicultural curricula that present the contributions of women and minorities is increasingly seen as a way of offering minority students and girls a sense of ownership in their schools. In Camden, New Jersey, for example, where the student body is only 1% white, the school board has proposed a shift from a curriculum that stresses European culture to an "Afro-centric" curriculum. Likewise, the Detroit public schools, which are 89% African American, are concerned about developing a curriculum that reflects the contributions of Africans and Afro-Americans.

Source: R. Rothman. (1988, December 14). Minnesota to mandate multicultural and gender fair curricula. *Education Week,* p. 15.

can have lasting effects on the academic performance of poor children. Many children and adolescents who attended preschool programs have shown greater cognitive gains, higher vocational goals, and lower teenage pregnancy, delinquency, dropout, and unemployment rates than children with no preschool training from similarly impoverished homes (Haskins, 1989; Riddle, 1988; Woodhead, 1988).

One of the most ambitious early childhood programs is the **Beethoven project,** being conducted in our nation's largest public-housing project, Chicago's Robert Taylor Homes (D. Cohen, 1989). Launched in late 1987, the program is located in one of our nation's poorest communities, where only one third of the parents have a high-school diploma and where 20,000 people live within a 2-mile area bordered by an expressway and railroad tracks. The Beethoven project combines prenatal care with a Head Start program, medical services, and a parent-education program in which mothers learn how to interact with their young children in ways that enhance the children's cognitive and social skills. The most striking benefit of the program thus far has been its success in improving parents' perceptions of themselves and raising their expectations about how they can positively influence their children's development. Nevertheless, the project is up against the overwhelming problems associated with poverty: parents' drug use, newborns' poor health and fetal alcohol syndrome, teenage mothers without husbands or education, and children's respiratory problems caused by the project's clogged incinerator chutes.

Given the economic odds against poor children, it is a wonder that preschool programs have had as much success as they have. Unfortunately, many of these children lose the cognitive and social gains they make in their preschool program. Such findings remind us that merely providing poor children with preschool education will not protect them indefinitely from factors at home and at school that again put them at risk of failure. Despite these debilitating factors, however, preschool programs can have a lasting effect on the cognitive skills and academic achievements of poor children.

SCHOOL VIOLENCE AND VANDALISM

Another problem facing at-risk students is the unsafe conditions under which they and their teachers usually work. Our nations' inner-city schools are often riddled with drug peddling, theft, vandalism, and violence. Even in more affluent schools, school safety has become a matter of concern. How safe are our secondary schools? Do most teachers and students fear going to school? Why do some schools have so much more vandalism and violence than others? How can principals and teachers make their schools safer?

Such questions are at the heart of several nationwide surveys of our secondary schools. On the basis of one sample of 11,000 adolescents, it is estimated that in 1987 about half of the boys and one third of the girls were involved in a fight with another student, and nearly 15% were robbed. According to these estimates, one fifth of the boys had carried a knife to school at least once during the year, and 7% carried one daily (American School Health Association, 1988).

Although these figures may leave us with the impression that our schools are unsafe, other surveys show that in the vast majority of schools violence is not considered a major problem either by students or by teachers. For example, in a nationally representative sample of 58,000 sophomores and seniors, tardiness, truancy, refusing to do homework, and refusing to follow the teachers' directions were far more prevalent problems than robbery or fighting (Diprete, 1981). Similarly, in the most recent national survey of teachers, less than half felt there was a problem with violence in their school, although nearly 70% felt that theft and vandalism were problems. In contrast, nearly 85% felt absenteeism was a problem (Carnegie Foundation, 1987. See Table 7.1). Other nationwide surveys have also shown that fighting, robbery, and vandalism are less prevalent than tardiness, truancy, apathy, and disrespect toward teachers (Boyer, 1983; Godlad, 1983; Powell, Farrar and Cohen, 1985).

Nevertheless, in a number of inner-city schools, students and teachers do feel threatened by the violence, theft, and vandalism that surround them. As a consequence, educators have worked toward finding innovative ways of making their schools safer. As Boxes 7.3 and 7.4 illustrate, many schools have succeeded in creating a safer environment by using contingency contracts, reinforcing students for appropriate behavior, and maintaining closer ties with parents.

Surveys have also shown us that junior high schools are generally more dangerous than high schools—a finding that can be partially explained by the fact that many disruptive students drop out of school when they are 16, thus leaving a more motivated, cooperative group of students to go on to high school. We also know that students who make the poorest grades and those who come from the poorest families are the most likely to steal, fight, and vandalize their schools. Understandably, students with low grades have low self-esteem in school as a consequence of not receiving the reinforcement that comes from being successful students. Lacking self-confidence and embarrassed by their academic failures, these young people may deface and destroy school property and lash out against other students and teachers with their fists and weapons.

A CLOSER LOOK 7.3

Reducing School Violence, Vandalism, and Academic Failure

Each of the following techniques has succeeded in improving adolescents' conduct or academic performance in schools. Which of these strategies are being used in your community's school system? Why do you believe these methods would or would not be successful in your community?

SCHEDULE CHANGES Discipline problems are recorded to determine how often and when they occur. Class periods are then rotated so that the same course does not always occupy the least or most desirable time of the day.

TEACHER RELEASE TIME Teachers who are the least effective in motivating and managing their classes are released from teaching for a day or 2. They are assigned to accompany some of their most disruptive students throughout the day so they can see school from the students' viewpoint.

SMOKING CLINIC Students who would otherwise be suspended from school for violating nonsmoking policies are assigned to evening seminars. A parent must accompany the student to each seminar. During these classes health professionals present the hazards of smoking and methods for quitting. One school district reduced its suspensions from 45% to 13% after 4 years with this method.

STUDENTS' HANDBOOKS A handbook stating the school's policies is given to all students. This must be signed by the parents at the beginning of the school year to ensure that they, too, know the rules and the penalties for infractions. The book is written at a fifth-grade level so that all parents and students can comprehend it.

SCHOOL SURVIVAL TRAINING Disruptive students learn to use behavior modification for relating more effectively to their teachers. Students learn to record their behavior and to reinforce teachers with smiles, eye contact, verbal praise, and attentive posture.

PHOTOGRAPHY PROJECT Several dozen of the most disruptive, unmotivated students are photographed when they are "caught" studying or behaving appropriately. These photos are enlarged to poster size and hung in the main corridors. Contrary to teachers' expectations, the students did not destroy the posters. In fact, 75% of the photographed misfits improved their conduct in school. Apparently they received peer approval and self-satisfaction from "being caught being good."

COMMUNITY CARDS AND STROKE NOTES The school gives students business cards that read:

continued

Some educators and citizens would have us believe that the best way to make schools safer is by running them in a more authoritarian, dictatorial way. In this "spare the rod and spoil the child" vein, the film *Lean on Me* achieved its nationwide success, in part, because people believed a tough-fisted, intimidating principal could whip students into line, resolving both their academic ills and their bad conduct (see Box 7.5).

In reality, however, the research shows that authoritarian, heavy-handed, nonegalitarian methods have the least success in improving students' behavior or academic work (Boyer, 1983; Godlad, 1983; Houlihan, 1988; Lipsitz, 1984; Sizer, 1984). Vandalism, theft, and violence are most likely to be reduced in schools where students are given some voice in the rules and disciplinary procedures. In these schools, the rules are clearly specified at the outset, as are the specific penalties for each type of infraction. This clearcut code helps students feel protected

Box 7.3 continued

"You have just been served by ________, a student at Jefferson High School." A student who performs a service for a fellow citizen leaves a card. Many principals receive complimentary phone calls and letters from citizens, which they share with the students. "Stroke notes" follow this same principle. When teachers or principals observe good conduct in school, they send a flattering note home to the adolescent's parents.

TELEPHONE SERVICES The teacher tape-records a 2-minute telephone message each day that gives the homework assignment and summarizes the day's class activities. The recording also provides daily attendance figures and information about special school events. As a result of this project, many students' homework and grades improved.

MONEY IN ESCROW The school system creates a special fund for students at the beginning of the school year. Whatever money is left at the end of the year, after paying to repair the damage created by vandals, is returned to that school's government. The students then use the money for entertainment or other items they want to buy for their own pleasure at school. Using this method, Oakland, California, reduced its vandalism bill from $433,205 in 1977 to $133,306 in 1978.

STUDENT TUTORS In San Antonio, Texas, 45% of Hispanic students drop out of school before graduating, more than half before the ninth grade. To stop this loss, the Valued Youth Partnership Program trains potential dropouts as tutors and assigns each three to five elementary school children to tutor several hours each week. As a result, of the total number of tutors, all of whom had failed at least 1 year in school before entering the program, only 2% have quit school. Disciplinary problems have also become less severe, their grades have improved, and attendance has soared. Recognition ceremonies, with T-shirts and rewards, give the tutors status at school and in their community.

CONFLICT RESOLUTION PROGRAM In 15 San Francisco middle schools and high schools, students resolve their disputes in a designated room. Students in conflict have the choice of going before two peer conflict managers or an adult. The student conflict managers are nominated by other students, receive 16 hours of training from their teachers (who have been trained by the CRP staff), and work in pairs so they can discuss cases and arrive at fair decisions.

Sources: Carnegie Council on Adolescent Development. (1989). *Turning points: Preparing American youth for the 21st century.* Washington, DC: Author. M. Casserly, S. Bass, & J. Garrett. (1980). *School vandalism.* Lexington, MA: Lexington Books. L. Nielsen. (1982). *How to motivate adolescents: A Guide for parents, teachers, and counselors.* Englewood Cliffs, NJ: Prentice-Hall.

from the subjective whims of teachers or principals who may change the rules periodically and dole out punishment differently for the same offenses. Although the rules are consistently enforced, these schools provide ample opportunities for all students to be reinforced and treated with esteem. In short, a school in which students are given some voice, yet where misbehavior is consistently punished, is superior to a school in which students are treated like pawns in a dictatorship.

Truancy

Although truancy may at first appear to be a rather trivial problem, absenteeism more than doubled in many urban schools during the 1970s. Nearly 10% of all 12- to 15-year-olds are absent from school without excuse. Moreover, chronic absenteeism takes the heaviest toll on those students who can least afford to be

A CLOSER LOOK 7.4

Contingency Contracting With Adolescent Students

Let's assume that Homer is a high-school sophomore who must learn to read at an eighth-grade level if he wants a diploma. Because he is presently reading at only a fifth-grade level, Homer is short-tempered or bored when asked to do the classwork necessary to improve his reading skills. His temperament is making life pretty difficult for his English teacher, Mr. Snodgrass. If Homer could ever improve his reading skills, he would probably begin to find reading intrinsically reinforcing. He might eventually be motivated to read because of the intrinsic pleasure that comes from the activity of reading. Until that happens, Mr. Snodgrass and Homer's parents can use extrinsic, or external reinforcement to motivate him to do the tedious assignments that will eventually improve his reading skills.

Mr. Snodgrass decides to set up a **contingency contract** with Homer for each small improvement in his classwork. This process of rewarding each small step is called shaping. Many adults make the mistake of expecting too much from the adolescent too soon and of being too stingy with external rewards. Therefore, Homer's teacher uses a continuous schedule of reinforcement, so that the youngster will receive rewards for each day's improvement. In order to design the contract, Mr. Snodgrass and Homer make a written record of the baseline behavior. Baseline is the period of time before any external incentives are introduced to motivate Homer. Homer's baseline charts show that for the last 2 weeks he has worked on his assignment only 10 minutes of each class period. The ultimate goal is for him to work 50 of the 60 minutes. Mr.

continued

missing their teachers' help and instruction—students with the poorest academic skills. Not surprisingly, students who are truant are more involved in delinquency and drug abuse than those attending school (Nursten & Carroll, 1981; Sommer, 1985).

Not all truants, however, are poor students. In fact, some very successful students avoid school out of fear of disappointing their parents or teachers. Having become "star" students, these young people encounter the stress of having to be perfect in all their school endeavors. Rather than risk imperfection or failure, they cut school. Likewise, some successful students avoid school because of problems with their peers. Feeling rejected or embarrassed or intimidated, they play hooky rather than face their problems with classmates.

Suspensions and Corporal Punishment

In response to truancy, vandalism, and violence, schools often resort to policies allowing hitting or suspending students. Although this happens to students of every race and socioeconomic class, minority students bear the brunt of these disciplinary tactics (Children's Defense Fund, 1985; Hyman, 1989). African American and Hispanic students, especially males, are disciplined more harshly and more frequently than whites and Asian Americans for similar offenses. For example, in 1986 although African American students constituted only 16% of the school population, they accounted for nearly 35% of the cases of corporal punishment and 25% of all suspensions. Similarly, Hispanic students, who represented about

Box 7.4 continued

Snodgrass proposes to Homer that Homer should try to accomplish this goal within 6 weeks from the time that the contingency contract begins.

The teacher allows Homer to choose his own reward for each day's progress. The teacher also provides social reinforcement by complimenting him for any improvement. Whenever Homer is not doing his work, the teacher avoids and ignores him, so that Homer will not learn to gain the teacher's attention by misbehaving. Both Homer and his teacher keep daily records of the time Homer works in class. On the days when he fails to reach his goal, he loses 4 points on his contract. His contract specifies that for every 5 additional minutes over his previous day's record that he works in class, he will receive 4 points. At the end of each week these points can be "cashed in" for the following:

- 20 points—use of the family's car on Saturday night
- 15 points—15 minutes of free time in class on Friday
- 10 points—a complimentary letter that will be sent home to his parents describing his progress that week
- 5 points—permission to continue sitting next to whomever he chooses in class

Many adults would say that Homer is not truly motivated unless he gives up his reliance on this contract and completes his classwork without any external incentives. Another interpretation, however, is that external incentives motivate many of us to complete tasks that are not inherently pleasurable. Why else do employers offer us money to show up for a boring day's work, when we would rather be out on the tennis courts or home watching television?

Source: L. Nielsen. (1982). *How to motivate adolescents: A guide for parents, teachers, and counselors.* Englewood Cliffs, NJ: Prentice-Hall.

10% of the student population, were involved in 9% of the suspensions and 8% of corporal punishment cases. The largest racial discrepancies in corporal punishment were in Arkansas, Tennessee, Texas, Florida, and New Mexico (National Coalition of Advocates for Students, 1988).

FACTORS INFLUENCING ACADEMIC ACHIEVEMENT

As we have already seen, students' academic skills are affected by a number of factors within the school's control: mixed-ability or tracked classes, a multicultural curriculum, teachers' self-fulfilling prophecies, students' access to computers, cooperative rather than competitive learning strategies, schools within schools, mastery learning, and programs that teach students thinking skills. In addition, we have seen that preschool education can have a beneficial effect on students' later intellectual development and academic achievements. Other factors beyond the school's control, however, also have an impact on students' achievement.

Learning Disabilities

In order to explain why certain adolescents are having academic problems, some educators and psychologists have blamed **learning disabilities.** The learning disabled, or LD, child is supposedly handicapped by minimal brain dysfunctions

A CLOSER LOOK 7.5

The Make Believe World of Lean on Me

In 1988 the movie *Lean on Me* became the nation's number one box office earner. Based on the true story of an African American high school principal in New Jersey, the film portrays Joe Clark as a success in reforming an inner-city African American school. Using an authoritarian style in which uncooperative teachers and students are forced out of the school, Clark wastes little time on what he calls "fruitless egalitarianism." In real life Clark claimed to have doubled his students' proficiency test scores during his first year as principal, for which he received congratulatory phone calls from President Reagan and Secretary of Education William Bennett.

The realities, however, fall short of the film's inspiring and exciting story. To begin with, the scores of Clark's students on the New Jersey High School Proficiency Test were the lowest in the state for 1986, 1987, and 1988. Over this 3-year period, an average of only 24% of his students passed all three sections of this basic skills test. In contrast, the average for all other urban schools in the state was 48%. Moreover, Clark's dictatorial tactics for promoting stricter discipline contradict the findings of educational researchers showing that crime, violence, and underachievement are reduced by principals who are democratic, firm, and consistent—the antithesis of Clark. Although *Lean on Me* fulfills the hopes of many who yearn for a return to the "good old days" of authoritarian rule by principals and teachers, it is doubtful that principals who used Clark's tactics would be tolerated in middle-class, white schools or that, had he been white, his tactics would have been tolerated in an African American urban school.

Source: J. Clark. (1989). *Laying down the law:* Joe Clark's strategy for saving our schools. Washington, DC: Regnery Gateway; I. Hyman. (1989, April 26). The make believe world of "Lean on me." *Education Week,* p. 27.

or neurological disorders that interefere with his or her ability to master the standard school curriculum. **Dyslexia,** for example, is a learning disability in which the person sees letters and numbers backwards or in a jumbled order. Likewise, **attention deficit disorder** is supposedly a learning disability that prevents its victims from being able to concentrate on their classroom activities for any sustained period of time. Critics, however, contend that so-called learning disabilities were invented to account for the unexplainable academic failure of middle- and upper-class students. In this vein, only 120,000 children were identified as having learning disabilities in 1969, in contrast to 1,872,399 in 1987—a finding that some feel suggests that the label has become a catch-all phrase for any problem that students have in mastering school material (Coles, 1987).

More problematic still, educators and researchers have been unable to agree on what *learning disability* actually means. As a result, Congress established a federal task force in 1988 to come up with a definition of learning disabilities and a head count of how many people are afflicted. The task force was unable to reach a consensus and urged, instead, establishing a research center to bring together psychologists, physicians, and educators to devise a classification system for defining and diagnosing learning disabilities (Lander, 1987). The mystery thus remains: Are unsuccessful students actually afflicted by neurological disabilities, or is learning disability a fictional explanation for problems that actually reside in our schools and families?

Cognitive Styles

It appears that we learn through different **cognitive styles.** That is, some of us learn material best through silent reading—a visual style—while others learn best through listening—an aural style. Likewise, some of us seem to learn best in a more structured classroom with a somewhat more authoritarian teacher who provides us with clear, predetermined guidelines. Others of us prefer a more unstructured class in which we are left to our own means for mastering the material. As a result, our different learning, or cognitive, styles may affect our success as students. If we happen to be in a class with a teacher whose methods are not matched to our particular cognitive style, we might fail, or at least do more poorly than with another teacher. Given this possibility, teachers are being urged to use a variety of teaching methods in their classes to increase the likelihood that students with different learning styles can succeed (Carbo, Dunn, & Dunn, 1986).

Overexposure to Lead

Not only does our learning style affect our school performance, but so does our exposure to lead, which comes into our bodies through lead-based paints, unleaded gasoline, and bad drinking water. A longitudinal study of young adults who had been exposed to lead as children has shown that these people are seven times less likely to graduate from high school and six times more likely to read at least 2 years below grade level than people not exposed to lead. Although previous studies had shown that children exposed to lead have lower IQs and perform more poorly in school than "lead-free" children, this is the first study to demonstrate that these handicaps persist into adulthood. Even more disturbing, these individuals had shown no visible signs of lead poisoning as children or as adolescents, making the findings even more intriguing for those of us trying to prevent school failure (Needleman, et al., 1990).

The federal Agency for Toxic Substances and Disease now estimates that between 3 and 4 million children (16%) have enough lead in their blood levels to be harmful. Likewise, the Centers for Disease Control recommend that all children between the ages of 1 and 5 have a blood test to assess their lead levels. Given that children from low-income families are more likely than those from higher income families to be exposed to high levels of lead, these findings have special implications for our work with at-risk students. If we cleaned the lead out of these children's bodies (and there are medical treatments for reducing their lead levels), how might the lives of impoverished adolescents improve as a consequence of their succeeding in school?

Parents' Income and Education

As has been repeatedly pointed out throughout this chapter, no other variable predicts adolescents' academic performance as reliably as their parents' income and education. For example, more than half of the 1980 college freshmen had fathers with at least some college education, while only 15% had fathers without a high-school diploma (V. Grant & Snyder, 1984). Given that parents with higher incomes frequently are better educated, become parents later in life, and have fewer children than low-income parents, these findings are not particularly surprising. Understandably, parents with higher incomes can more easily provide

What accounted for your successes and failures in high school?

the kinds of experience that enhance their child's intellectual and educational skills: travel, summer camps, academic tutors, music lessons, home computers, well-balanced diets, a quiet environment in which to study. It makes sense, then, that almost 80% of the adolescents from high-income families expect to earn bachelor's or graduate degrees, in contrast to only 15% of those from low-income homes (Peng, Fetters, & Kolstad, 1981).

Unfortunately, since parents' educations and incomes are closely linked to their childrens' educational achievements, minority youths are placed in double jeopardy. For instance, only 50% of Hispanic and 63% of African American adults have a high-school degree, in contrast to 80% of white adults. Likewise, only 10% of Hispanic or African American adults graduate from college, in comparison to 21% of white adults (U.S. Bureau of the Census, 1988a). In terms of income, Hispanic poverty is expected to exceed that of African Americans by the end of this decade. Even in 1985 the per capita income for Hispanics was only $6,613 and for African Americans, $6,840, in contrast to $11,671 for whites (Miller, Nicolau, Orr, Valdivieso, & Walker, 1988). Given their parents' educations and incomes and what has been said in this chapter about the effects of these factors, it is not surprising that 45% of Hispanic and 40% of African Americans adolescents have failed at least 1 year in school, in contrast to only 25% of white students (U.S. Bureau of the Census, 1988a).

Although the issue of family poverty will be discussed in detail in the next chapter, it is important to note that most of our nation's poor children are not living in single-parent households in inner-city ghettos. In fact, fewer than 9% of our poor children live in large central cities. Moreover, most poor children live with two parents who are both employed, and 50% of all poor children are white (Bane & Ellwood, 1989). In short, the key to understanding poverty lies beyond focusing on the ghetto, nonwhite poor.

Despite the relationship between poverty and children's chances for succeeding in school, low-income children do not have to be doomed to academic failure.

7.6 ADOLESCENT VOICES

Dropouts Talk About School

SHEILA, 17 "In the 9th grade, I really started f---ing up. They were threatening my mom. If I didn't go to school, they were going to fine her 50 days in jail or something. My dad used to beat me up pretty bad. I had bruises. I wouldn't go to school because I was afraid. What could I say? 'Oh, I got in a fight.' Five fights a day? I finally went and told the school nurse what happened. They got me a social worker. I told them, 'Don't say anything to my dad until you get me out of the house.' They said, 'O.K., O.K., don't worry.' The motherf-----s told him, called him and let him know. He came home and beat the s--- out of me."

BRENT, 18 "I was 18 and a senior when I dropped out three weeks ago. I used to get harassed by the teachers and the whole student body because I was different. If you think that dropping out of school is best for you, then that's what you should do because you'll feel more happy about it. The problem is the drop-outs who don't know why they dropped out. I know why I dropped out, so I'm not a problem."

SARA, 15 "It doesn't make sense. That's what everybody says. Of course it doesn't make sense. How could it make sense? I mean, if you're looking for why we're dropping out to make sense, forget it. The young, gifted, middle-class and bored. Fits me well. What is my opinion of education? Do you mean education as Plato saw it or as I see it? I see it as learning and it doesn't matter how you do it as long as you learn something."

CARRIE, 17 "It's the fault of both teachers and students. Because you might have an excellent teacher who's willing to give it her best and some student comes in all wasted, doesn't want to do anything, tells her to f--- off or something. She bums out and loses her desire to teach. On the other hand, the student can go in there with a great desire to learn, but the teacher is not the best or something. And they bum out the kid, and the kid doesn't learn anything. We need something like Dropouts Anonymous, where teachers, students, parents, administrators and family members all get to talk about it. Because when you think about it, kids don't really drop out because of the school. They drop out because there's some other personal problem that is affecting the way they came to school."

Source: A. Sheffield & B. Frankel (Eds.). (1989). *When I was young I loved school: Dropping out and hanging in.* New York: Children's Express Foundation, Inc.

As we have seen, we have the know-how and the technology to help these students succeed, despite their economic plight. But we must recognize that the proportion of children growing up in poverty in our society is increasing and that, as a consequence, more and more young people will be at risk of academic and financial failure. The question remains: Will we commit energy and our financial resources to these young people?

CONCLUSION

Considering the thousands of hours that adolescents have spent in school, it is little wonder that educators and researchers have directed so much attention to the impact of education. At this time in the world economy, and in our personal lives, formal education has assumed a special significance. Without the basic academic skills that many adolescents now lack, our economy, as well as our young people, suffer. Whether we ourselves are directly involved in educating adolescents, none of us can escape the reality that improving our young people's academic skills will benefit each of us as citizens in a country that must remain competitive in the world economy. We will also shoulder the financial and moral responsibility for supporting those young people who have been too poorly educated to support themselves.

QUESTIONS FOR DISCUSSION AND REVIEW

Review Questions

Cite specific percentages, scores, and numbers to justify your answers.

1. How have our schools and teachers changed since the turn of the century?
2. How do adolescents and their teachers feel about school? What troubles them most and least?
3. How do the academic skills and educational attainments (high-school diplomas and college degrees) of white, African American, Hispanic, Asian-American, and Native American students compare?
4. How do the academic skills of students in our society compare to those of other industrialized nations in regard to science? math? reading?
5. Which students are at risk, and what types of programs, teaching techniques, and school policies have proved effective in helping them?
6. How extensive are school violence, theft, and vandalism, and how have educators successfully reduced these problems?
7. How committed is our society to adolescents in terms of educational spending? How do the various states compare in this regard?
8. What is the confluence model, and how has it been used to explain the trends in SAT scores?
9. In regard to SAT scores, how do males and females compare? whites and minorities? students today with those of the past?
10. What is curriculum tracking? What are its advantages and disadvantages? Why is it so popular?
11. What are cooperative learning strategies, schools within schools, mastery learning, programs that teach thinking, and multicultural curricula? How and why does each advance students' academic skills?
12. How successful is preschool education? In what ways? Why?
13. Which attitudes, policies, and teaching techniques in our schools are detrimental to our students' academic progress?

14. What are learning disabilities and cognitive styles? How might these account for students' problems in school?
15. Which students are most likely to be suspended or to have corporal punishment administered?

Questions for debate

1. Which problems do you consider most serious in our public schools? Why?
2. Other than the ways mentioned in this chapter, how can our secondary schools be improved? What changes have you observed in schools that you least and most respect?
3. How do you feel about revoking the driver's licenses of dropouts? Of the methods mentioned in this chapter for reducing our dropout rate and improving students' academic skills, which do you like most and why? Which do you like least and why?
4. How would you go about reducing school vandalism, violence, theft, and truancy? Which methods have you observed that are and are not effective in reducing these problems in schools?
5. How do you feel about curriculum tracking? Why?
6. As a high-school teacher, how would you go about making your students less apathetic? Which of your teachers were most motivating? Why?
7. How do you feel about the quality of your own education? In what ways would you have liked your schools' policies, the curricula, and the teachers to have been different?
8. How do you think you would have reacted to cooperative learning strategies, schools within a school, and a multicultural curriculum? How do you feel about incorporating these ideas into our suburban and inner-city schools?
9. Other than suspensions and corporal punishment, how could teachers and administrators punish adolescents? What are the most creative or the most effective punishments you have ever observed or experienced in school?
10. Would you be willing to be a secondary school teacher, counselor, or principal in the inner city if the pay were high enough? Why or why not? How does your answer make you feel about yourself?

GLOSSARY

at-risk youths Students who are at high risk of failing in school or of graduating without basic skills in reading, writing, and math.

attention deficit disorder (ADD) A syndrome in which the individual is excessively energetic, impulsive, and unable to concentrate on an activity for any sustained period of time.

Beethoven project An extensive early childhood enrichment program now underway for parents and children living in the nation's largest public housing project in Chicago.

cognitive style The characteristic style each individual generally uses when involved in cognitive tasks, for example, reflective or impulsive style. Synonym: learning style.

confluence model The theory that family size, birth order, and spacing of siblings are partially responsible for certain personality traits and cognitive abilities.

contingency contract A written or verbal agreement in which the parties concur on certain goals stated in terms of specific behaviors. The rewards and punishments for achieving or failing to achieve these goals are also clearly specified; a behavior modification technique.

dyslexia A condition causing problems in learning to read when no disorders—such as mental retardation, or cultural factors—such as coming from a home where English is not spoken, are apparent.

LD child *See* Learning disability.

learning disability In people of normal or above-average intelligence, difficulties in learning to read, write, or do math that are assumed to stem from some form of minimal brain dysfunction.

mastery learning A system of teaching and grading that allows students to work at their individual pace to master specifically stated criteria without competing against other students.

multicultural curriculum A curriculum that includes information about and the perspectives of various cultural groups rather than being restricted exclusively to the white middle class culture.

schools within schools Schools which assign students to small cooperative groups under the direction of a team of teachers who stay with them over a period of several years.

self-fulfilling prophecy A term used to refer to the fact that things often turn out just as one expected they would. For example, a math teacher expects female students to do poorly, so she treats them in ways that increase the likelihood that the prophecy is fulfilled.

tracking The traditional practice of segregating students into classes, such as college preparatory, vocational education, special education or general, on the basis of their academic skills or future interests.

REFERENCES

Adelman, C., & Alsalam, N. (1989). *High school graduates and mathematics.* Washington, DC: U.S. Department of Education.

American Council on Education. (1989). *Seventh annual status report on minorities in higher education.* Washington, DC: Author.

American School Health Association. (1988). *National adolescent health survey.* Washington, DC: Author.

Bane, M., & Ellwood, D. (1989). One fifth of the nation's children: Why are they poor? *Science, 245,* 1047–1054.

Bennett, D. (1986.) *Comprehensive multicultural education.* Boston: Allyn Bacon.

Berlin, G., & Sum, A. (1988). *Toward a more perfect union: Basic skills, poor families and our economic future.* New York: Ford Foundation.

Beyer, B. (1987). *Practical strategies for the teaching of thinking.* Boston: Allyn Bacon.

Blake, J. (1989). *Family size and achievement.* Berkeley, CA: University of California Press.

Boyer, E. (1983). *High school.* New York: Harper & Row.

Carbo, M., Dunn, R., & Dunn, K. (1986). *Teaching students to read through individual learning styles.* Englewood Cliffs, NJ: Prentice-Hall.

Carnegie Council on Adolescent Development (1989). *Turning points: Preparing American youth for the 21st century.* Washington, DC: Author.

Carnegie Foundation. (1987). *An imperiled generation: Saving urban schools.* Lawrenceville, NJ: Princeton University Press.

Carnegie Foundation. (1988a). *The condition of teaching.* Lawrenceville, NJ: Princeton University Press.

Carnegie Foundation. (1988b). *Report card on school reform: The teachers speak.* Lawrenceville, NJ: Princeton University Press.

Carnegie Foundation for the Advancement of Teaching (1987). *National survey of public school teachers.* Washington, DC: Author.

Carroll, D. (1980). *College persistence and degree attainment for 1980 high school graduates.* Washington, DC: Department of Education.

Catterall, J. (1987). On the social costs of dropping out of school. *The High School Journal, 71,* 19–30.

Center for Learning and Teaching Literature. (1988). *A study of book length works taught in high school English courses.* Albany, NY: Author.

Children's Defense Fund. (1985). *Black and white children in America.* Washington, D.C.

Children's Defense Fund. (1988). *Survey of state policies and programs in the middle grades.* Washington, DC: Author.

Chipman, S., Segal, J., & Glaser, R. (Eds.). (1985). *Thinking and learning skills.* Hillsdale, NJ: Erlbaum.

Clark, J. (1989). *Laying down the law: Joe Clark's strategy for saving our schools.* Washington, DC: Regnery Gateway.

Cohen, D. (1989, February 1). Beethoven staff pushing on. *Education Week,* p. 9.

Cohen, E. (1986). *Designing groupwork: Strategies for the heterogeneous classroom.* New York: Teachers College Press.

Coleman, J., et al. (1966). *Equality of educational opportunity.* Washington, DC: U.S. Government Printing Office.

Coles, G. (1987). *The learning mystique: A critical look at learning disabilities.* New York: Pantheon Books.

College Exam Board. (1988). *Scholastic Aptitude Test performance.* Princeton, NJ: Author.

Council of Chief State School Officers. (1988). *School success for students at risk.* Fort Worth, TX: Harcourt Brace Jovanovich.

Dillon, R., & Sternberg, R. (1986). *Cognition and instruction.* Orlando, FL: Academic Press.

Diprete, T. (1981). *Discipline and order in American high schools.* Washington, DC: National Center for Education Statistics.

Doyle, D., & Hartle, T. (1985). *Excellence in education: The states take charge.* Washington, DC: American Enterprise Institute.

Economic Policy Institute. (1989). *Shortchanging education: How U.S. spending on grades K–12 lags behind other industrial nations.* Washington, DC: Economic Policy Institute.

Education Commission of the States. (1988). *Securing our future: The report of the national Forum for Youth At Risk.* Denver, CO: Education Commission of the States.

Educational Research Information Clearinghouse. (1982). *School size: A reassessment of the small school.* Washington, DC: Educational Research Information Clearinghouse.

Godlad, J. (1983). *A place called school: Prospects for the future.* New York: McGraw-Hill.

Gollnick, D. & Chinn, P. (1986). *Multicultural education.* Columbus, OH: Charles Merrill.

Good, T., & Brophy, J. (1984). *Looking in classrooms.* New York: Harper & Row.

Grant, G. (1989). *The world we created at Hamilton High.* Cambridge, MA: Harvard University Press.

Grant, V., & Snyder, T. (Eds.). (1984). *Digest of education statistics.* Washington, DC: National Center for Education Statistics.

Hakuta, K. (1986). *Mirror of language: The debate on bilingualism.* New York: Basic Books.

Hampel, R. (1984). *American high schools since 1940.* Boston: Houghton Mifflin.

Hargis, C. (1989). *Teaching low achieving and disadvantaged students.* Springfield, IL: Charles Thomas.

Haskins, R. (1989). The efficacy of early childhood education. *American Psychologist, 44,* 274–282.

Holmes, B. (1989, May 17). A closer look at the shortage of minority teachers. *Education Week,* p. 29.

Houlihan, T. (1988). *School effectiveness: The key ingredients of schools with heart.* Springfield, IL: Charles Thomas.

Hyman, I. (1989, April 26). The make believe world of "Lean on me." *Education Week,* p 27.

Insel, P., & Jacobsen, L. (Eds.). (1975) *What do you expect: An inquiry into self-fulfilling prophecies.* Menlo Park, CA: Cummings Publishers.

International Association for the Evaluation of Education Achievement. (1988). *Science achievement in seventeen countries.* New York: Pergamon Press.

Jackson, A., & Hornbeck, D. (1989). Educating young adolescents. *American Psychologist, 44,* 831–836.

Johnson, D., & Johnson, R. (1987). *Learning together and alone: Cooperative, competitive, and individualistic learning.* Englewood Cliffs, NJ: Prentice-Hall.

Kavrell, S., & Petersen, A. (1985). Patterns of achievement in early adolescence. In M. Maehr and M. Steinkamp (Eds.), *Women and science,* pp. 283–301. Greenwich, CT: JAI Press.

Keizer, G. (1988). *No place but here: A teacher's vocation in a rural community.* New York: Viking.

Kohn, A. (1986). *No contest: The case against competition.* Boston: Houghton Mifflin.

Lakebrink, J. (Ed.). (1989). *Children at risk.* Springfield, IL: Charles Thomas.

Landers, S. (1987, December). LD definition disputed. *Education Week,* p. 35.

Levine, D. (Ed.). (1985). *Improving student achievement through mastery learning programs.* San Francisco: Jossey-Bass.

Lipsitz, J. (1984). *Successful schools for young adolescents.* New Brunswick, NJ: Transaction Books.

McKenna, T., & Ortiz, F. (1988). *The broken web: The educational experience of Hispanic American women.* Berkeley, CA: Floricanto Press.

McKnight, C. (1987). *The underachieving curriculum: Assessing U.S. mathematics from an international perspective.* Champaign, IL: Stipes Publishing.

Meyers, C. (1986). *Teaching students to think critically.* San Francisco: Jossey-Bass.

Miller, S., Nicolau, S., Orr, M., Valdivieso, R., & Walker, G. (1988). *Too late to patch: Reconsidering opportunities for Hispanic and other dropouts.* New York: Hispanic Policy Development Project.

Mitchell, A. (1988). Black adolescent novels in the curriculum. *English Journal, 77,* 95–97.

National Assessment of Educational Progress. (1988a). *The mathematics report card.* Princeton, NJ: Author.

National Assessment of Educational Progress. (1988b). *The science report card.* Princeton, NJ: Author.

National Assessment of Educational Progress. (1988c). *A world of difference: science achievement in industrialized nations.* Princeton, NJ: Author.

National Center for Education Statistics. (1983). *High school and beyond study.* Washington, DC: Author.

National Center for Education Statistics (1988). *School enrollment by age and race.* Washington, DC: Author.

National Center for Education Statistics. (1989a). *Moonlighting among public school teachers.* Washington, DC: Author.

National Center for Education Statistics. (1989b). *Public elementary and secondary current expenditures.* Washington, DC: Author.

National Coalition of Advocates for Students. (1988). *School discipline and race.* Boston: Author.

National Commission on Excellence in Education (1983). *A nation at risk.* Washington, DC: Author.

National Commission on Secondary Schooling for Hispanics. (1984). *Make something happen: A report on secondary schooling for Hispanics.* New York: Author.

National Education Association. (1968). *Ability grouping: A research summary.* Washington, DC: Author.

National Education Association. (1988). *Rankings of the states.* Washington, DC: Author.

Needleman, H., Schell, A., Bellinger, D., Leviton, A., & Alred, E. (1990). The long term effects of exposure to low doses of lead in childhood. *The New England Journal of Medicine, 322,* 83–88.

Nickerson, R., Perkins, D. & Smith, E. (1985). *The teaching of thinking.* Hillsdale, NJ: Erlbaum.

Nielsen, L. (1982). *How to motivate adolescents: A guide for parents, teachers and counselors.* Englewood Cliffs, NJ: Prentice-Hall.

Nursten, J., & Carrol, H. (1981). *Unwillingly to school: school phobia or school refusal.* New York: Pergamon Press.

Oakes, J. (1985). *Keeping track: How schools structure inequality.* New Haven, CT: Yale University Press.

Ornstein, A., & Levine, D. (Eds.). (1990). *Introduction to the frontiers of education.* Boston: Houghton Mifflin.

Peng, S., Fetters, W., & Kolstad, A. (1981) *High school and beyond: A national longitudinal study for the 1980's.* Washington, DC: National Center for Education Statistics.

Plisko, V. (Ed.). (1984). *The condition of education.* Washington, DC: National Center for Education Statistics.

Powell, A., Farrar, E., & Cohen, D. (1985). *The shopping mall high school: Winners and losers in the educational marketplace.* Boston: Houghton Mifflin.

Presseisen, B. (Ed.). (1988). *At-risk students and thinking: Perspectives from research.* Washington, DC: National Education Association.

Riddle, W. (1988). *Early childhood education and development.* Washington, DC: Congressional Research Service.

Rosenthal, R., & Jacobson, L. (1968). *Pygmalion in the classroom.* New York: Holt, Rinehart and Winston.

Rosser, P. (1988). *The S.A.T. gender gap.* Washington, DC: Center for Women's Policy Studies.

Rothman, R. (1989, October 11). Denver abolishes remedial classes. *Education Week,* p. 27.

Rothman, R. (1988, December 14). Minnesota to mandate multicultural and gender fair curriculum. *Education Week,* p. 15.

Schmitt, C. (1989). *Changes in educational attainment: A comparison among 1972, 1980 and 1982 seniors.* Washington, DC: U.S. Department of Education.

Schorr, L., & Schorr, D. (1988). *Within our reach: Breaking the cycle of disadvantage.* New York: Anchor Books.

Simmons, R., & Blyth, D. (1987). *Moving into adolescence: The impact of pubertal change and school context.* New York: Aldine de Gruyter.

Sheffield, A. & Frankel, B. (Eds.) (1989). *When I was young I loved school: Dropping out and hanging in.* New York: Children's Express Foundation.

Sizer, T. (1984). *Horace's compromise: The dilemma of the American high school.* Boston: Houghton Mifflin.

Slavin, R. (1985). *Learning to cooperate, cooperating to learn.* New York: Plenum Press.

Smith, R., & Lincoln, C. (1988). *America's shame, America's hope: Twelve million youth at risk.* New York: Charles Stewart Mott Foundation.

Sommer, B. (1985). Truancy in early adolescence. *Journal of early adolescence, 5,* 145–160.

Tiedt, P., & Tiedt, I. (1986). *Multicultural teaching.* Boston: Allyn Bacon.

U.S. Bureau of the Census. (1988a). *School enrollment and characteristics of students: 1986.* Washington, DC: U.S. Government Printing Office.

U.S. Bureau of the Census. (1988b). *The Hispanic population in the U.S.: March 1988.* Washington, DC: U.S. Government Printing Office.

Viadero, D. (1989). L.A. school embraces a West German import. *Education Week, 9,* 1.

Wang, M., & Walberg, H. (Eds.). (1985). *Adapting instruction to individual differences.* Berkeley, CA: McCutchan.

West, P. (1988, September 28). On line at home. *Education Week,* p. 20.

Wigginton, E. (1985). *Sometimes a shining moment: 20 years in a high school classroom, the Foxfire experience.* Garden City, NY: Doubleday.

Wilder, G., & Powell, K. (1988). *Sex differences in test performance: A survey of the literature.* New York: College Board Publications.

Wilson, W. (1987). *The truly disadvantaged.* Chicago: University of Chicago Press.

Woodhead, M. (1988). The case of early childhood intervention. *American Psychologist, 43,* 443–454.

Zajonc, R. (1986). The decline and rise of scholastic aptitude scores. *American Psychologist, 41,* 862–868.

8 Adolescents and Their Families

CHAPTER OUTLINE

GOALS AND OBJECTIVES

This chapter is designed to enable you to:

- Refute the myths regarding adolescence as a family "crisis"
- Identify the situations and issues that create the most conflict for adolescents and their parents
- Explain the father's role in adolescents' social, vocational, and cognitive development
- Examine the effects of sibling relationships and birth order
- Consider the advantages and disadvantages of various styles of parenting
- Discuss the changes in the American family in regard to poverty, divorce, single-parenting, and women's employment
- Examine the impact of child abuse, sexual abuse, and incest

CONCEPTS AND TERMINOLOGY

Aid to Families with Dependent Children (AFDC)
authoritarian parents
authoritative parents
confluence theory
deficit family model
intentionality
joint custody
joint residency
latchkey children
mediation
permissive parents

DYNAMICS WITHIN THE FAMILY

What comes to mind when you hear the phrase *the American family?* Do you envision a mother and a father sitting around the dinner table with their two children? Do you imagine an endless series of family fights and the rise of the generation gap as children enter adolescence? Do you see the "ideal" family as one in which a child has at least one sibling? Do you envision a father with a stable job, a mother who is a full-time homemaker while her children are young, and a future in which the children will attain a standard of living at least equal to that of their parents?

With such questions in mind, in the first half of this chapter we will examine the dynamics within the family: the impact of various styles of parenting, the types of conflict that most adolescents do—and do not—experience with their parents, the existence of the supposed generation gap, the father's role in adolescent development, and the relationships among siblings. Beyond these dimensions of a family, however, changes within our society have dramatically transformed our families: the rising rates of divorce, out-of-wedlock births, poverty, women's employment, child abuse, and incest. Each of these topics, therefore, will be examined in the second half of this chapter as a powerful force that has altered our very definition of family and has cast millions of adolescents into situations that baffle our schools, social service agencies, and politicians.

Adolescence as Family Crisis: Fact or Fiction?

The generation gap While very much alive and well, Mark Twain once wrote, "Reports of my death have been grossly exaggerated." The same can be said of the generation gap that supposedly exists between adolescents and their parents. Despite the fact that many parents fear their child's adolescence as a time when a huge gap will suddenly appear between them, data from the 1970s and 1980s have been remarkably consistent on this one point: The majority of teenagers accept their parents' religious, political, educational, and social values (Bachman, Johnston, & O'Malley, 1986; Hill, 1987; Offer, Ostrov, & Howard, 1981; Youniss & Smollar, 1985). Even at the height of protest in the 1960s during the Vietnam War, most parents and their adolescent or college-age children shared the same values (Gallatin, 1980; Yankelovich, 1981).

If these data are true, why do so many people continue to believe in a generation gap? In part, the idea of a gap between young and old was reinforced by the amount of publicity given to young protestors of the 1960s and early 1970s who were openly critical of the older generation and "the establishment." Less attention was paid to the fact, however, that only a small percentage of young people, most of whom were college students, participated in these protests. Moreover, most of these young people were acting out the beliefs of their own parents, not rebelling against their upbringing.

The belief in a generation gap is also reinforced by the fact that most adolescents and their parents do disagree on issues related to their day-to-day habits and tastes—the type of music and clothes that are acceptable, curfews, household chores, table manners, dating rules. These disagreements, which are often the subject of adults' conversations, understandably contribute to the general impression that adolescents and their elders just do not see eye to eye on anything. Then, too, adolescence is the time of life when children usually separate themselves more from their parents, being less physically affectionate with them, spending more time away from home with friends, falling in love, planning for a future away from the family nest. Unfortunately, these natural and healthy moves toward independence can be misconstrued as signs of a widening gap between adolescents and parents. What is often overlooked is that parents' choices of neighborhoods, churches, and adult friends influence the pool from which their own children select friends. Consequently, even though adolescents spend more time with their friends and less time with their parents, those teenage friends typically reflect the values and behavior of the parents (Hartup, 1983; Rubin & Sloman, 1984). Most adolescents do not reject their parents' values about those areas that will have the most impact on their adult lives: education, religion, politics, vocations, and family styles.

Conflict Between Adolescents and Their Parents

Degree of conflict Whether we are 15 or 50, most of us will experience some degree of conflict and stress with our parents. The question is not so much whether adolescents and their parents argue and create stress for one another as how the conflicts between them differ from those of older or younger children and their parents. Contrary to earlier notions, researchers now agree that most adolescents and their parents do not experience serious conflicts (Hill, 1987; Montemayor, 1986; Offer, Ostrov, & Howard, 1981; Steinberg, 1987). Moreover, as the comments in Boxes 8.1 and 8.2 demonstrate, adolescents can display an amazing sensitivity toward their parents and their elders. This is not to say that adolescence is a conflict-free period for children and their parents, but as adolescents age and their parents grant them more control over personal matters, the family's conflicts subside (Smetana, 1988).

More important, even though conflicts arise between adolescents and their parents, a strong bond remains between them (Grotevant & Cooper, 1983; Youniss & Smollar, 1985). For some time, sociological and psychological researchers viewed adolescence as the period in which young people severed their relationships with their parents. In fact, severing the relationship was considered a prerequisite for establishing autonomy. Today, however, researchers agree that most adolescents care deeply about their parents' opinions and maintain a loving relationship while forming an identity of their own. For example, a review of the literature shows that adolescents usually name their parents, not their peers, as the most influential people in their lives (Galbo, 1984).

8.1

ADOLESCENT VOICES

The Kids' Book about Parents

The adolescents at Fayerweather Street School have written a book for other young people about relationships with parents. The following excerpts from *The Kids' Book about Parents* represent the central theme underlying the text: "In the world we live in, we know that kids are no longer happy, simple little people who play in the park all day and do whatever their parents tell them to do."

Here are some of the flaws that we've noted in our parents: being impatient, yelling too easily, being a health nut, embarrassing you in public, having a closed mind, changing their minds a lot, being obnoxious in public, nagging, using old-fashioned words, being a bad cook, forgetting birthdays, acting too sweet, talking loudly, pretending to listen to you, letting people push them around, picking fights over nothing, making arrangements with kids and then breaking them, being stubborn, driving too slowly, never being home, being lazy (p. 23).

Sometimes you'll find that parents will surprise you with their generosity, even when you think they might give you a hard time about it. Calbe said, "Recently I asked my father if I could have a raise in my allowance which had been at about $1 for the past three years. Sometimes it's pretty hard to talk to my father about things like this, and I was all ready to compromise at around $3, but I was surprised when he offered $5. Afterward although I definitely like the raise I got, I felt a little guilty because of the size of the allowance" (p. 36).

It's important to be ready with a good excuse when you want to stay up later. Here's a list of excuses we've used: "I'm not tired." "I have homework to

continued

Early adolescence Although most adolescents and their parents maintain close bonds and do not undergo terrible stress and strain, the early years of adolescence are generally the most stressful for the family (Montemayor, 1986; Shave & Shave, 1989). The fact that parents usually grant adolescents more freedom as the adolescents age is not a sufficient explanation for why early adolescence can be such a stressful period. Thus, researchers are attempting to explain this stress from several theoretical perspectives: the sociobiological, the psychoanalytic, and the social learning theories.

From the sociobiological perspective, researchers are examining the impact of changes in the adolescent's physical appearance on the family's interactions (Brooks-Gunn & Warren, 1990; Hill, et. al., 1985; Steinberg, 1988). Among the sociobiologists' questions are: How does the adolescent's physical maturation affect the relationship with his or her parents, and does the adolescent's physical maturation affect mothers more than fathers? From these studies, several intriguing findings are emerging. First, despite the adolescent's actual age, physical maturation increases the conflict, distance, and dissatisfaction in the parent-child relationship. That is, once the child begins to look grown-up, the parental relationship generally changes for the worse.

Why might this be? One line of research argues that the parents' own developmental issues contribute to the stress associated with their child's entrance into adolescence (Steinberg, 1987). At that time, the parents are usually in their late 30s or early 40s, a period when many adults are reappraising their own lives and trying to come to terms with some painful realities: an unhappy marriage, a

Box 8.1 continued

do." "I went to bed early last night." "John gets to stay up as late as he wants." "I have to watch this TV show for my social studies class." But you should be prepared for your parents to give you one of these answers: "You'll be grouchy in the morning.""I let you stay up later than most kids. The least you can do is go to bed when I ask you to." "Because I said so." "Go to bed as a present to me" (p. 43).

We made a list of all the gross and disgusting foods we could think of that parents like kids to eat: artichokes, beets, broccoli, brussel sprouts, cabbage, cauliflower, clams, eggplant, kale, kidney beans, kiwi fruit, lamb, lentil soup, lima beans, liver, mushrooms, oatmeal, pea soup, poached eggs, quiche, salmon, spinach, squash, succotash, tofu, turnips, yogurt, zucchini. If your parents start to tell you that you only eat lousy food and you should eat more okra, you can tell them that you like some of these foods: apple juice, baked potatoes, bread, carrots, chicken, corn, grape juice, hamburger, hot dogs, milk, orange juice, pies, rice, salad, spaghetti, steak, turkey, veal (p. 54).

Not all situations turn out with parents and kids feeling good about the pet. Last year Jake's grandpa came for a visit from New York and took Jake to a pet store. Jake told us, "He bought me two lizards. My mom was not thrilled with this, so we made a deal. If either of the lizards ever escaped, my mom would check into an expensive hotel at my grandpa's expense" (p. 75).

We all have different ways of knowing when our parents are unhappy. Here is a list of common warning signals for kids to watch out for: eating a lot, not talking, going to sleep early, not saying hi when they come home from work, chain smoking, arguing with cashiers, constantly cleaning things, snapping at everyone, ignoring your questions, making fun of your friends, beating up on the pets, driving too fast, yelling at other drivers and beeping the horn unnecessarily, slamming doors, staring blankly at the TV (p. 93).

Source: Fayerweather Street School. (1984). ***The kids' book about parents.*** Boston: Houghton Mifflin.

deterioration of physical beauty, a loss of athletic prowess or sexuality, an unfulfilling career. Some writers have even suggested that parents begin this introspective process, in part, because their children are entering adolescence (Baruch, Barnett, & Rivers, 1983).

From a psychoanalytic perspective, it is argued that parents identify with and see themselves reflected in their children at the onset of their children's adolescence. As young adolescents assume an increasingly sexual appearance and begin to behave more autonomously, their parents may feel less satisfied with their own lives: "If only I were still young, energetic, and attractive, with all life's possibilities still ahead of me." Moreover, during the process of individuation, the young adolescents perceive them for the first time as people with their own particular flaws. As a consequence, parents may react to the adolescents with a certain defensiveness and hypersensitivity emanating from their own feelings of insecurity or dissatisfaction with their own adult lives.

A recent study of 129 nuclear families with children between the ages of 10 and 15 demonstrates this psychoanalytic viewpoint (Steinberg, 1987). Fathers experiencing a mid-life crisis were more likely to have sons who had a less idealized image of the fathers and had a more individuated sense of self than to have sons who were more dependent. Similarly, mothers whose daughters were more physically mature, socially active, and emotionally independent had lower self-esteem and felt more dissatisfied with their lives than did mothers with more dependent daughters.

Finally, from a social learning theorist's perspective, early adolescence is more

8.2
ADOLESCENT VOICES
An Adolescent Male's View on the Elderly

He stares for a moment at the magazine that lies open before him on the table. "Now take this ol' cat, will you," he says, as he leans forward and points to a large color photograph of an elderly Navajo shepherd. "Would you look at his hands. Now those are some man's hands, all right. They've got wisdom in 'em. You can see his whole accumulated life experience right there, in all them craggly ol' wrinkles." He places a finger on the photographed hand. His young hands, like his feet, seem disproportionately large for his small but solid frame.

"Old people, man. You know, we've gotta stop trashing them. They've got a lot they can teach us. Now, I know that probably sounds real crazy comin' from a teen such as myself, but it's really true. Straight up. Older people is real important for young dudes like myself, and even for the young women. They're the ones who can show us how to do things, and when and where to do 'em at. They're the ones who should be models for us to show us what's good and bad, desirable and undesirable in life. I bet this old Indian here had someone to show him how to do things so the could feel like somebody. Bet he didn't have no deep blue funks. I remember in school this teacher tellin' us how the Indians really prepared their kids for manhood and womanhood. It was hard work, probably, you know, goin' through all them rituals and all, but at least those kids always knew there was a place for 'em and that there was somebody who was gonna help them get there. I tell ya, man, guidance. That's what it's all about, guidance. Having people around who've been there and can help you through whatever you're contendin' with. Just this morning as I was walking over here I saw this old lady. Man, it just gave me such a good feelin' to see her. I didn't talk to her or nothin', I haven't in years. But she recognized me, too, and we waved to each other." He is smiling. "She used to baby-sit me when I was real little. Just knowin' she's around and that she still remembers lets me know I still have a place in her mind."

Source: D. Frank, (1983). *Deep blue funk: Portraits of teenage parents.* Chicago: Ounce of Prevention Fund. Reprinted by permission.

stressful than later adolescence because parents and children are establishing new rules regarding acceptable and unacceptable behavior. In other words, much of what was acceptable for a child to do is no longer acceptable for an adolescent and vice versa. As children make the transition into adolescence, both they and their parents are redefining roles and rules: What is a fair curfew and bedtime hour? What is a reasonable amount of adult supervision? Who is in charge of choosing the child's clothes, food, movies, music, and friends? Who should be responsible for seeing to it that the adolescents do their homework every night?

Special conflicts with mothers Although adolescence is not a tumultous ordeal for most families, both sons and daughters do tend to experience more conflict with their mothers than with their fathers (Montemayor, 1986; Steinberg, 1987). In part this can be accounted for by the fact that mothers tend to base more of their self-esteem on their family roles than do fathers (Baruch, Barnett, & Rivers, 1983; Steinberg, 1987). As a consequence, a mother may feel more overwrought than a father when conflicts occur with her children and more threatened by her teenage children's growing independence. In other words, the woman who is overly involved in her role as a mother may have more conflict and stress with her teenage children than do men or women whose self-esteem comes from sources other than those involving children.

An even more obvious reason why teenagers are more likely to have conflicts with their mothers than with their fathers is that women are generally more involved in household matters and in the day-to-day care of children. Given the male and female roles that most parents act out, mothers and teenagers are more likely to be the ones who hassle over such routine matters as doing household chores, obeying curfews, playing music too loudly, and keeping rooms clean. On the other hand, mothers generally have the more intimate relationships with their children. Indeed, most adolescents say that they feel closer to their mothers and that their mothers understand them better than do their fathers (Grotevant & Cooper, 1986; Youniss & Smollar, 1985).

The Father's Role

Father-child involvement Whether you believe fathers ought to take a more active part in their childrens' lives, the fact remains that the father's impact on his children's development has virtually been ignored in the research until recent years. This reality reflects the traditional consensus, both in our legal system and in our private lives, that fathers are considered more dispensable and less crucial than mothers to their children's development.

Despite our more liberal attitudes about masculinity and fatherhood, most children still interact far less with their fathers than with their mothers (Bornstein & Cowan, 1988; Cath, Gurwitt, & Gunsberg, 1989; Juster, 1990; Lamb, 1986, 1987; Lewis & O'Brien, 1987). Indeed, these reviews of the literature have generally concluded that today's typical father does not interact significantly more with his children than did the fathers of yesteryear. It seems that the change in fathers' roles has been restricted to particular areas of family life. For example, between 1960 and 1980, fathers did become more involved with children at the time of childbirth. The question then becomes: Why are most men not participating more fully in raising their own children?

The most obvious answer is that most fathers are too busy earning the family's primary income to have much time left for their children. If we accept this explanation, the solution lies in helping men's and women's incomes become more equivalent. This explanation, however, does not wholly account for men's lack of involvement with their children. For example, in Sweden, where government policies enable fathers to spend extensive time with their children without financial penalties, few fathers choose to do so (Lamb & Levine, 1983. See Box 8.3). In our own society, even when husbands and wives work an equal amount of time outside the home, the women still assume the major responsibility for childcare in most families. In fact, most men spend no more time with their children when their wives are employed than when their wives are full-time homemakers (Gilbert, 1985 & 1988; Pleck, 1985). Such findings make it clear that many men need more than financial incentives to entice them to assume more active roles in their children's lives.

A CLOSER LOOK 8.3

Do Fathers Want to Spend Time With Their Children?

Sweden is the only country in the world where the government has had an official commitment to involve fathers in raising their own children. Recognizing that traditional employment practices prevented men from participating in childcare, the government devised a policy that permitted both parents to care for their children.

The present policy entitles each couple to 6 months of paid leave, which may be taken any time within the first 9 months of each child's birth. The parents are free to decide for themselves how to divide the leave. The parent who is on leave receives 90% of his or her regular salary out of a national insurance fund. Each parent is then entitled to another 6 weeks' leave any time in the first 7 years of the child's life, which can be used to reduce an employed parent's workday from 8 to 6 hours. Both parents are also entitled to 12 days of paid leave per year to take care of sick children. In addition, employers are required to give parents their former jobs and their former salaries when they return to work.

When the paid parental leave was first introduced in 1974, its advocates expected fathers to respond favorably to the idea of spending time with their children without financial penalties. Instead, only 2% of the fathers took parental leaves. A nationwide advertising campaign was then launched, picturing wrestlers, soccer players, and other "masculine" men who were walking, feeding, or holding their babies. Booklets describing the policy were widely distributed.

continued

Could it be that fathers are less involved in their children's lives because they are less competent as caretakers, particularly during the early months of infancy? Could it be that women just have a natural instinct for caring for children? Although these notions still exist, the research shows that mothers and fathers are equally competent—or equally incompetent—in caring for children, even newborns (Lamb, 1987). That is, regardless of gender, parents gain childcare skills through on-the-job training, not through instinctive know-how. The differences between mothers' and fathers' confidence and competence do, however, become more marked as years pass, since fathers spend increasingly less time around their children. Given their lack of on-the-job experience with children—their own or anyone else's—most fathers do eventually become less competent than most mothers in caring for their children. Not surprisingly, by the time children reach adolescence, their relationships with their own fathers have usually become more awkward and less intimate than those with their mothers (Youniss & Smollar, 1985).

In an effort to encourage more male involvement in child rearing, the Fatherhood Project was established in 1981 as a national research, demonstration, and dissemination center (Levine & Pleck, 1983). For example, the project has helped elementary and high schools establish childcare classes in which boys learn to care for infants and toddlers, to express affection publicly toward children, and to perceive the father's role as more than that of breadwinner. The premise of such projects is that once boys develop confidence in their childcare skills, they will seek out more contact with their own children in their future roles as fathers. The project also sponsors programs to help adult men learn how to be more effective fathers (Levant & Kelly, 1989).

Box 8.3 continued

Despite the advertising campaign, in 1979 only 11% of the fathers took any leave in families where both adults were employed full time. Of those men who did take a childcare leave, half left their jobs for only 1 month. Fathers with the most education and the highest salaries were the most likely to take a childcare leave.

Why haven't Swedish fathers taken advantage of the chance to take care of their own children? According to researchers who interviewed the Swedish fathers, many men refused to leave their jobs for fear of losing future advancement opportunities, fear of diminishing their professional reputation, or fear of displeasing their employers. Men in lower-status jobs were particularly worried about losing their status or chances for advancement by taking time away from work to care for their children. Moreover, the researchers found that sex role stereotypes also discouraged Swedish men from taking care of their children. Like U. S. men, most Swedish males are still socialized to perceive childcare as "women's work."

In Sweden's case, the government't financial incentives and publicity campaigns have failed to entice most fathers to take time away from work in order to care for their own children. Most Swedish men have chosen to ignore their government's "pro-family" policy and to leave the child-rearing responsibilities to women. How do you think U. S. fathers would respond to a policy like Sweden's? How might U. S. children benefit from more time with their fathers during infancy, childhood, and adolescence?

Source: M. Lamb & J. Levine. (1983). The Swedish parental insurance policy: An experiment in social engineering. In M. Lamb & A. Sagi (Eds.), *Fatherhood and family policy* (pp. 39–48). Hillsdale, NJ: Erlbaum.

How can we encourage boys and men to become more involved in nurturing and raising children?

Does this mean that all fathers should be encouraged to become more involved with their children? No—at least not according to some empirical evidence. Surprisingly, studies have shown that increased involvement between fathers and their children is not ideal for all families. To the contrary, increasing a father's involvement with his children sometimes has negative consequences (Pleck, 1985). For example, it has been assumed that employed women would be more satisfied if their husbands played a greater role in the family and in childcare; yet some women claim not to want their husbands more involved. Presumably, this is not a sign of woman's love of household or childcare chores, but her anxiety about abdicating her "power" within the family. In the only longitudinal studies of men who had been primary caretakers for their children, many of the families returned to more traditional divisions of family roles because of both the men's and the women's negative reactions to their experience (Radin & Goldsmith, 1985). In these families where fathers and mothers tried to share the roles of breadwinner and childcare more equally, the men's careers often suffered. Unfortunately, such results suggest that a man's increased involvement with his children can inadvertently add to the family's financial stress.

Such studies should not be misconstrued to mean that fathers do not need to be more involved with their children. Rather, these results remind us that trying to force fathers to interact more with their children might work against the family's best interests. In cases where the wife feels uncomfortable with her husband's being more involved with their children or in cases where the father is not interested in being more involved, encouraging fathers and children to interact might be disruptive to the family's functioning.

Fathers and sons Although most research has focused on the relationship between children and their mothers, recent studies are offering us more insight into the ways in which fathers influence their childrens' development (Bornstein & Cowan, 1988: Cath, Gurwitt, & Gunsberg, 1989; Lamb, 1986, 1987; Lewis & O'Brien, 1987; Sulzberger, 1987). This research shows that sons and daughters whose fathers are more involved with them have more cognitive skills, less sex-stereotyped beliefs, more internal locus of control attitudes, and more empathy than those with less involved fathers. Some interesting differences have emerged, however, in the ways that fathers influence their sons and their daughters.

To begin with, most fathers are more interested in and more involved with their sons than with their daughters, regardless of the children's ages. Although boys generally get more of their fathers' time and attention, they sometimes choose not to model themselves after their fathers. In trying to determine why this happens, researchers learned that fathers who are nurturant, supportive, and emotionally close to their sons have more influence over the sons' social and cognitive development than do distant, domineering, and unaffectionate fathers. Moreover, punitive, rejecting, or disinterested fathers undermine their sons' social and intellectual development, as do fathers who are overly domineering or overly protective. In terms of helping their sons become socially, intellectually, and vocationally successful, the best fathers are the ones who support their sons' independence, encourage their curiosity, and build their self-esteem while still setting limits and offering advice. Finally, since some research suggests that adolescent boys generally have more conflict with their mothers than adolescent girls, the father/son relationship might assume a particularly important role during the teenage years (Steinberg, 1987).

What impact has your father had on your development?

Fathers and daughters Unfortunately, a daughter is less likely than a son to have the kind of relationship with her father that will benefit her intellectually, socially, or vocationally (Bronstein & Cowan, 1988; Cath, Gurwitt, & Gunsberg, 1989; Lamb, 1986, 1987; Lewis & O'Brien, 1987; Marone, 1988; Sulzberger, 1987).

To begin with, fathers generally spend less time with their daughters than with their sons. As a consequence, whatever benefits might accrue from interacting with fathers are less likely to be given to girls than to boys. Moreover, when fathers do interact with their daughters, they do so differently than with their sons, being more apt to discourage their daughters' independence, to punish their curiosity and assertiveness, and to discourage them from fulfilling their full intellectual and vocational potential. In being treated like "daddy's little girl," many daughters, unlike sons, learn attitudes and behaviors that interfere with their intellectual and vocational growth. In loving their daughters, many fathers still inadvertently encourage them to become overly dependent on other people's approval, overly cautious about risk taking, and overly concerned with their social roles in comparison to their roles as students and future wage earners.

As a consequence of the way he responds to her teenage sexuality, a father also has a dramatic impact on his daughter's future happiness with the men in her life (Chodorov, 1978; Leonard, 1985; Tessman, 1989). By accepting his daughter's sexuality, by supporting her relationships with boys, and by helping her feel proud of her maturing body, a father helps his daughter lay the groundwork for healthy relationships with males; but by mocking or denigrating her sexuality, by treating her like a little girl, or by instilling sexual attitudes based on shame and guilt, a father undermines his daughter's sexual confidence, as well as her ability to relate in healthy, independent ways to her male peers. Unfortunately, too often a father feels uncomfortable, jealous, or angered by his daughter's blossoming sexuality and by her emotional attachment to boys her own age. Responding out of his own insecurities and jealousies, this father may tease, insult, or try to make his daughter feel guilty about issues related to dating, sexuality, or women's bodies.

From a psychoanalytic viewpoint, adolescence is the time when a girl should relinquish her childhood vision of her father as the "Prince Charming" among men—a man without imperfections, a man who can "rescue" her from the responsibilities of her own life. Only by giving up this childhood image can the teenage girl be free to fall out of love with daddy and fall in love with her male peers. Some fathers, however, refuse to relinquish their image as the heroic prince. Rather than letting their daughters see their frailties and imperfections, these fathers work at having their daughters idealize them. The unfortunate consequence is that these daughters may never outgrow their childhood dependence on daddy.

In these regards, the father is perhaps the most influential person in helping a teenage girl learn to balance her erotic, sexual roles with her achievement-oriented, intellectual roles. He is the person who helps or hinders her in achieving **intentionality,** the tendency to direct one's own energies toward a goal that has evolved from that individual's inner motivation, rather than primarily as a reaction to the wishes and demands of others. Intentionality means making an inner choice or plan, actively participating in implementing it, and being able to resist wishes and expectations of others when those wishes and expectations are against the individual's own better judgment. The daughter whose father praises her intellectual skills but keeps himself emotionally distant or denigrates her sexuality is likely to become a woman who is academically and professionally successful but whose emotional and sexual life is fraught with difficulty. Conversely, if her father supports her sexual and emotional life but denigrates her independence and her intellectual activities, she is likely to become a woman who has no identity aside from her personal relationships, who has difficulty asserting herself, who is ambivalent about her intellectual abilities, and who lacks intentionality. In other words, she is incapable of directing her own life.

In sum, the best father in terms of the one whose daughter is most likely to be happy in her sexual, personal, vocational, and intellectual life is the one who encourages her intentionality (Chodorow, 1978; Leonard, 1985; Tessman, 1989). He is actively involved with her, shows excitement about her unique interests, and demonstrates trust in her abilities and her judgments. This father is not restrictive, overly protective, or disparaging. He does not feel threatened by his daughter's accomplishments, so he does not need to compete with or demean her. Indeed, as she ages, he is as eager to learn from her as to instruct her. Moreover, this father is not only willing to let his daughter disagree with him but is also willing to let her express her anger toward him. This father recognizes that with a daughter, as with a son, expressing anger is a natural part of growing up and of human relationships. Anger is not in his eyes a sign of rejection nor is it unfeminine just because it is being expressed by his daughter rather than by his son. Finally, he does not relate to his teenage daughter as if she were a wife by expecting her to fulfill his own needs for nurturance, affection, intimacy, or sexual attention. He has made clear to his daughter that his primary emotional relationship is with his wife, which enables the daughter to grow in her own ways and on her own terms. It is this father whose adult daughter is most likely to telephone him announcing her latest accomplishment with the loving voice of her childhood: "Daddy, Daddy, guess what!"

Adolescents and Their Siblings

The influence of birth order Whether we are daughters or sons, most of us grew up in families with siblings. Given this demographic reality, researchers have investigated the impact that family size and birth order have on our intellectual, vocational, and academic development. Those who support the **confluence theory** contend that our intelligence, success in school, and vocational achievements are at least partially determined by our birth order, the number of siblings we have, and the number of years separating the birth of each sibling (Blake, 1989; Zajonc, 1983). The data in support of confluence theory are, of course, correlational and cannot be interpreted as cause and effect studies. Nevertheless, the advocates of this theory contend that the correlations are strong enough to warrant our serious attention.

According to confluence theory, being the first-born child or coming from a small family gives children an advantage intellectually, academically, and vocationally over children from large families. Children from small families are more likely to have been read to early in life than children from large families and to have experienced advantages such as music and dance lessons as well as travel. Leisure time among children from small families is also used in ways that serve to enhance educational and intellectual skills. In regard to education, the greatest impact of family size is not on the chances of going to college but on the chances of graduating from high school. Moreover, children without any siblings generally achieve more in terms of IQ scores, academic achievement, and vocational success than other children.

The correlational studies supporting the confluence model show that first-born children, only children, and children from small families achieve more than

A CLOSER LOOK 8.4

Family Size and SAT Scores: A Connection?

Between 1963 and 1980, adolescents' scores on the College Board's Scholastic Aptitude Tests (SAT) steadily declined, leaving both researchers and educators perplexed and generating a host of hypotheses to explain the declines. According to some analysts, such as Hunter Breland of the Educational Testing Service, about 44% of the decline is a consequence of the fact that so many more adolescents, especially students from minority groups, apply for college than in previous decades. Others have argued, however, that the declines since 1971 cannot be wholly attributed to the greater heterogeneity of the students taking the SAT. Thus, some researchers have blamed the public schools, claiming that teachers have lowered their standards so dramatically that students' performance on the college boards has suffered. Still others are criticizing parents for not instilling the proper motivation and values in their children.

In contrast to these hypotheses, however, Richard Franke, a professor of management at Loyola College, and Hunter Breland are placing the blame on another phenomenon: bigger families. According to Franke and Breland's analysis of the data, birth order and the number of children in a family account for 87% of the decrease in SAT scores, with these scores dropping 20 points for each additional child after the first.

Moreover, Franke and Breland contend that the high divorce rate and women's employment have detracted from SAT scores by limiting the intellectual stimulation that preschool children receive from their parents. On the basis of their

continued

children from large families on a number of measures. These children have attained a disproportionate percentage of merit scholarships, doctorates, and fame in their professions. As Box 8.4 illustrates, some confluence theorists even believe the recent rise in S.A.T. scores can be partially accounted for by smaller family size (Zajonc, 1986).

Before you go out bragging to your five younger siblings, however, you need to familiarize yourself with the criticisms of confluence theory. First and foremost, the studies supporting the confluence model are correlational, not experimental. In this vein, it is possible that family income and parents' education, not family size or birth order, are primarily responsible for the differences found in confluence studies. Since upper-income and well-educated parents tend to have the fewest children, it would stand to reason that their children would have more educational and intellectual benefits. Moreover, not all researchers have found strong correlations between academic achievement, family size, and birth order (Smith, 1982).

The only child Although the confluence model can be attacked on these grounds, it is nonetheless true that children without siblings are generally high achievers and successful students. A recent review of 155 studies shows that being an only child is an advantage, not a deficit (Falbo & Polit, 1986). In fact, in the areas of achievement, intelligence, sociability, character, and adjustment, only children are not substantially different from firstborns or from chldren from small families. Although parents with only one or two children are initially more anxious

Box 8.4 continued

analyses of data from 1965 to 1984, which take divorce rates and mothers' employment into consideration, Franke and Breland estimate that 97% of the SAT decline can be explained. According to their analyses, SAT scores have decreased 1.4 points for each 1% increase in the divorce or employment rate for mothers with preschool children.

In support of their theory, Franke and Breland point out that SAT scores declined during the 1960s and 1970s, when families were larger than in the two preceding decades. They attribute recent increases in SAT scores to the fact that adolescents in the 1980s come from smaller families than their cohorts in the 1960s and 1970s. Robert Zajonc, whose research on children without siblings is well-known, also predicts that SAT scores will rise as children from smaller families reach college age. According to Zajonc's research, firstborn children develop more intellectual skills and are likely to have higher achievement scores as a consequence of being intellectually stimulated through their early childhood interactions with adults rather than with siblings. From this perspective, the only child and children with the fewest siblings are the most intellectually advantaged.

As predicted by these theorists, the SAT scores for 1983's high-school seniors did increase 1 point on the verbal scores and 3 points on the math scores. Since neither the divorce rates nor the rates of female employment are declining, however, the outcomes of the SAT and other achievement tests may come increasingly to depend on the quality of preschool children's day-care centers. Thus, the question arises, will the day-care experiences of today's preschoolers have any significant impact on the SAT scores of adolescents in the year 2000?

Source: R. Zajonc. (1986). The decline and rise of scholastic aptitude scores. *American Psychologist, 41,* 862–867.

and have higher expectations than parents with larger families, their anxiety and expectations appear to help their children become high achievers. Since parents tend to spend more time with their only child or firstborn children, these children tend to acquire more sophisticated intellectual skills than do children from larger families. Although only children spend more time in solitary, intellectual, and artistic activities, they do not report being lonelier than children with siblings. Neither do they affiliate with more group activities than other youngsters in an effort to make up for the absence of siblings. In short, in terms of intellectual, academic, and vocational development, growing up without siblings is more of an advantage than growing up in a large family.

Similarities among siblings Despite the advantages of being an only child, most adolescents are growing up in families with siblings. Not surprisingly, psychologists have examined the similarities and differences between siblings and have tried to determine the relative impact of heredity and environment on family members.

In general this research is demonstrating that siblings are far less similar than is often assumed. For example, siblings are most alike in regard to their IQ scores, yet the correlations only range from .35 to .50. In other words, 75% of the variability in siblings' IQ scores is not accounted for by their being siblings. Moreover, the average difference between siblings' IQ scores is 13 points, in comparison with an average difference of 18 points between total strangers (Scarr

How close are you to your siblings? How similar are you?

& Grajek, 1982). There are even fewer similarities between siblings on measures of personality, attitudes, or psychological disturbance (Daniels & Plomin, 1985; Scarr & Grajek, 1982). In the words of psychologist Sandra Scarr, an award-winning expert in the field:

> Upper middle class brothers who attend the same school and whose parents take them to the same plays, sporting events, music lessons and therapists and who use similar child-rearing practices are little more similar in personality measures than they are to working-class farm boys whose lives are totally different. Now perhaps this is an exaggeration of the known facts, but not by much (Scarr, 1983, p. 361).

What do social learning theorists make of these surprising findings? How does this research figure in to the nature/nurture debate? If heredity is primarily responsible for our personalities and IQ, why are brothers and sisters not more alike? On the other hand, if environment is primarily responsible, why do children raised in the same family turn out so differently? This apparent paradox can be explained from several rational perspectives. First, even if genes do influence our personalities and cognitive abilities, each child in a family receives only half of each parent's genes. As a consequence, the number of different genetic combinations that each sibling might receive is quite large.

Second, just because children are raised in the same family does not mean that they are being raised in the same "environment" in terms of the types of reinforcement, punishment, or modeling that they receive. Siblings are not treated alike by their parents, nor do they encounter identical experiences outside the home. The older sister, for example, might be reinforced by her parents for being verbally assertive and independent. Her sister, while only a year younger, might, however, be treated like the baby of the family and be reinforced for more passive, dependent behavior. Moreover, what happens to each sister at school, with peers, and in the world at large is shaping her personality and attitudes.

Third, genetic makeup may be partially responsible for how individuals respond to certain rewards, punishments, and environmental stimuli. In other words, even when two sisters are exposed to exactly the same family interactions and experiences, each one's genetic uniqueness will influence her responses to the situation. These responses will, in turn, elicit different reactions (rewards and punishments) and different expectations (self-fulfilling prophecies) from the people around her. For instance, if one sister has a genetic predisposition toward being aggressive, she might interpret a casual remark from her mother as an attack, which will, in turn, elicit a hostile response. The other sister, hearing the same comment from her mother and having a genetic predisposition toward passivity, might toss the remark off with a joke. Understandably, the mother will respond differently to each of her daughters on the basis of such experiences, coming to expect that the one will always respond aggressively and the other passively. In other words, parents learn to interact differently with each child in the family on the basis of initial distinctions that existed between the children. Yet, as family patterns and roles are established, these initial differences between children—which may have been quite small at the outset—become more exaggerated. In short, how similar or how different siblings are depends on both genetic and environmental influences.

Styles of Parenting

Another reason siblings may differ from one another is that their parents may use different styles of interacting with and disciplining them. Within the same family, both parents are aging, having their own personal and marital crises, and being exposed to new experiences and new information related to child rearing. As a consequence, their styles of parenting can change from child to child. Especially in cases where there is a large age difference between the oldest and the youngest child, parents' attitudes toward child rearing may have changed—either for better or for worse. If the oldest child "turns out bad," permissive parents might become overly strict and dictatorial with their younger children. Conversely, strict parents might mellow after the first child. Likewise, most parents tend to be more permissive with their sons than with their daughters.

Aside from the question of why one sibling differs from another, researchers are also interested in parenting styles in relation to such questions as, How do different styles of parenting affect a child's development? How much impact do parents' disciplinary techniques have on their children? Is there a "best" style for raising children? Can we change a person's parenting style, and if so, how?

Limitations of the research In examining current research on such issues, we should keep several shortcomings in mind (Jones, 1984). To begin with, even when studies demonstrate a correlation between a certain style of parenting and certain types of adolescent behavior, this does not prove that the parent's behavior "caused" the adolescent to develop those attitudes or behavior. For example, if we find that most adolescents with high IQs and high grade point averages have parents who relate to them in a democratic, relatively relaxed style, we should not infer that the parents' nonauthoritarian style is what caused their children to be intelligent and academically successful. It may just as well be the case that these youngsters were exceptionally bright, well-adjusted, and self-controlled from an early age and that, as a consequence, their parents were able to respond to them in more democratic, less dictatorial ways. Given that the research on parenting styles is almost all correlational, we have no way of knowing which comes first, the child's "bad" behavior, which forces his or her parents to be more heavy-handed from the outset, or the parents' strict, authoritarian ways, which causes the child to become "badly behaved."

A second shortcoming is that it is difficult to measure what actually goes on when family members interact. How are we to determine how "aggressively" a teenage boy is behaving toward his father—by the boy's reports? by his father's reports? by his mother's reports? Since outside observers are not privy to the day-to-day interactions within a family, our information about families has to come from the family members themselves. Yet each person in a family has his or her own lapses of memory or distortions of reality, depending on that individual's own needs and attentiveness at any given moment. Try to recall, for example, the last argument that occurred between you and your parents before you graduated from high school: Who did what to whom? Were your parents being too authoritarian or too permissive? Were you being aggressive? How would they describe the incident? In other words, researchers studying the interactions within a family are in the awkward position of having to rely on retrospective and subjective data.

Still another shortcoming is that researchers, observers, parents, and children have a problem agreeing on the definitions of permissive, democratic, and authoritarian parenting. What is permissive in one family is perfectly acceptable in the next, and what is democratic in one might be considered relatively authoritarian to their neighbors. Arriving at a clearcut operational definition for each style of parenting and then having the data for every study collected in accord with these definitions would be the ideal, but it is not the reality. As a result, our conclusions about the impact of various parenting styles on adolescents are based on studies that have used various measures for determining a parent's style.

In an effort to provide operational definitions for various parenting styles, Diana Baumrind has categorized parents' behavior into three basic styles: authoritarian, permissive, and authoritative (1990). Each style is also composed of two dimensions: demandingness and responsiveness.

Authoritarian parents According to Baumrind, whose typology is popular in the field, parents who are **authoritarian** place demands on their children without

As a teenager, what were your relationships like with your family?

establishing a reciprocal relationship in which children may also make certain demands of their parents. In these families, children are expected to suppress their needs and, in extreme cases, are denied the right to speak before being spoken to by adults. Rules are not discussed in advance or agreed to by consensus or by compromises. Authoritarian parents attach the greatest value to maintaining their authority and to punishing any deviations from their rules. These parents manifest the belief that "children are to be seen and not heard." In Baumrind's terms, they score high on demandingness and low on responsiveness.

As you might expect, authoritarian parents usually encounter difficulties once their children reach adolescence (Maccoby & Martin, 1983). With their more sophisticated mental skills, adolescents are able to see the shortcomings in the authoritarian style and to recognize the inequities of dictatorial systems. Moreover, adolescents are in the process of separating themselves from their parents and questioning authorities as a natural part of the process of becoming more independent. Consequently, authoritarian parents and their teenage children are bound to butt heads. Although these youngsters tend to be academically successful, they are, because of their parents' monitoring and control, usually less socially at ease with their peers, less spontaneous, and less self-confident than teenagers whose parents have less restrictive styles. Discouraged by their parents from experimenting with various roles and ideologies, while encouraged to maintain the status quo and to acquiesce to authorities, these young people are the most likely to adopt a foreclosed identity, rather than to develop an independent identity of their own (Marcia, 1980). Because authoritarian parents usually rely on more physical punishment than do other parents, it seems logical to suspect that their children might, in turn, behave more aggressively toward other people. Fortunately, however, this hypothesis has not been borne out in the research (Maccoby & Martin, 1983).

Permissive parents In direct contrast to authoritarian parents, the laissez-faire or **permissive parents** seldom monitor, regulate, or punish their children's behavior. Permissive parents place very few demands on the children, seldom use any punishment, and, whenever possible, avoid asserting their authority or imposing any restrictions. They are generally tolerant of their children's impulsive behavior and in many ways appear to be uninvolved in their childrens' lives. Although most of these parents are nurturant and supportive, many have been described as detached and uncaring. These overly indulgent parents may be either acquiescing to their children out of intimidation or trying to compensate for their own childhood deprivation or for an overly strict upbringing. In either case, adolescents sometimes report feeling unloved by their indulgent parents. Because permissive parents make so few demands yet are generally responsive toward their children, adolescents from these families tend to be impulsive, irresponsible, and undisciplined.

Authoritative parents According to psychologists such as Baumrind, the most ideal parenting is the democratic or **authoritative** style. While allowing their children to participate in decision making and to express their opinions, authoritative parents still enforce rules, dole out punishment when necessary, and set limits on their children's behavior. Adolescents from these families generally develop more self-confidence, more self-control, and more moral, social, and academic competence than their peers from permissive or authoritarian families. Having been accorded the right to disagree with their parents, these youngsters develop a respect for their parents without feeling that adults' rules are unfairly imposed on them without rhyme or reason. Although authoritative parents and their children are more likely to argue with one another than are members of authoritarian families, their conflicts build rather than destroy their bonds with one another. As an added advantage, these give-and-take arguments and compromises help adolescents build their own identities.

Is it possible to teach authoritarian parents to be more democratic, which would benefit both parents and adolescents? Fortunately, with expert trainers to help them, yes. For example, after 10 years of working with the families of aggressive and maladapted children, Gerald Patterson and his colleagues devised a training program for authoritative parenting. In the program, parents learn how to state their rules clearly and to establish clearcut rewards and punishments for acceptable and unacceptable behavior. In learning to reward their children frequently, consistently, and immediately for "good" behavior, parents who once resorted to punishment as their only recourse for controlling their children's behavior learn that "you can catch more flies with honey than with vinegar" (Patterson, 1982).

Parenting styles are but one of the many aspects that affect the interactions within our families. As we have seen, siblings also play significant roles in adolescents' development. Beyond this, however, economic and social changes in society also have a far-reaching impact on adolescents' lives within their families. It is to these forces—divorce, out-of-wedlock births, poverty, and physical and sexual abuse, that we now turn our attention.

CHANGES IN THE FAMILY

How do you score on the quiz in Box 8.5? Do you have an accurate view of today's families? Ironically many of us cling to the belief that the nuclear family (one that includes both biological parents) is the ideal and the norm because we mistakenly

ARE YOU SURE? 8.5

The Family: Facts and Fictions

How accurate is your vision of the family in our present-day society? When envisioning the typical family of today's adolescents, do you permit your own family experiences to obscure the statistical realities of the 1990s?

True or false?

1. About 55% of all children are presently living with both parents.
2. In 1960 nearly 75% of all children were living with both parents.
3. By the end of the 1990s, about 30% of all children are expected to be living with both parents throughout their teenage years.
4. Nearly 10% of all children are living alone with their father.
5. About 15% of children live with adoptive parents, foster parents, or grandparents.
6. Close to 15% of all children are living with their widowed mother.
7. Nearly one-third of all women with preschool-age children are employed.
8. Nearly half of all adolescents' mothers are employed.
9. Only half of the children who are eligible for welfare assistance receive Aid to Families With Dependent Children (AFDC) payments.
10. The average child-support payment made by divorced fathers is $5,000 per year for two children.
11. More than half of all Hispanic, African American, and Native American children are living in poverty.
12. In 1985 half of all nonwhite children were born to unmarried mothers.
13. About 50% of first marriages and 60% of second marriages end in divorce.
14. Births to unmarried mothers have increased twice as much for white women as for minority women in recent years.
15. Hispanic adolescents living in rural areas are more likely to be living with both parents than are white adolescents living in central cities.
16. Single-parent families are almost as common among white Americans as among Cubans and Mexican Americans.
17. During this decade, nearly one-fourth of all children will live some part of their childhood with only one parent.
18. One-third to one-half of all children will be living in a blended family before the end of their adolescence.
19. Between 85% and 95% of African American children will live at least 1 year in a single-parent family before the age of 18.
20. Adolescents are more likely to be living in poverty now than in the past two decades.

Answers: All are true except #4 = 2%, #7 = 55%, #8 = 70%, and #10 = $2,300.

believe that the nuclear family was more common in the past than it is in the present. Consequently, many feel we have lost something of value and that our families are deteriorating. In fact, however, because of high rates of mortality, desertion, and lengthy separations due to economic hardships, until World War II most children in our society did not spend most of their childhood with both biological parents. Single-parent households, blended families, and abandoned children were at least as common in 1800 as in 1960 (Phillips, 1989). In sum, fears that the family has come apart are grossly exaggerated.

Children of Divorce

Limitations of the research Attempting to answer questions about the impact of divorce and single-parent families on adolescents is a complicated venture. In examining the literature we will often find notable contradictions, leaving us to wonder whether we can make any valid generalizations about the differences between adolescents in nuclear, single-parent, or blended families. Although we cannot eliminate these contradictions, we can try to appreciate the difficulties that social scientists confront in this domain.

To begin with, most research reflects an inherent bias against adolescents from single-parent or blended families in that most data have been collected from a **deficit family model** orientation (Clingempeel, Brand, & Segal, 1987; Ganong & Coleman, 1986). That is, children in any type of family other than the nuclear family have traditionally been studied with the presupposition that these families were deficient. For example, until recently very few studies attempted to identify the benefits of living in a blended family (Coleman, Ganong, & Gingrich, 1986).

Second, many of our assumptions about blended and single-parent families are based on reports that are clinical and descriptive in nature rather than quantitive or empirical. Since clinical data are typically drawn from nonrandom samples of troubled families seeking help from therapists, they offer a skewed vision of the divorced or blended family. Unfortunately, many of our assumptions about adolescents in single-parent or blended families are based on impressionistic reports from these nonrepresentative samples rather than on empirical studies using more randomized samples (Ganong & Coleman, 1987). For instance, the clinical literature supports the view that children experience loyalty conflicts between their parents and stepparents; yet, when empirically tested with quantitative measures, this hypothesis is not supported (Lutz, 1983).

A third limitation is that many confounding variables have been ignored when comparing nuclear, blended, and single-parent families. As you recall from chapter 1, confounding variables interfere with our interpretations of the relationship between the independent and the dependent variables. As the data in Box 8.6 demonstrate, we have historically made generalizations about single-parent and blended families without considering the impact of confounding variables such as socioeconomic status or family size.

Moreover, our impressions about children from divorced families are too often influenced by the media, as was the case with Judith Wallerstein's study, popularized on the covers of both *Time* and *Newsweek* (Wallerstein & Blakeslee, 1989). Despite the fact that Wallerstein's study received much attention nationally, it was methodologically flawed in several respects. First and foremost, the data were gathered from 60 well-educated, suburban families in northern California, not from a

A CLOSER LOOK 8.6

What We Don't Know About Blended Families

What are your beliefs about blended families in comparison to nuclear families? Do you consider adolescents living in blended families "deprived" or "advantaged"? The following list represents a sample of questions that have not yet been empirically verified. How many of your assumptions about blended families are reflected in this list?

1. What effect does the relationship between the formerly married parents have on adolescents' adjustment to their blended family?
2. What effects do stepsiblings have on each other?
3. How do income and residential space affect an adolescent's adjustment to the blended family?
4. What impact does joint custody have on adolescents, and under what circumstances are other types of custody more beneficial?
5. Do young people experience loyalty conflicts in blended families, and if so, how are these conflicts resolved?
6. Are adolescents bothered by their parents' displays of affection toward a new spouse, and if so, how can this be resolved?
7. How long do members of blended families need to adjust to their new roles?
8. What, if any, is the relationship between adolescents' adjustment to the blended family and the number of siblings or the birth of new children?
9. How should adolescents be prepared for their parents' remarriage?
10. How do our society's myths about nuclear families and our media and literary portrayals of the blended family (the "wicked stepmother") affect adolescents' adjustment to their blended family?

Adapted from: L. Ganong & M. Coleman. (1987). Effects of parental remarriage on children. In K. Pasley & M. Ihinger-Tallman (Eds.), *Remarriage and stepparenting: Current research and theory.* (pp. 109–112). New York: Guilford Press.

nationally representative sample. Second, although the study is commendable for its longitudinal design, the absence of a control group weakens any assertions that divorce causes permanent damage to children and adults. Third, the data were gathered by a descriptive method through interviews with family members, rather than by quantitative methods. Moreover, Wallerstein's study failed to take into account confounding variables, such as a child's age when the divorce occurred or the financial or emotional circumstances involved in the divorce.

This is not to say that Wallerstein's research is without merit, but to remind us that the media too often inflate the value of one particular study and ignore the empirical literature. For example, the media might well have publicized Zill's recent study with a nationally representative sample of 1,500 children that included many variables overlooked in Wallerstein's study. On the basis of Zill's findings, the public would have been informed that children from wealthier divorced homes have neither more nor fewer behavioral problems than those from poorer divorced families, children who see their fathers on a regular basis are not more well adjusted than those who never see their fathers, and children of college-educated parents exhibit more behavioral problems than children of high-school-educated parents if they live with their father and his new wife after a divorce (Zill, 1988). Although Zill's results are intriguing, neither his findings nor Wallerstein's are supported by the majority of research studies (Ganong & Coleman, 1987; Hetherington, Stanley, & Anderson, 1989).

In sum, our understanding of the impact of divorce and single-parent families on adolescents is still quite limited. Keeping these limitations in mind, we can begin to understand why there are inconsistencies in the data and to appreciate those studies that are more carefully designed to control for the confounding variables.

Statistics on the family The statistics on divorce and out-of-wedlock births testify to the dramatic changes in adolescents' families since the 1960s (Hernandez, 1988). In 1960 nearly 75% of all children were living with both biological parents, but by 1990 this figure had fallen to 56%. Although the divorce rate declined by 6% between 1979 and 1984, 50% of all first marriages and 60% of second marriages still end in divorce. Moreover, between 1940 and 1985, births to unmarried mothers increased by 725% for white women and by 306% for minority women. In 1985, 14% of all white newborns and 51% of all minority newborns were born to unwed mothers. Indeed, as Figure 8.1 illustrates, nearly one third of all African American children are living with an unmarried mother.

Although the number of divorces and single-parent families overall have risen dramatically, there are significant differences between racial and ethnic groups, as well as between urban and rural families, (Laosa, 1988). For example, Native, Hispanic, and African American adolescents in rural areas are more likely to be living with both parents than are white adolescents living in central cities. Not all groups should be considered alike, however, solely on the basis of religion or race when interpreting these statistics. For instance, single-parent families are more than three times more prevalent among Puerto Rican and African Americans than among whites, whereas single families are only slightly more common among Cuban and Mexican Americans than among whites. Likewise, although Jewish Americans are only half as likely to divorce as white Protestants, religiously

FIGURE 8.1
Living arrangements of children under 18

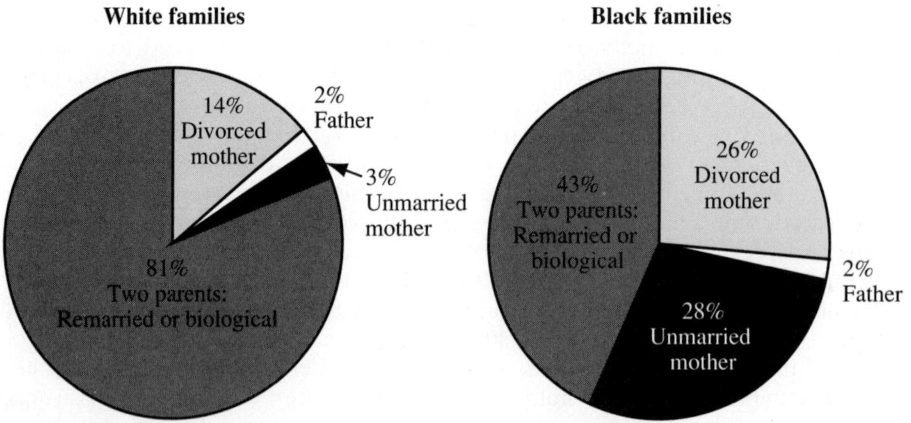

Source: D. Hernandez. (1988). Demographic trends and living arrangements of children. In E. Hetherington & J. Arasteh (Eds.), *Impact of divorce, single parenting and stepparenting on children* (p. 28). Hillsdale, NJ: Erlbaum.

unaffiliated Jews divorce at four times the rate of Orthodox Jews (Brodbar, 1984). Since most data are not analyzed according to these subgroups, we need to bear this shortcoming in mind when generalizing about racial or ethnic differences among adolescents' families. (See Figures 8.2 & 8.3)

Nonetheless, it is now estimated that in the 1990s only 20% to 30% of all children will be living with both bioligical parents throughout their teenage years, while 25% will be living with only one parent (Glick & Linn, 1986; Hernandez, 1988; Norton & Moorman, 1987). Between 50 and 70% of white children and between 85% and 95% of African American children will spend at least 1 year in a one-parent family by age 18. Stated differently, white children are expected to spend 30% and African American children 60% of their childhood in a single-parent household (Hofferth, 1985). Given that 80% of divorced parents remarry, between one third and one half of all children will live in a blended family before the end of their adolescence. In short, adolescents living with one parent or in a blended family are fast becoming the norm in our country.

Understandably, our nation's high incidence of divorce and remarriage has spawned numerous questions, perhaps the most seminal and controversial being what impact divorce and remarriage have on children, and if the impact is negative, whether it is long-lived. Many unhappily married parents contemplating divorce phrase the question more succintly: "Should we stay married for the sake of our children?" Answering this question is a ticklish enterprise, encumbered both by shortcomings of the research and by the emotional, and sometimes religious, nature of the question.

Psychological and emotional impact Social scientists are, however, offering at least tentative answers to some of our most pressing questions regarding divorce. First and foremost, the data consistently show that children generally suffer less from their parents' divorce than from living in a conflict-ridden nuclear family (Block, Block & Gjerde, in press; Hetherington, Stanley & Anderson, 1989; Long & Forehand, 1987; Pasley & Ihinger-Tallman, 1987; Stolberg, Camplain, et al, 1987). For example, even after declaiming the negative consequences of divorce in her nationally publicized research, Wallerstein concluded by reiterating that unhappily married adults should not stay married for the sake of their children: "A divorce undertaken thoughtfully and realistically can teach children how to confront serious life problems with compassion, wisdom, and appropriate action" (Wallerstein & Blakeslee, 1989, p. 305). This is not to say that adolescents sail through their parents' divorce without any distress. As the adolescents' comments in Box 8.7 demonstrate, most young people do feel angry and sad about their parents' divorce (Krementz, 1984; McGuire, 1987). Nevertheless, the research cautions against trying to predict how any particular adolescent will react or to assume that divorce permanently handicaps most youngsters.

Despite the growing prevalence of divorce, most adolescents still feel angry, resentful, depressed, guilty, or anxious in the period immediately following their parents' divorce (Hetherington, 1990; Pasley & Ihinger-Tallman, 1987; Stolberg, Camplain, Currier, & Well, 1987). In the process of giving up their fantasies of reconciliation, adjusting to their parents' new life-style as a single adult, and adapting to innumerable changes in household routines and living arrangements, adolescents can become defiant, aggressive, withdrawn, or apathetic. Yet these reactions vary considerably from child to child. In trying to determine why, researchers have identified a number of variables that influence a young person's

FIGURE 8.2
Change in family composition, 1970–1988

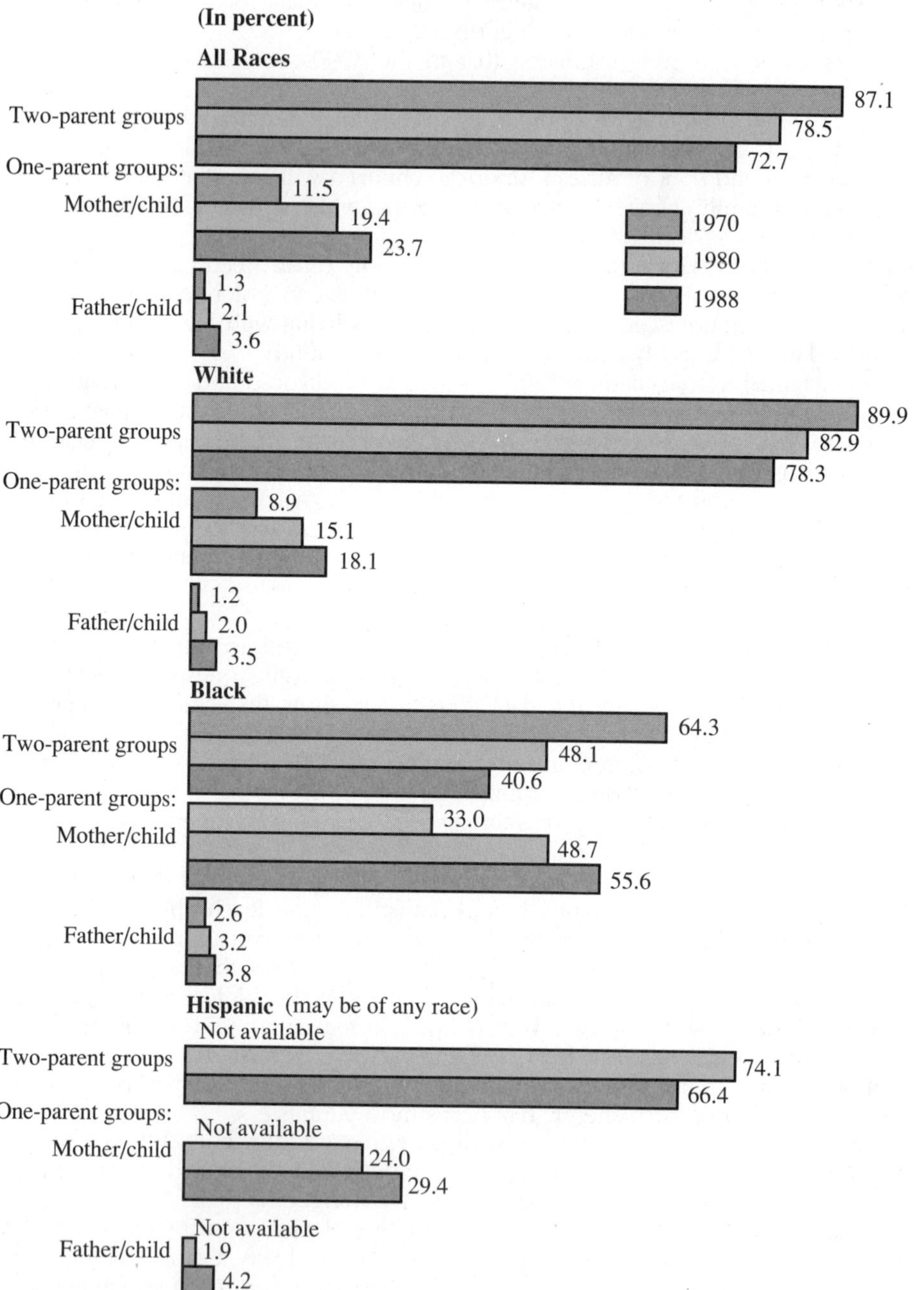

Source: D. Hernandez. (1988). Demographic trends and living arrangements of children. In E. Hetherington & J. Arasteh (Eds.), *Impact of divorce, single parenting and stepparenting on children* (p. 3-22). Hillsdale, NJ: Erlbaum.

FIGURE 8.3

Children under 18 by parent's education, marital status, and race

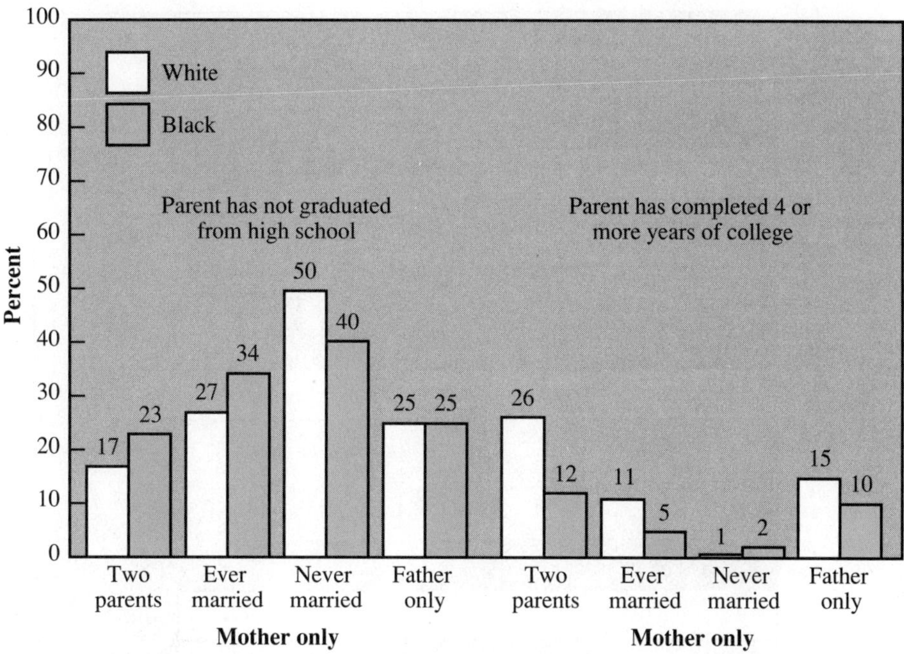

Source: D. Hernandez. (1988). Demographic trends and living arrangements of children. In E. Hetherington & J. Arasteh (Eds.), *Impact of divorce, single parenting and stepparenting on children* (pp. 3–22). Hillsdale, NJ: Erlbaum.

success in adjusting to divorce, three of the most important being money, contact with both parents, and conflict between the parents.

The financial impact As Figure 8.4 demonstrates, one of the most immediate and far-reaching losses in the aftermath of a divorce is a dramatic drop in the family's standard of living. For example, 80% of white children and 70% of African American children living with both parents enjoy a family income of at least $20,000, while only 25% of white children and 15% of African American children living with a divorced mother have a family income above $20,000. More disturbing still, 43% of all divorced mothers have annual incomes of less than $10,000. In contrast, most fathers maintain or improve their standard of living after divorce (Hernandez, 1988).

This discrepancy between divorced men and women can be attributed to several factors (Weitzman, 1985). First, women are less able to earn incomes equivalent to men's, averaging only 60% of men's earnings. In addition, 30% of all women do not work while they are married and are, as a consequence, handicapped when they try to find jobs after their divorce. Further, many former husbands fail to pay or pay only minimal child support. Nearly 65% of all mothers receive no child support whatsoever from the children's father (Bane & Ellwood, 1989).

FIGURE 8.4
Family incomes by race and marital status.

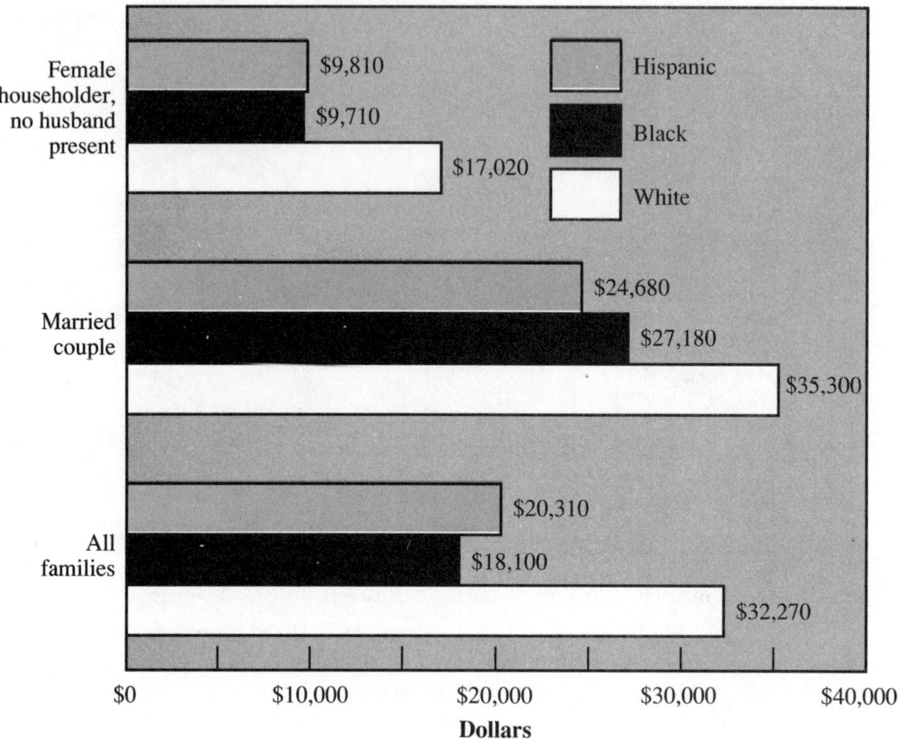

Source: Bureau of the Census. (1987). Washington, DC: Author.

In the wake of these financial losses, is it any wonder that many adolescents feel angry or depressed after their parents' divorce? The economic pinch often entails moving from a familiar home to a more modest dwelling, sharing smaller quarters with siblings, and forfeiting recreational activities and possessions to which they had become accustomed. To worsen matters further, even after the divorce most adolescents are still subjected to their parents' ongoing arguments over money: "Your father isn't paying us enough to get by on." "Your mother is trying to take the shirt off my back." (Fayerweather Street School, 1984; Krementz, 1987).

The father-child relationship While having to adjust to financial losses, most adolescents also lose something else after a divorce—their father. Despite the increasing popularity of joint custody, 95% of all children still live with their mother after a divorce. Fewer than 2% go to live with their fathers, and most do not split their time equally between their father's and their mother's homes (Hernandez, 1988).

Although many fathers maintain regular contact with their children in the first few months following the divorce, they become increasingly less available. The typical pattern is illustrated by two recent studies with large, nationally representative samples. The first, a longitudinal study, included nearly 2,200 children between the ages of 7 and 11. Only half of these children had seen their father within the past year, and only 15% had seen him at least once a week. Daughters had even less contact with their fathers than did sons (Furstenberg, 1988). In the second study, based on data from 1,300 children aged 1 to 17, only 8% of the children living with their mothers saw their fathers as often as once a week, and more than 75% saw their fathers less than once a month or never. Given our notions about maternal instincts and the special bonds that supposedly exist between children and their mothers, it is worth noting that when children were living with their father after a divorce, only 40% of their mothers saw them more than once a month (Zill, 1988).

Why is this? Contrary to what we might expect, remarrying has relatively little influence on whether the nonresidential parent continues to see his or her children after the divorce. The two most influential factors are income and the father's or mother's geographic proximity to the children. Parents with better incomes who live relatively near their former spouse are the most likely to maintain contact with their children. Interestingly, however, the parents' incomes, new marriages, and geographic proximity are not strongly related to the amount of collaboration or communication between the divorced couple in matters related to their children. After a divorce, most parents do not continue to communicate or collaborate on matters related to their children (Furstenberg, 1988).

Parental conflicts In addition to losing contact with their fathers, many adolescents must also cope with the continued anger and conflict between their divorced parents. Both before and after divorce, teenagers too often witness their parents' quarrels and tears. This is especially distressing since one of the best-documented findings is that children whose parents cooperate with one another after a divorce suffer the fewest negative reactions (Camara & Resnick, 1988; Forehand, Long & Brody, 1988; Pasley & Ihinger-Tallman, 1987; Wallerstein & Blakeslee, 1989). Understandably, the more conflict between the parents, the more likely the nonresidential parent is to avoid contact with his or her children after the divorce. In fact, it now appears that the parents' hostility toward one another, not the divorce per se, is probably the primary cause of children's behavioral problems during and after divorce (Hetherington, Stanley & Anderson, 1989). In other words, adults who are contemplating divorce would be well advised not to ask, "Will our divorce affect our children?" but "How cooperatively can we behave during and after our divorce in our life-long roles as parents?"

Child's age and divorce Most parents also wonder whether it is better to postpone an impending divorce until their children reach adolescence or to divorce while their children are young. The research on this question is mixed. Some studies show that children who are younger at the time of a divorce exhibit more problems, since their cognitive immaturity creates more anxiety, more confusion, and more inflexibility about new family roles. In contrast to adolescents, younger children tend to harbor more fantasies about their parents' reconciling, to feel more responsible personally for the divorce, to assign blame to one parent, and to feel torn between their loyalties to each parent. Young children are also less able than adolescents to profit from the support of peers and to focus their attention on establishing independence and interests beyond the family (Furstenberg, 1988; Wallerstein & Blakeslee, 1989; Zill, 1988).

On the other hand, teenagers tend to be more upset than younger children by

8.7

ADOLESCENT VOICES

Adolescents' Feelings About Divorce and Remarriage

"Even though I live with my dad, and my sister lives with my mom, my parents have joint custody, which means we can switch around if we feel like it. I think that's the best possible arrangement because if they had fought over us, I know I would have felt I was a check in a restaurant—you know, the way it is at the end of a meal when two people are finished eating and they both grab for the check. But secretly neither one really wants it, they just go on pretending until someone finally grabs it, and then that one's stuck." Zach, age 13

"When my parents were married, I hardly ever saw my dad because he was always busy working. Now that they're divorced, I've gotten to know him more because I'm with him every weekend. My mom got remarried and divorced again, so I've gone through two divorces so far. And my father's also gotten remarried—to someone I don't get along with all that well. And one thing I really worry about is that I think they want to have a baby, and I know that if they do, it will be just like a replacement for me. It could be a lot like what happened with my dog Spunker. I've had him for about six years and I've always said I'll never love any dog as much as I love him. Well, a year ago I picked up a little black Labrador puppy from the pound, and now I find I'm not as friendly with Spunker as I used to be." Ari, age 14 (male)

"Now that I'm older I do think it would be good for my mother to find someone—I mean, I feel sorry for her because I'm always going out on weekends and she hardly ever goes out. It's as if she's spending all her time with us because she can't seem to break the emotional tie. My father, on the other hand, is married to my present stepmother, Vana, and they've been together for about three and a half years. She and I have a great relationship. I never feel jealous of her because she's done so much for my dad and he's so happy now. They don't have any children, and the truth is, I hope they don't have any. It's funny, but I see a lot of kids whose parents aren't divorced and somehow they don't seem as independent and self-assured as I am and a lot of them don't have as good a relationship with their parents as I have. So, strange as it might sound, I can't say that I have serious regrets about my parents' divorce."
Corinne, age 16

"I think that if parents are going to divorce and not scar their children for life, they should keep them out of what's going on as much as possible. I'm not saying parents should lie to kids or anything, but they shouldn't make them suffer for what they've done and they don't have to give them all the details of what went wrong. Or try to make them hate the other parent. One of the reasons I may have bad feelings now toward

continued

the sexual issues surrounding their parents' divorce. In coming to terms with their own newly discovered sexuality, adolescents may be hypervigilant about and highly sensitive to their parents' new life-style as unmarried people (Hetherington, Stanley & Anderson, 1989). They may also be in the grips of the "imaginary audience," presuming that "everyone" is noticing their parents' sexuality—who their parents date, their new hairstyles and clothes, their new life-styles as single people. This imaginary audience can heighten a young adolescent's embarrassment over matters concerning their divorced parents' conduct in social situations with their dates or new spouses. Moreover, from a Freudian perspective, young adolescents are in

Box 8.7 continued

my mother is that I feel she tried to turn me against my father. It was such a bad time for my mother that she started holding on to me for her own security and I felt as if she was pulling me down with her. Finally I asked my dad if I could go to a child psychiatrist to sort out my problems. Looking back, I think it was Dr. Schwartzberg who pulled me through. He told me that I had to separate the past from what was happening now and that I had to realize what was best for me—that I shouldn't worry about hurting my parents' feelings." Nancy, age 15

"Sometimes I think it would be good if my mother got remarried. It's hard to go to your mother for advice about things, and sometimes my father isn't available, although he tries hard when he's around. Also, to tell the truth, it's hard living with just one person. There's no appeal system—your mother says no, and there's no father to go to, hoping he'll say yes!
Malik age 14 (male)

"The last couple of years have been really painful for me because I've tried so hard to have a good relationship with my father and it hasn't worked out very well. He only visits us about once a year, and because I hardly ever see him I always feel that I have to be on my best behavior and it's hard to be natural. Even though I thought the divorce was a good idea, it still made me feel sick inside for the first few years. I was so sick that I'd throw up, and it got to the point where I had to stay out of school for two months. But the worst thing by far about my parents' divorce is that it's still going on. I mean, my parents don't talk. If they talk, it's like screaming." Tracy, age 16

"My little sister had just been born, so their divorce seems especially weird. I mean, God, it's so hard for me to imagine how people who've just had a baby can turn around and split up. They used to have the most terrible fights on the phone which I can still remember vividly—they would have these violent conversations which were mostly about money. Sometimes I look at pictures of them together, back in the 1960s, and I can't imagine why they got married in the first place. It's one of the mysteries of my life." Nelson, age 16

"I was only eight years old at the time, and even though no one used the word divorce, I knew what was happening. After my dad told me, I put my arms around him and said, "I feel sorry for you, Daddy." We both cried for about two hours. As things are now, we have a great arrangement. I stay six months with my Mom, six months with my Dad, and I alternate weekends, so I'm never really away from either of them for very long. One of my friends even got his parents to try a similar arrangement. Unlike other divorced families, I don't feel I've lost one of my parents. But the most painful thing by far has been dealing with my parents' dating other people. I feel jealous, and then I end up feeling guilty because even though I know I'm entitled to my feelings, I also know I'm being unfair to everyone." Bartle, age 12 (male)

Source: J. Krementz. (1984). *How it feels when parents divorce.* New York: Knopf.

the midst of resolving their Oedipus or Electra complex with the opposite-sex parent, a process that fans jealousies and resentment toward anyone receiving their parent's sexual attention. Woe be it to mom's or dad's dates who have to pass the young adolescent's trials by fire! What will be overlooked by a 6-year-old in these situations will seldom be overlooked by the teenager.

Moreover, too many divorced parents rush their children into adulthood by disclosing too much about their own personal lives (Elkind, 1981). By seeking their child's counsel or by disclosing intimate details of issues related to the divorce or their new life, these parents are burdening their children with adult responsibilities. Even in cases where the reason for the divorce was a parent's homosexuality, parents sometimes disclose too much to their children regarding one another's private lives (Gantz, 1983).

In sum, there do not appear to be clearcut benefits to postponing divorce until children become adolescents. On the basis of our present research, the family's income, cooperation between the parents, and the amount of contact nonresidential parents maintain with their children are more important than the child's age at the time of the divorce.

Sons versus daughters If age has not yet been established as a crucial variable in terms of a child's reactions to divorce, how about gender? Are boys any more or less adversely affected by their parents' divorce than girls? Despite our stereotypes about girls' being more sensitive than boys, boys from divorced families perform more poorly in school, behave more aggressively, have less self-esteem, and have more difficulties with their peers than do girls from divorced families (Hetherington, Stanley & Anderson, 1989; Rutter, 1987). Why? First, children who live with their same-sex parent are usually more socially competent, mature, cooperative, and self-confident than children who live with their opposite-sex parent (Camara & Resnick, 1988; Furstenburg, 1988; Guidubaldi, 1990; Zill, 1988). Second, mothers are more likely than fathers to encounter problems with their sons even in nuclear families (Youniss & Smollar, 1985). Since almost all children live with their mothers after a divorce, it follows that boys would tend to be at a greater disadvantage than girls in these regards.

Some data also suggest that parents fight more in front of their sons than their daughters (Hetherington, Stanley & Anderson, 1989). As a result, boys would witness more of their parents' arguments and, in some cases, physical violence both before and after a divorce. Boys have also been found to react more aggressively than girls after witnessing their parents' conflicts (Forehand, Long & Brody, 1988). Taken together, these findings might explain, in part, why most boys have more behavioral problems than girls after their parents' divorce.

Before presuming that boys do suffer more than girls, however, a number of shortcomings in the existing research need to be addressed (Zaslow, 1988). First, girls may be more likely to internalize their reactions to their parents' divorce by sulking, developing health problems, or becoming withdrawn or depressed. In contrast, boys may express their sadness by externalizing their feelings through more publicly aggressive or defiant behavior. If this is the case, the research would be representing girls unfairly as less disturbed by divorce, since their symptoms are subtle and more private.

Taking these shortcomings into consideration, Zaslow (1988) analyzed only those studies that were quantitative rather than descriptive, only studies that specifically addressed the question of sex differences, and only studies that included a control group. Although the majority of the 27 studies focused on young children and failed to consider the amount of time that had elapsed since the divorce, the results of Zaslow's review are noteworthy. First, girls reacted more negatively to their mother's remarrying than did boys. Second, girls fared less well than boys if they lived with their father rather than with their mother. Third, boys were more negatively affected than girls by their parents' divorce only when they were living with a mother who did not remarry.

Considering the conflicting findings, what can we safely conclude about adolescents' reactions to divorce? First, that living with unhappily married parents in a conflict-ridden home is more debilitating than undergoing the trials and tribulations of divorce; second, that most young people are not permanently handicapped by their parents' divorce and are not significantly different in the long term from their friends in nuclear families; and, third, that having enough money, continuing to have regular contact with both parents, and having parents who cooperate with one another are more important than the child's age, gender, or whether the parents remarry in helping adolescents adjust to their parents' divorce.

The Blended Family

Since 80% of divorced adults remarry, 30% to 50% of today's youth will be living in a blended family before the end of their adolescence (Hernandez, 1988). Historically referred to as stepfamilies, the blended, or reconstituted, family is composed of one biological parent, his or her new spouse, and, in almost all cases, children from each spouse's former marriage. Since almost all children live with their mother after a divorce, most blended families consist of the adolescent's mother, her husband, and his children who live with his former spouse. In making generalizations about adolescents from blended families, remember that researchers typically clump all types of blended families under one category without considering the differences among them. For example, if Herbert is living with his father, his father's new wife, and her two preschool children by a former marriage, Herbert is considered a member of a blended family; but so is Samantha, who is living with her mother and her mom's new husband who has no children. Although both Herbert and Samantha are categorized by most researchers as living in blended families, their life-styles and family dynamics are quite different. Keeping this shortcoming in mind helps explain, in many instances, why the research shows that some adolescents adapt more easily than others to their new blended family.

Surprisingly, most studies have found no significant long-term differences between children from nuclear and from blended families on such variables as cognitive performance, psychosomatic complaints, personality characteristics, social and sexual behavior, family relationships, or attitudes about marriage and divorce (Ganong & Coleman, 1987; Hetherington, Stanley, & Anderson, 1989). This is not to say that adolescents do not encounter some difficulties adapting to their new roles in a blended family. It appears, however, that if youngsters do develop problems after their parent remarries, their reactions are usually a consequence of stress associated with the divorce, not the new marriage (Furstenberg, 1987, 1988; Zill, 1988).

A 1983 study with a sample of almost 2,300 children, aged 12 to 16, is representative of what seems to happen in many blended families (Furstenberg & Spanier, 1984). Most children and adults in these blended families said they enjoyed one another and had close relationships. Moreover, the household routines, family rules, and family activities were very similar to those in nuclear families. These results are consistent with what most other studies have found: Remarrying does not generally erase the negative effects of a divorce, but it does not aggravate or increase them either (Ganong & Coleman, 1987, in press; Hetherington, Stanley & Anderson, 1989). In fact, adolescents whose parents remarry generally benefit more than those whose parents remain single. First, the new marriage almost always improves their financial situation. Further, children who experience moderate levels of stress during divorce and remarriage seem to become better able to cope with later challenges in their lives. Learning how to adapt to stressful experiences while still young is also related to attributes in later life such as being independent, having an internal locus of control, and having sufficient self-esteem (Rutter, 1987).

Given that a parent's remarrying generally benefits adolescents, it is noteworthy that minority youths are handicapped in this respect. For example, African American women have only a .60 probability of remarrying, in contrast to .75 for white women—a probability that has remained fairly constant for white women but has declined for African American women (Hofferth, 1985). As a result, minority adolescents are more likely than whites to be deprived of the benefits of a blended family.

The advantages of blended families notwithstanding, it should come as no surprise that everyone initially needs time to adjust to the new living arrangements. As mentioned earlier, adolescents' newly developing sexuality may make the new marriage a more complicated matter for them than for younger children. Furthermore, in the process of establishing their independence and identities, most adolescents become increasingly less interested in certain kinds of family togetherness. For example, even in nuclear families most adolescents will choose to spend a good part of their free time with their own friends rather than with their parents. Unfortunately, this adolescent independence can be at odds with the newly married couple's efforts to create intimacy and cohesion in their blended family. What the couple might interpret as rejection or dissatisfaction with the blended family is often just the adolescent's healthy interest in his or her friends.

On the other hand, some adolescents do initially resent losing some of the special power or status they enjoyed with their parent before he or she remarried (Pasley & Ihinger, 1987). For example, adolescents may not like abdicating their role as their parent's confidant or as the caretaker of younger siblings. This resentment or jealousy may be especially felt by daughters toward their father's new wife, since some studies show that girls are encouraged more than boys to attend to their fathers' emotional needs (Greif, 1985). Not surprisingly, the adjustments are usually easier when the parent's new spouse has no children of his or her own (Beer, 1989; Santrock & Sitterle, 1987; Zill, 1988). The absence or presence of step-siblings, however, seems to be less important than variables such as family income (Ganong & Coleman, 1987).

It is not quite so clear, however, whether adolescents are any more accepting of living with a stepmother than with a stepfather. Most of the literature shows no difference (Ganong & Coleman, 1987). Other studies, however, find that children who live with their father are more reluctant to accept his new wife than those who live with their mother are to accept her new husband (Furstenberg, 1988; Hobart, 1987; Santrock & Sitterele, 1987). In part, these reactions may be influenced by the fact that our media and literature present a more negative image of stepmothers than of stepfathers (Santrock & Sitterle, 1987). Indeed, you would probably have a hard time recalling any portrayals of stepfathers, good or bad. Although some psychologists defend the presentation of "wicked" stepmothers as a useful device for giving children a way to deal with their ambivalent feelings about their own mothers (Bettelheim, 1977), others argue that we should portray stepmothers more positively (Radomisli, 1981). Teenagers who are more resistant to living with a stepmother than with a stepfather are probably reacting to the fact that more children live with their mother and stepfather. That is, adolescents living with their father and his new wife are more likely than those living with their mother and her new husband to feel that their family arrangement is "odd."

Ironically, children who live with their father and a highly educated stepmother seem to have a harder time adapting than children living with their mother and her highly educated husband (Zill, 1988). Zill suggests that the well-educated stepmother may be more likely to play an active role in child rearing than the well-educated stepfather, inadvertently creating more resentment in her husband's children. Then, too, the highly educated woman may pose more of a threat to the former wife, whose jealousy and insecurity would then be reflected in the children's behavior toward their stepmother. Finally, given our culture's emphasis on the importance of mothering, a mother and a stepmother are probably more likely than a father and a stepfather to compete for children's attentions. In support of these hypotheses, children who spend a lot of time with their mother do tend to have more difficulty relating to their new stepmother, which is not the case toward the stepfather when children spend a lot of time with their own father (Furstenberg, 1988; Santrock & Sitterle, 1987; Zill, 1988).

We might also wonder whether boys or girls have an easier time adjusting to their parents' new marriage. From a review of the studies that used quantitative methods rather than mere descriptive data, it appears that daughters have a more difficult time than sons adjusting to their mother's new husband (Zaslow, 1988). Given that we have so little research about the 2% of children who live with their father and his new wife, we do not yet have enough data to determine whether this type of family affects sons differently than daughters. We also lack the data to determine whether a parent's new marriage has any substantially different impact on younger children than on adolescents.

Joint Custody

Since 1979, when Kansas and Oregon adopted the first joint custody statutes, more adolescents are growing up under joint custody agreements (Koel, et al, 1988). Despite its growing popularity, however, joint custody has not appreciably altered the traditional arrangement in terms of a child's residence: Almost all children live with their mothers after a divorce, spending time in their fathers' homes only on weekends, for special occasions, or during school vacations. It is important not to confuse joint custody with joint residence. **Joint custody** does not require that children live with both parents an equal amount of time. In fact, joint custody may not require a child to live in the other parent's home at all. Although almost all adolescents in both joint custody and single custody homes live with their mothers, either type of custody agreement can be written so that adolescents spend equal time living in each parent's household, which is referred to as **joint residency** (Kolko, 1985).

When parents sign a joint residency agreement, the question then arises: Do adolescents living in two households feel torn asunder? Most data suggest not. Young people residing in two homes generally maintain strong bonds with both parents and adjust to—even thrive on—the differences between their parents' households, despite the logistics involved (Krementz, 1984; Luepnitz, 1986).

Although joint custody initially was most popular among well-educated couples with relatively high incomes, the concept is gaining a more widespread appeal. As a result, we have become more interested in gathering data to answer the question of whether joint custody is the best alternative for all families. In considering this question, it is important to differentiate between the idea that both parents should have an equal legal right in all matters related to their child's upbringing—which is joint custody—and the idea that children should spend equivalent time with both parents after a divorce—which is not an issue of legal custody but of visitation rights and living arrangements. Despite what our instincts might suggest, research has not yet demonstrated that joint custody is more beneficial for children than single custody.

Unfortunately, joint custody is not as ideal an option in many cases as its proponents had once hoped. Indeed, as its disadvantages become increasingly apparent, some child advocates are cautioning us against holding joint custody up as the ideal toward which all divorced couples should strive (Hagen, 1987; Koel, et al, 1988). First of all, joint custody almost always involves more contact between the former spouses than single custody—and more contact can mean more conflict. Given that many divorced couples are not cordial to or cooperative with one another, joint custody can create more stress for both adults and children. It can also add more stress when the divorced parents remarry, as 80% do, since continual contact between the formerly married couple can complicate the new marriage. Given these complications, it is worth noting that children's adjustment to divorce is generally unrelated to the type of custody agreement between their parents (Luepnitz, 1986). That is, whether a divorced couple shares custody jointly has less impact on their children's well-being than whether both parents maintain regular contact with their chldren.

On the other hand, joint custody does have it merits. Parents with joint custody are less likely to return to court than those with single custody (Roman, 1987). In this sense, then, joint custody may be worth the extra hassles, since the family is less likely to be involved in future legal battles. Moreover, just because parents were unable to get along well enough to stay married does not necessarily mean they cannot cooperate in their roles as parents after the divorce—in some cases, perhaps even better than while married (Elkin, 1987). Finally, joint custody may, at the very least, encourage cooperation between the divorced adults where animosity might otherwise prevail.

Whether adolescents' parents opt for joint or single custody, more divorcing couples are now seeking the help of a mediator. In **mediation,** parents try to negotiate their disagreements through the help of a trained counselor rather than through lawyers. The goal of mediation is to help parents resolve their differences in a more cooperative manner, rather than assume an adversarial position toward one another. The mediator's role is to help former spouses become problem-solving partners who focus their energies on creating a postdivorce, nonmarital family. In most cases, mediation reduces the likelihood of having to go back to court in the future and reduces the animosity between the parents. Even in cases where they have to resort to lawyers to resolve their differences, many couples also report that the mediation process helped them re-evaluate their ideas about cooperative parenting. Moreover, because mothers who go to court with a custody dispute are likely to win the contest, mediation has been found particularly beneficial to fathers in giving them greater access to their children after the divorce (R. Emery, 1988; Koopman & Hunt, 1988).

Father Custody

Although only 2% of all children live with only their fathers, the courts are more willing than in the past to consider the father's needs and his importance in his children's psychological well-being (R. Emery, 1988). Research is already contradicting the traditional notion that awarding custody to the mother is always in the "best interests" of the child (Grief, 1985; Hanson, 1988). For example, in one nationally representative study, custodial fathers reported better family adjustment and fewer problems with their children than did custodial mothers two years after their divorce (Furstenberg, 1988). Although single fathers initially feel confused and apprehensive about their new role, they report increased confidence and satisfaction as time passes. Indeed, some custodial fathers say their relationshhips with their children are more intimate and more satisfying than before the divorce.

POVERTY AND THE FAMILY

Economic Statistics

Not only are today's adolescents more likely to be living in a blended or a single-parent family, they also are more likely to be living in poverty than adolescents in the 1970s and 1980s. Among people of all ages, poverty increased from 11.6% in 1979 to 14% in 1985 (Ross & Danziger, 1987). The hardest hit are our nation's children. By 1986, 35% of all children were living below the poverty level, with nearly half of all Native, African, and Hispanic American children living in poverty (U.S. Census Bureau, 1987). As Figures 8.4 and 8.5 illustrate, the likelihood of an adolescent's being rich or poor is correlated with his or her parents' race, education, income, and marital status. For example, 45% of white children and 72% of Hispanic children from one-parent families are living below the poverty level in contrast to only 27% of Hispanic and 10% of white children in two-parent families (Hernandez, 1988).

More disturbing still, the situation is not likely to improve for those children who will become adolescents in the 1990s. Indeed, young parents suffered an economic setback between 1973 and 1986 that is, by some comparative measures, greater than the setbacks during the Great Depression (Johnson, Sum, & Weill, 1988). Adjusted for inflation, the median income for families headed by people younger than 30 shrank by 26% during these 13 years—a figure virtually identical to the 27% drop during the Great Depression of 1929. Moreover, the ability of these young parents to improve their children's standard of living by improving their own education is diminishing. For example, earnings of African American college graduates who head young families have declined by one third since 1973, and more than half the African American high-school dropouts heading families reported no earnings whatsoever in 1986. Similarly, despite Hispanics having attained higher levels of education than ever before, the median income for their households has dropped by 30% since 1973. Stated differently, in 1973 the median family income for all families in our society was $29,604, compared to only $29,401 in 1986 (−1%). During the same period of time, the median income of families headed by parents between the ages of 25 and 30 dropped from $29,074 to $25,000 (−8.3%). As a point of reference, in 1987 for a family of four the poverty line was roughly $12,000 and the median income was $36,800 (Bane & Ellwood, 1989). The sad reality is that an increasing number of adolescents and their parents can not achieve the "American dream"—the dream of having a higher standard of living than their own parents.

Why is it that one-fifth of our nation's children are poor? Why has poverty risen so dramatically in our society? In part the answer lies in the greater number of divorces and out-of-wedlock births that have meant that more children are growing up in households with only one parent to earn the family's income, and in part the answer lies in the fact that very few fathers make adequate child support payments after a divorce or in the case of out-of-wedlock pregnancies. For example, 65% of all mothers receive no child support from their children's fathers. Yet, contrary to popular opinion, the rise in poverty is not primarily the result of our rising divorce rates and out-of-wedlock births. In fact, roughly half of all poor children live in two-parent homes and virtually all the increases in poverty in the 1980s can be traced to losses within these two-parent homes (Bane & Ellwood, 1989).

In short, most poor children do not fit the popular stereotype: a minority child in an urban ghetto home with an unemployed, young, unmarried mother. Nearly half of all poor children are white, and fewer than 9% of all poor children live in urban ghetto areas. Moreover, poverty rates for female-headed families remained relatively constant at around 50% throughout the 1980s, as did the number of single parents receiving welfare benefits. By contrast, poverty among children in two-parent homes jumped dramatically in the 1970s and 1980s. The reasons? First, real wages (meaning what our money is actually worth from year to year after inflation is taken into account) declined in our society, reflecting the sharp slowdown in productivity of the economy as a whole. In terms of buying power, the median income of a full-time male wage earner is lower today than it was in 1973. Put differently, the minimum wage would have to be raised from its present rate of $3.35 per hour to $5.40 in order to equal its 1973 level. Second, more children are poor because of our nation's lack of medical protection, lack of governmental support for childcare, and stricter eligibility rules for welfare assistance, such as food stamps. Were it not for women's incomes, the legalization of abortion, the greater use of birth control, and the postponement of childbearing, poverty rates would be even higher. The new reality is that living with two parents who both work no longer guarantees that children will escape poverty (Bane & Ellwood, 1989).

Impact of Unemployment

Moreover, children who are now entering adolescence are being raised in families that have experienced the highest rates of unemployment in four decades (McLoyd, 1989). In 1982 the unemployment rate of 10.6% was the highest since the Great Depression (Flaim & Sehgal, 1985). Although the high rates of unemployment during the 1980s affected fathers at almost all socioeconomic levels, African American fathers were most adversely affected, given their predominance in central cities and the manufacturing industries, where the most retrenchment occurred. Although the 1980s also increased unemployment for women, females were less affected because their employment was concentrated in the service industry, which experienced fewer cutbacks.

Unfortunately, it now appears that a father's economic losses can also handicap his teenage children in that his behavior toward them changes for the worse (Elder, Nguyen, & Caspi, 1985; Galambos & Silbereisen, 1987; Isralowitz & Singer, 1986; Lempers, Clark & Simons, in press; McLoyd, 1989). Unemployed fathers are generally more depressed, anxious, hostile, suicidal, and psychotic than employed fathers. The unemployed man also tends to consume more alcohol, have poorer physical health, and develop a pessimistic attitude toward life. Not surprisingly, these fathers are more punitive, explosive, and irritable with their children. Their children, therefore, become more depressed, lonely, distrustful, emotionally sensitive, and withdrawn than youngsters from economically stable families. Adolescents with unemployed fathers are also more likely to become pessimistic about their own future, to lower their educational aspirations, and to perform poorly at school.

This research does not conclude, however, that all unemployed fathers mistreat their children. As you might expect, a father's reactions to unemployment are less severe if his wife is employed, if his self-esteem is not based solely upon his role as a breadwinner, if his job is middle class rather than blue collar, and if his unemployment is temporary rather than chronic. Nevertheless, a father's unemployment or a cut in income does appear to affect his children in ways other than lowering the family's standard of living—an important finding in these times of increased poverty and high unemployment.

Assisting Indigent Families

How is our society attempting to help adolescents living in poverty? One of the most widely utilized methods is the financial assistance provided through the **Aid to Families With Dependent Children (AFDC).** Established in 1935, AFDC is the most widely used welfare program in our society for providing food, shelter, and clothing to the indigent. In 1987, about 11 million people, 8 million of whom were children, received AFDC payments. These payments vary considerably from state to state, since each state supplements the federal government's payments. For example, a family of three in Alabama receives $118 per month, whereas in California the same family would received $617 (Richardson, 1987).

Unfortunately, AFDC has been subject to substantial cutbacks in recent years, and states have not increased benefits to match inflation. As a consequence, the real purchasing power of AFDC payments fell by almost one-third between 1970 and 1985. As more stringent guidelines for receiving AFDC benefits were imposed, only half of our nation's poor children received these benefits in 1985, in contrast to more than 80% in 1970 (U.S. House of Representatives, 1985). Moreover, until a federal reform bill was passed in 1988, 25 states refused AFDC to two-parent families, regardless of their level of poverty (U.S. Senate Finance Committee, 1988). Since AFDC was intended as only a temporary solution for indigent families, the goal has been to help its recipients get into the labor force. Since one third of all AFDC parents have only a ninth-grade education and three fourths have never been employed, helping them find jobs requires massive training. In this vein, the Welfare Reform Bill of 1988 now requires single parents who receive AFDC to participate in an education or employment program (U.S. Senate Finance Committee 1988). Since teenage mothers receive about half of all AFDC payments, this legislation should particularly benefit adolescents both by reducing poverty in the families in which they are raised and by improving their situations as teenage parents (Sawhill, 1987).

Given the difficulties with AFDC, other alternatives for helping indigent children are being explored (Stipek & McCroskey, 1989). One of the most promising is a program that automatically withholds a father's child support payments from his paycheck. Wisconsin is implementing such a system, which is projected to reduce poverty among children by 30% (Garfinkle, 1988). When the data from such programs eventually become available, they are sure to influence our nation's welfare and child support policies.

While we search for ways to help our nation's poor escape the ravages of poverty, millions of adolescents continue to grow up in families plagued by economic hardship. Indeed, as Box 8.8 illustrates, at least 750,000 of our nation's children are so poor that they must seek shelter in temporary housing for the homeless or live in the streets (Jennings, 1989; Kozol, 1988). While there have never been any quick or easy cures for poverty, our understanding of today's adolescents must confront the harsh, and perhaps embarrassing, reality that millions of our wealthy nation's youth live in a world of poverty that most of us have encountered only in brief glimpses, if at all.

MOTHERS' EMPLOYMENT

Considering the poverty rates and declining standard of living for most families, it is not surprising that most adolescents' mothers are employed. Today nearly 70% of all mothers work outside the home, in contrast to less than 30% in 1950 (U.S. Bureau of Labor Statistics, 1986). Although some people may still believe that women work primarily for emotional satisfaction or in response to the feminist movement, the reality is that most women work for their family's economic

Children are among the fastest growing group of homeless. What special problems do you think they face?

A CLOSER LOOK 8.8

The Homeless

It is now estimated that between 500,000 and 750,000 school-age children in our nation are homeless—estimates that many believe represent only a third of the actual numbers. Until passage in 1987 of the Homeless Assistance Act, which is attempting to determine the severity of and solutions for the problem, states were not required to count their homeless.

Distressingly, children are among the fastest growing group of the homeless. Only 43% of them attend school regularly. As a consequence, cities across the nation are experimenting with ways to educate homeless youngsters. For example, the Tacoma, Washington, school district joined with the Young Women's Christian Association to set up a school exclusively for homeless children. Houston's school system tried an unprecedented, although short-lived, program by providing overnight housing for homeless children in school buildings equipped with beds.

Why do so few homeless children attend school? First, there are difficulties in transferring school and immunization records quickly and in transporting students across school district lines. Many homeless parents are also reluctant to enroll their children in school, and the children themselves often feel too stigmatized by not having adequate clothing, a permanent address, or basic social and academic skills to interact with their classmates. Given the stress and poverty in which they live, homeless students often feel out of place in regular public schools. "We've had kids who just cry all day," says the director of the Tacoma program. "How would a regular school teacher deal with that, and 30 other students?" As might be expected, we are now confronted with the debatable question of whether it is better for homeless children to be educated in regular schools or in special schools designed exclusively for them.

Source: L. Jennings, (1989, February). Report expected to sharpen policy debate on homeless. *Education Week,* p. 19.

survival. For example, one-fourth of all employed women have husbands who earn less than $10,000 a year, and 35% more two-parent families would live below the poverty line if the wives were not employed (U.S. Bureau of Labor Statistics, 1986).

But would children be better off if their mothers did not have to work outside the home? Traditionally, there have been two opposing views on this question. The first is that an employed woman is more satisfied with her own life and serves as a positive role model for her children. The second is that being both a mother and a wage earner creates stress that interferes with the quality of a woman's relationship with her children.

In general, the first hypothesis wins out. The bulk of the research shows that both mothers and children derive certain benefits from a mother's employment (Gottfried & Gottfried, 1987; Hoffman, 1989; Zaslow, 1987). In part, these benefits to mothers and children might be explained by the fact that mothers in both professional and blue-collar jobs report being more satisfied with their lives than nonemployed mothers. Employed mothers also tend to score lower on measures of depression, stress, and psychosomatic illness. On the other hand, neither women nor children are likely to benefit when the husband opposses his wife's employment

What is your image of an "ideal" family? What changes would you most like to see in today's families?

or when he assumes none of the childcare responsibilities (Crosby, 1987; Pleck, 1985).

Adolescents also benefit from their mother's employment as a consequence of her attitudes toward children's independence and sex roles. In general, employed mothers have less stereotyped attitudes about sex roles and encourage their children to be more independent than do nonemployed mothers. Moreover, husbands and wives in two-income families are more likely to share household roles, thus modeling more androgynous behavior for their children. Some men whose wives are employed also tend to be more involved with their children, which is correlated with greater cognitive and social gains for their sons and daughters. Daughters, however, seem to benefit more than sons from their mothers' employment in terms of their future vocational and educational accomplishments. Moreover, daughters with employed mothers are more likely than those whose mothers are full-time homemakers to name their mother as the person they most admire and most want to emulate.

Childcare and Latchkey Children

Given that most mothers and virtually all fathers must work outside the home, millions of families are now confronting the problem of childcare; a problem involving adolescent as well as preschool children. Indeed, many adolescents whose parents work are left unsupervised after school and during school vacations.

As a consquence, the term **latchkey children** has risen to describe youngsters who are responsible for their own care at home until their employed parents return. It is now estimated that there are 2 to 7 million such children between the ages of 6 and 11 (Friedman, 1986).

Given that the average cost of day care is $3,000 per child per year, only a limited number of families can afford this option. Moreover, those most in need of childcare are single mothers whose incomes average only $10,000 a year (Friedman, 1986). The primary source for helping poor families with childcare expenses is provided through Title XX. These funds, however, served fewer than 15% of eligible families in 1981—a percentage that has further diminished as a result of more funding cuts (Kahn & Kamerman, 1987). Even California, which provides our nation's most comprehensive support for childcare, serves fewer than 10% of the 1.1 million eligible children (Children's Defense Fund, 1987). As a consequence, in both single- and two-parent households, many mothers cannot afford to seek employment in order to improve their familiy's income.

Why have we not provided more extensive childcare programs for adolescents and young children? Indeed, why are we the only industrialized nation in the world without a policy guaranteeing parents some time off from work for the care of their newborn children without a risk of jeopardizing their jobs or advancement at work (Stipek & McCroskey, 1989)? In part, we have failed to enact childcare legislation on the premise that such government support would "destroy the American family." Many in our society are also still tyrannized by the belief that any option other than a mother's care will adversely affect a child's development. To the contrary, however, high-quality childcare has not been found to have detrimental effects on a child's intellectual, social, or linguistic development. Nor do the bonds formed between children and their caregivers replace the child's attachment to his or her parents (Kahn & Kamerman, 1987; Lande, Scarr, & Guzenhauser, 1989; Scarr, 1983).

Fortunately, our society is slowly coming to understand these realities. We are also beginning to recognize that childcare is a necessity, not a luxury, for employed parents, as well as for parents who are trying to get off welfare. For example, within the past decade 2,500 businesses have begun helping employees defray childcare expenses, although this represents only a fraction of our country's 6 million businesses (Friedman, 1986). Nevertheless, we have a long way to go before catching up with the rest of the industrialized world in terms of family policies and childcare legislation.

PHYSICALLY ABUSED CHILDREN

An increasing number of adolescents are physically or sexually abused by their own parents, step-parents, or other relatives. Although we like to view ourselves as a child-loving society, the fact remains that each year at least 10% of our children are reported as having been physically abused by their own parents, and another 10% are reported as sexually abused by another relative (E. Emery, 1989; Russell, 1988). These figures, however, are considered gross underestimates of the amount of physical and sexual abuse that adolescents and younger children are actually experiencing in their families.

Why do parents physically abuse their own children? Are abusive parents more likely to come from lower socioeconomic classes, and were they abused as children? As the problem of physical abuse has become more public, researchers have shed new light on some of our former assumptions about abusive parents (Emery, 1989; Gelles & Straus, 1989; Wolfe, 1987). The motives underlying child abuse, however, have not been narrowed to a single cause. Given that the data are correlational, establishing cause and effect is problematic. Moreover, our information is skewed by the fact that not all cases of child abuse are reported and that, when abuse does exist, it is more likely to be discovered and reported in poorer than in richer familes.

These limitations notwithstanding, having been abused as a child is highly correlated with becoming an abusive parent. From the social learning theorists' viewpoint, this finding is not surprising in that people model their behavior after that of their own parents when they themselves become parents—"monkey see, monkey do." In this way, the cycle of family violence is passed from generation to generation. Nevertheless, thousands of parents who were abused as children do not abuse their own children. From these findings, it is clear that factors other than having been the victim of child abuse are also at play.

In this vein, research shows strong correlations between child abuse and a parent's low self-esteem. Since marital stress, financial crises, having a large family, or becoming parents at an early age tends to increase stress and decrease self-esteem, it is not particularly surprising that fewer cases of child abuse are reported among the wealthier, the happily married, parents with the fewest children, and those who become parents later in life. Some researchers, having found a slight decrease in family violence since 1975, attribute the decline to the fact that later marriages and legalized abortions lead to smaller families and to more wanted children. Moreover, women's increased participation as wage earners helps rectify the balance of power between adults in the family and thereby lessens the kind of stress that leads to family violence (Gelles & Straus, 1989). Contrary to earlier assumptions, child abusers do not seem to have an "abusive personality." They are, instead, people whose circumstances have created an undue amount of stress or whose backgrounds have given them limited knowledge about child rearing.

Although no single reaction characterizes abused children, their reactions can manifest themselves as aggressive behavior, depression, lack of empathy toward others, inability to trust anyone, or a decline in school performance. Many abused children also turn against their nonabusive parent for not having protected them from the physically abusive parent. Feeling that they have somehow "asked for it," abused children are also likely to suffer the guilt or self-incrimination of believing they are responsible for the abuse from their parents. As a consequence, the children's self-esteem is often damaged well into adulthood from feeling that if they had only been better or different, their parent would not have beaten them.

In a relatively new line of research, it now appears that just witnessing family violence, without actually being the victim, can disturb a child's development. In these studies, adolescents who have watched their fathers hitting their mothers develop psychological problems, and younger children often react as if they themselves had been the victims (E. Emery, 1989).

INCEST VICTIMS

While it has been difficult for many of us to admit that child abuse is such a problem in our society, it has been even more painful and embarrassing for us to come to terms with another form of family violence—incest. Not until 1983 was a national television network willing to air a movie about incest, entitled *The*

Trouble with Amelia. In 1984 and 1985, however, stories began to appear in the media and in books as incidents of incest, child pornography, and sexual abuse in preschools and elementary schools came to our nation's attention. As a consequence of our heightened awareness, some school systems are now requiring that preschoolers, as well as adolescents, be taught how to report incidents of rape, incest, and molestation.

Fortunately, despite the shame and secrecy that have surrounded incest, victims have been willing to publicize the trauma of "the best-kept family secret" (Bass & Thornton, 1983; Blume, 1990; Fraser, 1988; Russell, 1988; Tower, 1989). As a consequence of these revelations and of researchers' growing interest in the topic, we have gained a clearer understanding of these sex offenders and their victims.

We know, for example, that incest seldom occurs between biologically related individuals. The vast majority of cases involve a stepfather and his wife's daughter, followed by incest between other relationships established through marriage and divorce. Almost all victims, however, are female. Contrary to earlier stereotypes, the stepfather or other male relative who forces himself sexually on a young female family member is usually not a violent man, nor is he typically different from other men in terms of having a history of emotional, sexual, or psychological disorders. Instead, these men usually appear unremarkably ordinary to outsiders, as well as to the family. In fact, many researchers now evaluate the dynamics of the entire family, rather than merely analyzing the personality of the sex offender himself, in trying to determine the motives underlying the incestuous relationship. For example, How do the husband and wife relate to one another sexually and emotionally? How is the mother abdicating her emotional role as a "wife" to her daughter? How well do the mother and daughter communicate? Is a son feeling emotionally distant or angry at his own father and, as a consequence, seeking revenge by forcing himself sexually on his stepsister? Given the complications involved in studying such family dynamics, it has been difficult to uncover any single underlying cause for incest.

Although most of us think of incest as an exclusively female problem, boys are by no means spared this form of abuse. Boys are sexually abused by their uncles, stepfathers, and other male relatives. Moreover, the male victim's plight is complicated by the fact that he must deal with our society's loathing for male homosexuality. The male victim feels the shame and confusion associated with homosexuality as well as the trauma of having been sexually used by a male relative. As a result, male incest victims are often more reluctant than female victims to disclose their experiences or to seek help in recovering from their ordeal (Lew, 1990; Sonkins, 1988).

Whether male or female, incest victims are besieged by emotional and psychological difficulties during their adolescence and, most often, well into their adulthood. Understandably, these young victims separate sex from love, sometimes becoming promiscuous or unable to experience sexual pleasure even years after the incestuous relationship has ended. Not surprisingly, many run away from home, attempt suicide, become chronically depressed, act aggressively toward their teachers and friends, and lose their ability to concentrate on their schoolwork. Some female incest victims even adopt attitudes associated with the male gender role and hold negative views of females in general. These findings offer support for the hypothesis that incest victims have to identify with their aggressor psychologically and emotionally to subdue or repress their own rage and guilt. Given that many adults, above all family members, are reluctant or refuse to believe a child's reports of incest, many victims also come to doubt their own perceptions of reality—a doubt that can undermine their perceptions of reality in other domains as well. One of the most difficult challenges for these young victims, then, is trust. How are they to trust people they love in the future? Above all, how are they to trust or relate to the offender himself? Then, too, there is the matter not only of trusting the parent who seemingly permitted the incest to occur but also of dealing with the rage and betrayal felt toward that "innocent" parent: How could you let this happen to me? Why didn't you protect me from him?

Given the tragic consequences of this form of sexual abuse, it is fortunate that more therapists and books are now available to help victims recover from this childhood ordeal. More important still, we as individuals must adopt the attitude that incest is not the victim's fault and that incest victims are not somehow soiled in ways that make us uncomfortable in their presence. When someone has the courage to reveal this tragic part of his or her past, it is our responsibility to respond with the empathy and respect that will enable the person to rebuild his or her dignity, self-love, trust, and sexuality.

CONCLUSION

In many respects, the changes our families have undergone since the 1950s and the problems we now confront have been reflected by our television screens (Taylor, 1989). We have moved from "Leave it to Beaver," in which the all-knowing father resolved the family's problems, unchallenged by his wife, to "All in the Family," where the father could no longer be counted on to know best and where the entire family almost came to blows over issues such as racism, sexism, rape, and impotence. Ironically, amidst the worsening economic conditions and growing concerns about issues such as incest, divorce, and child abuse, the 1980s ended with television once again churning out images of healthy, happy, consumer-oriented families with "The Cosby Show" and its imitators. In this regard, we might well wonder what the television programs of the 1990s will reflect in terms of our realistic and unrealistic portrayals of the family.

Given what we know as we enter this decade, we might at the very least expect this much realism in popular portrayals of our families: that most families will not be nuclear, yet most children will adapt to their single parents or step-parents without permanent damage; that most families will be struggling economically, yet most parents will not lose their teenage children to the peer group or to the generation gap; that most fathers will remain relatively uninvolved with their children's upbringing in comparison to most mothers, but that more men will come to recognize the powerful impact they can have on their sons and daughters; and that incest and child abuse will continue, yet our diligence in confronting these problems publicly and privately will diminish their force.

QUESTIONS FOR REVIEW AND DISCUSSION

Review questions

1. How are the families of today's adolescents different from those of previous decades? Cite specific statistics to justify your answers.
2. What evidence supports and what evidence refutes the belief that children suffer irreparable damage as a result of their parents' divorce?

3. In regard to the generation gap and the "turmoil" created by adolescence, what do most teenagers and their parents experience? Where do our unfounded stereotypes regarding these issues come from?
4. How involved are most fathers with their teenage or young children? What accounts for this? What myths have the media perpetuated about the father's role in parenting?
5. Describe the ideal father in terms of the behaviors and attitudes that are most beneficial for a child's cognitive, social, and sexual development. How does this differ for sons and for daughters?
6. In what ways do many fathers undermine their daughters' cognitive, vocational, social, and sexual well-being?
7. To what extent do birth order and family size influence our cognitive and social development?
8. How similar and dissimilar are biological siblings? What accounts for their differences, assuming that they were raised in the same family?
9. How does the only child compare to children with siblings in terms of cognitive development, achievement, sociability, and loneliness?
10. What are the limitations of the research on parenting styles and divorce?
11. What are the various styles of parenting, and what impact does each seemingly have on adolescents' behavior and attitudes?
12. How prevalent are nuclear families, single-parent families, and blended families? How have these statistics changed during the past two decades, and what is the forecast for the 1990s?
13. What impact does divorce have on adolescents' cognitive, social, and personal development?
14. What variables affect adolescents' reactions to their parents' divorce? How can schools, parents, and counselors help to diminish the negative impact of divorce on adolescents?
15. What variables need to be taken into consideration in predicting how well any given adolescent will adjust to the blended family? How do most adolescents seem to fare?
16. What are the potential advantages for children living in blended families? What popular images of adolescents from divorced or blended families do not fit with the actual data?
17. "The American family has fallen apart in recent years." What evidence supports and what evidence refutes this assumption?
18. How prevalent is poverty in our society? What variables account for its rise? What stereotypes about poor people are not justified by the data? Describe the average poor adolescent in our society in terms of race, parents' marital status, family income, and geographic locale.
19. How prevalent is employment among mothers? What accounts for the greater numbers of employed women? How does a mother's employment affect her children?
20. How prevalent are child abuse and incest? What seems to account for these forms of aberrant behavior? What impact do physical abuse and incest have on adolescents' development?
21. What are the advantages and the disadvantages of joint custody, joint residency, and father custody? When is joint custody not in the best interests of the children or the adults? How does mediation differ from the traditional ways of resolving divorce and custody disputes?
22. How does our society rank with the rest of the world in terms of childcare policies? What accounts for this?
23. How successfully is our present welfare system providing for the needs of children and their families?
24. Using the questions in Box 8.5 and the data in Figures 8.1–8.5, describe the families in our society in terms of race, income, marital status, and parents' education.

Questions for Discussion and Debate

1. What types of conflict did you have with your parents during your adolescence? In retrospect, what might you or your parents have done to lessen these conflicts? In what ways have your conflicts with your parents changed or remained the same?
2. In what ways has your father had a positive and a negative impact on your development? What roles did your father play in your family? How did the two of you typically spend your time together? How did he react to your growing independence and sexuality? What would you

change about your relationship with your father if you had the power to do so? How might those changes have made a difference in your life now?

3. What is your picture of the ideal family in terms of the roles the father and the mother should play? How should preschool children be cared for?
4. Recall several television programs, children's stories, and popular movies that have shaped your images of the family, marriage, and child rearing. How do these images compare with the statistical realities presented in this chapter? In what ways are your expectations regarding family and marriage overly idealized or unrealistic?
5. How do you feel about preschool children being in day care centers while both their parents work? What role should employers and the government play in providing day care for the children of working parents? What are the pros and cons of day care? How was your own development affected by the type of childcare you received as a young child?
6. Why do most men not take a more active role in caring for and interacting with their own children? How would you go about changing men's and women's attitudes about their roles with their children? What are the advantages and disadvantages of the traditional nuclear family in which mom rocks the cradle and dad brings home the bacon?
7. How do you feel about your siblings or about being an only child? In what ways would you change your relationship with your siblings? How has your relationship with one another changed from childhood to the present? How would you account for the differences and the similarities between you and your siblings?
8. What style of parenting did each of your parents use with you and with the other children in your family? What were the positive and the negative effects of their parenting styles? If you could change anything about each of their styles, what would it be and why?
9. How do you feel about divorce and blended families? As a child of divorced parents, or as someone who has a friend from a divorced family, how has the divorce affected each of the people in the family? How would you feel if your parents got a divorce, or how did you feel when your parents got divorced?
10. What do you feel are the best custody arrangements for adolescent-aged children? How do you feel about fathers having the primary legal and residential custody?
11. What findings, statistics, or stories have you found most disturbing in this chapter? Why?
12. What do you feel needs to be done for the benefit or the betterment of families in our society?

GLOSSARY

Aid to Families with Dependent Children (AFDC) Welfare program.

authoritarian A dictatorial, excessively strict style of parenting in which essentially "children are to be seen and not heard."

authoritative A democratic yet disciplined style of parenting in which parents provide rules, giving rationales for them, but also let children have some say in the rules and punishments.

confluence theory The belief that family size and birth order are at least partially responsible for our personalities and attitudes.

deficit family model The premise that any family other than the nuclear family is somehow deficient and inferior.

intentionality The tendency to direct your own goals that have evolved from your own inner motivation rather than primarily as a reaction to the wishes or demands of others.

joint custody A legal agreement in which both divorced parents retain the right to be consulted about decisions related to issues concerning their children's well-being, such as education, health care, and religion.

joint residency A legal agreement, separate from joint custody, providing for children to spend roughly equal amounts of time living in each parent's home after a divorce.

latchkey children Children who are left unsupervised in their homes after school or during vacations because their parents work.

mediation A process in which a divorcing couple attempts to reach agreements about the terms of the divorce by meeting with a mediation counselor rather than resorting exclusively to lawyers.

permissive parents A style of parenting in which parents are either uninvolved with their children or in which the children are permitted to rule the roost. Synonym: laissez-faire parents.

REFERENCES

Bachman, J. Johnston, L., & O'Malley, P. (1986). *Monitoring the future.* Ann Arbor: Institute of Social Research.

Bane, J., & Ellwood, D. (1989). One fifth of the nation's children: Why are they poor? *Science, 245,* 1047–1053.

Baruch, G., Barnett, R., & Rivers, C. (1983). *Lifeprints.* New York: McGraw-Hill.

Bass, E., & Thornton, L. (Eds.). (1983). *I never told anyone: Writings by women survivors of child sexual abuse.* New York: Harper & Row.

Baumrind, D. (1990). Rearing competent children. In W. Damon (Ed.), *New directions for child development.* pp. 318–341. San Francisco: Jossey-Bass.

Beer, W. (1989). *Strangers in the house: The world of stepsiblings and half siblings.* New Brunswick: Transaction Press.

Bettelheim, B. (1977). *The uses of enchantment: The meaning and importance of fairy tales.* New York: Vintage.

Blake, J. (1988). *Family size and achievement.* Berkeley: University of California Press.

Block, J., Block, R., & Gjerde, P. (in press). Parental functioning and the home environment in families of divorce. *Journal of the American Academy of Child Psychiatry.*

Blume, S. (1990). *Secret Suvivors.* New York: Harper & Row.

Boose, L., & Flowers, B. (Eds.). (1989). *Daughters and fathers.* Baltimore: Johns Hopkins University Press.

Brodbar, J. (1984). Divorce in the Jewish community. *Journal of Jewish Communal Service, 61,* 150–159.

Bronstein, P., & Cowan, C. (Eds.). (1988). *Fatherhood today: Men's changing roles in the family.* New York: Wiley.

Brooks-Gunn, J., & Warren, M. (in press, 1990). The psychological significance of secondary sexual characteristics in 9 to 11 year old girls. *Child Development.*

Camara, K., & Resnick, G. (1988). Interparental conflict and cooperation. In E. Hetherington & J. Arasteh (Eds.), *Impact of divorce, single-parenting and stepparenting on children* (pp. 169–196). Hillsdale, NJ: Erlbaum.

Cath, S., Gurwitt, A., & Gunsberg, L. (Eds.). (1989). *Fathers and their families.* Hillsdale, NJ: Analytic Press.

Children's Defense Fund. (1987). *A children's defense budget.* Washington, DC: Author.

Chodorow, N. (1978). *The reproduction of mothering.* Berkeley: University of California Press.

Clingempeel, W., Brand, E., & Segal, S. (1987). A multilevel multivariable developmental perspective for future research on stepfamilies. In K. Pasley & M. Ihinger (Eds.), *Remarriage and stepparenting: Current research and theory* (pp. 65–93). New York: Guilford Press.

Coleman, M., & Ganong, L. (1988). The cultural stereotyping of stepfamilies. In K. Pasley & M. Inhinger (Eds.), *Remarriage and stepparenting: Current research and theory* (pp. 19–41). New York: Guilford Press.

Coleman, M., Ganong, L., & Gingrich, R. (1986). Strengths of stepfamilies identified in professional literature. In S. Van Zandt (Ed.), *Building family strengths* (pp. 439–451). Lincoln: University of Nebraska Press.

Coleman, M., Marshall, S., & Ganong, L. (1986). Beyond Cinderella: Relevant reading for adolescents about stepfamilies. *Adolescence, 21,* 553–560.

Crosby, F. (Ed.). (1987). *Spouse, parent, worker: On gender and multiple roles.* New Haven, CT: Yale University Press.

Daniels, D., & Plomin, R. (1985). Differential experience of siblings in the same family. *Developmental Psychology, 21,* 747–760.

Dunn, J. & Plomin, R. (1990). *Separate lives: Why siblings differ.* New York: Basic Books.

Elder, G., Nguyen, T., & Caspi, A. (1985). Linking family hardship to children's lives. *Child Development, 56,* 361–375.

Elkin, M. (1987). Joint custody: Affirming that parents and families are forever. *Social Work, 32,* 18–24.

Elkind, D. (1981). *The hurried child: Growing up too fast too soon.* Reading, MA: Addison Wesley.

Emery, E. (1989). Family violence. *American Psychologist, 44,* 321–328.

Emery, R. (1988). Mediation and the settlement of divorce disputes. In E. Hetherington & J. Arasteh (Eds.), *Impact of divorce, single-parenting and stepparenting on children* (pp. 53–72). Hillsdale, NJ: Erlbaum.

Falbo, T., & Polit, D. (1986). Quantitative review of the only child literature. *Psychological Bulletin, 100,* 176–189.

Fayerweather Street School (1982). *The kids' book of divorce: By, for, and about kids.* New York: Vintage.

Flaim, P., & Sehgal, E. (1985). Displaced workers of 1979–83. *Monthly Labor Review, 108,* 3–16.

Forehand, R., Long, N., & Brody, G. (1988). Divorce and marital conflict. In E. Hetherington & J. Arasteh (Eds.), *Impact of divorce, single-parenting and stepparenting on children* (pp. 155–167). Hillsdale, NJ: Erlbaum.

Frank, D. (Ed.). (1983). *Deep blue funk: Portraits of teenage parents.* Chicago: The Ounce of Prevention Fund.

Fraser, S. (1988). *My father's house: A memoir of incest and healing.* New York: Ticknor & Fields.

Friedman, D. (1986). Child care for employees' kids. *Harvard Business Review, 64,* 28–32.

Furstenberg, F. (1987). The new extended family. In K. Pasley & M. Ihinger (Eds.), *Remarriage and stepparenting: Current research and theory* (pp. 42–61). New York: Guilford Press.

Furstenberg, F. (1988). Child care after divorce and remarriage. In E. Hetherington & J. Arasteh (Eds.), *Impact of divorce, single parenting and stepparenting on children* (pp. 245–261). Hillsdale, NJ: Erlbaum.

Furstenberg, F., & Spanier, G. (1984). *Recycling the family.* Beverly Hills, CA: Sage.

Galambos, N., & Silbereisen, R. (1987). Income change, parental life outlook, and adolescent expectations for job success. *Journal of Marriage and the Family, 49,* 141–149.

Galbo, J. (1984). Adolescents' perceptions of significant adults: A review of the literature. *Adolescence, 18,* 951–970.

Gallatin, J. (1980). Political thinking in adolescence. In J. Adelson (Ed.), *Handbook of adolescent psychology* (pp. 344–82). New York: Wiley.

Ganong, L., & Coleman, M. (1986). A comparison of clinical and empirical literature on children in stepfamilies. *Journal of Marriage and the Family,48,* 309–318.

Ganong, L., & Coleman, M. (1987). Effects of parental remarriage on children. In K. Pasley & M. Ihinger (Eds.), *Remarriage and stepparenting: Current research and theory* (pp. 94–140). New York: Guilford Press.

Ganong, L., & Coleman, M. (in press). Stepchildren's perceptions of their parents. *Journal of Genetic Psychology.*

Gantz, J. (1983). *Whose child cries: Children of gay parents talk about their lives.* Rolling Hills Estates, CA: Jalmar Press.

Garfinkle, I. (1989). The evolution of child support policy. *Focus, 11*(1), 11–16.

Gelles, R., & Straus, M. (1989). *Intimate violence.* New York: Simon and Schuster.

Gilbert, L. (1985). *Men in dual career families: Current realities and future prospects.* Hillsdale, NJ: Erlbaum.

Gilbert, L. (1988). *Sharing it all: The rewards and struggles of two career families.* New York: Plenum.

Glick, P., & Linn, S. (1986). Recent changes in divorce and remarriage. *Journal of Marriage and the Family, 48,* 737–747.

Gottfried, A., & Gottfried, A. (Eds.). (1987). *Maternal employment and children's development: Longitudinal research.* New York: Plenum.

Grief, G. (1985). *Single fathers.* Lexington, MA: Heath.

Grotevant, H., & Cooper, C. (Eds.). (1983). *Adolescent development in the family.* San Francisco: Jossey-Bass.

Grotevant, H., & Cooper, C. (1986). Individuation in family relationships. *Human Development, 29,* 82–100.

Guidubaldi, J. (1990). Differences in children's divorce adjustment across grade level and gender. In S. Wolchik & P. Karoly (Eds.), *Children of divorce: Perspective on adjustment.* Lexington, MA: Lexington Books.

Hagen, J. (1987). Proceed with caution: Advocating joint custody. *Social Work, 32,* 26–30.

Hanson, S. (1988). Divorced fathers with custody: Review of the research. In P. Bronstein & C. Cowan (Eds.). *Fatherhood today* (pp. 166–194). New York: Wiley & Sons.

Hareven, T. (1986). Historical analysis of the family. In M. Sussman & S. Steinmetz (Eds.), *Handbook of marriage and the family* (pp. 37–57). New York: Plenum Press.

Hartup, W. (1983). The peer system. In E. Hetherington (Ed.), *Handbook of child psychology.* pp. 186–224. New York: Wiley.

Hernandez, D. (1988). Demographic trends and the living arrangements of children. In E. Hetherington & J. Arasteh (Eds.), *Impact of divorce, single-parenting and stepparenting on children* (pp. 3–22). Hillsdale, NJ: Erlbaum.

Hetherington, M., Stanley, M., & Anderson, E. (1989). Marital transitions: A child's perspective. *American Psychologist, 44,* 303–312.

Hill, J. (1987). Research on adolescents and their families. In C. Irwin (Ed.), *Adolescent social behavior and health* (pp. 13–31). San Francisco: Jossey-Bass.

Hill, J., & Holmbeck, G. (1986). Attachment and autonomy during adolescence. In G. Whitehurst (Ed.), *Annals of child development* (p. 3). Greenwich, CT: JAI Press.

Hobart, C. (1987). Parent child relations in remarried families. *Journal of Marriage and the Family, 47,* 93–115.

Hofferth, S. (1985). Updating children's life course. *Journal of Marriage and the Family, 43,* 120–132.

Hoffman, L. (1989). Effects of maternal employment in the two parent family. *American Psychologist, 44,* 283–292.

Isralowitz, R., & Singer, M. (1986). Unemployment and its impact on adolescent work values. *Adolescence, 21,* 145–158.

Jennings, L. (1989, February). Report expected to sharpen policy debate on homeless. *Education Week,* p. 19.

Johnson, C., Sum, A., & Weill, J. (1988). *Vanishing dreams: The growing economic plight of America's young families.* Washington, DC: Children's Defense Fund.

Jones, D. (1984). Family influences on cognitive development and school achievement. In E. Gordon (Ed.), *Review of research in education.* pp. 308–320. Washington, DC: American Educational Research Association.

Juster, F. (Ed.). (1990). *Studies in the measurement of*

time allocation. Ann Arbor, MI: Institute for Social Research.

Kahn, A., & Kamerman, S. (1987). *Child care: Facing the hard choices.* Dover, MA: Auburn House.

Koel, A., Clark, S., Phear, W., & Hauser, B. (1988). A comparison of joint and sole legal custody agreements. In E. Hetherington & J. Arasteh (Eds.), *Impact of divorce, single-parenting and stepparenting on children* (pp. 73–90). Hillsdale, NJ: Erlbaum.

Kolko, S. (Ed.), (1985). *Family law handbook.* Washington, DC: Bureau of National Affairs.

Koopman, E., & Hunt, J. (1988). Child custody mediation. *American Journal of Orthopsychiatry, 58,* 379–386.

Kozol, J. (1988). *Rachel and her children: America's homeless.* New York: Crown.

Krementz, J. (1984). *How it feels when parents divorce.* New York: Knopf.

Lamb, M. (Ed.). (1986). *The father's role: Applied perspectives.* New York: Wiley.

Lamb, M. (Ed.). (1987). *The father's role: Cross cultural perspectives.* Hillsdale, NJ: Erlbaum.

Lamb, M., & Levine, J. (1983). The Swedish parental insurance policy: An experiment in social engineering. In M. Lamb & A. Sagi (Eds.), *Fatherhood and family policy.* (pp. 39–48). Hillsdale, NJ: Erlbaum.

Lamb, M., & Sagi, A. (Eds.). (1989). *Fatherhood and family policy* (pp. 39–48). Hillsdale, NJ: Erlbaum.

Lande, J., Scarr, S., & Guzenhauser, N. (Eds.). (1989). *Caring for children: Challenge to America.* Hillsdale, NJ: Erlbaum.

Laosa, L. (1988). Ethnicity and single parenting in the U.S. In E. Hetherington & J. Arasteh (Eds.). *Impact of divorce, single-parenting and stepparenting on children* (pp. 23–49). Hillsdale, NJ: Erlbaum.

Lempers, J., Clark, D., & Simons, R. (in press). Economic hardship, parenting and distress in adolescence. *Child Development.*

Leonard, L. (1985). *The wounded woman: Healing the father-daughter wound.* Boston: Shambhala.

Levant, R., & Kelly, J. (1989). *Between father and child: How to become the kind of father you want to be.* New York: Penguin Books.

Lew, M. (1990). *Victims no longer: Men recovering from incest.* New York: Harper & Row.

Levine, J., & Pleck, J. (1983). The fatherhood project. In M. Lamb & A. Sagi (Eds.). *Fatherhood and family policy* (pp. 101–113). Hillsdale, NJ: Erlbaum.

Lewis, C., & O'Brien, M. (Eds.). (1987). *Reassessing fatherhood: New observations on fathers and the modern family.* Beverly Hills, CA: Sage.

Long, N., & Forehand, R. (1987). The effects of divorce and marital conflict on children. *Journal of Developmental and Behavioral Pediatrics, 8,* 292–296.

Luepnitz, D. (1986). Comparison of maternal, paternal and joint custody. *Journal of Divorce, 9,* 1–12.

Lutz, P. (1983). The stepfamily: An adolescent perspective. *Family Relations, 32,* 367–375.

Maccoby, E., & Martin, J. (1983). Socialization in the context of the family: Parent-child interaction. In P. Mussen (Ed.), *Handbook of child psychology* (pp. 37–101). New York: Wiley.

Marcia, J. (1980). Identity in adolescence. In J. Adelson (Ed.), *Handbook of adolescent psychology* (pp. 159–187). New York: Wiley.

Marone, N. (1988). *How to father a successful daughter.* New York: McGraw-Hill.

McGuire, P. (1987). *Putting it together: Teenagers talk about family breakup.* New York: Delacorte Press.

McLoyd, V. (1989). Socialization and development in a changing economy. *American Psychologist, 44,* 293–302.

Montemayor, R. (1986). Family variation in parent-adolescent storm and stress. *Journal of Adolescent Research, 1,* 15–31.

Norton, A., & Moorman, J. (1987). Marriage and divorce patterns of U.S. women. *Family Issues, 8,* 259–277.

Offer, D., Ostrov, E., & Howard, K. (1981). *The adolescent: A psychological self-portrait.* New York: Basic Books.

Pasley, K., & Ihinger-Tallman, M. (Eds.). (1987). *Remarriage and stepparenting: Current research and theory.* New York: Guilford Press.

Patterson, G. (1982). *Coercive family process.* Eugene, OR: Castalia Press.

Phillips, R. (1989). *Putting asunder: A history of divorce in western society.* Cambridge, England: Cambridge University Press.

Pleck, J. (1985). *Working wives/working husbands.* Beverly Hills, CA: Sage.

Radin, N., & Goldsmith, R. (1985). Caregiving fathers of preschoolers. *Merrill Palmer Quarterly, 31,* 375–381.

Radomisli, M. (1981). Stereotypes, stepmothers and splitting. *The American Journal of Psychoanalysis, 41,* 121–127.

Richardson, J. (1987). *Food stamps: 1987 issues.* Washington, DC: Congressional Research Service.

Roman, M. (1987). Joint custody fathers. In J. Jacobs (Ed.), *Divorce and fatherhood: The struggle for parental identity* (pp. 84–95). Washington, DC: American Psychiatric Press.

Ross, C., & Danziger, S. (1987). Poverty rates by state. *Focus, 10,* 1–5.

Rubin, Z. & Sloman, J. (1984). How parents influence their children's friendships. In M. Lewis (Ed.), *Beyond the dyad.* New York: Plenum Press.

Russell, E. (1988). *The secret trauma: Incest in the lives of girls and women.* New York: Basic Books.

Rutter, M. (1987). Psychosocial resilience and protective mechanisms. *American Journal of Orthopsychiatry, 57,* 316–331.

Santrock, J., & Sitterle, K. (1987). Parent child relationships in stepmother families. In K. Pasley & M. Ihinger (Eds.),

Remarriage and stepparenting: Current research and theory (pp. 135–154). New York: Guilford Press.

Sawhill, I. (1987). *Anti-poverty strategies for the next decade.* Washington, DC: Center for National Policy.

Scarr, W. (1983). *Mother care/other care.* New York: Basic Books.

Scarr, S., & Grajek, S. (1982). Similarities and differences among siblings. In M. Lamb & B. Smith (Eds.), *Sibling relationships* (pp. 357–383). Hillsdale, NJ: Erlbaum.

Shave, D., & Shave, B. (1989). *Early adolescence and the search for self.* New York: Praeger.

Smetana, J. (1988). Adolescents' and parents' conceptions of parental authority. *Child Development, 59,* 321–335.

Smith, B. (1982). Birth order and sibling status effects. In M. Lamb & B. Smith (Eds.), *Sibling relationships* (pp. 153–166). Hillsdale, NJ: Erlbaum.

Sonkins, D. (1988). *Wounded men: Healing from childhood abuse.* New York: Harper & Row.

Steinberg, L. (1987). Recent research on the family at adolescence. *Journal of Youth and Adolescence, 16,* 191–197.

Steinberg, L. (1988). Reciprocal relations between parent-child distance and pubertal maturation. *Developmental Psychology, 24,* 122–128.

Stipek, D., & McCroskey, J. (1989). Investing in children: Government and workplace policies for parents. *American Psychologist, 44,* 416–423.

Stolberg, A., Camplain, C., Currier, K., & Well, M. (1987). Individual, familial and environmental determinants of childrens' post-divorce adjustment and maladjustment. *Journal of Divorce, 11,* 51–70.

Sulzberger, C. (1987). *Fathers and children.* New York: William Morrow.

Taylor, E. (1989). *Prime-time families: Television culture in post-war America.* Berkeley: University of California Press.

Tessman, L. (1989). Fathers and daughters: Early tones, later echoes. In S. Cath, A. Gurwitt, & L. Gunsberg (Eds.), *Fathers and their families.* (pp. 197–223). Hillsdale, NJ: Analytic Press.

Tower, C. (1989). *Secret scars: A guide for survivors of child sexual abuse.* New York: Penguin Books.

U.S. Bureau of Labor Statistics. (1986, February). *Monthly labor review.* Washington, DC: U.S. Government Printing Office.

U.S. Census Bureau (1987). *Family incomes by race and marital status.* Washington, DC: U.S. Government Printing Office.

U.S. House of Representatives, Committee on Ways and Means. (1985). *Children in poverty.* Washington, DC: U.S. Government Printing Office.

U.S. Senate Finance Committee. (1988). *Data and materials related to welfare programs for families with children.* Washington, DC: U.S. Government Printing Office.

Wallerstein, J., & Blakeslee, S. (1989). *Second chances: Men, women and children a decade after divorce.* New York: Ticknor & Fields.

Weitzman, L. (1985). *The divorce revolution: The unexpected social and economic consequences for women and children in America.* New York: Free Press.

Wolfe, D. (1987). *Child abuse: Implications for child development and psychopathology.* Beverly, Hills, CA: Sage.

Yankelovich, D. (1981). *New rules: Searching for self-fulfillment in a world turned upside down.* New York: Random House.

Youniss, J., & Smollar, J. (1985). *Adolescent relations with mothers, fathers and friends.* Chicago: University of Chicago Press.

Zajonc, R. (1983). Validating the confluence model. *Psychological Bulletin, 93,* 457–480.

Zaslow, M. (1987). *Sex differences in children's response to maternal employment.* Washington, DC: National Research Council.

Zaslow, M. (1988). Sex differences in children's response to parental divorce. *American Journal of Orthopsychiatry, 46,* 355–378.

Zill, N. (1988). Behavior, achievement and health problems among children in stepfamilies. In E. Hetherington & J. Arasteh (Eds.), *Impact of divorce, single-parenting and stepparenting on children* (pp. 325–368). Hillsdale, NJ: Erlbaum.

Zuckerman, D. (1985, January). Too many sibs put our nation at risk? *Psychology Today,* p. 5.

9 Adolescents and Their Peers

CHAPTER OUTLINE

GOALS AND OBJECTIVES

This chapter is designed to enable you to:

- Discuss the limitations of the research on adolescents' peer relationships
- Explain the factors influencing an adolescent's popularity
- Explore the relative influence of parents and peers during adolescence
- Delineate the differences between childhood and adolescent friendships
- Examine the distinctions between male and female friendships
- Consider the ways in which schools influence adolescents' friendships
- Explore ways of encouraging interracial friendships
- Examine ways of helping adolescents overcome shyness and loneliness

CONCEPTS AND TERMINOLOGY

assertiveness training
date rape
friends
jigsaw teaching
peers
teams achievement divisions

THE VALUE OF THE PEER GROUP

Perhaps no aspect of adolescence provokes as much anxiety among adults as the presumed power of the peer group over young people's values and behavior. Given that adolescents spend more time with their friends and less time with their parents than they did as young children, adults' concerns about the influence of friends is understandable. Thus, in their study of adolescent friendships, researchers have asked: How much influence do friends have compared to that of the adolescents' parents? How do adolescents choose their friends? How do adolescent friendships differ from those of children and adults?

In comparison to their children's friends, even the most nurturant and empathic parents cannot provide the experiences that ultimately enhance adolescents' self-confidence, social skills, and self-understanding. It is their friends, not adults, who will teach the many necessary lessons—both painful and pleasurable—so that the adolescents can fashion their own identities and establish the kind of independence that will enable them to enter the adult world.

Limitations of the Research

In trying to determine the relative impact that peers and parents have on our development and in studying our adolescent friendships, researchers have encountered a number of problems that limit our understanding of these important issues (Cohen, 1983; Hallinan, 1983). First, when adolescents and their friends are found to behave in similar ways, researchers have usually assumed that this is a result of peer influence. In actuality, however, most of us—as adults and as adolescents—choose to interact with people who are already similar to us: "Birds of a feather flock together." Ignoring or downplaying these initial similarities, most researchers have overestimated the significance of peer influence. It has also been typical to assume that if peers are found to influence one another's decisions in one domain, they must be exerting as much influence in other domains as well. Therefore, for example, when we find that adolescents do generally influence one another's opinions about when to start dating and what kinds of clothes to wear, we assume they are exerting an equal influence over decisions about using drugs or graduating from school. Yet, as we will see in this chapter, this is not usually the case.

Understandably, researchers have also had a difficult time agreeing on operational definitions for the terms **friend** and **peer.** In some studies, for example, adolescents who spend a lot of time in the same classes or on athletic teams have been categorized as friends, while in other studies a *friend* is someone whom the adolescent identifies as such. In most studies, people of the same age are categorized as peers, yet in others people sharing the same activities are considered peers, even though their ages differ. Why is it important that researchers clarify these terms before gathering their data? First, because the amount of influence our friends have over us is probably more than that of our peers. But without a clear definition of these terms, we actually have no way of testing this hypothesis or of determining which kinds of decision our friends and our peers tend to influence. Second, our behavior is probably different around our friends than around our peers. Again, however, without a clear definition of these terms in the research, we have no way of verifying this hypothesis.

Moreover, almost all the existing research has been conducted with white, middle-class youths, ignoring family variables that might affect peer influence and peer selection. Such factors as the family's income and the degree of intimacy between adolescents and their parents have not usually been taken into account. Gender is also typically overlooked. Do male and female friends have different types of influence over one another? If so, how and why? Do males and females choose their friends and peers differently? If so, how and why? Finally, most studies rely on adolescents' self-reports of their feelings and behavior toward friends and peers, rather than on actual observations of their behavior. We need more studies that record and compare adolescents' actual behavior with that of their peers, friends, and parents.

The Parent-Peer Conflict?

Although adolescents' parents generally worry about the impact that the peer group will exert over their children, most of their worries are unfounded. As chapter 8 demonstrated, most adolescents continue to live by their parents' values regarding religion, education, politics, and careers. In the vast majority of families there is no generation gap that isolates adolescents from their parents or causes adolescents to reject their parents' values by yielding to peer pressure. Although adolescents spend less time with their parents and more time with their friends than they did as children, they still turn to their parents for advice and guidance on the important issues in their lives. Moreover, when asked who is most influential and most important in their lives, most adolescents name their parents, not their friends (Blyth, Hill & Thiel, 1982; Coleman, 1980; Galbo, 1984; Greenberg, Siegel, & Leitch, 1983; Marcia, 1980; Montemayor, 1983; Williamson & Campbell, 1985; Youniss & Smollar, 1985).

Why, then, do so many parents worry about losing their influence to their adolescent child's friends? In part, their worries may be founded on events during the 1960s and 1970s, such as demonstrations against the war in Vietnam, the rising use of drugs, and the increase in premarital sex. These highly publicized events served to highlight the seeming differences between the young and their parents, while failing to point out that the older generations' values on sexual and political issues were also becoming more liberal. Although there was not much of a generation gap even during those more politically charged times, today's adolescents appear to be seeking even more advice on social issues from their parents than did youths in the 1960s and 1970s (Sebald, 1986).

Parents may also worry unnecessarily about the influence of the peer group because peers do exert considerable influence over issues that are a daily annoyance to many parents—their child's clothes, hairstyles, music, curfews, allowance, and dating. Moreover, during the early years of adolescence, conflict between parents and children is usually at its height. The typical 13-year-old is overly concerned about establishing his or her independence, making a good impression on friends, being physically attractive, and being treated with trust and respect by older people—particularly by his or her parents. At the same time, the young adolescent's parents are usually overly concerned with maintaining control and respect so that the presumed peer pressure will not threaten their influence over their child. What the parent, often trying to exert more control, sees as advice, the young adolescent, wanting more independence, sees as criticism. As young adolescents and their parents work out these new roles, their conflicts generally increase. Parents then worry that this first year or so of adolescence is only the tip of the iceberg, that their conflicts are going to get worse rather than better. In reality, however, the reverse usually occurs after that first year or two.

ADOLESCENT FRIENDSHIPS

Choosing Friends

As mentioned briefly, it may also be a comfort to parents to know that most adolescents choose their friends from classmates or neighbors who are similar to themselves in socioeconomic class, intellectual abilities, family backgrounds, values, and interests (Berndt, 1982b; Duck, 1983; Epstein, 1983; Rubin & Sloman, 1984). It is unlikely, therefore, that parents will "lose" their children to an adolescent peer group whose values or lifestyle is totally at odds with those at home.

Unfortunately, in cases where adolescents are living in neighborhoods where crime, drugs, and violence are the community's predominant life-style, the peer group will reinforce these values; but the adolescents' peer group is not replacing the predominant adult culture. It is reflecting, not overturning, the most prevalent adult attitudes and behavior.

Popularity

Although most adolescents are able to find a group of friends who accept them, having friends does not eradicate their worries about being popular. We can have friends and still worry about how our behavior affects our popularity with them on a day-to-day basis. Understandably, therefore, even adolescents who have plenty of friends can wonder what it takes to "be popular." On what grounds are they judging one another as winners and losers on the social playing fields? Who has the advantage in the dating game? What does it take to make it as a popular person?

As is the case with adults, adolescents who are cheerful, have a good sense of humor, and assume the initiative in talking to or playing with others are generally more popular than their shy, withdrawn peers (Coleman, 1980; Hartup, 1983). It also appears that adolescents who can recognize other people's emotions and can empathize with others' feelings are well liked (Adams, 1983).

Fortunately or unfortunately, depending on your point of view, being athletic is still better than being scholarly in terms of boosting a boy's popularity among

Who were your closest teenage friends? How did you become friends? What's happened to each of those friendships?

both his male and his female peers (Savin-Williams, 1980; Weisfeld, Block & Ivers, 1983). Moreover, in schools with athletic teams that win frequently, being an athlete is more crucial in determining a boy's popularity than in schools with average or losing teams (Williams & White, 1983). Despite our supposedly more liberated views regarding masculinity, the key to popularity for high-school men is still making the grade on the playing field rather than in the classroom.

In contrast to the situation with boys, being athletic places the adolescent girl's popularity in jeopardy. If a teenage girl decides to participate in a sport, she had best choose one that is considered ladylike, such as tennis or gymnastics, if she wants to enhance her popularity. Being athletic, especially in sports such as basketball or soccer that have historically been male turf, jeopardizes a girl's popularity in most adolescent groups (Colley, Nash, O'Donnell, & Restorick, 1987; Desertrain & Weiss, 1988; Kane, 1988; Williams & White, 1983).

Moreover, as was the case with her mother's generation, being physically attractive is still one of the most important assets a girl can possess on the social playing field (Duck, 1983). Despite our reassurances to adolescent girls that "beauty is only skin deep," most of her male and female peers will judge her, in large part, on the basis of her appearance. Although being attractive also contributes to a boy's popularity, it is generally a more important criterion in determining a girls' social standing. Having recognized this unfortunate reality, girls are more concerned about, and more dissatisfied with, their appearance than are boys. Underscoring the importance of physical appearance, one study of eighth-grade students showed that both boys and girls preferred to be with attractive classmates, even if the classmate was shy and unfriendly (Zakin, 1983). Before chastising or mocking adolescents for their "superficial" standards, however, adults should recall that they also take serious account of others' physical appearance in choosing dates and friends.

CHANGES IN FRIENDSHIPS DURING ADOLESCENCE

As childhood bodies transform at adolescence, so do the children's definitions of a friend (Asher & Gottman, 1981; Coleman, 1980; Duck, 1983; Epstein, 1983; Seltzer, 1982; Youniss & Smollar, 1985). Young children choose their friends on the basis of relatively simple, concrete characteristics: "Suzie is my friend because she has nice toys." Before adolescence, friends are primarily people who share activities: "Friends are easy to make. All you have to do is go up to a guy, say hello, and ask him if he wants to play ball; then he's a friend. If he don't want to play ball, then he's not a friend unless you decide to play something else" (Smollar & Youniss, 1982, p. 281).

During adolesence, however, children begin to expect more from friends than just sharing an activity. They want someone to help them resolve personal problems, to share their innermost thoughts with, and to empathize with their feelings. Adolescents look for emotional support, mutual acceptance, and non-judgmental approval from those who claim to be friends. As a result, adolescents become concerned with whether someone is trustworthy, honest, unselfish, and reliable before deciding whether a friendship might develop. Then, too, instead of focusing exclusively on what their friends can offer them, adolescents awaken to the reality that friendships are reciprocal arrangements in which each partner must compromise and contribute. In this process, adolescent friends are learning how to recognize one another's feelings and to decipher one another's verbal and nonverbal messages.

According to cognitive psychologists such as Jean Piaget and David Elkind, these changes in friendship are directly related to the adolescent's entering a new cognitive stage (Elkind, 1980; Josselson, 1980; Piaget & Inhelder, 1969). Moving from the concrete to the formal stage of reasoning enables adolescents to be less egocentric in relating to others. Likewise, being able to think more abstractly enables them to focus on aspects of friendship other than the immediate here and now matters of who can be an entertaining playmate for a few brief hours. As the imaginary audience gradually loosens its grip on young adolescents, they also become more able to focus on their friends' feelings and needs, rather than worrying about how everyone else is judging them. In other words, as adolescence progresses, we become more empathetic and less self-centered as friends. For example, as Box 9.1 illustrates, adolescents are generally less judgmental toward peers with physical or mental handicaps than are young children (Whalen et al., 1983).

According to the ego psychologists, adolescents also become better friends to

A CLOSER LOOK 9.1

Adolescents' Perceptions of Aggressive and Retarded Peers

What do adolescents think of their mildly retarded classmates? How do they perceive their obstreperous, aggressive peers? Would adolescents be more critical of a retarded, a hyperactive, or an antisocial classmate? To answer these questions, several researchers presented 654 students in grades 4 through 10 with a description of four hypothetical classmates: The first is a normal, well-adjusted boy who succeeds academically and interacts with his classmates in a cooperative, enjoyable manner. The second is a mildly retarded boy who has trouble remembering things and needs help in class. He often acts younger than his age and behaves in an odd manner, but nonetheless enjoys being with other people. The third is a hyperactive male; impatient, easily frustrated, inattentive, impulsive, and moody. The fourth boy is antisocial and aggressive—showing off, dominating others, being argumentative, occasionally stealing and picking on his classmates. How do adolescents feel about these four boys?

Of the four, adolescents described the antisocial, not the retarded, boy as the one most likely to have problems in his future life. Not surprisingly, adolescents expected the normal boy to become the wealthiest, the most famous, and the most acceptable to others. The mildly retarded boy, however, was seen as more likely than the antisocial one to become rich and to become like other people as an adult. In addition, adolescents said they would be more willing to befriend the retarded boy than the antisocial one. In terms of treating the boys with leniency, the ratings for the mildly retarded and the normal boy were similar. In other words, most adolescents did not recommend that adults should be stricter with the retarded boy, in contrast to their recommendations for dealing with the hyperactive and antisocial boys.

Even more surprisingly, most adolescents described the antisocial boy as they did the retarded boy on the categories of "brain damaged" and "mentally retarded." They did, however, recommend that both the retarded and the aggressive boys be provided with professional help. Adolescents were less likely than younger children to use labels like "mentally ill" or "bad" to describe any of the atypical boys. Likewise, adolescents were less likely to suggest as solutions to the boys' problems that adults should be stricter or that the boys should seek professional help. Males and females generally agreed in their descriptions of the four boys, although girls were somewhat less likely to recommend that parents should be stricter and to label any of the boys as mentally retarded.

Source: C. Whalen, B. Henker, S. Dotemoto, & S. Hinshaw. (1983). Child and adolescent perceptions of normal and atypical peers. *Child Development, 54,* 1588–1598.

one another as they age as a consequence of having established more of their own personal identities (Erikson, 1968; Marcia, 1980). During the early years of adolescence, most of us are too concerned with establishing our own sense of self to establish truly intimate friendships. Trying to figure out who he or she is, the typical 13-year-old has less interest and less energy to invest in getting to know other people than the typical 17-year-old. Likewise, a 13-year-old is usually too busy experimenting with his or her own roles and values to focus primarily on friends' needs and feelings. As the adolescent's own sense of self develops, however, he or she is able to devote more attention to friends in the sense of being more intimate, unselfish, and supportive.

MALE AND FEMALE FRIENDSHIPS

Another interesting aspect of adolescents' friendships is that they are sex segregated. In fact, friendships between adolescent boys and girls are less common than among younger children. Although dating is certainly acceptable, being friends with someone of the other gender is rare. In fact, throughout adolescence and adulthood, individuals are more likely to befriend someone of another race than someone of the other sex. Friendships between males and females are rarest, however, in our early adolescent years—the time when our sex role stereotypes

How do your male and female friendships differ?

are exerting their fullest power over our identities and expectations (Hartup, 1983; Hill & Lynch, 1983; Karweit & Hansell, 1983b; Schofield, 1981).

Given that males and females seldom become friends, we might wonder whether there is something about the ways in which adolescent males and females relate to their friends that makes friendships between the sexes so rare. Is it true, in the words of one seventh-grade boy, that "the boys talk about football and sports and the girls talk about whatever they talk about" (Schofield, 1981)? Unfortunately, most of our present research does suggest that boys and girls, as well as men and women, have different approaches to and expectations of friendship (Blyth & Clark, 1987; Coleman, 1980; Crockett, Losoff & Petersen, 1984; Hartup, 1983; Hill & Lynch, 1983; Hinde, 1984; Karweit & Hansell, 1983; Savin-Williams, 1986; Wright, 1982; Youniss & Smollar, 1985). What, then, are these differences?

To begin with, females' friendships tend to focus more on sharing feelings and offering one another emotional support, while males' friendships are more often based on sharing activities and helping one another achieve specific goals. Girls are also more likely than boys to disclose their most intimate feelings and fears to their friends and to ask for advice and nurturance. In this sense, the stereotypical view of males getting together with friends to play or to talk about sports has a certain validity. In further contrast to boys, girls tend to invest more time and energy in their friendships and to worry more about being rejected. Not all research, however, has found these sex differences. For example, some studies have found that males and females are equally likely to have intimate knowledge of their best friend (Diaz & Berndt, 1982; Reis, Senchak, & Solomon, 1985).

Given the prevalence of sex role stereotypes in our society, these differences in male and female friendships are not particularly surprising. As previous chapters have already demonstrated, most boys in our society are socialized to establish their independence from other people and to keep their emotions to themselves. The very foundations for intimacy between people—disclosing feelings, asking for help, admitting weakness—are at odds with our general notions of masculinity. For instance, both male and female high-school students have judged girls far more harshly than boys for not expressing enough sensitivity toward people who need help (Barnett, 1987). Unlike girls, boys must also contend with accusations of homosexuality if they appear to be too close to another male. This fear, which arises from our society's having harsher attitudes toward gay males than toward gay females, undermines intimacy between adolescent boys (Herek, 1984; Kite, 1984). In contrast, most girls are socialized to establish intimate relationships and to base their self-esteem and their identities, in large part, on the success or failure of their relationships.

In sum, one of the reasons males and females seldom become friends with one another seems to be their different definitions of friendship. Still another reason, of course, is that sexual feelings often impose themselves on friendships between heterosexual males and females, transforming the friendship into something more complicated with a totally new set of expectations and rules. Our sexual feelings, however, cannot be held entirely accountable for why friendships between males and females are so rare throughout the life span. Clearly our society's traditional sex role stereotypes are partially responsible for the scarcity of friendships between males and females of all ages. By presuming that the primary interest between males and females has to be sexual if the two people are "normal," we often discourage friendships between the sexes. Indeed, being "just friends" is often met with the wink of an eye response, "Yeah, sure you are!". Indeed, being told by someone of the other gender that "I just want to be friends" is construed as the ultimate insult. Perhaps, as our society's sex role stereotypes become less restrictive and as boys and girls grow up engaged in more activities together, nonsexual friendships between males and females will become the norm rather than the exception.

INTERRACIAL FRIENDSHIPS

Although interracial friendships are more common than friendships between males and females, they too are still relatively rare among adolescents and adults in our society. Since school desegregation was declared illegal by the Supreme Court in 1954, many have hoped that desegregation would bring about more interracial friendships. Most adolescents, however, still segregate themselves along racial lines when it comes to choosing their friends and dates (Epstein, 1983b).

This is not to say that school desegregation has had no impact whatsoever on students' friendships. In fact, one of the most carefully designed longitudinal studies assessing the long-range impact of school desegration shows that integration does increase the number of interracial friendships. Moreover, minority students who attend desegregated schools are more likely to attend predominantly white colleges and to live in integrated neighborhoods as adults. Most minority and white students in desegregated schools develop more positive attitudes toward other races than do students who attend primarily segregated schools (Braddock, Crain & McPartland, 1984; Crain & Strauss, 1984; Merritt, 1983).

Nevertheless, merely integrating our schools has not necessarily led to less racial prejudice or more interracial friendship. To the contrary, under certain conditions desegregation can actually increase racial tensions and confirm negative racial stereotypes (Allport, 1958; Schofield, 1981). For example, situations in which minority students are interacting exclusively with white students with vastly superior academic skills, greater economic advantages, and higher social status in the school tend to increase racial stereotypes and prejudice. In cases where white students are in the positions of power and dominance in the classroom hierarchy, racial differences are exaggerated and negative stereotypes are often confirmed. In situations where everyone's skills are fairly equal, however, such as playing together on the school's athletic teams, racial prejudice generally decreases. In such cases, interracial friendships form as a consequence of each person's working toward a mutually beneficial goal and each making roughly the same contributions, regardless of race or economic background.

Keeping these findings in mind, teachers have had success with a number of classroom techniques designed specifically to enhance interracial friendships and to diminish prejudice (N. Miller, 1983; Slavin & Hansell, 1983). In the student **teams achievement divisions** approach, the teacher lectures on the academic materials and then assigns students to racially integrated teams to complete work sheets together. Each team is composed of four or five students with different academic abilities. After working together on their written assignments, the students each take a quiz over the materials. These quiz scores are then converted into a team score, which takes into account each student's improvement over his or her previous performance. Teams' rankings are then publicized in a newsletter or on the bulletin board. In a similar approach, **jigsaw teaching,** each student in a six-member interracial team is assigned a particular portion of the material to teach his or her teammates. Those students from the different teams who have the same assignment meet to discuss the material, then return to their own team to teach the information to their teammates. Everyone is then quizzed over the material and receives an individual grade. Both methods rely on giving minority and white students equal positions of power in which everyone gets a chance to be a teacher and in which each team works toward a mutually beneficial goal.

Students participating in these classroom activities form more interracial friendships both in and outside of class than those in the traditional curriculum, where students work individually and competitively against one another. Teachers using these cooperative, team methods have also reported fewer interracial fights in their schools. These results have been found in studies with Asian American, Mexican American, white, and African American adolescents. Interestingly, white students' attitudes toward minorities improved more than the minorities' views of whites. This suggests that students whose racial attitudes are the most negative at the outset may make the greatest improvements as a consequence of such cooperative team activities.

In sum, schools can promote interracial friendships by providing opportunities for students to interact in situations where everyone is accorded equal status. Since minority students often do have fewer academic skills than their white classmates, it is critical that we not exacerbate these differences by relegating minority students to roles in which they are always being tutored or being lead by their white classmates. Techniques such as "jigsaw teaching" minimize these status differences and increase the chances for mutual respect among different racial and socio-economic groups. With more widespread use of such techniques, our schools might be more effective in reducing racial prejudice—prejudice which, as Box 9.2 illustrates, is still very much alive among both adolescents and adults in our society.

LONELINESS AND SHYNESS

The Lonely and the Shy

Some adolescents, regardless of race and gender, have a difficult time making friends. Since adolescents are beginning to expect more from friends than just sharing activities, they tend to feel lonelier during these years than ever before. In addition, they begin to demand more from their friends in terms of intimacy and mutual support, which may lead to feelings of disappointment and misunderstanding. As adolescents, they are also becoming aware both of their separateness from their parents and of their own growing independence. While delighted by this independence, adolescents may feel lonelier as they become more individuated from adults. Working in conjunction, these changes can make the teenage years some of the loneliest of people's lives. As a result, researchers have tried to identify the reasons underlying adolescent loneliness and ways to alleviate this feeling (Brennan, 1982; Marcoen, Goossens, & Caes, 1987; Mijuskovic, 1986; Moore & Schultz, 1983; Woodward & Frank, 1988).

Of course, feeling lonely is affected by more than whether people have friends. Even people with friends can find themselves in situations that suddenly make

9.2 ADOLESCENT VOICES

Adolescents Talk About Prejudice

"The only reason that my special friend and I stopped dating each other is because I am a Mexican American, and her parents are very prejudiced. They demanded her to stop talking to me and never to see me again. Well, as it turned out, we had no other choice. . . . We had to hide to just talk to each other. Whenever I would call her, I would have to use another name so that her parents wouldn't know that it was me. Well, this went on for one whole year. Finally, we realized that we would have to see each other a different way. As it turns out now, we're the best of friends, just like two loving brothers and sisters. Her parents don't mind. I think they're finally getting to like me. There might still be hope." (Ricky Mendez, 17, Lubbock, Texas)

"In my family, there is prejudice everywhere. My dad just doesn't like blacks. Even if they are nice to him, he swears at them and still hates them. When someone murders some blacks, he's happy. I think that is just sick to wish someone dead. . . . I grew up hating blacks. That's all anyone ever told me—that they were bad people and to hate them always. But as I grew older, I grew smarter. Now I don't judge people by color. I really wish there was no prejudice in the world. It would be a happier place to live." (14-year-old female, Illinois)

"An example of being prejudiced against a black person found inside the high school would be letting a fellow black borrow a personal item such as a comb, hat, or lip balm, then later, after it is returned, treating it with disinfectant or even throwing the borrowed item away for fear of catching germs. If one feels this way about blacks causing germs, then maybe they would be better off not lending anything out. A common example of prejudice against the Trainable Mentally Retarded students would be not eating lunch in the lunch room because the only table left is the one which is for the TMRs. . . . Not everyone in McMinnville High shows prejudice against others. In fact, some even try to live without it. An example of where it might not exist in McMinnville High would be volunteering to become a peer tutor to let someone special know that they are cared for. Another example might be choosing a partner for sports who is unaccepted by society in P.E." (Kimberly Ault, 18, McMinnville, Oregon)

continued

them feel unloved and lonely. For example, adolescents report feeling lonelier on the weekends than during the week. With more leisure time on their hands and without immediate access to school friends on weekends, they tend to be more aware of being alone and more worried about whether they have been left out of the good times they assume everyone else is having. On the other hand, an adolescent's race, number of siblings, parents' marital status, and economic class seem to have very little impact on how lonely he or she feels.

Adolescents cope with their loneliness in different ways. Some become overly attached to a romantic relationship, trying to compensate for their loneliness by clinging to one person in a way that is often suffocating to the beloved. Others fantasize about being in love with famous people—rock stars, athletes, television heroes, or other unattainable people. Then there are those who combat their loneliness by redirecting their attention to their school work, sports, or television.

Box 9.2 continued

"I think a lot of people are prejudiced even though they think they're not. If you ask a white girl if she is prejudiced against blacks, she will probably say no, but then she will never go out with a black guy." (Laurel MacLaren, 15, Kirkwood, Missouri)

"I feel that prejudice is discriminating against a particular group or its beliefs. Prejudice happens all the time, all around us. In our beautiful state of Hawaii, there is a wide assortment of different racial groups and beliefs. At my school of Kamehameha, students must have Hawaiian blood in order to attend. This was part of the will of the school's founder, a Hawaiian princess. In the past, many opposed Kamehameha's requirements of claiming Hawaiian ancestry to attend, saying it was racial prejudice. However, Kamehameha was founded solely to benefit children of Hawaiian and part-Hawaiian ancestry. Racial groups in Hawaii must learn to interact to survive. The Chinese, the Filipinos, the Japanese, the Samoans, the Hawaiians, the Caucasians—although all have the ability to interact, many do not. Business in Hawaii thrives when all groups cooperate with each other to survive. In Hawaii many different groups have learned long ago to do just that. There are many different religions in Hawaii also. Roman Catholics worship next door to Buddhists in some parts of our islands. By interacting to help each other, all are happy." (Amy Soares, 16, Honolulu, Hawaii)

"An example of prejudiced people is the use of one of our gas stations around the corner from my house. This gas station is owned by a Chinese family so only Chinese men work there. The people that live in my neighborhood would rather drive an extra mile or two just so they won't have to be served by Chinese gas attendants. I feel that this is very wrong. A Chinese gas attendant can serve gas just as well as any other nationality gas attendant." (Sandy Scalise, 15, Chicago, Illinois)

"I know plenty of people who claim that they aren't prejudiced because they have a black friend or a Jewish friend. But when they are in downtown Boston, they don't hesitate to yell racial remarks out of their car window at them. It doesn't say much for those people. They must feel so threatened by those different people in order to say things like that. I think anyone that allows a public showing of prejudice should wake up to today's society. Why anyone ever lets the KKK march is still confusing to me and stirs up an unquenchable anger inside me." (Kathleen McKie, 17, Newton, Massachusetts)

Source: Glenbard East *Echo.* (1984). *Teenagers themselves.* New York: Adama Books.

The more unfortunate individuals attempt to overcome loneliness by resorting to drugs, sexual promiscuity, or delinquency.

Although everyone feels lonely from time to time, young people who suffer from extreme loneliness often feel physically unattractive, are least willing to risk initiating contact with others, and have relatively low self-esteem. Some data also suggest that adolescent boys who have a more feminine sex role orientation are lonelier than boys who have masculine or androgynous orientations. These findings, however, must be viewed tentatively, since boys who score high on the femininity scales may simply be more willing to admit their loneliness than boys with the so-called masculine attitude of not disclosing such feelings (Avery, 1982).

Clearly, not all adolescents who feel lonely are shy. In fact, being outgoing to the point of being obnoxious can be a way to compensate for feeling lonely. On the other hand, a number of lonely adolescents are excessively shy (Peplau &

When in your life have you felt loneliest?

Perlman, 1982; Zimbardo, 1981). Unfortunately, the shy adolescent is usually misperceived by his or her peers as aloof, snobbish, apathetic, or bored. As a result, peers often avoid the shy adolescent for fear of being rejected or disliked, further increasing the shy person's belief that "nobody likes me." Shyness, of course, can range from an occasional timidity to an almost neurotic phobia. Some shy adolescents are usually comfortable with other people but feel timid and withdrawn from time to time or in a particular type of situation. At the other extreme are those who are so terrified of interacting with people that they are unable to develop the social skills necessary for making friends.

Overcoming Shyness

One of the common problems that besets many lonely adolescents is their inability to assert themselves (Peplau & Perlman, 1982). These young people are too timid to express their opinions, their objections, or their desires. The unassertive adolescent is afraid to ask someone for a date, to speak up against aggressors, or to defend a position.

While the term *assertive* is often used synonymously with the term *aggressive,* those who train adolescents to become more assertive distinguish between the two concepts. Being assertive means expressing oneself in an honest, straightforward manner without resorting to angry, obscene, or manipulative methods. In contrast, begin aggressive means disregarding the feelings and opinions of others by dominating through angry, hostile, or coercive measures. For example, an assertive adolescent might calmly but firmly assert, "Yes, I do mind if you smoke because I'm very allergic to it and I'd really have a much better time this evening if you didn't smoke." An aggressive adolescent might say in an angry, sarcastic tone, "If you don't put out that disgusting cigarette, I'm going to leave this damn restaurant right now!"

Several recent studies demonstrate the utility of **assertiveness training** for shy and lonely adolescents. For example, after a month-long assertiveness training program conducted by their school counselor, 13-year-olds earned higher self-concept scores (Waksman, 1984). Their 4-week treatment included role playing, group compliment sessions, modeling of assertive behavior, observation of their assertive peers, and homework assignments on assertive and passive behavior. Activities were designed to teach the difference between assertive, aggressive, and passive behavior and to demonstrate the social and emotional beneifits of behaving assertively. These adolescents learned to use eye contact, body posture, voice, and self-praise in ways that enhanced their assertiveness. Seven weeks after the original post-testing, the students were retested to determine whether the positive effects of the assertiveness training persisted. A third of the students had even higher self-concept scores in the second testing, a finding that suggests that the benefits of assertion training may become most apparent as time passes.

Assertiveness training programs have also helped adolescents become more confident and more willing to speak up in their classes (Wehr & Kaufman, 1987). Even with as little as 12 hours of assertiveness training, high-school girls have improved their self-esteem and their relationships with teachers. Moreover, the girls with the lowest self-esteem scores at the outset made the greatest improvements (Stake, Deville & Pennell, 1983).

As an adolescent, how did you feel about spending time alone? How do you feel about it now?

Another way of helping shy adolescents is through classroom activities specifically designed to build social skills and to encourage friendship (Epstein, 1983a). Group techniques, such as jigsaw teaching, mentioned earlier in this chapter, place shy students in situations where they are forced to assume positions of leadership. Rather than isolating students doing individual assignments at their desks, teachers who incorporate small-group activities and peer tutoring into their curriculum are encouraging shy students to participate in ways that are less threatening than having to speak up in front of a whole group of 30 students.

In order to identify the behavior that promotes or destroys friendship, researchers have observed the ways in which popular and unpopular adolescents interact with their peers (Duck, 1983; LaGaipa, 1981). From these observations, counselors are then able to teach shy youngsters the specific skills that put others at ease and that attract people. For example, whether working or playing with others, popular youngsters generally offer other people several alternatives when a decision has to be made, whereas unpopular youngsters tend to give orders without allowing anyone else's input. People with friends also tend to give lots of reinforcement to others, both verbally and nonverbally. By smiling, maintaining eye contact, and looking interested when others are talking, these youngsters make others feel good about themselves and subsequently are perceived as friendly people. By watching videotapes of people interacting and by then analyzing the videotapes with a counselor, young people can learn to recognize the specific kinds of behavior that attract others. Through rehearsing these skills with a counselor, young people have learned how to interact with their peers in ways that help them make friends.

ADOLESCENT DATING

Although the "right" time to start dating varies somewhat from community to community, most adolescents have had a date by time they are 15. Most have also been involved in at least one serious romantic relationship by the time they reach 19 (Bell, 1988; Dornbusch, et al, 1981). Most adolescents, however, spend less time dating than we might initially expect. For example, national surveys show that half the high-school seniors have only one date a week and that only one third date more than once a week (Bachman, Johnston, & O'Malley, 1980). It also appears that dating has become more informal, somewhat less sex role stereotyped, and less oriented to a competitive form of popularity. Girls and boys are more likely than they used to be to make mutual decisions about what to do on a date and to share the financial burdens of dating (R. Miller & Gordon, 1986).

Perhaps what is most evident, however, about adolescents' social lives is the diversity of opinion regarding "having a good time." For example, one adolescent girl said, "My favorite way to have a good time is going to church or to Bible study and praising the Lord." On the other hand, a 16-year-old boy said, "My favorite way to have a good time is to go out with some friends and get wasted. My parents hate it when I come home stoned or drunk or when I party at my house." Yet another male responded, "One of my favorite ways to have a good time is to go out to eat with my girlfriend, stop at the store to get a couple of beers, and go back to my house and make sweet, beautiful love when nobody is there" (Glenbard East *Echo,* 1984, pp. 90–91).

As the research in Box 9.3 illustrates, our definitions of love and friendship differ pretty dramatically during adolescence (Davis, 1985). We tend to be more critical, have higher expectations, and be more jealous of people we date than of our friends. As we move through adolescence, however, we generally choose our dates less for superficial factors, such as appearance and popularity, and more for attributes, such as honesty, dependability, and reciprocity (Roscoe, Diana, & Brooks, 1987). Although some of us continue to date primarily to meet our sexual needs or for the novelty of sexual experimentation, we generally consider companionship and intimacy of growing importance as we enter late adolescence and early adulthood.

Despite the supposed sophistication of today's adolescents, most young adolescents still feel shy about asking someone for a date (Bell, 1988; Glenbard East *Echo*, 1984). As one young adolescent male explained, "I'm already in the tenth

A CLOSER LOOK 9.3

A Comparison of Friends and Lovers

What distinguishes a friendship from a sexual relationship, other than the sex itself? Psychologists such as Keith Davis and Michael Todd are attempting to find out. In their surveys with college students and young adults, these researchers developed a profile of the characteristics that distinguish friends from lovers. Friends and lovers are very much alike in terms of their mutual respect and trust, confiding in each other, offering mutual assistance, and enjoying one another's company. People also tend to feel as much freedom to be themselves with their lovers as they do with friends. Friends, however, are much less fascinated with one another and view their relationship as more stable than that of lovers. Surprisingly, almost one third of the people in these studies named a person of the opposite sex as their best friend, and nearly 60% of the men and 45% of the women named a person of the opposite sex as one of their close friends. Friends of the same sex, however, were more likely than those of the opposite sex to reveal personal information, offer practical assistance, and perceive their relationship as stable. A third of the people in Todd and Davis's studies said their friends had not lived up to their expectations. For example, some best friends had violated a confidence or tried to seduce a friend's lover. Despite these problems, sexual relationships have the greater potential for conflict, insecurity, and ambivalence. Relationships between lovers demand more problem-solving discussions and include more conflict than friendships. Lovers also seem to be less willing than friends to accept one another as they are and to refrain from criticizing each other. Like Dorothy Tennov, who defined the differences between love and "limerence" in her research, Davis and Todd agreed that people who are "in love" often have an acute longing for reciprocal passion and let their moods depend on their lover's conduct toward them.

Is being in love less likely to enhance a youngster's happiness than "loving" someone? Can friendships with members of the same sex provide benefits that those with the opposite sex cannot? Do adolescents need to learn to have less idealistic expectations of their lovers in order to have more realistic and more satisfactory relationships as adults? Is our society encouraging adolescents to confuse the feelings associated with "falling in love" with the realities of maintaining loving relationships, once the newness wears off?

Sources: K. Davis. (1985). Near and dear: Friendship and love compared. *Psychology Today, 19,* 22–28; D. Tennov, *Love and limerence.* New York: Stein and Day, 1978.

grade and I've never even gone out with a girl and that bugs me. I'm shy to an extent, but I think I could overcome it if I knew there were some girls who liked me. Then I could probably ask them out or something; but I haven't been able to be friends enough with a girl to give her a reason to like me." Yet a young teenage girl lamented, "It always blows me away when I run into a guy who says, 'I can't go out with you because you asked me and I didn't ask you' " (Bell, 1988, p. 67). The problem of who asks whom to what, where, and when is still very much in the minds of young adolescents.

On a more serious note, the incidence of physical violence and rape during a date seems to be on the rise—a phenomenon that has come to be known as **date rape** (Carlson, 1987; Levine & Kanin, 1987; O'Keeffe, Brockopp, & Chew, 1986; Warshaw, 1990). According to these reports, a growing number of young men and teenage boys are forcing their dates to have intercourse or perform other sexual acts against their will, often by using physical force. The accumulating evidence indicates that this increase may be related to our society's overemphasis on alcohol and the ways in which our mass media and popular culture feature sexuality. Indeed, drinking, having "fun," and having sex are often linked in advertising and in television programming. Although the reasons for date rape are still not altogether clear, this research reminds us that teenage girls must be helped to understand that just knowing someone well enough to date him is not a failsafe guarantee against rape or physical assault.

INTERRACIAL DATING

Young people who have grown up in metropolitan areas or in communities where schools have been integrated for many years are more likely to approve of and to engage in interracial dating than those who have grown up in racially segregated areas where minorities seldom achieve equal social or economic status with whites. Moreover, prejudice against a particular race in some areas of the country can be virtually nonexistent in other regions. For example, white and Native American adolescents in the Southwest may have acquired certain prejudices toward one another that would be considered bizarre by adolescents raised in the Southeast, where interracial experiences are primarily limited to African Americans and whites.

Despite such regional differences, however, African American adolescents still experience more discrimination in regard to interracial dating and marriage than Asian, Indian, or Mexican American youths (Bass, 1982). Interracial dating is still an incendiary issue for many of today's adolescents and their parents. Considering that only in 1967 was interracial marriage ruled legal by the Supreme Court and that, as recently as 1976, 30% of the adults in one national survey wanted to outlaw marriage between whites and African Americans, the attitudinal differences between many adolescents and people their parents' age is understandable (McLemore, 1980). Racial barriers seem to be diminishing somewhat in social domains, however. For example, marriages between African Americans and whites doubled during the 1960s, so that by 1977 there were 350,000 such marriages (Glick, 1981). It appears from adolescents' own comments, such as those in Box 9.2, that interracial dating is also becoming more acceptable among the young (Bell, 1988; Glenbard East *Echo,* 1984). Having recently conducted their national study of U.S. high schools, Theodore Sizer (1984) and his colleagues concluded that interracial dating is "an accepted exception" among today's adolescents.

Unfortunately, most studies on interracial dating have been conducted with college students. Since college students are generally more liberal in their social attitudes than their peers who choose other options after high school, the generalizability of the data to adolescents in secondary schools is limited. There appears to be a general tolerance toward interracial dating on predominantly white campuses. African American males tend to be more willing than African American females to date and marry someone of another race. African American females are more apt to express anxiety over peer rejection for interracial dating. There has been little support for the stereotypical asumption that minority males would rather date white females than females from their own race. In fact, in several studies, minorities have expressed biases against dating whites. White females have been described as more materialistic, sneakier, and more masculine than African American females, and white males have been described as more effeminate, self-centered, and complacent than African American males (Clark & Pearson, 1985; Lampe, 1981).

One reason some African American females may oppose interracial dating is demographic: There simply are not enough African American males to go around. Among African Americans, females outnumber males by 11% at age 18 and by 20% at age 30. In contrast, white females do not have to confront the problem of outnumbering white men until after the age of 30. To complicate matters further, African American males are twice as likely as African American females to marry outside their race. Only about 5 percent of African American males and 2.4 percent of African American females have a spouse of a different race—almost always white. In contrast, only 7⁄10 of a percent of whites marry outside their race, with less than half of these interracial marriages involving African Americans. In short, interracial dating and marriage are presently working against the black female by detracting from, more than adding to, her pool of marriageable candidates (Spanier & Glick, 1980).

What ramifications might these demographic facts have on African American adolescent girls? Given the shortage of African American males, do African American girls feel more pressured than whites to form a committed relationship during their adolescence or to marry young? Are they readier than white females to marry males with less education and those who are divorced? Are they more willing than white girls to engage in premarital intercourse, perceiving it as a means to build bonds that will lead to matrimony? Using data from the 1975 Census, researchers have confirmed these hypotheses. African American females marry younger and are more likely to marry a less educated man than are white females. Among whites, the husband is more educated in 31% of the couples and less educated in 24%; but among African Americans, the husband is more educated in only 18% of the couples and is less educated in 36%. In addition, African American women are more than twice as likely as whites to marry a divorced man (Spanier & Glick, 1980).

While the shortage of African American males is one possible factor influencing interracial dating, there are others. Many white adolescents are still being socialized to adopt unfounded sexual stereotypes about members of other races. For example, African Americans are often stereotyped as being more sexual and more desirous of intermarriage or interracial dating than whites. In a similar vein, reactions to a white girl who dates an African American male are often still laced with remnants of the old assumption that minority males are in pursuit of white females. As a consequence, the white girl with an African American boyfriend is still not immune from racist comments and innuendos: "What's wrong with her that she would want to date him? I understand why he wants to be seen with her but why would she want to date him?" (Bass, 1982).

In sum, strong prejudices and stereotypes still come to the fore when adolescents date, have sex with, or plan to marry someone of another race. White and minority parents who endorse school integration and avidly support integrated athletic teams often feel uncomfortable when their adolescent son or daughter dates a member of another race. While many adults may have encouraged children to treat all races equally, the situation often changes once sex or marriage is introduced into the situation. That children of different colors play together in a sandbox or on a basketball court is often cited as evidence that the United States has overcome its racial prejudices, but this is a misrepresentation of the realities confronting many adolescents who choose to interact socially or sexually with young people of other races.

CONCLUSION

Among the services we might render to adolescents' parents is to reassure them that the infamous peer group is not going to steal their children away, destroying all the family's values in the process. Although peers do influence one another's behavior, adolescents generally choose friends who reflect their parents' values about the most important issues in their lives. Moreover, most adolescents continue to seek their parents' counsel and to maintain good rapport with adults during their teenage years. As we will see in the next chapter, sexuality is one of the domains in which adolescents and their parents may most often disagree. Yet, even in matters of sex, most adolescents choose friends with values similar to their own—values instilled by their family and by our culture, not primarily by their peers.

In the age-old struggle to learn how to make friends and how to be popular, adolescents will continue to discover their own frailties, as well as those of their peers. They will experience the agonies of embarrassment, of shyness, of broken hearts, and of rejection—and the pleasures of being loved and of discovering unknown dimensions of themselves through their interactions with their peers.

QUESTIONS FOR DISCUSSION AND REVIEW

Basic Concepts and Terminology

1. How much influence does the peer group exert over adolescents in comparison to the amount of influence exerted by their parents?
2. How does being an athlete affect a male and a female adolescent's popularity?
3. How can teachers and counselors help adolescents overcome shyness and loneliness?
4. How do adolescents choose their friends, and what characteristics are most likely to make an adolescent popular?
5. How do male and female friendships differ, and what might account for these differences?
6. How do nontraditional teaching techniques, such as jigsaw teaching, affect adolescents' friendships? Why do the more traditional teaching methods lack these effects?
7. How do extremely lonely adolescents and those without any friends differ from other adolescents?
8. In what ways does dating seem to be changing,

and in what ways does it seem to have remained unchanged?

9. How and why do our friendships change from childhood through adolescence?
10. What increases and what decreases the chances of adolescents' forming interracial friendships? How does school desegregation sometimes increase racial prejudice?

Questions for Discussion and Debate

1. Given your own experiences with interracial friendships, how do you believe society could encourage more social interaction between adolescents of different races?
2. In what regards are your present friends similar and dissimilar to the friends you had as a young adolescent? How have your own views of friendship changed as you have aged?
3. Considering your own shyness, past or present, how could teachers, counselors, parents, or friends help shy adolescents?
4. When did you feel loneliest during your adolescence and what might have helped alleviate your feelings? How do your present feelings of loneliness differ from the feelings you experienced as an adolescent?
5. How have your own relationships with males and females corroborated or failed to corroborate the researchers' findings?
6. How do your own experiences with peer pressure confirm or refute the data cited in this chapter? What factors influenced your own susceptibility to peer pressure and parental influence as a young adolescent? How do your peers and your parents influence your present behavior?
7. Recalling some of the foolhardy decisions you made as an adolescent in response to peer pressure, how do you believe adolescents could be more liberated from peer pressure?
8. Since your first date, in what ways have your dating experiences changed, and in what ways have they remained the same? How have your criteria for a "good date" and your own behavior and feelings during a date changed as you have matured? What advice would you offer today's young adolescents about dating?
9. How do you feel about interracial dating and interracial marriage? How do your present feelings compare with those you had 10 years ago? Who or what has influenced your attitudes?
10. How could you have made yourself more "popular" during your adolescence? What advantages or disadvantages might have accrued to you if you had been more popular? How do the standards for popularity on this college campus compare with those at your high school?

GLOSSARY

assertiveness training A model based on social learning theory that teaches participants to be more outspoken. Not synonymous with aggressiveness.

date rape Sexual acts that a male forces his date to perform, either by physical force or by verbal threats.

friends People who are more than peers in that they are attached to one another by feelings of affection or personal regard.

jigsaw teaching A method of teaching in which students are assigned to interracial teams for cooperative learning assignments.

peers People who regard one another as equal with respect to some particular skill (for example, athletic teams), a characteristic (for example, income), or a shared situation (for example, all members of the same math class). Sometimes used loosely to refer to people of the same age.

teams achievement divisions *See* Jigsaw teaching.

REFERENCES

Adams, G. (1983). Social competence during adolescence. *Journal of Youth and Adolescence, 12,* 203–211.

Allport, G. (1958). *The nature of prejudice.* Garden City, NY: Doubleday.

Asher, R., & Gottman, J. (Eds.). (1981). *The development of children's friendships.* New York: Cambridge University Press.

Avery, A. (1982). Escaping loneliness in adolescence: The case for androgyny. *Journal of Youth and Adolescence, 11,* 451–459.

Bachman, J., Johnston, L., & O'Malley, P. (1980). *Monitoring the future: Questionnaire responses from the nation's high school seniors, 1981.* Ann Arbor, MI: Institute for Social Research.

Barnett, M. (1987). Adolescents' evaluations of peers' motives for helping. *Journal of Youth & Adolescence, 16,* 579–586.

Bass, B. (1982). Interracial dating and marital relationships. In B. Bass (Ed.), *The Afro-American family* (pp. 347–356). New York: Grune and Stratton.

Bell, R. (1988). *Changing bodies changing lives: A book for teens on sex and relationships.* New York: Random House.

Berndt, T. (1982a). Fairness and friendship. In K. Rubin and H. Ross (Eds.), *Peer relationships and social skills in childhood* (pp. 251–278). New York: Springer Verlag.

Blyth, D., & Clark, F. (1987). Gender differences in perceived intimacy with different members of adolescents' social networks. *Sex Roles, 17,* 689–719.

Blyth, D., Hill, J., & Thiel, K. (1982). Early adolescents' signfiicant others. *Journal of Youth and Adolescence, 11,* 425–450.

Braddock, J., Crain, R., & McPartland, J. (1984, December). A long term view of school desegregation. *Phi Delta Kappan,* pp. 259–265.

Brennan, T. (1982). Loneliness at adolescence. In L. Peplau & D. Perlman (Eds.), *Loneliness: A sourcebook of current theory, research and therapy* (pp. 269–290). New York: Wiley Interscience.

Carlson, B. (1987). Dating violence: A research review. *Social Casework, 68,* 16–23.

Clark, M., & Pearson, W. (1985). Racial stereotypes revisited. *International Journal of Intercultural Relations, 6,* 381–393.

Cohen, J. (1983). The relationship between friendship selection and peer influence. In J. Epstein & N. Karweit (Eds.), *Friends in school* (pp. 163–174). New York: Academic Press.

Coleman, J. (1980). Friendship and the peer group in adolescence. In J. Adelson (Ed.), *Handbook of adolescent psychology* (pp. 408–432). New York: Wiley.

Colley, A., Nash, J., O'Donnell, L., & Restorick, L. (1987). Attitudes to the female sex role and sex typing of physical activities. *International Journal of Sport Psychology, 18,* 19–29.

Crain, R., & Strauss, J. (1984). *School desegregation and black occupational attainments: Results from a long term experiment.* Baltimore: Johns Hopkins University, Center for Social Organization of Schools.

Crockett, L., Losoff, M., & Petersen, A. (1984). Perceptions of the peer groups and friendship in early adolescence. *Journal of Early Adolescence, 4,* 155–181.

Davis, K. (1985). Friendship and love compared. *Psychology Today, 19,* 22–28.

Desertrain, G., & Weiss, M. (1988). Being female and athletic: Cause for conflict. *Sex Roles, 18,* 567–582.

Diaz, R., & Berndt, T. (1982). Children's knowledge of best friends. *Developmental Psychology, 18,* 787–794.

Dornbusch, S., Carlsmith, L., Gross, R., Martin, J., Jenning, D., Rosenberg, R., & Duke, D. (1981). Sexual development, age and dating. *Child Development, 52,* 179–185.

Duck, S. (1983). *Friends for life: The psychology of close relationships.* New York: St. Martin's Press.

Elkind, D. (1980). Strategic interactions in early adolescence. In J. Adelson (Ed.), *Handbook of adolescent psychology* (pp. 341–375). New York: Wiley.

Epstein, J. (1983). *Choice of friends over the life span.* Baltimore: Johns Hopkins University, Center for Social Organization of the Schools.

Erikson, E. (1968). Identity: Youth and crisis. London: Faber.

Galbo, J. (1984). Adolescents' perceptions of significant adults: A review of the literature. *Adolescence, 76,* 951–970.

Glenbard East *Echo* (1984). *Teenagers themselves.* New York: Adama Books.

Glick, P. (1981). Demographic picture of black families. In H. McAdoo (Ed.), *Black families.* (pp. 119–125). Beverly Hills, CA: Sage.

Greenberg, M., Siegel, J., & Leitch, C. (1983). Nature and importance of attachment relationships to parents and peers. *Youth and Adolescence, 12,* 373–386.

Hallinan, M. (1983). New directions for research on peer influence. In J. Epstein & N. Karweit (Eds.), *Friends in school.* (pp. 215–234). New York: Academic Press.

Hartup, W. (1983). Peer relations. In P. Mussen and E. Hetherington (Eds.), *Handbook of child psychology* (pp. 103–196). New York: Wiley.

Herek, G. (1984). Beyond homophobia. *Journal of Homosexuality, 10,* 1–21.

Hill, J., & Lynch, M. (1983). The intensification of gender related role expectations during early adolescence. In J. Gunn & A. Petersen (Eds.), *Girls at puberty.* (pp. 87–120). New York: Plenum Press.

Hinde, R. (1984). Why do the sexes behave differently in close relationships? *Journal of Social and Personal Relationships, 1,* 471–501.

Josselson, R. (1980). Ego development in adolescence. In J. Adelson (Ed.), *Handbook of adolescent psychology.* (pp. 188–210). New York: Wiley Interscience.

Kane, M. (1988). The female athletic role as a status determinant within the social systems of high school adolescents. *Adolescence, 23,* 253–264.

Karweit, N., & Hansell, S. (1983). Sex differences in adolescent relationships: Friendship and status. In J. Epstein & N. Karweit (Eds.), *Friends in school.* (pp. 141–153). New York: Academic Press.

Kite, M. (1984). Sex differences in attitudes towards homosexuals: A meta analytic review. *Journal of Homosexuality, 10,* 69–81.

LaGaipa, J. (1981). Children's friendships. In S. Duck & R. Gilmour (Eds.), *Developing personal relationships.* (pp. 81–95). London: Academic Press.

Lampe, P. (1981). Interethnic dating. *International Journal of Intercultural Relations, 6,* 115–126.

Levine, E., & Kanin, E. (1987). Sexual violence among dates: Trends and implications. *Journal of Family Violence, 2,* 55–65.

Marcia, J. (1980). Identity in adolescence. In J. Adelson (Ed.), *Handbook of adolescent psychology.* (pp. 159–188). New York: Wiley.

Marcoen, A., Goossens, L., & Caes, P. (1987). Loneliness in pre through late adolescence. *Journal of Youth and Adolescence, 6,* 561–577.

McLemore, D. (1980). *Racial and ethnic relations.* Boston: Allyn Bacon.

Merritt, R. (1983). Comparison of tolerance of white graduates of racially integrated and segregated schools. *Adolescence, 69,* 67–70.

Mijuskovic, B. (1986). Loneliness: Counseling adolescents. *Adolescence, 21,* 941–950.

Miller, R., & Gordon, M. (1986). The decline in formal dating: A study in six Connecticut high schools. *Marriage and Family Review, 10,* 139–156.

Montemayor, R. (1983). Parents and adolescents in conflict: All families some of the time and some families most of the time. *Journal of Early Adolescence, 3,* 83–103.

Moore, D., & Schultz, N. (1983). Loneliness at adolescence: Correlates, attributions and coping. *Journal of Youth and Adolescence, 12,* 95–100.

O'Keefe, N., Brockopp, K., & Chew, E. (1986). Teen dating violence. *Social Work, 31,* 465–468.

Peplau, L., & Perlman, D. (Eds.). (1982). *Loneliness: A sourcebook of current theory, research and therapy.* New York: Wiley Interscience.

Piaget, J., & Inhelder, B. (1969). *The psychology of the child.* New York: Basic Books.

Reis, H., Senchak, M., & Solomon, B. (1985). Sex differences in intimacy of social interaction. *Journal of Personality and Social Psychology, 48,* 1204–1217.

Roscoe, B., Diana, M. & Brooks, R. (1987). Early, middle and late adolescents' views on dating. *Adolescence, 22,* 59–68.

Rubin, Z., & Sloman, J. (1984). How parents influence their children's friendships. In M. Lewis (Ed.), *Beyond the dyad.* (pp. 85–115). New York: Plenum Press.

Savin-Williams, R. (1980). Dominance hierarchies in groups of middle to late adolescent males. *Journal of Youth and Adolescence, 9,* 75–85.

Savin-Williams, R. (1986). *Adolescence: An ethological perspective.* New York: Springer Verlag.

Schofield, J. (1981). Complementary and conflicting identities: Images and interaction in an interracial school. In S. Asher & J. Gottman (Eds.), *The development of children's friendships.* New York: Cambridge University Press.

Sebald, H. (1986). Adolescents' shifting orientation towards parents and peers. *Journal of Marriage and the Family, 48,* 5–13.

Seltzer, V. (1982). *Adolescent social development: Dynamic functional interaction.* Lexington, MA: Lexington Books.

Sizer, T. (1984). *Horace's compromise: The dilemma of the American high school.* Boston: Houghton Mifflin.

Slavin, R., & Hansell, S. (1983). Cooperative learning and intergroup relations: Contact theory in the classroom. In J. Epstein & N. Karweit (Eds.), *Friends in school.* (pp. 93–114). New York: Academic Press.

Smollar, J., & Youniss, J. (1982). Social development through friendship. In K. Ruin & H. Ross (Eds), *Peer relationships and social skills in childhood* (pp. 279–298). New York: Springer Verlag.

Spanier, G., & Glick, P. (1980). Mate selection differentials between whites and blacks in the United States. *Social Forces, 58,* 707–725.

Stake, J., Deville, C., & Pennell, C. (1983). The effects of assertive training on the performance and self-esteem of adolescent girls. *Journal of Youth and Adolescence, 12,* 435–443.

Tennov, D. (1978). *Love and limerance.* New York: Stein & Day.

Waksman, S. (1984). Assertion training with adolescents. *Adolescence, 73,* 123–130.

Warshaw, R. (1990) *I Never Called it Rape.* New York: Basic Books.

Wehr, S., & Kaufman, M. (1987). The effects of assertive training on performance in highly anxious adolescents. *Adolescence, 22,* 195–205.

Weisfeld, G., Block, S., & Ivers, J. (1983). A factor analytic study of peer perceived dominance in adolescent boys. *Adolescence, 18,* 229–243.

Whalen, C., Henker, B., Dotemoto, S., & Hinshaw, S. (1983). Child and adolescent perceptions of normal and atypical peers. *Child Development, 54,* 1588–1598.

Williams, J., & White, K. (1983). Adolescent status systems for males and females at three age levels. *Adolescence, 70,* 381–389.

Williamson, J., & Campbell, L. (1985). Parents and their children comment on adolescence. *Adolescence, 20,* 745–748.

Woodward, J., & Frank, B. (1988). Rural adolescent loneliness and coping strategies. *Adolescence, 23,* 559–565.

Wright, P. (1982). Men's friendships, women's friendships and the alleged inferiority of the latter. *Sex Roles, 8,* 1–20.

Youniss, J., & Smollar, J. (1985). *Adolescent relations with mothers, fathers and friends.* Chicago: University of Chicago Press.

Zakin, D. (1983). Physical attractiveness, sociability, athletic ability and children's preferences for their peers. *Journal of Psychology, 115,* 117–122.

Zimbardo, P. (1981). *The shy child.* New York: McGraw-Hill.

10 Adolescent Sexuality

CHAPTER OUTLINE

MALE AND FEMALE ATTITUDES

ADOLESCENT SEXUAL BEHAVIOR

Age and Frequency
Racial Differences
Socioeconomic Status
Religiosity
Family Characteristics
Peer Influence

TEENAGE CONTRACEPTION

Habits and Trends
Influential factors
Males' Attitudes
New Contraceptives

TEENAGE PREGNANCY

Rates and Trends
Racial Differences
Birthrates
Abortion

TEENAGE PARENTS

SEXUALLY TRANSMITTED DISEASES

AIDS

Herpes
Gonorrhea
Syphilis
Yeast Infections

SEX EDUCATION

In the Schools
Beyond the Schools
Reaching Adolescent Males

HOMOSEXUALITY

Prevalence
The Determinants of Sexual Orientation

Problems Confronting Homosexual Adolescents

CONCLUSION

GOALS AND OBJECTIVES

This chapter is designed to enable you to:

- Describe the sexual attitudes and behavior of today's adolescents
- Explore the issues related to abortion, homosexuality, teenage pregnancy, and sex education
- Describe the symptoms, treatments, and consequences of adolescents' sexually transmitted diseases
- Consider the pros and cons of the various methods of contraception available to adolescents
- Debunk some of the popular misconceptions about teenagers' sexual behavior, contraceptive habits, and sexual attitudes
- Consider the issues confronting heterosexual and homosexual adolescents

CONCEPTS AND TERMINOLOGY

acquired immune deficiency syndome (AIDS)
asymptomatic carriers
bisexual
cervical sponge
chancres
gonorrhea
herpes
homophobia
homosexual
human immuno-deficiency virus (HIV)
intrauterine device (IUD)
"morning after" pill
rhythm method
sexually transmitted disease (STD)
syphilis

Are today's adolescents part of a sexual revolution? How is the threat of AIDS affecting young people's sexual behavior? How have legalized abortions and easier access to contraceptives changed young people's sexual lives? Have adolescents become too sexually promiscuous, and if so, why?

Researchers are trying to unravel the answers to these and many other questions to give us a clearer understanding of adolescent sexuality. Unfortunately, most of our data regarding sexual behavior and attitudes have been gathered from college students—a population that is not representative of younger adolescents, minorities, or high-school dropouts. This chapter, however, will focus on the information about young people between the ages of 11 and 20, rather than on college students.

MALE AND FEMALE ATTITUDES

As happened with couples in their parents' generation, most of today's teenage boys see sex differently from the ways girls do (Bell, 1988; Juhasz & Schneider, 1987; P. Miller & Simon, 1980). Boys are more likely to see intercourse as a way of establishing their maturity and of achieving social status, whereas most girls see intercourse as a way of expressing their love and of achieving greater intimacy. As a consequence, boys are more apt to have sex with someone who is a relative stranger, to have more sexual partners, and to disassociate sex from love. Even in their sexual fantasies, boys are more likely to imagine sexual adventures detached from love and emotional intimacy.

Given their different sexual motives, boys generally expect sex sooner in a relationship than girls. Many teenagers, for example, still believe that males have a greater "innate need" for sex than females and that it is physically or psychologically dangerous not to satisfy a male's sexual needs (Allgeier & McCormick, 1983; Lewin, 1985). Since girls usually want to wait until an emotional commitment and intimacy have developed, many say they feel pressured into having sex before they are ready. Although more girls are now having intercourse and at a much earlier age than did girls in their mothers' generation, they are apparently not as comfortable with their decision as we might initially presume.

Why, given society's more relaxed sexual standards, are girls still more reluctant to express their sexuality than boys? Why do most males and females still attach a different meaning to sex? One hypothesis is that, as a consequence of their hormonal or genetic differences, boys are more easily aroused or have greater sexual needs than girls. This position, however, fails to explain why girls have become so much more sexually active in recent decades. Moreover, females do become as sexually aroused as males when erotic material is designed to meet female, not male, standards of erotica. For example, when erotica includes romance and emotional involvement, girls become more sexually aroused than when the erotica involves sex between strangers, forcible sex, or explicit sexual scenes (P. Miller & Simon, 1980).

It appears, then, that males and females generally feel differently about sex because of the different ways in which they are socialized—specifically, our society's sexual double standard. Historically, our society has expected a teenage boy to have sexual experiences as part of "becoming a man" and "sowing his wild oats." In contrast, "good girls" were to remain virgins until marriage since no husband wants "spoiled goods." Although this standard has changed somewhat in that most males no longer expect a woman to remain a virgin until marriage, other aspects of the double standard remain well entrenched. For example, although a young woman no longer needs to be a virgin, she is usually still expected to be less sexually experienced than her partner and to engage in sex only with boys she loves. If she is "too" sexually active or engages in casual sex, she is still likely to be marked as a "slut," an "easy lay," or "promiscuous." In contrast, a male with similar tastes and habits is usually looked up to and

10.1

ADOLESCENT VOICES

Adolescents' Sexual Experiences

"When I was in junior high school I found that my fantasies were a lot more pleasurable than the reality. In my imagination I could make things work perfectly and be with just who I wanted to be with but the reality of it at the time wasn't anywhere near as great. In fact I was really awkward with girls and had trouble getting it on with them—but in my fantasy world it was really smooth."

"I've never been in an experience where I might have to compromise my morals, because most of the people I hang out with feel the same way I do. I know I want to be a virgin when I get married, and that's all there is to it."

"In sixth grade my friends and I made a pact that we would never ever French-kiss anyone because it was such a gross thing to do. Needless to say, we all broke the pact sooner or later."

"When I was 16 I learned about sex all the wrong ways. I never knew what I was doing and I never got any pleasure out of it. And I was always so afraid everyone would see I didn't know what I was doing, so I had to get drunk and stoned to get me through."

"It's like a game. My friends told me that when a girl says no she doesn't really mean it. So if a girl tells me quietly to stop, and doesn't yell out loud about it and hit me over the head with it, I'm not supposed to listen. It's a game to find out if she really means it."

"Can you imagine making out with a guy and being able to say, 'Oh, I don't like that. Oh, I wish you would do this.' I think that's ridiculous. I'm not comfortable enough with my own body to be able to tell some other person about it."

"The first time I had intercourse I was lying there thinking, You mean this is IT? Am I supposed to be thrilled by this? It wasn't that it hurt me or anything because it didn't. It just didn't feel like anything to me. I figured there must be something wrong with me so I didn't say a word to him."

"Everyone's going around wondering why they aren't having the greatest sexual experiences in the world and nobody's saying anything about it."

Source: R. Bell. (1988). *Changing bodies, changing lives: A book for teens on sex and relationships.* New York: Random House.

appreciated for being a "stud" and an "experienced lover." Indeed, girls who seem to enjoy sex "too much" or who have "too many" partners are sometimes accused of being nymphomaniacs, meaning that they have abnormal and uncontrollable sexual desire. Interestingly, there is no equivalent word of insult leveled against boys with similar sexual habits. In short, most girls are still discouraged from being as sexually active as boys, which understandably accounts for girls' having different sexual attitudes.

Whom did you first fall in love with? And when?

ADOLESCENT SEXUAL BEHAVIOR

Age and Frequency

Given our society's double standard of sexuality, it is not surprising that boys engage in more sexual intercourse and masturbation than girls (P. Miller & Simon, 1980). Before the age of 20, nearly 90% of all boys and 60% of all girls have masturbated. Although our sexual attitudes have grown more lenient, most adolescents still feel embarrassed or guilty admitting that they engage in this form of sexual pleasure.

Contrary to popular belief, it appears that teenage boys' sexual activity may actually have declined somewhat in the early 1980s (all statistics are from Hayes, 1987, and Hofferth & Hayes, 1987, unless otherwise cited). Nevertheless, nearly 80% of all males and 70% of all females have had intercourse by the time they are 20. In other words, 22 million teenagers are sexually active by their 19th birthday. In contrast, in the 1940s, 25% of the male and 80% of the female 19-year-olds were still virgins (Kinsey, Pomeroy, & Martin, 1948). Clearly, then, a sexual revolution has occurred—but only among teenage girls! Indeed, somewhat fewer teenage boys are having intercourse today than in the 1940s and 1950s, whereas the percentage of sexually active teenage girls has doubled.

During the 1970s and 1980s, when adolescents were becoming more sexually active, the sexual attitudes of their elders were also undergoing dramatic change. For example, 60% of the adults in our society approved of premarital sex in 1985, compared with only 24% in 1969. Notably, Catholics were more approving of premarital sex than Protestants, probably because of the growing influence of the fundamentalists among Protestants (Gallup, 1985). Similarly, television programs became increasingly sexual during the 1970s and 1980s, reflecting our society's growing tolerance for premarital and extramarital sex. Given the more liberal sexual attitudes of their elders, the introduction of the birth control pill, and easier access to contraceptives, it is hardly surprising that young people have become more sexually active (see Figure 10.1).

As you would expect, most young people first have sex in the later, not the earlier, years of adolescence. Only 5% of teenage girls and 17% of teenage boys report having had intercourse by their 15th birthday, whereas more than 80% of the 19-year-old boys and 70% of the girls are no longer virgins. Most adolescents have intercourse infrequently. For example, a 1982 national survey showed that nearly one fifth of the sexually active girls had not had intercourse during the past three months (Zelnik & Shaw, 1983).

Racial differences

African American adolescents have been more sexually active than other racial groups. For example, by age 16, African Americans are about four times more likely than whites to have had intercourse (Furstenberg et al., 1987). One noticeable trend since the 1980s, however, is that sexual activity among African Americans is declining faster than among whites. For instance, in 1976 there were 30% more sexually active African American than white teenagers, compared with only 10% more in the late 1980s. At every age, however, African Americans are still more likely than whites or Hispanics to be sexually active. Also, African American children

FIGURE 10.1
Teenage sexual behavior, contraception, and births

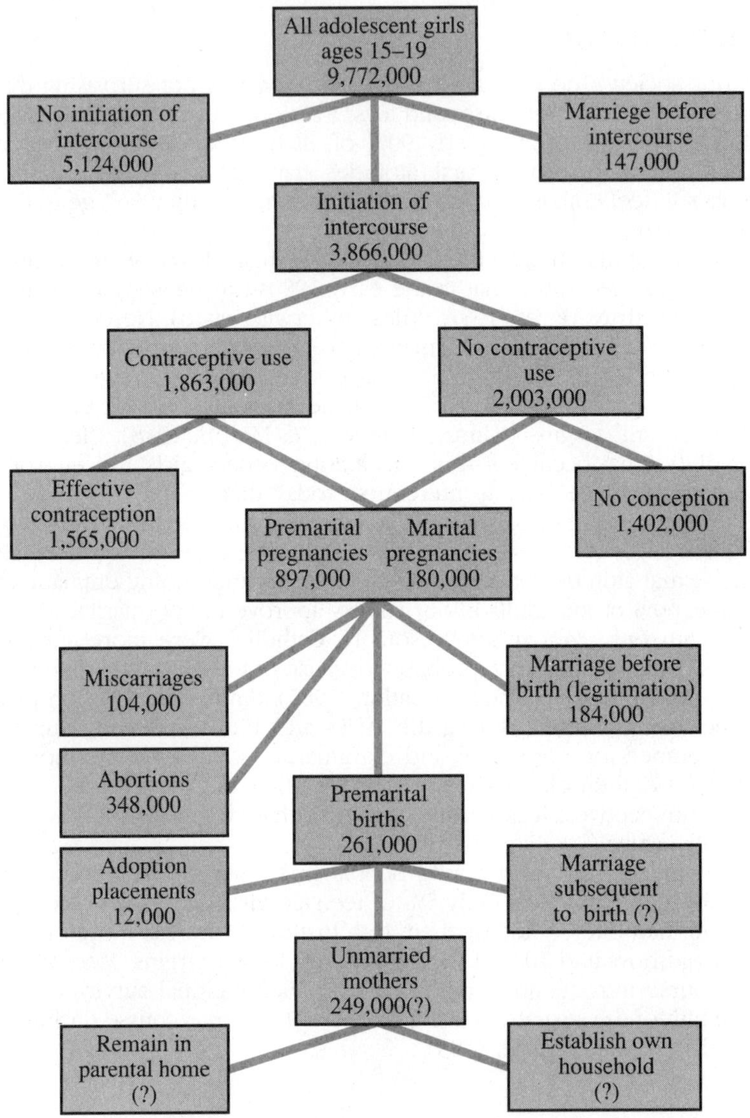

Source: S. Henshaw. (1989). *Teenage pregnancy in the U.S.* New York: Alan Guttmacher Institute.

become sexually active sooner than other racial groups as Table 10-1 shows. In this respect, however, it is worth noting that adolescents who mature physically at an early age tend to have sexual intercourse before their later maturing peers (Zelnick, Kantner, & Ford, 1981). The fact that African American adolescents mature somewhat earlier than children of other races may contribute to their becoming sexually active at a younger age.

Table 10.1

Percentages of Never-Married Males Aged 15–19 Who Have Had Sexual Intercourse, by Age, According to Race/Ethnicity, United States, 1988

AGE	ALL RACES *(N = 1,880)*	AFRICAN AMERICAN *(N = 676)*	WHITE *(N = 752)*	HISPANIC *(N = 385)*
15–19	60.4	80.6	56.8	59.7
15	32.6	68.6	25.6	32.8
16	49.9	70.1	46.7	47.2
17	65.6	89.6	59.1	87.6
18	71.6	82.5	71.4	52.8
19	85.7	95.9	84.5	82.2

Source: F. Sonenstein, J. Pleck, & L. Ku. (1989). Sexual activity, condom use and AIDS awareness among adolescent males. *Family Planning Perspectives, 21,* 152–158.

In addition African Americans report a greater acceptance of sexual activity and teenage childbearing than do other minorities and whites. These attitudes, however, may not indicate that African American parents are any happier than other parents when their teenage children become pregnant. Rather, African Americans may have adapted to the high teenage birthrates by offering a supportive community when adolescents do become pregnant (Moore, 1986). In this regard it is interesting that several studies have found African American students from poor families who attend primarily white schools to be less sexually active and to have lower pregnancy rates than African Americans with similar economic backgrounds who attend primarily African American schools. These findings suggest that the peer group at school can exert some influence over the sexual attitudes and behavior of impoverished African American teenagers (Braddock, Crain & McPartland, 1984; Furstenberg et al., 1987).

Socioeconomic status

The fact that so many more African American than white adolescents live in poverty has also been offered as a partial reason for their earlier initiation of sex. Regardless of race, children from poor families generally become sexually active at earlier ages than children from more affluent environments. Since impoverished children are usually less successful in school, they may understandably be less motivated to postpone sex and pregnancy than their more successful classmates whose educational and financial goals serve as incentives to postpone parenthood. Poor children's parents are also likely themselves to have been sexually active and become pregnant at an early age. In contrast, children with well-educated, wealthier parents tend to be more future oriented, to place a higher value on their educational and vocational achievement, and to be better prepared to delay gratification—all of which serve as incentives to postpone sex or to protect themselves against pregnancy if they choose to be sexually active.

Religiosity

Youngsters who become sexually active at an early age also tend to be less involved in organized religion than those who wait until later in adolescence. It is not, however, a question of what particular religion an adolescent is affiliated with as much as how traditional, devout, and fundamentalist his or her involvement is. In other words, you cannot predict which adolescents will be least or most sexually active on the basis of whether they are Catholic, Jewish, or Protestant. Instead, you should look at how fundamentalist or how liberal they are in the practice of their particular religion.

Family characteristics

The relationship between teenage sex, how well adolescents and their parents communicate, and the parents' own attitudes about premarital sex are not, as many of us might assume, clearcut. Although some studies show that adolescents who are close to their parents remain virgins longer, other research shows that children who communicate best with their parents feel more comfortable expressing their sexuality. Neither is it clear whether a close relationship and good communication with the father is any more or less influential than with the mother in determining adolescents' sexual decisions. Similarly, we do not know whether parents who supervise their children's behavior closely are any more successful in postponing their children's sexual activities than those who leave their teenage children relatively unsupervised. In other words, as a parent you would not be justified in assuming that establishing good communication, keeping a careful eye on your children's social activities, or explaining how much you personally disapprove of teenage sex will necessarily prevent your children from becoming sexually active teenagers.

There is, however, a high correlation between a mother's own sexual experiences and her daughter's. The earlier the mother's first sexual experience and the birth of her first child, the earlier the daughter's will be. On the other hand, having parents who are divorced does not seem to affect adolescent's sexual decisions. Some evidence does suggest, however, that having sexually active older siblings encourages younger adolescents to follow suit (Hofferth & Hayes, 1987).

Peer influence

Surprisingly, research on peer influences on teenage sexual decisions is relatively rare. Despite this lack of data, we frequently cite peer pressure as one of the most influential factors affecting teenagers' sexual decisions. The research that does exist, however, shows that the peer group's power has probably been overrated, particularly among African Americans and white males. In short, adolescents vary considerably in their susceptibility to peer pressure on sexual matters. Irrespective of race, girls tend to be more swayed by the opinions of their male friends or boyfriends than by those of their girlfriends. White girls, however, seem to be more susceptible to their peers' opinions in making their sexual decisions than African American males and females or than white males (Bill & Udry, 1985). Even so, a teenager's sexual behavior is not primarily determined by pressure from his or her friends (Hofferth & Hayes, 1987).

This is not to say that peer pressure can never influence an adolescent's sexual behavior. As the horrifying story in Box 10.2 illustrates, a group can generate an environment that encourages reprehensible acts of sex and aggression. Nevertheless, for the vast majority of adolescents it is not peer pressure that determines

A CLOSER LOOK 10.2

Gang Rape in the Suburbs

Not many months after a group of black teenage boys from Harlem were arrested for assaulting and raping a white female jogger in Central Park, another group of high-school boys were charged with raping and sodomizing a mildly retarded 17-year-old girl. This time, however, the boys were all white, were star athletes in their school, and were from an affluent New Jersey suburb. The students, including twin brothers who co-captained the football team, lured the girl from a city park to one of their wealthy homes. Then, while eight of the boys watched, they forced the girl to perform sexual acts and raped her with several objects. County authorities took over the case after it was discovered that the 18-year-old son of the police lieutenant assigned to the case was one of the boys who participated by witnessing the assault. When a television news producer tried to ask the policeman's son about the case, the boy responded, "She wanted it."

In the New Jersey incident, the two 17-year-olds were charged as juveniles rather than as adults, meaning that their names were not released to the press. In the Central Park incident, however, all the African American males' names were released to the press because they were charged as adults. In the midst of the concern over teenage violence and rape, these two incidents also focus attention on racial issues: Is the media as willing to cover a story about the brutality of white, affluent high-school athletes as it is about African American males from the ghetto? Are we less willing to prosecute white 17-year-olds as adults than we are African American males?

Source: B. Turque & S. Hutchison. (1989, June 5). Gang rape in the suburbs. *Newsweek,* p. 26.

their sexual decisions but a combination of factors: the family's socioeconomic status, the age at which the mother became sexually active and gave birth to her first child, religiosity, educational and vocational goals, and, perhaps, the age at which sexual maturation began.

TEENAGE CONTRACEPTION

Habits and trends

Unfortunately most adolescents who have chosen to become sexually active have also chosen not to use contraceptives on a regular basis (Hayes, 1987; Hofferth & Hayes, 1987). The good news is that during the 1980s nearly 85% of sexually active teenagers said they had used a contraceptive at some time, compared with only 65% in the 1970s. The bad news is that 40% only use a contraceptive "sometimes" and 20% "never." Moreover, the least effective methods—withdrawal, the diaphragm and spermicidal foam—are on the increase, while the most effective methods—the IUD and the pill—are on the decline. Approximately 60% of the girls who do use a contraceptive are on the birth control pill, 20% have boyfriends who wear condoms and 6% use a diaphragm. Not surprisingly, the youngest adolescents are the worst at assuming any responsibility for using contraceptives.

When they do, they are the most likely to use unreliable methods like douching or the "rhythm method." It is little wonder then why more than half of all teenage pregnancies occur with the first six months of first having sex (Morrison, 1985).

Before we assume, however, that adolescents are the only ones who are irresponsible when it comes to contraception, note that 40% of married adult women say their pregnancies were accidental (Thornburg, 1981). Similarly, on the campus where the famous Kinsey Institute for Sex Research is housed, only one-third of the sexually active college students said they used contraceptives regularly (Byrne & Fisher, 1983).

Sadly, a 37-country study shows that our adolescents do not use contraceptives as effectively as teenagers in other industrialized nations (Jones, et al., 1986). Although we might think that this is because our young people are more sexually active or become sexually active at an earlier age, neither is the case. In fact, Swedish teenagers have the lowest pregnancy rates even though they have intercourse at the earliest age. Moreover, birthrates among adolescents are not lower in other countries because of more frequent use of abortion. On the contrary, where the pregnancy rate is low, the abortion rate is also low. In other words, teenagers in other countries are not relying on abortion as their main contraceptive even though their abortion policies are generally more lenient than our own. Neither can our high teenage pregnancy be attributed mainly to the high birthrate among our African American teenagers. In fact, the pregnancy rate and the birthrate of our white teenagers are higher than those of teenagers in any western European country. Simply put, our young people are not using contraceptives as responsibly as those in other industrialized nations where teenage sex is as popular as it is in the United States.

This embarrassing and distressing situation has been accounted for by the fact that we provide less thorough sex education, make contraceptives less accessible and more expensive, and sensationalize sex while maintaining a puritanical attitude about contraception. Other countries also offer adolescents more confidentiality in regard to their sexual lives. For example, Swedish doctors are specifically forbidden to inform parents about an adolescent's request for contraceptives, and Dutch physicians are required to keep visits confidential if the teenager requests it. Several countries have also waged more active campaigns aimed at encouraging young men to use condoms. Then, too, other nations are less reluctant to prescribe birth control pills for adolescents. In contrast, teenagers' use of the pill dropped during the 1980s in the United States as a consequence of the negative publicity regarding its potential side effects—effects that many experts believe have been exaggerated, especially in comparison to the risks involved in adolescent pregnancy (Ory, Forrest, & Lincoln, 1983). In short, the 37-country study provides convincing evidence that many of our widely held beliefs about teenage pregnancy cannot explain the high rate of teenage pregnancy in our society.

Influential Factors

Why do adolescents in the United States not use contraceptives more regularly? Among their reasons are: "We thought it was the safe time of the month so we didn't need birth control." "We didn't plan to have sex so we didn't have anything with us." "We don't have sex very often so we didn't think there was much chance of getting pregnant." "We were too embarrassed to go to the drugstore or to a doctor to get stuff." "My friends told me you couldn't get pregnant the first time you did it." "It's unromantic to use contraceptives." "If a boy wears a rubber, he can't enjoy sex." "It's the girl's responsibility to do the birth control, so I just figured she was using something." "I just didn't think pregnancy could happen to people like us" (Alan Guttmacher Institute, 1989; Bell, 1988).

As these statements clearly demonstrate, many adolescents are still misinformed regarding conception and contraception. Even more distressing, most sexually active youngsters who are not using birth control have completed so-called sex education courses in their schools (Hayes, 1987; Moore, Simms, & Betsey, 1986; Vinovskis, 1988). As we will see later in this chapter, however, what passes for sex education in our schools is usually too little and too late. Indeed, sex education classes, when poorly done, often leave students dangerously misinformed.

Moreover, we have not made it particularly easy for our young people to obtain contraceptives, as have other industrialized countries (Jones et al., 1986). The most reliable contraceptives, the IUD and the pill, require a visit to the doctor, which puts the youngster at risk of having her parents discover that she is sexually active. The other alternative is hardly preferable: going into a drugstore, often having to ask an adult to hand you the package from behind the counter, then making your purchase with a dozen other customers looking on. This ordeal is embarrassing enough to many adults, let alone to a 16-year-old whose date is waiting outside and who is hoping not to run into anyone who knows his or her parents.

Other factors influencing teenagers' decisions to use contraceptives include the age at which they lost their virginity, their academic success, their self-esteem, and their parents' attitudes about contraception (Hayes, 1987). The longer an individual waits to become sexually active, the more likely he or she is to use contraceptives and to use them regularly. Young adolescents are the most likely to be sporadic and to rely on condoms, if using any birth control at all. Since a higher proportion of African Americans are very young when they become sexually active, they are most at risk of becoming pregnant or causing pregnancy. As you might expect, adolescents who have sex sporadically with a number of partners are less likely to use contraceptives than those who are involved in a committed relationship with one partner.

Among both African Americans and whites, girls who have clear educational goals and expectations and who are performing well in school are the most likely to use contraceptives. In the same vein, girls with high self-esteem who feel they have a large measure of control over their lives are more likely to use birth control than girls who feel inferior or who believe that what happens to them is essentially beyond their control. Similarly, the better educated her parents and the more her mother encourages her to use birth control, the more likely a girl is to use contraceptives reliably. Understandably, those girls who admit to themselves and to their friends that they are sexually active are better contraceptors than those who are still denying the reality by pretending "this won't happen again because I'm not 'that kind of girl.' "

Male Attitudes

Unfortunately, one of the major stumbling blocks to effective contraception is that most males abdicate their responsibility, leaving adolescent girls to shoulder this burden alone. Quite simply, most teenage boys do not or will not see birth

control as their "problem" (Hofferth & Hayes, 1987; Pleck, 1989). In contrast to teenage males in western European countries, most American males have a prejudice against using condoms, a particularly distressing attitude since a condom provides protection not only against pregnancy but against disease (Jones et al., 1986).

Although more males are now using condoms as a consequence of their fear of acquired immune deficiency syndrome (AIDS), they still use them infrequently and inconsistently. For example, in a 1988 national survey of adolescent males, only slightly more than half reported that they had used a condom the last time they had had intercourse. On the other hand, among youths aged 17 to 19, their rates of reported condom use more than doubled between 1979 and 1988. Even more optimistically, the odds of using a condom increased 110% among males who first had intercourse during 1987 and 1988 in comparison to males who first had intercourse between 1975 and 1982. Interestingly, African American males had higher rates of condom use when they last had sex (66%) than white (54%) or Hispanic (53%) respondents. Unfortunately, however, African American males were the least likely to have used a condom the first time they had sex, a finding that reflects the fact that they become sexually active at an earlier age than whites or Hispanics and that young adolescents are the least likely to use contraceptives (Sonenstein, Pleck, & Ku, 1989). Among older adolescents, however, African American, Hispanic, and white males seem about equally likely to use condoms (Moore, Simms & Betsey, 1986; Morrison, 1985; Pleck, Sonenstein, & Swain, 1988).

In this vein, a number of critics have pointed out that the media should take an active role in encouraging boys and men in our society to use condoms (Margulies, 1987). For example, while advertisements for beer, feminine hygiene products, and hemorrhoid medications are acceptable, TV advertisements for prophylactics or any other type of birth control are forbidden. In fact, not until 1987 was the word *condom* used in any prime-time television drama. Although television offers a vast array of premarital and extramarital sexual experiences, the topic of contraception is still downplayed or totally ignored.

New Contraceptives

As Box 10.3 illustrates, a number of contraceptives are already available for adolescents, if they can be motivated to use them and to use them consistently. New birth control devices are also coming onto the market with special features that might make them particularly appealing to adolescents (Adler, 1989). For example, Norplant uses six capsules implanted under the skin of the woman's upper arm and slowly releases a long-acting progesterone, preventing pregnancy for up to 5 years. Already approved by the Food and Drug Administration (FDA), these capsules are now in use in other countries. Another new device, the vaginal ring, introduces steroids into the woman's body in order to prevent pregnancy. Different versions of the ring are now being tested, including one that uses a natural steroid produced by the woman's own body. A female condom is also under FDA review. It is a combination of the diaphragm and male condom with a loose-fitting polyurethrane sheath held in place by two flexible plastic rings attached to the ends. The woman would insert the sheath like a diaphragm.

And for males? Research is being conducted on the hormone LHRH, which releases gonadotropin, the hormone that stimulates the testes. LHRH blocks the production of sperm. Since it stops testosterone production, however, its users will have to take testosterone supplements. At present LHRH has been successfully tested as a nasal spray, although its producers are working on other ways of introducing this drug into the body. Also promising is an injection that replaces the operation required to have a vasectomy (Adler, 1989).

A CLOSER LOOK 10.3

Contraceptives for Adolescents

DIAPHRAGM OR CERVICAL CAP

A diaphragm is made of soft rubber in the shape of a shallow cup and is inserted into the vagina so that it covers the cervix. The cervical cap is a smaller covering that fits snugly over the cervix. A spermicide must be applied to the inside of the diaphragm or cap.

Advantages: No side effects other than that a particular brand of spermicide may irritate the vagina or the penis; offers protection against certain sexually transmitted diseases.

Disadvantages: Requires a visit to a physician so that the correct size diaphragm can be prescribed; requires that girls feel comfortable touching their genitals.

Effectiveness: 98% effective when properly fitted, when used with a proper amount of spermicide, and when used during every incidence of intercourse.

CONDOMS (RUBBERS, PROPHYLACTICS, "SAFES")

Worn as long ago as 1350 B.C. by Egyptian men as decorative covers for their penises, the condom is a sheath made of thin, strong rubber or of lamb membrane, which fits over the penis to keep semen from entering the vagina.

Advantages: Offers protection against certain sexually transmitted diseases; requires no visit to a physician; is readily available at drug stores; is inexpensive.

Disadvantages: Limits the spontaneity of intercourse; is perceived as old-fashioned by many males.

Effectiveness: 98% effective when used as directed.

SPERMICIDES

Spermicidal jelly, cream, or aerosol foams that are inserted into the vagina act as contraceptives by killing sperm.

Advantages: Require no prescription; are easily available in drugstores; offer some protection against certain sexually transmitted diseases.

Disadvantages: High rate of pregnancy when used without a diaphragm or a condom; allergic reactions to a particular brand of spermicide; must be inserted immediately before intercourse for maximum effectiveness.

Effectiveness: Limited effectiveness unless used in conjunction with a diaphragm or condom.

CERVICAL SPONGE

Functioning on the same principle as the diaphragm and the cervical cap, the recently developed contraceptive sponge is presaturated with spermicide, which is activated by dampening the sponge with water before inserting it into the vagina. While covering the cervix, the sponge releases spermicide into the vagina. Several hours after intercourse, the sponge is removed and thrown away.

Advantages: Requires no prescription; is available at drugstores; offers some protection against sexually transmitted diseases; can be disposed of in privacy several hours after intercourse.

Disadvantages: Spermicide may irritate vagina or penis; no data available on possible long-term side effects; relatively high failure rate in comparison to other methods.

Effectiveness: Failure rate of nearly 17%.

BIRTH CONTROL PILLS

By releasing synthetic estrogen or progesterone into the female's body, birth control pills inhibit the development of the egg so that fertilization cannot occur.

Advantages: Provide continual protection without the necessity of preplanning immediately before intercourse; lessen menstrual bleeding, cramping, and acne; regulate irregular periods; offer the most protection against pregnancy of all contraceptives.

continued

Box 10.3 continued

Disadvantages: Require a doctor's prescription; side effects include heart attack, strokes, nausea, swelling and weight gain, high blood pressure, cervical cancer, headaches, depression, fatigue vaginitis, urinary tract infection, and aggravation of diseases such as epilepsy.

Effectiveness: Almost 100% effective for women who remember to use the pill daily.

INTRAUTERINE DEVICE

A small device made of plastic or copper, the **IUD** is inserted into the uterus by a doctor, where its presence prevents pregnancy. Although it is not yet clearly understood how the IUD works, the most widely accepted theory is that the IUD causes an inflammation or chronic low-grade infection in the uterus, thereby causing an elevated number of white cells that destroy sperm or fertilized egg.

Advantages: Offers continual protection without preplanning immediately before intercourse; alleviates worry about forgetting to take a pill.

Disadvantages: Spontaneous expulsion of the IUD; perforation of the uterus; increased incidence of ectopic pregnancies; vaginal and uterine infections; heavier menstrual bleeding and cramping; high miscarriage rate if pregnancy occurs while IUD is present; irritation to the penis from the plastic string that extends into the vagina; less effective with women who have not yet borne a child.

Effectiveness: 97% effective.

THE "MORNING AFTER" PILL

Within 3 days of unprotected intercourse, a series of very high doses of synthetic estrogens (DES), progesterones, or combination pills (Ovral) known as the 'morning after" pill, can be injected; this pill prevents a fertilized egg from implanting itself in the uterine wall.

Advantage: Less expensive than an abortion.

Disadvantages: Long-range effects of DES not yet studied; side effects of Ovral and DES include nausea and vomiting, high incidence of ectopic pregnancy and birth defects, if the drugs fail; heart attack or stroke.

THE RHYTHM METHOD

By keeping track of her daily temperature, her daily cervical secretions, and the dates of her last menstrual period, a woman can try to estimate the day on which she is fertile. The 7 days preceding and the 3 days following this day of ovulation are the days on which she abstains from intercourse.

Advantage: No immediate or long-term physical side effects.

Disadvantages: High incidence of failure; requires careful daily measurement of bodily functions and great familiarity with one's own body; irregularity of menstrual cycle makes predictions by the calendar highly unreliable; particularly impractical for adolescent-age girls whose physiological knowledge of their own bodies is limited; sperm can survive for 5 or 6 days in the uterus, and thus the couple must refrain from intercourse for a week before the day of ovulation as well as for 3 days thereafter.

BIRTH CONTROL PILLS FOR MALES

Although not yet available on the market and not a high priority among researchers, gossypol (extracted from cottonseed) has been found effective in stopping sperm production and in changing sperm motility. Pills made from gossypol have been researched in the People's Republic of China but have not yet been clinically tested in the United States. Given the tradition of allocating the responsibility for birth control to females, there appears little incentive at present for developing pills or shots that would permit males to share in the responsibility of contraception.

Source: Boston Women's Health Collective. *Our bodies, ourselves.* New York: Simon and Schuster. 1988.

TEENAGE PREGNANCY

Rates and Trends

In the United States each year, 1 in 10, or 1 million, teenage girls become pregnant—the highest rate of any industrialized nation in the world (Alan Guttmacher Institute, 1989; Jones et al., 1986). As Figure 10.2 illustrates, almost half of our teenage women have sex before the age of 19, half of them without using birth control. Consequently, nearly 20% of white females and 40% of African American females become pregnant before turning 18. As Figure 10.3 shows, pregnancies are most frequent among older adolescents, although more than 10,000 girls under the age of 15 become pregnant each year.

Although our teenage pregnancy rate is alarmingly high, it has actually declined since the 1970s (Hayes, 1987). As a consequence of teenagers' increased use of contraceptives, a smaller percentage of adolescents are now becoming pregnant

FIGURE 10.2

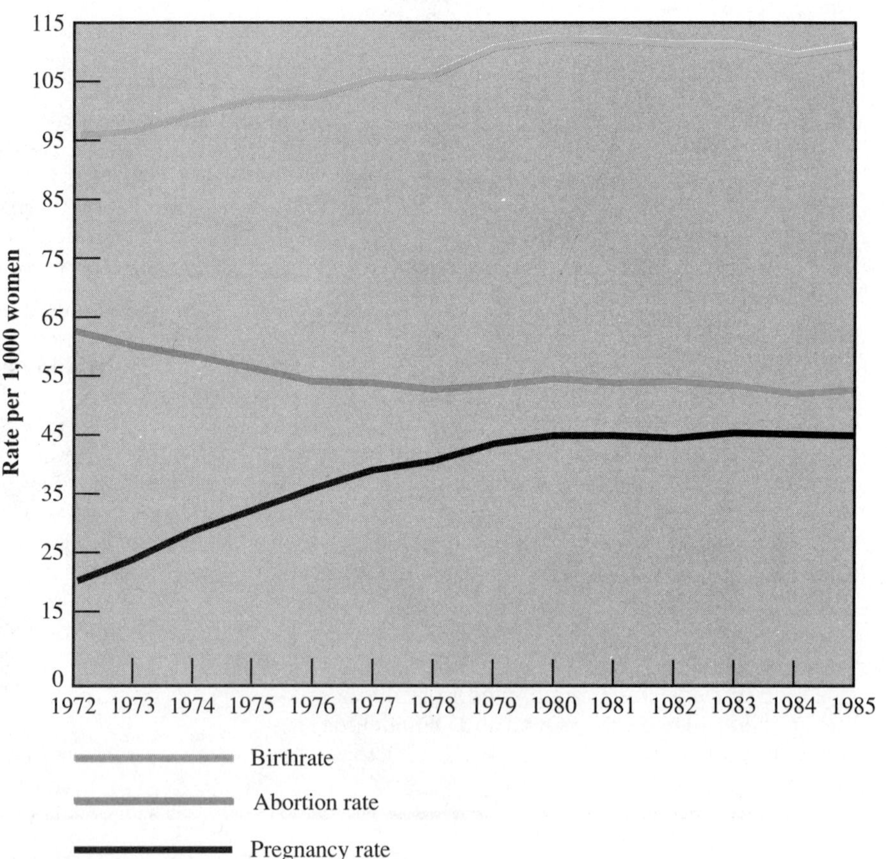

Source: S. Henshaw. (1989). *Teenage pregnancy in the U.S.* New York: Alan Guttmacher Institute.

FIGURE 10.3
Births to teenage mothers

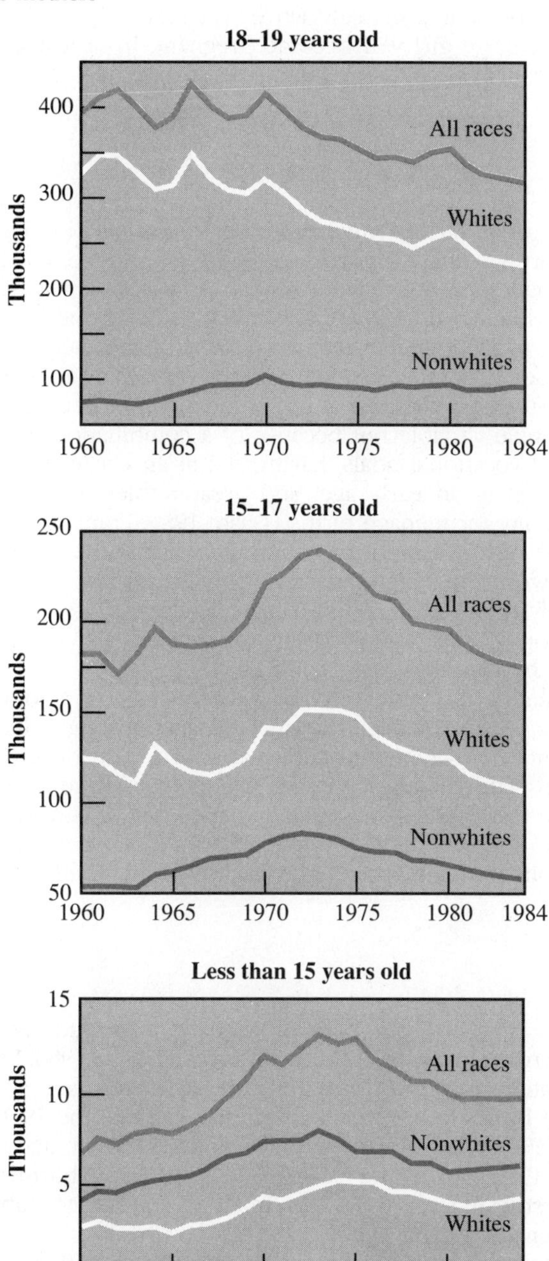

Source: National Center for Health Statistics. (1985). Washington, DC: Author.

than ever before. Despite this improvement, however, the problem has become worse in that many more young teenagers, who are the least likely to use contraceptives, are becoming sexually active. As a result, the odds are now greater than ever that a teenage girl will become pregnant. In fact, it is now estimated that 43% of all girls will become pregnant at least once before their 20th birthday (Forrest, 1986).

Racial Differences

Worse yet, 63% of all African American girls are estimated to become pregnant at least once before turning 20 (Forrest, 1986). For example, in a survey of more than 13,000 teenage girls, 40% of the African Americans, 30% of the Hispanics, and 23% of the whites said they would consider single motherhood. Regardless of race, however, the higher the girl's educational expectations, the less willing she was to consider becoming a single mother (Abrahamse, 1988). To reiterate, African American teenage girls are at the highest risk of becoming pregnant not because of any single variable but because of a combination of factors: poverty, low academic and vocational goals, having sex at an earlier age, their mothers' having had children at an early age, and greater tolerance within the African American community for teenage births (Dash, 1989; Franklin, 1988). Given that nearly half of the African American children in our society are growing up in poverty, it is noteworthy that high-income African Americans, Hispanics, and Native Americans actually have fewer children than do their white counterparts in the general population—a fact underscoring the impact that poverty has on our attitudes toward childbearing (Sowell, 1981).

Teenage pregnancy has also reached alarming levels among the Hispanic population (Lopez, 1987). Although Hispanic teenagers are more likely than African Americans to be married when their babies are born, Hispanic girls are less likely to complete high school than any other group of teenage mothers. It is also important to note that the teenage pregnancy rates differ considerably from one Hispanic group to the next. For example, Puerto Rican teenagers have proportionately more births than Cuban, Mexican, or Central and South American Hispanics.

Birthrates

Fortunately, the growing numbers of sexually active adolescents have not resulted in an increase in the adolescent birthrate (Hayes, 1986; Vinovskis, 1988). Given the legalization of abortion and the increase in teenagers' use of contraceptives, the teenage birthrate has steadily diminished since the 1970s. In 1984, for example, only 13% of all births were to mothers under age 20, the lowest proportion since 1957. During the past decade, the teenage birthrate has dropped by 8% to its lowest level since the 1940s. In short, contrary to public opinion, no "epidemic" of teenage pregnancy or births has occurred.

Why, then, is there a general impression that adolescents are giving birth to more children than ever before? One reason is that teenage pregnancy and births have become far more visible in our communities. In the "good old days" of shotgun weddings and until 1972, when it became illegal to expel a pregnant student from school, pregnancies and teenage sexuality in general were easier to ignore. Moreover, the sheer number of teenagers in the population—the result of the post-World War II baby boom—has focused more of our attention on teenagers' sexual behavior. There are now proportionately greater numbers of pregnant girls and teenage births, although the percentage has steadily declined since the end of the 1950s.

Perhaps even more noticeably, the rate (40%) of out-of-wedlock births has skyrocketed, even though the overall teenage birthrate has declined. Between 1950 and 1978, for instance, out-of-wedlock births tripled among girls under the age of 15 and during the 1960s increased by 30% among all teenagers. The rise, however, is almost entirely among whites, with African American teenagers having fewer out-of-wedlock births than in recent decades. For example, during the 1970s, African American adolescents' out-of-wedlock births decreased by 7% while whites' increased by 13%. Nevertheless, close to two-thirds of all white teenage mothers and almost 97% of all African American teenage mothers are single (Furstenberg, Brooks-Gunn, & Chase, 1989).

Abortion

Rates The Supreme Court's *Roe v. Wade* decision, which legalized abortion in the United States in 1973, has helped reduce our teenage birthrate, despite our rising rates of out-of-wedlock births. In conjunction with adolescents' increased use of contraceptives, legalized abortion has helped to lower the teenage birthrate by nearly 25% since the Court's decision. The number of teenage abortions more than doubled in the five years following the Court's ruling, until by the 1980s approximately 40% of all teenage pregnancies were being terminated. Teenage mothers now account for more than one-fourth of all abortions performed in the United States. Contrary to what some opponents of legalized abortion predicted, however, adolescents have not become less responsible about using contraceptives. In fact, since abortion was legalized, teenage contraceptive use has increased by 35% (Hofferth & Hayes 1987). Moreover, the rates of teenage pregnancies, births, and abortions have remained relatively unchanged since 1979 (Henshaw, et al, 1989).

In 1985, of approximately 1 million teenage girls who became pregnant, about 45% had abortions, including 16,970 under the age of 15. Of the 18- and 19-year-olds who had abortions, 60% already had at least one child. If these 1985 rates continue, 8.8% of all girls will have at least one abortion and 8.7% will have one or more births by their 18th birthday. Moreover, our teenage abortion rate is more than twice as high as any other nation's (Henshaw, Kenney, Somberg, & Van Vort, 1989).

As with contraception, the girl who is most likely to terminate an unplanned pregnancy is from a middle- or upper-income family. The higher her parents' level of education, the more likely a girl is to terminate her unplanned pregnancy (Hofferth & Hayes, 1987). She is also more educationally ambitious, a better student, and more likely to have parents and friends who support terminating unwanted pregnancies than the girl who carries her pregnancy to term. In contrast, the girl who chooses not to abort her pregnancy is likely to be poor, to have relatives or friends who had children as teenagers, or to come from a very religious family. For these reasons, white teenagers are far more likely than African Americans or Hispanics to terminate an unplanned pregnancy.

A CLOSER LOOK 10.4

An Effective Abortion Pill

The controversial issue of abortion assumed an even more complicated twist in the fall of 1986, when a team of French researchers reported their latest results with RU 486. The so-called once-a-month contraceptive pill has been proved effective in safely inducing abortions in women who have just become pregnant. The controversy, however, is that RU 486 makes it possible for girls and women to abort their pregnancies in the privacy of their own homes, rather than in an abortion clinic or hospital. The drug blocks the action of progesterone, the hormone that prepares the uterine wall for the implantation of a fertilized egg. In effect, the drug brings on a menstrual period even after a woman has become pregnant. Although the pill was not designed as a contraceptive, a woman could take the pill routinely each month and abort a pregnancy she never is aware of. Although the drug is now available in France and other countries, it has been banned by the U.S. government in the midst of the abortion controversy.

Source: M. Clark, K. Springen, & B. Alderman. (1986, December 29). An effective abortion pill. *Newsweek,* p. 47.

Psychological and physical consequences One of the many issues surrounding adolescents' abortion rights is whether having an abortion causes permanent psychological or physical damage. The research has not demonstrated that girls who terminate a pregnancy have more negative psychological or physical consequences than girls who carry their accidental pregnancy to term. When negative reactions do occur after an abortion, they are almost always mild and transitory. Indeed, among both minors and adults the most common reaction after terminating an unplanned pregnancy is relief, not depression. Moreover, most adolescents are able to make well-reasoned, logical decisions in choosing to abort a pregnancy (Landers, 1989; Lewis, 1987; Marecek, 1987; Melton, 1986).

In regard to the physical well-being of teenage girls, death and physical complications are far more common among girls carrying a pregnancy to term than among those who terminate a pregnancy. Unfortunately, the youngest adolescents are the most likely to delay their abortions until after the first trimester, thereby increasing their physical risks. Fearing their parents' reactions and pretending that the pregnancy really does not exist (the personal fable), young adolescents need the most help in confronting the fact that they are indeed pregnant and in making an early decision about their pregnancy. Whichever decision a girl makes, the earlier the better, since the first trimester is the most critical time for medical checkups and dietary changes if the pregnancy is to be continued. Sadly, however, most young adolescents who complete their pregnancy seldom see a physician during the first trimester, when the fetus is most vulnerable to birth defects due to poor prenatal care.

Although parental consent is not required for abortions in all states, many girls still consult their parents in making their decisions. Indeed, adolescents who are most confused seem to be the most likely to involve their parents. Consequently, younger adolescents are more likely than older teenagers to seek their parents' advice. Because younger adolescents are making the transition from concrete to abstract thinking, they generally need more help assessing the future consequences of their pregnancy decision. Receiving information about the social, physical, and economic risks of teenage parenting is thus especially important at this young age.

Legal regulation of abortion As a result of the Supreme Court's 1989 ruling that accords individual states the right to impose more restrictive abortion laws, adolescents' access to abortion will inevitably be made more difficult in some areas of the country. Before the Court's 1989 ruling, 13 states permitted adolescents to terminate an unwanted pregnancy without parental consent; 7 required either the parents' or the court's consent; and 6 gave a minor the option of either notifying her parents or asking the court's permission to abort. Both from a legal and a psychological perspective, at least two seminal questions remain unresolved: Are all adolescents mature enough to make their pregnancy decisions without parental approval? If not, how should the courts or psychologists determine which adolescents are and which are not capable of making such decisions (Melton, 1987)? As a consequence of the Court's more restrictive 1989 ruling, however, these two issues have now become secondary once again to the legal and ethical controversy of whether a woman has the right to determine the outcome of her pregnancy—an issue that will inevitably affect the lives of poor women and teenagers whose access to legal abortions will be most restricted by the more conservative laws in certain states.

TEENAGE PARENTS

Teenage Mothers and Children

The 600,000 teenage girls who choose to become mothers pose a different set of legal and psychological questions: Who should support the children born to teenage mothers? Should pregnant teenagers be encouraged to get married or are they better off remaining single? What types of service should we provide for teenage parents and their children? What are the consequences for mother, father, and child of teenage childbearing?

Unlike the differing viewpoints concerning many of the other questions regarding teenage sexuality, the research is remarkably consistent in documenting the negative consequences of teenage parenthood (Bolton, 1983; Furstenberg, Brooks-Gunn & Morgan, 1987; Hayes, 1987; Hofferth & Hayes, 1987; Lancaster & Hamburg, 1986). Teenage mothers suffer more social, educational, and economic disadvantage throughout their lives than girls who delay childbearing until their 20s. They are also less likely to complete high school, to be employed, to limit the size of their families, and to be happily married. In fact, teenage mothers are only half as likely to complete high school and have more than twice as many children as older mothers. Because of their educational and financial situation, families in which mothers gave birth as teenagers cost taxpayers about $20 billion a year in food stamps, Medicaid, and Aid to Families with Dependent Children. For example, if the teenage births in 1988 had been delayed until the mother was at least age 20, we would have saved more than $2 billion in welfare costs (Center for Population Options, 1989). This is not to say that teenage girls can never recover from the disruptions created by early motherhood. Some teenage parents do marry and raise their children in a financially stable family. These couples, however, are the exception, not the norm.

The children of teenage parents are also more handicapped economically, intellectually, and physically. These children have more childhood diseases, a higher infant mortality rate, and more physical and cognitive deficits than children of older mothers. As a consequence, the children of teenage mothers have more academic problems, a higher school dropout rate, and more pregnancies when they themselves become teenagers. Fortunately, however, the once-popular assumption that teenage parents are more likely to abuse their children physically has not been borne out (Bolton, 1985; S. Miller, 1983).

These problems have been partially accounted for by the fact that teenage mothers generally receive poor prenatal care, especially during the first trimester of pregnancy, which, as mentioned previously, is the most crucial period for fetal development. Since teenage mothers usually have less education and come from lower socioeconomic backgrounds, they are also usually unable to provide the kinds of experience that foster a child's intellectual and emotional development, particularly during the years of early childhood. In addition, most teenage mothers are unmarried, so their children are deprived of having two parents to attend to their intellectual, educational, and emotional needs. As the stories in Box 10.5 illustrate, many teenage fathers and mothers are barely beyond their own childhood and, therefore, are unable to assume responsibility for the development of their children.

Teenage Marriages

If a 15-year-old girl is about to have a baby, will she benefit more from getting married than from staying single? Would marriage benefit her boyfriend? their baby? Since teenage marriages are much more likely to end in divorce and since few teenage boys are able to support a family, should we encourage teenage parents to get married?

In addition to the fact that teenage marriages are less likely to last than are marriages of older couples, teenage mothers who get married are less likely than those who remain single to finish high school. This may be partially accounted for by the fact that single mothers may receive more help with the childcare and more encouragement to finish school from their relatives than from a teenage husband. Once married, a teenage mother may also fool herself into believing that she no longer has to worry about finishing school or preparing herself for a job. Whatever the reasons, teenage mothers are generally better off educationally if they remain single (Alan Guttmacher Institute, 1989; Moore, Simms, & Betsey, 1986). On the other hand, some surveys have found that teenage marriages to legitimize a birth are more stable and long-lasting than we might expect (McLaughlin, 1986). The basic question thus remains unresolved: Is marriage an asset or a liability in terms of the needs of children, teenage parents, and the rest of society?

Teenage Fathers

Much less is known about teenage fathers than about teenage mothers. We do know that most teenage fathers do not take part in raising their child or in providing emotional or financial support for their child's mother. Since most teenage couples do not get married, we have generally discouraged young fathers

10.5 ADOLESCENT VOICES

Comments From Adolescent Mothers

Thirteen-year-old mother: "You know, sometimes I look at him and he don't seem like he's mine. I guess I'm not used to him yet. Even in the hospital, right after he was born he didn't seem like he was mine. It's hard to think he's what I had in me for nine months. After he came out of me, the doctor put him on my stomach. 'Get that messy thing off me!' I yelled at that doctor. Maybe he don't seem like he's mine 'cause he can't talk yet. Now, my little cousin, he's different. He's three years old and he seems like he's mine, but he ain't. It's funny, I know he ain't a baby doll, but he don't yet seem like he's a real baby, like my cousin. He's sorta in between" (Frank, 1983, p. 54).

Fifteen-year-old mother: "Here's to all those doctors and teachers who said I couldn't raise a baby at my age, let alone graduate from school early. I had to prove to all of them, my grandmother, other teens, that not all teens are dumb and ignorant about makin' good choices for themselves. I love proving people wrong, I was gonna be a good example. I knew all about raising children. I had stored up in me all this knowledge about babies and with my own baby I felt I could apply it to my own instead of always telling others what I know. When I was seven, my cousins were having babies. I've been around babies all my life. I'm still the same person I was before I was a parent. Only thing that's changed is that I have a baby. Same ol' me, though" (Frank, p. 76).

Eighteen-year-old mother: "But one thing I'll never do is get married. No way. Too much divorce in my family. My mother's been divorced twice, my uncle twice, my grandmother twice. I've learned that marriage just doesn't work. I'll have plenty of boyfriends, but no husbands. Women got to be careful of men. The reason I don't let my baby's father see our son is because he's not helpin' support him financially. If the father wants rights, he's got to live up to his responsibilities. No responsibilities, no rights. I won't let no man just barge in here and start ordering me around whenever he damn pleases. Not with me. I'm not one of those girls! No man's gonna beat me or push me around. My girl friend couldn't say no to her boyfriend and I found her all bloody and beat up with her blouse torn off. Any man who raises a hand to me is gone, and I mean fast!" (Frank, p. 96).

Fifteen-year-old mother: "I was lucky in that the labor was short in duration, only five and a half hours, because I don't think I could have stood any more. And then sharing a room. My roommate's husband was a minister and he was awful to me. He embarrassed me, he said wise comments, which just made me lie there and cry—made me feel even more awful" (McGuire, p. 90).

Source: D. Frank. (1983). *Deep blue funk and other stories: Portraits of teenage parents.* Ounce of Prevention Fund; P. McGuire. *It won't happen to me: Teenagers talk about pregnancy.* (1983). New York: Delacorte.

from being involved with their child or the child's mother. As a consequence, a number of young fathers feel guilty, depressed, and emotionally isolated from both their child and the child's mother.

It remains to be discovered whether teenage fathers exert a major influence on teenage girls' decisions to have a child. It is also still unclear why some teenage fathers assume a larger role in childcare and financial support than others (Elster & Lamb, 1986). Moreover, our legal system has virtually ignored unmarried teenage fathers in terms of trying to collect child support payments. Likewise the Bureau of the Census does not include questions related to child support for mothers under the age of 18. As a consequence, we lack statistics describing teenage fathers' economic support for their children (Kahn & Kamerman, 1988).

What we do know is that of all women with court orders for child support payments, about 40% receive full payment, 30% partial payment, and 30% no payment. Men are most likely to make their payments during the first few years of the child's life, although the average total payment throughout the nation is still only $2,460. Even without official statistics, it is clear that teenage fathers are less likely than older fathers to provide child support (Kahn & Kamerman, 1988). Interestingly, however, it seems that African American males are no less likely to provide child support when they are unmarried than when they are married. (Furstenberg, Brooks-Gunn, & Morgan, 1987).

As is the case with teenage mothers and their childless peers, teenage fathers also achieve less educationally and financially than boys who are not fathers, even when they do not marry their child's mother. Some of these differences, of course, are not a result of becoming a father per se. That is, boys who become teenage fathers tend to have performed less well academically and to come from poorer socioeconomic backgrounds than other boys. Having become fathers, therefore, these young men are more in need than ever of educational and vocational training that will enable them to offer some financial and emotional support for their family (Elster & Lamb, 1986; Hendricks & Solomon, 1987; Zayas, Schinke, & Casareno, 1987).

SEXUALLY TRANSMITTED DISEASES

In terms of sheer numbers, **sexually transmitted diseases** (STDs) pose an even more widespread threat than teenage pregnancy and childbearing. Nearly one-fourth of all adolescents have genital herpes and more than 1% have gonorrhea, which, when adjusted for adults' higher rates of sexual activity, means that teenagers have the highest rates of gonorrhea of any age group. Likewise, one-fifth of the AIDS cases have been found in people in their 20s, meaning that most of these victims were infected as adolescents (Centers for Disease Control, 1989).

AIDS

Rates and trends Although far rarer than any other sexually transmitted disease, **AIDS** is unrivaled in terms of the terror it has generated since the 1980s. Caused by the **human immunodeficiency virus (HIV),** AIDS kills its victims by destroying the body's immune system. As a result, AIDS victims die of diseases, such as pneumonia, that a healthy immune system can usually defeat. Having first come to the general public's attention in the early 1980s as a disease presumably confined to homosexuals and intravenous drug users, AIDS created alarm among heterosexuals as it became apparent that the virus can be contracted through blood transfusions and through sex with bisexual or heterosexual partners. For example, in Africa, AIDS kills males and females in equal proportions. Sadder still, children are born with AIDS as a consequence of having mothers with the infection. In short, no segment of our population—above all, not adolescents—is immune to HIV.

As a consequence, in the 1980s our nation had to confront the issues involved in permitting children with AIDS to attend school. Having contracted the virus through contaminated blood transfusions or from their own mothers at birth, these students' lives have been torn asunder, as have the lives of their families and friends (Kirp, 1988; Moffatt, 1988). For example, Ricky, Robert, and Randy Ray, three brothers who contracted the HIV virus through treatment for hemophilia, were refused admission to their elementary school in Arcadia, Florida, in 1986 and 1987. In August 1987, the boys were permitted to enroll in school under a federal court order, but the family fled to Sarasota after other students' parents staged a boycott and their house was burned by an unknown arsonist. The family was ultimately awarded $1.1 million in their settlement with the school district (Three AIDS, 1988).

Table 10.2

AIDS Cases Among U.S. Children by Sex and Race, Reported Through 1989

AGE AT DIAGNOSIS (YEARS)	WHITE	AFRICAN AMERICAN	HISPANIC	ASIAN/ PACIFIC ISLANDER	AMERICAN INDIAN/ ALASKAN NATIVE	TOTAL
Males:						
Under 5	142	436	209	3	2	794
5–12	117	62	39	3	—	222
13–19	171	97	62	5	3	339
Subtotal	430	595	310	11	5	1355
Females:						
Under 5	127	426	176	1	2	733
5–12	25	55	28	2	—	110
13–19	16	50	14	1	1	82
Subtotal	168	531	218	4	3	925
Total	598	1126	528	15	8	2280

Source: Centers for Disease Control (1989). *HIV/AIDS Surveillance Report.* Atlanta, GA: Author.

Since the disease was first recognized in 1979, the number of AIDS victims has more than doubled every year. By the end of May 1989, 97,193 people in our society were reported to have AIDS, and between 1.0 and 1.5 million are estimated to be infected with the virus (Centers for Disease Control, 1989). More frightening still, as Table 10.2 shows, adolescents are at a particularly high risk of contracting AIDS. Although teenagers presently account for less than 1% of all reported AIDS cases, their sexual behavior, including intercourse with multiple partners and infrequent use of condoms, may make them more vulnerable than many adults. For example, 7% of one sample of 1,000 homeless youths in New York City had the HIV virus. Moreover, because the average length of time between infection and the onset of symptoms is 8 to 10 years, the fact that 20% of all people now diagnosed with AIDS are in their 20s means that many of these infections were contracted during adolescence. Since the rates of other sexually transmitted diseases are higher among teenagers than among adults, the teenage population has been identified, even by the surgeon general, as especially vulnerable to AIDS (Centers for Disease Control, 1988, 1989; Guinan, 1986, Koop, 1987).

Indeed teenage girls are now more likely than adult females to contract AIDS. Most teenage girls contract the virus through intercourse with a boyfriend. Nearly three fourths of the female AIDS victims, however, are either Hispanic or African American, a finding that has been attributed to the greater popularity of intravenous drugs among minority males. Nevertheless, white young people are certainly not safe from the disease, and neither are the well educated. For example, in 1988, in the first national survey of college students concerning AIDS, 0.2% of the 16,861 blood samples from the 19 schools tested positive for AIDS. Similarly, 0.1% of the 17- to 19-year-old military recruits tested positive (Centers for Disease Control, 1988a; 1989).

Awareness and education Despite the increasing threat of AIDS, most adolescents continue to behave in ways that do little to protect them from this deadly virus. For example, in a sample of 860 Boston teenagers, only one fifth used condoms and only 15% said they had changed their sexual behavior in response to their fear of AIDS (Strunin & Hingson, 1987). Similarly, in San Francisco, where the risks of contracting AIDS are especially high, nearly 80% of the 1,326 adolescents surveyed said they were worried about contracting AIDS; but only 60% were aware that using a condom might reduce their chances of contracting the virus (DiClemente, Zorn, & Temoshok, 1987). Other surveys have also found that teenagers' incomplete knowledge; their infrequent use of condoms, even though more adolescents are now using them; and their becoming sexually active at earlier ages and with multiple partners increase their risks of contracting AIDS (Becker & Joseph, 1988; Centers for Disease Control, 1988a, 1989; Kegeles, Adler, & Irwin, 1988; Quackenbush, 1987; Sonenstein, Peck, & Ku, 1989).

Before we jump to the conclusion that teenagers are just downright irresponsible and stupid, let's consider how adults have dealt with the AIDS problem. For example, although 38 public service announcements were prepared by the Centers for Disease Control and were distributed to the major television networks in the fall of 1987, only one was shown during the following month. During the next few months, nearly 90% of all AIDS messages were aired during nonprime-time hours (General Accounting Office, 1988). Likewise, only 16 states require AIDS education to begin in elementary school, and only 3 states require teachers to discuss condoms as a way of preventing AIDS (National Association of State Boards of Education, 1989). How, then, can we be surprised to find that adolescents treat AIDS in such a cavalier fashion and that they are so poorly informed?

Herpes

Although AIDS has undoubtedly become the nation's most frightening disease, **herpes** remains the more distressing illness in terms of its prevalence. About one fifth of the U.S. population is currently infected with genital herpes, with more than half a million new cases being reported each year (Centers for Disease Control, 1989). The typical herpes victim is white, well educated, and financially well-off. About 50% of herpes victims are female, 95% are white, 50% have at least a college degree, 80% are between 20 and 39 years old, and 56% earn at least $21,000 a year. As health specialists have noted, however, the incidence of herpes is undoubtedly higher than officially reported among minorities and the poor who cannot afford medical services.

Although not identified until 1940 as a virus, herpes is not a new disease. The Roman Emperor Tiberius supposedly banned kissing because of the epidemic of lip sores created by herpes. Not until the late 1960s, however, did researchers discover that there were two types of herpes virus. One strain, called Type I herpes virus, causes chicken pox, shingles (a painful skin disease), and common cold sores that appear around the mouth.

The strain responsible for genital herpes is the Type II herpes virus—a virus that continues to mystify researchers in terms of both prevention and cure. Type I herpes can be transferred from cold sores to the genitals by finger or mouth, thereby causing genital herpes. Thus, while hoping to avoid herpes by refraining from intercourse, adolescents may contract the virus through oral-genital sex and other intimate forms of foreplay. Researchers are still debating whether young people can protect themselves from herpes by using condoms, since the virus may be small enough to penetrate a prophylactic. Some evidence suggests that herpes can be spread by contaminated towels and toilet seats, since live viruses have been found on some objects up to 72 hours after contact with a herpes victim. Although the data are still inconclusive on this point, some doctors warn herpes victims and their friends not to share towels or bathroom facilities.

Once a person contracts Type II herpes, he or she is infected for life. Although researchers have developed medications for the treatment of the herpes blisters, neither a vaccine nor a cure is available. While not everyone exposed to the herpes virus will contract the disease, those who do first experience an itching or tingling sensation around their genitals. These initial symptoms may also be accompanied by a slight fever, headache, swollen glands, and general achiness—all of which are easily ignored by naive young people who may mistake the symptoms for a simple case of the flu. Although the incubation period may last up to a year, most individuals develop the small, painful, red blisters around the genital area within 2 to 20 days after contact.

The initial outbreak of blisters can last as long as 2 weeks, after which they usually return periodically throughout the individual's lifetime. Unfortunately, many adolescents deceive themselves into believing they are cured after the blisters disappear, as they inevitably do even without any medical treatment. The virus, however, is alive and well, traveling up the nerves to the base of the skull, the spinal column, or the ganglia to live in a dormant state until the next outbreak.

Some people are **asymptomatic carriers,** meaning that they show no external symptoms of having the disease. Because girls' sores may erupt only inside the vagina, the virus is often harbored unknowingly and transmitted innocently to others. Similarly, boys may carry the virus without symptoms.

Although the first attack is usually the most severe and most painful for both male and female adolescents, the virus poses far more serious threats to the female. For unknown reasons, females tend to have more painful and more frequent attacks than males. More seriously, girls with herpes are eight times more likely than uninfected females to develop cervical cancer. For this reason, females with herpes should have a PAP test for the early detection of cancer twice a year for the rest of their lives. More sadly still, a baby can contract the herpes virus as it passes through the birth canal of an infected mother. Consequently, a female whose herpes virus is in its active state near the time of delivery is advised to have a Caesarean section. Herpes can also cause miscarriages, birth defects, and brain damage to the unborn infant.

Although we cannot offer adolescents a cure for herpes, we can offer them advice for diminishing the severity and the frequency of their attacks (Bell, 1988). When an adolescent is under stress, sick, upset, tired, or exposed to too much sun, the herpes virus tends to be reactivated. Avoiding junk foods, staying out of the sun as much as possible, and getting enough sleep and exercise are also advised. Friction from clothing can also trigger an attack, so herpes victims are advised to dispose of their skin-tight jeans, snug-fitting underwear, and pantyhose. Prescribed drugs are available to reduce the blisters' pain during an attack, although it has been argued that topical creams can spread the infection, and some physicians refuse to prescribe them. Some doctors recommend applying ice and keeping the sores as clean and dry as possible.

Unknowingly, infected adolescents can spread the virus to their friends in the days before the actual appearance of the sores. Therefore, it is of utmost importance that young people learn to recognize their preattack symptoms, which may include tingling or tenderness around the mouth or genital area, a dry or red spot on the skin, fever, swollen glands, flulike aches, and depression. Although condoms cannot be considered absolute safeguards, adolescents who have herpes or who are having intercourse with someone who has herpes are advised to use prophylactics. Adolescents must be made to understand, however, that using condoms is no substitute for honesty.

Understandably, adolescents with herpes often experience considerable remorse, guilt, anger, sadness, and stress. Some become seriously depressed and impotent, while others feel "dirty" and become obsessed with constant bathing. Living in shame and social isolation, many fear that nobody except another herpes victim would want to have sex with or marry them. By way of empathizing, we might ask ourselves: Would I have sex with someone who was honorable enough to tell me that he or she had herpes? Would I date someone who I knew had herpes? Would I feel comfortable sharing a bathroom with a roommate who had herpes?

Gonorrhea

Less worrisome than herpes, because it can be cured with antibiotics, **gonorrhea** nevertheless continues to affect thousands of adolescents. Also known as "the clap," "dose," "drip," "morning dew," "gleet," and "the whites," gonorrhea is caused by the gonococcus bacteria. Since these bacteria die on contact with air, there is no truth to the myths that gonorrhea can be contracted from swimming pools, clothing, door knobs, or toilet seats. Adolescents contract this disease in two ways: through anal or vaginal intercourse and through oral-genital sex. Even though gonorrhea can be cured, its consequences are serious if left untreated.

Since the gonococcus bacteria grow well in the vagina, penis, mouth, throat, and anus, adolescents who perform fellatio or cunnilingus can contract gonorrhea of the throat. The bacteria can also be spread through anal sex. Though most symptoms show up within 2 weeks after contact, almost 80% of all infected females and 10 to 20% of infected males are asymptomatic. As a consequence, gonorrhea is more easily spread than herpes. If symptoms do occur, the infected girl will experience frequent urination, lower abdominal pain, swollen glands, sore throat, or a discharge from the anus or vagina. The most common symptoms among males are a discharge from the penis (sometimes noticed as a drip before urinating in the morning); burning, itching, or pain when urinating; sore throat, swollen glands, or a discharge from the anus. A doctor must diagnose the disease by taking cultures from the affected area or by conducting a test on the male's discharge.

Fortunately for adolescents who detect the disease, it is as mentioned above, curable with antibiotics. Unfortunately, too many fearful youngsters borrow antibiotics or divide their own prescription with a friend without realizing that the medicine is effective only if taken in its full dose for the full period of time prescribed. Even after taking the medicine correctly, adolescents should return to their doctors for another test to be certain that all the bacteria have been destroyed. Since, like those of herpes, gonorrhea's symptoms will disappear on their own without medical treatment, many adolescents never seek a doctor's counsel and continue to spread the bacteria. Unlike herpes, untreated gonorrhea can inflict permanent, irreversible damage to the reproductive organs, rendering both males and females infertile. If the gonococcus bacteria infect the eyes, blindness can result.

Unlike the herpes and AIDS viruses, the gonococcus bacteria can definitely be barricaded by condoms and spermicides. Using a diaphragm in conjunction with a spermicide or using the vaginal sponge (which is already presaturated with spermicide) affords additional protection. Also gargling with salt water immediately after oral sex acts as a deterrent to gonorrhea of the throat. Squeezing the penis for signs of any suspicious discharge also provides some assurance regarding the absence or presence of an infection (Bell, 1988).

Syphilis

If an adolescent catches a venereal disease, it is not likely to be **syphilis** since only about 100,000 new cases are reported annually (Centers for Disease Control, 1988c). Caused by spiral-shaped bacteria, syphilis can be cured with antibiotics. Sometimes called "siff," "the pox," "lues," "bad blood," "Old Joe," or "haircut," syphilis first appears as sores, called **chancres,** around the genitals or mouth. Unlike herpes sores, syphilis sores are painless. A rash may also appear on the body, especially on the hands and feet. The sores usually appear within 10 to 90 days after oral sex, anal sex, or vaginal intercourse with an infected person. The sores gradually disappear without any medication, but the bacteria continue to thrive inside the victim's body. Several months after the sores disappear, some people notice other symptoms: fever, aches, sore throat, mouth sores, swollen glands, rash, loss of hair. These symptoms also disappear without any treatment, yet during these first two stages the disease is highly contagious.

Unfortunately, as with herpes and gonorrhea, many victims are asymptomatic. Consequently, no matter how carefully an individual visually inspects a sexual partner, there is no way to be absolutely certain whether he or she has syphilis, gonorrhea, or herpes. More distressing, some people never consult a doctor because the symptoms gradually disappear without medical treatment. The same kinds of prophylactic measures that reduce our chances of catching the gonococcus bacteria also offer some protection against syphilis. On the basis of a blood test or an examination of the rash or chancres, doctors can reliably diagnose and treat the bacteria. Unfortunately, too many victims stop taking their medicine as soon as they start feeling better and never return for a second examination to determine whether all the bacteria have been destroyed. If not completely destroyed, the syphilis bacteria can cause heart disease, blindness, deafness, insanity, paralysis, and death.

Yeast Infections

Although many people assume that any form of discharge or genital irritation indicates the presence of a venereal disease, this is not the case. A number of infections in both males and females can be caused by an overproduction of yeast in the reproductive or urinary tracts. Yeast and bacteria are always present in the healthy vagina and around the male's penis and anus. Sometimes, however, due to changes in diet, excessively hot weather, nylon underwear, or deodorant soaps and douches, these micoorganisms get out of balance and multiply beyond their natural limits. Although these infections can be extremely uncomfortable, often accompanied by painful urination, itching, and burning, they cause no permanent damage even when untreated. Nevertheless, these infections seldom disappear without treatment and are easily communicated to sexual partners. Depending on the type of infection, the affected individual is treated with oral medicines, vaginal suppositories, or topical creams applied to the penis. Nonprescription treatments, such as douches and anti-itching creams, only mask the symptoms and may even spread the infection. Unless both sexual partners are treated, these annoying infections continue to recur as the untreated partner continues to reinfect the other.

In sum, we must somehow convince more adolescents to seek medical advice whenever signs of a genital infection appear or whenever they suspect they have been exposed to a disease. Given their understandable embarrassment, our task is to help the young overcome their shyness in regard to protecting their own health and the health of their sexual partners. Only by being helped to overcome their timidity and their discomfort can young people learn to ask their dates the appropriate questions before having sex, to seek medical advice when necessary, and to notify their sexual partners of any signs of disease. Medical handbooks written especially for young people, such as *Changing Bodies, Changing Lives,* should be made visible in every school library and at home in order to keep adolescents well-informed and healthy (Bell, 1988).

SEX EDUCATION

In the Schools

Considering the millions of adolescents being affected by sexually transmitted diseases and pregnancy, you might wonder why sex education programs have had

ARE YOU SURE? 10.6

Adolescents' Misconceptions About Sexually Transmitted Diseases

True or False?

1. If the symptoms of the disease go away, it means I am cured.
2. Wearing a condom is a fail-safe way to protect against the herpes and HIV viruses.
3. Diaphragms and contraceptive jellies offer no protection against sexually transmitted diseases.
4. If someone has herpes, gonorrhea, or syphilis, I can see the sores or a discharge or some other visible sign that he or she is infected.
5. Once people have had a sexually transmitted disease and have been cured, they cannot contract it again because they are immune.
6. The only sexually transmitted diseases are gonorrhea, herpes, and syphilis.
7. I cannot contract or transmit a disease through oral sex.
8. Homosexuals do not have to worry about catching diseases except AIDS.
9. If a person catches a disease, he or she will definitely know about the infection from the symptoms.
10. Penicillin and other modern drugs can cure herpes.
11. Urinating before and after sex will protect me from a sexual disease.
12. If a female has a vaginal discharge, this means she has an infection.
13. You cannot infect other people with herpes unless you have visible sores.
14. Symptoms of a sexual disease will always show up within a month or so of contracting the infection.
15. You cannot catch genital herpes from kissing someone who has cold sores on the lips.
16. You can catch AIDS from toilet seats, towels, swimming pools, or door knobs.
17. No permanent damage can be done from herpes.
18. Douching immediately after intercourse reduces a female's risk of contracting a disease.
19. Birth control pills and the IUD reduce a girl's chances of catching a sexual disease.
20. Once you have finished taking the medicine prescribed by a doctor for a sexual disease you can be sure it is safe to have sex again.

Answers: All 20 statements are false.

Source: R. Bell. (1988). *Changing bodies, changing lives: A book for teens on sex and relationships.* New York: Random House.

so little impact. The main reason is that sex education is too little and too late. As the map in Figure 10.4 illustrates, even with the growing concern over AIDS and pregnancy, most states still do not require sex education in their schools. Moreover, in those that do, the most thorough sex education classes are restricted to high-school students, most of whom have been sexually active for months or years. Even in many so-called sex education courses, information about contraception, abortion, and homosexuality is omitted or glossed over. Most teachers who do broach these subjects say they feel resistance from parents and the community. Although the AIDS crisis has spurred many schools to adopt some form of sex education, only 60% of all students receive any sex education before graduating from high school (Forrest & Silverman, 1989; Kenney, Guardada, & Brown, 1989).

More unfortunate still, although most states agree that students should be given information about how AIDS is contracted, only seven states require instruction about pregnancy prevention. The sex education curricula of Alabama and New York, for example, focus on the failure rate of condoms. In contrast, Michigan's curriculum discusses where condoms can be purchased, and New Jersey is proposing a classroom activity for teaching students how to use a condom.

FIGURE 10.4
Teaching about sex

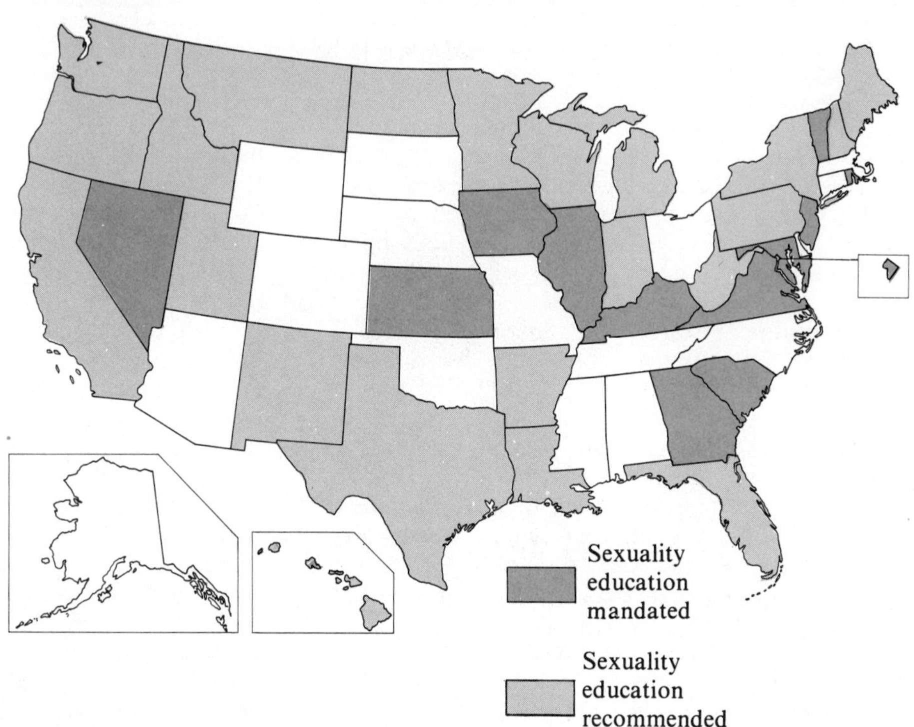

Source: M. Kenney, S. Guardado, & L. Brown. (1989). Sex education and AIDS in the schools. *Family Planning Perspectives, 21,* 58.

In brief, states are more willing to educate students about AIDS than about contraceptives.

On a more optimistic note, only 10 states have taken no action whatsoever in regard to recommending or requiring sex education in their schools. While only 3 states required sex education in 1980 (Kentucky, Maryland, and New Jersey), 17 did so by 1988. Moreover, the largest school districts in urban areas are the most supportive of educating students about contraception and are the most likely to provide this information in earlier grades. Despite vocal opposition from religious fundamentalists, the vast majority of parents have supported sex education in our schools since the late 1970s. While some adults still believe that informing adolescents about birth control will cause them to become sexually active, the evidence does not support their fear. Adolescents who are choosing to be sexually active are doing so whether or not they receive information about contraceptives in school.

Beyond the Schools

Even the experts agree, however, that sex education should not be the exclusive responsibility of our schools. Parents should be encouraged to discuss sex and contraception with their children, which may mean providing television programs that give parents, teachers, and counselors accurate and up-to-date information. Merchants could also help by displaying contraceptives in private, yet easily accessible, sections of their stores so that young customers will feel less embarrassed selecting them. Putting contraceptive dispensers in men's and women's bathrooms, especially in places frequented by teenagers, such as movie theaters and discos, would also encourage their use.

Television, radio, and movie theaters could advertise contraceptives and highlight the risks involved in being sexually active. Furthermore, movies and television shows could stop promoting irresponsible sexual behavior by portraying sex as an unpremeditated, carefree activity. Instead, more movies and TV programs could include scenes like the one in *Saturday Night Fever* in which John Travolta zips up his jeans and makes a hasty retreat from his date's car when she makes it clear that she is not interested in using any contraceptive.

Reaching Adolescent Males

Perhaps even more important, our attempts at sex education, both in and out of school, have to reach the male audience. Until teenage boys are taught to assume equal responsibility with girls for contraception, the rate of sexually transmitted diseases and pregnancy will remain alarmingly high. Unfortunately, even many girls have bought into the notion that birth control is solely a female responsibility. Indeed, some young men report that when they are foresightful enough to bring a condom with them on a date, their girlfriends reprimand them for "planning to have sex" or for "ruining the romance" (Bell, 1988).

Boys and men must be encouraged to change their antiquated attitudes about using condoms. Until 1965, condoms were the most popular method of birth control in our society. With the advent of the pill and the IUD, however, males came to view the condom as an outmoded contraption, rather than as our best protection against sexual diseases and relatively good protection against pregnancy. Many boys refuse even to try condoms, having been told that their sexual pleasure will be reduced. Instead, our schools and the media might be teaching boys that wearing a condom increases their pleasure, as well as their partner's, by reducing the fear of disease and pregnancy. Then, too, advertisements could help males and females understand that today's sophisticated and varied styles of condoms do not rob a male of sexual pleasure. To the contrary, many are designed to enhance it. Other industrialized nations have been more successful than ours in convincing boys and men that condoms are not for sissies, nor are they outdated contraptions that rob men of their sexual pleasure (Jones et al., 1986).

One Planned Parenthood program, for example, sponsored a Condom Couplet Contest to encourage teenage boys to use prophylactics. Among the boys' winning couplets were: "At first a condom may seem a bother, but it prevents an unwanted father" and "From using a condom you will learn, that no deposit means no return!" Another program was aimed at helping teenage boys view manhood in a new context. Rather than encouraging boys to use condoms or to refrain from sex merely for the girl's sake, the program emphasized the personal benefits of condoms and restraint: "I owe it to myself to protect myself against disease even if the girl is using a contraceptive." "As a man, I have the right to say no to a girl if I'm worried about pregnancy or disease." "I have the right to have a friendship with a girl that doesn't include sex" (Scales & Beckstein, 1982).

HOMOSEXUALITY

Prevalence

It is now estimated that approximately 20–25% of all males and 6% of all females have at least one sexual experience with someone of their own sex before the age of 20. After adolescence, somewhere between 5 and 10% of the population is **homosexual,** while a larger percentage is estimated to engage in **bisexual** activity (Tripp, 1987). Contrary to many heterosexuals' opinions, however, the percentage of homosexuality in our society has remained relatively constant since the 1940s, when such data were first collected (Kinsey, Pomeroy, & Martin, 1948; Kinsey, Pomeroy, Martin, & Gebhard, 1953).

Why, then, do many of us have the false impression that homosexuality has become more prevalent? In large part this impression has been created by the fact that homosexuals are now legally and socially permitted to live more openly in our society. Legislation enacted during the 1970s and 1980s has offered homosexuals more protection against being thrown out of school, evicted from their apartments, and fired from their jobs. As a consequence, gay people are more visible in our communities. Our society is also gradually becoming more aware that homosexuality is not an illness or a pyschological disorder that must be cured. In fact, the American Psychiatric Association no longer categorizes homosexuality as a mental disorder (1987). Through more openness and education, most of us are also coming to understand that a person's sexual orientation, whether homosexual, bisexual, or heterosexual, does not preclude him or her from living a fulfilling life or from making significant contributions to our world—as witnessed by the lives of such homosexuals as Walt Whitman, Oscar Wilde, and Gertrude Stein (Duberman, Vicinus, & Chauncey, 1989; Greenberg, 1988).

The Determinants of Sexual Orientation

More sophisticated research methods, particularly in the medical sciences, are also helping us understand that being homosexual, heterosexual, or bisexual is probably not a choice that any of us makes. Rather, our sexual orientation appears to be determined by a complex combination of genetic, hormonal, and environmental components (Money, 1988; Savin-Williams, 1988; Tripp, 1987).

Social learning theory Historically, social learning theorists have investigated the possibility that our sexual orientation, like other aspects of our personalities, is determined by environmental influences—particularly interactions with our parents and other sexual experiences with our peers. Contrary to these assumptions, however, the families of homosexuals and heterosexuals have not been found to differ in ways that could cause a child to develop any particular sexual orientation. For example, gay males do not have mothers who are any more domineering or overly protective than do heterosexual males. Neither do lesbians have fathers who are any more overbearing, oppressive, or unloving than do heterosexual females. Although some gay adolescents do come from such families, so do some heterosexuals. Like heterosexuals, some homosexual teenagers have terrible relationships with their parents and have had unpleasant sexual experiences with members of the other sex. Moreover, evidence now suggests that male homosexuals

How do you feel about homosexuality?

exhibit signs of their homosexuality very early in their childhood, at a time before their parents or friends could have had any appreciable impact on their sexual orientation (Green, 1987). In other words, our sexual orientation does not appear to be determined by our parents' behavior or by the nature of our first sexual experiences.

To reiterate this point, the research has repeatedly shown that a child with a lesbian mother does not model himself or herself after the mother's sexual orientation or develop any more psychological or sexual problems than does a child with a heterosexual mother (Bozett, 1987; Falk, 1989). This is not to say that adolescents whose mothers are lesbian or whose fathers are gay never experience the pain and embarrassment of society's cruelty. Understandably, adolescents with a gay parent may feel the need for secrecy and may feel anxious, fearing reprisals against themselves or their family. Nor is this to say that children with a gay parent never feel confused, or even temporarily shocked, when they first discover their parents' homosexuality. Nevertheless, these discoveries do not determine a child's sexual orientation or undermine the quality of an otherwise good parent-child relationship.

Biological theories In contrast to social learning theorists, other researchers have pursued the possibility that our sexual orientation is determined by biological

10.7

ADOLESCENT VOICES

Homosexuality: Experiences and Reactions

How do you feel about these adolescents' experiences and reactions to homosexuality?

"When Ed first said he was gay, I thought, 'Let me out of here!' But I knew the guy. We were friends already. I knew what he did in his spare time, what kinds of fights he had with his mother, what kind of movies he dug. I mean, he's a person. So by now his being gay is just something else I know about him. I never thought I'd hear myself saying that."

"In a straight person's mind, getting a homosexual guy in bed with a girl is going to be all he needs to make a miraculous change into being a heterosexual. It's funny. Some people think that the only reason you're gay is because you had a bad experience with a woman. Like a woman laughed at you or something. So they think all you need is a good experience to turn you straight."

"I had more enjoyment with guys than I did with girls and it just confirmed what I had already been thinking. I cried about it a lot. I said to myself, you're a homosexual. And I didn't want to be, not then anyhow. I called myself all sorts of names: 'You're a fag, you're a freak.' Where was my belief in God? Where was my future with a wife and kids? All this was going through my mind at that time."

"After people at school found out that I was gay, a lot of them kind of kept a distance from me. I think they were scared that I was going to do something to them. You know, the old fears about gay people attacking you and that junk. I

continued

factors—prenatal hormones, adolescent hormones, or our genetic inheritance (Savin-Williams, 1988). The fact that homosexuality is generally more common among people who are biologically related than in society at large suggests a biological link. On the other hand, these family studies do not rule out environmental explanations since relatives tend to be reared in households with similar values and styles of interacting. Nevertheless, twin studies have lent support to the notion that sexual orientation is, in part, genetically determined. For example, there is a considerably higher incidence of homosexuality among identical twins (conceived from the same egg) than among fraternal twins (conceived from two separate eggs). There are, however, many methodological problems with these studies, such as small sample sizes and how to separate genetic from environmental influences (Savin-Williams, 1988).

Likewise, studies of prenatal and adolescent hormones have yielded inconclusive and contradictory results, leaving us without enough evidence to determine that there is a relationship between hormones and our sexual orientations. Although there is general agreement that prenatal developments do influence our later development, the connection between prenatal hormones and homosexuality is still relatively controversial. Most researchers do agree, however, that the hormonal shifts occurring during our adolescence do not affect our sexual orientation. That is, our adolescent hormones increase our interest in sex, but they do not determine whether we are homosexual, bisexual, or heterosexual.

Although the causes of heterosexuality or homosexuality are still unknown, it

Box 10.7 continued

guess that was one of the reasons why I didn't come out sooner, because I was afraid that they would be scared of me."

"For me, it was a real lonely experience. I could never show the real me, especially that part of me, to anyone, because I felt that would mean no one would want to be with me. I was sure that if I told them about my homosexual feelings, no one would care about me. The loneliness was awful."

"Finally, just about when I was graduating from high school, I looked at myself and just accepted the fact that I was gay. I looked in the mirror and said, not "You're a homosexual," but "I'm a homosexual." And from that point on I could admit to myself who I was, and that made me a man in my own feelings. It's funny, because a lot of people think that being a homosexual robs a guy of his manhood. But for me, admitting my own homosexuality gave me my manhood."

"The only other gay guys I knew in my high school were both jocks—real macho, on the football team and all that. I was clearly not as masculine as they were. In fact, I look more like the stereotype many people have of homosexuals. It's one thing to be gay and macho, and another to be gay and effeminate. I felt really isolated."

"My mother said, 'You didn't need to tell me. I knew it all the time.' But I wanted to tell her, because it was coming from me. I needed to tell her, even if she already knew."

"I've always been proud that I wasn't embarrassed about being a lesbian. I always enjoyed being able to open up other people's minds about it. Being different for me was a way of teaching people to respect others and to open their minds."

Source: R. Bell. (1988). *Changing bodies, changing lives: A book for teens on sex and relationships.* New York: Random House. For more commentaries from adolescent homosexuals you may want to read S. Alyson's *Young, gay and proud;* A. Heron's *One teenager in ten: Writings by gay and lesbian youth;* and A. Fricke's *Reflections of a rock lobster: A story about growing up gay* (Boston: Alyson Publications). (1980).

is now agreed that our sexual orientation cannot be changed through therapy, behavior modification, or such shame-invoking approaches as harassment and ridicule (Coleman & Remafedi, 1989; Gonsiorek, 1988). Assumptions by counselors, religious personnel, or parents that homosexuals can somehow be converted into heterosexuals are as erroneous as assumptions that heterosexuals can be converted into homosexuals. The goal of teachers, counselors, physicians, and others who work with gay adolescents and their families, therefore, is to help them come to terms with homosexuality in a homophobic society.

Problems Confronting Homosexual Adolescents

Like heterosexuals, homosexuals present the full range of emotional and sexual adjustment—from the happy and well adjusted to the unhappy and severely disturbed. Although being homosexual does not of itself cause psychological problems, living in a homophobic society does adversely affect many gay and lesbian youths. In fact, many of the problems that these young people experience stem directly from the cruelty and lack of support in our society, ranging from physical and verbal abuse to benign neglect (Coleman & Remafedi, 1989).

Homophobia As the adolescents' comments in Box 10.7 illustrate, we are still a long way from being a society in which homosexuals can feel safe and accepted. Despite our having become more tolerant, our culture still expresses hostility, both overtly and covertly, toward gays. Our biases range from a denial that homosexuals exist, especially among teenagers, to indictments of gays as diseased or criminal people. Most schools, religious institutions, neighborhoods, and employers make clear that homosexuals are unwanted. Well before adolescence, children have learned that being called a "fag" or a "dyke" is a supreme insult, even without being quite certain what the terms actually mean.

Much of the cruelty and prejudice to which gay teenagers are subjected stems from our **homophobia,** the irrational fear or hatred of homosexuals. This term, literally meaning "fear of man," is used to describe those of us who have an excessive dislike or excessive fear of homosexuals. Not surprisingly, as occurs with other forms of prejudice, homophobic people are generally the least likely to have had any interactions with gays—a finding that suggests that one way to reduce this fear and hatred is to bring gay and heterosexual people into more, not less, contact with one another (Gonsiorek, 1988). Among heterosexuals, homophobia is most commonly manifested as prejudice toward or discomfort with homosexuals. Among gays, who are, of course, also raised in a homophobic society, homophobia is typically manifested as self-hatred and shame.

Peer rejection Given that we are more restricted by gender roles as teenagers than at any other period of our lives, gay teenagers are in a particularly precarious position. Both gay and heterosexual males experience intense peer pressure to be tough and act like a man, while females are equally pressured into being feminine by heterosexual standards. Even for heterosexuals who do not fit these stereotypes, rejection and teasing from peers can be heartbreakingly cruel; but for gay teenagers, the failure to fit these gender stereotypes can be felt as a total rejection of the self.

Moreover, gay teenagers are often forced to withdraw from the social experiences that help individuals form their identities during adolescence. For some, socializing with either males or females can be difficult. Interacting with people of the same gender may arouse strong sexual or emotional feelings, and interacting with the other gender may be a painful reminder of not being heterosexual. The net effect is that gay teenagers often have to resort to protective strategies to avoid these painful encounters. They may retreat from interacting with their peers, withdrawing to relatively conflict-free activities, such as schoolwork or hobbies. Just at the time of life when our sexual needs increase, they are often forced to hide or deny their needs for sex and companionship.

Inevitably, as teenagers most of us have to face the confusion and heartbreak associated with learning to date, falling in and out of love, and coming to terms with our own sexuality. For gay teenagers, however, these experiences and feelings are compounded by living in a society where they are usually made to feel that they are "sick," "deviant," or "queer." As a consequence, in many communities gay youths have had to form their own social organizations in order to create some semblance of the sexual and social world that we all need as a normal part of our adolescence. Fortunately, literature and counseling are now available to help gay teenagers examine the struggles that characterize same-sex partnerships and help them create loving, stable, satisfying relationships (Berzon, 1990; Preston & Swann, 1989). For the most part, however, gay adolescents must resolve their social and sexual issues alone in a society that typically ignores or ridicules their needs for love, acceptance, and companionship.

Lack of role models In the midst of their confusion, when they could most benefit from the guidance of well-adjusted, older gay people, most gay adolescents are either denied role models or encounter adults who are not positive models (Gonsiorek, 1988). Because of our lingering myth that homosexuals intentionally seek out children and teenagers for sex, older gay adults have feared reaching out to younger gay people who could profit from their counsel and guidance. (In fact, most of the adults who sexually exploit children and teenagers are heterosexual men.) Isolated from well-adjusted adult role models, many gay teenagers are forced to resort to frequenting bars or other public meeting places, where they are most likely to meet gay adults who are intoxicated, are emotionally or sexually exploitative, or carry a sexual disease (which is also the case for heterosexuals who frequent places like public bars).

Family tensions In addition to being without role models, most gay people have a painfully difficult time telling their own families about this aspect of their identities—or, as painfully, having to keep this aspect of themselves secret from those they love. Fortunately, there are now support groups, books, and counselors for parents coming to terms with their gay children's lives (Borhek, 1988; Griffin, Wirth, & Wirth, 1986; Muller, 1987; Rafkin, 1987). From this literature we have learned that before "coming out" to their parents, gay children should first question their motives. If they need their parents' approval to feel at ease about being gay, the disclosure is not likely to succeed. In other words, the young person who still feels ashamed of his or her homosexuality and announces, "Mom and Dad, I have something awful I want to tell you" is not likely to receive as positive a response as those who have already arrived at a level of self-acceptance that enables them to say, "Mom and Dad, I've been wanting to share something with you because it's important to me and I care about you."

Unfortunately, many young people are deprived of telling their parents because their parents learn the news from other sources. Moreover, when the issue of homosexuality emerges, both parents and teenagers often hold it responsible for all the family's difficulties. The choice of coming out to parents is seldom a choice between pain and no pain. Regardless of the circumstances, there is almost always pain. In some cases, this initial pain gives way to greater intimacy and understanding, while in too many others, the pain destroys what few bonds existed between parents and children.

Even for those families that do make it through the transition of adjusting to their child's homosexuality, there is a period of grieving (Borhek, 1988). The gay person grieves for the losses of the benefits that we offer only to heterosexuals: the loss of job security, the loss of police protection (gays are vulnerable to harassment from police, as well as from their fellow citizens), and the loss of legal rights that heterosexual couples have in such matters as inheritance, marriage, and insurance benefits. Likewise, the parents of homosexual children also have losses to grieve: probably, though not always, the loss of being future grandparents, the loss of socially approved rituals such as marriage ceremonies for their children, and the loss of social status that usually accompanies having a gay child.

Religious development Most gay adolescents also have to tolerate religious condemnation as well. Since many people's homophobia is rooted in their interpretations of biblical passages that they believe condemn homosexuality as a sin, gay teenagers often feel cast aside by their religion. At some point, therefore, it can be helpful for gays and their families, as well as for society as a whole, to explore the impact that religious beliefs have on feelings and behavior. In this endeavor, religious personnel can help us examine the labeling of heterosexuality as good and homosexuality as bad. Instead, we can be helped to focus on the goodness or badness of such forms of behavior as sexual exploitation, sexual abuse, and sexual irresponsibility rather than on sexual orientation per se (Borhek, 1988; Griffin, Wirth, & Wirth, 1986; Scroggs, 1983).

Identity development Coming to terms with the religious aspects of being gay is only one part of the process of forming a healthy identity—an identity typically formed in four stages: sensitization, confusion, identity assumption, and commitment (Troiden, 1988). Before puberty, most lesbians and gay males have childhood experiences that give them the sense of being different from their peers. Although these childhood experiences are not related to sexuality per se, they do sensitize the gay child to the fact that he or she is not like other children.

Once puberty begins, however, this somehow being different feeling becomes more clearly identified as sexual. By middle to late adolescence, most gay teenagers have begun to recognize themselves as being sexually attracted to members of their own gender. Even at this point, however, the adolescent usually wonders whether it's "just a phase" or "just experimentation or curiosity," rather than clearly identifying himself or herself as homosexual. In fact, a large majority of lesbians and gay males have both heterosexual and homosexual interests and experiences as teenagers.

Interestingly, gay and heterosexual males share several patterns in their roles as males in our society. As a general rule, gay males are aware of their same-sex attractions sooner than gay females, usually at about the age of 13 for males and 16 for females. Just as heterosexual males are more likely to act on their sexual feelings sooner than heterosexual females, gay males act sooner than lesbians. Lesbians usually do not have their first homosexual experience until the age of 20, while most gay males have their first experiences between the ages of 14 and 16. Also like heterosexuals, gay males are more apt to have sex without having an intimate emotional relationship, while lesbians, like heterosexual girls, are more apt to have a close emotional bond with their lovers. In other words, whether heterosexual or homosexual, most boys become sexually active at an earlier age, have more partners, and have more casual sex than do heterosexual girls or lesbians.

While most gay males and females suspect as adolescents that they are homosexual, they usually do not incorporate their homosexuality into their identity until their 20s. That is, most gay teenagers do not identify themselves as homosexual to themselves or to other gays until after adolescence. The act of self-disclosure is not typical of adolescents. During adolescence, most gay youths experience so-called identity confusion, sometimes avoiding their sexuality altogether by directing their attention elsewhere or by trying to force themselves into being heterosexual. As teenagers, gays may vehemently ridicule homosexuals or make rigorous attempts to eradicate their homosexual feelings. In the ways we all use defense mechanisms, gay teenagers try to postpone the realization that they are gay in a heterosexual, homophobic culture.

After adolescence, however, most gay males and females come to accept their sexual orientation as part of their adult identities. Even during this time, gays may try passing as heterosexuals to all but their most trusted friends. Leading double lives, they protect themselves from persecution at work or at school by simply letting others assume they are part of the heterosexual majority. Once a serious, committed sexual relationship comes into their lives, however, most gay women and men begin to disclose their identities to some of their trusted heterosexual friends and family members. Although not ashamed of their homosexuality and not wishing they could become heterosexual, even with this well-adjusted and well-integrated identity, most gay adults wisely exercise caution regarding the disclosure of their sexual orientation. Not even in the case of family members is it always advisable or wise to disclose being homosexual. Indeed, it is not advisable to push gay teenagers into disclosing their sexual orientation to friends and family members as a way of demonstrating "self-acceptance" or "mental health." Although each person's circumstances are unique, most gay people choose not to come out as adolescents but to wait until later in their lives.

Suicide and AIDS Not surprisingly, given the multitude of problems confronting gay teenagers, many feel depressed and overwhelmed. Although studies of adolescent suicide seldom gather data about the individual's sexual orientation, data are now suggesting that gay teenagers do have a higher suicide rate than heterosexuals (Coleman & Remafedi, 1989). Moreover, gay adolescents are at a higher risk than heterosexuals of contracting AIDS, in part because their first sexual encounters often occur with partners who are 6 or 7 years older and who were met in bars or other public areas where the incidence of disease is highest. Then, too, gay adolescents are less likely than heterosexuals to have received applicable information in their sex education classes or from peers about how to prevent disease (Remafedi, 1988; Zenilman, 1988).

Helping gay teenagers Recognizing the emotional stress and disease to which so many gay teenagers are subjected, a number of professional organizations are now urging their members to change their behavior and attitudes. For example, the National Education Association adopted a resolution in 1989 stating that every school district should provide counseling by trained personnel for gay students or for those struggling with their sexual orientation (Flax, 1990). Some schools also provide special programs for heterosexual students in an effort to reduce homophobia and harassment against gay students. These schools also include issues about homosexuality in the curriculum and library materials, such as *The Truth about Alex,* a book for teenagers that shows how a high-school senior decides not to renounce a friend and football teammate who is gay (Snyder, 1988). Likewise, the American Academy of Pediatrics has urged physicians to provide relevant health care and information for those young patients who are gay (1983).

CONCLUSION

The issues involved in teenage sexuality are indeed complex: Should adolescents be given easier access to contraceptives, and if so, when? What types of sex education are appropriate for preteens and adolescents, and who should determine the curriculum? How can we create a society in which gay adolescents feel comfortable and accepted? Should pregnant adolescents be encouraged to terminate their pregnancies or to get married and try to raise their children?

Clearly, no simple answers are available when such controversial legal and ethical issues are at stake. Not everyone will be able to agree on the answers, nor will politicians and educators be able to find a way to please all their constituents when it comes to sensitive, inflammatory issues such as these. Nevertheless, each of us must stop sidestepping these questions in our efforts to protect our political or social positions or in our desire to keep the peace among our friends, co-workers, or family members. As have other industrialized nations of the world, we must somehow move forward in a less tentative and less contradictory manner in resolving the problems of teenage pregnancy, teenage childbearing, and sexually transmitted disease.

QUESTIONS FOR DISCUSSION AND REVIEW

Review questions

1. How do male and female attitudes toward sexuality differ, and what accounts for these differences?
2. Has there been a sexual revolution? Cite specific statistics from the past and present to support your answer. If there have been dramatic changes, what accounts for them?
3. How sexually active are our society's adolescents? How do gender, race, socioeconomic status, and education affect their sexual decisions?
4. What other factors contribute to adolescents' sexual decisions?
5. Which adolescents are the most likely to be sexually active? to use contraceptives? to terminate their unplanned pregnancies?
6. How have adolescents' contraceptive habits changed in recent decades? What accounts for these changes?
7. What types of contraceptive do most adolescents use? How responsible are adolescents in using contraceptives? What could our society do to encourage better contraception among the young?
8. How do our teenagers compare to those in other industrialized countries in regard to pregnancy and contraception? What accounts for these differences?
9. How do most male adolescents regard their role in contraception? What can be done to improve their attitudes and change their behavior?
10. What are the advantages and disadvantages of the types of contraceptive now available for teenagers? Explain exactly how each of these contraceptives prevents pregnancy.
11. How common are pregnancy, abortion, and teenage childbearing among African American, white, and Hispanic youths? How have these rates changed during the past two decades? Support your answer with specific statistics.
12. What are the psychological and physical consequences of terminating a pregnancy in comparison to becoming a teenage parent?
13. How does becoming a teenage parent affect the father, mother, child, and taxpayer?
14. How are each of the following diseases transmitted, recognized (the symptoms), prevented, and treated: AIDS, herpes, gonorrhea, syphilis, and yeast infections? How common is each? What are the physical consequences, if treated and if untreated, of each?
15. How seriously are adolescents treating AIDS? Why? What could be done to change their behavior and attitudes about this disease?
16. What is the present status of sex education in our society? What improvements could be made in educating our young people about sex?
17. What are some of the common misconceptions that adolescents have about sexually transmitted diseases, contraception, and conception?
18. What factors determine our sexual orientations?
19. How does being raised by a lesbian mother affect children?
20. How common is homosexuality, and what types of problems do gay adolescents face in our society? What might be done to alleviate some of these problems?

Questions for discussion and debate

1. How do you feel about adolescents' becoming sexually active? What is sexually "moral" and "immoral" for teenagers? for college students? for adults? What accounts for your personal attitudes on this subject?
2. What have you noticed about the differences or similarities in males' and females' sexual attitudes and behavior? How have your attitudes changed since adolescence? Why?
3. How would you design sex education in our society to reduce teenage pregnancy and sexually transmitted diseases? Remember that the media, merchants, and parents are also a part of sex education.
4. What role do you feel the schools and the media should play in sex education? For example, should contraceptives be advertised on TV? Should clinics be set up in schools to provide contraceptives for students? If so, for what age?
5. What contraceptive would you recommend that adolescents use? Why?
6. If you could relive your own adolescence in regard to your sexual attitudes and experiences, what would you change? What would you not change? Why?
7. How do you feel about males' sexual attitudes and contraceptive habits? If there are aspects you would like changed, how would you recommend our society bring about these changes?
8. How do you feel about adolescents' terminating an unplanned pregnancy? What laws would you like to see our society adopt in regard to teenage abortions? Do you think the "morning after" pill should be approved by the FDA?
9. Should we encourage teenage couples to get married and raise their child? Why or why not? If you were 16 and pregnant (or if your girlfriend were pregnant) what would you do? What would your parents recommend?
10. How do you feel about adolescents living with a mother or a father who is gay? Should gay parents be legally denied custody of their children or denied the right to adopt children?
11. How do you feel about the comments of the adolescent mothers and the gay students in Boxes 10.5 and 10.7, respectively? What experiences have you had with either pregnant or gay teenagers, and how have these affected your attitudes?
12. How have your attitudes and behavior, and those of your friends, been influenced by AIDS and other sexually transmitted diseases? In what ways have you or someone you know been sexually responsible or irresponsible?
13. What are the most instructive experiences you or any of your friends have had in regard to your sexual attitudes and behavior? How was sex education handled in your school? by your parents?
14. Who or what was most influential in determining your sexual attitudes and decisions as a teenager and now?
15. What experiences have you had with gay people, and how have these affected your attitudes and behavior? Which of your beliefs about gay people have you modified since your adolescence? Why?

GLOSSARY

acquired immune deficiency syndrome (AIDS) An incurable disease that is transmitted through infected hypodermic needles, sexual intercourse, or contact with infected blood and kills its victims by destroying their immune systems.

asymptomatic carriers People who have a disease but show no visible symptoms.

bisexual A male or female whose sexual preferences includes members of both genders.

cervical sponge A contraceptive device that covers the opening to the cervix, thus preventing sperm from entering the uterus.

chancres Body sores that are the initial symptoms of certain sexually transmitted diseases.

gonorrhea A sexually transmitted bacterial disease that can be cured with antibiotics but when left untreated can cause infertility and other complications of the urogenital tract.

herpes A sexually transmitted virus that causes an incurable disease whose initial symptoms include genital blisters and flulike symptoms.

homophobia Excessive fear or hatred of homosexuals, sometimes linked to a fear of one's own homosexual feelings or tendencies.

homosexual A male or female whose sexual desires are for members of his or her own gender.

human immunodeficiency virus (HIV) The virus that causes AIDS.

Intrauterine device (IUD) A contraceptive object, usually made of plastic but sometimes made of copper, that is inserted by a physician into the uterus to prevent implantation of a fertilized egg in the uterine wall.

"morning after" pill A contraceptive pill that, when taken soon after intercourse, prevents a fertilized egg from implanting in the uterine wall.

rhythm method An attempt to prevent pregnancy by abstaining from intercourse during the days when the woman is believed to be fertile.

sexually transmitted disease (S.T.D.) Any infection that is passed from person to person through oral, anal, or vaginal sexual activity.

syphilis A sexually transmitted disease that can be cured with antibiotics but that can cause death, blindness, and insanity if untreated.

REFERENCES

Abrahamse, A. (1988). Teenagers willing to consider single parenthood. *Family Planning Perspectives, 21,* 13–18.

Adler, T. (1989, June). New birth control ideas stalled. *APA Monitor,* p. 10.

Alan Guttmacher Institute. (1989). *Teenage pregnancy: The problem that hasn't gone away.* New York: Author.

Allgeier, E., & McCormick, N. (Eds.). (1983). *Changing boundaries: Gender roles and sexual behavior.* Palo Alto, CA: Mayfield.

Alyson, S. (1982). *Young, gay and proud.* Boston, MA: Alyson Publications.

American Academy of Pediatrics Committee on Adolescence. (1983). Homosexuality and adolescence. *Pediatrics, 72,* 249–250.

American Psychiatric Association. (1987). *Diagnostic and statistical manual of mental disorders.* Washington, DC: Author.

Becker, M., & Joseph, J. (1988). AIDS and behavioral change to reduce risk: A review. *American Journal of Public Health, 78,* 394.

Bell, R. (1988). *Changing bodies, changing lives: A book for teens on sex and relationships.* New York: Random House.

Berzon, B. (1990). *Permanent partners: Building gay and lesbian relationships that last.* New York: Dutton.

Billy, J., & Udry, R. (1985). The influence of male and female best friends on adolescent sexual behavior. *Adolescence, 77,* 21–32.

Bolton, F. (1983). *The pregnant adolescent: Problems of premature parenthood.* Beverly Hills, CA: Sage.

Borhek, M. (1988). Helping gay and lesbian adolescents and their families. *Journal of Adolescent Health Care, 9,* 123–129.

Boston Women's Health Collective (1988). *Our bodies, ourselves.* New York: Simon & Schuster.

Bozett, D. (Ed.). (1987). *Gay and lesbian parents.* New York: Praeger.

Braddock, J., Crain, R., & McPartland, J. (1984). A long term view of school desegregation. *Phi Delta Kappan, 43,* 259–265.

Byrne, D., & Fishser, W. (1983). *Adolescents, sex and contraception.* Hillsale, NJ: Erlbaum.

Center for Population Options. (1989). *Teenage pregnancy: Cost to taxpayers.* Washington, DC: Author.

Centers for Disease Control. (1988a). HIV related beliefs, knowledge and behavior among high school students. *Morbidity and Mortality Weekly Report, 37,* 394.

Centers for Disease Control. (1988b). Prevalence of AIDS virus antibody in U.S. military personnel. *Morbidity and Mortality Weekly Report, 37,* 461.

Centers for Disease Control. (1988c). *Sexually transmitted disease statistics.* Atlanta: Author.

Centers for Disease Control. (1989). *HIV/AIDS surveillance report.* Atlanta: Author.

Clark, M., Springer, K., & Alderman; B., (1986, December 29). An effective abortion pill. *Newsweek,* p. 47.

Coleman, E., & Remafedi, G. (1989). Gay, lesbian and bisexual adolescents. *Journal of Counseling and Development, 68,* 36–40.

Dash, L. (1989). *When children want children: The urban crisis of teenage childbearing.* New York: William Morrow.

DiClemente, R., Zorn, J., & Temoshok, L. (1987). A survey of knowledge, attitudes and beliefs about AIDS in San Francisco. *Journal of Applied Social Psychology, 17,* 216–230.

Duberman, M., Vicinus, M., & Chauncey, G. (Eds.). (1989). *Hidden from history: Reclaiming the gay and lesbian past.* New York: New American Library.

Elster, A., & Lamb, M. (Eds.). (1986). *Adolescent fatherhood.* Hillsdale, NJ: Erlbaum.

Falk, P. (1989). Lesbian mothers. *American Psychologist, 44,* 941–948.

Flax, E. (1990, February 7). Special problems of homosexual students need attention. *Education Week,* pp. 1, 24.

Forrest, J. (1986). *Women ever pregnant before age twenty.* New York: Alan Guttmacher Institute.

Forrest, J., & Silverman, J. (1989). What public school teachers teach about preventing pregnancy, AIDS and sexually transmitted diseases. *Family Planning Perspectives, 21,* 65–72.

Frank, D. (Ed.). (1983). *Deep blue funk and other stories: Portraits of teenage parents.* Chicago: University of Chicago Press.

Franklin, D. (1988). Race, class and adolescent pregnancy. *American Journal of Orthopsychiatry, 58,* 339–354.

Furstenberg, F., Brooks-Gunn, J., & Chase, L. (1989). Teenaged pregnancy and childbearing. *American Psychologist, 44,* 313–320.

Furstenberg, F. Brooks-Gunn, J., & Morgan, S. (1987). *Adolescent mothers in later life.* New York: Cambridge University Press.

Gallup, G. (1985). Premarital sex. *The Gallup Report, 237,* Princeton, NJ: Author.

General Accounting Office. (1988). *AIDS education: Reaching populations at higher risk.* Washington, DC: Author.

Gonsiorek, J. (1988). Mental health issues of gay and lesbian adolescents. *Journal of Adolescent Health Care, 9,* 114–123.

Green, R. (1987). *The "sissy boy" syndrome and the development of homosexuality.* New Haven, CT: Yale University Press.

Greenberg, D. (1988). *The construction of homosexuality.* Chicago: University of Chicago Press.

Griffin, C., Wirth, M., & Wirth, A. (1986). *Beyond acceptance.* Englewood Cliffs, NJ: Prentice-Hall.

Guinan, M. (1986). Sexually transmitted diseases may reverse the revolution. *Journal of the American Medical Association, 255,* 1665.

Hayes, C. (1987). *Risking the future: Adolescent sexuality, pregnancy and childbearing.* Washington, DC: National Academy Press.

Hendricks, L., & Solomon, A. (1987). Reaching black male adolescent parents through nontraditional techniques. *Child and Youth Services, 9,* 111–124.

Henshaw, S., Kenney, A., Somberg, D., & VanVort, J. (1989). *Teenage pregnancy in the U.S.* New York: Alan Guttmacher Institute.

Heron, A. (1983). *One teenager in ten: Writings by gay and lesbian youth.* Boston, MA: Alyson Publications.

Hofferth, S., & Hayes, C. (Eds.). (1987). *Risking the future* (Vol. 2). Washington, DC: National Academy Press.

Jones, E., Forrest, N., Goldman, S., Henshaw, R., Lincoln, J., Westoff, C., & Wulf, D. (1986). *Teenage pregnancy in industrialized countries.* New Haven, CT: Yale University Press.

Juhasz, A., & Schneider, M. (1987). Adolescent sexuality: Values, morality and decision making. *Adolescence, 22,* 580–590.

Kahn, A., & Kamerman, S. (Eds.). (1988). *Child support: From debt collection to social policy.* Newbury Park, CA: Sage.

Kegeles, S., Adler, N., & Irwin, C. (1988). Sexually active adolescents and condoms. *American Journal of Public Health, 78,* 460–466.

Kenney, A., Guardada, S., & Brown, L. (1989). Sex education and AIDS education in the schools. *Family Planning Perspectives, 21,* 56–64.

Kinsey, A., Pomeroy, W., & Martin, C. (1948). *Sexual behavior in the human male.* Philadelphia: Saunders.

Kinsey, A., Pomeroy, W., Martin, D., & Gebhard, P. (1953). *Sexual behavior in the human female.* Philadelphia: Saunders.

Kirp, D. (1989). *Learning by heart: AIDS and schoolchildren in America's communities.* New Brunswick, NJ: Rutgers University Press.

Koop, C. (1987). *Understanding AIDS: A message from the surgeon general.* Washington, DC: U.S. Public Health Service.

Lancaster, J., & Hamburg, B. (Eds.). (1986). *School age pregnancy and parenthood.* Hawthorne, NY: Aldine.

Landers, S. (1989, May). Severe stress after abortions is rare. *APA Monitor,* p. 32.

Lewin, M. (1985). Unwanted intercourse: The difficulty of saying no. *Psychology of Women Quarterly, 2,* 184–192.

Lewis, C. (1987). Minors' competence to consent to abortion. *American Psychologist, 42,* 84–88.

Lopez, N. (1987). *Hispanic teenage pregnancy.* Washington, DC: National Council of La Raza.

Marecek, J. (1987). Counseling adolescents with problem pregnancies. *American Psychologist, 42,* 89–93.

Margulies, L. (1987, February 7). David of TV's "Valerie" faces the issue of contraception. *Winston Salem Journal,* p. 17.

McLaughlin, S. (1986). The effects of sequencing of marriage and first birth during adolescence. *Family Planning Perspectives, 18,* 12–18.

Melton, G. (Ed.). (1986). *Adolescent abortion: Psychological and legal issues.* Lincoln: University of Nebraska Press.

Melton, G. (1987). Legal regulation of adolescent abortion. *American Psychologist, 42,* 79–83.

Miller, P., & Simon, W. (1980). The development of sexuality in adolescence. In J. Adelson (Ed.), *Handbook of adolescent psychology* (pp. 383–408). New York: Wiley Interscience.

Miller, S. (1983). *The influence of adolescent childbearing on the incidence, types and severity of child maltreatment.* New York: Child Welfare League of America.

Moffatt, B. (1988). *When someone you love has AIDS.* New York: Plume.

Money, J. (1988). *Gay, straight and in-between.* New York: Oxford University Press.

Moore, K., Simms, M., & Betsey, C. (1986). *Choice and circumstance: Racial differences in adolescent sexuality and fertility.* New Brunswick, NJ: Transaction.

Morrison, D. (1985). Adolescent contraceptive behavior: A review. *Psychological Bulletin, 98,* 538–568.

Muller, A. (1987). *Parents matter: Parents' relationships with lesbian daughters and gay sons.* Tallahassee, FL: Naiad Press.

National Association of State Boards of Education. (1989). *AIDS education survey.* Alexandria, VA: Author.

Ory, H., Forrest, J., & Lincoln, R. (1983). *Making choices: Evaluating the health risks and benefits of birth control methods.* New York: Alan Guttmacher Institute.

Pleck, J. (1989). Correlate of black adolescent males' condom use. *Journal of Adolescent Research, 4,* 247–253.

Pleck, J., Sonenstein, F., & Swain, S. (1988). Adolescent males' sexual behavior and contraceptive use. *Journal of Adolescent Research, 3,* 275–284.

Preston, J., & Swann, G. (1989). *Safe sex: The ultimate erotic guide.* New York: Plume.

Rafkin, L. (1987). *Different daughters: A book by mothers of lesbians.* Pittsburgh: Cleis Press.

Ramafedi, G. (1988). Preventing the sexual transmission of AIDS during adolescence. *Journal of Adolescent Health Care, 9,* 139–144.

Savin-Williams, R. (1988). Theoretical perspectives accounting for adolescent homosexuality. *Journal of Adolescent Health Care, 9,* 95–105.

Scales, P., & Beckstein, D. (1982). From macho to mutuality: Helping young men make effective decisions about sex, contraception and pregnancy. In I. Stuart & C. Wells (Eds.), *Pregnancy in adolescence* (pp. 264–290). New York: Van Nostrand.

Scroggs, R. (1983). *The New Testament and homosexuality.* Philadelphia: Fortress Press.

Snyder, A. (1988). *The truth about Alex.* New York: Signet.

Sonenstein, F., Pleck, J., & Ku, L. (1989). Sexual activity, condom use and AIDS awareness among adolescent males. *Family Planning Perspectives, 21,* 152–158.

Sowell, T. (1981). *Ethnic America: A history.* New York: Basic Books.

Strunin, L., & Hingson, R. (1987). AIDS and adolescents. *Pediatrics, 79,* 825–828.

Thornburg, J. (1981). Sex information obtained during adolescence. *Journal of Early Adolescence, 1,* 171–183.

Three AIDS carriers win school settlement. (1988, October 12) *Education Week,* p. 12.

Tripp, C. (1987). *The homosexual matrix.* New York: Meridian.

Troiden, R. (1988). *Gay and lesbian identity: A sociological analysis.* Dix Hills, NJ: General Hall.

Vinovskis, M. (1988). *An epidemic of adolescent pregnancy?* New York: Oxford University Press.

Zayas, L., Schinke, S., & Casareno, D. (1987). Hispanic adolescent fathers. *Children and Youth Services Review, 9,* 235–248.

Zelnick, M., Kantner, J., & Ford, K. (1981). *Sex and pregnancy in adolescence.* Beverly Hills, CA: Sage.

Zelnick, M., & Shah, F. (1983). First intercourse among young Americans. *Family Planning Perspectives, 15,* 64–72.

Zenilman, J. (1988). Sexually transmitted diseases in homosexual adolescents. *Journal of Adolescent Health Care, 9,* 129–139.

Resources for teaching about AIDS

AIDS Education Newsletter. National Professional Resources, Box 1479, Port Chester, NY 10573.

Frazer, K., & Mitchell, P. *Effective AIDS education: A policymaker's guide.* National Association of State Boards of Education, 1011 Cameron St., Alexandria, VA 22314.

Halleron, T., & Pisaneschi, J. *AIDS information resources directory.* American Foundation for AIDS Research, 40 West 57th St., New York, NY 10019.

Institute of Medicine. *Confronting AIDS: Update 1988.* National Academy Press, 2101 Constitution Ave., Washington, DC 20418.

National Safety Council. *Administrators' guide to AIDS* and *Guide to teaching about AIDS.* 444 North Michigan Ave., Chicago, IL 60611.

Quackenbush, M., & Nelson, M. *The AIDS challenge: Prevention education for young people.* Network Publications, Box 1830, Santa Cruz, CA 95061.

Schwartz, L. *AIDS answers for teens.* The Learning Works, Box 6187, Santa Barbara, CA 93160.

11 Adolescents and Vocations

CHAPTER OUTLINE

ADOLESCENTS' VOCATIONAL ATTITUDES

ADOLESCENT EMPLOYMENT

THE ADVANTAGES AND DISADVANTAGES OF ADOLESCENT EMPLOYMENT

ADOLESCENT UNEMPLOYMENT

REDUCING YOUTH UNEMPLOYMENT

VOCATIONAL PREPARATION

The Economic Forecast: A Nation at Risk?
High-School Vocational Education: The Pros and Cons
The Value of a College Education

THEORIES OF VOCATIONAL DEVELOPMENT

The Differentialist Perspective
The Developmentalist Perspective
A Challenge to Traditional Theories

FEMALES' VOCATIONAL DEVELOPMENT

CONCLUSION

GOALS AND OBJECTIVES

The materials presented in this chapter will enable you to:

- Compare the vocational values of contemporary adolescents to the values of adolescents in the 1960s and 1970s
- Present the advantages and disadvantages of employment during adolescence
- Enumerate the differences between the leading theories of vocational development
- Explain the differences between male and female vocational development
- Advise adolescents and their parents about the value of college or technical education
- Present a statistical profile of employed and unemployed adolescents in today's society
- Consider the roles that family, race, gender, and other sociocultural factors play in determining adolescents' vocational aspirations and achievements
- Present the arguments against the traditional theories of vocational development
- Describe several different approaches to vocational training being used in secondary schools today

CONCEPTS AND TERMINOLOGY

developmentalist perspective
differentialist perspective
Fair Labor Standards Act
Foxfire project
Holland's occupational types
satellite schools
Strong-Campbell Interest Inventory

ADOLESCENTS' VOCATIONAL ATTITUDES

How do adolescents feel about working? Do they think much about their future jobs? Are they making wise decisions in terms of preparing themselves for their future work? What should adults be doing to help teenagers prepare for their futures as wage earners? Should we encourage them to have part-time jobs and to enroll in vocational education classes? Such questions are the focus of vocational psychologists—and of our nation's leading economists. According to many economists, we are now a "nation at risk" in that our young work force is not educated enough to keep our society competitive in the world market. Worse still, the fastest growing groups of young people—the impoverished and the racial minorities—are the most poorly equipped to handle the demands of the jobs on which our society depends for its well-being. In other words, adolescents' attitudes about work and the way we are preparing them for their future jobs are more than just a matter of concern to the adolescents and their parents. Like it or not, all our financial futures are indirectly affected by the attitudes and skills of today's adolescents because we each depend upon a competent work force to maintain our country's place in the world market—a place that controls such vital day-to-day issues as the value of the U.S. dollar.

What, then, are adolescents' attitudes toward work? Are they a lackadaisical bunch who seldom think about the future, or are they concerned about and motivated to do well in their future jobs? One way of answering these questions is to look at the responses of 17,000 high-school seniors who were asked, "If you had all the money you could ever spend in your lifetime, would you still want to work?" Nearly 85% answered "yes" (Bachman, Johnston, & O'Malley, 1985). Also, more adolescents are now working, and those who work are putting in longer hours than at any time in the past 40 years. For example, in 1940 only 1 in 25 10th-grade boys and only 1 in 100 10th-grade girls worked while attending school, whereas today almost one third of all 10th-graders have part-time jobs. By the time they graduate from high school, almost 80% of all teenagers have held a job (Charner & Fraser, 1987). In short then, it seems that most adolescents are committed to working, both in word and in deed.

Whether for good or bad, high-school and college students do seem to have become more focused on the financial aspects of their future jobs. As Table 11.1 illustrates, today's high-school seniors are more concerned than youths in the 1970s about finding work that pays well and offers financial security (Bachman, Johnston, & O'Malley, 1985). Such findings have led some commentators to lament that the hippie mentality of the 1960s has given way to yuppie attitudes. At a time when Wall Street scandals have become national buzzwords, it appears that some adolescents have developed a "yuppie obsession" with making money (Jennings,

A CLOSER LOOK 11.1

Greed on Sesame Street?

Welcome to the Dollars and Cents summer camp in Marco Island, Florida, where adolescents attend lectures and seminars on mutual funds, the *Wall Street Journal,* and investment strategies. Playing games in which they invest their pretend money and in which they have to make ethical decisions about loaning money to friends, these young people are preparing themselves for their vocational futures. As one 14-year-old said, "I want to be a millionaire, and this is one way to get there." Or, in the words of a 17-year-old, who also happens to be the youngest stockbroker in the country, "I'd like to become a corporate raider or get involved with heavy-duty arbitrage."

Recognizing that our adult obsession with money and business is filtering down to the young, the Young Americans Bank in Denver features scaled-down teller windows and step-chairs for their young clients. The bank also offers loans to its young customers, a move that has raised the ire of local educators. The bank offers MasterCards with a $100 credit limit and an annual interest rate of 18.8% to its depositors who are age 12 or older. Although a parent's cosignature is required for those under 18, the young customers will receive credit directly and will be billed in their own names. Says the bank's founder, "Kids will learn that if they default on a bicycle, we're going to repossess it." In similar fashion, the First Women's Bank of New York is launching a venture to open its branches on the premises of Schwarz toy stores.

Even children's publications are tapping the market. *Junior Scholastic,* a 16-page biweekly newspaper for children between 11 and 14, now offers an economics page once a month. Another bimonthly publication, *Penny Power,* devotes itself exclusively to financial matters. This periodical features such articles as "How to ask your parents for more money" and "Eight ways to goof-proof your search for a summer job." Increasingly, youngsters are entering the marketplace as inventors and entrepreneurs. Three adolescents from Kansas, for example, have plans to distribute their frozen soy-based dessert, Ice Whip, nationwide given its success in the Kansas City area. Said one member of the trio, "We've got big dreams. We want fancy cars, spending money, and all the luxuries of being rich."

Source: Jennings. (1989, September 21). Financial educators take aim at bank's youth credit card. *Education Week,* p. 5; A. Miller & D. Tsiantar. (1987, July 20). Greed on Sesame Street? *Newsweek,* pp. 38–40.

1989). On the other hand, today's teenagers say they are less willing to sacrifice their personal happiness in pursuit of making money than were teenagers in the 1970s. Students who are planning to attend college, as well as those who are planning to get a job directly after high school, say they want more than just money from their future jobs. They also want personal satisfaction and intellectual challenge (Johnston, & O'Malley, 1985; Lewko, 1987).

ADOLESCENT EMPLOYMENT

Since so much of adolescents' time is spent at part-time jobs, we might well wonder what types of work they are doing. As you might guess, most teenagers work at fast-food places or as sales clerks and manual laborers. In a word, their

Table 11.1

Important Things in a Job (Percent Rating Very Important, Classes of 1976–1983)

	MALES					FEMALES				
	1976	*1978*	*1980*	*1982*	*1984*	*1976*	*1978*	*1980*	*1982*	*1984*
Interesting to do	84	87	85	85	86	92	91	91	91	89
Uses skills and abilities	65	69	68	68	66	76	74	76	76	76
Predictable, secure future	62	66	64	66	66	62	62	65	66	65
Good chances for advancement	59	67	65	66	67	54	59	61	65	64
See results of what you do	55	58	54	56	53	61	63	64	62	61
Chance to earn a good deal of money	54	56	58	61	61	40	44	50	52	54
Chance to make friends	47	47	47	46	45	61	61	59	57	58
Worthwhile to society	39	36	36	37	36	50	50	51	50	47
A job most people look up to and respect	32	33	36	36	38	36	39	39	43	43
High status, prestige	22	24	26	30	29	18	23	24	30	29

Source: J. Bachman, L. Johnston, & P. O'Malley. (1985). *Recent findings from Monitoring the Future.* Ann Arbor: University of Michigan, Institute for Social Research.

jobs are usually not very stimulating or challenging. As Table 11.2 illustrates, their jobs are also sex stereotyped in that most young adolescent girls are babysitters and maids, while the boys are laborers (Nilsen, 1984). Not surprisingly, given the types of jobs available on a part-time basis, many young people become disillusioned and cynical as a consequence of their experiences. The more fortunate ones, on the other hand, enjoy their work and feel a sense of pride and independence, as Box 11.2 illustrates (Cole, 1983; Glenbard East *Echo,* 1984; Lewko, 1987).

Why do we not offer adolescents more exciting work? Why are most of them having to do relatively boring, routine tasks? First, of course, their opportunities are limited by the fact that they are inexperienced and are only able to work part-time. In addition, our laws restrict adolescents to certain types of jobs. Enacted to protect children from physical and emotional abuse, child labor laws restrict the number of hours that minors can work as well as the types of work they can do. Under the federal **Fair Labor Standards Act,** children under the age of 14 cannot be employed in any manufacturing, mining, or processing occupation such as laundering clothes or dressing poultry. Minors are also prohibited from working for a public messenger service, from operating power-driven machinery, and from jobs involving transportation, warehousing, construction, or communications, with the exception of office or sales work. In most cases, state or federal laws also prohibit young teenagers from working in freezers or boiler rooms, loading and unloading heavy goods, or doing maintenance and repair work.

Table 11.2

Major Occupation Group of Employed Persons 16 to 24 Years Old: 1980 Annual Average (Percent of Civilian Noninstitutional Population)

	MALE		FEMALE	
	16–19 Years	*20–24 Years*	*16–19 Years*	*20–24 Years*
White collar workers	16.9	30.5	52.4	67.5
Professional, technical, and kindred workers	2.5	10.8	2.8	14.2
Managers and administrators, except farm	1.4	5.8	1.4	4.7
Sales workers	5.8	5.4	12.2	6.3
Clerical and kindred workers	7.2	8.5	36.0	42.2
Blue-collar workers	52.9	55.8	10.3	13.0
Craft and kindred workers	11.9	21.4	1.2	1.8
Operatives, including transport	18.2	22.8	6.6	9.6
Laborers, except farm	22.8	11.5	2.4	1.6
Service workers	24.0	10.4	35.9	18.8
Private household workers	0.2	(Z)	5.4	1.1
Service workers, except private household	23.8	10.4	30.5	17.7
Farm workers	6.2	3.3	1.5	0.7
Farmers and farm managers	0.5	1.0	(Z)	0.1
Farm laborers and supervisors	5.7	2.3	1.4	0.6
Total employed (thousands)	4,016	7,254	3,587	6,360
Percent	100.0	100.0	100.0	100.0

Note: (z) = 0.0
Source: U.S. Department of Commerce, Bureau of the Census, unpublished 1980 Current Population Survey data.

THE ADVANTAGES AND DISADVANTAGES OF ADOLESCENT EMPLOYMENT

Even though most adolescents' jobs are pretty boring, many of us still encourage them to work. In part, we are influenced by the belief that "idle hands are the devil's workshop." Then, too, we are influenced by the idea that jobs help adolescents develop a sense of responsibility, an understanding of the "real world," and invaluable lessons in budgeting and delayed gratification. But are our beliefs actually justified by the data we now have about adolescents' part-time jobs?

Undoubtedly some adolescents do profit from their part-time jobs. For those who have not done well in school or who have poor relationships with their parents, a job can be especially helpful in providing the opportunity to develop a sense of pride, responsibility, and independence. Others learn, perhaps for the first time in their lives, how to budget their time, how to communicate with adults, and how to manage money. Jobs that are connected to the school curriculum can also offer apprenticeship opportunities in which young people work closely with adults who serve as their mentors, not just as their employers. Teenage employment

11.2

ADOLESCENT VOICES

Adolescents' Views on Working

Charlotte, age 16, from Georgia:
"Well, the job that I had was not like I had expected it to be. I couldn't handle it. It was putting too many pressures on me. I mostly worked on the weekends, and that's when everything happens. I couldn't stand to see other people go out. I am not a lazy person. I just didn't like the job or the employers. They treatec me like I was a nobody. I was trained to work on a cash register, but as time passed they had me taking out trash, mopping a large floor, sweeping the floor, and cooking. They embarrassed me many times so I decided to just leave it alone."

Jason, age 17, from Kansas:
"Among my friends, maintaining a nice car is the primary reason for having a job. Others have jobs so they can get out of the house and away from mom and dad for a while. Also, having a job provides a form of independence from financial restrictions imposed by parents. My parents never allowed me to have a job during school. They say that they would rather give me an allowance than for me to be distracted from my studies. So far it has worked. My grade point average has been 3.8 to 4.0. In addition I have been able to participate in forensics, debate and the school plays. I feel that parents that allow and even encourage their teens to get an after school job for the experience are doing their children a great disservice. One's education and high school experience are much more important and valuable than the little bit of spending money acquired from minimum wage slave labor."

Kim, age 17, from Illinois:
"Teenage workers' biggest problem is that their

continued

also contributes to the economic well-being of local communities by increasing the purchasing power of the teenage consumer. From this somewhat mercenary viewpoint, employed adolescents are "good for business" because they have more money to spend on movies, records, cosmetics, clothes, and other youth-oriented products (Cole, 1983; Cook, 1983; Lewko, 1987).

Despite these potential advantages, however, the reality is that many adolescents do not reap many benefits from working. As a consequence, the value of working needs to be weighed against the benefits of not working for adolescents who are still in school. By way of illustration, a survey of 3,100 10th- and 11th-graders in California showed that working did not enhance their sense of social responsibility, their commitment to the welfare of others, or their tolerance of individual or cultural differences. In fact, the employed students expressed negative attitudes about working and had increased their use of marijuana and tobacco after going to work (Greenberger & Steinberg, 1986). Moreover, most jobs available to adolescents do not teach skills that can be applied in later life in the adult work force (Borus, 1984).

But don't jobs teach adolescents that "money doesn't grow on trees" and that "a penny saved is a penny earned"? Not often, according to the data. National surveys of high-school seniors suggest that most employed teenagers spend all their money on entertainment for themselves, save no money for the future, do

Box 11.2 continued

employers don't treat them with enough respect. One of my managers is constantly making plays at me. When I stand up for myself, he threatens me with my job."

Martin, age 18, from Nevada:
"I don't know why other teenagers work, but for me it is mainly parent pressure. I want to make them feel I'm good for something. Also I want to relieve them of some financial burden. I am a very materialistic person and very label conscious. I firmly believe you get what you pay for. Thus, I spend lots of money for the things I want."

Kevin, age 18, from Indiana:
"I work for a carpet cleaning company. My pay is good and my co-workers are real nice. I'm treated like an adult and a partner or co-worker. My only problem is when we clean a restaurant. I don't start until ten thirty or twelve at night so I usually get home from one thirty to three in the morning. This is a bit hard since I'll only get three to five hours sleep."

Sunni, age 15, from Indiana:
"I have a job training and showing horses for different farms. I can't imagine not having to go to the farm after school. Getting there on time, making sure all my horses I work are healthy and doing well is my way of being independent. It's not necessarily the money. It's more or less the way I try and earn respect for being responsible."

Brian, age 16, from Illinois:
"I think it's great to work. In my case I have to. My mother and father are divorced and I have to help my mom any way I can. So my brother and I got jobs. He works four nights a week at Woolworth's and I work for the city of Centralia as a sports director. We both make good money and we never have to ask for money. Sometimes we even give her money out of our checks. Don't get me wrong—my mom works too. We have made it for two years at our jobs and we love to work."

Source: Glenbard East *Echo*. (1989). *Teenagers themselves.* New York: Adama Books, pp. 77–87.

not contribute any money to their families, and do not budget even for their weekly expenditures. Ironically, part-time jobs might actually be teaching adolescents to have more self-centered, "give it to me now" attitudes. That is, adolescents who have worked during high school report being less satisfied with their standard of living after graduation than those who did not work as high-school students. These findings suggest that teenagers with part-time jobs become accustomed to an unrealistic standard of living as a consequence of being permitted to treat their money purely as discretionary income. Having become prematurely affluent, they are then discontented when confronted with the reality that most of our adult paychecks are spent for the basic necessities of food and shelter, not for our entertainment or personal whims (Bachman, 1983).

Another argument against part-time jobs is that they may contribute to delinquency by providing adolescents with too much mobility, privacy, and emotional distance from their parents (Greenberger & Steinberg, 1986; Hirschi, 1983). Adolescents with their own incomes may be in a better position to ignore their parents' advice and to disobey the family's rules (the "golden rule": "Those who have the gold make the rules"). Having a job may also provide the financial resources to indulge in vices that they otherwise could not afford, such as drugs and gambling. On the other hand, some surveys fail to find any relationships between employment and delinquency (Cook, 1983; Gottfredson, 1985). Answering

What experiences have influenced your educational and vocational choices?

the question of the value of part-time work is muddied by the fact that most research has failed to take before and after measurements to see whether students with and those without part-time jobs were different to begin with. Given this shortcoming, the results are still too contradictory to allow us to conclude that working causes students to become more delinquent, yet the possibility should not be totally discounted.

The more widespread concern, however, is whether having a part-time job while going to school interferes with grades, attendance, or achievement scores. Several large-scale surveys have found that students' grades and attendance fell after they started working (Borus, 1984; Greenberger & Steinberg, 1986). Other surveys, however, have found no detrimental effects on grades, homework, or commitment to education (Gottfredson, 1985). In the first nationwide study to examine the relationship between employment and achievement across a range of academic subjects, students who worked less than 20 hours a week were seemingly not harmed in terms of their achievement or absenteeism. Those who worked more than 20 hours, however, did have the lowest achievement scores in all academic areas (National Assessment of Educational Progress, 1989). Once again, however, this study did not take before and after measurements, so we do not know whether those working more than 20 hours a week were poorer students to begin with.

In sum, it would be overly simplistic to argue that all adolescents ought to have a part-time or summer job. For some, a job might interfere with their schoolwork or contribute to delinquency. It would be equally naive, however, to argue that working is always a relatively meaningless endeavor or that it always interferes with a young person's schoolwork. The pluses and minuses of a job depend on a number of variables—the hours, the type of work, the working conditions, the characteristics of the boss and co-workers. Rather than asking whether we should encourage adolescents to work, it is more to the point to ask: Is the youngster doing well enough in school to handle a job? What kind of people is the adolescent going to be working with? What skills or attitudes can be learned at this particular job? How is the adolescent going to be taught to budget money?

ADOLESCENT UNEMPLOYMENT

Beyond the question of whether adolescents should have part-time jobs looms a much more complex and serious question: What are we to do for the thousands of young people who have finished or have quit school and are unable to find work? These young people who are looking for work but are unable to find a job, or who can find jobs for only a few weeks or months of the year are referred to as the *chronically unemployed.* Unfortunately, the vast majority of these young people are, as we have seen in previous chapters, the "at risk" students who come primarily from minority and poor families and have poor academic skills, even though they may have a high-school diploma. In 1988 white teenagers' unemployment rate hovered around 13%, while African Americans' was nearly 35% and Hispanics' 22% (see Figure 11.1). In other words, coming from a poor family goes

FIGURE 11.1
Youth unemployment, 1955–1986

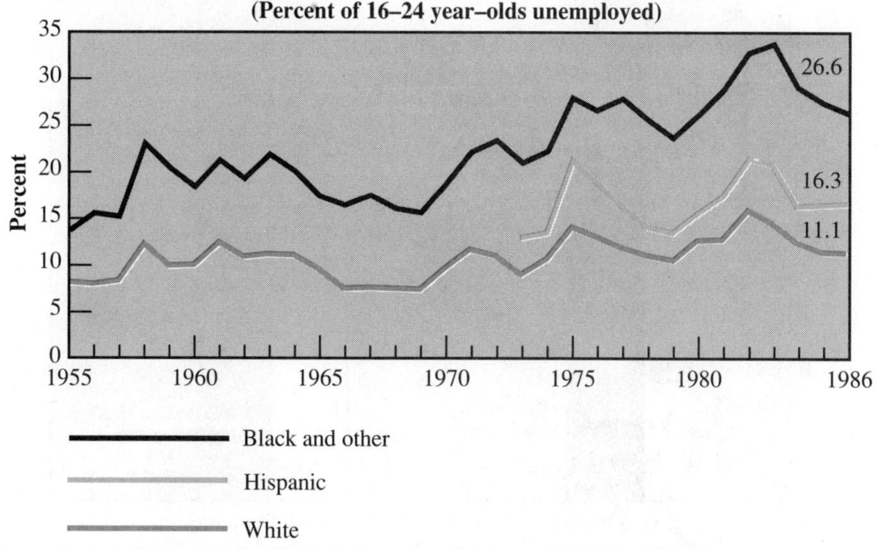

Source: Bureau of Labor Statistics. (1987). *Employment and earnings.* Washington, DC: Author.

hand in hand with a teenager's being unable to find part-time or full-time work. To underscore this point, the states with the highest poverty rates also have the highest rates of teenage unemployment—28% in Louisiana, 27% in Mississippi, and 26% in West Virginia (Government Printing Office, 1988. See Figure 11.2).

As a society our problem then becomes how to help these young people who want to work find jobs. Given that their families are too poor to afford more education and given their inadequate educational skills, where do we begin? Contrary to the assumption that these unemployed young people think most jobs are beneath them, most say they would accept any type of work, even for salaries below the minimum wage. Sadly, however, even having participated in a vocational education program in high school does not appreciably increase their chances of getting a job—a finding that the Labor Department's analysts conclude is a reflection of racial inequality in our society (Borus, 1984). Moreover, even when these young people do find temporary work, their employers often complain that their poor reading and math skills are an insurmountable handicap (Gottlieb & Driscoll, 1982).

Understandably, wanting to work but being unable to find a job eventually erodes a young person's self-esteem, hope, and motivation. Having lost a sense of control over the future and feeling that our society has cast them aside, most of these young people slip into the despair that ultimately destroys their motivation

FIGURE 11.2
Unemployment rates for high-school graduates and dropouts, 1986

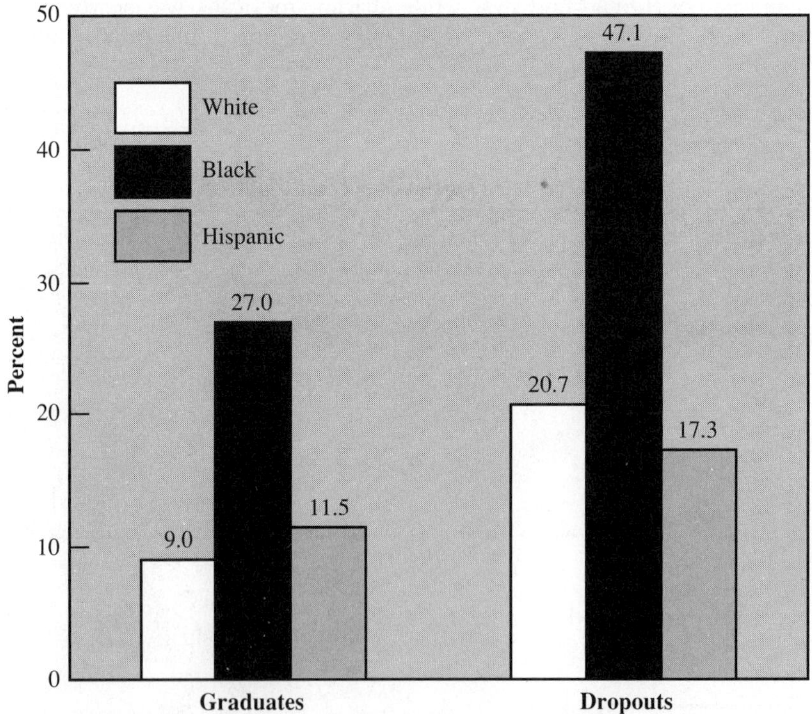

Source: Bureau of Labor Statistics. (1986). *Employment and earnings.* Washington, DC: Author.

to work. Not surprisingly, they become disillusioned and alienated from the social, political, and educational systems (Banks & Ullah, 1987; Breakwell, 1986).

REDUCING YOUTH UNEMPLOYMENT

What, then, are we doing about these high rates of unemployment among our young people? What have we learned from the programs we have developed for the chronically unemployed? To begin with, we know that the needs of unemployed young people in rural areas are not the same as the needs of those in urban areas. Although both groups are vocationally and educationally handicapped, they should not be treated as if they were a single conglomerate, "the unemployed." It is important to keep in mind that our country's worst poverty and our highest youth unemployment are in our rural, not in our urban, communities (Appalachian Regional Commission, 1987). Although describing the numerous programs aimed at reducing youth unemployment is beyond the scope of this chapter, a description of a few representative programs can demonstrate the creativity and dedication involved (for descriptions of other programs consult Grant Foundation, 1988; Kyle, 1987).

One example of the innovative approaches for helping rural youths trapped by the economic slump in their communities is North Carolina's REAL project (Mathis, 1989). No longer able or willing to follow their parents into the mills or mines or onto the farms, these young people often lack the skills needed to enter a more urban marketplace. To ease students into the world of business, the REAL program gives high-school students vocational training and the option of eventually buying the business they establish while in school. Students take courses in business management then develop a plan for establishing their own business in their local community. The capital for their business comes from loans made by the school district, the community, or REAL Enterprises. Under the direction of adult supervisors, the students actually develop a business that serves the community's needs and contributes to its economy. After the business is well-established, the school itself or the students can buy it from the school district.

Among the businesses established through the REAL program are a T-shirt shop, a boat rental business, an ice cream parlor, a day-care center, and a pig farm. The oldest of the projects is the Way Off Broadway Deli owned by four of the teenagers who helped set it up as part of their high-school program. Schools in several other states are studying the feasibility of establishing similar programs.

Programs in Dallas and Birmingham have succeeded in helping poor African American males gain entry into the marketplace of more urban communities (U.S. Department of Labor, 1988a). Among the more than 600 males enrolled, virtually all were reading below the eighth-grade level and 94% were high-school dropouts. Despite these educational handicaps, after only 17 weeks of individualized instruction and special motivational activities two thirds of these young men either found jobs or enrolled in other vocational programs for more training. As an added bonus, the programs were cost-effective in that only $2,128 was spent for each student's training in comparison to the Department of Labor's $4,900 standard.

In yet another urban program, the Work Scholarship Connection was developed by Wegman's supermarket chain in Rochester, New York, to help at-risk students finish high school while learning job skills. Wegman's provides part-time jobs to

14- and 15-year-olds recommended by their schools as capable of graduating but in danger of dropping out. Wegman's provides pre-employment workshops, on-the-job mentors who give advice and encouragement, free transportation to and from work, and academic tutors. In return, the students promise not to use illegal drugs or alcohol and to attend school regularly. As a final bonus, those who stay in the program until they graduate from high school are given a $5,000 a year scholarship to any accredited postsecondary school in the state (W. T. Grant Foundation, 1988).

Unfortunately, there are not enough innovative programs like these to serve those who need them. The largest federally funded vocational education program, the Job Training Partnership Act (JTPA), falls far short of meeting the needs of unemployed youths. The JTPA is currently only able to offer 18 weeks of vocational training with a restriction of only $2,321 per youth. With this limited budget, which is down 70% from its 1980 allocation, JTPA can serve only about 5% of the young people who are eligible for this type of vocational training (U.S. Department of Labor, 1988b.).

VOCATIONAL PREPARATION

The Economic Forecast: A Nation at Risk?

The high rates of unemployment among the young and the poor reading and math skills of so many adolescents have many economists worried about our society's future. In the 1990s, three out of every four jobs will require training beyond high school. Projections for the year 2000 are that new jobs will require a work force whose median level of education is 13.5 years (Smith & Lincoln, 1988). The troubling question is: Who will fill these jobs?

Not only are most of our future workers too poorly educated for the jobs that await them, but the number of young people available for work is declining. In 1978 people 16 to 24 years of age accounted for 23% of our population; but by 1995 6they will constitute only 16%. This means that as our demand for young workers is rising, their numbers are decreasing. Of those who will be available for work, an increasingly higher percentage are from minority cultures whose educational and vocational skills are weakest. For example, the fastest growing segment of our population, Hispanic Americans, has a school dropout rate of nearly 40%, with nearly one third of their total population now under the age of 15 (Smith & Lincoln, 1988). By the year 2000, one out of every three Americans will be a member of a racial minority.

A number of economic analysts are warning us that the basic skills in our work force, particularly at the entry level, are simply not good enough to allow us to compete successfully in the worldwide market (Berlin & Sum, 1988; National Commission on Excellence in Education, 1983; Smith & Lincoln, 1988; Grant Foundation, 1988). For example, it is estimated that if every child who reaches the age of 17 between now and the year 2000 could read sophisticated materials, write clearly, speak articulately, and solve complex problems requiring algebra and statistics, our economy could exceed a 4% growth rate (Johnston & Packer, 1987). Yet, despite these warnings, we are allocating only 5% of our state education funds for services to at-risk youths on whom our economy's well-being relies.

Instead of allocating our tax money to educate those whose poor academic skills are putting us at greatest economic risk, we continue to invest most of our money in educating college students and those planning to attend college. For example, the combined funds from local, state, and federal governments for educating noncollege-bound students is roughly only one seventh of our investments for the college bound (U.S. Department of Labor, 1988b.). A recent report by an economic-political think tank has reiterated this point by showing that our society spends proportionately less on precollegiate education than 13 other major industrialized nations. Only Australia and Ireland spend a smaller percentage of per capita income on educating students in grades K–12 (Economic Policy Institute, 1989. See Figure 11.3).

Not only are we not directing as much money toward preparing noncollege-bound students for their future roles in our work force, but we usually are not providing them with enough advice and direction either. Most high-school students are poorly informed regarding our society's economic needs and lack information about the high level of skills now necessary to succeed in blue-collar jobs. Even most high-school counselors admit feeling far less confident advising the noncollege-bound student than the college bound (Borus, 1984; Boyer, 1983; Mitchell,

FIGURE 11.3

K–12 expenditures per pupil as a percent of per capita income, 1985

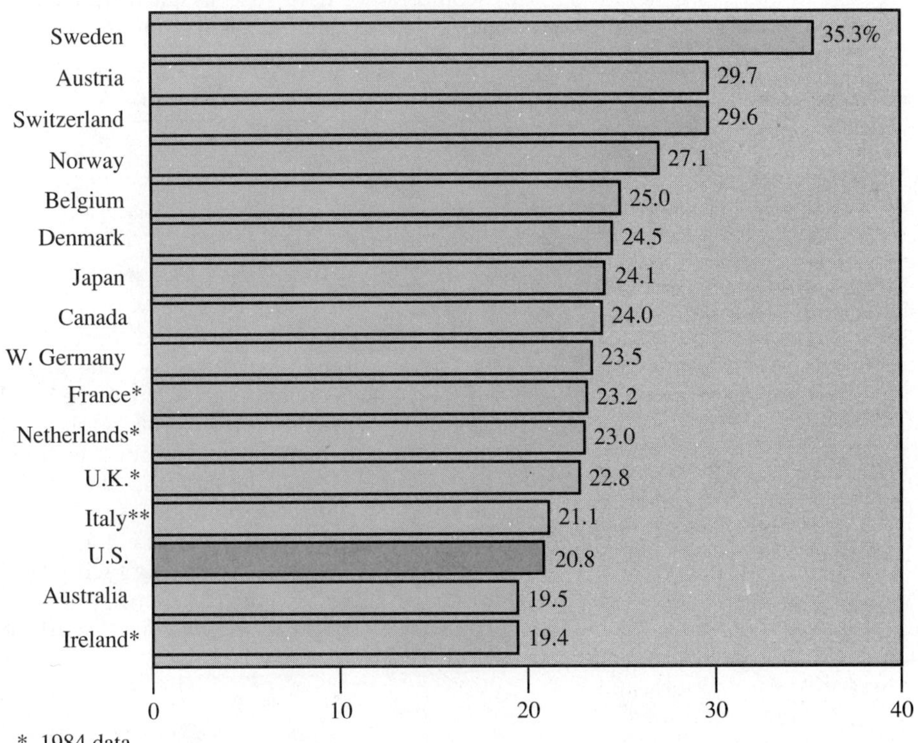

Source: Economic Policy Institute. (1989). *Shortchanging education.* Washington, DC: Author.

1988). Given most adolescents' lack of information, we might jump to the conclusion that what we need is more vocational education classes. This "solution," however, creates an entirely different set of sticky issues.

High-School Vocational Education

The idea of providing job training as part of the high-school curriculum is not new. It has been around since the 1950s, when "voc ed" classes came into vogue in the public schools. Some vocational education projects, such as Eliot Wigginton's **Foxfire Project,** have achieved international fame (see Box 11.3); but Wigginton's project is the exception to the rule. Given the situation as it exists in most high schools, vocational education does not appear to be our best tack in preparing adolescents for their future jobs.

Why not? To begin with, despite our best intentions vocational education programs have fallen short on too many counts (Boyer, 1983). First, the kind of training most schools can afford to offer and the actual skills needed in today's technological jobs are worlds apart. Given the expense of equipment such as computers and other high-tech tools, very few high schools have the money to expose students to state-of-the-art methods or materials. Even if schools did have the money, most employers prefer to train their own employees because their company has its own specialized equipment, procedures, and policies. For this reason, employers generally say they would rather have schools teach students to read, write, and do math well, leaving the specific job-skills training to the

A CLOSER LOOK 11.3

Foxfire: An Appalachian High School's International Success

In the 1960s, when Eliot Wigginton went to Rabun Gap, Georgia, in the Appalachian mountains, he expected to use his master's degree to teach the well-worn classics of the traditional high-school curriculum. His students responded with apathy and unruly behavior, eventually convincing Wigginton to replace the prescribed curriculum with one that captured his students' interest and excited the entire community. "Foxfire" was born. Curious about Appalachian culture, Wigginton convinced his students to preserve their community's oral history by interviewing their elders and writing down their stories. As the students ventured into the community with their tape recorders, notebooks, and cameras, they became increasingly motivated to learn reading and writing skills that would enable them to convey to others what they were learning. Trusting his students, Wigginton gave them the independence to pursue their projects beyond the school's boundaries. He permitted them to learn from the community's elders and to engage in activities that they considered relevant to their own lives. Since its beginning in 1966, adolescents in the Foxfire project have created four best-selling books, a magazine subscribed to in 50 states and a dozen foreign countries, a furniture-building business, and a record album of Appalachian music. This outstanding high-school program has indeed become like "foxfire"—a tiny organism that glows in the dark in shaded mountain coves.

Source: E. Wigginton. (1985). *Sometimes a shining moment: 20 years in a high-school classroom—The Foxfire experience.* Garden City, NY: Doubleday.

employer. In fact, "voc ed" students are often viewed by their teachers, peers, and future employers as intellectually inferior to students in the general curriculum. Although this stereotype is not always justified, it is true that in too many schools "voc ed" has become the dumping ground for those students performing far below average in their basic academic skills. Rather than working with these students in the general curriculum to help them catch up with other students, too many teachers or counselors advise them to change to the vocational track.

Could it be, then, that we ought to eliminate the vocational track in our schools and enroll all students in an academic curriculum where learning to read, write, and compute is the primary goal? According to a number of educational analysts, yes (Boyer, 1983). The single-track curriculum would provide all students with basic skills in reading, writing, communication, and mathematics. Rather than going to outdated vocational classes, all students would attend a course that would introduce them to the basic issues and information needed to make well-informed vocational choices. For those schools that refuse to abandon their vocational education track, **satellite schools** could take the place of vocational classes. There college-bound and noncollege-bound students receive their basic academic training at the same location, traveling to an off-campus school for specific job training. For example, students who wanted to prepare for nursing jobs might be educated in a local hospital.

Whatever the ultimate direction of vocational education, the present system has to be overhauled. Whether we should adopt the satellite concept or leave vocational training to future employers, we are clearly doing our young people a disservice by preparing them, as most schools now are, to make buggy whips in an age when there are no buggies.

The Value of a College Education

For those fortunate enough to have been well-educated adolescents and to have the money, a college education is still the best route to obtaining a good job with secure pay. As Table 11.3 illustrates, those having some college education or a

Table 11.3

Education, Unemployment, and Poverty

EDUCATIONAL LEVEL COMPLETED	PERCENT OF POPULATION AGE 25+ COMPLETING LEVEL	UNEMPLOYMENT RATES OF PERSONS AGE 25–64 (MARCH 1987)		FAMILY POVERTY RATE (MARCH 1987) (HEAD OF HOUSEHOLD AGE 25+)
		Male	*Female*	
College—4 or more years	19.4%	2.5%	2.1%	N.A.
College—1–3 years	16.9	5.0	4.0	4.0%
High school—4 years	38.4	6.7	5.8	9.5
High school—1–4 years	11.9	11.2	10.9	18.5
Averages		6.0%	5.2%	10.9%

Source: U.S. Bureau of the Census. (1988). *Statistical Abstract of the United States.* Washington, DC: U.S. Government Printing Office.

college degree are far more likely to be well paid and to have jobs than those with only a high-school education (U.S. Bureau of the Census, 1988). For example, high-school dropouts are five times more likely than college graduates to be unemployed. Moreover, male college graduates have lost the least ground financially as our economy has declined (see Table 11.4). In 1986, 30-year-old male college graduates earned 50% more money than 30-year-old male high-school graduates—triple the 16% difference between the salaries of college and high-school graduates in 1973 (Levy, 1989). This growing gap between male high-school and college graduates may reflect the increased demand for better educated workers in our work force, as well as the fact that a college education has become too expensive for many of our citizens. The income gap between college and high-school female graduates, however, has not widened as dramatically because women are concentrated primarily in service jobs where a college education makes less difference in their incomes (Murphy & Welch, 1987). Nevertheless, even for females, a college degree is beneficial.

It is unfortunate that recent cutbacks in federal aid have now put a college education beyond the reach of many academically qualified adolescents. Thanks to the expansion of federal aid for students during the 1960s and 1970s, college attendance rose by 30% for students from medium- and lower-income families. In contrast, between 1980 and 1986, when federal support was cut back, the proportion of college students from blue-collar families declined by 20%, African American enrollment fell from 34% to 25%, and Hispanic enrollment fell from 36% to 27%. Stated differently, since 1980 college expenses paid by students and their families have risen by 70% to 90%, and their personal debts from financing their education have increased by 60%. During the same period, federal aid for low-income college students, adjusted for inflation, rose by only 3% and shifted from grants to loans. In short, as Table 11.5 illustrates, a college education is fast

Table 11.4

Trends in the Real Mean Annual Earnings of 20- to 24-Year Old Civilian Males, 1973–1986, by Educational Attainment and Race/Ethnic Group (in 1986 Dollars)

	ALL MALES (20–24)		% CHANGE IN EARNINGS 1973–1986			
	1973	*1986*	*All*	*White*	*African American*	*Hispanic*
All males	$12,166	$ 9,027	−25.8	−21.0	−46.0	−29.0
Males with less than high-school education	11,815	6,853	−42.0	−42.3	−60.6	−27.3
High-school graduates	15,221	10,924	−28.2	−24.4	−43.8	−34.5
Some college	13,108	10,960	−16.4	−11.3	−42.7	−21.2
College graduates	14,630	13,759	−6.0	−5.6	+6.5	N.A.

Source: U.S. Bureau of the Census. (1988). *Statistical Abstract of the United States.* Washington, DC: U.S. Government Printing Office.

Table 11.5

College Participation Rates by Income, Race, and Sex, 1973 to 1988

	INCOME, RACE, AND SEX	1973	1976	1979	1982	1985	1987	1988
WHITE	**Total**	**47.9%**	**49.3%**	**46.2%**	**46.3%**	**47.3%**	**50.9%**	**52.9%**
	Low	36.8	37.0	35.8	32.5	31.7	36.4	38.8
	Middle	44.5	46.0	43.1	42.3	46.0	48.7	51.0
	Upper	59.9	60.9	56.4	59.3	57.2	62.0	63.2
	Men	**48.1**	**46.1**	**44.5**	**43.8**	**44.7**	**50.9**	**49.8**
	Low	37.9	34.9	33.8	29.9	29.1	36.4	32.1
	Middle	44.2	42.4	41.6	39.5	43.0	48.4	48.8
	Upper	60.2	57.3	53.6	56.7	55.0	62.0	60.6
	Women	**47.5**	**53.3**	**48.2**	**49.3**	**50.4**	**52.6**	**56.4**
	Low	35.4	39.4	38.1	35.3	34.8	38.0	46.4
	Middle	44.9	50.5	44.6	45.5	49.4	49.9	53.5
	Upper	59.4	65.5	60.1	62.4	60.0	64.8	66.1
AFRICAN AMERICAN	**Total**	**33.2**	**47.5**	**39.0**	**36.0**	**32.8**	**37.1**	**35.5**
	Low	31.7	39.8	34.2	29.2	27.9	31.1	30.3
	Middle	32.0	52.7	43.6	40.2	35.5	39.3	36.2
	Upper	*	*	*	*	*	*	*
	Men	**34.9**	**46.5**	**36.4**	**32.6**	**30.8**	**35.1**	**29.5**
	Low	*	37.2	36.1	23.0	29.0	26.8	23.0
	Middle	*	53.2	36.4	39.4	29.0	37.4	28.1
	Upper	*	*	*	*	*	*	*
	Women	**31.6**	**48.3**	**41.1**	**39.1**	**34.6**	**38.8**	**40.8**
	Low	*	41.7	32.9	34.2	27.1	34.1	35.6
	Middle	*	52.2	51.0	41.0	42.6	41.0	44.1
	Upper	*	*	*	*	*	*	*

* The number of cases in the sample is too small to produce reliable estimates for this population.

Note: Figures show the percentage of 18- to 24-year-old dependent high-school graduates who are dependent primary family members and enrolled in college as of October of that year.

Source: American Council on Education (1988b). *Status report on minorities in education.* Washington, DC: Author.

becoming an option limited primarily to those lucky enough to have been born into higher income families (American Council on Education, 1988a).

These declining college enrollments demonstrate the impact that our government's financial policies have on adolescents' educational and vocational opportunities (W. T. Grant Foundation, 1988). In contrast to our present policies, for example, in 1944 our government decided to increase educational opportunities for returning veterans under the GI Bill. By offering financial aid to any veteran who wanted to enroll in a postsecondary-school program, our government enabled more than 19 million young Americans to go beyond their high-school degree, with 45% of them going to college. As a consequence, our nation's pool of trained talent was expanded manyfold and a college education, once reserved primarily for the affluent, was democratized beyond that of any other industrialized country.

As this experience demonstrates, if people from nonaffluent families are given the chance financially to get more education, most will seize the opportunity. Unfortunately, however, our present policies are once again putting a college education beyond the reach of many adolescents who could otherwise succeed in college or in other forms of postsecondary education.

In response to federal cutbacks, some states are trying through financial incentive programs to help adolescents from poor and middle-income families further their education and their vocational training (W. T. Grant Foundation, 1988). In Michigan, for example, high-school graduates from low-income families are eligible for 2 years of free tuition at any community college within the state. Students who complete their community college program then receive an additional $2,000 credit for tuition at a 4-year college. Adolescents who find full-time jobs within a year after graduating from high school and who keep their job for 2 years receive a $1,000 bonus.

In another incentive program, San Francisco State University offers one free college credit course each semester for Mission High School seniors, most of whom are minority youths from low-income families. To overcome the students' transportation problems and parents' fears about letting their daughters leave the neighborhood after dark, the university's professors teach the courses after school on the high-school campus. Nearly 150 students are enrolled in the program, including one gang leader whose potential was recognized by the school's custodian. In spite of predictions that these seniors would not be able to do college level work, most of the students have an average grade point of 2.75 in college. Mission High School also pays 30 of its poorest freshmen $250 a semester to attend an after-school study hall 3 days a week instead of looking for part-time jobs (Canon, 1988).

Such programs serve as powerful reminders that if we are willing to help poor teenagers by offering them some financial assistance, these young people are highly motivated to continue their education. The question is not whether low-income students are "willing" or "motivated" to work hard toward an education or whether their families "value education." The question is whether taxpayers are willing to change their priorities, as they once did with the GI Bill, to provide financial aid for qualified students whose parents cannot afford to give them an education beyond high school.

THEORIES OF VOCATIONAL DEVELOPMENT

In addition to how to finance postsecondary education, most adolescents and their parents are interested in how to go about deciding what the adolescents will do for a living after getting out of school. Economists and psychologists also want to know the answer to this question, among others, such as: How do race, gender, and socioeconomic class affect job choices? How can schools and parents help adolescents with their future vocations? What variables play the biggest parts in influencing what individuals will do for a living?

The Differentialist Perspective

According to the **differentialist perspective,** individuals choose their jobs by the gradual process of matching their abilities, interests, and personalities to the rewards, demands, and prestige of different jobs (Holland, 1985). This perspective contends that one of the most important services adults can render to adolescents is to help them assess their own interests and skills and help them identify the types of job they are best suited for. One of the most popular ways of assessing these interests is the **Strong-Campbell Interest Inventory,** illustrated in Box 11.4 (Campbell, 1974). The results of such inventories are then compared with the characteristics of different jobs until good "fits" are found. One of the better known methods for matching jobs to personalities is **Holland's occupational types,** described in Box 11.5. In support of this approach, people generally say they are more satisfied with their work and tend to change jobs less often when their skills, personalities, and job requirements are congruent (Spokane, 1985).

Nevertheless, this match your traits to the job approach has its critics. First, an adolescent's score may not necessarily reflect his or her actual skills or future potential. Second, most adolescents are not very aware of the status or requirements of different jobs, so it is unlikely that these factors influence them in selecting their future work, as differentialists contend they do (Grotevant & Cooper, 1986). Then, too, teenagers may not express any interest in certain jobs simply from lack of knowledge. For example, Gertrude may be well suited for a future career as a surgeon, but she may not express any interest in medicine since she has never had experiences or encouragement in this direction. Conversely, merely because her parents have been encouraging her in this direction since she was 5 years old, Gertrude might express a lot of interest in becoming a surgeon without having had any relevant experiences. Once she cuts into her first frog in biology class, she might quickly discover that she has no interest in cutting into more amphibians or into mammals. The point is that career interest inventories can be very unreliable ways of assessing adolescents' actual interests or skills.

The Developmentalist Perspective

Another shortcoming of the differentialist view is that it does not take into account the different abilities that adolescents have to assess themselves or to assess different types of work. According to developmental psychologists such as Piaget, adolescents in, for example, the formal operational stage of reasoning can make more refined decisions about their future jobs than those in the concrete operational stage. In other words, from the **developmentalist perspective** adolescents' attitudes and decisions about jobs are influenced, in large part, by their stage of cognitive development.

Among the most renowned proponents of this developmentalist view are Donald Super (1976) and Eli Ginzberg (1972, 1980). According to Ginzberg, our vocational attitudes advance through three phases: the fantasy stage, the tentative stage, and the realistic stage. Naive fantasies shape the feelings young children have about the world of work. They might, for example, want to be astronauts because they fantasize about flying around in the heavens, peering aimlessly out the windows of their spacecraft. At this young age, they have not stopped to consider the unpleasant aspects of the job, such as the years of training or the physical stamina required for space travel. Just before adolescence, however, young people start evaluating their own talents and shortcomings and becoming more aware of the actual requirements of different types of work. In this tentative stage, they are still undecided about future jobs but are more realistic about the world of work than they were as younger children. During adolescence, however, individuals suppos-

A CLOSER LOOK 11.4

Excerpts From the Strong-Campbell Interest Inventory

Here are several pairs of activities or occupations. Show which one of each pair you like better: If you prefer the one on the *left,* mark in the space labeled *"L"* on the answer sheet; if you prefer the one on the *right,* mark in the space labeled *"R";* if you like *both the same,* or if you *cannot decide,* mark in the space labeled "=". Work rapidly. Make one mark for each pair.

Airline pilot	282	Airline ticket agent
Taxicab driver	283	Police officer
Headwaiter/Hostess	284	Lighthouse keeper
Selling things house to house	285	Gardening
Developing plans	286	Carrying out plans
Doing a job yourself	287	Telling somebody else to do the job
Dealing with things	288	Dealing with people
Taking a chance	289	Playing safe
Drawing a definite salary	290	Receiving a commission on what is done
Outside work	291	Inside work
Work for yourself	292	Carrying out the program of a superior whom you respect
Superintendent of a hospital	293	Warden of a prison
Vocational counselor	294	Public health officer
Physical activity	295	Mental activity
Dog trainer	296	Juvenile parole officer
Thrilling, dangerous activities	297	Quieter, safer activities
Physical education director	298	Free-lance writer
Statistician	299	Social worker
Technical responsibility (in charge of 25 people doing scientific work)	300	Supervisory responsibility (in charge of 300 people doing business-office work)
Going to a play	301	Going to a dance
Teacher	302	Salesperson
Experimenting with new grooming preparations	303	Experimenting with new office equipment
Being married to a research scientist	304	Being married to a sales executive
Working in a large corporation with little chance of being president before age 55	305	Working for yourself in a small business
Working in an import-export business	306	Working in a research laboratory
Music and art events	307	Athletic events
Reading a book	308	Watching TV or going to a movie
Appraising real estate	309	Repairing and restoring antiques
Having a few close friends	310	Having many acquaintances
Work in which you move from place to place	311	Work where you live in one place

Source: D. Campbell. (1974). *The Strong-Campbell Interest Inventory.* Palo Alto, CA: Stanford University Press.

A CLOSER LOOK 11.5

Holland's Personality-Occupational Types

Which of the following descriptions are most characteristic of your present and your past vocational orientation?

Realistic These people are robust, rugged, practical, physically strong, and often athletic. They have excellent motor coordination and skills but are weak in verbal, interpersonal skills. They perceive themselves as mechanically inclined and uncomfortable in social settings. They prefer concrete to abstract problems and are conventional in political or social matters. Rarely do they perform creatively. These realistic types enjoy practical occupations such as mechanics, engineering, farming, construction, wildlife specialties, and tool designing.

Investigative *or* Intellectual These people are typically task oriented, introspective, asocial, and unconventional. They are strongly inclined toward science and prefer to think through rather than act out problems. They prefer to work independently and they feel confident intellectually. Describing themselves as reserved, curious, and analytical, these people prefer jobs in the sciences, psychology, or technical writing.

Enterprising These individuals have verbal abilities that enable them to lead others and sell products or ideas. They tend to avoid situations that require long periods of intellectual effort, although they have a high energy level. They are concerned with power, status, and leadership, seeing themselves as assertive, self-confident, and sociable. Vocations for which they are well suited include real estate sales, retail merchandising, political or business management, or television production.

Artistic These people enjoy expressing themselves and are inclined toward impulsive, creative behavior. They prefer unstructured situations that permit introspection and individual expression. They avoid situations that are too structured or that require too much conformity. Perceiving themselves as creative, intuitive, independent, introspective, and expressive, these people's occupational preferences include musician, artist, author, composer, and stage director.

Social These individuals are sociable, humanistic, verbally skilled, and group oriented. They are often religious, have good interpersonal skills, and like structured activities. They prefer to solve problems through feelings and interpersonal manipulation of others, tend to avoid intellectual problem solving and physical exertion, and enjoy activities that inform, train, or enlighten others. Describing themselves as understanding, idealistic, and helpful, these people's occupational preferences include social worker, missionary, teacher, therapist, and counselor.

Conventional People of this type are usually conformists who prefer well-structured environments and subordinate rather than leadership roles. They avoid situations involving ambiguity, physical skills, or interpersonal relationships. Describing themselves as conscientious, efficient, obedient, calm, orderly, and practical, these individuals value status and money. Their vocational preferences include bank examiner, bookkeeper, clerical worker, financial analyst, traffic manager, and statistician.

Source: Adapted from D. Campbell and J. Hansen. (1988). *Manual for the Strong-Campbell Interest Inventory* (3rd ed.), Form T325, pp. 29–30. Stanford, CA: Stanford University Press. Reprinted with permission.

edly become able to appraise their own skills and to recognize the demands of various types of work. At this point, according to the developmentalists, they can make wise decisions regarding future jobs.

Ginzberg initially believed that individuals reach this realistic phase before the age of 25, which enables them to make a final decision about their lifelong careers. In later revisions of his theory, however, Ginzberg conceded that most people continue to assess their skills and the demands of various jobs throughout their lives. As a result, most people will probably change jobs several times as adults. On the other hand, Ginzberg admitted that many adolescents are not in the privileged position of being able to choose a job on the basis of their personal skills and interests. These young people have to accept virtually whatever job comes their way, given factors they cannot control, such as the needs of the economy or their family's socioeconomic status.

Like Ginzberg, Super maintained that people choose jobs on the basis of personal interests and skills. Super, however, believed that the self-concepts established in childhood are the forerunners of later career decisions. As a result of their parents' expectations and encouragement, individuals develop attitudes about the type of work they think best suits them. In other words, people may feel as though they have chosen their future jobs of their own free will when, in actuality, the messages they received as young children ruled their final choices.

A Challenge to Traditional Theories

Although the developmentalist and differentialist views have historically dominated vocational psychology, new research is now challenging their assumptions (Gottfredson, 1987). These reviews of the literature show that people's aspirations and skills are not primarily what determine the jobs they take. Instead, the evidence indicates that vocational choices are largely a response to beliefs regarding the appropriate roles for people of a certain race, gender, and socioeconomic class. In fact, if we could choose only one variable for predicting an adolescent's future job, his or her parents' socioeconomic status is usually more reliable than answers on career interest inventories (Schulenberg, Vondracek & Crouter, 1984). As important, the nation's economic needs appear to have more impact on an adolescent's future job than do his or her particular interests, skills, or personality.

According to older, more traditional theories, people who are unhappy in their jobs are primarily responsible for their own misery since they made their own choices. Newer theories, however, argue that individuals' future jobs will probably be determined by forces beyond their control—above all, the opportunities in the job market at the particular time they enter the work force. From this viewpoint, the best way to help young people prepare for the future is not to invest time and energy discussing their interests and personalities or steering them toward a job that "fits" them. Instead, the focus should be on educating them about the types of job that will most likely be available at the time they finish their education. By doing the latter, we would also be helping those who have unrealistic expectations to adopt more realistic plans.

FEMALES' VOCATIONAL DEVELOPMENT

Despite the popular assumption that women's liberation has changed the world of work for women and girls, the reality is that most teenage girls are still preparing themselves for the jobs that women have historically performed in our society: teaching, nursing, and secretarial work. Most girls still steer away from jobs involving science or math, the fields offering some of the best salaries and most needing qualified workers. For example, females actually lost ground during the 1980s in terms of college degrees earned in science and engineering, as Table 11.6 illustrates (U.S. Department of Education, 1988). Having prepared themselves for jobs that are among the most overpopulated and lowest paying, working women still earn roughly 40% less than men with the same levels of education (Murphy & Welch, 1987). Given that most adolescent girls will have to work outside the home as adults in order to support themselves and their children, these findings are discouraging.

Why are so many girls still making such traditional choices? To begin with, adolescent boys and girls are still usually encouraged to follow different paths in developing their attitudes about work (Gottfried, 1988; Williams, 1989). Unlike boys, many adolescent girls restrict their vocational choices by making their primary concern their future roles as wives and mothers. Worried about balancing the roles of wife, mother, and wage earner, most teenage girls are still encouraged to prepare themselves for flexible jobs, meaning part-time employment or jobs with shorter workdays and extended vacations, such as public school teaching. Contrary to the popular stereotypes about liberated women, most girls are continuing in the footsteps of their foremothers by preparing for jobs that will

Table 11.6

Who Got Science and Engineering* Degrees?

		BACHELOR'S		MASTER'S		PH.D.	
YEAR & GROUP		***Number***	**%**	***Number***	**%**	***Number***	**%**
Total	1985	204,064	100.0	43,910	100.0	11,821	100.0
	1987	203,055	100.0	47,947	100.0	13,040	100.0
Women	1985	62,448	30.6	9,724	22.1	2,135	18.1
	1987	61,487	30.3	11,443	23.9	2,442	18.7
African Americans	1985	8,019	3.9	788	1.8	133	1.1
	1987	9,205	4.5	1,055	2.2	137	1.1
Hispanics	1985	4,613	2.3	688	1.5	218	1.8
	1987	5,266	2.6	954	2.0	217	1.7
American Indians	1985	656	0.3	108	0.2	13	0.1
	1987	662	0.3	91	0.2	15	0.1
Asians	1985	9,903	4.9	2,631	6.0	619	5.2
	1987	13,112	6.5	3,239	6.8	662	5.1
Minority Subtotal	1985	23,191	11.4	4,195	9.6	983	8.3
	1987	28,245	13.9	5,339	11.1	1,031	7.9
Foreign	1985	10,628	5.2	9,638	21.9	2,878	24.3
	1987	11,345	5.6	11,557	24.1	4,054	31.1

* Includes agriculture, natural resources, computer and information sciences, life sciences, mathematics, physical sciences, and engineering.

Source: U.S. Department of Education. (1988). *Degrees and other formal awards conferred.* Washington, DC: National Center for Education Statistics.

come second to their future husbands' jobs and second to their roles as wives and mothers.

Those teenage girls preparing themselves for jobs historically held by men differ in several respects from their more traditional peers. First, they are less committed to having large families or to marrying young. Like boys, these young women typically come from homes in which their parents have encouraged them to be ambitious, independent, assertive, and intellectually competitive. Many of these young women have also had in their own families role models of independent, assertive, employed women. Their parents tend to be better educated, earn higher incomes, and have less sexist attitudes than the parents of girls who choose more traditional jobs (Hannah & Kahn, 1989; Hollinger, 1988; Houser & Garvey, 1985; Sandberg, 1987). In other words, their nontraditional career choices are encouraged and reinforced by the people closest to them.

Although girls' vocational choices are changing more slowly than many of us might imagine, new patterns are gradually emerging. First, more teenage girls are now working, with the proportion having part-time jobs nearly doubling in the past 30 years (Nilsen, 1984). Although parents are still more likely to encourage

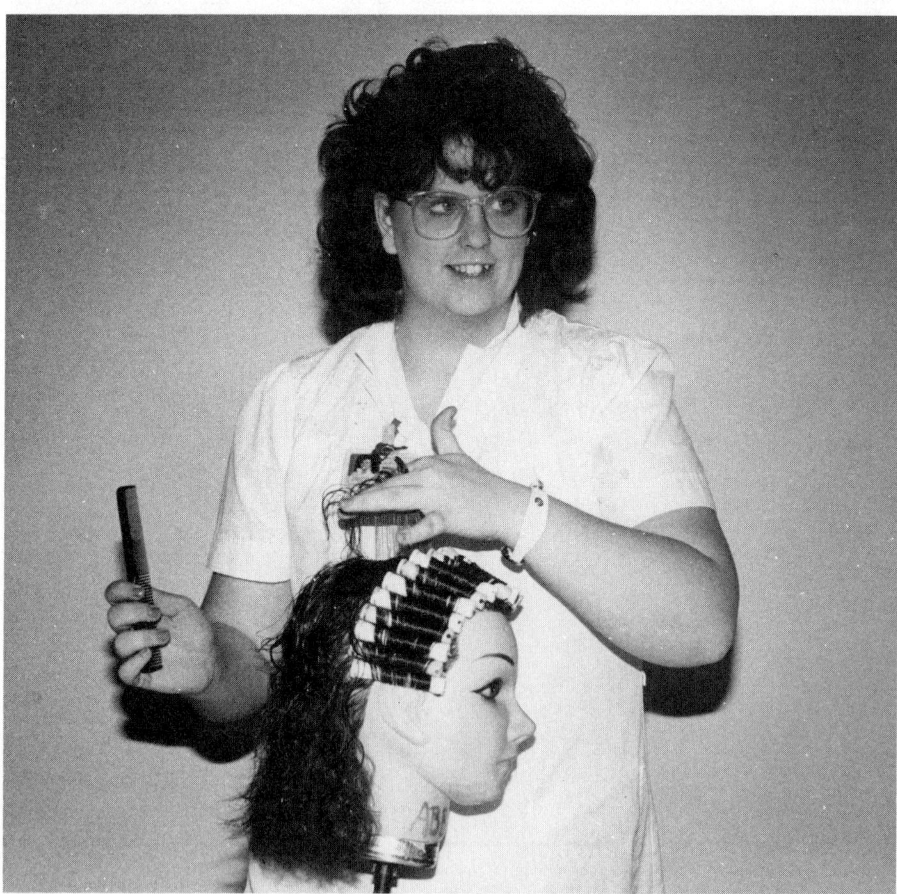

How has your being male or female influenced your vocational choices?

their teenage sons to work than their daughters, girls are now almost as likely as boys to have a part-time job (Peters, 1987). Second, more girls are entering jobs formerly reserved for men, as evidenced by their growing numbers in fields such as law, medicine, and industry (Gerstein, 1988).

As further evidence of the changing times, in 1975 female students were finally accorded the right to enter our nation's military academies. Indeed, in 1988 a female student became the First Commander of West Point's Corps of Cadets, a post formerly held by leaders such as Douglas MacArthur and William Westmoreland. Despite vehement opposition and upheaval, female cadets have established their reputations as scholars and as cadets in our armed service academies (see Box 11.6; Stiehm, 1981, 1988).

Unfortunately, teenage boys generally feel more restricted by sex-role stereotypes than girls when it comes to choosing jobs. That is, a girl is more likely to pursue a job that has historically been restricted to men than a boy is to pursue a job that has historically been restricted to women. Even in these times of less restrictive gender roles, boys usually choose jobs typically held by men (Alpert & Breen, 1989; Lee, 1985). These findings are not particularly surprising, however, since most "male" jobs have higher prestige and bigger paychecks than most "female" jobs. Then, too, our society has encouraged females to break free from sex role stereotypes in ways that it has not encouraged boys.

CONCLUSION

Given adolescents' attitudes toward work, the present condition of vocational education in our schools, and our nation's economic forecast, what can we conclude? First, most adolescents are not getting the kind of academic or vocational training that will prepare them for the jobs awaiting them in the future. In this sense, the analysts are correct in warning us that we are a nation at risk. Second, female adolescents and youths from poor and low-income families are the most in need of training and of our financial support to prepare themselves for better paying, more secure jobs. Third, the question is not whether we have the know-how to prepare our young people for the work force but whether we will deem these goals worthy enough to finance them.

QUESTIONS FOR DISCUSSION AND REVIEW

Basic Concepts and Terminology

1. In what ways are the vocational values of today's adolescents different from and similar to those of their counterparts in the 1960s and 1970s?
2. Considering wages, hours, and type of work, how would you describe the employment situation of most adolescents today? How do their jobs differ depending on the adolescent's age, sex, and race?
3. What are the relative advantages and disadvantages of part-time employment for adolescents?
4. How has the federal government's spending affected the educational level of the work force in the past and in the present?
5. In what ways are the differentialist and developmentalist views alike and different?
6. On what grounds are the developmentalist and differentialist theories being challenged?
7. Describe several programs that have been successful in improving adolescents' vocational skills.

A CLOSER LOOK 11.6

Military Training for Females

"The kind of women we want in the Air Force are the kind who will get married and leave."—A major at the U.S. Air Force Academy

"I disagree with the admittance of women to the academies. This is just another step taken for political reasons that will tend to weaken our combat capability."—An Air Force general stationed in the Midwest

"Maybe you could find one woman in 10,000 who could lead in combat, but she would be a freak, and the Military Academy is not being run for freaks."—General William Westmoreland

Despite such opposition, on May 21, 1975, the House of Representatives mandated by a vote of 303 to 96 that females be admitted to the Department of Defense academies for academic and military training. During the first 16 months of coeducation at West Point, data were collected to examine the transformation that the academy was undergoing in educating female cadets for the first time in its history.

The Department of Physical Education and Athletics was responsible for deciding how the physical training requirements needed to be altered. While the program rather consistently emphasized the differences in male and female upper-body strength, it did not bother to incorporate physical tests on which females typically perform better than males. Neither did the department question whether the tests on which females characteristically performed more poorly were actually related to skills required by their military jobs. For example, is the requirement to run 3 miles in 24 minutes related to any military activity, or is it merely a way of testing

continued

8. How do the vocational aspirations and achievements of male and female youths differ, and what factors contribute to these differences?
9. According to the statistics on unemployment and income, how valuable are a college education, a high-risk diploma, and vocational education?
10. Considering the projections for future jobs and the economy, what would adolescents be best advised to do in regard to their vocational futures?

Questions for Discussion and Debate

1. What do you feel the government's role should be in preparing adolescents for their future jobs, retraining disadvantaged youth, and helping young people obtain a college education?
2. What factors at school, at home, and in society influenced your occupational aspirations? How do these factors compare with the present influences on your career plans?
3. How should vocational education be implemented to serve the needs of college- and noncollege-bound students?
4. How would your occupational plans have differed had you been a member of the opposite sex? a lower socioeconomic class? another race?
5. Which experiences during your adolescence or childhood were most beneficial in helping you readjust your vocational and educational plans?
6. How do you feel about females' enrolling in military academies and their pursuing of careers in the armed services?
7. How would you attempt to resolve the problem of adolescent unemployment, particularly among youth in inner cities and in rural areas?
8. As a prospective employer of an adolescent, what characteristics or credentials would you be seeking?
9. What advice would you offer parents whose

Box 11.6 continued

a cadet's self-discipline and dedication to the academy? If the latter, must females be required to complete the same physical task as males in order to demonstrate their professional commitment or will power?

In a program designed exclusively for male students and faculty, a number of provocative questions arose. How were male cadets going to respond to academic competition and physical combat with females? Since the seminude pictures of "spacemates" in the academy's training manuals were intended to "motivate" the male cadets, how appropriate were these photographs once the academy became coeducational? Would male cadets learn to trust female cadets in situations where they believed their physical differences would somehow jeopardize them? If the role of "warrior" is no longer reserved exclusively for males, will men lose their feelings of masculinity? How would males respond to female leadership in combat situations?

Since the curriculum had been designed by and for males, unexpected dilemmas arose. For instance, the Air Force Academy's materials failed to inform the female cadets or their instructors that excessive physical exercise can result in amenorrhea (the cessation of menstrual periods). For those female cadets who had need to worry about pregnancy, this minor "omission" in the curriculum created considerable anxiety until accurate information about amenorrhea and physical exercise was eventually provided. In addition, male officers had to be made comfortable enough with issues related to female physiology that saying words such as *menstruation* did not embarrass them.

Source: J. Stiehm. (1981). *Bring me men and women: mandated change at the U.S. Air Force Academy.* Berkeley, CA: University of California Press.

adolescent child wanted their permission to get a part-time job during the school year?

10. Do you think today's adolescents are being adversely affected by premature affluence? How did part-time employment affect your adolescence?
11. Which of Holland's personality-vocational types best describes you as you were during your adolescence, and how does this compare with your present self-assessment?
12. Considering job projections for the future and the factors influencing career aspirations and achievements, how would you advise adolescents in regard to their vocational plans?

GLOSSARY

developmentalist perspective The assumption that our views about work advance in a sequence of stages from childhood through adulthood.

differentialist perspective The assumption that we choose our future jobs on the basis of matching our personalities, interests, and abilities to the characteristics of particular jobs.

Fair Labor Standards Act Federal legislation that mandates the hours and conditions under which adolescents may be employed.

Foxfire Project A program in Rabun Gap, Georgia, that has integrated regional culture into the high school's curriculum.

Holland's occupational types Personality types that are supposedly suited for specific types of jobs.

satellite schools Schools that are based away from the main high-school campus, often in actual business settings, and offer more specialized and updated vocational training.

Strong-Campbell Interest Inventory A written test for assessing vocational interests.

REFERENCES

Alpert, D., & Breen, D. (1989). Liberality in children and adolescents. *Journal of Vocational Behavior, 34,* 154–160.

American Council on Education. (1989b). *Status report on minorities in education.* Washington, DC.

Appalachian Regional Commission. (1987). *Dropout prevention in Appalachia: Lessons for the nation.* Knoxville, TN: Author.

Atkinson, R. (1988). *The teenage world: Adolescent self-image in ten countries.* New York: Plenum Press.

Bachman, J. (1983). Premature affluence: Do high school students earn too much? *Economic Outlook, 10,* 64–67.

Bachman, J., Johnston, L., & O'Malley, P. (1985). *Recent findings from Monitoring the Future.* Ann Arbor: University of Michigan, Institute For Social Research.

Banks, M., & Ullah, P. (1987). Political attitudes and voting among unemployed and employed youth. *Journal of Adolescence, 10,* 201–216.

Berlin, G., & Sum, A. (1988). *Toward a more perfect union: Basic skills, poor families and our economic future.* New York: Ford Foundation.

Borus, M. (Ed.) (1984). *Youth and the labor market: Analyses of the national longitudinal survey.* Kalamazoo, MI: Upjohn Institute for Employment Research.

Boyer, E. (1983). *High school: A report on secondary education in America.* New York: Harper & Row.

Breakwell, G. (1986). Political and attributional responses of the young unemployed. *Political Psychology, 7,* 575–586.

Campbell, D. (1974). *The Strong-Campbell interest inventory.* Palo Alto, CA: Stanford University Press.

Canon, A. (1988, February 13). Getting minorities into college. *San Francisco Chronicle,* p. A2.

Charner, I., & Fraser R. (1987). *Youth and work: What we know, what we don't know.* Washington, DC: National Institute for Work and Learning.

Cole, S. (1983). *Working kids on working.* New York: Lothrop, Lee & Shephard.

Cook, M. (1983). *Jobs and schooling.* Baltimore: Johns Hopkins University Center for Social Organization of Schools.

Economic Policy Institute. (1989). *Shortchanging education: How U.S. spending on grades K–12 lags behind other industrial nations.* Washington, DC: Author.

Gerstein, M. (1988). Occupational plans of adolescent women and men. *Career Development Quarterly, 36,* 222–230.

Ginzberg, E. (1972). Toward a theory of occupational choice: A restatement. *Vocational Guidance Quarterly, 21,* 169–176

Ginzberg, E. (1980). *The school work nexus.* Bloomington, IN: Phi Delta Kappan.

Glenbard East *Echo.* (1984). *Teenagers themselves.* New York: Adama Books.

Gottfredson, D. (1987). Youth employment, crime and schooling. *Developmental Psychology, 21,* 419–432.

Gottfried, A. (1988). *Maternal employment and children's development.* New York: Plenum Press.

Gottlieb, D., & Driscoll, E. (1982). *Entering the world of work.* Princeton, NJ: Educational Testing Service.

Government Printing Office. (1988). *Geographic profile of employment and unemployment: 1988.* Washington, DC: Author.

Grant Foundation, W. T. (1988). *The forgotten half: Pathways to success for America's youth and young families.* Washington, DC: Author.

Greenberger, E., & Steinberg, L. (1986). *When teenagers work.* New York: Basic Books.

Grotevant, H., & Cooper, C. (1986). Exploration as a predictor of congruence in adolescents' career choices. *Journal of Vocational Behavior, 29,* 201–215.

Hannah, J., & Kahn, S. (1989). The relationship of socioeconomic status and gender to occupational choices of twelfth grade students. *Journal of Vocational Behavior, 34,* 161–178.

Havighurst, R. (1972). *Developmental tasks and education.* New York: McKay.

Hirschi, T. (1983). Crime and the family. In J. Wilson (Ed.), *Crime and public policy* (pp. 55–64). San Francisco: Institute for Contemporary Studies.

Holland, J. (1985). *Making vocational choices.* Englewood Cliffs, NJ: Prentice-Hall.

Hollinger, C. (1988). Toward an understanding of career development among gifted and talented female adolescents. *Journal for the Education of the Gifted, 12,* 62–79.

Houser, R., & Garvey, C. (1985). Factors that affect nontraditional vocational enrollment among women. *Psychology of Women Quarterly, 49,* 105–117.

Jennings, L. (1989, September 20). Financial educators take aim at bank's youth credit card. *Education Week,* p. 5.

Johnston, W., & Packer, A. (1987). *Workforce 2000: Work and workers for the twenty-first century.* Indianapolis, IN: Hudson Institute.

Kyle, J. (Ed.). (1987). *Children, families and cities.* Washington, DC: National League of Cities.

Lee, C. (1985). An ethnic group and gender comparison of occupational choice among rural adolescents. *Journal of Non-white Concerns in Personnel and Guidance, 13,* 28–37.

Levy, F. (1989). Incomes of college and high school graduates. *The College Board Review, 152,* 35–38.

Lewko, J. (Ed.) (1987). *How children and adolescents view the world of work.* San Francisco: Jossey-Bass.

Mathis, N. (1989, June 14). Way off Broadway, school-based businesses thrive. *Education Week,* p. 7.

Miller, A. & Tsianter, D. (1987, July 20). Greed on Sesame Street? *Newsweek,* pp. 38–40.

Mitchell, C. (1988). Preparing for vocational choice. *Adolescence, 23,* 331–334.

Murphy, S., & Welch, F. (1987). *The structure of wages.* Washington, DC: Department of Labor.

National Assessment of Educational Progress (1988). *Earning and learning: The academic achievement of high school juniors with jobs.* Princeton, NJ: Author.

National Commission on Excellence in Education (1983). *A nation at risk.* Washington, DC: Author.

Nilsen, D. (1984). The youngest workers: 14 and 15 year olds. *Journal of Early Adolescence, 4,* 189–197.

Peters, J. (1987). Youth, family and employment. *Adolescence, 22,* 465–473.

Sandberg, D. (1987). The influence of individual and family characteristics on career aspirations of girls. *Sex Roles, 16,* 11–12.

Schulenberg, J., Vondracek, F., & Crouter, A. (1984). The influence of the family on vocational development. *Journal of Marriage and the Family, 46,* 366–374.

Smith, R., & Lincoln, C. (1988). *America's shame, America's hope: Twelve million youth at risk.* Chapel Hill, NC: MDC Corporation.

Spokane, A. (1985). A review of research on person-environment congruence. *Journal of Vocational Behavior, 26,* 306–343.

Stiehm, J. (1981). *Bring me men and women: Mandated change at the U.S. Air Force Academy.* Berkeley: University of California Press.

Stiehm, J. (1988). *Arms and the enlisted woman.* Philadelphia: Temple University Press.

Super, D. (1976). *Career education and the meanings of work.* Washington, DC: U.S. Office of Education.

U.S. Census Bureau (1980). *Current population survey data.* Washington, DC: U.S. Government Printing Office.

U.S. Census Bureau (1988). *Statistical abstract of the U.S.* Washington, DC: U.S. Government Printing Office.

U.S. Department of Education (1988). *Degrees and other formal awards conferred: 1986–87.* Washington, DC: National Center for Education Statistics.

U.S. Department of Labor (1988a). *Believing once again: Solutions addressing the plight of challenged youth.* Washington, DC: Department of Labor, Training and Employment Institute.

U.S. Department of Labor (1988b). *Annual status report for program year,* Washington, DC: Employment and Training Administration.

Wigginton, E. (1985). *Sometimes a shining moment: 20 years in a high school classroom—The Foxfire experience.* Garden City, NY: Doubleday.

Williams, C. (1989). *Gender differences at work: Women and men in nontraditional occupations.* Berkeley: University of California Press.

12 Adolescent Moral, Religious, and Political Development

CHAPTER OUTLINE

THE DEVELOPMENT OF MORAL REASONING

THE DEVELOPMENTAL PERSPECTIVE

Piaget's Theory

Kohlberg's Theory

The Six Stages of Moral Reasoning

Advancing Moral Reasoning

Criticisms of Kohlberg's Theory

THE SOCIAL LEARNING PERSPECTIVE

THE PSYCHOANALYTIC PERSPECTIVE

MALE AND FEMALE MORAL DEVELOPMENT

ADOLESCENTS AND RELIGION

Limitations of the Research

Religious Affiliation and Attitudes

Factors Influencing Religiosity

Age

Race, Gender, Income

Parents

Religiosity and Misbehavior

Conversion Experiences

ADOLESCENTS' POLITICAL DEVELOPMENT

CONCLUSION

GOALS AND OBJECTIVES

The information in this chapter should enable you to:

- Explain adolescents' moral reasoning from various theoretical viewpoints
- Discuss the controversies regarding male and female moral reasoning
- Describe adolescents' religious attitudes and behavior
- Identify factors influencing adolescents' political and religious views
- Explain the changes in political and moral reasoning from childhood through adolescence

CONCEPTS AND TERMINOLOGY

autonomous morality
born again
cognitive disequilibrium
conventional reasoning
Defining Issues Test (DIT)
Gilligan's "different voice"
moral dilemma
moral realism
postconventional reasoning
values clarification

THE DEVELOPMENT OF MORAL REASONING

How do our feelings about what is right and wrong change as we age? What influences our decisions and our attitudes on moral issues during our teenage years? Why is it that some adolescents seem to have much more sophisticated ways of reasoning about complicated moral issues than their peers? Do males and females have different ways of reasoning about moral issues, and if so, why? Are there ways to help teenagers develop more mature moral reasoning?

Such questions are at the heart of the research on moral development. By moral development we mean the ways people reason about the rules that guide them in situations involving ethical issues. In studying this reasoning, researchers also examine the types of experience and the cognitive skills that influence the individual's ethical principles and decision-making process. The study of moral development also includes an assessment of our feelings after we have behaved rightly or wrongly, according to our individual set of principles. Finally, by observing our behavior or by administering written tests, these psychologists are trying to identify and to explain the ways in which our behavior and our ethical reasoning change as we age. For example, in studying moral development, when Bertha cheats on her math test we might ask such questions as: What factors influenced her to cheat? How does she feel afterwards about having cheated? What reasoning was going on in her head when she made the decision to cheat? Would her reasoning have been different if she had been older, and if so, how? Does her cheating have anything to do with her gender?

In examining the issues related to moral reasoning, psychologists have assumed basically three different approaches: the developmental approach, the psychoanalytic approach, and the social learning approach.

THE DEVELOPMENTAL PERSPECTIVE

Piaget's Theory

The two most famous psychologists who influenced the developmental viewpoint were undoubtedly Jean Piaget and Lawrence Kohlberg. Piaget derived his theories from children's responses to hypothetical moral dilemmas (1932/1965). A **moral dilemma** is a situation in which the person is confronted with having to choose among two or more contradictory courses of action in such a way that choosing one option violates one set of moral principles and choosing the other violates another equally important set. For example, Piaget might present a young child with this moral dilemma: One little boy is trying to sneak jam out of the closet and, in the process, breaks a cup. Another little boy, through no fault of his own, accidentally breaks 12 cups. Which boy is "the naughtier"? Which violation is "worse"?

According to developmental psychologists such as Piaget, our moral development advances from moral realism to autonomous morality during adolescence. Moral realism, the less sophisticated reasoning, is associated with children between the ages of 4 and 7, while moral autonomy is associated with children older than 10. In the stage of **moral realism** a child determines the rightness or wrongness of behavior by considering only the consequences, not the motivations of the individuals. The younger the child, the more likely he or she is to say that the boy who broke the 12 cups by accident is naughtier and that his act is worse. Moral realists also believe that the rules set by authorities are absolute, unquestionable, and permanent. Rather than evaluating the rules on their own to determine whether they are fair or reasonable, children obey rules out of deference to and fear of authority. Morality is naively equated with obedience. The moral realist sees no shades of gray—an act is either right or wrong without consideration for motives or for extenuating circumstances. Then, too, they believe that whenever rules are broken, there will be swift and immediate punishment. They have not yet come to understand that not all of our wrongdoings are punished.

In contrast, adolescents advance into the stage of **autonomous morality,** a morality based on cooperation, reciprocity, motivation, and many shades of gray. Rather than categorizing acts as either right or wrong, adolescents will consider the motives and the circumstances surrounding the situation. This means, of course, that they are less willing to obey rules or adopt moral codes merely out of fear or respect for an authority. Instead, adolescents will take account of the impact of the rules and will empathize with the individuals involved in a moral dilemma. Back to the situation with the broken cups, for example, adolescents would conclude that the boy who broke 1 cup is naughtier than the one who broke 12 cups, since the motive of the former was to steal the jam, while the other boy, despite the fact that he broke more cups, was a well-meaning (although clumsy) fellow.

What causes children to advance to this more mature type of moral reasoning? Are there ways we can help youngsters move from one stage to the next? According to Piaget and his followers, two factors are primarily responsible for this change: our more advanced cognitive skills and the types of interactions we have with our friends and peers. As individuals move from concrete operational thinking to formal operational thinking, their childhood egocentrism slowly gives way to less egocentric ways of viewing the world. In other words, they gain the ability to empathize with other people and to see their perspectives even when those perspectives are different from their own. In dilemmas involving ethical issues, this means individuals can see the legitimacy or the "morality" of several different viewpoints and several different courses of action, even when they are contradictory. Therefore, for example, in the autonomous stage of moral reasoning, individuals are finally able to see both the pros and cons of ethical issues, such as terminating unwanted pregnancies or disobeying military leaders who order the massacre of civilians.

Interactions with childhood friends also help people move from moral realism toward moral autonomy. In working and playing with peers and friends, people learn to see others' viewpoints, to make up their own rules without the guidance of authorities, to determine their own penalties for infractions, and to modify the rules when necessary to suit their group's special needs or special circumstances. These experiences also cause people to examine the motives of others, rather than just to judge their behavior without regard for their intentions. As people work and play together, **cognitive disequilibrium** inevitably occurs. That is, new information and new situations will not fit into existing schemata, thus creating the uncomfortable feelings that accompany cognitive disequilibrium. In order to restore equilibrium, individuals accommodate the new information into their existing schemata, in the process creating more sophisticated moral reasoning.

For example, when a Christian girl from a small, rural, southern community goes off to college, she might be assigned to a suite with three other girls: a Jewish girl from a large, urban west coast city; an agnostic African American girl from a northeastern industrial city; and an Asian American girl from Hawaii. During their year together, they discuss their views and observe one another's behavior regarding birth control, religion, sex, dating, voting, and a host of other areas related to ethical issues. As they interact with and observe each other, each will question and reexamine some of her own beliefs. Each will also feel a certain amount of cognitive disequilibrium as her new experiences collide with some of her existing beliefs and expectations. In the process, according to Piagetians, each girl will advance toward more autonomous moral reasoning.

Kohlberg's Theory

The six stages of moral reasoning Like Piaget, Lawrence Kohlberg believed that we advance through distinct moral stages as we age (1983. See Table 12.1). Also like Piaget, Kohlberg tested his theory by asking children and adolescents to respond to various moral dilemmas. In these interviews, young people would explain their answers to the interviewee, thereby disclosing the types of reasoning they used in arriving at their decisions. One of the best-known of these dilemmas, the story of Heinz and his terminally ill wife, is presented in Box 12.1

According to Kohlberg's six-stage theory, we advance from preconventional reasoning to postconventional reasoning as we age. In the preconventional stage, our moral decisions are based on conforming to the rules in order to avoid punishment and on reciprocating for the sake of personal gain. For instance, a little boy might say he would not tell on his classmate who cheats because "someday she might see me cheating and I don't want her to snitch on me." In other words, it is acceptable to behave unethically as long as you do not get caught. This first level of reasoning ignores intentions and overlooks people's different perspectives.

As we age, however, we begin to base our decisions and our ethics on something other than fear of punishment or the desire for personal gain. In the stage of **conventional reasoning,** we still rely on society's or authorities' standards, but we also become concerned with the fairness of the rules and with other people's motives. Our behavior and our ethical standards are based on a desire to live up to the expectations of other people, to uphold society's goals, and to live by the Golden Rule. We also tend to reason that certain rules are justified for the good of the group or society by arguing that there can be no exceptions to the rule because of what would happen if everyone broke it. For the most part, then, we conform to the rules and ethics defined by others in order to gain their approval.

Table 12.1

Kohlberg's Stages of Moral Development

LEVEL ONE: PRECONVENTIONAL REASONING

Stage 1: Heteronomous Morality

Obeying rules out of fear of punishment and respecting authorities without question. Reasoning from an *egocentric point of view,* the individual does not recognize the perspectives and needs of other people as different from his or her own, nor consider others' needs in making moral decisions.

Stage 2: Individualism

Obeying rules in order to obtain immediate rewards. Although making decisions on the basis of meeting his or her own needs, the individual also lets the concepts of fairness, equal exchange, and keeping agreements serve as rationales for moral decisions. Reasoning from the *concrete individualistic perspective,* the person recognizes that people have different needs, a situation that creates conflicts.

LEVEL TWO: CONVENTIONAL REASONING

Stage 3: Interpersonal Expectations and Conformity

Living up to what others expect and showing concern for others constitute "being good." The individual tries to abide by rules and to make decisions that gain social approval. Abiding by the Golden Rule, the individual lets mutual agreements and societal expectations take precedence over individual interests.

Stage 4: Social System and Conscience

Fulfilling duties and abiding by laws that maintain a fixed order, whether social or religious. Contributing to a society, a group, or an institution is a manifestation of "being good." Through obeying the rules one tries to avoid any disruptions in the established order. Reasoning from a societal point of view, the person considers individuals' interests and interpersonal relationships as secondary to maintaining social order.

LEVEL THREE: POSTCONVENTIONAL REASONING

Stage 5: Social Contact

Being aware that people's opinions differ and that rules and values are relative to each group's idiosyncratic perspectives. Certain values, however, such as liberty, are presumed to be appropriate for all groups. Emphasis is upon equality and mutual obligation within a democratic order. Reasoning from a rational perspective, the person recognizes moral conflicts and finds it difficult to integrate moral, legal, and societal points of view.

Stage 6: Universal Principles

Believing that principles such as justice and equality take precedence over obedience to particular laws or agreements. When laws violate these principles, the person acts in accordance with the principle. Reasoning from the universal perspective, the person transcends any particular culture's perspective of morality.

Sources: L. Kohlberg. (1983). *Moral stages: A current formulation and a response to critics.* London: Karger: (1984). *The psychology of moral development.* San Francisco: Harper & Row.

A CLOSER LOOK 12.1

Kohlberg's Moral Dilemmas: The Story of Heinz

In trying to determine adolescents' stages of moral reasoning, Kohlberg asked them to respond to a series of questions about dilemmas such as this one faced by Heinz:

> In Europe a woman was near death from a special kind of cancer. There was one drug that the doctors thought might save her. It was a form of radium that a druggist in the same town had recently discovered. The drug was expensive to make, but the druggist was charging ten times what the drug cost him to make. He paid $200 for the radium and charged $2,000 for a small dose of the drug. The sick woman's husband, Heinz, went to everyone he knew to borrow the money, but he could only get together $1,000 which is half of what it cost. He told the druggist that his wife was dying and asked him to sell it cheaper or let him pay later. But the druggist said, "No, I discovered the drug and I'm going to make money from it." So Heinz got desperate and broke into the man's store to steal the drug for his wife.

Among the questions Kohlberg and his associates asked the adolescents were: Should Heinz have done that? Was it right or wrong? Why? It is a husband's duty to steal for his wife if he cannot get the money any other way? Did the druggist have the right to charge so much for the drug? Why? What would a good husband do?

Source: L. Kohlberg. (1969). Stage and sequence. In D. Goslin (Ed.), *Handbook of socialization theory and research* (p. 379). Chicago: Rand McNally.

Most adolescents, Kohlberg believed, function at this stage of conventional moral reasoning, as do most adults.

Beyond this, however, is the stage of **postconventional reasoning**—the most sophisticated level we can achieve, according to Kohlberg—a level that most of us reach only after adolescence, if at all. If we ever arrive at this level, we realize that rules and moral codes are relative and flexible, not permanent or written in stone. At this stage, we formulate our ethics and base our decisions on our own personal principles. Rather than feeling obliged to obey rules merely because they have been passed down by authorities, we follow self-chosen ethical principles. When laws violate our principles, we act in accord with the principles.

Advancing moral reasoning Like Piaget, Kohlberg believed that our moral reasoning can be advanced through interactions with our peers. In this spirit, a number of teaching techniques and programs have been designed to move adolescents toward postconventional reasoning (Berkowitz & Oser, 1985; Chazan, 1985; Damon, 1988; Kurtiness & Gewirtz, 1987). These techniques place adolescents in situations where they encounter a level of moral reasoning slightly higher than their own. The cognitive disequilibrium created in these situations is then supposed to help the youngster advance to a higher level of reasoning. Kohlberg also believed parents can help their children move toward more advanced reasoning by encouraging discussions about value-laden issues.

Two approaches focusing on the development of moral reasoning spread widely in our schools during the 1970s and 1980s (Damon, 1988). They are similar in that they use provocative questions and group discussions aimed at making students more thoughtful about the importance of values. The first approach, called **values**

clarification, was introduced in a 1966 book for classroom teachers (Raths, Harmin, & Simon, 1978.). These approaches are based on the assumption that young people should freely choose their own values. The activities, therefore, are designed to provoke students into thinking about their values—not to give them any specific set of moral principles or provide "correct" answers to any moral dilemma. In values clarification activities, students are encouraged to choose their values freely from among as many alternatives as possible, to affirm their own choices whatever they may be, and to behave in accord with their own values consistently in their day-to-day lives. In this approach, teachers ask questions and encourage students to discuss their values more fully but avoid criticizing, giving values, or evaluating the students' responses. The teacher is warned not to lead the student toward any of his or her notions of what is morally right and wrong. Box 12.2 gives an example of the type of discussion that might occur between students and teachers in a values clarification exercise.

A CLOSER LOOK 12.2

Values Clarification in the Classroom

Teacher: So some of you think it is best to be honest on tests, is that right? (Some heads nod affirmatively). And some of you think dishonesty is all right? (A few hesitant and slight nods). And I guess some of you are not certain. (Heads nod.) Well, are there any choices, or is it just a matter of honesty or dishonesty?
Sam: You could be honest some of the time and dishonest some of the time.
Teacher: Does that sound like a possible choice, class? (Heads nod.) Any other alternatives to choose from?
Tracy: You could be honest in some situations and not in others. For example, I'm not honest when a friend asks me about an ugly dress, at least sometimes. (Laughter).
Teacher: Is that a possible choice, class? (Heads nod again.) Any other choices?
Sam: It seems to me that you have to be all one way or all the other.
Teacher: Just a minute, Sam. As usual we are first looking for the alternatives that there are in the issue. Later you can discuss this and see if you are able to make a choice and if you want to make your choice part of your actual behavior. That is something you must do for yourselves.
Ginger: Does this mean that we can decide for ourselves whether we should be honest on tests in here?
Teacher: No, that means you can decide on the value. I personally value honesty, and although you may choose to be dishonest, I will insist that we be honest on our tests here. In other areas of your life, you may have more freedom to be dishonest, but one can't do anything any time, and in this class I will expect honesty on tests.
Ginger: But how can we decide for ourselves? Are you telling us what to value?
Teacher: Not exactly. I don't mean to tell you what you should value. That's up to you. But I mean that in this class, not elsewhere necessarily, you have to be honest on tests or suffer consequences. I merely mean that I can't give tests without the rule of honesty. All of you who choose dishonesty as your value may not practice it here, that's all I'm saying. Further questions anyone?

Source: L. Raths, M. Harmin, & S. Simon. (1978). ***Values and teaching*** (2nd ed.). Columbus, OH: Merrill.

Table 12.2

Three Stage Theories Related to Adolescents' Moral Reasoning

THEORETICAL VIEW	STAGE	MORAL CHARACTERISTICS
Psychoanalytic Theories		
Freud	Oedipal stage	Developing a morality individuated from our parent's values.
Ego Theories		
Erikson	Identity versus confusion	Developing independent ideologies by experimenting with roles and values
Marcia	Identity achieved	Developing a moral code independently
	Foreclosed identity	Adopting the morals of authorities
	Moratorium or diffused	Being uncertain of our own moral values
Cognitive Stage Theories		
Piaget	Formal operations	Developing a less egocentric view
Elkind	Formal operations	Becoming less controlled by the personal fable and imaginary audience
Kohlberg	Conventional reasoning	Becoming more empathetic and aware of others' motives and needs.

Values clarification has enjoyed some popularity in schools since it avoids the controversy about which values should be taught outside the home. On the other hand, the techniques have raised a number of other concerns: Are students being trained to tolerate all values? Are there not some values so central to our society that we should teach them to students? How can teachers not take a position on certain issues, such as cheating? Should adults not act as models for students rather than withholding judgment on moral issues?

Given these concerns, the cognitive-development approach takes a somewhat different tack concerning moral education (Damon, 1988). Unlike values clarification, this approach assumes that some moral views are better than others and that, as children age, they are able to adopt less self-centered values. The adult's responsibility, then, is to promote moral growth and to impart certain values. This is done by exposing the student to a level of moral reasoning just slightly beyond where he or she is presently functioning. So, for example, if a student has not yet learned to take account of other people's feelings and perspectives, the adult might ask a series of questions that would direct everyone's attention to empathy and unselfishness: "How would you feel if the situation were reversed? What do you think the other people in that particular case might be thinking and feeling?" In contrast to values clarification activities, however, in the cognitive-developmental approach, teachers make their own values known. By creating cognitive disequilibrium and by providing models of more advanced ways of reasoning, these methods introduce young people to new ways of thinking about moral issues.

Studies comparing these two approaches generally show that values clarification has less impact than the cognitive approach on changing students' values or ways of reasoning about moral issues (Damon, 1988). On the other hand, there is no convincing evidence that the cognitive approach has any significant impact on students' actual behavior. Also, the older the students, the less impact these cognitive approaches seem to have on their moral reasoning. In other words, at present we do not have evidence that any particular technique actually influences adolescents' behavior in situations calling for moral reasoning.

Criticisms of Kohlberg's theory As you might expect, Kohlberg's ideas have been the subject of considerable criticism and debate (Boyes & Walker, 1988; Gilligan, 1982; Modgil & Modgil 1986; Snarey, 1985). First, as is the case with other stage theories, Kohlberg's work is undermined by evidence showing that adolescents do not invariably pass through the stages in a predictable, universal pattern. Second, it appears that cultural differences do influence our ways of reasoning about moral issues. In this regard, Kohlberg's assertion that postconventional reasoning is superior to other types of moral reasoning has been attacked as ethnocentric and culturally biased. In other words, who is to say that abstract thinking, individualism, and democratic principles—the components of Kohlberg's most advanced stage—are more advanced forms of reasoning than concrete thinking, group-oriented decisions, and communal principles? In fact, the most sophisticated stages in Kohlberg's model tend to be found mainly in technological, democratic societies where the philosophy of individualism prevails. But are these societies more advanced in their moral reasoning than cultures with less individualistic philosophies? In this same vein, as we will see later in this chapter, Kohlberg has come under heavy attack from Carol Gilligan who, among others, finds his assumptions invalid for females.

Furthermore, like other stage theorists Kohlberg assumes that we advance from one stage to the next in such a way that our thinking is distinguishably different in each stage. He also presumes that our moral reasoning parallels our stage of cognitive development. That is, an adolescent who is in Piaget's stage of concrete operational thinking should not be capable of postconventional moral reasoning. Research contradicting these predictions, however, shows that our moral reasoning occasionally reverts to a former stage depending on the situations in which we find ourselves. Moreover, our cognitive development and our style of moral reasoning do not always go hand in hand. For example, even very young children have been found to use postconventional reasoning (Windmiller, Lambert, & Turiel, 1980).

Kohlberg's conclusions have also been criticized on methodological grounds. Because the questions used to determine an individual's stage of moral reasoning are open-ended, subjects must formulate their answers in the presence of an experimenter who then judges their responses. The danger inherent in this method is that subjects may give answers they think will please the experimenter, not answers that represent their own thoughts. Moreover, even Kohlberg agreed with his critics that the scoring procedures are sometimes inadequate or inconsistent.

Above all, Kohlberg has been criticized for assuming that the ways in which we go about reasoning on his hypothetical moral dilemmas reflect our own behavior in any particular real-life situation. In other words, how do we know whether our ways of reasoning about Heinz's situation with his terminally ill wife (see Box 12.1) have any relationship to the ways we actually behave when we are confronted with a moral dilemma in our own lives? We might, for example, have a class of adolescents with high scores on Kohlberg's tests but who are perfectly comfortable cheating on their final exams.

In response to some of these concerns, another alternative to Kohlberg's methods for assessing our styles of moral reasoning has been developed—Rest's **Defining Issues Test (DIT)** (Rest, 1979, 1986). Using multiple-choice questions that can be objectively scored, the DIT presents a series of dilemmas and a list of the major issues to be considered in making each decision. Subjects are then asked to rate the importance of each of the issues involved in making their decision. In the dilemma of Heinz and the druggist, for example, a multiple-choice question might ask us to rate the importance of each of five different issues involved in deciding what Heinz ought to do. According to Rest, his test offers us a more reliable and valid measure of moral thinking than Kohlberg's more subjectively scored personal interview method.

THE SOCIAL LEARNING PERSPECTIVE

In contrast to Kohlberg's and Piaget's cognitive views, social learning theorists start from the position that our moral attitudes and behavior are primarily determined by the ways in which we are punished and reinforced in particular situations. In this light, an adolescent's moral values and ways of reasoning about ethical issues depend on his or her particular history of reward and punishment. Through reinforcement, punishment, and modeling, we learn which behaviors are supposedly right and wrong. In other words, the types of reward given for being good and the likelihood of being punished for being bad in any given situation influence our moral decisions and reasoning (Damon, 1988; Eisenberg, 1987; Hoffman, 1984; Kurtiness & Gewirtz, 1987; Rest, 1986; Rich & Devitis, 1985).

Therefore, for example, the social learning theorist contends that Bernie cheats on his exam because he has been rewarded for this behavior in the past by getting higher grades when he cheats than when he is honest. Since he has not yet been caught for his wrongdoing, and since he sees other students in class cheating without getting punished, he figures that this unethical behavior is worth the risks. On the other hand, Bernie's classmate Dreyfus does not cheat, even though he is failing the course. Why? Perhaps because he has been convinced by his church group that God "sees all" and that there will be a heavy price to pay in the hereafter for behavior such as cheating and lying. Although he is "punished" for his honesty by failing the test, he is "rewarded" by his thoughts that he will be noticed and appreciated by his God. Then there is Gertrude, who does not cheat on the test even though her grades are bad, because the last time she cheated the teacher caught her and she had some heavy-duty punishment right here on earth when she got home and had to confess to her parents. Obviously, social learning theorists are critical of cognitive psychologists such as Piaget and Kohlberg for placing too little emphasis on the situational factors that influence us.

Social learning theorists also contend that our moral reasoning and moral behavior are, at least in part, shaped by our parents' ways of disciplining and communicating with us. Those whose parents used an overly authoritarian style of communication and discipline tend to base their moral decisions on the fear of external punishment. Accustomed to their parents controlling them through these excessively punitive, dictatorial methods, these individuals in turn, base their ethics on the principle that "might makes right." In these families, the sense of guilt comes about when the individuals are punished for their misdoings by others, not from the individuals' own internalized standards based on feelings of empathy or fairness or reciprocity. In contrast, those whose parents used a more democratic, yet authoritative, style usually base ethical decisions on their own internalized principles rather than on the fear of getting caught. In these families, individuals are more apt to learn to feel bad about their wrongdoings out of a sense of compassion and empathy for other people rather than merely in response to a fear of external punishment.

This is not to say that social learning theorists totally discount our cognitive abilities as having an influence on our moral behavior. Like cognitive psychologists, they agree that as we age we are better equipped cognitively to think into the future, to think abstractly, and to empathize with others. In general, we become less egocentric and more able to see the bigger picture in going beyond our own personal experiences in thinking about ethical issues. These cognitive advances, in turn, have an impact of their own, separate from the system of rewards and punishments that control our behavior. So, for example, back to Bernie—as he ages he is more likely to empathize with the teacher's position or with other students in his class. This greater ability to empathize might then influence his decisions about cheating. As Box 12.3 illustrates, and as both social learning theorists and cognitive theorists agree, we tend to become more aware of the principles of fairness and reciprocity as we move from childhood through adolescence.

THE PSYCHOANALYTIC PERSPECTIVE

A third perspective on the development of moral reasoning is the psychoanalytic approach. Within the traditional Freudian model the superego assumes a special significance during our adolescence (Josselson, 1980). As a child, the "contents" of your superego were the lessons and moral or religious ideologies given to you by others. You adopted these ideas of good and evil without question, and when you were bad, as defined by the authorities, you felt a scary, disquieting, uncomfortable feeling—guilt. Simply put, your superego is your conscience, the voice or feeling in you that says, "I'm good for doing what 'they' have told me is good" or "I'm bad for doing what 'they' have told me is bad." The "they" included your parents, religious institution, teachers, and any other authority figures in your life as a child.

During adolescence, however, a change occurs. The ego, the aspect of your personality that is most in contact with "reality," begins to evaluate the contents of your superego—to question whether all the standards from parents and other authorities are indeed "good." According to psychoanalytic theory, one of your primary tasks as an adolescent is to sort through your superego's contents and to

A CLOSER LOOK 12.3

Fairness and Friendship: How the Concept of Justice Dev.elops

• Two boys, a little one and a big one, once went for a long walk in the mountains. When lunchtime came, they were very hungry and took their food out of their bags, but they found that there was not enough food for both of them. What should have been done? Give all the food to the big boy or to the little one, or the same to both? (Piaget, 1932/1965)

• A class of schoolchildren drew pictures to sell at a fair. Some of the children were lazy and did not draw many pictures. Other children were poorer than their classmates. What should be done with the money collected by the class after the fair? Should everyone get the same portion of the money, or should those who worked hardest get more? Should the poor children receive more than others? (Damon, 1980).

• You and your friend have each been given a picture to color, but your friend's is twice as large as yours. The teacher tells you that rewards will depend on how much of the picture each person completes. Although you are told that you may help one another, you are also told that there will be no rewards for helping. What will you do? (Berndt, 1982)

• These three hypothetical dilemmas exemplify the types of question posed by researchers who study the development of such moral values as justice and fairness. From such research we have learned that the principles children apply in deciding what is fair or unfair change with age. Testing the theories of Piaget and Kohlberg, contemporary researchers are exploring questions about distributive justice: Does an adolescent treat a friend differently than a stranger when deciding what constitutes fair conduct? How do our concepts of justice change as we age?

• Piaget's work represented the first major attempt to explain the development of distributive justice. According to Piaget, young children are egocentric, lacking the ability to appreciate another person's point of view. Since they rely solely on authorities for their moral codes, young children will accept unfair treatment as fair, if it is condoned by an authority. As children age and have more experiences with peers, however, they begin to perceive fairness as synonymous with equity. For example, confronted with a

continued

figure out for yourself which standards to keep and which to jettison. This process is part of *individuation*—establishing a self that is more than just a reflection of your parents and developing a conscience based on your own standards of right and wrong. This does not mean rejecting every moral principle your parents and other authorities have given you, but sorting principles through on your own. As an adolescent, you will judge some of the authorities' ethical standards as good and keep them as ethical principles against which to judge yourself as good or bad. Others you will throw out like outgrown clothes: "That fit me as a child, but it doesn't fit me now."

According to the psychoanalytic view, this sorting out process is a healthy, desirable part of adolescence. Without it, you would stay bound to other people's ideas of morality, never establishing an ethical code of your own for yourself. As the psychoanalytic theorist James Marcia pointed out (1980), it is unfortunate that some of us as adolescents do adopt this foreclosed identity—we wear the identities of our parents and other authorities without trying on different identities of our own to see which fits us best. And, as we have seen in earlier chapters, it seems

Box 12.3 continued

hypothetical situation of the two boys and the sandwiches, most 6- and 7-year-olds say the bigger boy should get the most food because he is older, not because he is hungrier. Most 9- and 10-year-olds, however, say that the younger boy should have more food for such reasons as, "He will not be able to finish their walk without a good lunch, because he is little." Older children are more concerned with creating an equitable outcome.

• During the 1970s, Damon's investigations of children's moral reasoning focused extensively on the development of distributive justice. Furthermore, Damon believed that our childhood notions about distributive justice are primarily related to our abilities to engage in the classification and seriation of physical objects. In other words, our childhood beliefs about distributing rewards fairly depend on our ability to reason logically about physical objects. Consequently, in order to reason maturely about fairness, a child must be functioning at least in the stage of concrete operational thinking.

• Children reasoning at the lowest level of distributive justice make self-centered decisions without providing any logical rationale. "I should get most of the money because I want it." Children at the next higher level justify their decision by considering some external characteristics of other people. Nevertheless, the underlying rationale is still self-serving. Hence, a boy says: "The boys should get more money than girls because they're boys." Children then progress to equating fairness with equity: "Everyone should get the same amount of money, no matter how many pictures they drew." Finally, children equate fairness with distributing rewards on the basis of relative performance: "Those who drew the most pictures should get the most money."

• After the age of 9, a child can consider several principles simultaneously. A young person may then consider giving the most money to the poorest children in the class, giving the most to those who drew the most pictures, or giving everyone the same amount because it was a class project rather than an individual venture. While considering all these possibilities simultaneously, a child will eventually choose one principle on which to base his or her choice.

Source: T. Berndt. (1982). Fairness and friendship. In K. Rubin & H. Ross (Eds.), *Peer relationships and social skills in childhood,* New York: Springer Verlag; W. Damon, (1980). Patterns of change in children's social reasoning. *Child Development, 51,* 1010–1017.

that female adolescents are more apt than males to adopt this foreclosed identity, never examining the contents of their own superegos but instead adopting the superegos of those in authority (Josselson, 1987).

MALE AND FEMALE MORAL DEVELOPMENT

One of the most controversial new theories is Carol **Gilligan's "different voice"** concept (Gilligan, 1982; Gilligan, Ward, & Taylor, 1988). According to Gilligan, a developmental psychologist who initially worked with Kohlberg at Harvard, girls solve moral dilemmas using a different set of standards than boys. Given these differences, Gilligan and her advocates argue that Kohlberg's ways of determining the maturity or immaturity of our moral reasoning are inappropriate for females. Kohlberg assumed that moral decisions in which we put rules ahead of relationships or ahead of pleasing other people reflect the most mature and sophisticated kind of reasoning. Consequently, since most girls learn to define their goodness and their identity on the basis of maintaining close relationships and pleasing others, they usually show up as less mature and less advanced than boys on Kohlberg's scales. Gilligan, however, contends that females are socialized to base their ethical principles on interpersonal relationships, while males are socialized to base their ethics on individuation and separation from others. As a consequence, Gilligan changed Kohlberg's moral dilemmas to ones involving relationships and scored female responses from an interpersonal, caring perspective. Using this approach, Gilligan found that girls are just as mature in their moral reasoning as boys.

For example, in asking boys and girls what people should do when responsibility to themselves and responsibility to others are in conflict, a young boy answered, "You go about one fourth to the other and three fourths to yourself. The most important thing in your decision should be yourself. Don't let yourself be guided totally by other people, but you have to take them in consideration." In contrast, a girl answered, "Well, it really depends on the situation. If it's just your responsibility to your job or to somebody that you barely know, then maybe you go first—but if it's somebody that you really love and love as much [as] or even more than you love yourself, you've got to decide what you really love more, that person or the thing or yourself. You can't just decide, 'well, I'd rather do this or that' " (Gilligan, 1982, p. 36).

As a result of the different ways in which boys and girls are socialized, Gilligan believes that their moral development takes different paths. Boys feel that their primary responsibility is to themselves, considering their responsibility to others as secondary. Girls, on the other hand, consider their responsibilities to other people first, relegating their own well-being and needs to second place. Thus each sex has its own moral developmental tasks. For boys, moral development entails coming to see other people's needs as equal to their own, while for girls it entails coming to see their own needs as equal to other people's. While girls base their moral decisions on too much self-sacrifice, boys base theirs on too little. In other words, boys' moral reasoning ought to take other people into account more, and girls ought to consider themselves more. According to Gilligan, both males and females need to base their moral decisions on principles that incorporate both the masculine and the feminine perspective: Moral issues cannot always be resolved without someone being hurt. Moral behavior does not always have to involve self-sacrifice. Behaving in a moral or responsible manner does not mean totally ignoring your own needs and your own well-being. Caring for your own needs and asserting yourself are not necessarily the equivalent of selfishness.

As previous chapters have demonstrated, it does appear that girls are more likely than boys to base their identities on their relationships with other people. Gilligan's assertion that males and females operate by different standards regarding their moral decisions, however, has been criticized on a number of counts. Among these criticisms the most important is that the research, including meta-analyses and experimental studies, has not found differences between males' and females' moral reasoning when their occupations and educational levels are similar (Colby & Damon, 1983; Gibbs, Arnold, & Burkhart, 1984; Greeno & Maccoby, 1986; Luria, 1986; Thoma, 1986). For example, in 61 studies that used Kohlberg's methods for assessing moral reasoning, males did not generally score differently from females (Walker, 1984). Even when Gilligan's methods for measuring moral reasoning are used, males and females have been found to reason more alike than differently (Friedman, Robinson, & Friedman, 1987; Lowery & Ford, 1986).

Critics have also pointed out that the studies on which Gilligan based her theory were methodologically flawed. First, her original theory was based on only two studies—one in which only 29 women were asked to discuss their decisions regarding abortion, and the other in which only 16 boys and girls responded to Kohlberg's moral dilemma questions. Second, Gilligan did not study the actual behavior of her subjects or take into account the research showing that most of our moral decisions are situation specific. That is, we do not adopt one type of moral reasoning and apply it in all situations (Gibbs & Schnell, 1985). Instead, we usually make our decisions based on the particulars of each moral dilemma in which we find ourselves. These two criticisms, of course, also apply to the theories of Kohlberg and Piaget. As stage theorists, they also believed that our moral reasoning was consistent across all situations, and neither Piaget nor Kohlberg studied his subjects' actual behavior in real-life moral situations.

In this same vein, since most men and women live under different conditions, notably in their access to money and power, our moral sense of responsibility to other people versus our sense of responsibility to ourselves may depend more on our social and economic position than on our sex. Could it not be that people in positions of power, whether male or female, tend to be more self-centered and to focus more on rules and rationality than those with less power (Hare-Mustin & Maracek, 1986)? For example, poor African American men and women have been found to have similar ways of reasoning in that they are less self-centered and more focused on interpersonal relationships—a finding suggesting that even if Gilligan's theory regarding sex differences is applicable to white, middle-class people, it does not necessarily apply to other groups with less access to power and money (Stack, 1986).

Why, then, have Gilligan's assertions been met with such widespread acceptance, particularly among women themselves? In part, this is because her findings reflect the traditional sex role stereotypes of females being more altruistic, empathic, and self-sacrificing than males. Intuitively we feel that Gilligan must be right, yet both males and females have been trapped into sex role stereotypes by this same willingness to trust our personal intuitions and to discount the actual research data. The different voice is also part of a currently popular category of theory, sometimes referred to as *cultural feminism,* that argues on behalf of females' special, and even superior, nature (Scott, 1988). To assume that all girls and women are more empathetic and less self-centered than all boys and men is to adopt the false premise that people of the same sex share the same perspectives and moral values regardless of their economic or social differences (Eisenstein, 1983).

ADOLESCENTS AND RELIGION

Limitations of the Research

In trying to understand how adolescents feel about religion, how religion influences their behavior, and how they develop their religious attitudes, we are limited by a number of shortcomings in the research (Benson, Donahue, & Erickson, 1989). First, most of what is known about young people's involvement in religion comes from college students or other young adults, not from adolescents.

In this same vein, the information we have about people who have undergone religious conversion experiences, such as born again Christians or Moonies, comes from people older than 18. Second, studies attempting to describe how our religious views change as we age have used cross-sectional, not longitudinal, designs. That is, the researchers have not followed the same group of children or adolescents as they age but have instead compared different groups of people who are different ages. Third, race and ethnicity have seldom been considered, nor has the relative effect of parents versus peers on adolescents' religious attitudes or behavior. Although it seems reasonable to assume that peers have an impact in this area, we do not have research to substantiate this hunch. Then, too, since attendance at religious services and denominational affiliation are not usually under the control of the adolescent until after he or she moves away from home, measuring teenagers' attitudes by asking them what church or synagogue they belong to and how often they attend is not a particularly valid assessment of their own feelings or beliefs. Whether adolescents attend religious services and where they attend are usually their parents' decisions, not their own. Finally, we have virtually no information about the relationship between religion and a teenagers' personality, self-esteem, or behavior. In other words, we have not collected data that enable us to determine how religiosity is related to such important teenage behavior as drug use, sex, pregnancy, racism, altruism, empathy, or volunteerism. Perhaps most surprising is the failure to explore the possible connections between religion and an adolescent's level of moral reasoning. Given these limitations, we cannot yet answer such intriguing questions as: Are religious adolescents more likely than other teenagers to avoid drugs, abstain from sex, be less racist, be more altruistic, be more empathetic? Other than going to church or temple, is the behavior of religious teenagers different in any appreciable way from anyone else's?

Given these limitations, we can examine the data that identify adolescents' religious affiliation, their attendance at religious services, and the ways in which our religious ideas seem to change throughout our childhood and adolescence.

Religious Affiliation and Attitudes

Among adults in our society, nearly 85% of the people identify themselves as Christians, 35% of whom are Catholics, 21% Baptist, 10% Methodist, 7% Lutheran, 3% Presbyterian, 2% Episcopalian, 2% Church of Christ, and 2% Disciples of Christ. Another 3% of the population identifies itself as Jewish, while the remainder say they have no religious affiliation. In contrast to their elders, in Gallup's nationwide poll of 13- to 18-year-olds, 50% said they are Protestants, 40% Catholics, 3% Jewish, 3% other, and 6%-no preference."

Attendance at churches and synagogues has remained fairly consistent during the past 50 years, with approximately 40% of all adults attending a service weekly. The highest rates of attendance, nearly 50%, were reached in 1955 and 1958, and the lowest rate, 37%, in 1940. Since 1969, however, the rates have not changed by more than two percentage points from year to year. More females attend than males, and more people living in the East attend than in other regions of the country—a finding that has been attributed to the large Catholic population in the eastern states.

As you would expect, not all adolescents share the same degree of commitment to organized religions, even though they may identify themselves as having a

What role does religion play in your life?

religious affiliation. The majority of adolescents in Gallup's nationwide surveys describe themselves as "moderately religious," meaning they attend a religious service at least once a month. The 10% who reported themselves as "highly" religious attended services at least once a week. Nearly one-third labeled themselves as "low" in religiosity, meaning that they attend a service only on rare occasions. Nearly 95% of these adolescents profess belief in "God or a universal spirit," about the same percentage as among adults. Additionally, 58% believe in life after death and 87% pray at least occasionally.

Are today's adolescents less religious than those in previous decades? According to most surveys, yes (Benson, Donahue, & Erickson, 1989). Today's teenagers are less likely than those in the 1970s to attend a religious service, read the Bible, have a religious preference, or pray. The most thorough, long-term study of trends in adolescents' religious beliefs, which has surveyed a nationally representative sample of 16,000 high-school seniors each year since 1976, shows that the importance of religion declined between 1980 and 1985 (See Figure 12.1; Johnston, Bachman, & O'Malley, 1986). For example, in 1985 only 35% of the adolescents attended a religious service weekly.

Factors Influencing Religiosity

Age Although the data are limited in that they come from cross-sectional studies, it does appear that our religious beliefs change as we leave childhood and pass through adolescence (Benson, Donahue, & Erickson, 1989; Heller, 1988; Nye & Carlson, 1984). As we become more proficient at abstract thinking, most of us develop more sophisticated religious concepts. For example, as teenagers we are less likely than we were as young children to believe in literal translations of the Bible or to believe in a God who actually exists in some humanlike form in a location somewhere in the sky. Our reasons for believing in a deity also change as we age. For instance, when asked why they believe in a God, young children typically give answers that rely exclusively on what they have been told to believe by those in authority: "I believe in God because the Bible says so." "I know there's a God because my daddy told me there was." In contrast, adolescents

FIGURE 12.1
Adolescents' religiosity

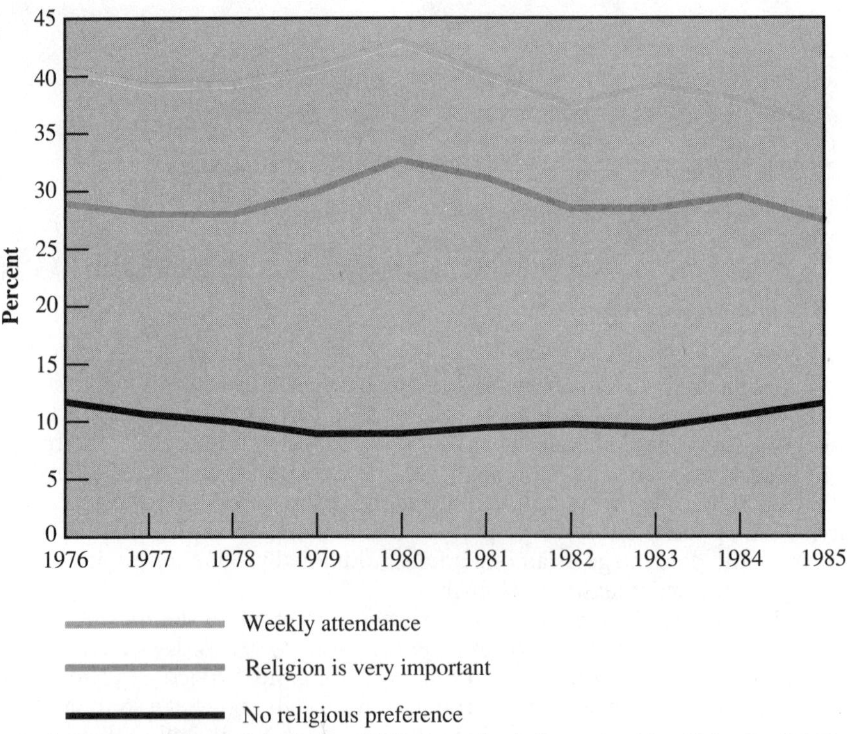

Source: L. Johnston, J. Bachman, & P. O'Malley. (1986). *Monitoring the Future*. Ann Arbor: University of Michigan, Institute for Social Research.

rely on more rational thinking: "There must be a God because the universe is so orderly."

Among the more extensive studies of how religious thinking changes as people age is the work of James Fowler (1981). By interviewing people between the ages of 4 and 84 from a variety of socioeconomic and racial backgrounds, Fowler delineated six stages of faith. The third stage, occurring in early adolescence, relies on the ability of people to think abstractly and to reflect on their own thinking. A principal task for individuals in this stage is to adapt their own religious views with the incompatible views of other people. In other words, they must have the maturity to recognize the disparities and incongruities among various religions, yet to hold views of their own simultaneously. In the next stage, later in adolescence, people begin to reexamine their own viewpoints and to examine objectively how their religious beliefs evolved.

As individuals move from early to late adolescence, their involvement in religion also usually declines (Benson, Donahue, & Erickson, 1989; Johnston, Bachman, & O'Malley, 1986). Young adolescents are more likely to attend a religious service and to consider religion important than are older adolescents. In addition to having more advanced cognitive skills, the older adolescents have generally been given more control over their own decisions as they aged, which may, at least in part, account for these changes.

Race, gender, income In terms of race and gender, teenage girls are generally more involved in religion than boys, as is the case with adult men and women, and African American youths and their parents generally attach more importance to religion than do whites. Regardless of race, however, adolescents living in rural areas, those with less education, and those with lower incomes are the most likely to attend religious services and to consider religion an important part of their daily lives (Benson, Donahue, & Erickson, 1989; Gallup, 1984).

Parents Not surprisingly, young people are more likely to remain affiliated with their parents' denomination than to convert to another faith. Indeed, parents are among the strongest influences on adolescent religious behavior. Similarly, attending a Catholic school that involves at least 1,000 hours of classroom instruction in religion seems to have a long-term impact on adolescent religiousness among Catholic youth (Spilka, Hood, & Gorsuch, 1985). It is difficult, however, to assess the effects of religious education, since most parents who send their children to religious schools are themselves very religious people. Although little research has investigated the effect of parents and peers, it seems that the peer group probably has less overall impact on adolescents' religiosity than cultural folklore suggests (Benson, Donahue, & Erickson, 1989).

Religiosity and Misbehavior

How do attending religious services and affiliating with a church or synagogue affect adolescents' behavior? Are religious teenagers any less likely than others to "misbehave" in terms of drug use, sex, delinquency, or racism? In contrast to other types of behavior, the literature concerning the effects of religiousness on sexual intercourse is sufficiently large and consistent in its findings (Benson, Donahue & Erickson, 1989). In regard to white adolescents, attending religious services is highly correlated with abstaining from sexual intercourse. In regard to

African American adolescents, however, this does not seem to be the case (McCormick, Izzo-Folcik, 1985). In other words, African American adolescents, even those who are churchgoers, tend to be more sexually active than whites. These findings suggest that African American and white cultural attitudes toward teenage pregnancies and sexuality may have an impact separate from that of religion.

The research findings on the relationship between religiosity and other forms of adolescent behavior, however, are less clear (Benson, Donahue, & Erickson, 1989). Most of the evidence seems to indicate that religion inhibits drug use, although less so with alcohol than with other drugs. Nevertheless, the findings are more contradictory than those regarding religion and sex. In regard to religion and delinquency the correlations are weaker still. The most frequent explanation for these findings is that religious values have their greatest effect when they differ from the values of the society at large. Since our society is more accepting of teenagers having sex and drinking than it is of delinquency, being religious would make less difference to a teenager's decisions about delinquency than to his or her decisions regarding sex and alcohol.

Conversion Experiences

In later adolescence, some young people undergo conversion experiences, returning to their Christian faith or being converted from a mainline religious group into a religious sect, such as the Hare Krishnas. The phenomenon now popularly known as being **born again,** an abrupt, rapid change to an enthusiastic religious attitude with highly emotional experiences, is not new to those who study the psychology of religion (Ellwood, 1988; Meadow & Kahoe, 1984; Spilka, Hood & Gorsuch, 1985). In fact, conversion may be the best-researched single topic in the psychology of religion. There is even a standard model of the conversion process: conflict, crisis, conversion, contentment. The traditional consensus among researchers has been that most conversions come about during adolescence as a result of confusion in values and lack of purpose in life and that the adolescent tries to resolve these issues by "making a decision for Christ" or adopting some other religious system in toto.

More recent research, however, has challenged some of these earlier assumptions. For example, conversion experiences are not as limited to adolescents as had once been assumed. That is, older adults also have these experiences. It now seems that the supposition that conversions typically took place during adolescence came about because most researchers had restricted their samples to college students. Unfortunately almost all our information about conversion experiences is still based on college students or older adults, not on adolescents (Benson, Donahue, & Erickson, 1989).

ADOLESCENTS' POLITICAL DEVELOPMENT

Recognizing that religious beliefs usually undergo changes from childhood through adolescence, researchers have also examined the changes in political thinking during this period. Once again, however, our information is limited in that most studies about political values have been restricted to college students. The few that do exist with adolescent samples do, however, illustrate the changes that seem to occur as youths move through adolescence (Adelson, 1982; Gallatin, 1980).

As is the case with religious attitudes and ways of reasoning about religion, individuals think more abstractly about political issues as they age. Equipped with the more advanced mental skills that accompany formal operational thinking, they start to understand more complicated political ideologies and to appreciate political viewpoints that differ from their own. It is worth noting, however, that adolescents' tolerance toward other people's political views seems to vary in accord with their cognitive maturity. For example, seventh- and ninth-graders who are the most willing to grant political rights to people whose views differ from theirs are those with the most advanced reasoning abilities and the most experience with political issues (Avery, 1988). Older adolescents, however, are generally more tolerant and less apt to see only their own political views as the ideal. Regarding the enforcement of laws, young adolescents are also more inclined to recommend harsh punishments for violations. For example, younger adolescents are more likely to endorse the death penalty than are older adolescents. Even in cross-cultural studies of younger and older adolescents, researchers have concluded that the youngest adolescents are the most likely to have a system of political justice similar to that of Attila the Hun (Adelson, 1982). Similarly, older adolescents' opinions regarding our country's

How politically active are you? Why?

military involvement in Latin America are less punitive, harsh, and extremist than are younger adolescents' views (Roscoe, Stevenson, & Kennedy, 1988).

Given the number of hours most adolescents spend watching television, it is not particularly surprising that their knowledge of political matters is primarily gleaned from that medium (Garramone & Atkin, 1986). Perhaps the impact of television, which has become more widespread throughout the country among all socioeconomic groups, helps account for the finding that the political attitudes of southern and northern youths have become more similar in recent years (Corbett, 1988).

CONCLUSION

Whether we endorse the cognitive or the psychoanalytic or the social learning views, it is nontheless clear that most adolescents' political, religious, and moral reasoning is more advanced than that of younger children. Their attitudes and their behavior generally become more tolerant, more empathetic, and more compassionate. Able to appreciate the perspectives and the motives of other people, adolescents adopt a more flexible, more independent moral code—a code that, as the next chapter demonstrates, will affect some of the most important decisions they will confront during their teenage years—whether to use and abuse drugs.

QUESTIONS FOR DISCUSSION AND REVIEW

Basic Concepts and Terminology

1. Explain Piaget's theories of moral development by providing definitions and specific examples of moral realism, cognitive disequilibrium, and autonomous morality.
2. Explain Kohlberg's theory of moral development by providing definitions and specific examples of preconventional, conventional, and postconventional reasoning, heteronomous morality, and individualism.
3. How do Carol Gilligan's theories of moral development differ from Kohlberg's and Piaget's? On what bases have her theories been criticized?
4. How are children's and adolescents' moral reasoning skills assessed in the research by Piaget, Kohlberg, Rest, and Gilligan? What are the strengths and weaknesses of this approach?
5. Define *values clarification* by giving specific examples of how this would be used by a classroom teacher. What are its goals? How effective has it been shown to be?
6. How does the cognitive developmental approach to moral education differ from values clarification? How effective has it proved to be?
7. What are the criticisms leveled against Kohlberg's theories and those leveled against Gilligan's theories?
8. According to Piaget and Kohlberg, how can we help adolescents develop more advanced moral reasoning skills?
9. How do Marcia's identity statuses relate to adolescents' moral reasoning skills?
10. How do the social learning theorists' views differ from those of the cognitive developmental psychologists, such as Piaget and Kohlberg?
11. How do empathy and self-centeredness generally change from childhood through adolescence? How are these changes related to the ways in which an individual reasons about moral dilemmas?
12. According to psychoanalytic theory, how do the

ego, superego, and individuation affect our moral reasoning? What changes should occur during adolescence?

13. How do males and females generally differ in regard to empathy and the importance of interpersonal relationships? How might this affect moral reasoning?
14. What limitations restrict our knowledge about adolescents' religious views and the development of religious thinking?
15. Describe the adolescent population in terms of religious affiliation and their degree of religiosity.
16. What factors influence adolescents' religious beliefs and their degree of religiosity? Which seem to be the most influential?
17. How closely related is an adolescent's religiosity to his or her use of drugs, delinquency, sexual behavior, drinking?
18. What is a conversion experience? According to traditional theories, when and why do these typically occur? How have these views been somewhat modified by more recent research?
19. How do our political views and ways of reasoning about political matters typically change during adolescence? Give specific examples of children's and adolescents' responses to support your answer.
20. How do our views of God and our ways of reasoning about religious matters usually change as we age? What factors account for these changes?

Questions for Discussion and Debate

1. How do you feel about Carol Gilligan's assertions that females make their moral decisions and form their ethical standards from a less self-centered position than males? On what experiences are you basing your feelings?
2. Which of Kohlberg's stages best describes your moral reasoning as an adolescent? How have your ways of reasoning about moral dilemmas changed, if at all, since your adolescence? What has accounted for these changes or the lack of change?
3. Which moral dilemmas did you find most difficult as an adolescent? How do these differ from the moral dilemmas that now confront you?
4. On what principles do you base your moral decisions and your ethical code? How have these changed since your childhood? What brought about these changes?
5. Which experiences and which people have been most influential in shaping your political and religious ideologies? How much impact did your peers and your parents have on your beliefs as an adolescent?
6. How would you describe yourself as an adolescent and now in terms of your religiosity? How do your religious views and activities compare to those of the adolescents and young adults in Gallup's national polls?
7. How do you think schools, parents, and religious institutions should handle the issue of moral education? How do you feel about values clarification methods versus the cognitive-developmental approach? Why?
8. In what specific instances have you experienced cognitive disequilibrium? How did these experiences with cognitive dissonance change your ways of reasoning about moral issues, your religious beliefs, and your political ideologies?
9. Using a psychoanalytic approach to explain your own moral development, how did your superego change during your adolescence? How did your parents react to your individuation?
10. In the story of Heinz (Box 12.1), how did you respond? What moral principles underlay your decision? Do you think our analyzing your responses to Heinz's situation is a valid way of assessing your level of moral reasoning? Why or why not?
11. If you were the teacher in the example in Box 12.2, how would you have responded to your students' comments? How do you feel about this teacher's responses? Why?
12. Using the social learning theorists' perspective, how would you explain the development of your religious and political beliefs and your ways of reasoning about religious or political issues? How adequately does the social learning perspective account for the changes in your moral, religious, or political thinking during adolescence?

13. Have you or anyone you know ever had a conversion experience? How did this affect your life or theirs? What do you think accounts for these experiences?
14. How do you personally differentiate between a religion and a cult and between brainwashing and socializing a child into adopting certain religious viewpoints? Should parents have the legal right to stop an adolescent from joining a religious group they oppose? Why?
15. How have the media and religious institutions influenced your religious and political viewpoints since early adolescence?

GLOSSARY

autonomous morality According to Piaget, the stage of moral reasoning generally achieved during adolescence and characterized by reciprocity, questioning authorities, empathy, and abstract thinking.

born again Undergoing an emotional and abrupt conversion to a religion.

cognitive disequilibrium According to Piaget, the process that occurs when new events or new information cannot be handled by existing schemata; thus, new learning takes place so that cognitive equilibrium can be restored.

conventional reasoning According to Kohlberg, the stage of moral reasoning in which our behavior and values are primarily determined by external rewards, punishments, and the rules of "the authorities."

Defining Issues Test (DIT) A test used to assess adolescents' stages of moral reasoning.

Gilligan's different voice Carol Gilligan's theory that males and females base their moral values and behavior on different principles.

moral dilemma A situation in which the person is confronted with having to choose among two or more alternative courses of action, in such a way that choosing one violates one set of moral principles and choosing the other violates another, equally important set.

moral realism According to Piaget, the stage of moral reasoning characteristic of childhood that is based on authorities' viewpoints, clearcut notions of right and wrong, and external reward and punishment.

postconventional reasoning According to Kohlberg, the most sophisticated level of moral reasoning in which we see rules and moral codes as relative and flexible.

values clarification Classroom activities designed to help adolescents examine and evaluate their moral values and behavior.

REFERENCES

Adelson, J. (1982, Summer). Rites of passage: How children learn the principles of community. *American Educator,* pp. 60–67.

Avery, P. (1988). Political tolerance among adolescents. *Theory and Research in Social Education, 16,* 183–201.

Benson, P., Donahue, M., & Erickson, J. (1989). Adolescence and religion: Review of the literature from 1970–1986. *Research in the Social Scientific Study of Religion, 1,* 153–181.

Berkowitz, M. & Oser S. (1985). (Eds.). *Moral education: Theory and applications.* New York: Erlbaum.

Berndt, T. (1982). Fairness and friendship. In K. Rubin and H. Ross (Eds.), *Peer relationships and social skills in childhood.* pp. 252–278. New York: Springer Verlag.

Boyes, M., & Walker, L. (1988). Implications of cultural diversity for the university claims of Kohlberg's theory of moral reasoning. *Human Development, 31,* 60–64.

Chazan, B. (1985). *Contemporary approaches to moral education.* New York: Columbia Teachers College.

Colby, A., & Damon, W. (1983). Listening to a different voice: A review of Gilligan. *Merrill Palmer Quarterly, 29,* 473–481.

Corbett, M. (1988). Changes in noneconomic political attitudes of Southern and Northern youth. *Journal of youth and adolescence, 17,* 197–210.

Damon, W. (1988). *The moral child.* New York: Macmillan.

Damon, W. (1980). Patterns of change in children's social reasoning. *Child Development, 51,* 1010–1017.

Eisenberg, R. (1987). *Empathy and its development.* Cambridge, England: Cambridge University Press.

Eisenstein, H. (1983). *Contemporary feminist thought.* Boston: G. K. Hall.

Ellwood, R. (1988). Religions and spiritual groups in modern America. Englewood Cliffs, NJ: Prentice-Hall.

Fowler, J. (1981). *Stages of faith.* New York: Harper & Row.

Friedman, E., Robinson, A., & Friedman, B. (1987). Sex differences in moral judgments? *Psychology of Women Quarterly, 11,* 37–46.

Gallatin, J. (1960). Political thinking in adolescence. In J. Adelson (Ed.), *Handbook of adolescent psychology* (pp. 344–383). New York: Wiley.

Gallup, G. (1984). *Religion in America.* Princeton, NJ: Princeton Religion Research Center.

Garramone, G., & Atkin, C. (1986). Mass communication and political socialization. *Public Opinion Quarterly, 50,* 76–86.

Gibbs, J., Arnold, K., & Burkhart, J. (1984). Sex differences in the expression of moral judgment. *Child Development, 55,* 1040–1043.

Gibbs, J., & Schnell, S. (1985). Moral development versus socialization. *American Psychologist, 40,* 1071–1080.

Gilligan, C. (1982). *In a different voice: Psychological theory and women's development.* Cambridge, MA: Harvard University Press.

Gilligan, C., Ward, J., & Taylor, J. (Eds.). (1988). *Mapping the moral domain.* Cambridge, MA: Harvard University Press.

Greeno, C., & Maccoby, E. (1986). How different is the "different voice"? *Signs, 11,* 310–316.

Hare-Mustin, R., & Maracek, J. (1986). Autonomy and gender. *Psychotherapy, 23,* 205–212.

Heller, D. (1988). *The children's God.* Chicago: University of Chicago Press.

Hoffman, M. (1984). Empathy, its limitations and its role in comprehensive moral theory. In W. Kurtiness & J. Gewirtz (Eds.), *Morality, moral behavior and moral development* (pp. 283–302). New York: Wiley.

Johnston, L., Bachman, J., & O'Malley, P. (1986). *Monitoring the future: Questionnaire responses from the nation's high school seniors.* Ann Arbor: University of Michigan, Institute for Social Research.

Josselson, R. (1960). Ego development in adolescence. In J. Adelson (Ed.), *Handbook of adolescent psychology* (pp. 188–211). New York: Wiley.

Josselson, R. (1987). *Finding herself: Pathways to identity development in women.* San Francisco: Jossey-Bass.

Kaslow, R. & Sussman, M. (1982). *Cults and the family.* New York: Haworth Press.

Kohlberg, L. (1969). Stage and sequence. In D. Goslin (Ed.) *Handbook of socialization theory and research.* Chicago: Rand McNally.

Kohlberg, L. (1983). *Moral stages: A current formulation and a response to critics.* London: Karger.

Kohlberg, L. (1984). *The psychology of moral development.* San Francisco: Harper & Row.

Kurtiness, W., & Gewirtz, J. (Eds.). (1987). *Moral development through social interaction.* New York: Wiley.

Lowery, C., & Ford, M. (1986). Gender differences in moral reasoning. *Journal of Personality and Social Psychology, 50,* 777–783.

Luria, Z. (1986). A methodological critique. *Signs, 11,* 316–321.

Marcia, J. (1980). Identity in adolescence. In J. Adelson (Ed.), *Handbook of adolescent psychology.* (pp. 159–188). New York: Wiley.

McCormick, N., Izzo, A., & Folick, J. (1985). Adolescents' values, sexuality and contraception. *Adolescence, 20,* 385–395.

Meadow, J., & Kahoe, R. (1984). *Psychology of religion.* New York: Harper & Row.

Modgil, S. & Modgil, C. (Eds.). (1986). *Lawrence Kohlberg: Consensus and controversy.* Philadelphia: Jalmer Press.

Nye, W. & Carlson, J. (1984). The development of the concept of God in children. *Journal of Genetic Psychology, 145,* 137–142.

Piaget, J. (1965). *The moral judgment of the child.* New York: Free Press. (Original work published 1932.)

Raths, L., Harmin, M., & Simon, S. (1978). *Values and teaching: Working with values in the classroom* (2nd ed.). Columbus, OH: Merrill.

Rest, J. (1979). *Development of judging moral issues.* Minneapolis: University of Minnesota Press.

Rest, J. (1986). *Moral development: Advances in research and theory.* New York: Praeger.

Rich, J., & DeVitis, J. (1985). *Theories of moral development.* Springfield, IL: Charles Thomas.

Roscoe, B., Stevenson, B., & Yacobozzi, B. (1988). Conventional warfare and the U.S. military involvement in Latin America: Early adolescents' views. *Adolescence, 23,* 357–372.

Scott, J. (1988). Deconstructing equality versus difference. *Feminist Studies, 14,* 33–50.

Snarey, J. (1985). The cross-cultural universality of social-moral development: A critical review of Kohlbergian research. *Psychological Bulletin, 97,* 202–232.

Spilka, B., Hood, W., & Gorsuch, R. (1985). *The psychology of religion.* Englewood Cliffs, NJ: Prentice-Hall.

Stack, C. (1986). The culture of gender: Women and men of color. *Signs, 11,* 321–324.

Thoma, S. (1986). Estimating gender differences in the comprehension and preferences of moral issues. *Developmental Review, 6,* 165–180.

Walker, L. (1984). Sex differences in the development of moral reasoning: A critical review. *Child Development, 55,* 677–691.

Windmiller, M., Lambert, N., & Turiel, E. (Eds.). (1980). *Moral development and socialization.* Boston: Allyn Bacon.

13 Adolescents and Drugs

CHAPTER OUTLINE

ADOLESCENT DRUG USE: INCREASING OR DECLINING?

FACTORS INFLUENCING ADOLESCENT DRUG USE

ADOLESCENT DRUG ABUSERS

ALCOHOL

Effects

Teenage Usage

Sex and Race Differences

Children of Alcoholics

NICOTINE

MARIJUANA

COCAINE

AMPHETAMINES

BARBITURATES

HALLUCINOGENS: PCP

HALLUCINOGENS: LSD

HALLUCINOGENS: MESCALINE AND PSILOCYBIN

HEROIN

INHALANTS

DRUG PREVENTION

CONCLUSION

GOALS AND OBJECTIVES

This chapter is designed to enable you to:

- Compare and contrast the various drugs used by adolescents
- Discuss the changes that have occurred in adolescents' drug use
- Identify the differences between drug users and drug abusers
- Describe the differences between effective and ineffective drug abuse prevention programs
- Discuss the various factors that influence adolescents' drug use and drug abuse

CONCEPTS AND TERMINOLOGY

acid
Al-Anon
Alateen
alcohol
amphetamines
amping
angel dust
barbiturates
caffeine
children of alcoholics (COAs)
cocaine
codependent
Codependents Anonymous
crack
cross-tolerance
downers
drug addiction
drug dependence
drug tolerance
ecstasy
fetal alcohol syndrome
flashbacks
free basing
hashish
ice
LSD
MDA
Mothers Against Drunk Driving (MADD)
nicotine
paper
PCP
popping
quaaludes
smokeless tobacco

Key terms continued.

Key terms continued.

speed uppers
THC withdrawal

ADOLESCENT DRUG USE: INCREASING OR DECLINING?

The United States is a drug culture. We use caffeine to wake us up; alcohol, nicotine, and tranquilizers to relax; amphetamines to lose weight; and a host of illegal drugs to give us a temporary high. In the midst of this, adolescents have no difficulty recognizing the hypocrisy of our urging them to "just say no to drugs." Added to our hypocrisy, we have historically shifted the focus of our concerns about drugs from decade to decade. In the Roaring Twenties, for example, we attempted to ban the use of alcohol, in the 1960s we focused our concern on marijuana and LSD, and in the 1980s we turned our attention to cocaine and crack. Yet relatively little attention has historically been focused on the two drugs that do the most damage to the largest number of people in our nation—alcohol and nicotine. Indeed, young people are too often given the message that drugs such as marijuana and cocaine are bad, while simultaneously seeing their idols on television holding a drink in one hand and a cigarette in the other. Moreover, as Table 13.1 illustrates, adolescents have a vast array of drugs from which to choose.

Given the frequency with which adults use drugs, it is little wonder that researchers are trying to keep careful track of adolescents' drug habits. The largest project of its kind, Monitoring the Future, has been gathering data from several thousand high-school seniors and college students since 1975, giving us our most complete information on adolescent drug use (Johnston, O'Malley & Bachman, 1989. All statistics in this chapter regarding prevalence of drug use are from this source unless otherwise noted. See Tables 13.2, 13.3). Unfortunately, these surveys include only young people currently enrolled in high school. Since dropouts are not in the sample, we need to keep in mind that these statistics probably underestimate adolescents' drug use, particularly among the poor.

The best news is the steady decline in overall use of drugs among high-school and college students since 1980. Although 39% of the seniors polled in 1988 reported using an illegal drug within the past year, this represented a 3% decrease from 1987 and a 15% decrease from 1979, the peak year for teenage drug use. Although 57% of high-school seniors have tried an illegal drug at some time in their lives, their use of marijuana, stimulants, and sedatives has declined, as has the use of these drugs among college students and young adults. On the other hand, the bad news is that adolescents' drug use is still high—among the highest

Table 13.1

Facts About Drugs

	NAME	ALTERNATIVE TERMS	SOURCE	INTAKE METHOD
DEPRESSANTS	Alcohol	Booze, juice, shot	Fruits, grains	Swallowed
	Methaqualone	Quaaludes	Synthetic	Swallowed
	Barbiturates	Blue devils, downers, yellow jackets, reds, goofballs, phenies, blue heavens	Synthetic	Swallowed, injected
	Tranquilizers	Valium, librium	Synthetic	Swallowed
NARCOTICS	Heroin	Horse, smack, scag, stuff, scat	Opium	Injected, sniffed, smoked
	Codeine	Cough syrup	Opium	Swallowed
	Demerol	——	Synthetic	Swallowed
	Morphine	White stuff	Opium	Swallowed
	Methadone	Dolly, meth	Synthetic	Swallowed, injected
HALLUCINOGENS	LSD	Acid, sugar, cubes	Semisynthetic	Swallowed
	PCP	Angel dust, tic-tac, hog	Synthetic	Swallowed, injected, smoked
	Mescaline	Mesc	Peyote	Swallowed
	Psilocybin	Magic mushroom	Mushrooms	Swallowed
STIMULANTS	Amphetamines	Speed, uppers, bennies, pep pills, dexies, hearts	Synthetic	Swallowed, injected
	Cocaine	Snow, coke, flake, Bernice, star dust, crack	Coca leaves	Injected, swallowed, sniffed
	Caffeine	——	Coffee plant	Swallowed
	Nicotine	A smoke, a chaw	Tobacco plant	Chewed, smoked
RELAXANTS, EUPHORIANTS	Marijuana	Mary Jane, grass, pot, hash, tea, dope, reefer, joint	Cannabis plant	Smoked, sniffed, swallowed
INHALANTS	Glue, gasoline, paint thinner, lighter fluid, toluene	——	Synthetic	Sniffed

in all industrialized nations. The other bad news is that the use of some drugs, such as cocaine, is on the rise. Perhaps even more important, drinking among high-school and college students remains alarmingly high.

FACTORS INFLUENCING ADOLESCENT DRUG USE

As you might expect, and as social learning theorists would predict, a strong relationship exists betweeen children's and parents' use of drugs. Children are more likely to drink, to smoke, or to use other drugs if their parents do.

Table 13.2

High-School Seniors' Drug Use: 1988

	EVER USED	PAST MONTH	PAST YEAR, NOT PAST MONTH	NOT PAST YEAR	NEVER USED
Marijuana/hashish	47.2	18.0	15.1	14.1	52.8
Inhalants	16.7	2.6	3.9	10.2	83.3
Amyl & butyl nitrites	3.2	0.6	1.1	1.5	96.8
Hallucinogens	8.9	2.2	3.3	3.4	91.1
LSD	7.7	1.8	3.0	2.9	92.3
PCP	2.9	0.3	0.9	1.7	97.1
Cocaine	12.1	3.4	4.5	4.2	87.9
Crack	4.8	1.6	1.5	1.7	95.2
Other cocaine	12.1	3.2	4.2	4.7	87.9
Heroin	1.1	0.2	0.3	0.6	98.9
Other opiates	8.6	1.6	3.0	4.0	91.4
Sedatives	7.8	1.4	2.3	4.1	92.2
Barbiturates	6.7	1.2	2.0	3.5	93.3
Methaqualone	3.3	0.5	0.8	2.0	96.7
Tranquilizers	9.4	1.5	3.3	4.6	90.6
Alcohol	92.0	63.9	21.4	6.7	8.0
Cigarettes	66.4	28.7	(37.7)		33.6

Source: L. Johnston, P. O'Malley, & J. Bachman. (1989). *Drug use, drinking and smoking: National survey results from high school, college and young adult populations 1975–1988.* Rockville, MD: National Institute on Drug Abuse.

Nevertheless, factors other than our parents' habits also influence our decisions about drugs (Halebsky, 1987; Jaynes & Rugg, 1988; Rhodes & Jason, 1988).

Many adolescents first use drugs, especially alcohol and nicotine, to feel more at ease in social situations. Then, too, using drugs in social situations serves as a modern-day rite of passage—it is adolescents' way of signifiying to themselves and to their peers that they are "grown-up." In this regard it is noteworthy that adolescents who use alcohol but avoid other drugs do tend to have more self-confidence and feel less lonely than their peers who use harder drugs (Newcomb & Bentler, 1988). Adolescence is also the time during which individuals experiment with a wide range of behaviors and values as part of the natural process of becoming more independent from their parents. In developing a sense of autonomy and in trying out new identities, young adolescents are particularly likely to experiment with recreational drugs with their friends. They are also particularly likely in early adolescence to be under the spell of their personal fable, ignoring the potential risks of drugs because they believe they are invulnerable to injury, let alone death.

Another variable influencing adolescents' use of drugs, particularly alcohol and cigarettes, is the media. Although cigarette advertisements were banned from television in the 1970s, alcohol commercials are an integral part of prime-time TV. The sexy, vibrant young people in these ads sell alcohol as if it were essential for every activity from sex to family picnics. Given the thousands of hours that

Table 13.3

College Students' Drug Use: 1988

	PERCENT WHO USED IN LIFETIME									
	1980	***1981***	***1982***	***1983***	***1984***	***1985***	***1986***	***1987***	***1988***	***'87–'88 change***
N =	(1040)	(1130)	(1150)	(1170)	(1110)	(1080)	(1190)	(1220)	(1310)	
Marijuana	65.0	63.3	60.5	63.1	59.0	60.6	57.9	55.8	54.3	−1.5
Inhalants	10.2	8.8	10.6	11.0	10.4	10.6	11.0	13.2	12.6	−0.6
Hallucinogens	15.0	12.0	15.0	12.2	12.9	11.4	11.2	10.9	10.2	−0.7
LSD	10.3	8.5	11.5	8.8	9.4	7.4	7.7	8.0	7.5	−0.5
Cocaine	22.0	21.5	22.4	23.1	21.7	22.9	23.3	20.6	15.8	−4.8
Crack	NA	NA	NA	NA	NA	NA	NA	3.3	3.4	+0.1
Heroin	0.9	0.6	0.5	0.3	0.5	0.4	0.4	0.6	0.3	−0.3
Other opiates	8.9	8.3	8.1	8.4	8.9	6.3	8.8	7.6	6.3	−1.3
Stimulants	29.5	29.4	NA	NA	NA	NA	NA	NA	NA	NA
Stimulants, adjusted	NA	NA	30.1	27.8	27.8	25.4	22.3	19.8	17.7	−2.1
Sedatives	13.7	14.2	14.1	12.2	10.8	9.3	8.0	6.1	4.7	−1.4
Barbiturates	8.1	7.8	8.2	6.6	6.4	4.9	5.4	3.5	3.6	+0.1
Methaqualone	10.3	10.4	11.1	9.2	9.0	7.2	5.8	4.1	2.2	−1.9
Tranquilizers	15.2	11.4	11.7	10.8	10.8	9.8	10.7	8.7	8.0	−0.7
Alcohol	94.3	95.2	95.2	95.0	94.2	95.3	94.9	94.1	94.9	+0.8

Source: L. Johnston, P. O'Malley, & J. Bachman. (1989). *Drug use, drinking and smoking: National survey results from high school, college and young adult populations 1975–1988.* Rockville, MD: National Institute on Drug Abuse.

most children watch television, it is inevitable that their attitudes toward drinking and smoking are at least partially shaped by the media (Defore & Breed, 1988).

Then, too, adolescents' peers influence their decisions about using drugs. Peer influence, however, primarily affects adolescents' decisions about using drugs for occasional recreational purposes, whereas drug abuse is primarily determined by the youngsters' own psychological, economic, or family problems, not by peer pressure (Newcomb & Bentler, 1988). Moreover, blaming peer pressure for adolescent drug use is an oversimplification that obscures the many other factors that affect teenage behavior. For example, one survey of 5,000 adolescents found that the majority had never felt pressured by their friends to use marijuana (Sheppard, 1985). Similarly, peer pressure may differ among racial groups. For instance, in a sample of almost 2,000 young adolescents, whites reported more encouragement from their friends to drink and to use marijuana than did African Americans (Newcomb & Bentler, 1986). This is not to say that adolescents' friends have no influence over their using drugs. Indeed they do. Research has clearly demonstrated, however, that other variables, such as ethnic norms and the relationship between parents and their children, can be as influential as the peer group.

Yes, parents are justified in assuming that their children's friends will more than likely influence them to take their first drink, use marijuana, or smoke a cigarette. We are not justified, however, in assuming that the peer group converts children from emotionally healthy families whose parents do not abuse drugs into drug abusers. Remember, too, that adolescents generally choose friends who are like themselves in terms of family backgrounds and values. As a result, when adolescents do encourage one another to try a drug, it is very likely that they are all reflecting their parents' values to a certain degree.

Taking all drugs into consideration, how are age, gender, income, college attendance, and geographic locale related to teenage drug use (Johnston, O'Malley, & Bachman, 1989)? First, with the exception of cigarette smoking, high-school and college males use more drugs and use them more frequently than females. Second, seldom is any drug other than alcohol or cigarettes tried before the 6th grade. Marijuana and inhalants are used at the earliest ages, with the peak rate reached in the 9th grade. The peak rates for using cocaine and hallucinogens are reached in 10th and 11th grades. Third, drug use among college students and their same-age peers not in college is remarkably similar. The one exception is cigarette smoking: Young people not in college smoke far more than do college students. This is also true at the high-school level, where college-bound students have far lower smoking rates than their noncollege-bound classmates. In regard to all drugs, college-bound high-school students have somewhat lower drug use than those not planning to go to college. Once these adolescents are in college, however, they catch up with those who do not attend college in the use of all drugs except cigarettes.

As to regional differences, it is not particularly surprising to find that young people living in large metropolitan areas throughout the country are more likely to use drugs than those in less urban areas. These differences, however, pertain mostly to the use of cocaine. For example, in 1988 twice as many high-school students in the West (12%) had tried cocaine as in the South (6%). On the other hand, heavy cigarette smoking is lowest in the West and highest in the Northeast.

And income? Surprisingly, for most drugs there is not much association with the family's socioeconomic status, which illustrates the extent to which illicit drug use has permeated all social levels. There are a few exceptions to this rule. Heroin and PCP, for example, are most often used by low-income youths.

FIGURE 13.1

Percentage of high-school seniors reporting illicit drug use

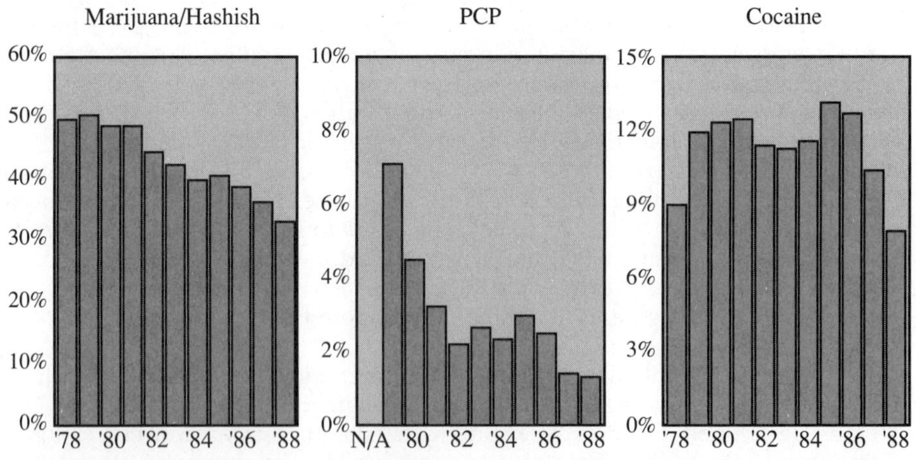

Source: L. Johnston, J. Bachman, & P. O'Malley. (1989). *Monitoring the Future*. Ann Arbor: University of Michigan, Institute for Social Research.

ADOLESCENT DRUG USERS

As many adults know from first-hand experience, not all teenagers who experiment with a given drug will become regular users, nor will they necessarily progress to using more dangerous drugs after using alcohol or marijuana. In other words, there is a difference between drug use and drug abuse. In contrast to teenagers who only use a drug on occasion out of curiosity or for recreational reasons, those who abuse drugs, meaning that they use drugs regularly or use multiple drugs simultaneously, generally have serious personal or family problems. Young drug abusers are usually more impulsive, more delinquent, more depressed, more suicidal, less successful in school, and less self-confident than occasional drug users. Abuse is also highly correlated with poverty and with parents' drug addictions and abuse (Jaynes & Rugg, 1988; Long & Schert, 1984; Newcomb & Bentler, 1988; Wright, 1985).

Adolescents who use drugs on a regular basis or use them in heavy doses often build up a tolerance to the drug. **Drug tolerance** occurs when repeated use of a drug causes a diminished response to the effects of a given amount of the drug. As a result, increasingly larger doses of the drug are needed to produce the same effects. In some cases, tolerance can be so dramatic that no amount of the drug can induce its original effects. Some drug users can also develop **cross-tolerance,** meaning that tolerance to one type of drug results in decreased sensitivity to the effects of another. For example, heavy drinkers who have developed a tolerance to alcohol's sleep-inducing properties may not get sleepy when taking a dose of a barbiturate (sleeping pill, tranquilizer) that would normally put someone to sleep.

Adolescents who abuse drugs can also become psychologically or physically dependent on the drug, a condition once commonly referred to as **drug addiction.** Distinguishing between physical and psychological dependence, however, is difficult because the symptoms are similar and because the two often occur together. Psychological dependence refers to a person's strong compulsion for the drug because it produces pleasure or reduces psychic discomfort. Basically, psychological dependence occurs because taking the drug is followed by the reinforcing effects of the drug. Physical dependence is characterized by physical disturbances that occur when the drug is not being used; that is, when the person cannot have the drug, his or her body begins to manifest **withdrawal** symptoms. In almost all cases, the effects of withdrawal are the opposite of the effects induced by the drug. For example, although barbiturates usually produce a calm, sleepy feeling, the withdrawal symptoms are characterized by anxiety, inability to sleep, and convulsions.

ALCOHOL

Effects

A popular drug in ancient and modern times, **alcohol** is made by a distilling or fermenting process that involves any number of fruits and vegetables. The final product can contain as little as 5% alcohol, as in some light beers and blush wines, or as much as 50% alcohol, as in 100 proof whiskey. Alcohol consumed on an empty stomach enters the bloodstream more quickly than when the stomach is full. Likewise, the smaller the drinker's body, the more dramatically the alcohol will affect him or her. Limited by their lack of experience and misinformation, many adolescents are unaware of these important details. As a result, a 130-pound boy may discover, much to his chagrin, that he can only handle three or four beers without getting nauseatingly drunk, while his 160-pound friend can consume a six-pack without the slightest hangover.

Many young drinkers are also unaware that alcohol can be physically addictive (Coffey, 1988). What begins as one carefree social drink can result in a lifetime of addiction for those children who have inherited alcoholism from a parent. Even when young drinkers do not become physically addicted, however, thousands are killed and maimed each year in traffic accidents. Excessive drinking has also been shown to cause damage to the liver, kidneys, brain, and cardiovascular system. Moreover, it has recently been confirmed that pregnant women who drink as little as 3 ounces of alcohol a day can retard the mental and physical development of their unborn children, a condition referred to as **fetal alcohol syndrome** (Light, 1988).

Of particular concern is adolescents' driving while under the influence. In response to drunk driving, some schools have gone so far as to suspend students who are merely in the presence of others who are drinking (see Box 13.1). Also, mothers of crippled or fatally injured adolescents have founded the **Mothers Against Drunk Driving (MADD)** campaign in an effort to curtail drunk driving. There is now also a BADD campaign, initiated in 1983, to address the drunk

A CLOSER LOOK 13.1

Minnesota Students Suspended From School Activities

More than 10% of the 365 students who attend Olivia (Minnesota) High School have been barred from extracurricular activities following a fatal automobile accident after a party that violated the school's drinking policy.

Thirty-eight students from the high school attended the party, which took place in a public park near Olivia on September 23, 1984. Todd Mathiowetz, aged 17, was killed when the car he was driving ran off the road as he left the party that night.

"Not all the students were drinking," said Jerry Bass, superintendent of the high school. "But our rule states that 'a student shall not consume, possess, or be in the presence of others who are consuming or in possession of an alcoholic beverage.'"

The rule covers all circumstances, not just gatherings related to school activities, according to Delbert J. Altmann, principal of Olivia High School.

The students, who were members of the band, the National Honor Society, and school athletic teams, were suspended for 4 to 8 weeks.

The reaction to the suspensions has been generally favorable, Mr. Bass said. "The majority of the people I've been in contact with are supportive of the decision. Some said that it was something that should have been done years ago, that could possibly have averted this tragedy."

Source: Minnesota Students Suspended. (1984, October 27). *Education Week*, p. 3.

driving problem from an African American cultural perspective (Womble & Bakeman, 1986).

Teenage Usage

Among high-school and college students, alcohol is still the most popular of all drugs. Despite the fact that it is illegal for virtually all high-school students and most college students to drink, only 8% of the high-school seniors and 5% of college students have never had a drink. Among high-school seniors, 66% have had at least one drink within the past month. More serious is the frequency of "occasional heavy drinking," defined as having five or more drinks in a row at least once in the past 2 weeks. Among high-school seniors, 35% put themselves in this category, 4% drink daily, and 37% said they were drunk within the past month. Among college students 43% categorize themselves as "occasional heavy drinkers" and 5% drink daily.

Although drinking rates are still high, they have fallen somewhat among high-school seniors since 1980. The monthly use of alcohol among high-school seniors declined from 72% in 1980 to 64% in 1988. Daily use also declined from a peak of 7% in 1980 to 64% in 1988, and the prevalence of heavy drinking fell from 41% in 1983 to 35% in 1988. On the other hand, college students' drinking patterns have remained relatively unchanged since 1980. In most surveys, about 5% of college students drink daily, a rate about 2% lower than that of people of the same age who are not in college. This suggests that college students probably confine more of their drinking to weekends than do people not enrolled in school.

Sex and race differences Interestingly, African American high-school students are less likely to drink than whites (Harper, 1988; Singer & Petchers, 1987). For example, in a survey of 140,000 students in Alabama, only 40% of the African American high-school juniors reported having had a drink within the past 3 months in contrast to 55% of the whites (Black students, 1989). Likewise, in a survey of 27,335 adolescents in New York State, African American students reported drinking less than whites, Hispanics, and Native Americans (Welte & Barnes, 1987a). Nevertheless, serious drinking problems still exist among young people of all minorities (Harper, 1988; Watts & Roosevelt, 1989).

Regardless of race, however, males generally drink more heavily and more often than females (Beck & Summons, 1987; Gibbons, 1986; Johnston, O'Malley, & Bachman, 1989). College men (7.2%), for example, are more than twice as likely as college women (3.3%) to drink daily. Likewise, 43% of the high-school senior boys drink heavily on occasion compared to only 27% of the girls (Johnston, O'Malley, & Bachman, 1989). Interestingly, both males and females who identify with the masculine gender role drink more and use more drugs than those who have more feminine gender roles (Horwitz & White, 1987). This suggests that our society's notions regarding masculinity inadvertently encourage many males to abuse drugs and alcohol as a way of proving their manhood.

Children of Alcoholics

Thousands of adolescents are also damaged by their parents' abuse of alcohol. As researchers have taken more careful note of the **children of alcoholics (COAs),** we have learned that having an alcoholic parent changes the family's interactions in ways that cripple each of its members psychologically and emotionally (Ackerman, 1989; Hope, 1988; Ryerson, 1985; Seixas, 1985). As Box 13.2 illustrates, adolescents with alcoholic parents suffer not only at home but at school and with their friends.

Moreover, the damage incurred from living with an alcoholic parent extends beyond adolescence. Forced by their parent's alcoholism into roles such as the caretaker or family peacemaker, many COAs develop unhealthy patterns of reacting to and coping with life. Even after leaving home, they continue as adults to behave as they did within the family—to behave as codependents. **Codependent** people are individuals who are obsessed with taking care of and feeling responsible for another person's well-being. Codependent people have adopted these self-destructive attitudes in reaction to the lies, indirect communication, denial of reality, and anger that enabled their families to survive the parent's alcoholism. As a consequence, many COAs grow up to be insecure, self-sacrificing souls who

A CLOSER LOOK 13.2

When Your Parent Drinks Too Much

Eric Ryerson begins his book for adolescents: "I am the child of an alcoholic. For 11 years I lived under the dark, horrible cloud of a parent's drinking problem. It was the most difficult time in my life and, looking back, it's not hard to see why: I was growing up in a place where all the things we need most from our families—love, support, stability—were washed away in a tidal wave of alcohol. Even as things get worse, the alcoholic typically will deny that any problem exists. In fact, he will likely become very angry at the slightest hint by you or someone else that alcohol is causing difficulties. I heard in my home for years, "I'm just going through a hard time. Why can't you show me some sympathy instead of getting on my case about having a drink to relax?" In his book Ryerson goes on to empathize with and to advise young people, on the basis of his own painful adolescent experiences:

- You didn't cause your parent's drinking. You can't control it. And you can't cure it.
- I had little time or energy left for understanding myself better, or for coming up with plans or solutions to lessen my unhappiness.
- This concept of separating ourselves emotionally from the ups and downs of our parent's drinking is commonly known as "detachment." It means looking at and caring for ourselves, instead of devoting our life's energy to dreaded thoughts of what will become of the alcoholic. Detaching doesn't mean you're selfish or disloyal.
- It took me a long time to get past thinking that my mother was nothing other than a "bad girl" whenever she got drunk, particularly when she acted up in front of other people.
- It made me angry to feel so manipulated. I also felt angry that she was so needy and childlike. I feel like I never had a childhood.
- It's okay to feel cheated, because you are being cheated.
- We have to be careful about devoting ourselves too much to "fixing" things, about trying too hard to make our sober or our alcoholic parent happier.
- Cold hearted as it sounds and as hard as this can be, not rushing to the problem drinker's rescue is the greatest act of love we can give him.

Source: E. Ryerson. (1985). *When your parent drinks too much: A book of help and hope for teenagers.* New York: Warner Books.

seek out relationships with seriously troubled people whom they destructive devote themselves to "saving." Unfortunately, the codependent's idea of "helpin and "loving" others is to adopt the self-destructive roles they were forced into children living with an alcoholic parent—trying to "cure" their loved one problems, assuming the blame for problems not within their control, and feelin excessive shame or guilt when things go wrong in their own life or in someon else's.

In an effort to help the children of alcoholics recover from these disabling roles and attitudes, organizations such as **Al-Anon, Alateen,** and **Codependents Anonymous** have grown in popularity (Al-Anon, 1981). A primary goal of these programs is to help codependents overcome their patterns of equating love with pain, centering their lives exclusively around other people, seeking out relationships with individuals who are incapable of loving, and staying in abusive relationships.

NICOTINE

Effects

Nearly 300,000 people in the United States die each year from cancer, heart attacks, and strokes caused by smoking cigarettes. A stimulant and a carcinogen, nicotine has devastating effects on the human body. Moreover, after reviewing more than 2,000 scientific papers and consulting more than 50 experts, the Surgeon General concluded that nicotine is every bit as addictive as heroin and cocaine. Continued use may lead to tolerance and the need to increase the dosage; and cessation leads to withdrawal symptoms, including irritability, poor concentration, and sleep disturbances. Given nicotine's destructive effects on the body, the Surgeon General recommended that states take cigarettes as seriously as liquor and require sellers to obtain a license. He also suggested that warnings on cigarette packs include a mention of the potential for addiction (Koop, 1989). More disturbing still, in the quantities typically used by adolescent smokers, cigarettes can have a more negative effect on their health than does alcohol, marijuana, or hard drugs (Newcomb & Bentler, 1989).

Among the dangers of cigarette smoking are heart attacks, strokes, cancer, emphysema, and chronic bronchitis. Because nicotine is a stimulant, it increases the heart rate and constricts the blood vessels, limiting the flow of oxygen to all parts of the body. In addition, females who smoke and take birth control pills run a much higher risk of cancer and strokes than do nonsmokers. Pregnant smokers also have more miscarriages, stillbirths, premature births, and unhealthy babies than nonsmokers. Aside from these health hazards, nicotine also has its social drawbacks—a fact that many antismoking programs have tried to stress to teenage smokers. In terms of physical appearance, smoking stains the teeth, fouls the breath, and dries the skin, creating tougher, leathery looking, more wrinkled skin.

Teenage Usage

Although many adolescents have heeded the message that smoking is hazardous, millions of young people still smoke. Among high-school seniors, nearly 20% smoke daily, 10% smoke half a pack or more a day, 30% smoke sometimes, and 65% have tried smoking at least once. Although the daily smoking rate for high-school seniors dropped from 29% in 1977 to 20% in 1981, it has dropped very little in the 9 years since then despite the downturn in most other drug use during this period. Also, more teenage girls are now smoking than ever before, with some experts estimating that females will soon be outsmoking males (Gritz, 1982; Koop, 1989). It is interesting to note that minority teenagers are less likely to smoke than whites (Black students, 1989; Welte & Barnes, 1987b; Zabin, 1986). It is also noteworthy that college-bound high-school students and college students are far less likely to smoke than their peers who do not attend college (Johnston, O'Malley, & Bachman, 1989).

Chewing tobacco (also called **smokeless tobacco**), for example, is almost exclusively confined to white males and is a habit on the rise (Chassin, 1988; Elder, 1988; McCarthy, 1986). Believing that tobacco is harmless if it is not smoked, these adolescents chew wads of tobacco to get the effects of the nicotine. Released into the body by chewing, however, nicotine reeks the same damage as cigarettes, with the exception that it cannot pollute the lungs; and tobacco's direct contact with the skin contributes to mouth cancer.

Antismoking Programs

The most successful antismoking programs for adolescents have appealed to the here and now issues of bad breath, yellow teeth, and loss of sex appeal, rather than to the long-range health hazards (DelGreco, 1986; Murray, Luepker, & Mittlemark, 1984). Programs taught by adolescents themselves, rather than by adults, also have higher success rates. Others have had success by appealing to nonsmokers to help their friends who smoke. For example, a Save a Sweetheart campaign disseminated buttons and posters with antismoking slogans on Valentine's Day to help adolescents make the connection between loving someone and helping them kick the habit. Most adult smokers say they smoke to relieve tension or because it is a habit (addiction) that they just cannot give up. In contrast, most adolescents say they smoke in order to appear more grown up and to win peer approval. Not surprisingly, almost all teenage smokers say that at least one of their best friends smokes. Knowing this, the most effective programs focus on teaching young people how to resist a friend's offer to light up.

As is the case with drinking, teenagers who smoke usually have parents who smoke (Elder, 1988; Welte & Barnes, 1987b). Ironically, however, teenagers who know the most smokers or whose parents smoke know the least about the destructive effects of nicotine. They downplay the risks of getting sick from smoking and defend against the thought that they, their friends, or their parents have an uncontrollable, destructive, and addictive habit (Leventhal, 1987). Given the connection between children's and parents' smoking habits, many of the most successful antismoking programs have involved both teenagers and their parents.

MARIJUANA

Effects

One of the other popular drugs for smoking among both adults and adolescents is marijuana. Derived from the dried leaves of the Indian hemp plant, marijuana provides fiber for rope and birdseed as well as "dope" ("grass," "weed") for smoking or eating. When the leaves and flowering tops of the plant are dried and crushed, they can be smoked in pipes, rolled into "joints," or eaten. The drug varies in potency, depending on the type of plant, the climate in which it grew, and which part of the plant is used. For example, **hashish** is the most potent form of marijuana, gathered from the dark brown resin at the tops of high-quality plants. Whatever the quality of the drug, **THC** (tetrahydrocannabinal) is the chemical within the plant that is actually responsible for marijuana's effects. Since the concentration of THC differs in different qualities of marijuana, the drug's effects can vary considerably from one use to the next. That is, a person needs larger amounts of low-quality "grass" to produce the same high he or she gets with smaller amounts of high-quality hashish.

The effects of marijuana generally include impaired memory and cognitive functions, such as loss of attention, fragmented speech, and difficulty solving problems. Events or thoughts that are of no particular significance appear to take on special meaning and to provide special insights while a person is under the influence of THC. Individuals respond to marijuana in a wide variety of ways, often depending upon the type of setting, self-fulfilling prophecies, and the expectations of other people. Although there are no studies directly assessing the effects of marijuana on classroom learning experiences, the types of impairment it generally causes, particularly in both long-term and short-term loss of memory, suggest that it interferes with classroom functioning. It also interferes with users' motor skills. This interference makes it especially dangerous for them to drive a car, for example. Moreover, it appears that the effects may last for up to 24 hours after use.

Acute feelings of panic and anxiety can also occur when strong marijuana is used. More serious forms of psychoses and intellectual deficiencies have been reported in countries where marijuana use is extensive, although these reactions have not been commonly reported in North America. Not enough evidence exists to support the hypothesis that marijuana causes aggressive behavior or brain damage. On the other hand, chronic marijuana use is associated with lung disorders, including cancer, and with lower testosterone levels and less vigorous sperm motility which interferes with reproduction. Although marijuana is less addictive than alcohol and other sedative-hypnotics, people can become psychologically dependent on this drug. Some users have become physically addicted, but this is rare.

Teenage Usage

As the dangers of marijuana have become more well-known, its popularity among high-school students has decreased steadily since 1978. Between 1975 and 1978 there was an almost twofold increase in daily use of marijuana among high-school students, reaching a high of 11% in 1978. By 1988, however, only 2.7% of the adolescents smoked daily. Similarly, among college students in 1988 only 35% had used marijuana within the past year in contrast to 51% in 1980. Nevertheless, marijuana comes in second to alcohol in terms of the number of adolescents who have tried the drug. By their senior year, about one-third of the adolescents still in school had tried grass.

COCAINE

Effects

Although nicotine is by far the most widely used and abused stimulant, **cocaine** captured our society's attention during the 1980s (Grilly, 1989. All the information in the following sections is based on this source unless otherwise cited). Derived from the leaves of the South American coca plant, cocaine is a white, powdery substance that can be swallowed, sniffed ("snorted"), or rubbed on the inside of the gums. Cocaine has been used throughout the ages in a variety of contexts: among the Incas for religious ceremonies, among South American Indians to increase their physical endurance and reduce fatigue and hunger, and by the Europeans in the 1800s in patent medicines and wines. In 1886 an Atlanta, Georgia, pharmacist patented a popular medicinal cola containing coca and hailed it as a remedy for an assortment of ailments. Capitalizing on his new elixir, he called his marvel medicine Coca-Cola. Long before it was marketed as today's "Coke" drink, however, the coca was replaced with other substances. Cocaine has also been used as an anesthetic and an antidepressant. As was well-known among his friends and colleagues, at one period of his life Sigmund Freud used and endorsed cocaine as a wonder drug for relieving depression.

As the dangers of cocaine became increasingly apparent, however, experts who once praised it as the "perfect drug" in terms of its supposedly harmless side effects changed their tune. We now know that cocaine is a highly addictive drug. Although moderate doses and occasional use usually increase alertness and lift the spirits, larger doses and prolonged use can cause hallucinations, convulsions, and death. Even Freud became disillusioned with the drug as his own work showed tremendous variability in the ways individuals responded to its impact. With few exceptions, the responses to cocaine are very similar to those for amphetamines. Indeed, most studies have found that when cocaine and amphetamines are administered intravenously, users are unable to distinguish between them except that the effects of amphetamines usually last 2 or 3 hours, whereas cocaine's dissipate in about 30 minutes.

Although most reports before 1980 indicated that cocaine had relatively benign effects on most people, the majority of reports in the 1980s reached a different conclusion. Like amphetamines, in low to moderate doses cocaine usually improves performance on tasks that depend on sustained attention, such as detecting objects on a radar screen. In proper doses cocaine also increases physical quickness and strength, although it interferes with tasks requiring smooth, accurate motions. In part, this helps to explain why golfers and tennis players invariably avoid this drug, while linemen and linebackers, swimmers, and track competitors find cocaine more tempting. In larger doses cocaine interferes with alertness and causes the user to feel depressed and withdrawn. Continued exposure to these high doses can cause psychological symptoms similar to those of paranoid schizophrenia. The person may engage in a repetitious thought or meaningless act for hours, seemingly fascinated with his or her own thought processes and with philosophical concerns on a grand scale. The person may also get very suspicious, antisocial, and violent.

We also know now that cocaine is highly psychologically addictive. As a result, it is estimated that 10% of all people who started out as casual, recreational users become psychologically addicted. The deaths of well-known athletes, such as basketball player Len Bias and football player Don Rogers, have also emphasized cocaine's potential lethality. It is not clear, however, how many of these deaths are directly due to cocaine overdoses. The majority of cocaine-related deaths can be attributed to suicide or to combining cocaine with other drugs. Nevertheless, about one-fourth of these deaths seem to have occurred when the user was using only moderate doses for recreational purposes. These sudden deaths occur from cerebral hemorrhaging (bleeding within the brain), convulsions, or heart attacks caused by an insufficient supply of blood to the heart.

Given its addictive properties and harmful side effects, we have even further cause for alarm since the arrival of the newer, more potent form of cocaine, "crack." **Crack** is cocaine that has been converted from its powdery, white form into its crystalline form, giving it the appearance of large crystals of salt. In this crystallized form the drug's effects are magnified, meaning that crack is more addictive and causes a greater "crash" after coming down off the drug than does cocaine in its powdered form. The practice of smoking crack by putting the crystals into a small pipe is called **free basing.** People using crack or high doses of powdered cocaine usually develop a tolerance for the drug, causing them to need it in larger and larger doses to produce the same highs as the last time. As a consequence, the social problems associated with cocaine—crime, bankruptcy, family disruption—come about because of the user's preoccupation with an extremely expensive drug.

In trying to overome their addiction, people experience the pains of withdrawal. In the first few hours after using the drug, the person feels depressed and agitated, loses his or her appetite, and craves more cocaine. In the next several hours or days, the need to sleep and extreme hunger are overwhelming. Soon the sleep patterns and mood return to normal and the craving subsides. Then, however, the user starts to feel anxious, loses energy, and becomes unable to enjoy normal daily activities. The craving returns.

Teenage Usage

Despite its high price and addictive properties, cocaine did gain popularity among high-school students during the 1980s. Betweeen 1977 and 1981, for example, the number of high-school seniors who had tried cocaine doubled from 6% to 12%, reaching a high of about 13% in 1986. Fortunately, this trend seems to have abated, with only about 8% of the high-school seniors and 9% of college students in 1988 having used cocaine within the past year.

Without question the most important developments in 1988 were the drop in crack use among high-school seniors for the first time and the continued decline in the use of other cocaine. In 1988 only 4.8% of the high-school seniors and 10% of college students had ever tried crack. The fact that these percentages are almost identical to those of 1986 suggests that crack has not continued to spread in the high-school population as had been widely feared. It is important to note, however, that crack use may be disproportionately located in the out-of-school population, as is likely true for PCP and heroin as well. Interestingly, too, the use of crack among college-bound high-school seniors is about half of what it is for those not bound for college. Regionally, students in the West are twice as likely as those in other parts of the country to have used crack, and nationwide those living in metropolitan areas are almost twice as likely to have used crack as those in smaller cities.

AMPHETAMINES

Effects

The most frequently used stimulants are the **amphetamines.** These pills, popularly known as **uppers** or **speed,** are physically addictive, as well as lethal if taken in large doses or mixed with alcohol. As its street names suggest, an amphetamine speeds up the body's systems in such a way that users feel more alert and awake—a reaction that explains the popularity of this drug among students who need the extra boost of energy supplied by uppers while trying to pull all-night study sessions. The newest addition to the line, **ice,** (methamphetamine) is as addictive as crack cocaine and is slowly making its way into the mainland United States via Hawaii. The effects of amphetamines are described under the "Cocaine" heading since the body responds in such similar ways to both drugs.

Teenage Usage

Despite their dangers, amphetamines remain relatively popular among students. In the class of 1988 nearly one fifth of the high-school seniors had used these stimulants at least once in their lives. Fortunately, the rate for those who had used amphetamines within the past year fell from 20% in 1982 to 11% in 1988 among high-school seniors and from 21% to 6% among college students. The use of nonprescription "stay-awake" pills, which usually contain **caffeine** as their active ingredient, more than doubled from 12% to 26% among seniors, a finding that suggests that students are turning to these far less dangerous pills to keep themselves awake. Another nonprescription stimulant that remains popular, at least among girls, is diet pills. Nearly one-third of all girls have used these stimulants by their senior year in high school.

BARBITURATES

Effects

The opposite of amphetamines, **barbiturates** slow down the body, creating a calm, sleepy effect. These tranquilizing drugs, known as **downers,** goof balls, or blue devils, are depressants that, in excessive doses or when mixed with alcohol, can be lethal. In low doses the depressant drugs can be used as muscle relaxants, sedatives, or tranquilizers. Within this category of tranquilizing drugs, methaqualone or **quaaludes** were recently withdrawn from the market because of their almost purely recreational use and rates of abuse.

Teenage Usage

Barbiturates have been declining in popularity among high-school and college students since 1975. In 1988 only about 3% of the seniors reported having used a barbiturate, in contrast to almost 11% in 1975. Similarly, only about 1% of college students in 1988 had used this kind of drug. On the other hand,

A CLOSER LOOK 13.3

The Fire of "Ice"

Twenty years old and fresh out of college, he saw a good future for himself. So when he was offered a puff from the small glass pipe—a little something to help him survive the grueling 20-hour shift—he felt he couldn't refuse: "I felt alert, in control. It didn't seem to have a downside." No wonder so many people in his office were using it.

The Japanese call it "shabu"; to Koreans it is "hiroppon." To Americans this highly addictive new drug is known as ice. As addictive as crack cocaine, ice—a type of methamphetamine, or speed, whose crystals resemble tiny particles of ice—is a drug with a high lasting anywhere from 8 to 24 hours. Unlike cocaine, which comes from a plant, ice can be conjured up in a laboratory using easily available chemicals. Prolonged use can cause fatal lung and kidney disorders, as well as long-lasting psychological damage even up to 2 years after quitting the drug. The drug also tends to make users violent. Ice originated in Asia, where it was used by Japan's military leaders during World War II to energize weary soldiers and munitions plant workers. In Korea, experts estimate that 130,000 citizens, including students, housewives, and businessmen, are addicted to ice. Although its spread to the United States has primarily been limited to the Hawaiian Islands, in just over 4 years, ice has surpassed marijuana and cocaine as Hawaii's main drug problem. A penny-sized bag, called a **paper,** costs about $50 and when smoked can keep a new user high for up to a week. Addicts call the high **amping** for the amplified euphoria it gives them. Odorless and hard to detect, ice is used as much for recreation as for staying alert on the job or while studying. As occurs when they use cocaine, pregnant women who use ice are giving birth to addicted babies. Also, like cocaine, ice is proving difficult for addicts to kick.

Source: M. Lerner. (1989, November 27). The fire of "ice." *Newsweek,* pp. 37–40.

methaqualone rose steadily in popularity from 1975 to 1981, when its use among high-school and college students reached 8%. It then fell rather sharply, however, to its present level of 1.3% among high-school seniors and 0.5% among college students. This drop is probably due to the fact that it is no longer legal to manufacture quaaludes, so they have become unavailable in the market.

HALLUCINOGENS: PCP

Effects

Among the hallucinogens, phencyclidine **(PCP)** gained popularity during the 1970s, leading some to conclude that it was becoming one of the more widely used drugs among young adolescents (Young, 1987). Even now the average age at which most people first use PCP, or **"angel dust",** is 14. A synthetic drug, PCP can be swallowed, injected, or smoked. Like those of LSD, the effects of PCP depend on the amount consumed and the kind of substance it has been mixed with. First used as an anesthetic and still used as an animal tranquilizer, PCP can be classified both as a depressant and as a hallucinogen. It simultaneously has the properties of a sedative, a stimulant, a convulsant, and a hallucinogen. The effects range from sensory distortions, euphoria, depression, short-term memory loss, and hallucinations to uncontrollably violent and self-destructive behavior.

Teenage Usage

Fortunately, PCP's popularity among teenagers seems to be on the decline. In contrast to 7% of the high-school seniors who had used PCP in 1979, only 1% of the seniors in 1988 reported using this drug.

HALLUCINOGENS: LSD

Effects

During the 1960s the hallucinogen **LSD** (lysergic acid diethylamide) captured the public's attention. Rock musicians and people such as Timothy Leary, a Harvard psychologist, were among those publicizing the importance of LSD in "raising consciousness" and producing profound insights. For others, LSD was simply used to intensify sensory experiences and produce pleasurable hallucinations—tripping. Eaten as a tablet or as a small square of gelatin or saturated on paper, LSD takes effect within 30 minutes, and the effect lasts between 7 and 10 hours. While some users experience "good trips," the less fortunate have frightening hallucinations that create psychotic and violent reactions. During a "bad trip," users suddenly feel that they are losing complete control and may never return to normal. People and objects, including the person's own body image, may become so distorted that they seem grotesque and threatening. Weeks or months after having taken the drug, some users also experience brief episodes similar to the LSD trip—**flashbacks.** While some people view them as novel, curious phenomena, others find these flashbacks extremely upsetting.

The effects of LSD are very dependent on the context in which the users take the drug and on their expectations. Users may feel deeply religious at one moment, sexual another, and then sad, frightened, or paranoid. Bizarre thoughts can alter users' perceptions of reality to the point they believe they can fly, stop cars at will, or perform other life-threatening feats that have led to the deaths of some. In many instances, users report having developed insights that never occurred to them before. Visual and auditory distortions are also common, so that with the eyes closed the users experience a virtual kaleidoscope of changing patterns and intense colors.

A chemically related drug, **MDA** (known as **ecstasy**), possesses both amphetamine-like and LSD-like effects. Users claim it leaves them feeling more empathetic, insightful, and aware without the hallucinations produced by LSD. Some psychotherapists who have used MDA in their practice also claim that it is useful in facilitating more direct communication and that it reduces anxiety and lowers defensiveness. The effects, however, are not uniformly predictable nor uniformly controllable. The most common negative effects are higher blood pressure, fatigue, insomnia, loss of motor coordination, anxiety, and blurred vision. It appears, however, that with continued use of MDA the positive effects often decrease and the negative ones often increase. Most users limit the situations in which they take the drug and the amount they take so that their drug use does not lead to drug dependence or to significant psychopathology, although use of high doses can lead to physical and psychological reactions such as anxiety.

Teenage Usage

LSD use has remained fairly constant over the last several years among high-school and college students. In 1988 fewer than 5% of the high-school seniors had used LSD within the past year, and slightly fewer than 8% had ever tried it. Among college students, fewer than 4% had used LSD within the past year, and about 8% had tried it at some time.

HALLUCINOGENS: MESCALINE AND PSILOCYBIN

Two other hallucinogens, mescaline and psilocybin, are far less powerful than PCP or LSD. Derived from plants indigenous to Mexico and parts of the Southwest, these mild hallucinogens have been used in religious ceremonies by some Indian tribes for centuries. Mescaline is taken from the mescal bud of the peyote cactus, and psilocybin from the psilocybe mushroom. Once ingested these drugs cause mild distortions and intensify sensory experiences. Official statistics on their use are not available because the percentage of the population involved is small and the effects of the drugs are mild.

A CLOSER LOOK 13.4

Facts and Fictions About Drugs

Can you give adolescents up-to-date information about drugs? Test yourself. Which of these statements are true?

1. Alcohol and nicotine can be physically addictive.
2. Hashish and marijuana are essentially the same drug.
3. Uppers and downers can be lethal when mixed with alcohol.
4. Nicotine, caffeine, diet pills, and amphetamines are stimulants.
5. Cocaine and crack are essentially the same drug but in different form.
6. PCP and THC are synonyms for the same drug.
7. Nicotine and alcohol can both be physically addictive.
8. Mescaline and psilocybin are recently discovered synthetic drugs.
9. Smoking marijuana can have damaging effects on the lungs.
10. Heroin comes from the poppy plant.
11. Angel dust is a newly developed form of cocaine.
12. Barbiturates generally decrease your alertness and wakefulness.
13. Speed and ecstasy are street names for MDA.
14. Ice is more closely related to speed than to cocaine.
15. Ice and crack are somewhat similar in terms of their appearance.

Answers: 6, 8, 11, and 13 are false.

HEROIN

The most frequently used opiate, heroin, can be sniffed or smoked. Most users, however, inject it directly into a vein (shooting up) or just under the skin's surface **(popping).** The pleasurable rush is soon followed by lethargy and sleep. Although addiction is not inevitable, most users do become physically dependent. Given its expense, the heroin habit also generally leads users to crime, including prostitution, to support their addiction.

Adolescents seldom use heroin or other narcotics. In fact, among middle- and upper-income families, heroin use is almost nonexistent. Most teenage users come from poor families in large, urban areas, and one or both parents often are heroin users. Although heroin use is undoubtedly higher among teenagers who have dropped out of school, only 0.5% of all high-school seniors report using heroin, a figure that has remained constant since 1976.

INHALANTS

Given their convenience for young adolescents who cannot afford or do not have access to other drugs, inhalants continue to attract a small percentage of the teenage population. Users get high by inhaling substances such as gasoline, paint thinner, or glue. A specific class of inhalants sold on the street as "poppers" or "snappers" has been tried by roughly 3% of high-school seniors; yet fewer than 4% of high-school seniors and college students have used inhalant drugs.

DRUG PREVENTION

The fact that some adolescents buy hemp seeds to smoke for a high (see Box 13.5) reminds us that drug prevention programs have to keep abreast of a variety of new products available to young people today. Indeed, drug education and prevention programs based on outdated information are doomed to fail. Not only do we have to present data that is up-to-date, we have to present the information in a way that avoids the exaggerated scare tactics that have caused many young people to distrust medical experts and other adults warning them against the dangers of drugs.

From both an intuitive and a rational perspective, it would seem that the best way to deter drug abuse would be to educate children about the dangers of drugs before they begin experimenting with them. This approach is based on the premise that adolescents begin smoking, drinking, or using other drugs because they lack enough knowledge about the dangers of drugs to make rational decisions. Programs based on this premise, however, have met with decidedly mixed and rather unimpressive results (Price, et al., 1988; Newcomb & Bentler, 1989). Efforts to control drug traffic or to preach against drug use have also been relatively ineffective in preventing drug use among the young (Schinke & Gilchrist, 1985).

A meta-analysis of the research has, however, identified the most and least effective strategies in drug education (Tobler, 1986). Two indirect approaches have been quite popular in recent years. In the first, educators try to enhance adolescents' self-esteem and social skills. In the second, job training and academic

A CLOSER LOOK 13.5

Hemp Seeds Are for the Birds . . . Or Are They?

In Palm Beach County, Fla., what started out as just another student fad has turned into a murky legal issue that has district officials grappling with how to deal with students who are smoking bird seed to get high.

When Johnny McKenzie, director of security for the Palm Beach County School Board, heard that some youths in his 73,000-student district were mashing, rolling, and smoking hemp seeds—a high-quality bird seed that is sold in local pet stores—he decided to investigate further.

First, labrador retrievers used by the district to sniff out narcotics in the schools successfully detected hemp seeds in the schools. Next, a crime-lab criminal-evaluation test found that the seeds contained three psychoactive ingredients that are found in marijuana, including tetrahydrocannabinol (THC). And the test found that the seeds are capable of germination. "Those seeds that the kids can go out and buy—they can also grow them," Mr. McKenzie said.

The seeds, which sell in West Palm Beach pet stores for $1.25 to $1.40 a pound, are said to give students one-third to one-half the high that marijuana produces, Mr. McKenzie said.

After sharing the test results with Superintendent Thomas J. Mills, Mr. McKenzie last week sent a letter to the district's 102 principals stating that "it is illegal to possess hemp seeds on school grounds." Furthermore, he said, the district intends to treat students who are found to be in possession of hemp seeds in the same way as those who have marijuana—they will suspend them for up to 10 days.

Robert S. Schwartz, assistant state attorney for juvenile justice, said last week that any substance that contains THC or cannibis is covered in the statute that relates to marijuana possession and use.

Under the statute, Mr. Schwartz said, "if someone is caught with the seeds, it would be violative of the section. We would treat it as possession of marijuana. . . . There is no reason we wouldn't prosecute."

Mr. Schwartz did note that there would be a problem of proving an individual in possession of the hemp seed intended to use it to get high, not to feed his or her birds.

In recent weeks, a number of pet-store operators and veterinarians in the Palm Beach County area have said the only thing the seeds do is make birds fat. And one bird specialist wrote in a newspaper column that it is impossible to get high by smoking the seeds.

"The kids could smoke that and chew it and eat it until they're blue in the face," he said. "You can't get stoned on it."

Source: Hemp Seeds. (1984, October 31), *Education Week,* p. 3. Reprinted by permission.

tutoring are given to those young people at greatest risk of abusing drugs in hopes that increasing their chances for success in school and in the work force will decrease their drug use. There are also the more direct approaches: to give children information about the dangers of drugs and to teach them how to "say no" to peer pressure. The latter approaches focus on assertiveness training, building self-esteem, and social skills training.

In general, offering children information about the dangers of drugs and trying to build their self-esteem have had relatively no effect on their use or abuse of drugs. Programs in which students learn to assert themselves have been the most successful in reducing recreational drug use but have had little impact on more serious drug abuse. Once again, these results indicate that drug use and drug abuse are not synonymous. Adolescents who abuse drugs are generally reacting to severe distress in their personal lives, such as poverty or chronic depression, whereas most adolescents use drugs only on occasion. On a more pessimistic note, a more recent meta-analysis of drug prevention programs found that no particular approach to drug education had any appreciable effects. Taken together, these findings underscore the reality that most of our drug education programs need a major overhaul (Bangert, 1988).

There is also growing concern that for various reasons, not the least of which is the profit motive, some privately owned treatment programs are purposefully blurring the distinction between the use and the abuse of drugs. Relatively ignorant about drugs other than alcohol, too many parents are persuaded to commit their teenage children to drug abuse programs for infractions such as smoking a joint. Given this criterion, well over half of this nation's youth would be in therapy for drug use (Peele, 1986). Nevertheless, private drug treatment programs are growing in popularity, although their methods and results have not been carefully studied (Newcomb & Bentler, 1989).

In an effort to determine the success of outpatient drug clinics, Friedman and his colleagues (1986) analyzed data from more than 5,000 adolescents who had been treated for drug problems. The drug users who profited most from these programs were those who were still enrolled in school, who used only one drug, who began their drug use at an older age, and who spent the longest time in treatment. These programs were also more successful with white than with minority youths.

Some drug prevention strategies that are now being tested, however, differ from traditional approaches in several important respects (Botvin, 1986). First, they are based on a more complete understanding of the causes of the use and abuse of drugs, including tobacco and alcohol. Second, they are using a combination of behavioral and cognitive techniques that have been shown to be effective in bringing about changes in human behavior. Third, their methods are being tested using rigorous evaluation techniques that enable us to identify the most and the least effective portions of each program.

One example of these newer drug prevention programs is called Life Skills Training (LST), a system that has been successful with young adolescents in a variety of multiethnic settings (Botvin & Tortu, 1988). LST is based on the research findings that most adolescents first use drugs in a social situation and that their decisions are influenced by not just one factor, but by a variety—their attitudes, personalities, cognitive maturity, and the particulars of the social situation in which they find themselves. The program has also recognized that many individuals first experiment with drugs during the preadolescent or early adolescent years. Therefore, drug education programs are needed well before senior high school.

The techniques used in the LST program are primarily based on social learning theory. From this perspective, decisions regarding drug use are shaped by models and by reinforcement as well as by beliefs and cognitive reasoning. Some individuals may be motivated to smoke, drink, or use other drugs as a way of coping with failure or alleviating tension. Others may use drugs as a means of enhancing their popularity or self-esteem. Then again, they might be influenced by observing the models around them. Susceptibility to these outside influences, however, is mediated by aspects of people's personalities such as self-confidence and locus of control attitudes; that is, those with the least self-esteem and the most external

A CLOSER LOOK 13.6

Drug-Abuse Program Focuses on Athletes

Citing the likelihood that student athletes may become involved in drug or alcohol abuse, the U.S. Justice Department in June announced a drug-abuse-prevention program that it hopes will reach more than 5 million such athletes. The program stresses the influential role school coaches can have in educating their students about alcohol and drug abuse. Coaches "have loyalty, commitment, and dedication in athletics which may not be present in other areas of the school," a promotional booklet said. Through training clinics and literature, the department's Drug Enforcement Administration plans to target 48,000 coaches and 5.5 million student athletes in 20,000 high schools. The program is expected to run for at least three years at an estimated cost of $5 million, said Ronald Trethric, preventive programs coordinator at the D.E.A.

"Our goal is to reach every coach and student athlete in the country," Francis M. Mullen Jr., the D.E.A. administrator, said. Federal officials stress that educating athletes is especially significant since the pressure to succeed and the influence of peers can make drugs and alcohol look more tempting for such students than for others. Printed literature for coaches stresses that they should not ignore evidence of substance abuse, but should instead "open a dialogue" with their athletes. "The bottom line is that the coaches will train their athletes to serve as role models in the area of drug-abuse prevention," said Carey McDonald, a spokesman for the National High School Athletic Coaches Association, which cosponsors the program.

Other organizations sponsoring the program are the International Association of Chiefs of Police, the National Football League Players Association, and the National Football League.

Source: Drug abuse program focuses on athletes. (1984, August 22). *Education Week,* p. 6. Reprinted by permission.

locus of control attitudes are more easily swayed by others to use drugs. For these reasons, the LST program combines approaches designed to reduce adolescents' motivation for using drugs as well as to teach assertiveness skills for saying no to peer pressure.

Although merely providing information about the dangers of drugs has proved fairly fruitless, some knowledge about drugs can be a deterrent to their use. For example, adolescents typically overestimate the prevalence of smoking and drinking. By providing the statistics showing that the majority of people in our society today are nonsmokers, we might help adolescents perceive the "reinforcement" available to them for not smoking. The information, however, must be presented in ways that take account of adolescents' cognitive abilities. For example, since most adolescents are making their decisions in terms of the present, warning them about the long-range consequences of smoking is pretty fruitless.

As Table 13.4 illustrates, the LST program includes training in decision making, behavior change, social skills, and coping with anxiety, as well as information about the dangers of drugs (Botvin, 1983). The 18 sessions include such activities as using apparatus to demonstrate the immediate effects of nicotine: increased heart rate and carbon monoxide in the smoker's exhaled breath. Another session explains the techniques used by advertisers to manipulate our decisions as consumers. Those enrolled in the program also learn ways to relax, other than smoking, such as deep breathing and mental rehearsal. Brief refresher courses

Table 13.4

Life Skills Training Program Description

	NUMBER OF SESSIONS	TOPIC	DESCRIPTION
I. KNOWLEDGE AND INFORMATION	4	Substance use: myths and realities	Common attitudes and beliefs about tobacco, alcohol, and marijuana use; current prevalence rates of adults and teenagers; social acceptability of using these substances; process of becoming a regular (habitual) user and the difficulty of breaking these habits; one immediate physiological effect of smoking.
II. DECISION MAKING	2	Decision making and independent thinking	Discussion of routine decision making; description of a general decision-making strategy; social influences affecting decisions; recognizing persuasive tactics; the importance of independent thinking.
	2	Media influences and advertising techniques	Discussion of media influences on behavior; advertising techniques and manipulation of consumer behavior; formulating cognitive strategies for resisting advertising pressure; cigarette and alcohol advertising as case studies in the use of these techniques.
III. SELF-DIRECTED, BEHAVIOR CHANGE	2	Self-image and self-improvement	Discussion of self-image and how it is formed; the relationship between self-image and behavior; the importance of a positive self-image; alternative methods of improving one's self and self-image; beginning a self-improvement project.

are offered during the eighth and ninth grades to help students cope with new pressures and to reinforce the main points of their seventh-grade LST program.

The LST approach has proved successful with students at junior and senior high schools in several suburban school districts in the Northeast. The program has reduced these young adolescents' use of nicotine, alcohol, and marijuana. More impressive still, the 1-year follow-up data indicate that these changes are long lasting. Large-scale trials are now being conducted using the LST approach with urban minority students, with preliminary evidence indicating its success in these environments as well (Botvin & Tortu, 1988). The program's designers remind us, however, that teachers' rapport with students and their commitment to the program are crucial to its success. Teachers must be carefully selected and thoroughly trained in order to ensure the success of the LST techniques.

Other innovative prevention programs also utilize strategies similar to those of LST (for a listing and brief description, see Rhodes & Jason, 1988). What these share is their emphasis on specific skills training. Rather than merely presenting data about the dangers of drugs or merely admonishing young people to "just say no to drugs," these programs are taking a more realistic approach: Teach adolescents

Table 13.4 *(Continued)*

Life Skills Training Program Description

	NUMBER OF SESSIONS	TOPIC	DESCRIPTION
IV. COPING WITH ANXIETY	2	Coping with anxiety	Discussion of common anxiety-inducing situations; demonstration and practice of cognitive-behavioral techniques for coping with anxiety; instruction on the application of these techniques to everyday situations as active coping strategies.
V. SOCIAL SKILLS	2	Communication skills	Discussion of the communication process; distinguishing between verbal and nonverbal communication; techniques for avoiding misunderstandings.
	1	Social skills (A)	Discussion on overcoming shyness; initiating social contacts, giving and receiving compliments; basic conversational skills: initiating, sustaining, and ending conversations.
	1	Social skills (B)	Discussion of boy-girl relationships and the nature of attraction; conversations with members of the opposite sex; social activities and asking someone out for a date.
	2	Assertiveness	Situations calling for assertiveness; reasons for not being assertive; verbal and nonverbal assertive skills; resisting peer pressures to smoke, drink, or use marijuana.

Source: G. Botvin. (1983). *Life Skills Training: Teacher's Manual.* New York; Smithfield Press.

the specific behavioral techniques for building self-esteem, resolving personal problems, reaching a specific goal, and resisting peer pressure.

The issues involved in drug use and drug education are far from simple. As the story in Box 13.7 illustrates, resolving drug-related problems can literally tear families apart. Despite the complexity of the situation, we moved forward against drugs in 1988 by establishing the first National Commission on Drug-Free Schools in our nation's history (Flax, 1989). As this commission implements its multimillion dollar plan, we can only hope that adolescents will glean from it the skills needed to resist drug abuse in a culture that too often promises effortless highs and painless cures through pills, liquids, and smoke.

CONCLUSION

Given our society's attitudes toward drugs, as evidenced by our own adult drinking and smoking habits, it is little wonder that most adolescents have, at least on occasion, used drugs. Fortunately, however, drug use seems to have been on the

A CLOSER LOOK 13.7

Adolescent "Drug Bust": Turning in Your Parents

After listening to an anti-drug lecture at her church, 13-year-old Deanna Young returned home, dumped her parents' pills, pot, and cocaine into a trash bag, and shortly before midnight took her evidence to the police station. As a result, her parents were arrested and Deanna was placed in a foster home, despite her pleas to return home. Facing the possibility of a 3-year jail sentence, the Youngs were allowed to enter a drug program rather than face charges. In a similar incident, an 11-year-old reported her stepfather to police for growing a marijuana plant in their backyard. While no case was made against him and the girl was returned home, her stepfather commented, "This wasn't about drugs. It was about a family feud that ended up on the 6 o'clock news."

Source: Kids' crusade. (1986, December 1). *Newsweek,* p. 8.

decline in recent years, and most young people continue to limit their use to occasional recreational situations. Nevertheless, nicotine and alcohol still pose the most serious hazards to millions of adolescents and their parents, while drugs such as cocaine and crack have become problems of epidemic proportions among the poor. We want to avoid creating stereotypes, however, regarding the types of adolescents who use drugs. For example, white youngsters tend to drink more than minorities, and more girls than boys are now smoking.

While keeping in mind the distinctions between adolescents who use drugs and those who abuse them, it is nonetheless true that most of our approaches to drug education have had relatively little success. On a more optimistic note, however, some of the most recent approaches utilizing cognitive and behavioral techniques do seem to be making an impact, especially on adolescents' use of nicotine and alcohol. There is little doubt that most young people will continue to try drugs, at the very least out of curiosity in recreational settings. Nor is there any doubt of the futility of merely warning them about the long-range consequences of drug abuse. Nevertheless, by offering accurate information without resorting to scare tactics and by teaching specific ways to resist the temptations of our drug-oriented culture, we are helping adolescents exercise the kind of caution that may indeed save their lives and the lives of their friends.

QUESTIONS FOR DISCUSSION AND REVIEW

Basic Concepts and Terminology

1. How does each of these drugs affect the body: alcohol, amphetamines, barbiturates, angel dust, crack, ice, nicotine, cocaine, marijuana, inhalants, LSD, heroin, MDA, PCP?
2. How has adolescent drug use changed since the 1970s? Provide specific statistics on the use of different drugs to support your answer.
3. In what ways do adolescents who abuse drugs differ from those who use drugs in moderation?
4. What methods have been most effective and which have been least effective in reducing adolescents' use of nicotine, alcohol, and marijuana? Why have so many programs failed to have much impact?

5. What are the variables that influence adolescents' decisions to smoke, drink, or use other drugs? How are age, gender, income, geographic location, and college attendance related to the use of various drugs?
6. How concerned should parents be that peer pressure will turn their adolescent children into drug users or drug abusers? Explain your answer with the research or statistics.
7. Why do most adolescents say they start drinking or smoking? How are these two habits similar and how are they different in terms of their impact on the body and the type of person who uses them?
8. How are adolescents affected by living with an alcoholic parent? What is codependency, and how does it develop?
9. Describe the Life Skills Training program. What components of this program and others like it have accounted for their success?
10. How does our society contribute to adolescent drug use and drug abuse? In what ways are our sex roles related to drug use?

Questions for Discussion and Debate

1. On what grounds can you argue for and against lowering the legal drinking age again to 18?
2. Since most adolescents and adults continue to use drugs in moderation for recreational purposes, which drugs do you think create the least damage? the most? Why?
3. How would you design a program to help adolescents quit smoking? reduce their drinking? use other drugs cautiously? What role would you have the media and the legal system play?
4. How did your experiences with nicotine, alcohol, and other drugs affect your adolescence? What, if anything, do you wish you had known then that you know now?
5. What did you find most depressing and most heartening in this chapter?
6. Why do you think we are such a drug-oriented culture? In what ways, if any, do you think we could change our behavior and attitudes?
7. How do you feel about adolescents reporting their parents to the police for using illegal drugs?
8. If you had an adolescent child, what would your policy be regarding his or her use of drugs? (Remember that nicotine and alcohol are drugs.)
9. How have you or any of your friends suffered as a consequence of having an alcoholic family member?
10. What are the biggest mistakes you feel our society is making in regard to dealing with drugs? How would you go about improving our situation?

GLOSSARY

acid *See* LSD.

Al-anon National organization designed to help members deal with and recover from a family member's alcoholism.

Al-a-teen National organization for teenagers with an alcoholic family member.

alcohol The most frequently used drug; an addictive sedative-hypnotic that in moderate doses relaxes the muscles but in large doses causes both loss of muscle control and sleep.

amphetamines "Uppers." Synthetic drugs that speed up the body's heart rate and blood pressure. When taken in low to moderate doses, increase energy, alertness, and self-confidence.

amping The "high" that comes when using "ice."

angel dust Phencyclidine. *See* PCP.

barbiturates "Downers." Synthetic sedatives that relax the muscles, slow down the heart rate, and cause drowsiness or sleep.

caffeine The most widely used stimulant in the world, a drug that induces wakefulness. In large doses can cause insomnia, mild sensory disturbance, muscle tenseness, or anxiety.

Children of Alcoholics (COAs) People who develop certain attitudes and behaviors that undermine their well-being as a consequence of having lived with an alcoholic parent.

cocaine Made from the leaves of the coca plant, a highly addictive drug that can be fatal, especially when introduced intravenously or smoked.

codependent People who are obsessed with taking care of and being responsible for other people.

Codependents Anonymous An organization designed to help codependents overcome their self-destructive ways of relating to other people.

crack The crystalline form of cocaine, induces stronger effects than cocaine in powdered form.

cross-tolerance The phenomenon in which developing a tolerance to one type of drug results in diminished sensitivity to the effects of another drug.

downers *See* barbiturates.

drug addiction The older term for drug dependence. *See* drug dependence.

drug dependence Psychological dependence refers to a strong compulsion to use a drug because it produces pleasure or reduces anxiety. Physical dependence occurs when the user's body undergoes withdrawal symptoms when he or she is not using the drug.

drug tolerance A condition occurring after prolonged and heavy use of a drug, wherein the user becomes less affected by the doses and has to increase the amount in order to experience the original effects.

ecstasy *See* MDA.

fetal alcohol syndrome A condition occurring in infants in which they are born with mild to moderate mental retardation, low birth weights, and excessive irritability or hyperactivity during childhood due to their mother's alcohol consumption during pregnancy.

flashbacks Unexpectedly re-experiencing the effects of LSD several weeks or months after use of the drug.

free basing Introducing cocaine to the body by smoking, rather than eating or injecting it.

hashish Concentrated form of marijuana that has more THC and thus causes a stronger reaction.

ice A type of "speed" (methamphetamine) that produces a "buzz" for up to 24 hours and is more addictive than cocaine.

LSD Lysergic acid diethylamide. A synthetic drug causing hallucinations.

MDA "Ecstasy." A synthetic drug producing amphetaminelike and LSD-like effects that is associated with feeling more insightful, empathic, and aware.

Mothers Against Drunk Driving (MADD) National organization working to increase public awareness on the hazards of driving while intoxicated and lobbying for stricter legislation on the issue.

nicotine The active ingredient in tobacco (smoked or chewed). A physically addictive drug that has a mild stimulant effect.

paper A penny-sized bag of "ice."

PCP Phencyclidine, "angel dust." A synthetic hallucinogen that causes distortions of body image and a sense of timelessness.

popping Introducing a drug to the body by putting the needle just slightly under the skin's surface.

quaaludes A tranquilizer recently withdrawn from the market by the pharmaceutical manufacturer due to its dangers and abuse.

smokeless tobacco Chewing tobacco.

speed *See* amphetamines.

THC The chemical in marijuana responsible for its psychoactive effects.

uppers *See* amphetamines.

withdrawal The physical reactions that people who are physically addicted to a drug experience when they stop using the drug. The symptoms are usually directly opposite of the effects induced by the drug.

REFERENCES

Ackerman, R. (1989). *Perfect daughters: Adult daughters of alcoholics.* Deerfield Beach, FL: Health Communications.

Al-Anon. (1981). *Al-Anon's twelve steps and twelve traditions.* New York: Al-Anon Family Group Headquarters.

Bangert, R. (1988). The effects of school based substance abuse education: A meta-analysis. *Journal of Drug Education, 18,* 243–264.

Beck, K., & Summons, T. (1987). Adolescent gender differences in alcohol beliefs and behaviors. *Journal of Alcohol and Drug Education, 33,* 31–44.

Black students found to use drugs less often than whites. (1989, September 6). *Education Week,* p. 2.

Botvin, G. (1986). *Life skills training: Teacher's manual.* New York: Smithfield Press.

Botvin, G., & Tortu, S. (1988). Preventing adolescent substance abuse through life skills training. In R. Price,

E. Cowen, R. Lorion, & J. Ramos (Eds.), *Fourteen ounces of prevention.* Washington, DC: American Psychological Association.

Chassin, L. (1988). The social image of smokeless tobacco use in three different types of teenagers. *Addictive Behaviors, 13,* 107–112.

Coffey, W. (1988). *Straight talk about drinking: Teenagers speak out against alcohol.* NY: Plume.

Defoe, J., & Breed, W. (1988). Youth and alcohol in television stories. *Adolescence, 23,* 533–550.

DelGreco, L. (1986). Four year results of a youth smoking prevention program using assertiveness training. *Adolescence, 21,* 631–640.

Drug abuse program focuses on athletes. (1984, August, 22). *Education Week,* p. 6.

Elder, J. (1988). Predictors of chewing tobacco and cigarette use in a multiethnic school population. *Adolescence, 23,* 689–702.

Flax, E. (1989, September 6). Campaign against drugs beginning to take shape. *Education Week,* p. 24.

Friedman, A., Glickman, N., & Morrissey, M. (1986). Prediction of successful treatment outcome by client characteristics in adolescent drug treatment programs. *Journal of Drug Education, 16,* 149–65.

Gibbons, S. (1986). Patterns of alcohol use among rural and small town adolescents. *Adolescence, 21,* 887–900.

Grilly, D. (1989). *Drugs and human behavior.* Boston: Allyn Bacon.

Gritz, E. (1982). *Cigarette smoking by adolescent females.* Washington, DC: American Psychological Association.

Halebsky, M. (1987). Adolescent alcohol and substance abuse: Parent and peer effects. *Adolescence, 22,* 961–967.

Harper, F. (1988). Alcohol and Black youth: An overview. *Journal of Drug Issues, 18,* 7–14.

Hemp seeds. (1984, October 3). *Education Week,* p. 3.

Hope, P. (1988). *Lovebounds: Recovering from an alcoholic family.* New York: New American Library.

Horwitz, A., & White, H. (1987). Gender role orientations and styles of pathology among adolescents. *Journal of Health and Social Behavior, 28,* 158–170.

Jaynes, J., & Rugg, C. (1988). *Adolescents, alcohol and drugs: A practical guide for those who work with young people.* New York: Charles Thomas.

Johnston, L., & Bachman, J. (1989). *Drug use, drinking and smoking: National survey results from high school, college and young adult populations 1975–1988.* Rockville, MD: National Institute on Drug Abuse.

Kids' crusade. (1986, December 1). *Newsweek,* p. 8.

Koop, E. (1989). *The health consequences of smoking.* Washington, DC: U.S. Department of Health, Education, and Welfare, Office of the Surgeon General.

Lerner, M., (1989, November 27). The fire of "ice." *Newsweek,* pp. 37–40.

Leventhal, H. (1987). Adolescent smokers. *Journal of the American Medical Association, 257,* 3373–3376.

Light, W. (1988). *Alcoholism and women: genetics and fetal development.* New York: Charles Thomas.

Long, J., & Schert, D. (1984). Developmental antecedent of compulsive drug use: A report on the literature. *Journal of Psychoactive Drugs, 16,* 169–182.

McCarthy, W. (1986). Smokeless tobacco use among adolescents. *Journal of Drug Education, 16,* 383–402.

Minnesota students suspended. (1984, October 27). *Education Week,* p. 3.

Murray, D., Luepker, R., & Mittlemark, M. (1984). The prevention of smoking in children. *Journal of Applied Social Psychology, 14,* 274–285.

National Institute on Drug Abuse. (1987) *National household survey on drug abuse.* Rockville, MD: Author.

Newcomb, M., & Bentler, P. (1987). Substance use and ethnicity. *Journal of Psychology, 120,* 83–85.

Newcomb, M., & Bentler, P. (1988). *Consequences of adolescent drug use.* Newbury Park, CA: Sage.

Newcomb, M., & Bentler, P. (1989). Substance use and abuse among children and teenagers. *American Psychologist, 44,* 242–248.

Peele, S. (1986). The "cure" for adolescent drug abuse: Worse than the problem? *Journal of Counseling and Development, 65,* 23–24.

Price, R., Cowen, E., Lorion, R., & Ramos, J. (Eds.). (1988). *Fourteen ounces of prevention.* Washington, DC: American Psychological Association.

Rhodes, R., & Jason, L. (1988). *Preventing substance abuse among children and adolescents.* New York: Pergamon Press.

Ryerson, E. (1985). *When your parent drinks too much: A book of help and hope for teenagers.* New York: Warner Books.

Schinke, S., & Gilchrist, L. (1985). Preventing substance abuse with children and adolescents. *Journal of Consulting and Clinical Psychology, 55,* 596–602.

Seixas, J. (1985). *Children of alcoholism.* New York: Harper & Row.

Sheppard, M. (1985). Peer pressure and drug use: Exploding the myth. *Adolescence, 20,* 949–958.

Singer, M., & Petchers, M. (1987). A biracial comparison of adolescent alcohol use. *Journal of Drug and Alcohol Abuse, 13,* 461–474.

Tobler, N. (1986). Meta analysis of 143 adolescent drug prevention programs. *Journal of Drug Issues, 16,* 537–568.

Watts, T., & Roosevelt, W. (1989). *Alcoholism in minority populations.* New York: Charles Thomas.

Welte, J., & Barnes, G. (1987a). Alcohol use among adolescent minority groups. *Journal of Studies on Alcohol, 48,* 329–336.

Welte, J., & Barnes, G. (1987b). Youthful smoking. *Journal of Adolescence, 10,* 327–340.

Womble, M., & Bakeman, C. (1986). A culturally specific approach to drunk driving for blacks. *Alcoholism Treatment Quarterly, 3,* 103–113.

Wright, L. (1985). High school polydrug users and abusers. *Adolescence, 20,* 853–861.

Young, T. (1987). PCP use among adolescents. *Child Study Journal, 17,* 55–66.

Zabin, L. (1986). Substance use and its relation to sexual activity among inner city adolescents. *Journal of Adolescent Health Care, 7,* 320–331.

14 Atypical Adolescent Problems

CHAPTER OUTLINE

DELINQUENCY

Prevalence and Trends
Contributing Factors
IQ and Academic Success
Learning Disabilities
Self-Esteem
The Parent-Child Relationship
Peer Relationships
Race and Income
Gender Roles
Prevention and Rehabilitation

RUNAWAYS

SUICIDE

Prevalance and Trends
Contributing Factors
Depression
Conceptions of Death
Societal Factors
Gender Roles
Family Factors
Prevention and Rehabilitation

EATING DISORDERS

Anorexia Nervosa
Bulimia
Prevention and Treatment

COPING WITH DEATH AND DYING

Bereavement
Death Education

CHRONICALLY ILL ADOLESCENTS

CONCLUSION

GOALS AND OBJECTIVES

This chapter is designed to enable you to:

- Discuss the factors contributing to delinquency, suicide, eating disorders, and running away from home
- Consider the various methods for treating and preventing delinquency, suicide, eating disorders, and depression
- Become familiar with the statistics on the prevalence of various adolescent problems
- Identify the special problems of chronically ill and terminally ill adolescents and their families
- Explain how we might help adolescents cope with their own death and the death of people they love

CONCEPTS AND TERMINOLOGY

anomie
anorexia nervosa
binge
bulimarexia
bulimia
cluster suicides
DSM III-R
purging

In previous chapters we have seen that most adolescents' problems are related to their schoolwork, their parents, and their friends. Unfortunately, however, thousands of our young people are confronted with far more serious concerns: delinquency, suicidal depression, eating disorders, and chronic or terminal illness. It is important to note that the number of adolescents affected by these disorders is relatively small when compared to the number affected by problems such as poverty and pregnancy. For example, the number of adolescents affected by drug abuse, suicidal depression, and anorexia combined does not equal the number affected by teenage pregnancy (see Table 14.1). In other words, these problems are not typical of adolescents. Nevertheless, unlike the more prevalent teenage problems, eating disorders, chronic depression, delinquency, and certain teenage

Table 14.1

Adolescent Problems in Perspective

PROBLEM	PERCENT OF ADOLESCENTS AFFECTED
Deaths from suicide	.0002
Arrests for drunk driving	.001
Anorexia and bulimia	.3
Chronic illness	2
Official arrests	5
Runaways	2
Girls who become pregnant	10
Girls who abort pregnancies	5
Victims of child abuse	10
Cigarette smokers	30
Drinkers	70
School dropouts	
Native Americans	40
African Americans	20
Hispanic	
White	12
Poverty	
Native American	50
African American	53
Hispanic	45
White	20

Population of adolescents aged 12–17 = 22.3 million (1985).

illnesses are often fatal. Moreover, the data suggest that suicide, delinquency, and eating disorders are on the rise, destroying the lives of thousands of young people and their families.

DELINQUENCY

Prevalence and Trends

How common is delinquency among our adolescent population? It is estimated that about 12% of all juveniles today will have a police record before the age of 20. Put differently, about 1.4 million juveniles are arrested each year for nonindex crimes, such as vandalism, running away from home, or drug abuse, and about 900,000 are arrested for index crimes, such as theft, robbery, or rape. Although people under 18 account for nearly half of our nation's arrests for vandalism, car theft, burglary, and arson, they account for very few crimes such as rape, murder, or assault. For example, as Table 14.2 illustrates, only about 1,000 of the 1,543,372 people arrested for murder in 1984 were under 18 (FBI, 1987).

It is important to note, however, that these figures reflect the number of official arrests, not the number of actual crimes committed. Indeed, adolescents' self-reports indicate that police records may account for as little as 2% of all juvenile offenses (Dunford & Elliot, 1982). Moreover, since 1960 arrests of adolescents for serious crimes such as murder have escalated faster than their overall arrest rates for less serious offenses, such as vandalism (FBI, 1987). As Box 14.1 illustrates, disturbed adolescents are clearly capable of gruesome and heinous crimes—acts that have brought the controversial issue of the death penalty for minors to the forefront. The Supreme Court's 1989 decision to lower the age to 16 for the death penalty has been met with cries of outrage from those who consider this cruel and unusual punishment (McDaniel, 1989).

Furthermore, adolescent gangs are posing an increasing threat to inner-city communities and to adolescents themselves. (Johnstone, 1983; Lander, 1988). While gang members once wielded switchblades and iron pipes, today's gangs have expanded their arsenals to include grenades, Uzis, and other automatic weapons. Worse yet, these weapons are often purchased with money made from selling drugs, which involves adult criminals and nationwide drug traffickers. In many poor, urban neighborhoods, children as young as 10 are clinging to the fringes of a gang, hoping to prove themselves worthy of membership by the age of 12. By offering a sense of family, income, and status, gangs are able to lure adolescents in ways that leave their parents and police feeling virtually helpless. Despite this, our urban police departments rarely have any specialized units to deal with juvenile gangs (Needle & Stapleton, 1983).

As a consequence of both the growing involvement of gangs in drug traffic and the general rise in juvenile crime, adolescents are more likely than ever to witness or to be the victims of, crime. Adolescents are now about twice as likely to be the victims of a violent crime as are adults. At greatest risk are older adolescent males, and African American teenagers of either sex. Homicide is now the leading cause of death among African American adolescent males and the third leading cause among the entire adolescent population (Whitaker, 1986). Surrounded by more violence, children are also now more likely to witness a serious crime. For example, in a 1986 survey of 536 elementary school students in Chicago, one-

Table 14.2

Total Arrests of Adolescents in 1984, by Race

	ARRESTS UNDER 18	PERCENT DISTRIBUTION			
Offense Charged	*Total*	*White*	*African American*	*American Indian or Alaskan Native*	*Asian or Pacific Islander*
Murder and manslaughter	1,004	53.7	45.2	.7	.4
Forcible rape	4,394	45.2	53.8	.7	.3
Robbery	27,788	30.3	68.5	.2	.9
Aggravated assault	31,126	59.5	39.3	.7	.6
Burglary	127,521	76.0	22.4	.8	.7
Larceny-theft	338,235	71.2	26.5	1.1	1.2
Motor vehicle theft	33,795	72.0	25.9	1.0	1.0
Arson	6,235	84.8	13.6	1.0	.7
Violent crime	64,312	45.8	53.0	.5	.7
Property crime	505,786	72.7	25.3	1.0	1.1
Other assaults	66,809	66.6	31.4	.8	1.2
Forgery and counterfeiting	6,172	83.2	15.7	.7	.4
Fraud	16,992	51.3	46.7	.2	1.7
Stolen property; buying, receiving, processing	22,963	66.9	32.0	.5	.5
Vandalism	87,040	84.7	14.1	.6	.6
Weapons, carrying	20,644	69.7	29.0	.4	.9
Sex offenses (except rape and prostitution)	13,385	75.1	24.0	.4	.5
Drug abuse violations	66,484	79.0	19.6	.5	1.0
Driving under the influence	18,391	96.4	2.2	1.1	.4
Liquor laws	101,662	95.9	2.4	1.2	.4
Drunkenness	23,510	93.2	4.9	1.7	.2
Disorderly conduct	73,478	75.1	24.1	.5	.3
Curfew and loitering	67,073	70.4	28.0	.6	1.0
Runaways	114,059	85.5	12.3	.9	1.2

Source: U.S. Department of Justice. (1985, July). *Crime in the United States* (p. 181). Washington, DC: Author.

fourth had seen someone shot and one-third had seen a stabbing. In a more recent Chicago survey of 1,000 elementary and secondary students, 40% had seen a shooting and nearly one fourth had witnessed a murder. Likewise, in a Detroit study of one half of the 1985 murder cases, nearly one fifth of the murders were witnessed by children under the age of 18 (Flax, 1989).

Contributing Factors

The lives that are destroyed or damaged by crime and delinquency have naturally motivated a search for the factors that contribute to juvenile crime. Although the data are often contradictory, a number of findings have emerged rather consistently.

(Unless otherwise cited, the research in the following sections is from Goldstein, Glick, Irwin, & Rubama, 1989; Holin, 1989; Johnson, E., 1987).

IQ and academic success Are delinquents less intelligent than nondelinquents? Does academic failure somehow make a young person more susceptible to delinquency? Although it is true that delinquents are usually poorer students than nondelinquents, IQ scores in and of themselves are not very reliable predictors of which children will become delinquent. In other words, children with lower IQ scores are not necessarily at greater risk of committing a delinquent act than those with better IQ scores. Nevertheless, it is the case that delinquents are seldom successful students (Hawkins & Lishner, 1987). Since most of our data are correlational, however, we cannot conclude that academic problems cause a student to become delinquent. It is possible, for example, that children do poorly in school as a consequence of their already being aggressive, noncompliant, or emotionally disturbed in ways that eventually lead them into delinquency. In fact, this argument is well supported in that research has repeatedly demonstrated that programs that do improve student's academic skills have had little impact on decreasing their delinquent or other antisocial behavior.

This is not to say, however, that preventing students from becoming failures at school has no impact on later delinquency. To the contrary, adolescents from ghetto areas who attended Head Start's preschool program have been found to be more successful academically and less delinquent than their classmates with similar socioeconomic backgrounds who did not attend a preschool enrichment program (Barrueta-Clement, et al, 1984; Consortium for Longitudinal Studies, 1983). Such findings suggest that being a successful student may be a deterrent to becoming delinquent. The key seems to be to take measures in early childhood to prevent students who are at a high risk of becoming delinquent from becoming failures at school in the first place.

Learning disabilities In a similar line of reasoning, researchers have wondered whether children with learning disabilities are more likely to become delinquent than their nondisabled classmates. Two conflicting findings appear in the literature. The first is that adolescents who have been arrested are more likely to have a learning disability than those who have never been arrested. The second is that among adolescents who have never been arrested, those with learning disabilities have no higher incidence of delinquency than those without learning disabilities (Grande, 1988; Perlmutter, 1987). Our best guess, then, is that most students with a learning disability compensate for their handicapping condition without resorting to delinquency. Yet students with severe learning disabilities who experience enough school failure may try to compensate for their failures through delinquent acts. The evidence is not strong enough for us to conclude, however, that having a learning disability, in and of itself, puts an adolescent at risk of becoming delinquent.

Self-esteem It has also seemed logical to presume that adolescents with low self-esteem will be more likely to become delinquent than youngsters with positive self-images and self-confidence. Since most of the research is correlational, however, the question has to be examined cautiously. Merely finding, as we have, that delinquents usually earn lower self-esteem scores than nondelinquents does not prove that the low self-esteem causes the delinquency. Nor do these correlations

A CLOSER LOOK 14.1

Children Who Kill

In 1989, by a five-to-four vote, the Supreme Court concluded that the Eighth Amendment ban on cruel and unusual punishment does not prohibit the execution of murderers who are mentally retarded or who are as young as 16. Approximately 1,300 children under 18, most of them 16- and 17-year-olds, are arrested each year for murder. According to Amnesty International, the United States, Pakistan, Bangladesh, Bwanda, and Barbados are the only countries that have executed teenaged murderers since 1979. Is our society's execution policy "barbaric" or "cruel and unusual" punishment? If so, what should be done with adolescents who kill?

Arthur Bates Fourteen-year-old Arthur Bates did not set out to kill. He was planning to burgle a house. Once inside, however, he strangled and raped the 60-year-old resident, then helped himself to some butter-pecan ice cream from his victim's freezer. When arrested an hour later, he immediately confessed and added, matter-of-factly, "You can't do anything to me. I'm just 14." Before he turned 4, Arthur's mother had asked welfare workers for help with her troubled son; and by the age of 10, Arthur was taken over as a ward of the state as an abused child, spending time in detention centers and mental hospitals. Although doctors at a Houston hospital had agreed that Arthur needed treatment, they refused to admit him because he was not "out of touch with reality." The state had invested $113,000 in Arthur by providing him with private psychiatric care for 2 years, yet he was released to the

continued

prove that the low self-esteem necessarily preceded the delinquency. For example, in a study involving 1,658 adolescents over a 3-year period, those who started out low in self-esteem were no more delinquent than those who started out with high self-esteem. In fact, there was a slight tendency for a person's self-esteem to fall after he or she became delinquent, contradicting the long-standing assumption that delinquents raise their self-esteem through their criminal activities (McCarthy & Hoge, 1984). Moreover, a number of studies have failed to find correlations between delinquency and self-esteem (Byner, O'Malley, & Bachman, 1981). In short, there is too much inconsistency for us to jump to the conclusion that having low self-esteem causes adolescents to resort to delinquency as a way of improving their self-image or boosting their self-confidence.

The parent-child relationship Working from the hypothesis that violence begets violence, researchers have also explored the relationship between child abuse and delinquency. Although the impact of physical abuse is still not altogether clear, the research does suggest that delinquents are more apt than nondelinquents to be physically abused by their parents. The data also suggest that the parents of delinquents behave more aggressively toward one another and toward their children (Kratovsky, 1982). On the other hand, the research has not consistently demonstrated a relationship between child abuse and delinquency (Paperney & Deisher, 1983).

Studies related to dimensions of the family other than child abuse, however,

Box 14.1 continued

custody of his stepmother shortly before he committed the murder.

Dartagnan Young Fifteen-year-old Dartagnan Young died in 1988 at Chicago's DuSable High School after accusing a 16-year-old classmate of slapping his girlfriend. The schoolmate pulled out a .32 revolver and started shooting. As other students watched in horror, Dartagnan staggered through the crowded hallway, blood pouring from his chest. He died hours later.

Chester Jackson In the spring of 1987, Chester Jackson, a talented linebacker at Murray-Wright High School in Detroit and a local hero, fell into an argument with a 14-year-old freshman during lunch hour. Chasing the football player into the school parking lot, the younger boy gunned Jackson down with a .357 magnum, injuring two other students in the shoot-out. After the incident, the city's mayor said he was prepared to send city police into the schools again to search for weapons. But an American Civil Liberties Union lawsuit, filed after a high-school coed was "patted down" by a male police officer even though she had passed the metal detector test, had put a halt to sweep searches in the Detroit schools in 1985.

Yvette and Janet Weaver Seventeen-year-old Yvette Weaver, a star pupil and the family favorite, had argued with her 15-year-old sister, Janet. As a result, Janet and her 22-year-old girlfriend stabbed Yvette to death in her bedroom. For 3 days Janet remained silent, watching cartoons while the police searched the house for clues. Eventually Janet and her friend were charged with the murder, recounting for the police Yvette's last word: "Why?"

Sources: G. Hackett, (1988, January 11). Kids: Deadly Force. *Newsweek,* pp. 18–19; A. Press. (1986, November 24). Children who kill. *Newsweek*, pp. 93–94; E. Salholz (1987, May 11). In Detroit, kids kill kids. *Newsweek*, pp. 74–75.

have yielded more consistent findings. Delinquents' parents are more likely to resort to excessively harsh discipline, to make extreme threats, and to let their children roam freely without adult supervision. They are also less involved in their children's lives and communicate poorly with them. As the research in chapter 8 demonstrated, adolescents whose parents are more communicative, supportive, affectionate, and democratic are more swayed by their parents' opinions than those whose parents are critical, authoritarian, indifferent, and uncommunicative. Some evidence also shows that the type of relationship adolescents have with their fathers may be a better predictor of delinquency than their relationship with their mothers (R. Johnson, 1987). Although some research has failed to find differences between the parenting styles of delinquents and nondelinquents, most studies find delinquents' parents to be more authoritarian, more emotionally distant, and more uncommunicative.

Underscoring the importance of parents' disciplinary styles is a series of studies monitoring the impact of those styles on the sons' antisocial behavior (Baldwin & Skinner, 1988; Patterson, Reid, & Dishion, 1990). The parents of boys who were behavioral problems typically used coercion, threats, and punishment to control their sons. They also tended to ignore their sons' good behavior. When these parents were trained to use positive reinforcement and contingent punishment, however, their sons' behavior improved. Further demonstrating the family's influence is the high degree of similarity from generation to generation in terms of a family's antisocial, aggressive, or criminal behavior (Huessmann, 1984;

Patterson, 1989). Aggressive, antisocial, or delinquent adolescents tend to have parents and grandparents who behaved similarly and who disciplined their children in an explosive, irrational way.

Given the parents' power in shaping a child's behavior, it is not particularly surprising that the signs of juvenile delinquency are usually apparent early in childhood (see Figure 14.1). Most delinquents were recognized as troubled, antisocial children by their grade school teachers or parents. Very seldom do well-adjusted children mysteriously or suddenly surprise us by becoming delinquent at the onset of adolescence. The harbingers of future trouble are usually apparent from an early age—excessive truancy, poor grades, and poor relationships or outright rejection by their peers (Farrington, Ohlin, & Wilson, 1986; Kazdin, 1987; Shinn, et al, 1987; Wahler & Dumas, 1984).

One unique study demonstrated the tenacity of aggressive and antisocial behavior by examining the behavior of 400 males and females over a 22-year period (Huesmann et al., 1984). Starting when the participants were in the third grade, the researchers collected data from the subjects, their parents, and eventually their spouses. Although the kind and amount of aggression changed with age, those individuals who were aggressive and antisocial as children remained that way throughout their adolescence and adulthood. In other words, the "bad" kids grew up to be the "bad" teenagers who became the "bad" adults.

Not surprisingly, the earlier children become involved in delinquent activities, the more likely they are to be chronic offenders and adult criminals. Only about half of all children who behave in antisocial ways during grade school go on to become juvenile delinquents, yet roughly half to three quarters of the delinquents become adult offenders (Blumstein, Cohen & Farrington, 1988).

Peer relationships Would poor social skills contribute to a youngster's becoming delinquent? Is it possible that children who have only a few or no friends might be more susceptible to delinquency than those who are well liked and socially skilled? Can we lower the delinquency rate by teaching adolescents how to relate to their peers in ways that make them more socially acceptable?

FIGURE 14.1

A developmental progression for antisocial behavior

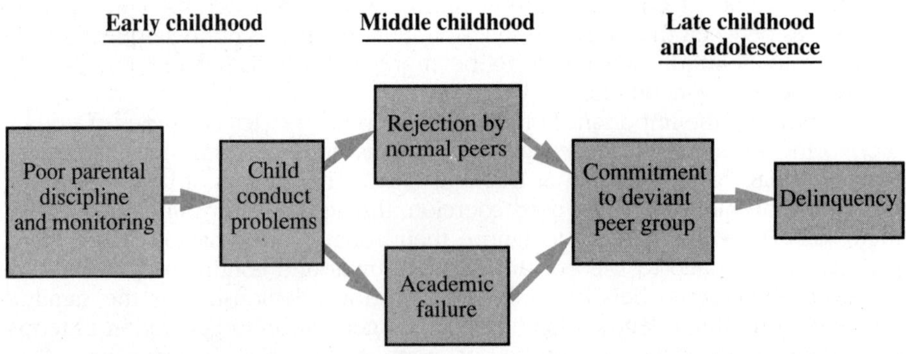

Source: G. Patterson, B. DeBaryshe, & E. Ramsey. (1989). A developmental perspective on antisocial behavior. *American Psychologist, 44,* 329–335.

Some evidence does suggest that delinquents have poorer interpersonal skills than nondelinquents (Gaffney, 1984; Short & Simeonsson, 1986). Specifically, the delinquents had trouble assuming the perspectives of other people. The delinquents were also less able to empathize with others and expressed less confidence about their interpersonal skills. Although not all researchers have found these differences (Mullis & Hanson, 1983), it appears that many delinquents have poor social skills. In this vein, experimental studies of children forming their peer groups show that aggressive behavior leads to rejection, not the reverse. In other words, children do not become delinquent because their peers have rejected them; rather, they have been rejected by their peers because they are behaving in aggressive or antisocial ways (Coie & Kupersmidt, 1983; Dodge, 1983).

Race and income For reasons already examined in previous chapters, we know that children living in poverty are the most likely to abuse drugs, to have poorly educated parents who are seldom available to supervise their children's activities, to have problems with their schoolwork, to be deprived of contact with their fathers, and to live in violent, crime-ridden neighborhoods—all of which are contributing factors to delinquency. We have also seen that most minority children in our society now live in poverty. It stands to reason, then, that minority youths would account for a disproportionate share of the juvenile crime rate, and they do. For example, African American youths account for about 55% of the arrests for violent crimes and 25% of all arrests for people under the age of 18, although they represent only 10% of the population (FBI, 1987).

It is important to note, however, that when adolescents are asked to report on their own delinquent acts, these racial and socioeconomic differences diminish (Gold & Petronio, 1980). These self-reports, in conjunction with the statistics regarding arrests and sentencing, reflect yet another reason for minorities being more likely than whites to be labeled delinquents—racial prejudice. African Americans, Hispanics, and Native Americans are arrested more often and are given harsher sentences than their white counterparts. Coupled with the fact that so many minority youths live in poverty, racial discrimination puts minority males at high risk for being arrested and sentenced for their crimes and misdemeanors.

Gender roles During the past two decades, arrests for female delinquency have risen steadily. For example, between 1960 and 1972 arrests for major crimes increased 82% for adolescent males and 306% for adolescent females. Although boys still commit nearly four times as many delinquent acts as girls, both the official police records and adolescents' self-reports confirm that girls have entered the world of delinquent crime (Gold & Petronio, 1980; Rutter & Giller, 1983).

Since our society's gender roles have become somewhat more androgynous in recent years, these statistics on female delinquency have caused us to wonder how gender roles and crime might be related. Have girls become more delinquent, at least in part, as a consequence of our being more accepting of female independence and aggressiveness? In order to test this hypothesis, researchers have compared the types of crime committed by males and females with adolescents' descriptions of themselves in terms of their masculinity and femininity. If gender roles and criminal behavior are related, the most violent and aggressive offenses should be committed by those males and females with the most masculine self-descriptions in terms of their behavior and values. Those with the most masculine traits should also commit more delinquent acts than those with more feminine orientations. Intriguing as these hypotheses may be, the data are too inconsistent either to adopt or to reject. Some researchers have found correlations between gender roles and type of crime committed (Horwitz & White, 1987), while others have not (Thornton, 1982).

Another hypothesis regarding female crime is that police and juvenile justice workers are now more willing than in former times to arrest and to prosecute girls for their delinquent acts. For example, in the past a girl who was with her boyfriend while he robbed a store was more likely to be classified merely as his accomplice, whereas today she is more likely to be charged and sentenced as his partner. In this sense, then, gender roles may be partially accountable for females' higher arrest rates, since most law enforcement officers and court officials are less sexist in that they are more willing to perceive girls as capable of and responsible for crime. While the reasons for the increase still remain somewhat a mystery, it is nonetheless a sad reality that female delinquency is on the upswing.

Prevention and Rehabilitation

Until recently we have had relatively little success in preventing delinquency or rehabilitating adjudicated youths (E. Johnson, 1987; Kazdin, 1987). Our efforts to reduce delinquency through training offenders' parents to use more effective styles of discipline have produced, at best, short-term effects that are usually lost within a year or two after the training stops. Even within halfway-house programs in which behavior modification procedures have improved delinquents' behavior, these improvements are generally lost after the youths return to their homes and communities. The most successful parent-training programs are those starting well before the children reach adolescence and relying on behavior modification techniques. In these programs delinquents' parents learn to use positive reinforcement in lieu of their usual patterns of criticizing, belittling, hitting, yelling at, and threatening their children. In general, parent training based on behavioral principles does improve children's predelinquent behavior if the intervention occurs early enough.

Given that most juvenile detention centers are not able to provide intensive rehabilitation programs, incarcerating delinquents seldom improves their behavior. Indeed, jails and detention centers often exacerbate delinquents' problems by putting them in contact with more hardened criminals, drug abusers, and sexual molesters. Moreover, when adolescents are jailed with adult prisoners, their suicide rates are more than three times as great as those of adolescents jailed with other juveniles (Flaherty, 1983). A number of studies indicate that when first-time juvenile offenders are given suspended sentences or put on probation, they are less likely to repeat their offenses than delinquents who are incarcerated for similar offenses. Data from recent experimental studies, as well as reviews of the literature, also show that punishment or the threat of punishment is one of the least effective ways of deterring juvenile crime (Schneider, 1989).

The few programs that have succeeded in rehabilitating delinquents or preventing troubled youths from becoming delinquent rely on a combination of cognitive and social learning techniques (Goldstein, et al, 1989; Holin, 1989). Specifically, these programs teach delinquents new ways of behaving through positive reinforcement and contingency contracts. For example, at Camp Wediko troubled children who are headed toward delinquency learn to control their own behavior through written contracts and through the staff's daily monitoring of their behavior (see Box 14.2). Like other programs for troubled and aggressive youths, the Wediko program uses ample amounts of daily reinforcement for appropriate behavior and for improvements in behavior. Although the staff does not hesitate to punish those who violate their contracts, the guidelines are clearly specified at the outset so that the children know exactly what type of behavior will be punished and what the punishments will be.

Although it is discouraging that so few programs have succeeded in helping delinquents, it is important to note that most of the attempts have been mainly rehabilitative rather than preventative. That is, most programs become available to adolescents only after they have already become delinquent. The most promising approach is to reach those children who are at highest risk of becoming delinquent well before their teenage years. For example, programs such as the Beethoven Project discussed in chapter 6 are teaching low-income parents more effective ways of disciplining and communicating with their young children. Likewise, the methods discussed in earlier chapters for improving the academic and vocational skills of impoverished students can be perceived as delinquency prevention programs, as are our efforts to reduce poverty. In short, programs aimed at increasing indigent children's chances for economic and educational success are probably our most effective delinquency prevention measures. The question is not whether such methods work but whether we will opt to make them our priority in allocating our money and our human resources.

RUNAWAYS

While many adolescents respond to their problems at home and school by becoming delinquent, thousands take another course—they run away. To many of us the term *runaway* may still conjure up carefree images of Huckleberry Finn, leaving home and finding friendship, adventure, and laughter before returning to the welcoming arms of his relatives. Most real-world runaways, however, are a far cry from such fictionalized characters. In fact, runaways might more accurately be described as throwaways, given that many of them leave home as a consequence of physical or emotional abuse (Garbarino, Wilson, & Garbarino, 1986; Janus, et al, 1987).

Somewhere between 730,000 and 1.3 million young people are classified as runaways. Of these, 500,000 are for all intents and purposes homeless. Although only 3 or 4% of all children run away from home, those who do often become victims of prostitution, drug abuse, physical assault, and pornography. It is estimated that in New York City alone nearly 30,000 runaway youths roam the streets, living without shelter or in temporary housing for the homeless. Contrary to the old stereotype, most runaways are not merely disobedient children who capriciously leave home over minor squabbles with their parents. Rather, most are children from troubled families who, having left home, have no place else to go.

Moreover, when runaways return to their families, only a small portion receive any help to alleviate the problems that motivated them to leave in the first place. Certainly there are those who run away in reaction to temporary problems at home or at school that have been resolved by the time they return home. Those who repeatedly run away from home, however, are often trying to protect themselves from sexual or physical abuse or from a family that is otherwise

A CLOSER LOOK 14.2

A Successful Program for Predelinquent and Disturbed Youths

Just after breakfast, outside the dining hall near the lake, a 17-year-old boy hurls a bench at a camp counselor. While several staff members restrain him, and while he is screaming threats and insults, his counselor talks to him calmly. Within an hour the boy is apologizing for losing control and trying to tell his counselor how afraid he is about his mother's upcoming visit. Clearly, Wediko is not your ordinary summer camp.

Located in a forest retreat in New Hampshire, Wediko has demonstrated that it can turn disturbed youngsters' lives around in 45 days and achieve this for one-fifth to one-seventh the average daily cost of a stay in a psychiatric hospital. Started in 1934, Wediko is one of the nation's oldest therapeutic camplike programs for emotionally disturbed adolescents, most of whom are inevitably headed toward delinquency. Using a combination of behavioral and cognitive approaches, the counselors first get young people to stop their antisocial behavior and then, after the behavior is under control, to try to understand the reasons for their outbursts. One third of the children at Wediko do not live with either of their parents, and 90% are enrolled in special education programs at school. Many have been sexually or physically abused and have alcoholic parents.

Each child's behavior is recorded daily to identify the specific activities he or she engaged in during a day. This behavior tracking system enables the researchers and counselors to determine what stimuli and what responses influ-

continued

dysfunctional. Finding out why a young person has left home before returning him or her to the parents' custody, therefore, is a practice that can protect a number of young people from potentially life-threatening situations.

SUICIDE

Prevalence and Trends

While some adolescents react to their problems by running away from home, others choose a more drastic measure—suicide. Although accurate statistics on suicide are difficult to obtain, it appears that today's young people are attempting and committing more suicides than those in earlier decades. Among 15- to 19-year-olds, the suicide rate in 1950 was between 2.7 and 3.5 per 100,000—a figure that had risen to 14.2 by 1977. Similarly, the number of suicides in the 15- to 24-year-old age group rose from 4,760 in 1985 to 5,120 in 1986. By 1986 there were 1,896 reported deaths by suicide among 15- to 19-year-olds, an average of 5 a day (Centers for Disease Control, 1989). Given that many families report their child's suicide as an accidental death, the actual suicide rate among adolescents is no doubt higher than these official statistics indicate. In fact, some analysts believe the actual rate may be three times as high as the official statistics and that for every successful adolescent suicide there are 10 unsuccessful attempts (Husain & Vandiver, 1984). Nevertheless, suicide is still rare among the young, affecting only 0.0002% of all adolescents (Centers for Disease Control, 1989).

Box 14.2 continued

ence each child's behavior: How did Joe react to a peer's teasing? How did Jane react when her counselor warned her to straighten up? How did Alex respond when his friend complimented him? How did Marlene respond to her counselor after she was punished?

An important part of each child's program is the use of behavioral contracts, which are often written as metaphors so the children can easily remember and relate to them:

"My name is James," one contract reads. "I am a wonderful boy but I have a broken heart. This heart of mine has been broken many, many times. But I haven't given up. Sometimes my broken heart gets in the way and I do things which make people mad, particularly my foster parents. But I want to get along. But most of all, I want shoes!!! I am going to start to fix my heart and I am going to earn hearts for listening, being cooperative and not being silly. I can earn up to 15 hearts a day. Five big whole heart stickers earn me one pair of shoes. Can James have a big, mended heart?"

Another contract reads: "My name is Aaron and I am a kid who has two big parts to him. One part is called the Team Player. When I am a Team Player, I listen, share, try, talk, and don't hit. But there are times when I foul out. I foul out when I push others, when I am sneaky and when I ignore my coaches (parents). Like in the NBA, I get benched when I foul out. My coaches (parents) will always tell me when I am benched. My coaches can also tell me I am being a team player by the points I earn on my daily check list. For every check I earn, I get two minutes of basketball time with my dad."

Source: J. Buie. (1988, October). Wediko leads kids out of the woods. *APA Monitor,* pp. 22–23.

When have you felt most like running away from home?

14.3 ADOLESCENT VOICES

Mark: An Adolescent's Account of His Attempted Suicide

I was nine years old when I first started drinking, but I didn't get into it seriously till I was twelve. I'm seventeen now. All my troubles started off with my drinking. Things just weren't working out for me, and I'd just take it out on myself with booze. After drinking for a couple of weeks I'd get sick. Sometimes I'd end up in the hospital.

I started drinking because both my parents were alcoholics. My mother died when I was six. My father turned into a real alcoholic then. You'd think that seeing such a bad example, I would want to stay away from it; and when I was ten I tried. When I got to be eleven I started back into it, nipping beer off my father and my uncle. Then, when I was twelve, I started getting into trouble. I started fighting and stealing things to drink. That just got me into deeper trouble and it kept on building up.

When I look back I see that I started drinking more or less because I was unhappy, and it was a way to make me feel better. I knew from watching older people that if you were really down, booze could make you feel better. Just before my father passed away he said he didn't want me to drink. I thought about it for a while, then I said that's a bunch of garbage. He went out drinking, why can't I? I just kept repeating to myself, "I'm really alone now," and it got drilled into my skull that I was gonna become a loner. Nobody could tell me what to do. I did my own thing and just kept on going.

When I was about fifteen I made an attempt at suicide by jumping out of a window. I landed in the hospital for that. I remember everything except right after jumping out the window. I split my head open and got twelve stitches across my forehead. I was in the hospital for three weeks, in the psychiatric ward. I really freaked out there. I was kind of mad that I failed. I guess I wanted to be dead with my parents. I thought I'd be happier that way. As an Indian, my view of death or life after death may be different from yours. I really believe that when you die you still live. You come back in a different form. So in suicide I was just ending this life, not all life, so I wasn't afraid to do it.

It wasn't really planned. The night before I was drinking and talking to a friend and I said I should kill myself because I want to be with my parents. He said that was no way to go about it. So I started to get mad at him and I left. I kept on drinking and I went back to his place that night. I passed out there and started drinking again the next morning. I passed out and got up again and drank some more. That's when I jumped out of the window. It was about nine o'clock I guess. I don't remember getting to the hospital or anything. It's kind of hard to describe what happened in the psychiatric ward. After a couple of days I came back to my mind and wondered why I was there. I was mad because I had failed.

Source: B. Rabkin. (1979). ***Growing up dead: A hard look at why adolescents commit suicide*** (p. 70). Nashville, TN: Abingdon Press.

The increase in youth suicide is primarily a result of the dramatic change in the male suicide rate. From 1970 to 1980, male suicides increased by 50%, with only a 2% increase among females. Almost 90% of all male suicide victims are white, although no significant racial differences exist among female suicide victims. Because males choose more lethal methods for trying to kill themselves, such as shooting and hanging, more boys than girls succeed at suicide. Sadly, however, an increasing number of girls and women are now resorting to using guns. For example, in 1970 fewer than one third of young women's suicides were committed with a firearm, whereas 42% used lethal drugs. By 1984, however, more than half of young women's suicides were committed with a firearm and only one fifth with drugs (Centers for Disease Control, 1989).

In addition to the rise in the overall suicide rate, the number of apparent **cluster suicides** during recent years also causes concern (Tugend, 1984). In these incidents, one adolescent's suicide seems to set off a rash of related suicides. In response to public concern, the national Centers for Disease Control have begun extensive research on cluster suicides, which should provide valuable data about this phenomenon. In the meantime, the uncertainty over whether publicity contributes to these multiple suicides has made researchers proceed cautiously about directing too much public attention to the matter.

Except in regard to these cluster suicides, the suicidal behavior of adolescents and adults is similar in several respects (Fremouw, Perczel, & Ellis, 1990). Irrespective of age, three times as many males as females commit suicide, although females attempt suicide three times more often than males. More suicides occur among whites than among minorities, among urban than among rural dwellers, among the wealthy than among the poor, and among Protestants than among Catholics or Jews. Older adolescents and adults usually kill themselves by hanging or shooting, while younger adolescents and children usually take an overdose of drugs. Most people who fail in their attempted suicide have taken poisonous drugs, a method that works slowly enough to increase the chances of their being discovered before dying.

Contributing Factors

Depression As you might expect, many adolescents who attempt or succeed at suicide are severely depressed. Although the association between depression and suicidal behaviors in younger children is not as firmly established as it is among adults, depressive disorders and suicidal behavior generally go hand in hand by adolescence (Brent, 1988; Fremouw, Perczel, & Ellis, 1990; Patros, 1988; Robins & Aless, 1985). Children and adolescents can experience various degrees of depression, some episodes lasting only a few months and others lasting several years. Unfortunately, chronically depressed children are often suffering from several psychiatric disorders simultaneously, which makes finding an effective treatment especially difficult. Although youngsters with major depressive disorders can recover with treatment, their depression generally returns. In fact, nearly two thirds of adolescents with a history of childhood depression develop a new episode while still in their teens. Fortunately, however, severe depression is very rare among the young, affecting less than 2% of the adolescent population (Kovacs, 1989).

Although all of us occasionally get the blues and refer to ourselves as depressed, the chronic depression that leads some adolescents to commit suicide is of a different nature. Adolescents with a potentially life-threatening depression have extremely external locus of control attitudes that leave them feeling helpless about improving their situations or resolving any of their problems (Nolen, Girgus & Seligman, 1986). They also have negative views of themselves, of the future, and of their own performance in all their endeavors. Moreover, clinically depressed adolescents have severe problems with relating to other people. They are typically unable to assume the initiative in social interactions, to maintain friendships, or to recognize how their own inappropriate behavior adversely affects other people. As a result, their depression leads them to conclude "I'm bad and can't do anything right, but everyone else is okay" (Kovacs, 1989; Rutter, Izard, & Read, 1986).

Of course, not all adolescents express their depression in the same way, which has been part of the problem in distinguishing those young people who are suicidally depressed from those who are just experiencing life's normal ups and downs. Nevertheless, some symptoms of severe depression are common enough to serve as warning signals of potentially suicidal behavior (Kovacs, 1989; Ryan, 1987). Severely depressed adolescents are likely to have sleep disturbances, either sleeping excessively or rarely being able to sleep. Their cognitive development also may appear to slow down for no apparent reason, particularly in regard to their acquisition of verbal skills appropriate to their age group. An inexplicable drop in school grades can, thus, be a symptom of depression. Excessive self-criticism, inexplicable crying spells, and isolation from other people can also be manifestations of depression. Since almost all adolescents will behave in these ways from time to time, the changes must be dramatic and persistent before we should presume that the adolescent is seriously depressed.

It is also important to note that depression is not the only factor contributing to adolescent suicide. In fact, not all sucidal adolescents are depressed as our stereotypes might lead us to believe. It is overly simplistic to assume that if an adolescent commits suicide, someone should feel guilty for not having recognized the symptoms of his or her depression. Although most suicidal youths do manifest symptoms of depression, others attempt to kill themselves without ever having experienced or shown such symptoms (Husain & Vandiver, 1984).

Unrealistic conceptions of death Among the factors other than depression that may contribute to suicidal thoughts are a young person's unrealistic conceptions of death (Husain & Vandiver, 1984; Rabkin, 1979). Especially during early adolescence, cognitive limitations can distort a young person's understanding of death. In our culture, where death is often presented in euphemistic, vague, or romanticized terms, the realities of death are too often hidden from the young. The melodramatic or emotionless portrayals of death in the media often sustain the image that suicide is somehow an instructive act that teaches our enemies and our careless loved ones some lesson. As a result, a teenage girl may naively believe that in killing herself she will cause her former boyfriend to pine away for her forever and to regret having broken her heart. Or a teenage boy might imagine that by attempting suicide he will live on forever in the minds and hearts of his 13-year-old peers who have heretofore ignored him.

This kind of "magical thinking" about death reflects the limitations of young adolescents' cognitive skills. Their belief in the imaginary audience and their egocentric thinking tend to mystify suicide, to lend it a drama and an appeal based on unrealistic thinking. For example, a number of those who failed at their suicide attempts have later explained that they believed they would remain aware of events on earth after they died. They believed they would somehow be able to look down on the living and enjoy the effects of their suicide on those left on earth. Some imagined their suicides would radically transform the lives of everyone who knew them. Others believed their suicide would reunite them with a deceased friend or relative. Conceiving death in terms of these fantasies, they had not ever thought of their death as a permanent end to life and to all contact with the living.

Societal factors Does living in a highly technological, competitive society contribute to suicidal thinking? According to some analysts, yes (Husain & Vandiver, 1984). Suicide rates tend to be higher in societies with a high degree of anomie than in societies with low anomie. **Anomie** is a condition that manifests itself as feelings of alienation and detachment from other people and from society. Anomie is said to arise in situations where personal bonds are secondary to other values. Societies with the most anomie are those that stress such values as competitiveness, mobility, rapid change, and materialism at the expense of family, intimacy, and interpersonal relationships. From this perspective, in response to their feelings of anomie, more adolescents in highly competitive societies (such as Japan and the United States) commit suicide than those in more rural, religious, and traditional societies.

In support of this argument, the suicide rates of Native American youths are instructive (Berlin, 1984). Reported suicides among Native American youths have increased by almost 1000% during the past 2 decades, becoming the second leading cause of death among 10- to 20-year-olds. Societal factors contributing to this increase include a breakdown of tribal traditions and a decline in the importance of religion. It has also been noted that the lowest suicide rates exist in tribes with the most traditional customs and in areas where the opportunities for employment and education exist within the tribal community itself. As Indian communities have become more acculturated, the factors contributing to anomie and the suicide rate have skyrocketed.

Interestingly, however, a country's overall standard of living does not appear to be related to teenagers' suicide rates. International surveys show an increase in suicide in 23 nations between 1970 and 1980. Norway, where the standard of living is relatively high, had the largest percentage increase of teenage suicide. Although each nation's adult suicides were related to the overall standard of living, teenage suicides were not (Lester, 1988). These findings clearly suggest that teenagers' motives for committing suicide are not the same as adults'—an understandable difference when we consider that most adults' self-esteem and daily problems (unemployment, low wages, medical care policies) are closely linked to their society's standard of living.

Gender roles Given that three times as many girls as boys attempt suicide, we have naturally wondered why. Several hypotheses have been offered, although none has been unilaterally accepted as the definitive answer. To begin with, adolescent girls report feeling more depressed than adolescent boys, which would account at least in part for girls' higher rates of attempted suicide. These findings, however, need to be viewed somewhat cautiously since girls seem to be more willing than boys to admit feeling depressed, whereas boys may be more apt to mislabel their feelings of depression as anger or frustration.

Moreover, when boys feel depressed they tend to react by developing behavioral problems, such as drinking, smoking, or fighting, which we are less likely to recognize as symptoms of depression. In contrast, when girls feel depressed, they tend to turn their feelings inward, developing sleep disorders, headaches, and other symptoms that we generally associate with being depressed (Baron & Perron, 1986; Choquet & Menke, 1987; Worchel, 1987). In other words, it is possible that girls are no more depressed than boys but that we are more likely to recognize the signs of depression in girls.

One representative study in support of this hypothesis surveyed 5th-, 9th-, and

11th-graders about their emotions (Stapley & Haviland, 1989). Although both adolescent boys and girls reported the same intensity of emotions, the types of emotion they felt and the situations in which they felt them were quite different. Girls felt their strongest emotions in their relationships with other people, frequently, in fact, in their relationship with a boyfriend. Boys, on the other hand, experienced most of their emotions during activities in which their performance was being assessed, such as sports events and school activities. Moreover, the boys were much more likely to deny feeling sad, guilty, or depressed and to keep their feelings to themselves. Joy was the only emotion boys did not deny in their retrospective reports of how they had felt during the past month. When the girls felt depressed, they directed their negative emotions inward in the form of self-hostility. In contrast, when the boys felt depressed, they directed their negative feelings toward others, most often in the form of anger. To summarize, research indicates that girls tend to become depressed about personal relationships, to admit to their depressed feelings, and to turn their depression inward. In contrast, boys tend to become depressed about experiences having to do with their personal perfomance, to deny their feelings, and to turn their depression against others in the form of anger.

Family factors As is the case with delinquency, family factors have been found to be highly correlated with adolescent suicide (Husain & Vandiver, 1984; Rutter, Izard, & Read, 1986). Once again, however we should not presume that these family variables are necessarily the cause of suicidal behavior since the data are correlational, not experimental. Drug abuse, child abuse, and marital conflict are more common in the families of suicidal than nonsuicidal youths. Many suicidal youths also say they feel unloved and unwanted, suggesting that their parents, even if they do love the children, have been unable to create an atmosphere of love and acceptance in their home. Many of these young people also say that they often feel criticized and that their parents have excessively high expectations in terms of the children's vocational or academic achievements.

Studies are also being conducted on the possible link between suicidal behavior and genetic factors within a family (Tugend, 1984). Since children who come from families where someone has committed suicide are six times more likely to kill themselves than are other children, researchers are examining both the genetic data and the family's style of interacting. One possibility is that a predisposition toward depression may be inherited. If this is found to be the case, suicidal behavior will occur more often within certain families. Given the difficulty in separating genetic from environmental influences, however, these hypotheses are still highly speculative.

Less speculatively, however, we do know that, as a consequence of modeling and reinforcement certain types of family interaction that contribute to depression and to aggression tend to be handed down from generation to generation (Patterson, 1989). This being the case, suicidal behavior would tend to run in families, not as a consequence of genetics but as a result of mimicking and being rewarded for unhealthy ways of interacting within the family. However, rather than worrying about the possibility of inheriting suicidal tendencies, people should focus on relating to their own children and other loved ones in ways that help them feel loved and accepted. In this regard, if a suicide has occurred, therapists can help the survivors examine the family's interactions in search of patterns that may inadvertently be contributing to suicidal behavior. If such patterns are discovered, the individuals have the opportunity to learn new ways of relating that can break the family's cycle. Keep in mind, however, that not all suicides occur as a result of dysfunctional family interactions. Jumping to such a conclusion would be both foolhardy and mercilessly unkind toward those who may be inflicting blame on themselves for a suicide that was in no way related to the family.

Prevention and Rehabilitation

With adolescent suicides coming more to the public's attention in the early 1980s, a number of schools began offering suicide prevention programs (Johnson & Maile, 1988). Given the stigma attached to the word *suicide,* some schools present this information under the guise of stress management programs. By whatever name, hundreds of school districts now offer these programs. Each is aimed at teaching students to recognize suicidal tendencies in themselves and in their friends and to seek help when feeling suicidal or depressed. Most programs offer strategies for reducing stress and for resolving personal problems. At present suicide prevention programs are required in school by five states: Florida, California, Louisiana, Wisconsin, and New Jersey. Many schools now also require teachers to be trained to recognize students' suicidal tendencies. Interestingly, in 1989 a jury in Munster, Indiana, ordered the school district to pay $50,000 to the parents of a 15-year-old boy who committed suicide in 1986. Though school officials had tried to warn the boy's parents that he was suicidal, the jury found the school at fault because it did not have a formal policy on suicide intervention in operation (Suicide report, 1989).

Unfortunately, although there is a flood of material available to educators, the lack of data on what works has left school officials confused about what they can or should do. Only in 1989 did the American Association of School Administrators release a guidebook on preventing teenage suicide, the first of its kind for educators. In addition, the Centers for Disease Control are collecting data on the effectiveness of various suicide prevention classes in an attempt to evaluate our existing school-based programs (Suicide report, 1989).

A four-volume government report on adolescent suicide tells us what to look out for in trying to recognize students at high risk of committing suicide. Most suicide victims have a history of disruptive behavior characterized by impulsivity and aggression, yet seldom are they mentally ill. Their antisocial behavior is, however, often aggravated by drug abuse. The 10 stressful events reported most often by those who attempt suicide are, in order of frequency: breakup with a boyfriend or girlfriend, trouble with a brother or sister, change in the parents' financial status, parents' divorce, losing a close friend, trouble with a teacher, changing to a new school, personal injury, failing grades, and arguments with parents (U.S. Department of Health and Human Services, 1989).

With those adolescents diagnosed as depressed, therapists have had the most success using a combination of cognitive and behavioral approaches (Matson, 1989). Cognitive techniques are used to alter the adolescents' thinking patterns and attitudes, while behavioral strategies are employed to improve the youngsters' problem-solving skills and to reduce tension. In cases where neither the cognitive nor the social learning techniques are effective, antidepressant drugs are used to alleviate severe depression.

Finally, it bears repeating that, despite the symptoms that suicidal adolescents often display, some young people kill themselves without manifesting any behavior

A CLOSER LOOK 14.4

Suicide: The Warning Signs

- Dramatic changes in eating or sleeping habits
- Spending increasingly longer periods of time alone, away from family and friends
- Giving away valued possessions or making comments about "getting my life in order"
- Talking excessively or asking many questions about suicide
- A sudden interest in religion and the afterlife
- Experiencing recent losses, such as breaking up with a boyfriend or girlfriend, a relative's death, a personal injury, or chronic illness
- An inexplicable and dramatic drop in grades at school
- Complaining often about feeling tired
- Expressing excessive concern over physical health (hypochondria)
- Frequent breakdowns of communication with parents or friends
- A history of repeated "accidents"
- Being unable to make any friends
- Truancy, delinquency, drug abuse, or sexual permissiveness
- Appearing constantly bored, restless, or hyperactive
- Expressing feelings of helplessness: "It just doesn't matter anymore what I say or do"
- Expressing excessive shame or guilt

that could clearly be recognized as a warning signal. All too often the family and friends of suicide victims chastise themselves for having overlooked the warning signals when, in reality, none may have existed. Since everyone has bad days and feels down from time to time, each individual could be said to have manifested a "symptom" of suicidal behavior at some time in his or her life. Likewise, the friends and family of a suicide victim can scrutinize the events of the weeks or months preceding the death and inevitably find some clue foretelling their future tragedy. Yet, in retrospect what appears as a clear call for help, may, at the moment it occurs, be rightfully or innocently perceived as nothing more than a passing mood or a momentary fit of anger. In such cases both the bereaved and those around them must recognize that not all suicide victims send us signals of distress before taking their lives.

EATING DISORDERS

Anorexia Nervosa

While thousands of adolescents take their own lives with pills and guns and ropes, others end their lives through self-starvation. **Anorexia nervosa** became "the disease of the 1970s," popularized in the media as the bizarre "starving disease." In fact, however, anorexia nervosa was adopted into the medical vocabulary in the late 1800s both in the United States and abroad. Even in 1873 physicians were suggesting, as do most psychologists today, that this disorder arose from conflicts between the maturing girl and her parents. Unlike anorexic girls in the Victorian era, who usually presented themselves as ill and who were listless and physically inactive, many of today's anorexics are physically active and refuse to see themselves as sick. In fact, today's anorexics are often hyperactive and engage in rigorous physical activities in their never-ending battle to lose more weight (Brumberg, 1988).

According to the official definition in the revised edition of the American Psychiatric Association's diagnostic manual of mental disorders (**DSM III-R**), anorexia nervosa is a potentially life-threatening disorder in which the victim eats so little that he or she eventually starves to death. Anorexia is diagnosed when a person weighs at least 16% less than his or her expected body weight, has an intense fear of gaining weight, has a distorted image of himself or herself as fat, and, in females, has missed at least three consecutive menstrual periods as a consequence of the severe weight loss. Anorexics typically begin by dieting, a practice so prevalent that it arouses no particular suspicion. Once having lost so much weight that people start confronting them about being too thin, anorexics adamantly deny the problem and continue their self-starvation. In their attempt to lose weight, many anorexics resort to self-induced vomiting or to using laxatives after they eat in order to prevent their body from absorbing any calories. Using these strategies in secret, they appear to be eating normally, leaving their parents and friends mystified about why they are continuing to lose weight.

It is estimated that approximately 0.4% of all females and 0.02% of all males are anorexic (Lachenmeyer & Muni, 1988). When the disorder does occur in males, it is typically viewed as a by-product of other pathology, rather than as a disorder in and of itself. Male anorexia has been attributed to excessive athletic training (Gwirtsman, et al, 1984), to schizophrenic disorders (Svec, 1987), and to the perception among male homosexuals that being thin is sexually desirable (Herzog, 1984).

To this day, therapists disagree about the family's role in the development of anorexia nervosa (Brumberg, 1988; Chernin, 1985; Romeo, 1986; Thompson, 1990; Williamson, 1990). American and British physicians of the Victorian era attributed anorexia in part to a girl's craving for attention and to her parents' failure, her mother's in particular, to assert their "moral authority." Likewise, today there are those who contend that anorexia arises partly because some mothers find it difficult to be empathic with and supportive of their daughters. Others contend that anorexics' parents are overly protective, overly critical, and overly perfectionistic people who are threatened by the idea of their daughters' becoming independent. In reaction to their parents' unhealthy attitudes, anorexics thus may resort to excessive dieting in order to feel in control of at least one aspect of their own lives. Seen from this perspective, anorexia is a response to a dysfunctional family. The data, however, have been too contradictory to support this hypothesis fully. For example, a recent study of white adolescent girls and their mothers found no differences between the mother-daughter relationships of those with and those without anorexia (Attie & Brooks-Gunn, 1989).

Moreover, there is evidence that anorexia may be linked to neurochemical abnormalities (Fava, 1989). People with eating disorders may lack a hormone thought to induce the feeling of fullness after eating. These hormonal abnormalities have even been found after the anorexics have regained their normal weight. The cause of these chemical abnormalities, however, is difficult to determine since it is impossible to test people's chemical levels before and after they have become anorexic. In other words, the anorexia may cause the chemical abnormalities, rather than the other way around.

A third factor implicated in anorexia is our society's obsession with female thinness and beauty. Since anorexia is far more prevalent among females than males, it seems logical to presume that our notions of masculinity and femininity are somehow linked to this disorder. Pursuing this line of reasoning, researchers have consistently found that adolescent girls and women are far more critical of their physical appearance than are boys and men. Moreover, unlike males, females of all ages tend to see themselves as overweight even when their weight is actually normal or less than normal. Teenage girls who are the most dissatisfied with their appearance have the most distorted, inaccurate notions of how "fat" they are. That is, girls who like their bodies can accurately assess whether they are "too fat" or "too skinny," whereas girls who dislike their bodies are at high risk of becoming anorexic and almost always see themselves as overweight (Desmond, et al, 1986; Rosen, 1988; Stewart & Brook, 1983; Storz & Greene, 1983; VanThore & Vogel, 1985). Taken together, these findings leave little doubt that our society's overemphasis on female beauty, particularly on females' being thin, contributes to girls' disliking their bodies which reinforces attitudes that can lead to anorexia.

Bulimia

A disorder closely allied with anorexia is **bulimia** or binge eating (R. Hawkins, Fremouw, & Clement, 1984). Although the literature has traditionally treated bulimia and anorexia as facets of the same disorder, the DSM III-R now classifies bulimia as a separate disorder. The essential features of bulimia are episodic binge eating triggered by intense emotional experiences and followed by **purging** the body of the unwanted calories. In order to be clinically diagnosed as bulimic, a person must meet three of the following criteria: (1) consuming large quantities of high-calorie foods in a single sitting—a **binge;** (2) keeping these binges a secret; (3) ending each binge because of abdominal pain or by self-induced vomiting; (4) repeatedly attempting to lose weight by severe dieting, self-induced vomiting, or using laxatives and diuretics (drugs that rid the body of its fluids) and (5) frequent fluctuations in weight greater than 10 pounds as a result of binging, purging, and fasting (American Psychiatric Association, 1988).

Some adolescents with bulimia are overweight, while others are of normal weight or anorexic. Although bulimics are not necessarily anorexic, it appears that about one fourth of all anorexics are also bulimic, a disorder referred to as **bulimarexia.** To distinguish the bulimic from the anorexic instruments such as the Eating Attitudes Test (EAT) and the Binge Scale are used. Bulimarexics tend to have the most distorted perceptions of their own body weight and the most serious emotional disturbances. Consequently, the prognosis for recovery from bulimarexia is poorer than from either bulimia or anorexia.

Little information exists concerning the causes of bulimia, since it has not traditionally been studied as a disorder separate from anorexia. Each of the hypotheses related to anorexia has, therefore, also been used to also explain the development of bulimia. Although some bulimics are male, it is a condition almost exclusively limited to white females with a poor self-image and a distorted view of themselves as overweight. It is estimated that 1 to 2% of all teenage girls are bulimic, although as many as 10% of the female students on some college campuses have expressed attitudes on the EAT that are characteristic of bulimics (R. Hawkins, Fremouw, & Clement, 1984). Moreover, in some samples as many as 20% of the young adolescents have scored high enough on the EAT to suggest an orientation toward developing bulimia (VanThore & Vogel, 1985), and in other samples as many as 4% of the high-school students were bulimic (Howat & Saxton, 1988).

Prevention and Treatment

Given the disagreement concerning the causes of bulimia and anorexia, therapists have used a variety of approaches to treat these disorders. Although no drug has proved consistently effective in treating anorexia, antidepressant drugs have been successful in treating bulimia. Although scientists are unsure exactly why or how these drugs work, we know they affect the brain's neurotransmitters (Fava, 1989).

The social learning view contends that eating disorders are closely allied with our society's attitudes about female beauty and with a family's methods of relating to one another. These theorists' approaches to treating these disorders, therefore, rely on forms of family therapy that examine the victims' relationships with their parents. Family therapy is thus seen as a way of alleviating some of the tensions that presumably underlie anorexia and bulimia. Social learning techniques are also used to teach adolescents ways to enhance their self-esteem and to express frustration or depression other than through overeating, purging, or self-starvation. Rather than expressing their emotions through the abuse of food, these young people are taught how to express their feelings, to avoid anxiety-producing situations, and to seek reinforcement and a sense of self-control through means other than food and body image.

One of the puzzles about anorexia nervosa is its sudden occurrence in seemingly normal children who have grown up in privileged, stable homes and have caused little or no trouble for their parents. Once therapists explore the "real" family behind this happy facade, however, a number of less pleasant realities emerge: that the anorexics often feel that their parents' love is contingent on their being perfect; that expressing emotions, especially anger, is forbidden or punished in the family; that the children's independence is discouraged; and that pleasing others without asking anything in return is one of the overriding family rules. As Box 14.5 illustrates, one of the routes to recovery through therapy is for the anorexics to recognize that they are lovable despite their human shortcomings. The therapist's goal is also to help the anorexics see the family realistically, rather than pretending to themselves and to others that everything is perfect. During the course of therapy, the anorexics must come to recognize the family's role in creating the unrealistic need to be perfect, always to please others, to keep their unpleasant emotions to themselves, and, to assume the responsibility for making everyone else happy.

COPING WITH DEATH AND DYING

Although most anorexics recover from their illness through therapy, some succeed in starving themselves to death. Thousands of other adolescents die of terminal illnesses, suicide, and fatal injuries associated with delinquency, alcohol, drugs, and accidents. Even those adolescents who do not themselves undergo a life-threatening experience are often confronted with the pain of someone else's death—the death of a parent, a sibling, or a friend. Although we are quick to applaud those who work on oncology (cancer) wards and to praise parents with terminally ill children, most of us are not willing to read about or to discuss death.

Adolescents suffering from anorexia feel a need to be in control. How could such feelings come about in a well-meaning home?

Our awkwardness around the terminally ill, unwillingness to answer children's questions about death candidly, and discomfort with a person whose loved one has recently died attest to society's tradition of avoiding topics related to death whenever possible. Unfortunately, this attitude too often leaves us unequipped to respond to adolescents and their families who have had to confront the inescapable realities of death.

A CLOSER LOOK 14.5

Anorexia Nervosa: The Road to Recovery

When Annette weighed 106 pounds at age 15, her pediatrician was only somewhat concerned about her weight in comparison with other girls her height, 5′7″. When her weight had dropped to 85 pounds as a high-school senior, and then to 70 pounds during her first year at a prestigious eastern college, she was forced to take a medical leave and seek the help of a therapist. Among Annette's remarks during her years in therapy:

- "I have found myself most dependent on, and in rebellion against, my parents, most especially my mother. . . . I feel a failure and have a need to be in control."
- "I'm frightened by the idea of getting well. I still want to be part of my parents' lives. But I am no longer part of them, but not of anything else either."
- "When I cried, I was afraid they would be annoyed. Of course they wouldn't ever show it. But I would feel that they were."
- "Only when absolutely everything has been given, when I really cannot give anymore, have I done my duty. I was not giving anything to the world, so I did not have the right to eat."
- "When I was a little kid, I couldn't be a child. I had to act as if I was this adult. I had to talk to my father about business and finance and something on his level when I was eight years old."

Among Annette's therapist's remarks:

- "This is one of the tragedies of your life, that in this well-meaning home into which you were born, you experienced 'I am only an appendix, they don't give me genuine recognition.'"
- "I'm glad your true feelings are coming into the open. You've spent so much time maintaining that your family was perfect and you never talked about what had hurt you, out of fear that it might sound as if you were 'blaming' them."
- "If I understand what you are telling me, you feel your whole life has been a facade performance where you would show only sweet, compliant, submissive behavior. Isn't that what you called 'the great put-on'?"
- "Your problem is not feeling anger; your problem is that you never dare to express these feelings. You reacted to this by becoming sick."
- "You always held back with the feeling 'I mustn't tell them because it will upset them.' We might define as the real horror of your childhood the fact that you could never honestly complain."

Source: D. Czysewski & M. Suhr (Eds.). (1988). *Conversations with anorexics: Hilde Bruch.* New York: Basic Books.

Bereavement

In her provocative books on death and dying, Dr. Elisabeth Kübler-Ross criticizes our attitudes toward both those who are dying and their survivors (Kübler-Ross, 1969, 1983). On the basis of her work with dying patients and their families, Kübler-Ross has identified stages that both the dying and their loved ones undergo: denial, anger, bargaining, depression, and acceptance. As Box 14.6 illustrates, adolescents' reactions to a parent's death poignantly demonstrate these stages of grieving (Krementz, 1982).

From her own work with children and adolescents dying of terminal illnesses and with families of those who commit suicide, Kübler-Ross addressed a number of provocative questions: How are children different from adults when faced with

14.6

ADOLESCENT VOICES

Two Adolescent Boys' Reactions to Their Mothers' Deaths

FIRST BOY:

Shortly after my mother died, I wrote down my feelings and felt much better.

What Am I: I Am My Mother's Spirit

I am my mother's slow-moving footsteps as she walks down to the hospital to get her cancer check-up, her utter despair as she finds the results, and her trouble in finding the words to tell Dad. I am the slow and reluctant boy who takes a couple of Mom's things to the hospital where she will stay before the operation. I am Mother's loneliness in her hospital bed as she patiently awaits Father's next visit. I am her joy to find us with him as he walks near her bed, her curiosity to learn of the day's events, and her sorrow as a very short visiting period ends. I am my mother's frail, ever-weakening body as Mom slips into a coma. I am the sparkling tear that runs down her stiff face as the words of a friend's letter roll out. I am the disbelief of everyone as the news reaches us that Mom has died. I am not the pounds of make-up that hide the painful expression on her cold, still face, nor am I her whole shell that lies in an open casket, but I am her spirit walking somewhere about the room. I am the sorrow of all as the casket is being lowered into the ground. I was my mother, I am her spirit.

SECOND BOY:

I'm still glad I knew how sick she was because even if it didn't make it that much easier, it did give me a chance to make the most of the time we had left. I got very close to my mother that last year. Before she was sick, she always used to want me to go hiking with her and do things with her and I never did because—I hate to say it, but—who wants to do something with a mother, especially if you're a boy and your friends are saying, "Oh, c'mon Dave, let's go bike-riding or skiing, or whatever"? It's hard to do something with your mother because they're stick-in-the-mud old fogeys. And the sad thing is that I didn't realize what it would be like *not* to be able to do something with her if I wanted to until after she couldn't do things like that. Actually, I did go hiking with her a couple of times before I knew she had cancer. We went across some of the White Mountains and we climbed Mount Madison. I had started doing more things with her because I realized I too would become an old-fogey stick-in-the-mud myself one day. But when she got sick, I guess I got closer to her because I paid more attention to her. I realized she wouldn't be around to be ignored.

Source: J. Krementz. (1982). *How it feels when a parent dies.* New York: Knopf. pp. 80–84.

terminal illness? Do little ones also go through the five stages of dying? Are they aware of their impending death even if parents or hospital staff do not mention the seriousness of the illness? What is their concept of death at different ages, the nature of their unfinished business? How can we best help them and their parents, grandparents, and siblings during this time of parting? (Kübler-Ross, 1983).

During the period of bereavement, honest communication can be especially beneficial to members of the family. Although feelings such as anger and guilt are often difficult to express, sharing them can prevent more serious depression and greater disruption within the family. For example, in some families a deceased sibling is portrayed by parents as the "perfect" child, thereby creating a sense of jealousy, anger, guilt, and confusion in the surviving children. Or if one child has a terminal illness, the other siblings may need help working through their feelings of jealousy and resentment over the inordinate amounts of attention bestowed upon a victim of a long-term illness.

In the case of a parent with a terminal illness, it can sometimes be useful for children to express their anger, fear, or sadness to the parent before he or she dies, as a way of diminishing their feelings of guilt or anger. Bereaved adolescents and adults also become more susceptible to alcohol and drug abuse in an attempt to cope with their sadness, guilt, and anger. Given the upheaval created by death, it is perhaps not surprising that between 70% and 90% of all couples separate or divorce after the death of a child.

Although it is often presumed that friends help the bereaved through their grief, the reality often falls short of this expectation. Both adolescents and adults have explained that many friends avoid them during their period of mourning. Because most of us feel uncomfortable about death, we act in ways that exacerbate the bereaved's feelings of loneliness, anger, or guilt. Not knowing how to behave, we too often avoid any topic even remotely related to the death or take the opposite tack by dwelling incessantly on the topic. In the words of one adolescent whose father died, "I guess my friends didn't know what to say because they felt kind of embarrassed, so they'd just look at me and no one would say hello. But it got to be a little too much—like no one would say the word 'father' in front of me. So I finally transferred to a different school" (Krementz, 1982, p. 92). The most supportive friends somehow manage to achieve a delicate balance between a willingness to discuss the death and an eagerness not to condescend or to pity.

The grieving process is especially difficult for young people who have witnessed a murder or for those who have known a victim of murder (Turkington, 1984). For youngsters in either of these positions the process of bereavement often includes feelings of revenge and anger toward the murderer or toward police who seem indifferent about apprehending the murderer. Although the data have been relatively scant on the responses of children after witnessing or learning of a murder of a loved one, the existing data show that rage often overshadows expressions of sadness. A child whose loved one or friend has been murdered often regresses to bedwetting, aggression, and other forms of childish behavior. Violent deaths also leave the bereaved with the depressing conviction that society is an orderless, chaotic, and frightening place in which to live.

Although Kübler-Ross is probably the most renowned researcher on the topic of death and dying, others have gathered data of special relevance to adolescents and their families (Cook & Oltjenbruns, 1989). For example, a study of adolescents who had experienced the death of a sibling showed that older adolescents felt angrier about the death than younger adolescents. Those from the least cohesive families also felt angrier and guiltier than those from more intimate families. Likewise, adolescents whose parent had died adapted best when they had an intimate relationship with the surviving parent and a lot of support from friends (Gray, 1987).

Death Education

A number of educators besides Elisabeth Kübler-Ross are urging us to educate childen about death and dying from an early age. Authors are now writing books on topics related to death in an effort to help parents explain death to young

14.7 ADOLESCENT VOICES

Adolescents' Views of Death

"A young girl of my community was murdered. She was murdered six months ago. The police are having a difficult time figuring out the killer. The feeling that is in the air at school, in town, and even in my own home is unreal. It is a creepy feeling. Sometimes I wonder if the killer is sitting next to me in class or if he is passing me on the streets. The girl died in a way that I hope no one ever has to again. I hope and pray for her and her family. I know that I cannot bring her back, but maybe my prayers will help others." *(Jeri Parvin, 17, Mannford, Oklahoma)*

"I remember the day 'Phil' died. November 11, 1980 was a cold and windy day. I felt the coldness running through my blood as I began to realize that he was gone forever. 'Phil shot himself last night,' I said to one of my friends, only half believing and half hearing the words I said. 'He's gone.' With those words as my stepping stone, I knew I would make it through, for that was the first time I had admitted what had happened to my best friend several hours earlier. For weeks my thoughts wandered. I felt as though I was walking through each memory in my mind, seldom being able to return to reality. . . . Phil has been gone for two years now. I still miss him very much. There are times I want him to come back so badly to help me through, but I know he is gone. Many other people take death in such a way that it is hard for them to ever carry on. Life, of course, will be different without them, but a person never really dies if their memories live on in your heart." *(Michelle Skinner, 17, Lincoln, Nebraska)*

"Death is a natural part of life. It is hard to accept sometimes, but I have learned to accept death. I experienced the death of a boyfriend in 1981. I really took it hard. He was really too young, only 16. It made me a stronger person though. When someone close to you dies, it always takes a part of you. But the best thing to do is always remember the good times you shared with them." *(Cheryl Browder, 17, Winston-Salem, North Carolina)*

"I don't understand death, but I know it affects people when they are involved indirectly or directly. I wrote a poem to a friend of mine that was killed in a car accident. His name was Raschelle. I went to the wake and to the funeral. It was so weird seeing him lie in the coffin up at the front of the room. I felt like all I had to do was close my eyes and he'd be alive again. I sometimes still go back to a classroom, where I had him in class, hoping he'll be sitting there, laughing and telling jokes. Over this last Christmas vacation, I knew Raschelle was dead, but I said to myself, aloud, 'I'm going to call Raschelle and wish him a very merry Christmas.' I only said that to myself, knowing he was dead, because he was a friend I'll never forget. I wanted him to have a very merry Christmas, wherever he was." *(Christi Pennel, 17, Independence, Missouri)*

Source: Glenbard East *Echo*. (1984). *Teenagers themselves* (pp. 196–198). New York: Adama Books.

children (Wass & Coor, 1984). Books for adolescents are also available on topics such as a parent's death, funerals, terminal illness, and suicide (Krementz, 1982; Kübler-Ross, 1983; Rabkin, 1979). Some books not only provide information about topics such as the body's decomposition after death but also tackle the kinds of philosophical question reflected in the title of the best-seller *When Bad Things*

Happen to Good People, written by a rabbi about his son's death (Kushner, 1981). It has been suggested that high schools implement courses in death education, which will help students ask questions about death and dying in an atmosphere that is both sensitive and objective (Schvaneveldt, 1982).

One of the most impressive and controversial attempts to educate children about death was the 1984–1985 exhibit at the Boston Children's Museum—Endings: An Exhibit about Death and Loss (Weld, 1984). The first of its kind, the exhibit taught children about death through experiences such as touching a tombstone, looking into a coffin, hearing funeral music from around the world, and watching a speeded-up videotape of a dead mouse's body being eaten by insects with a sign saying, "Everything that is alive now will die, decompose and return to life." Also on display were the chemicals used to embalm bodies, burial clothes, and signs asking questions such as: "Do you remember the death or birth of anyone in your family?" "Were you named for someone who died?"

One goal of the exhibit was to help children understand the difference between fantasies and realities about death. On one videotape children viewed a director and an actor enacting a death scene replete with fake blood and ending with, "Ok, cut, that's a take." Another videotape showed live scenes from the fighting in Lebanon and concluded with the narrator's comment, "Sometimes it's hard to tell the difference between what's real and what isn't." As a general theme, the exhibit tried to dispel children's myths about death. One puppet in a videotaped show said, "Dying isn't a vacation. It's not like going to visit your grandmother. You don't come back again."

How were you introduced to the topics of death and dying?

The youngest children at the exhibit tended to spend time with their parents mastering the differences between "living" and "dead." Older children and adolescents spent most of their time on the more advanced sections of the exhibit. Janet Kamien, the exhibit's creator, hoped the experience would provide children and their parents with a reference point from which to discuss death with one another. As you might expect, however, the exhibit elicited mixed reactions from parents: "How dare you present this topic in a children's museum!" "Thank you so much for being brave and courageous enough to do this." And mixed reactions from children: "I hate thinking about death." "I like this exhibit because I love my grandmother dearly and the doctor said she might die and I don't want her to, so this makes it a little easier."

According to Kübler-Ross and others who share her views, children and adolescents should be allowed to participate in funerals, to relate to their dying parents and siblings, and to have the facts about death and dying. After a death each family member, including very young children, should be allowed to say their private farewells to the deceased. This may sometimes mean rocking, singing to, bathing, and dressing the body before it is removed from the home. Opponents of this view argue that adolescents and children should be shielded from the unpleasantries associated with death because they are incapable of coping with such distress. In response, Kübler-Ross and her supporters argue that adolescents and children would be better equipped to cope with their own death and the deaths of loved ones if given honest information and if included in conversations and events related to death and dying. Without this information, young people are more likely to respond to death by denial, aggression, withdrawal, and other self-destructive means of grieving.

In coming to terms with their own deaths, some terminally ill adolescents have prepared their own wills and have helped make arrangements for their own funerals (Powell, 1982). Adolescents seem to be particularly interested in deciding how they are to be dressed, what music will be played, and who will be speaking during their service. In some families an older sibling has even asked to help plan the funeral for a deceased younger brother or sister. Conversations and preparations of this sort require an accepting, communicative family in which parents and children have somehow come to terms with the impending death. Those who advocate a more open attitude and a more formal system of instruction about death contend that those who have difficulty facing death cannot offer much guidance or comfort to grieving children. If adults were more willing to come to terms with their own dying and the deaths of those they love, they could offer better care and advice to the young.

CHRONICALLY ILL ADOLESCENTS

Having to deal with their impending death or having narrowly escaped death is also part of living for the thousands of chronically ill adolescents in our society. As our medical technology has become more advanced, children with otherwise fatal diseases are surviving. For example, 30 years ago children diagnosed with cancer were given only months to live, whereas today 63% of young cancer patients survive, an improvement of 40% since the early 1970s. Such illnesses, however, usually involve prolonged and painful treatment that disrupts not only the young victims' lives but the lives of their parents and siblings as well. Given that about 2% of all children are afflicted by a severe chronic illness and that 40,000 young adults who fought childhood cancer are still alive to tell about it, there has been a sustained growth in research on how these life-threatening and chronic illnesses affect the emotional and psychological development of children and their families (Gregg, Robertus, & Blair, 1989; Koocher & O'Malley, 1987).

This research has dispelled many stereotypes, among them the myth that severe illnesses, such as diabetes, cancer, sickle cell anemia, and chronic asthma, always

How do you feel and behave in the presence of physically handicapped or terminally ill people?

leave indelible psychic scars on their victims. Gone too is the belief that each illness affects children in a predictable way by creating a "diabetic personality" or an "asthmatic personality." Nevertheless, children with these chronic illnesses do, as a group, have higher rates of emotional and social difficulties. Separation from parents, days missed from school, painful medical procedures, and changes in their appearance are among the obstacles they must overcome. For example, although most school districts now provide in-home tutoring for students who miss 2 consecutive weeks of school due to illness, almost no school system makes special arrangements for students who are periodically hospitalized for several days of treatment for a chronic illness. Thus their parents are faced with having to find special tutors who are willing and able to work with their sick child.

Such problems need not debilitate these families, however, if communities choose to address the needs of chronically ill children. For example, in Baltimore part-time teachers are assigned to students with chronic illnesses. When the student misses school, these teachers take homework assignments to the students' homes and tutor them on the day's work. The Baltimore program also sponsors a peer program that matches older chronically ill students with younger ones, providing a role model for dispirited children. Likewise, the program helps teachers by sensitizing them to the needs of chronically ill students. For example, many well-intentioned teachers are overly cautious, coddling these students in ways that further isolate them from their classmates. When teachers are taught more about their students' illnesses, however, they are better able to adapt their classroom techniques to the needs of their special students without condescending to or overprotecting them.

Not surprisingly, siblings are also affected by their brother's or sister's illness. Many parents are so focused on the hospitalized or sick child that they are, understandably, unaware of how their healthy children are coping. In many families the healthy children feel left out or jealous of the attention or special privileges bestowed on their sick sibling. Simultaneously, they may also feel guilty about their resentful feelings. Ironically, feeling left out is sometimes made worse by parents' well-intentioned efforts to spare their healthy children from having contact with the sick child when the illness is at its worst. For example, most parents are reluctant to have their healthy children visit the sibling in the hospital; yet, when asked about their feelings, most siblings agree that they want to be included in these visits. With this new understanding, many counselors and physicians are now urging that healthy and sick siblings communicate with each other in person, in writing, or by telephone when hospitalization occurs.

In preparation for hospital visits, however, parents should make sure the siblings understand that their brother or sister may look and act differently. Especially when children are young, they should be prepared ahead of time for the strange odors or equipment they will encounter during their hospital visits. Above all, parents need to encourage their healthy children to ask questions about the illness, while listening carefully to their questions in order to clear up misconceptions, fears, and fantasies. Then, too, parents need to make extra efforts to schedule time alone with their healthy children to diminish their jealousies and insecurities.

As we gather more data from adolescents with chronic illnesses, we will inevitably become more sensitive to their needs. A number of surveys, for example, have shown that at least one in four victims of childhood cancer has been discriminated against, shunned at work, and avoided at school. A case in point is that until 1986, when the Department of Defense adopted anti-discrimination guidelines, the U.S. armed services generally rejected applications from cancer survivors (Monmaney, 1988). It is hoped that society is becoming more enlightened about and empathic to those who have survived a life-threatening disease, live with chronic illness, or battle daily to survive.

CONCLUSION

Although thousands of adolescents struggle with problems such as chronic illness or depression, these problems are relatively rare among the young. Far more prevalent and more destructive are the less "sensational" problems, such as poverty, drinking, smoking, dropping out of school, and pregnancy—problems that tend to be less publicized by the media and politicians. Thousands more adolescents lose their lives because of traffic accidents caused by drunk driving and from diseases caused by smoking cigarettes than from suicide, anorexia, child abuse, and drugs combined. Keeping these realities in mind can help society view the various problems affecting young people in a clearer perspective.

Because of limited human and financial resources, our society is continually confronted with the philosophical and political dilemma of choosing which problems ought to receive top priority. Like it or not, everyone is forced to prioritize the issues that are most important to them in regard to our country's adolescents. As a taxpayer and a voter, as a volunteer and a donator to charity, as someone preparing for a future vocation, each person is faced with having to choose where to invest his or her time, money, and focus. Will the individual be dedicated to the concerns of pregnant teenagers? the poor and homeless children? young drug abusers? the educationally disadvantaged? delinquents? chronically ill youths? young people with terminal illnesses? runaways? suicidal youths? No one can dictate anyone else's choices in these matters, and no one can give anyone else a "correct" list of priorities based solely on the statistics showing how many adolescents are affected by each of these problems. For each person, these decisions are not merely questions of statistics but questions of the heart.

QUESTIONS FOR DISCUSSION AND REVIEW

Review Questions

1. How do each of these factors contribute to juvenile delinquency: IQ, academic problems, self-esteem, the parent-child relationship, socioeconomic status, gender roles, peer relationships, family violence, parenting styles?
2. How prevalent is delinquency and what types of crime do most adolescents commit? Provide specific statistics to support your answers.
3. How do gangs today differ from those of earlier times? Why are adolescents enticed to join a gang?
4. What might account for the rise in female delinquency?
5. What methods have been least and most effective in preventing delinquency and in rehabilitating delinquents? Why?
6. Why do young people run away from home, and how serious is the problem?
7. What factors might contribute to youth suicide? Considering each of these, how could a suicidal adolescent be helped by the school, a counselor, a friend, and a parent?

8. How can serious depression be distinguished from our normal downs and temporary moodiness? What are the symptoms of suicidal thinking?
9. How are anorexia nervosa and bulimia clinically defined? How prevalent are these disorders?
10. What are the various hypotheses that have been offered to explain the development of anorexia and bulimia, and what approaches are used in treating these disorders?
11. What issues and specific problems confront chronically ill adolescents and their families? How can each of these be somewhat alleviated by schools, friends, legislation, and health care professionals?
12. What is death education. What forms has it taken, and what rationale underlies it?
13. According to Kübler-Ross, what stages do we undergo when confronted with our own impending death or the death of someone we love?
14. How can adolescents who have experienced a death in the family be helped to cope with their grief?
15. What are the 10 most serious problems facing adolescents in terms of the numbers of teenagers they affect? Approximately what percentage of the adolescent population is affected by each?

Questions for Discussion and Debate

1. What do you feel should be done with adolescent murderers? How do you feel about the Supreme Court's ruling on the death penalty for minors?
2. How would you design a delinquency prevention program and a rehabilitation program for delinquents? What kind of training do you think people in the juvenile justice system need?
3. How has suicide personally affected your life or the life of one of your friends? Why are shame, guilt, and embarrassment so much a part of our reaction to suicide?
4. How do you feel about euthanasia ("mercy killing")? the Boston Museum's exhibit on death for children? adolescents with a terminal illness planning their funerals and writing wills? siblings and friends visiting a dying adolescent?
5. What makes you most uncomfortable in reading the sections of this chapter on death, illness, and suicide? Why? How have your own family and friends affected your feelings on these topics?
6. What do you feel friends, schools, and parents should be doing about adolescent suicide?
7. What do you think is responsible for anorexia and bulimia? How have these issues affected your life or the lives of people you know? How do your feelings about your own body and your eating habits relate to these topics?
8. How have your own serious illnesses or those of your friends and family affected your life? How do you imagine your life would be different if you had lived through childhood cancer (also consider your friends' and family's lives)?
9. What myths or stereotypes about suicidal, runaway, and delinquent adolescents did you let go of while reading this chapter? How had your stereotypes been formed?
10. Of the many issues discussed throughout this book, which adolescent problems do you feel most committed to personally and professionally? Why? How have your attitudes toward the relative importance of each of these problems changed since the beginning of this course?

GLOSSARY

anomie A condition in which the members of a society feel isolated and disconnected as a result of excessively specialized social structures that limit closeness and intimacy.

anorexia nervosa An eating disorder characterized by intense fear of becoming fat, obsessive concern with weight, and the belief that one is fat when of normal weight or even when emaciated.

binge Consuming large quantities of high calorie foods in a single setting, often part of bulimia or anorexia.

bulimarexia A combination of the disorders of bulimia and anorexia.

bulimia An eating disorder characterized by repeated episodes of binge eating followed by self-induced vomiting, usually accompanied by guilt and depression.

cluster suicides Incidents in which one youngster's suicide seems to motivate others to commit suicide.

DSM III-R *The Diagnostic and Statistical Manual,* revised edition. Manual that describes mental disorders as defined by professionals in psychology.

purging Forcing oneself to vomit or using laxatives to force food quickly out of the body so that calories will not be absorbed after eating. A symptom of bulimia.

REFERENCES

American Psychiatric Association. (1988). *Diagnostic and statistical manual of mental disorders* (rev. 4th ed.). Washington, DC: Author.

Attie, I., & Brooks-Gunn, J. (1989). Development of eating problems in adolescent girls. *Developmental Psychology, 25,* 70–79.

Baron, P., & Perron, L. (1986). Sex differences in the Beck Depression Inventory scores of adolescents. *Journal of Youth and Adolescence, 15,* 165–171.

Barrueta-Clement, J., Schweinhart, L., Barnett, W., Epstein, A., & Weikart, D. (1984). *Changed lives.* Ipsilanti, MI: High Scope.

Berlin, I. (1984). *Suicide among American Indian adolescents.* Washington, DC: National American Indian Courts Judges Association.

Blumstein, A., Cohen, J., & Farrington, D. (1988). Criminal career research. *Criminology, 26,* 1–35.

Brent, D. (1988). Risk factors for adolescent suicide. *Archives of General Psychiatry, 45,* 581–588.

Brumberg, J. (1988). *Fasting girls: The emergence of anorexia nervosa as a modern disease.* Boston: Harvard University Press.

Buie, J. (1988, October). Wediko leads kids out of the woods. *APA Monitor,* pp. 21–24.

Bynner, J., O'Malley, P., & Bachman, J. (1981). Self esteem and delinquency revisited. *Journal of Youth and Adolescence, 10,* 407–441.

Centers for Disease Control (1989). *Adolescent suicide.* Atlanta: Author.

Chernin, K. (1985). *The hungry self.* New York: Harper & Row.

Choquet, M., & Menke, H. (1987). Development of self-perceived risk behavior and psychosomatic symptoms in adolescents. *Journal of Adolescence, 10,* 291–308.

Coie, J., & Kupersmidt, J. (1983). A behavioral analysis of emerging social status in boys' groups. *Child Development, 54,* 1400–1416.

Consortium for Longitudinal Studies (1983). *As the twig is bent: Lasting effects of pre-school programs.* Hillsdale, NJ: Erlbaum.

Cook, S., & Oltjenbruns, K. (1989). *Dying and grieving.* New York: Holt, Rinehart and Winston.

Czysewski, D. & Suhr, M. (Eds.) (1988). *Conversations with anorexics: Hilde Bruch.* New York: Basic books.

Desmond, S., Price, J., Gray, N., & O'Connell, J. (1986). The etiology of adolescents' perceptions of their weight. *Journal of Youth and Adolescence, 15,* 461–473.

Dodge, K. (1983). Behavioral antecedents of peer social status. *Child Development, 54,* 1386–1399.

Dunford, F., & Elliot, D. (1982). *Identifying career offenders with self-reported data.* Washington, DC: National Institute of Mental Health.

Farrington, D., Ohlin, L., & Wilson, J. (1986). *Understanding and controlling crime.* New York: Springer Verlag.

Fava, M. (1989, August). Neurochemistry and anorexia. *Journal of American Psychiatry,* pp. 118–126.

Federal Bureau of Investigation (1987). *Crime in the United States: 1986.* Washington, DC: U.S. Government Printing Office.

Flaherty, M. (1983, Summer). The national incidence of juvenile suicide in adult jails and juvenile detention centers. *Suicide and Life Threatening Behavior,* pp. 85–94.

Flax, E. (1989, May 24). Panel hears testimony on causes of violent acts by nation's teenagers. *Education Week,* p. 13.

Fremouw, W., Perczel, M., & Ellis, T. (1990). *Suicide risk: Assessment and response guidelines.* Riverside, NJ: Pergamon Press.

Gaffney, L. (1984). A multiple choice test to measure social skills in delinquent and nondelinquent adolescent girls. *Journal of Consulting and Clinical Psychology, 42,* 911–912.

Garbarino, J., Wilson, J., & Garbarino, A. (1986). The adolescent runaway. In J. Garbarino & J. Sebes (Eds.), *Troubled youth, troubled families.* (pp. 315–351), New York: Aldine.

Gold, M., & Petronio, R. (1980). Delinquent behavior in adolescence. In J. Adelson (Ed.), *Handbook of adolescent psychology.* pp. 495–536. New York: Wiley.

Goldstein, A., Glick, B., Irwin, M., & Rubama, I. (1989). *Reducing delinquency.* Riverside, NJ: Pergamon Press.

Grande, C. (1988). Delinquency: The learning disabled students' reaction to academic school failure? *Adolescence, 23,* 209–219.

Gray, R. (1987). Adolescent response of the death of a parent. *Journal of Youth and Adolescence, 16,* 511–525.

Gregg, C., Robertus, J., & Blair, S. (1989). *The psychological aspects of chronic illness.* New York: Charles Thomas.

Gwirtsman, H., Roy, R., Lerner, L., & Yager, J. (1984). Bulimia in men. *Journal of Clinical Psychiatry, 45,* 78–81.

Hackett, B. (1988, January 11). Kids: Deadly Force. *Newsweek* pp. 18–19.

Hawkins, J., & Lishner, D. (1987). Schooling and delinquency. In E. Johnson (Ed)., *Handbook on crime and delinquency prevention* (pp. 179–221). New York: Greenwood Press.

Hawkins, R., Fremouw, S., & Clement, L. (Eds.). (1984). *The binge-purge syndrome.* New York: Springer Verlag.

Herzog, D. (1984). Sexual conflict and eating disorders in males. *American Journal of Psychiatry, 14,* 989–990.

Holin, C. (1989). *Cognitive behavioral interventions with young offenders.* Riverside, NJ: Pergamon Press.

Horwitz, A., & White, H. (1987). Gender role orientations and styles of pathology among adolescents. *Journal of Health and Social Behavior, 28,* 158–170.

Howat, P., & Saxton, A. (1988). The incidence of bulimic behavior in a secondary and university school population. *Journal of Youth and Adolescence, 23,* 221–231.

Huesmann, L. (1984). Stability of aggression over time and generations. *Developmental Psychology, 20,* 1120–1134.

Husain, S., & Vandiver, T. (1984). *Suicide in children and adolescents.* New York: SP Medical and Scientific Books.

Janus, M., McCormack, A., Burgess, A., & Hartman, C. (1987). *Adolescent runaways.* Lexington, MA: Lexington Books.

Johnson, E. (Ed.). (1987). *Handbook on crime and delinquency prevention.* New York: Greenwood Press.

Johnson, R. (1987). Mother's versus father's role in causing delinquency. *Adolescence, 22,* 305–315.

Johnson, S., & Maile, L. (1987). *Suicide and the schools.* Springfield, IL: Charles Thomas.

Johnstone, J. (1983, March). Recruitment to a youth gang. *Youth and Society,* pp. 281–300.

Kazdin, A. (1987). Treatment of antisocial behavior in children: Current status and future direction. *Psychological Bulletin, 102,* 187–203.

Koocher, R., & O'Malley, J. (1987). *The Damocles syndrome.* New York: McGraw-Hill.

Kovacs, M. (1989). Affective disorders in children and adolescents. *American Psychologist, 44,* 209–215.

Krementz, J. (1982). *How it feels when a parent dies.* New York: Knopf.

Kübler-Ross, E. (1969). *On death and dying.* New York: Macmillan.

Kübler-Ross, E. (1983). *On children and death.* New York: Macmillan.

Kushner, H. (1981). *When bad things happen to good people.* New York: Avon.

Lachenmeyer, J., & Muni, P. (1988). Eating disorders in a nonclinical adolescent population. *Adolescence, 23,* 313–322.

Lander, S. (1988, May). Gangs attract youngsters who've grown up in solitude. *APA Monitor,* p. 31.

Lester, D. (1988). Youth suicide. *Adolescence, 23,* 955–958.

Matson, J. (1989). *Treating depression in children and adolescents.* Riverside, NJ: Pergamon Press.

McCarthy, J., & Hoge, D. (1984). The dynamics of self-esteem and delinquency. *American Journal of Sociology, 90,* 396–410.

McDaniel, A. (1989, July 10). The court: Reagan's legal legacy. *Newsweek,* pp. 19–20.

Monmaney, T. (1988, July 18). Young survivors in a deadly war. *Newsweek,* pp. 50–51.

Mullis, R., & Hanson, R. (1983). Perspective taking among offender and nonoffender youth. *Adolescence, 18,* 831–836.

Needle, J., & Stapleton, W. (1983). *Police handling of youth gangs.* Sacramento, CA: American Justice Institute.

Nolen, S., Girgus, J., & Seligman, M. (1986). Learned helplessness in children. *Journal of Personality and Social Psychology, 51,* 435–442.

Paperney, D., & Deisher, R. (1983). Maltreatment of adolescents: The relationship to a predisposition toward violent behavior and delinquency. *Adolescence, 18,* 499–506.

Patros, P. (1988). *Depression and suicide in children and adolescents.* Boston: Allyn-Bacon.

Patterson, G. (Ed.) (1989). *Depression and aggression in family interactions.* Hillsdale, NJ: Erlbaum.

Patterson, G., DeBaryshe, B., & Ramsey, E. (1989). A developmental perspective on antisocial behavior. *American Psychologist, 44,* 329–335.

Patterson, G., Reid, J., & Dishion, T. (1990). *Antisocial boys.* Eugene, OR: Castalia.

Perlmutter, B. (1987). Delinquency and learning disabilities. *Journal of Youth and Adolescence, 16,* 89–95.

Powell, C. (1982). *Adolescence and the right to die: Issues of autonomy, competence and paternalism.* Washington, DC: American Psychological Association.

Press, A. (1986, November 24). Children who kill. *Newsweek,* pp. 93–94.

Rabkin, B. (1979). *Growing up dead: A hard look at why adolescents commit suicide.* Nashville, TN: Abingdon Press.

Robins, D., & Aless, N. (1985). Depressive symptoms and suicidal behavior in adolescents. *American Journal of Psychiatry, 142,* 588–592.

Romeo, F. (1986). *Understanding anorexia nervosa.* New York: Charles Thomas.

Rosen, J. (1988). Eating attitudes test and eating disorders inventory: Norms for adolescent girls and boys. *Journal of Consulting and Clinical Psychology, 56,* 305–308.

Rutter, M., & Giller, H. (1983). *Juvenile delinquency: Trends and perspectives.* Baltimore: Penguin.

Rutter, M., Izard, C., & Read, P. (Eds.) (1986). *Depression in young people.* New York: Guilford.

Ryan, N. (1987). The clinical picture of major depression in children and adolescents. *Archives of General Psychiatry, 44,* 854–861.

Salholz, E. (1987, May 11). In Detroit, kids kill kids. *Newsweek,* pp. 74–75.

Schneider, A. (1989). *Deterrence and juvenile crime.* New York: Springer Verlag.

Schvaneveldt, J. (1982, March). Developing and implementing death education in high schools. *High School Journal,* pp. 189–197.

Shinn, M., Ramsey, E., Walker, H., O'Neill, R., & Steiber, S. (1987). Antisocial behavior in school settings. *Journal of Special Education, 21,* 69–84.

Short, R., & Simeonsson, R. (1986). Social cognition and aggression in delinquent adolescent males. *Adolescence, 21,* 159–176.

Suicide report urges a new search for safeguard (1989, September 21). *Education Week,* p. 20.

Svec, H. (1987). Anorexia nervosa: A misdiagnosis of the adolescent male. *Adolescence, 87,* 617–623.

Thompson, K. (1990). *Body image disturbance: Assessment and treatment.* Riverside, NJ: Pergamon Press.

Thornton, W. (1982). Gender traits and delinquency involvement of boys and girls. *Adolescence, 15,* 749–768.

Tugend, A. (1984, October 31). Researchers begin to examine youth suicide as a national problem. *Education Today,* p. 1.

Turkington, C. (1984, December). Support urged for children in mourning. *APA Monitor,* 16–17.

U.S. Department of Health and Human Services. (1989). *Youth and suicide.* Washington, DC: Secretary's Task Force on Youth Suicide.

VanThore, M., & Vogel, F. (1985). The presence of bulimia in high school females. *Adolescence, 20,* 45–51.

Wahler, R., & Dumas, J. (1984). Family factors in childhood psychopathology. In T. Jacob (Ed.), *Family interaction and psychopathology.* New York: Plenum Press.

Wass, H., & Coor, C. (1984). *Helping children cope with death: Guidelines and resources.* New York: Hemisphere.

Weld, E. (1984, October 3). Seeing death as part of life. *The Boston Globe.*

Whitaker, C. (1986). Teenage victims: A national crime survey report. Washington, DC: Department of Justice.

Williamson, D. (1990). *Assessment of eating disorders.* Riverside, NJ: Pergamon Press.

Worchel, F. (1987). New perspectives on child and adolescent depression. *Journal of School Psychology, 25,* 411–414.

15 Communicating With Adolescents

CHAPTER OUTLINE

GOALS AND OBJECTIVES

This chapter is designed to enable you to:

- Improve your listening skills
- Design effective contingency contracts for adolescents
- Communicate in a more specific, behavioral style
- Interpret conversations from the perspective of transactional analysis
- Learn some of the techniques of rational emotive therapy

CONCEPTS AND TERMINOLOGY

contingency contracts
extrinsic rewards
intrinsic rewards
rational emotive therapy
reality therapy
transactional analysis

Throughout this text we have explored many of the problems confronting adolescents. Although strategies for counseling and for communicating with adolescents have been integrated into each chapter, an extensive explanation of any single approach to counseling, teaching, or parenting is beyond the scope of an introductory text in adolescent psychology. Thus, this final chapter is intended only as a brief introduction to several of the most prevalent strategies for communicating with, and for modifying the behavior of, adolescents. As this chapter's references demonstrate, a number of books elaborate on the general principles introduced in the following pages. After reading this chapter, you may wish to pursue additional information through these sources.

ACTIVE LISTENING

On the basis of the views of the phenomenologists, a number of theorists have developed models for training professional counselors to listen effectively to their clients. Undoubtedly two of the most renowned educators in this domain are Carl Rogers (1961) and Richard Carkuff (1969). The basic premise underlying the Rogers and Carkuff models is that warmth, openness, and genuineness are crucial to establishing rapport with adolescents. Fortunately, both Rogers and Carkuff agree that these communication skills can be learned by parents and teachers as well as by professional therapists.

The first step in establishing effective communication is to accept the adolescent with unconditional positive regard. Authoritarian behaviors such as advising, directing, urging, forbidding, warning, moralizing, or commanding impede discourse and serve as obstacles to effective communication. For example, at 2 A.M., frightened parents may confront their daughter coming in the front door with an accusatory statement about her whereabouts, rather than stating their fears and asking her for an explanation. The first response is authoritarian. In contrast to this reaction, Carkuff and Rogers believe we must master the skills of active listening.

The first step in active listening is to rephrase or reflect the youngster's statements: "If I understand you correctly, you're feeling that your dad and I are being unfair to you by staying awake until 2 A.M. to talk to you, and this makes you feel both sad and angry." The second step is clarifying: "Do you mean that you feel angry because you don't think we trust you enough to go to bed even though you're not home? I'm not really sure what the source of your anger and sadness is so can you explain it to me?" The third step is to acknowledge the youngster's perspective even though it may differ from our own: "I can understand that from your viewpoint our staying up until you came home seems foolish and unnecessary." And the final step is an exchange of feelings and perspectives: "Now let me tell you my feelings. Let me start by telling you how afraid I was because I love you so much, and then let me tell you why I feel angry at you."

Active listening demands more than simply comprehending the meaning of the speaker's words. Empathetic active listening involves interpreting the speaker's nonverbal gestures—his or her facial expressions, breathing, eye movements, tone of voice, and posture. When these nonverbal messages contradict the adolescent's verbal statements, the active listener elicits more information before accepting the youngster's verbal comments for their literal meaning. For example, if an adolescent is scowling, slumped over in her chair, and taking shallow breaths while saying that she is not upset about being suspended from school, you might respond, "I sense there's really a part of you that doesn't agree with what you've just said to me. Would you like to tell me a little more about how you're feeling?"

Another important component of these models of communication is that both the adult and the adolescent "own their feelings." We often hear an adolescent's parents and the adolescent expressing their feelings in the guise of aggressive, critical statements leveled against someone else. For example, the parent standing at the door at 2 A.M. when her daughter walks in may yell, "Where have you been? Why are you so immature and irresponsible? Don't you have any respect for me?" And the adolescent may retort, "You're unreasonable and you treat me like a 2-year-old! Get off my back!" When people are taught to express their feelings by using "I" messages and to avoid blaming the other person, the exchange is altered considerably: "I have been waiting for you since midnight because I was so afraid that something terrible had happened to you, and I could feel my heart sinking into my stomach as the hours passed. I even had a terrible vision of your lying alongside the road in an overturned car. Then I started to get angry at you for not phoning to let me know that you were safe somewhere." These "I" messages avoid putting the other person on the defensive. The exercise in Box 15.1 illustrates the types of response considered appropriate and inappropriate in terms of the principles espoused by Carkuff and Rogers.

BEHAVIORAL LANGUAGE

A number of methods for helping adolescents depend on our ability to communicate by using behavioral terminology. Behavioral statements rely exclusively on words that represent observable, measurable behavior, rather than referring to aspects of the adolescent's character or to vague generalities such as "attitudes" and "will power." From this perspective the most efficient way to bring about changes in adolescents's behavior is to state our compliments, our criticisms, and our expectations in behavioral terms.

The purpose of a behavioral statement is to identify the specific behavior that is being criticized, praised, or desired. For example, instead of saying, "I want you to improve your attitude here around the house, young man," you would specify the particular behavior you want changed: "I want you to empty the garbage at least three times a week without my nagging you." Likewise, if you want to maintain an adolescent's behavior through praise, your compliments should be stated in behavioral terms, rather than in vague generalities: "I really feel happy when I see that you have taken the garbage out and cleaned your room three times this week without my having to remind you at all," instead of "I like your new attitude

A CLOSER LOOK 15.1

Active Listening and Empathetic Communication

Which of the following exchanges with an adolescent represent the principles of active, empathetic communication espoused by phenomenological theorists such as Carl Rogers, Abraham Maslow, and Richard Carkuff?

1. *Client:* I really don't want to go back into that class because I know that teacher hates me.
   Counselor: You seem really worried about interacting with this teacher, and I can understand that that must make you reluctant to stay in the class. Can you tell me what the teacher does that makes you feel she doesn't like you?
2. *Daughter:* I had a terrible day at school with that big math test and all.
   Mom: You really shouldn't be so negative about school all the time. Life is hard, you know, and you really have it good.
3. *Son:* I couldn't help it, Dad. I just didn't see the post and I backed the car right into it.
   Dad: Why don't you watch where you're going? Do you have to be so irresponsible?
4. *Student:* I guess I need to talk to you about my grade, Mr. Snodgrass. I don't seem to be doing so hot.
   Teacher: I can tell you're feeling pretty tense about this, and it must have been hard for you to muster the courage to come in to talk.
5. *Father:* I feel angry when you promise to do your household chores without my nagging you and then you go out with your friends all weekend without doing a single chore.
6. *Teacher:* You make me angry when you don't come to class because it shows what an irresponsible person you are.
7. *Client:* My boss is on my back all the time and I want to quit that job before it gets worse.
   Therapist: What I seem to hear you saying is that you're feeling frustrated and confused right now about your relationship with your boss and you're not sure how to make things better without quitting the job.
8. *Adolescent boy:* I'm just not cut out for any sport. I try because I want to be popular and I know I ought to get in better shape, but it just seems too useless.
   Adult friend: Well, give it a while and everything will work out.
9. *Adolescent girl:* You just don't seem to appreciate anything I do for you, and I can't seem to do anything right anymore.
   Adult friend: You don't make me feel very good about myself either, as a matter of fact. I've been wondering what's gotten into you lately.

Answers: 1, 4, 5, and 7 represent active, empathetic listening skills. The other statements represent an inattentive, critical, judgmental, or authoritarian attitude toward the adolescent.

here around the house." Box 15.2 demonstrates the differences between behavioral and nonbehavioral statements.

Behavioral language can also be valuable in designing strategies for improving unpleasant situations that arise in the adolescent's life. For example, assume you have an adolescent client who is constantly complaining about "unfair treatment" from her math teacher, which is causing her to feel depressed and frustrated. You could ask your client any number of questions to identify the specific behaviors underlying her frustration and the specific behaviors that would remedy the situation: What does your teacher actually do that makes you feel she does not like you? Describe her behavior to me in detail during the last incident when you

A CLOSER LOOK 15.2

Behavioral and Nonbehavioral Communication

Which of the following statements use behavioral terminology to communicate a message?

STATEMENTS ABOUT ADOLESCENTS:

1. Susan has no will power or self-discipline at home or at school.
2. That boy just isn't cooperative.
3. This student demonstrates an attitude that bothers me by wearing a hat in class and by never getting here on time.
4. Why can't my son get along with his brother?
5. I really want the whole team to be able to run eight consecutive laps before the end of the semester.
6. George and I have an argument every time I ask him to babysit for his younger sister.
7. Young people today don't respect their elders.
8. I can't be happy unless he cleans up his room without my nagging.
9. I keep telling him to read at least 30 minutes a night, but he won't.

STATEMENTS BY ADOLESCENTS:

10. I'm just an aggressive person, so what you're asking is almost impossible for me, you see?
11. I have to learn to speak up in class when I don't understand the material, or I'm going to fail. Can you help me?
12. Shyness just runs in my family.
13. I seem to have an attitude problem, don't I?
14. I'm going to have to do something to make myself run laps after school, or I'll never get in shape before the season starts.
15. I want to be able to talk to my sister without our yelling at each other.

Answers: Statements 3, 5, 6, 8, 9, 11, 14, and 15 are using behavioral terminology. The underlined words in each statement indicate either behavioral or nonbehavioral terms. For example, in number 12 the term *shyness* would have to be changed to a phrase indicating specific behaviors in order to qualify as a behavioral statement: "Everybody in my family seems unable to speak up in a group of more than two people."

felt unliked. How are you behaving when the teacher does or does not seem to like you? How do the students she likes behave in class? How do you think you would have to change your behavior in order to make her like you?

Teaching adolescents to use behavioral statements in their own language facilitates communication and enhances the effectiveness of certain kinds of behavioral therapy. Adolescents who learn to express their feelings and to identify their needs in behavioral terms can more effectively set goals for themselves, improve their interactions with other people, and avoid catastrophizing events in ways that make them seem impossible to remedy (Nielsen, 1982; Williams & Long, 1990).

TRANSACTIONAL ANALYSIS

Another approach frequently used to improve communication between adolescents and adults is **transactional analysis** (Berne, 1964). Transactional analysis, commonly referred to as *TA,* is a model for analyzing verbal communication that categorizes our statements as representing the perspective of either the "child," the "adult," or the "parent" in us. Statements representing a child's perspective merely impart emotion and are typically impulsive and self-serving. In contrast, statements representing the parent in us are typically reprimanding, restrictive, authoritarian, and judgmental. They are intended to make others feel guilty. According to the TA model, the best statements are those that come from the perspective of the "adult" in us. These statements are rational, nonjudgmental, and nonmanipulative in the sense that they represent honest feelings and reasonable expectations. The comments in Box 15.3 demonstrate these principles of transactional analysis.

In addition to providing a way to analyze conversations, transactional analysis also teaches us to recognize the "games" we play with each other. According to TA, a game is an exchange in which one person is verbally manipulating the other into a predictable and inescapable position, rather than communicating in an honest manner about the real problem. A game is an attempt to evade personal responsibility by casting the burden onto another person. For example, in the game entitled "Uproar," the adolescent stockpiles all the real or imagined insults she believes her teacher has been sending her. When she collects enough of these

A CLOSER LOOK 15.3

Transactional Analysis: A Model for More Effective Communication

According to the principles of transactional analysis, all comments in a conversation can be categorized according to one of three perspectives: that of a child, of a parent, or of an adult. How would you classify each of the following statements—as that of the child, the parent, or the adult within the speaker?

1. My parents don't love me because they make me come home so early and don't give me much allowance.
2. I'm your father and as long as I pay the bills, you'll do exactly as I say without needing to know the whys and wherefores!
3. This assignment is frustrating me and is making me feel stupid. Can you show me how to do it?
4. I'm fed up with your behavior and your brother's and I don't intend to discuss any of this with you, so get out of here!
5. You know that your behavior is wrong and you are violating the principles of the school.
6. You ought to feel ashamed of yourself, young man!
7. What you've done makes me very angry, and we need to sit down and discuss the situation to devise some sort of remedy.
8. Nothing ever goes right for me, and I just don't see any need to try anymore!
9. I can't believe you did that, given all we've done for you all these years.
10. Let's talk about this after we both calm down.

Answers:

Spoken from the perspective of a child who is impulsive, irrational, emotional, and self-centered: 1, 4, 8.

Spoken from the perspective of a parent who is critical, judgmental, threatening, authoritarian, and guilt-producing: 2, 5, 6, 9.

Spoken from the perspective of an adult who is rational, candid, and emotionally expressive, yet nonaccusatory: 3, 7, 10.

insults she feels justified in creating an uproar in front of the whole class, during which she lambasts her teacher with her stockpile.

In the game "Make Me," the student tries to force the adult into an adversary position by complaining, "You just don't like me and that's why I'm making a D in here." The teacher can refuse to play the game by saying: "If you choose to make a passing grade in here, you may do the following things. If you choose to do otherwise, that is totally your right and your responsibility. I'm not here to force you to do things against your will." The games that adolescents typically play are comically yet candidly described in the books *Transactional Analysis for Teens and Other Warm Important People* and *Games Students Play* (Freed, 1976; Ernst, 1972).

BEHAVIORAL CONTRACTING

In terms of providing specific methods for improving our communication with adolescents, the social learning models have been among the most popular and most successful. In brief, this perspective contends that an adolescent's negative self-judgments and emotions, such as depression or anxiety, can best be alleviated through systematically altering the rewards, punishments, setting events, and models in the environment. Hence, the best way to help adolescents is to utilize the principles of behavioral psychology. Furthermore, self-control is a learned skill that involves applying the principles of behavioral psychology to one's own life. This means we can teach adolescents the principles of behavioral psychology and thereby give them skills for self-management and self-control.

Reality Therapy

One of the more popular behavioral approaches is William Glasser's *Reality Therapy* (1965). Originally designed during his work with delinquents, Glasser's principles have been successfully used with adolescents in public schools, detention centers, and special education classes. Basically, in **reality therapy** the adult functions as a guide and discusses a series of prescribed questions with the adolescent: (1) What are you doing? This question demands a description in behavioral terms of the problem. (2) How is your behavior helping you? (3) Since in some cases the adolescent's behavior is harming other people the next question is often necessary: How is your behavior helping other people—your family, your classmates, your girlfriend? (4) What plan can you and I devise to remedy this situation? (5) Will you commit yourself to this plan? (6) Will you check back with me in a week to reevaluate this plan so we can determine whether it needs to be modified?

Contracts are then written stating each person's expectations and promises to the other. In an effort to avoid misunderstanding and to prevent future arguments, the contract serves as an important vehicle in communication. The contract agreed to between the adolescent and the adult may be either verbal or written, but Glasser recommends written contracts so that misunderstandings will be minimized. Although the contract may take a variety of forms, the guidelines suggested in Table 15.1 ensure that both the adolescent and the adults will understand the contingencies clearly from the outset.

Contingency Contracts

Although Glasser's reality therapy represents one form of contracting, another option, referred to as **contingency contracts,** has repeatedly demonstrated its success in improving adolescents' behavior both at home and at school. Contingency contracts have improved communication and behavior. Moreover, contracting has proved itself successful with delinquents, retarded youths, and learning-disabled students, as well as with normal adolescents (Nielsen, 1982).

A contingency contract specifies the behavioral goals toward which the adolescent is working, as well as the daily system of rewards and punishments for each day's progress toward the ultimate goal. Thus, contingency contracts are excellent means through which to communicate our expectations to adolescents and to specify each person's commitments without relying on forms of communication that can later be misconstrued. Table 15.1 summarizes the recommendations for designing contingency contracts.

Contracts have advantages seldom found in other communication strategies. Because contracting requires people to be specific and candid with each other, disputes are less likely to arise. Most adults have an unwritten contract of sorts etched inside their heads during their conversations with adolescents. Contingency contracts are ways to transfer these plans into public, written form for the

Table 15.1

Self-Management Contracting Checklist

In helping adolescents learn to create their own self-management programs, use the following statements as guidelines for writing effective contingency contracts:

1. State your goal in behavioral terms.
2. Choose only one goal at a time to work toward.
3. Allow yourself ample time to achieve your goal.
4. Be certain you possess the skills necessary to achieve your goal.
5. Choose a goal that is within your power to control and not one that is dependent upon changes in other people.
6. Determine your daily rewards and punishments.
7. Record your behavior daily.
8. Reward yourself for accomplishing goals on a daily basis.
9. Arrange the physical environment to help you reach your goal.
10. Increase your goal very gradually at the end of each week.
11. Do not choose the most difficult problem in your life as your first self-management project.
12. Provide role models for yourself, even if these are just characters in a book you have read.
13. Get someone to help you design your self-management contract. Select a person who knows your skills and can help you set reasonable goals for each day.
14. Arrange to have friends reward you for your progress each day.
15. Talk to others who have succeeded in meeting goals similar to yours.
16. Rehearse your new skill first in the presence of people you trust.

Source: L. Nielsen. (1982). *How to motivate adolescents: A guide for parents, teachers and counselors.* Englewood Cliffs, NJ: Prentice-Hall.

adolescents' benefit. Contracts also oblige adults who are confused about their objectives or who are communicating contradictory messages to adolescents to come to terms with these discrepancies and confusion. As Box 15.4 illustrates, contingency contracts can be designed to communicate with adolescents on academic, social, or familial issues. The contracts can be as elaborate or as simple as necessary for the adolescents' particular needs.

Contracting is especially beneficial when communicating with adolescents who are not motivated by internal or **intrinsic rewards.** When an activity is not intrinsically pleasurable, people must rely on external or **extrinsic rewards** to motivate themselves. For example, society gives us external rewards for our work by offering paychecks, promotions, or special awards, such as "salesperson of the month." These external rewards often motivate us to complete tasks that are less pleasurable and less appealing than other alternatives—such as sleeping late or watching television instead of getting up on a rainy Monday morning to go to a dreary job. Contracts also help us with adolescents who—intentionally or unintentionally—tend to misunderstand or forget what has been communicated to them. In other words contracts between adolescents and adults are meant to serve the same purposes as contracts between employers and employees in terms of facilitating communication and avoiding misunderstandings.

A CLOSER LOOK 15.4

Contract Between Teacher and Student

POINTS I EARNED TODAY					MAXIMUM POSSIBLE		
Mon.	***Tues.***	***Wed.***	***Th.***	***Fri.***	***Daily***	***Weekly***	**ACTIVITY**
2	0	2	2	0	2	10	Attending class
5	0	3	3	0	5	25	Completing the assigned work in class
3	0	3	3	0	3	15	Turning in last night's homework assignment
			5			5	Making fewer than two mistakes on the weekly quiz
My weekly total: 31					Total:	55	

Weekly totals will be recorded in the teacher's gradebook as follows:
50–55 points = A; 45–50 points = B; 40–45 points = C; 35–40 points = D.

CONTRACT BETWEEN PARENT AND CHILD:

If Susan (1) makes up her bed each morning this week without being reminded, (2) babysits with baby Joey for 3 hours during the week without complaining, and (3) washes the dishes after two dinners, Mom will (a) let her have the car for 4 hours on the weekend without complaining, (b) let her have an extra hour on Friday or Saturday night's curfew, and (c) refrain from nagging or reminding her about these three chores.

Signed: ________________ Mom ________________ Susan

RATIONAL EMOTIVE THERAPY

Our attempts to communicate with adolescents may show us that a young person's feelings and judgments are being based on illogical thinking or on data that do not coincide with the actual facts. For example, some students may be convinced that a teacher is singling them out for discriminatory treatment, even though objective observers note that these students are being treated just like the others. Trying to communicate with adolescents who are basing their behavior on irrational thinking or erroneous data is a frustrating exchange.

One approach for helping people reexamine the data on which they are basing their feelings and judgments is **rational emotive therapy.** Developed by Albert Ellis (1974) during his work as a psychoanalyst, rational emotive therapy is based on the assumption that many emotional disturbances result from illogical thinking. Unconsciously, some individuals indoctrinate themselves repeatedly with negative, irrational "self-talk" that governs their behavior. The task of rational emotive therapy is to make individuals aware of the covert messages they are sending themselves and to confront them with the irrational messages.

According to Ellis, many neurotic people believe illogical thoughts such as: "It is essential for a person to be loved and approved of by everyone." "There is always a solution to every problem and unless it is found, the results will be catastrophic"; "I must be perfectly adequate and competent at all times or people will not like me." The first task, then, is to identify these internal messages. Once the counselor has helped an adolescent identify his or her self-talk, the task of replacing the old messages with new ones begins. The objective is to replace the debilitating, irrational messages with self-talk that is more reasonable.

In the cleverly illustrated and witty book *Talk to Yourself,* the principles of rational emotive therapy are presented to adolescents in comprehensible terms (Zastrow, 1979). Among the book's suggestions is that the person should look for objective evidence that supports or refutes his or her beliefs. For example, the adolescent is instructed to write down one of his or her self-talk statements: "Doing homework is a waste of time because it doesn't help me pass the course." Then he or she must write the thought as a testable hypothesis: "My belief that doing homework is a waste of time is true if most people in this class who did their homework still fail tomorrow's test, but false if most people who did their homework pass the test."

Another technique suggested for adolescents is to write "counter cards." On a small card the adolescent writes the irrational thought, followed by three or four rational statements that counteract it. For example, "The coach hates me and forces me to do things nobody else has to do" might be followed by these countering statements: "The coach did give me a compliment last week, which isn't compatible with my idea that she hates me. The coach does make everyone run laps, not just me, which is inconsistent with the belief that she is singling me out for unkind treatment." Methods based on rational emotive therapy are being used effectively by teachers, parents, and counselors to help adolescents gain more control over their own irrational feelings and behavior (Bernard, 1984).

ADOLESCENTS' OWN VOICES

In an apocryphal story about the limits of empirical investigations and sophisticated methods for gathering data, a psychology professor asks her class of graduate students, "What is your most reliable and valid method for determining whether a woman is homosexual?" The students respond enthusiastically, "With projective tests." "With a psychological profile." "With an intensive investigation of her past." And the grinning professor answers, "No. Just ask her." In a similar vein, a joke about statistics asks, "Did you hear about the 6-foot man who couldn't swim and drowned because he confidently tried to cross a stream that a statistician told him had 'an average' depth of 4 feet?" Both stories are intended to underscore the fact that statistics and sophisticated psychometric techniques can lead to misinterpretations about adolescents.

Without disregarding the information gleaned from research, we can expand our understanding of adolescents by venturing into another domain—books written by adolescents and books whose authors recount stories in adolescents' own words. One advantage of this approach is that it permits us more detailed views of the lives of adolescents, whose personal stories are overlooked in research. Both descriptive and experimental research present data on groups of adolescents, rather than detailing the personal experiences of any single individual. The poignancy, humor, and wisdom often revealed through an individual adolescent's own poetry, commentary, or essay is thus lost to us in the process of averaging scores and sampling large groups—much like the 6-foot man who drowns in a stream whose average depth is only 4 feet, but whose deepest water is obviously well above the 6-foot mark!

The number of books containing writings by adolescents is still rather limited. Although excerpts from several of these books have been included in previous chapters, their titles and topics bear repeating as a reminder of their value to students and practitioners of adolescent psychology. As a continuing source of the current topics most affecting the young, Chicago's *New Expression* magazine provides new stories and information of relevance to both young and old. Written and published by adolescents, the newspaper is the largest teen newspaper in the nation. In addition to the benefits that accrue to the adolescents on the staff, the newspaper's readers profit from the fact that teenage reporters gain access to information from other adolescents, which would otherwise be inaccessible to adults. For example, among *New Expression*'s headlines have been: "Teen Alcoholics Break Out of the Bottle," "Bisexuality: Breaking Out of the School Closet," "Will Teens from Divorced Families Self-Destruct?," and "Tables Turned: Males Expose Their Side of Sex Issues" (*New Expression,* 1986).

Publications such as *New Expression* are testimony to the fact that adolescent writers are willing to tackle issues that are both controversial and emotion laden. Adolescents at the Fayerweather Street School in Cambridge, Massachusetts, have written two books under the direction of their teacher Eric Rofes. The first, *The Kids' Book of Divorce,* presents stories of children's and adolescents' reactions to their parents' divorce (Rofes, 1982). The second, *The Kids' Book about Death and Dying,* reflects these adolescents' interviews with parents, children, hospice workers, veterinarians, funeral directors, cemetery workers, religious leaders, and medical personnel (Rofes, 1985). In the process of writing that book, these adolescents visited hospitals, funeral homes, graveyards, and health-care centers. The result is a text that treats such topics as reincarnation, the death of a pet, funeral customs, and immortality with a poignancy and candor that equal those of many adult books on death and dying.

Also written by adolescents for a teenaged audience, *Teenagers Themselves* offers cartoons, short stories, interviews, and poetry by young people across the nation (Glenbard East *Echo,* 1984). The adolescents on the staff of the *Echo* at

Glenbard East High School in Lombard, Illinois, gathered responses to a number of open-ended questions over the period of a year. Choosing the best cartoons and writings from nearly 9,000 responses from every state in the nation, the student writers and editors developed a 20-chapter text that includes such topics as religion, interracial dating, work, honesty, violence, death, prejudice, drinking, and drugs. Written by and for adolescents, it presents an insightful glimpse of the many facets of adolescence in our contemporary society.

In a similar vein, *Changing Bodies, Changing Lives* offers a number of comments and stories from adolescents about their views and experiences regarding relationships with parents and peers (Bell, 1988). In their efforts to create a book for adolescents on sex and relationships, the adult authors interviewed hundreds of young people from various socioeconomic, racial, and religious backgrounds. The stories and commentaries represent the views of homosexuals and heterosexuals, of males and females, of younger and older adolescents, and of those with liberal and conservative perspectives on social and sexual issues. The authors state that their two main goals are to give adolescents accurate information about sex and physical development and to give them the opportunity to learn about other adolescents' experiences and feelings.

Other adult authors have interviewed adolescents and transcribed the conversations into texts. Among these are *How It Feels When a Parent Dies* (Krementz, 1983) in which adolescents and children have recounted their feelings about their confrontation with death, and *Growing up Dead* in which young people who have attempted suicide express their feelings and experiences (Rabkin, 1979). In a different vein, *Whose Child Cries* recounts the concerns of adolescents with gay parents (Gantz, 1983). In regard to adolescents' vocational experiences, nonfiction books are scarce. One valuable source, however, is *Working Kids on Working* in which 25 children between the ages of 9 and 15 describe their work experiences (Cole, 1980). Cole's book poignantly presents the stories of adolescents working in situations far removed from the suburbs and the fast-food restaurants.

Deep Blue Funk is a collection of stories about black adolescents' experiences as mothers and fathers that captures both the dialect and the emotional fervor of these young parents. Above all, this book distinguishes itself for its portrayals of teenage fathers, a group typically excluded from both the empirical and the nonfictional literature on pregnancy and parenting (Frank, 1983). In a somewhat different vein, *It Won't Happen to Me* recounts the author's interviews with pregnant adolescent girls and with professionals who work with teenage mothers (McGuire, 1983). Perhaps most dramatic, however, is an adolescent girl's own autobiography based on excerpts from her journal during her pregnancy and first year of motherhood—*The Magic Washing Machine* (Slapin, 1983).

CONCLUSION

To reiterate, the suggestions offered in this chapter for improving your communication with adolescents and for helping adolescents modify certain dimensions of their behavior are not intended as an exhaustive presentation of contemporary therapies. However, the chapter may have achieved several purposes.

First, the fact that these techniques have been effective in altering adolescents' behavior undermines skeptics' assertion that nothing can be done with today's adolescents. To the contrary, we are in the fortunate position of having techniques at our disposal for alleviating many of the problems that contemporary adolescents most frequently encounter. The problem is not so much that we lack the methods for improving communication or for helping adolescents change certain aspects of their behavior. The greater problem is that we have not disseminated the available information to most parents or to adults who are interacting with adolescents in a professional capacity.

Second, the data in this chapter should not be construed to mean that there is a cure-all for every possible problem that an adolescent in today's society might confront. Such a view would be both spurious and foolhardy. Moreover, to assert unequivocally that "where there's a will, there's a way" is to create guilt in cases where parents and professionals are indeed unable to alleviate the problems of an adolescent whom they love. Unquestionably, some adolescents are besieged with such serious problems that not even the most skilled professionals or most loving parents can eliminate their pain or suffering.

QUESTIONS FOR DISCUSSION AND REVIEW

Basic Concepts and Terminology

1. According to the models of Rogers and Carkuff, what specific skills enhance communication with adolescents?
2. In what ways can behavioral language facilitate communication?
3. How do the principles of transactional analysis explain the miscommunication that often occurs in conversation?
4. In helping adolescents design contingency contracts, what criteria can be applied to increase the likelihood of the contract's success?
5. Employing rational emotive therapy, how can adolescents be helped to interpret their experiences more rationally and less subjectively?
6. What advantages might accrue to adults who read materials produced by adolescents themselves, rather than those that rely on empirical data?

Questions for Discussion and Debate

1. How could active listening skills and behavioral contracting have facilitated communication between you and your parents during your adolescence? In answering this question, recount a specific incident between you and your parents as it actually occurred and then as it might have been improved.
2. How could you respond to each of the adolescent's statements in Box 15.1 in a way that demonstrates active listening skills?
3. What do you see as the advantages and disadvantages of reality therapy and transactional analysis in communicating with adolescents?
4. How could you convert each nonbehavioral statement in Box 15.2 into a behavioral comment?
5. If you were given the power and the money to create three new community services for youths, what kinds of organization would you establish? Why?
6. What writings by adolescents have affected you most profoundly and why? With whom have you shared your feelings concerning these writings?

GLOSSARY

contingency contracts Written or verbal agreements in which the parties agree to certain goals stated in terms of specific behaviors and in which the rewards and punishments for achieving or failing to achieve these behaviors are clearly specified; a behavior modification technique.

extrinsic rewards A reward, external to the activity itself, that is offered as a way of maintaining a behavior that the person does not find intrinsically pleasurable. Examples: salary, grades.

intrinsic rewards Pleasurable feelings derived from engaging in an activity without having to receive external rewards of any sort. Examples: the pleasure of eating when you are hungry.

rational emotive therapy An approach to changing human behavior based on the principles of social learning theory and cognitive psychology in which people reexamine the rationality of the thoughts influencing their behavior.

reality therapy A counseling and teaching method based on contingency contracting developed by William Glasser through his work with troubled adolescents.

transactional analysis A method for improving communication in which conversations are analyzed according to the "roles"—the "child," the "parent," or the "adult"—each statement represents.

REFERENCES

*Bell, R. (1988). *Changing bodies, changing lives: A book for teens on sex and relationships.* New York: Random House.

Bernard, M. (1984). *Rational emotive therapy with children and adolescents.* New York: Wiley.

Berne, E. (1964). *Games people play: Theories of transactional analysis.* New York: Grove Press.

Carkuff, R. (1969). *Helping and human relations.* New York: Holt, Rinehart and Winston.

*Cole, S. (1980). *Working kids on working.* New York: Lothrop & Lee.

Ellis, A. (1974). *Disputing irrational beliefs.* New York: Institute for Rational Living.

Ernst, K. (1972). *Games students play.* Milbrae, CA: Celestial Arts.

*Frank, D. (1983). *Deep blue funk and other stories: Portraits of teenage parents.* Chicago: Ounce of Prevention Fund.

Freed, A. (1976). *Transactional analysis for teens and other warm important people.* Sacramento, CA: Jalmar Press.

*Gantz, J. (1983). *Whose child cries: Children of gay parents talk about their lives.* Rolling Hills Estates, CA: Jalmar Press.

Glasser, W. (1965). *Reality therapy.* New York: Harper & Row.

*Glenbard East *Echo* (1984). *Teenagers themselves.* New York: Adama Books.

*Krementz, J. (Ed.). (1983). *How it feels when a parent dies.* New York: Knopf.

*McGuire, P. (1983). *It won't happen to me: Teenagers talk about pregnancy.* New York: Delacorte.

Nielsen, L. (1982). *How to motivate adolescents: A guide for parents, teachers and counselors.* Englewood Cliffs, NJ: Prentice-Hall.

*Rabkin, B. (1979). *Growing up dead: A hard look at why adolescents commit suicide.* Nashville, TN: Abingdon Press.

*Rofes, E. (Ed.). (1982). *The kids' book of divorce: By and for kids.* Boston: Little, Brown.

*Rofes, E. (Ed.). (1985). *The kids' book about death and dying.* Boston: Little, Brown.

Rogers, C. (1961). *On becoming a person.* Boston: Houghton Mifflin.

*Slapin, B. (1983). *The magic washing machine: A diary of single motherhood.* Mesquite, TX: Ide House.

Williams, R., & Long, J. (1990). *Toward a self-managed lifestyle.* Boston: Houghton Mifflin.

Zastrow, C. (1979). *Talk sense to yourself.* Englewood Cliffs, NJ: Prentice-Hall.

**Books written mainly by adolescents themselves.*

Glossary

accommodation As used by Piaget, the change in an existing schema to one that enables us to understand a new concept or new experience.

acculturation The adopting of the values and behaviors of the majority culture.

achieved identity An independent identity that we acquire as a consequence of experimenting with different roles and values during adolescence and early childhood.

acid *See* LSD.

acquired immune deficiency syndrome (AIDS) An incurable disease that is transmitted through infected hypodermic needles, sexual intercourse, or contact with infected blood and kills its victims by destroying their immune systems.

adipose tissue Fat.

aggregate data The summing of each person's data together to form group averages.

Aid to Families with Dependent Children (AFDC) Welfare program.

Al-anon National organization designed to help members deal with and recover from a family member's alcoholism.

Al-a-teen National organization for teenagers with an alcoholic family member.

alcohol The most frequently used drug; an addictive sedative-hypnotic that in moderate doses relaxes the muscles but in large doses causes both loss of muscle control and sleep.

amenorrhea The cessation of the menstrual period.

amphetamines "Uppers." Synthetic drugs that speed up the body's heart rate and blood pressure. When taken in low to moderate doses, increase energy, alertness, and self-confidence.

amping The "high" that comes when using "ice."

anal stage According to Freudians, the period, usually between 2 and 3 years old, when the child makes the shift from deriving pleasure from defecating to learning self-control.

androgen Any of the steroid hormones that develop and maintain masculine secondary sex characteristics.

androgyny State of possessing masculine and feminine personality traits simultaneously. Example: being both nurturant and independent.

angel dust Phencyclidine. *See* PCP.

anomie A condition in which the members of a society feel isolated and disconnected as a result of excessively specialized social structures that limit closeness and intimacy.

anorexia nervosa An eating disorder characterized by intense fear of becoming fat, obsessive concern with weight, and the belief that one is fat when of normal weight or even when emaciated.

anovulatory When the ovaries do not release an egg during the monthly cycle.

areola The dark-colored area of skin around the nipple.

assertiveness training A model based on social learning theory that teaches participants to be more outspoken. Not synonymous with aggressiveness.

assimilation The merging of groups with different backgrounds into one group with a common identity.

assimilation As used by Piaget, the process of fitting new concepts or new experiences into our existing schema.

associativity According to Piaget, the idea that the sum is independent of the order in which things are added. $4 + 2 + 3 = 9$, and so does $2 + 3 + 4$.

asymptomatic carriers People who have a disease but show no visible symptoms.

attention deficit disorder (ADD) A syndrome in which the individual is excessively energetic, impulsive, and unable to concentrate on an activity for any sustained period of time.

attribution theories Theories that assign responsibility for one's own successes or failures either to oneself (internal attributions) or to something outside oneself (external attributions). These beliefs then influence our responses to reinforcement and punishment. Related concepts: learned helplessness, locus of control, self-efficacy.

at-risk youths Students who are at high risk of failing in school or of graduating without basic skills in reading, writing, and math.

authoritarian A dictatorial, excessively strict style of parenting in which essentially "children are to be seen and not heard."

authoritative A democratic yet disciplined style of parenting in which parents provide rules, giving rationales for them, but also let children have some say in the rules and punishments.

autonomous morality According to Piaget, the stage of moral reasoning generally achieved during adolescence and characterized by reciprocity, questioning authorities, empathy, and abstract thinking.

banana syndrome Asian Americans who have become so assimilated into white culture that they have little sense of a separate ethnic or racial identity.

barbiturates "Downers." Synthetic sedatives that relax the muscles, slow down the heart rate, and cause drowsiness or sleep.

basal metabolism rate The rate at which the body converts calories into sugar for energy.

Beethoven project An extensive early childhood enrichment program now underway for parents and children living in the nation's largest public housing project in Chicago.

behaviorism A school of psychology that examines only observable behavior and that believes our personalities and attitudes are primarily determined by how we are rewarded and punished.

behavior modification Altering a person's attitudes or behavior through the rearrangement of reinforcements and punishment. Related concepts: contingency management, operant conditioning, behaviorism, Skinnerian methods.

bicultural Having equal familiarity with two cultures, usually as a consequence of having been raised in a bicultural family.

bilateralized The brain's capacity to process certain types of information in either hemisphere.

bilingual The ability to speak or write in two languages.

binge Consuming large quantities of high calorie foods in a single setting, often part of bulimia or anorexia.

biosocial theories Beliefs that human behavior is determined by biological influences, such as genes and hormones.

bisexual A male or female whose sexual preferences includes members of both genders.

born again Undergoing an emotional and abrupt conversion to a religion.

brain lateralization The separation of mental and physical functions between the left and right hemispheres of the brain. Synonyms: hemisphericity, left and right brain thinking.

bulimarexia A combination of the disorders of bulimia and anorexia.

bulimia An eating disorder characterized by repeated episodes of binge eating followed by self-induced vomiting, usually accompanied by guilt and depression.

Bureau of Indian Affairs (BIA) The federal governmental agency that oversees American Indian affairs.

caffeine The most widely used stimulant in the world, a drug that induces wakefulness. In large doses can cause insomnia, mild sensory disturbance, muscle tenseness, or anxiety.

cervical sponge A contraceptive device that covers the opening to the cervix, thus preventing sperm from entering the uterus.

cervix The tip of the uterus extending into the vagina.

chancres Body sores that are the initial symptoms of certain sexually transmitted diseases.

Children of Alcoholics (COAs) People who develop certain attitudes and behaviors that undermine their well-being as a consequence of having lived with an alcoholic parent.

circumcised When the skin covering the penis glans is surgically removed.

classical conditioning A form of learning by association that involves pairing a "conditioned stimulus" (such as a bell ringing) with an "unconditioned stimulus" (such as food), thereby eliciting a "conditioned response" (such as salivation) to the conditioned stimulus. Example: Pavlov's dog experiment.

class inclusion The ability to reason simultaneously about parts of a whole and the whole itself.

client-centered therapy *See* Rogerian counseling.

clitoris The female's center of sexual excitation

and source of orgasms whose small, pea-shaped glans (head) is protected by a small covering of skin within the folds of the labia; swells during sexual excitation. Slang/synonyms: "joy button," "clit."

cluster suicides Incidents in which one youngster's suicide seems to motivate others to commit suicide.

cocaine Made from the leaves of the coca plant, a highly addictive drug that can be fatal, especially when introduced intravenously or smoked.

Codependents Anonymous An organization designed to help codependents overcome their self-destructive ways of relating to other people.

codependent People who are obsessed with taking care of and being responsible for other people.

cognitive disequilibrium According to Piaget, the process that occurs when new events or new information cannot be handled by existing schemata; thus, new learning takes place so that cognitive equilibrium can be restored.

cognitive style The characteristic style each individual generally uses when involved in cognitive tasks, for example, reflective or impulsive style. Synonym: learning style.

cohort A person who has experienced the same events during the same interval of time as another person; generally refers to people born at about the same time.

concrete operations stage According to Piaget, the cognitive stage between the ages of 7 and 11 during which we learn the rules of equivalence, reversibility, class inclusion, and associativity.

confluence model The theory that family size, birth order, and spacing of siblings are partially responsible for certain personality traits and cognitive abilities.

confounding variable Factor other than the experimental treatment that might account for changes in the subject's attitudes or behavior.

conservation According to Piaget, the concept grasped by about age 7 that the amount of something stays the same regardless of changes in its shape or the number of parts into which it is divided.

contingency contracts Written or verbal agreements in which the parties agree to certain goals stated in terms of specific behaviors and in which the rewards and punishments for achieving or failing to achieve these behaviors are clearly specified; a behavior modification technique.

continuous culture A society in which children move gradually from childhood to adulthood without defined periods such as adolescence being marked along the way.

control group The group of people who are not exposed to any treatment in an experiment.

conventional reasoning According to Kohlberg, the stage of moral reasoning in which our behavior and values are primarily determined by external rewards, punishments, and the rules of "the authorities."

convergent thinking Thinking along conventional lines in order to find a single best answer or solution.

correlational research Studies comparing the strength of the relationship between two or more variables but not able to determine cause and effect.

correlation coefficient The number that indicates the strength of the relationship between two variables in correlational studies.

counter conditioning *See* desensitization.

crack The crystalline form of cocaine, induces stronger effects than cocaine in powdered form.

cross-sectional studies A way of designing research in which subjects from two or more age groups are measured at the same point in time on the same dependent variables.

cross-tolerance The phenomenon in which developing a tolerance to one type of drug results in diminished sensitivity to the effects of another drug.

date rape Sexual acts that a male forces his date to perform, either by physical force or by verbal threats.

defense mechanisms According to Freudians, the methods by which the ego protects itself from threatening ideas or from external dangers: denial, projection, rationalization, reaction formation, regression, repression, and sublimation.

deficit family model The premise that any family other than the nuclear family is somehow deficient and inferior.

Defining Issues Test (DIT) A test used to assess adolescents' stages of moral reasoning.

denial A defense mechanism in which we refuse to believe that something that threatens or offends us is true.

dependent variable The variable that changes as a consequence of the treatment being administered by the experimenter.

desensitization A form of behavior therapy that helps a person overcome a fear by presenting the threatening stimuli in small doses and then gradually increasing the doses, while simultaneously teaching the person to relax.

developmentalist perspective The assumption that our views about work advance in a sequence of stages from childhood through adulthood.

differentialist perspective The assumption that we choose our future jobs on the basis of matching our personalities, interests, and abilities to the characteristics of particular jobs.

diffused identity An identity that is based on not yet having chosen one's values or goals ("diffused" literally means being spread widely or thinly).

discontinuous culture A society like the United States in which childhood, adolescence, and adulthood are clearly delineated in terms of roles and responsibilities for each age group.

disequilibrium In Piagetian theory, the unpleasant feeling that arises when we encounter new information that contradicts the information in our existing schema.

displacement A defense mechanism in which the person attributes his or her feelings to the wrong source.

divergent thinking Thinking that is creative and original in that it deviates from the obvious and produces several solutions or answers.

downers *See* barbiturates.

drug addiction The older term for drug dependence. *See* drug dependence.

drug dependence Psychological dependence refers to a strong compulsion to use a drug because it produces pleasure or reduces anxiety. Physical dependence occurs when the user's body undergoes withdrawal symptoms when he or she is not using the drug.

drug tolerance A condition occurring after prolonged and heavy use of a drug, wherein the user becomes less affected by the doses and has to increase the amount in order to experience the original effects.

DSM III-R *The Diagnostic and Statistical Manual,* revised edition. Manual that describes mental disorders as defined by professionals in psychology.

dyslexia A condition causing problems in learning to read when no disorders, such as mental retardation, or cultural factors, such as coming from a home where English is not spoken, are apparent.

dysmenorrhea Excessive pain during menstruation.

ecological fallacy Drawing conclusions from group data and trying to apply them to an individual or to a smaller group.

ecstasy *See* MDA.

ectomorph Tall, skinny body type.

ego The part of the personality that attempts to balance the id's unconscious drives and the superego's unrealistic rules and regulations.

egocentrism The inability to see things from another person's point of view or to imagine several different perspectives simultaneously.

eidetic memory Memory of the explicit details of an event as a consequence of the emotionally charged nature of the situation.

Electra complex A daughter's unconscious desire to have sex with her father and her consequent jealousy toward her mother.

empirical data Data that can be confirmed by experiments or gathered in surveys.

endomorph Stocky, short, round body type.

endorphins Chemicals released by the brain that act as natural pain killers and mood elevators.

English as a second language (ESL) A term referring to the study of English by people whose native language is something different.

environmental theories Theories contending that factors external to the individual are primarily responsible for human behavior.

estrogen The hormone in both males and females that, at high enough levels, produces female secondary sex characteristics in either sex.

ethnocentrism The tendency to view one's own ethnic or racial group and its standards as the basis for judging others, usually seeing others' standards and behavior as inferior.

experimental group The people who are subjected to a specific treatment in an experiment.

experimental research Studies that are designed in such a way that cause and effect can be examined.

external locus of control The belief that the successes or failures in our lives are primarily determined by sources beyond our personal control, resulting in a "why bother" attitude.

Related concepts: attribution theory, learned helplessness.

extinction The weakening of a particular behavior by withholding reinforcement.

extraneous variable *See* confounding variable.

extrinsic rewards A reward, external to the activity itself, that is offered as a way of maintaining a behavior that the person does not find intrinsically pleasurable. Examples: salary, grades.

Fair Labor Standards Act Federal legislation that mandates the hours and conditions under which adolescents may be employed.

Fallopian tubes The small tubes that connect the ovaries to the uterus and through which the egg passes midway through each monthly cycle. The place where the egg is fertilized by sperm during a pregnancy. Synonym: oviducts.

fear of success Being afraid to succeed at tasks or in jobs that have traditionally been considered appropriate for the other gender.

fetal alcohol syndrome A condition occurring in infants in which they are born with mild to moderate mental retardation, low birth weights, and excessive irritability or hyperactivity during childhood due to their mother's alcohol consumption during pregnancy.

field research Studies in which the researcher observes and describes the behavior of a group in its natural social environment.

field theory A set of theories developed from Gestalt psychology that views human behavior as a consequence of the interactions between the field of our psychological forces and the field of our environment.

flashbacks Unexpectedly re-experiencing the effects of LSD several weeks or months after use of the drug.

flashbulb memory See eidetic memory.

foreclosed identity A person who has adopted an identity based on the viewpoints and values of their parents and other authorities without first examining other roles and values.

foreskin The skin that covers the end of the penis and is cut and folded back during a circumcision.

formal operations stage In Piagetian theory, the fourth stage of cognitive development, which is supposed to occur during adolescence and in which we become capable of logical reasoning and abstract thinking.

Foxfire Project A program in Rabun Gap, Georgia, that has integrated regional culture into the high school's curriculum.

free association The process whereby a therapist presents a list of words or phrases and the therapist interprets the client's answers in accord with Freudian theory.

free basing Introducing cocaine to the body by smoking, rather than eating or injecting it.

Freudian theory Theory contending that human behavior is primarily determined by childhood conflicts, primarily sexual in nature, within the family.

friends People who are more than peers in that they are attached to one another by feelings of affection or personal regard.

Gestalt psychology A type of field theory formed in reaction against behaviorism, contending that our experiences are like "gestalts" (pictures) that can be interpreted differently, depending on the viewer's particular perspectives. See Figure 4.3.

Gilligan's different voice Carol Gilligan's theory that males and females base their moral values and behavior on different principles.

gender roles The behaviors and attitudes prescribed by a society as appropriate for males and for females. Synonym: sex roles.

gender schema theory A cognitive theory stating that sex-typed behavior is influenced by fitting our experiences into our existing systems of beliefs (schema).

generativity According to Erikson's personality stages, the last stage in life when we want to guide and advise younger people and leave something of value to others before we die.

genital stage In Freudian theory, the final stage, lasting from puberty throughout adulthood, in which we focus our sexual energy on love and work.

glans The head of the penis or the tip of the clitoris.

gonadotropins Hormones released by the pituitary gland that cause the ovaries and the testes to increase the amounts of estrogen in girls and testosterone in boys during puberty.

gonads The ovaries and the testes.

gonorrhea A sexually transmitted bacterial disease that can be cured with antibiotics but, when left untreated, can cause infertility and other complications of the urogenital tract.

hashish Concentrated form of marijuana that has more THC and thus causes a stronger reaction.

hemisphericity The brain's organization in which each side of the brain is generally responsible for a specific type of motor or cognitive task.

herpes A sexually transmitted virus that causes an incurable disease whose initial symptoms include genital blisters and flu-like symptoms.

Holland's occupational types Personality types that are supposedly suited for specific types of jobs.

homophobia Excessive fear or hatred of homosexuals, sometimes linked to a fear of one's own homosexual feelings or tendencies.

homosexual A male or female whose sexual desires are for members of his or her own gender.

human immunodeficiency virus (HIV) The virus that causes AIDS.

humanistic psychology Largely the creation of Abraham Maslow, the view that psychology should be concerned with higher human motives such as self-actualization.

hymen The fold of mucous membrane partially closing the external opening to the vagina. Slang/synonyms: "maidenhead," "cherry."

hypothalamus The upper brain stem, which signals the pituitary gland to release the hormones that begin puberty.

ice A type of "speed" (methamphetamine) that produces a "buzz" for up to 24 hours and is more addictive than cocaine.

id The part of the personality that houses those drives that are most in touch with a person's biological nature—above all, sex and aggression.

identity status In Erikson's and Marcia's theories, the four types of identity statuses—foreclosed, achieved, diffused, and moratorium—that people can adopt in the process of creating their adult personalities.

imaginary audience The false belief that a person is continually being noticed and critiqued by other people; hypersensitive self-consciousness.

independent variable A factor that remains constant throughout a study, such as the subject's gender or race.

individuation According to Freudians, the process, typically occurring during adolescence, of forming a more independent identity by examining and modifying the contents of the superego, particularly the values adopted in childhood from our parents.

information processing approach An approach concerned with how we process the information and experiences around us. It involves perception, memory, thinking, and problem solving.

intentionality The tendency to direct your own goals that have evolved from your own inner motivation rather than primarily as a reaction to the wishes or demands of others.

internal locus of control The belief that the successes and the failures in our lives are primarily determined by sources within our personal control. Synonym: self-efficacy.

Intrauterine device (IUD) A contraceptive object, usually made of plastic but sometimes made of copper, that is inserted by a physician into the uterus to prevent implantation of a fertilized egg in the uterine wall.

intrinsic rewards Pleasurable feelings derived from engaging in an activity without having to receive external rewards of any sort. Examples: the pleasure of eating when you are hungry.

inverse correlation A relationship in which as one factor increases, the other decreases.

jigsaw teaching A method of teaching in which students are assigned to interracial teams for cooperative learning assignments.

joint custody A legal agreement in which both divorced parents retain the right to be consulted about decisions related to issues concerning their children's well-being, such as education, health care, and religion.

joint residency A legal agreement, separate from joint custody, providing for children to spend roughly equal amounts of time living in each parent's home after a divorce.

Klinefelter's syndrome Chromosomal abnormality in males that prevents their secondary sex characteristics from developing at puberty.

labia The folds of skin surrounding the vulva.

latchkey children Children who are left unsupervised in their homes after school or during vacations because their parents work.

latency stage The fourth stage in Freud's theory (roughly ages 6–12), in which the child concentrates on forming satisfying peer relationships and identifying with the same-sex parent.

LD child *See* Learning disability.

learned helplessness The view that depression

and lack of motivation arise from prolonged exposure to failure and losses over which we have no control, resulting in the belief that whatever good or bad happens to us is beyond our control: "Why bother trying?"

learning disability In people of normal or above-average intelligence, difficulties in learning to read, write, or do math that are assumed to stem from some form of minimal brain dysfunction.

life space In field theories, the field that includes the individual and all significant other people.

Limited English Proficiency (LEP) Students whose abilities in writing or speaking English are limited by their having learned another language as their native tongue.

locus of control The beliefs we carry with us about who or what controls the successes or failures in our lives. *See* external locus, internal locus. Synonyms: attribution theory, self-efficacy.

longitudinal study Research in which people from the same cohort group are measured on the same dependent variables over a period of time.

LSD Lysergic acid diethylamide. A synthetic drug causing hallucinations.

machismo Among Hispanics, the belief that men should assume responsibility for the emotional and financial well-being of their families and should instill in children a respect for their mothers. In its anglicized meaning, to be overly aggressive and dominant, to be "macho."

mammary glands The milk-producing glands in the breast.

Maslow's hierarchy of needs According to Maslow, the set of basic and more sophisticated needs that motivate an individual.

mastery learning A system of teaching and grading that allows students to work at their individual pace to master specifically stated criteria without competing against other students.

MDA "Ecstasy." A synthetic drug producing amphetamine-like and LSD-like effects that is associated with feeling more insightful, empathic, and aware.

mean The mathematical average. Example: 10 is the mean of the numbers 12, 2, 13, 8, and 15.

median The number that divides a group of scores in half, with half the scores falling above the median and half falling below the median. Example: 10 is the median for the numbers 12, 2, 8, 15.

mediation A process in which a divorcing couple attempts to reach agreements about the terms of the divorce by meeting with a mediation counselor rather than resorting exclusively to lawyers.

menorrhagia Excessively heavy menstrual flow.

mental rotation The result of imagining what a two- or three-dimensional figure would look like from different angles or in its mirror image if it were rotated in space. See Figure 5.1.

mesomorph Muscular, relatively tall body that is not too heavy or too lean.

meta-analysis A statistical technique that permits more sophisticated analyses of data by considering variables such as gender and socioeconomic class that influence the results.

metacognition The ability to think about the strategies we use in thinking.

Minnesota Multiphasic Personality Inventory (MMPI) A written test used to identify personality traits.

modeling Learning that occurs by our watching the ways in which other people are reinforced or punished and, on that basis, deciding whether we want to copy their behavior. Synonym: observational learning.

moral dilemma A situation in which the person is confronted with having to choose among two or more alternative courses of action in such a way that choosing one violates one set of moral principles and choosing the other violates another, equally important set.

moral realism According to Piaget, the stage of moral reasoning characteristic of childhood that is based on authorities' viewpoints, clearcut notions of right and wrong, and external reward and punishment.

moratorium According to Marcia, the stage in which an individual has not yet adopted any specific identity.

"morning after" pill A contraceptive pill that, when taken soon after intercourse, prevents a fertilized egg from implanting in the uterine wall.

Mothers Against Drunk Driving (MADD) National organization working to increase public awareness on the hazards of driving while intoxicated and lobbying for stricter legislation on the issue.

multicultural Reflecting the perspectives of more than two cultures simultaneously.

multicultural curriculum A curriculum that includes information about and the perspectives of various cultural groups rather than being restricted exclusively to the white middle class culture.

negative correlation A relationship in which an increase in one variable is related to a decrease in the other variable.

neo-Freudian Freudian theories that deviate from Freud's original ideas in that they place less emphasis on early childhood and unconscious sexual conflicts as the explanations for human behavior.

neo-Nazi Recently organized groups based on Hitler's Nazi doctrines that preach and practice violence against Jews and racial minorities.

neo-Piagetian The updated or modified theories based on the work of Piaget.

nicotine The active ingredient in tobacco (smoked or chewed). A physically addictive drug that has a mild stimulant effect.

nocturnal emissions Male ejaculation during sleep. Synonym: "wet dreams."

nonconscious ideology Values and beliefs so ingrained in a society's institutions and habits that people are unaware of being subjected to them.

object permanence In Piagetian theory the awareness that comes before the age of 7 that even when an object or person is out of view, it still exists.

observational learning *See* modeling.

Oedipus complex In Freudian theory the son's unconscious desire to have sex with his mother and his jealousy and hatred toward his father.

operant conditioning *See* behaviorism, behavior modification.

operant psychology *See* behaviorism.

operational definitions Concepts that are defined in terms of specific, observable behavior, rather than in terms of abstractions that cannot be specifically measured.

oral stage According to Freudians, the first psychosexual stage (birth to 12 months) in which we must learn to be less dependent on our mothers.

organismic theories Theories that attribute human behavior and attitudes primarily to influences within the individual, rather than in the environment.

os The opening in the cervix through which menstrual fluid flows and which expands during birth for the baby's passage.

ovulation The release of the egg from the ovary each month, usually occurring about two weeks after menstruation.

panel study *See* Longitudinal study.

paper A penny-sized bag of "ice."

PCP Phencyclidine, "angel dust." A synthetic hallucinogen that causes distortions of body image and a sense of timelessness.

peers People who regard one another as equal with respect to some particular skill (for example, athletic teams), a characteristic (for example, income), or a shared situation (for example, all members of the same math class). Sometimes used loosely to refer to people of the same age.

permissive parents A style of parenting in which parents are either uninvolved with their children or in which the children are permitted to rule the roost. Synonym: laissez-faire parents.

personal fable The erroneous belief, typifying early adolescence, that we are immune from any type of harm.

phallic stage The Freudian stage (ages 4–5) in which our essential conflict is created by our sexual desire for our opposite-sex parent and by our jealousies toward our same-sex parent.

Piagetian theories Theories contending that our cognitive skills advance in relatively predictable, universal stages, each of which is associated with specific new skills primarily determined by our chronological age, not by environmental influences.

popping Introducing a drug to the body by putting the needle just slightly under the skin's surface.

postconventional reasoning According to Kohlberg, the most sophisticated level of moral reasoning in which we see rules and moral codes as relative and flexible.

premenstrual syndrome (PMS) A condition causing an extreme shift in mood and behavior in some females before each menstrual cycle.

preoperational stage According to Piaget, a stage of cognitive development between the ages of 2 and 7 in which we develop such new skills as object permanence but during which we are still handicapped by our egocentristic thinking.

prepuce The protective hood of skin covering the end of the clitoris or the end of the penis.

primary reinforcers Objects or activities, such as food and sex, that "naturally" motivate us because they satisfy our biological needs.

progesterone Female hormone secreted before implantation of the fertilized egg in the uterine lining.

projection Denying one's own feelings or tendencies by ascribing those traits or feelings to other people.

projective techniques Any test or procedures designed to provide insight into an individual's personality by allowing him or her the chance to respond in an unrestricted manner to ambiguous objects or situations.

prostate gland The male gland that produces semen.

protein loading Consuming large quantities of proteins in the erroneous belief that it will build muscles.

pseudostupidity The seemingly "stupid" behavior of adolescents that ego psychologists believe is the consequence of their rapidly expanding cognitive abilities in combination with their lack of experience.

psychoanalytic theory *See* Freudian theory.

psychometric approach A method of studying human intelligence through measurements such as IQ tests.

psychosexual stages According to Freudians, the stages of childhood and adolescence during which we must resolve certain psychological conflicts of a sexual nature in order to form a healthy adult personality.

psychosocial stages According to Erikson, the stages people undergo in which the personality is shaped primarily by the interaction between the person and the physical and social environment.

purging Forcing oneself to vomit or using laxatives to force food quickly out of the body so that calories will not be absorbed after eating. A symptom of bulimia.

Q-sort A technique used in personality assessment based on a series of statements which the subject sorts into categories from "most characteristic of me" to "least characteristic of me."

quaaludes A tranquilizer recently withdrawn from the market by the pharmaceutical manufacturer due to its dangers and abuse.

random sample Sample of people participating in a study who possess characteristics similar to those of people to whom the results are going to be generalized. Also called a representative sample.

rational emotive therapy An approach to changing human behavior, based on the principles of social learning theory and cognitive psychology, in which people reexamine the rationality of the thoughts influencing their behavior.

rationalization A defense mechanism in which a person creates reasons to justify his or her behavior and attitudes but that conceals the person's true motives.

reaction formation A defense mechanism in which a person replaces his or her anxiety-producing feeling with its opposite feeling.

reality therapy A counseling and teaching method based on contingency contracting developed by William Glasser through his work with troubled adolescents.

regression A defense mechanism in which a person who feels threatened or frustrated reverts to ways of behaving that were characteristic of a less mature stage of development.

reinforcement Any object or activity that increases the likelihood that a person will repeat a particular behavior.

reliability The ability of a measuring device or a test to yield consistent scores or results over time.

representative sample *See* random sample.

repression The defense mechanism of forgetting unpleasant incidents.

reversibility The ability to work backward or forward, rotate objects in your mind, and undo activities that have been completed in actuality or in thought.

rhythm method An attempt to prevent pregnancy by abstaining from intercourse during the days when the woman is believed to be fertile.

Rogerian counseling A type of therapy developed by Carl Rogers in which clients can presumably resolve their own problems without the counselor's advice through self-disclosures and feeling "accepted without any judgments" by the counselor. Synonym: client-centered therapy.

Rorschach test The "ink-blot" projective test for

diagnosing unconscious traits or problems. See Figure 4.1.

rule of equivalence According to Piaget, the ability to understand the equivalent relationships between seemingly different objects or ideas (if $A = B$, and $B = C$, then $A = C$) acquired during the stage of concrete operations.

satellite schools Schools that are based away from the main high-school campus, often in actual business settings, and offer more specialized and updated vocational training.

schema The existing mental framework (ideas, ways of analyzing data) into which new information or new experiences are integrated as we mature.

schools within schools Schools which assign students to small cooperative groups under the direction of a team of teachers who stay with them over a period of several years.

scrotum The pouch of skin that contains the testes.

secondary reinforcers Activities or objects that become rewards only as a consequence of someone's teaching a person that they are important or because that person discovers that he or she can exchange the activities or objects for primary rewards.

self-actualization In Maslow's theory of personality, the final level of psychological development that can be achieved when all the basic and higher level needs are fulfilled and the "actualization" of the person's full potential occurs.

self-fulfilling prophecy A term used to refer to the fact that things often turn out just as one expected they would. For example, a math teacher expects female students to do poorly, so she treats them in ways that increase the likelihood that the prophecy is fulfilled.

semantic differential A technique in which subjects reveal their feelings by rating specific words along a scale of opposite words such as "strong-weak."

semen The fluid, containing both sperm and seminal fluids, that is released when a male ejaculates. Not synonymous with sperm.

seminal fluid Semen.

seminal vesicles Tubes where the sperm is stored.

sensorimotor stage According to Piaget, the earliest cognitive stage from birth to 2 years in which we learn to use primitive symbols.

serialization The arrangement of objects in proper order according to some dimension, such as weight or length, attained during the concrete stage of thought according to Piaget.

Sexually Transmitted Disease (S.T.D.) Any infection that is passed from person to person through oral, anal, or vaginal sexual activity.

shaft The part of the penis below the glans that becomes engorged during an erection.

skinheads Loosely organized gangs of neo-Nazi teenagers and young adults known for shaving their heads.

Skinnerian psychology *See* behaviorism.

smokeless tobacco Chewing tobacco.

social learning theory The view that our behavior and attitudes are primarily the consequence of reinforcement, punishment, and modeling but are also influenced by such cognitive variables as our preconceived expectations.

sociobiology The study of theories contending that human behavior is in large part determined by biological factors, such as hormones, and by genetic changes that have evolved for the good of a species.

spatial perception The ability to locate the horizontal or the vertical while ignoring other distracting, irrelevant visual cues. See Figure 5.1.

spatial visualization The ability to analyze the relationship between different spatial representations of an object. See Figure 5.1.

speed *See* amphetamines.

stage theories Theories contending that human behavior changes as a consequence of maturation occuring in distinct, universal stages that are basically unaffected by environmental influences.

Stanford Binet An IQ test.

state-dependent memory Information that the individual memorizes in one mood is difficult to retrieve unless the individual is in a similar mood.

steroids Sex hormones that contribute to muscle bulk.

Strong-Campbell Interest Inventory A written test for assessing vocational interests.

superego According to Freud, the part of the personality that has internalized society's values, particularly the values of one's parents, and controls behavior by invoking guilt feelings. Synonym: the conscience.

survey research Gathers information through written or personal questionnaires but cannot establish cause and effect.

syphilis A sexually transmitted disease that can be cured with antibiotics but that can cause death, blindness, and insanity if untreated.

System of Multicultural Pluralistic Assessment (SOMPA) An IQ test that takes account of ethnicity and environmental variables, such as family income.

teams achievement divisions *See* Jigsaw teaching.

testicles The male sex glands that hang inside the scrotum. Slang/synonyms: "balls," "nuts," "family jewels," "rocks."

testosterone The hormone in males and females that, at high enough levels, produces male secondary sex characteristics in either sex.

THC The chemical in marijuana responsible for its psychoactive effects.

Thematic Apperception Test A psychoanalytic technique in which the therapist asks the client to tell a story based on viewing a series of pictures and then interprets the story from a Freudian viewpoint.

Title IX Federal law passed in 1972 stating that no person in the United States shall, on the basis of sex, be excluded from participating in, be denied the benefits of, or be subjected to discrimination under any educational program or activity receiving federal money. See Table 5.2.

tracking The traditional practice of segregating students into classes, such as college preparatory, vocational education, special education or general, on the basis of their academic skills or future interests.

transactional analysis A method for improving communication in which conversations are analyzed according to the "roles"—the "child," the "parent," or the "adult"—each statement represents.

tubal ligation A method of birth control in which the female's Fallopian tubes are either clamped shut or cauterized so that the egg, after it is released from the ovary, cannot meet with a sperm. Synonyms: a tubal, sterilization.

Turner's syndrome A chromosomal abnormality in females that prevents the development of secondary sex characteristics at puberty. The equivalent of Klinefelter's syndrome in males.

uppers *See* amphetamines.

urethra In the female, the tube that carries urine from the bladder to the outside of the body; in the male, the tube that carries both urine and seminal fluid to the outside of the body.

uterus The organ, about the size of a fist and the shape of an upside-down pear with a thick wall of strong, stretchy muscles, in which the fetus develops during pregnancy. Synonym: womb.

vagina The passageway from the uterus to the outside of the body whose walls touch unless separated by an external object, such as a tampon or a penis; produces mucous for cleansing the body and for lubrication during intercourse. Synonym: birth canal.

validity The ability of a test or an instrument to measure accurately what it claims to be measuring.

values clarification Classroom activities designed to help adolescents examine and evaluate their moral values and behavior.

vas deferens The tubes that carry sperm from the testicles to the seminal vesicles.

vasectomy A method of birth control in which the vas deferens are surgically cut or cauterized so that sperm cannot be mixed with the seminal fluid before ejaculation.

vulva The external female genitals.

Wechsler Adult Intelligence Scale (WAIS) An IQ test.

Wechsler Intelligence Scale for Children-Revised (WISC-R) An IQ test.

withdrawal The physical reactions that people who are physically addicted to a drug experience when they stop using the drug. The symptoms are usually directly opposite of the effects induced by the drug.

zygote An egg that has been fertilized by the sperm.

Index

3.1 p. 78 Dr. Bob Jones, **3.2 p. 83** Susan Lapides/Design Conceptions, **3.3 p. 105** Winston Salem/Forsyth County Schools, **3.4 p. 108** Wake Forest University Office of Public Affairs/Bill Ray III

4.1–4.6 p. 114–141 Dr. Bob Jones, **4.7 p. 145** © 1985 Ruth Anne Clarke-Mason

5.1–5.3 p. 162–189 Dr. Bob Jones, **5.4 p. 196** Courtesy of North Carolina School of the Arts, Winston Salem, **5.5 p. 199** Winston Salem/Forsyth County Schools

6.1 p. 210 © 1985 Ruth Anne Clarke-Mason, **6.2 p. 217** © 1985 Ruth Anne Clarke-Mason, **6.3 p. 228** Winston Salem/Forsyth County Schools, **6.4 p. 232** © 1985 Ruth Anne Clarke-Mason

7.1 p. 250 Dr. Bob Jones, **7.2 & 7.3 p. 256, 268** Winston Salem/Forsyth County Schools, **7.4 p. 280** Paul Ribisl

8.1 p. 288 Dr. Bob Jones, **8.2 & 8.5 p. 297, 307** Bob Beck, **8.3, 8.4, & 8.6 p. 299, 304, 328** Dr. Bob Jones, **8.7 p. 330** © 1985 Ruth Anne Clarke-Mason

9.1 & 9.2 p. 341, 347 Dr. Bob Jones, **9.3 p. 350** Wake Forest University Office of Public Affairs, **9.4 & 9.5 p. 356–357** Dr. Bob Jones

10.1 p. 368 © 1985 Ruth Anne Clarke-Mason, **10.2 p. 372** Dr. Bob Jones, **10.3 & 10.4 p. 380, 392** Reproduced with permission of The Children's Defense Fund, **10.5 p. 403** Bob Beck

11.1 p. 416 © 1986 Susan Lapides/Design Conceptions, **11.2 p. 424** Courtesy of the North Carolina School of the Arts, Winston Salem, **11.3 p. 440** Winston Salem/Forsyth County Schools

12.1 p. 446 © 1986 Bill Aron/Photo Researchers, Inc., **12.2 p. 449** Bill Anderson/Monkmeyer Press, **12.3 p. 467** Wake Forest University

13.1 p. 472 Dr. Bob Jones

14.1 & 14.2 p. 504, 517 Dr. Bob Jones, **14.3 p. 528** © George S. Zimbel/Monkmeyer Press, **14.4 p. 533** Richard Duggan/Boston Children's Museum, **14.5 p. 535** Wake Forest University Office of Public Affairs

15.1 p. 542 Dr. Bob Jones